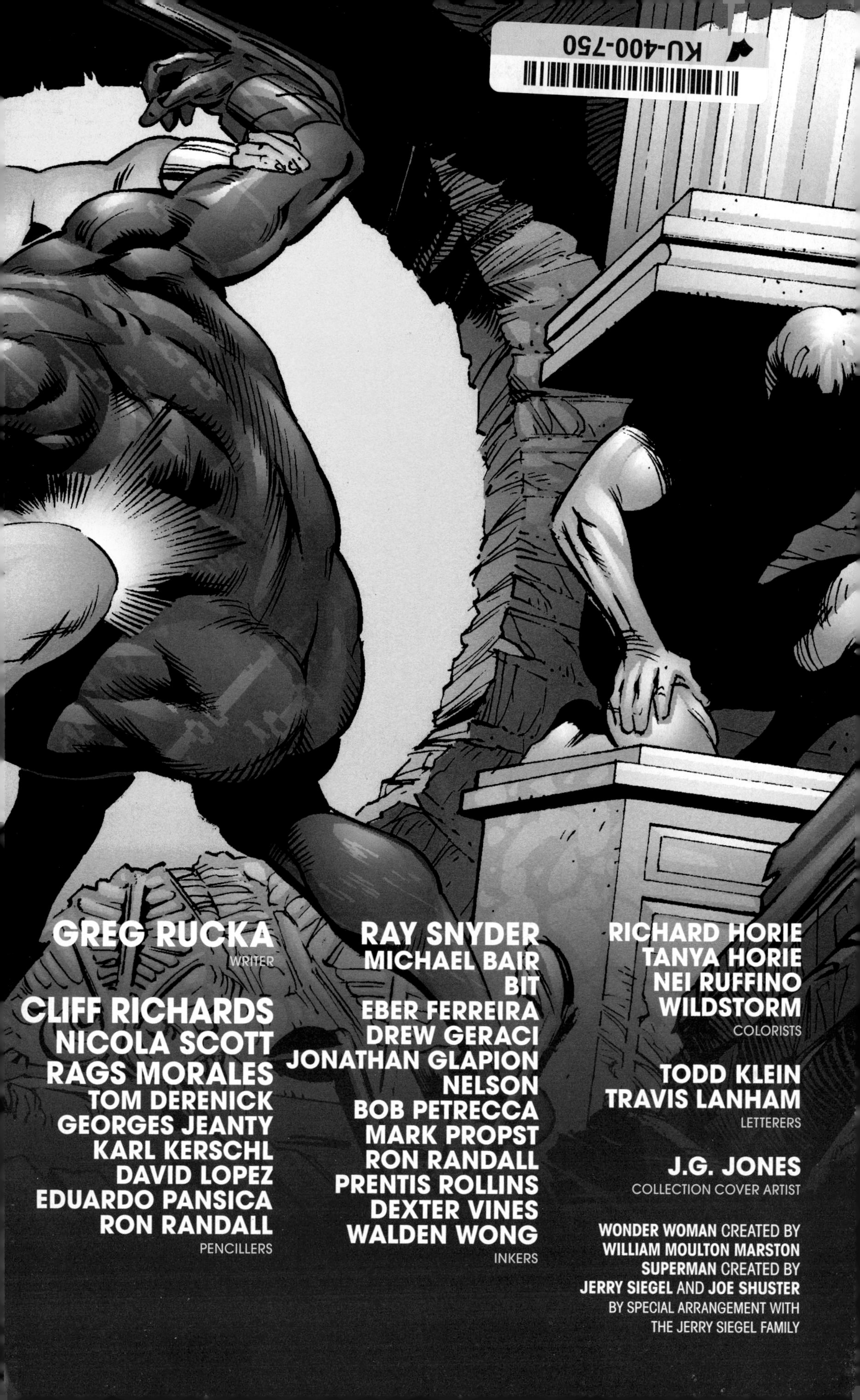

GREG RUCKA
WRITER

CLIFF RICHARDS
NICOLA SCOTT
RAGS MORALES
TOM DERENICK
GEORGES JEANTY
KARL KERSCHL
DAVID LOPEZ
EDUARDO PANSICA
RON RANDALL
PENCILLERS

RAY SNYDER
MICHAEL BAIR
BIT
EBER FERREIRA
DREW GERACI
JONATHAN GLAPION
NELSON
BOB PETRECCA
MARK PROPST
RON RANDALL
PRENTIS ROLLINS
DEXTER VINES
WALDEN WONG
INKERS

RICHARD HORIE
TANYA HORIE
NEI RUFFINO
WILDSTORM
COLORISTS

TODD KLEIN
TRAVIS LANHAM
LETTERERS

J.G. JONES
COLLECTION COVER ARTIST

WONDER WOMAN CREATED BY
WILLIAM MOULTON MARSTON
SUPERMAN CREATED BY
JERRY SIEGEL AND **JOE SHUSTER**
BY SPECIAL ARRANGEMENT WITH
THE JERRY SIEGEL FAMILY

IVAN COHEN
EDDIE BERGANZA Editors – Original Series
ADAM SCHLAGMAN Associate Editor – Original Series
JEB WOODARD Group Editor – Collected Editions
ERIKA ROTHBERG Editor – Collected Edition
STEVE COOK Design Director – Books
MEGEN BELLERSEN Publication Design
CHRISTY SAWYER Publication Production

BOB HARRAS Senior VP – Editor-in-Chief, DC Comics
PAT McCALLUM Executive Editor, DC Comics

DAN DiDIO Publisher
JIM LEE Publisher & Chief Creative Officer
BOBBIE CHASE VP – New Publishing Initiatives & Talent Development
DON FALLETTI VP – Manufacturing Operations & Workflow Management
LAWRENCE GANEM VP – Talent Services
ALISON GILL Senior VP – Manufacturing & Operations
HANK KANALZ Senior VP – Publishing Strategy & Support Services
DAN MIRON VP – Publishing Operations
NICK J. NAPOLITANO VP – Manufacturing Administration & Design
NANCY SPEARS VP – Sales
MICHELE R. WELLS VP & Executive Editor, Young Reader

WONDER WOMAN BY GREG RUCKA VOL. 3

Published by DC Comics. Compilation and all new material Copyright
© 2019 DC Comics. All Rights Reserved. Originally published in single
magazine form in WONDER WOMAN 218-226, BLACKEST NIGHT: WONDER
WOMAN 1-3. Copyright © 2005, 2006, 2010 DC Comics. All Rights
Reserved. All characters, their distinctive likenesses and related
elements featured in this publication are trademarks of DC Comics. The stories,
characters and incidents featured in this publication are entirely fictional. DC
Comics does not read or accept unsolicited submissions of ideas, stories or
artwork. DC – a WarnerMedia Company.

DC Comics, 2900 West Alameda Ave., Burbank, CA 91505
Printed by LSC Communications, Kendallville,
IN, USA. 7/5/19. First Printing.
ISBN: 978-1-4012-9342-0

Library of Congress Cataloging-in-Publication
Data is available.

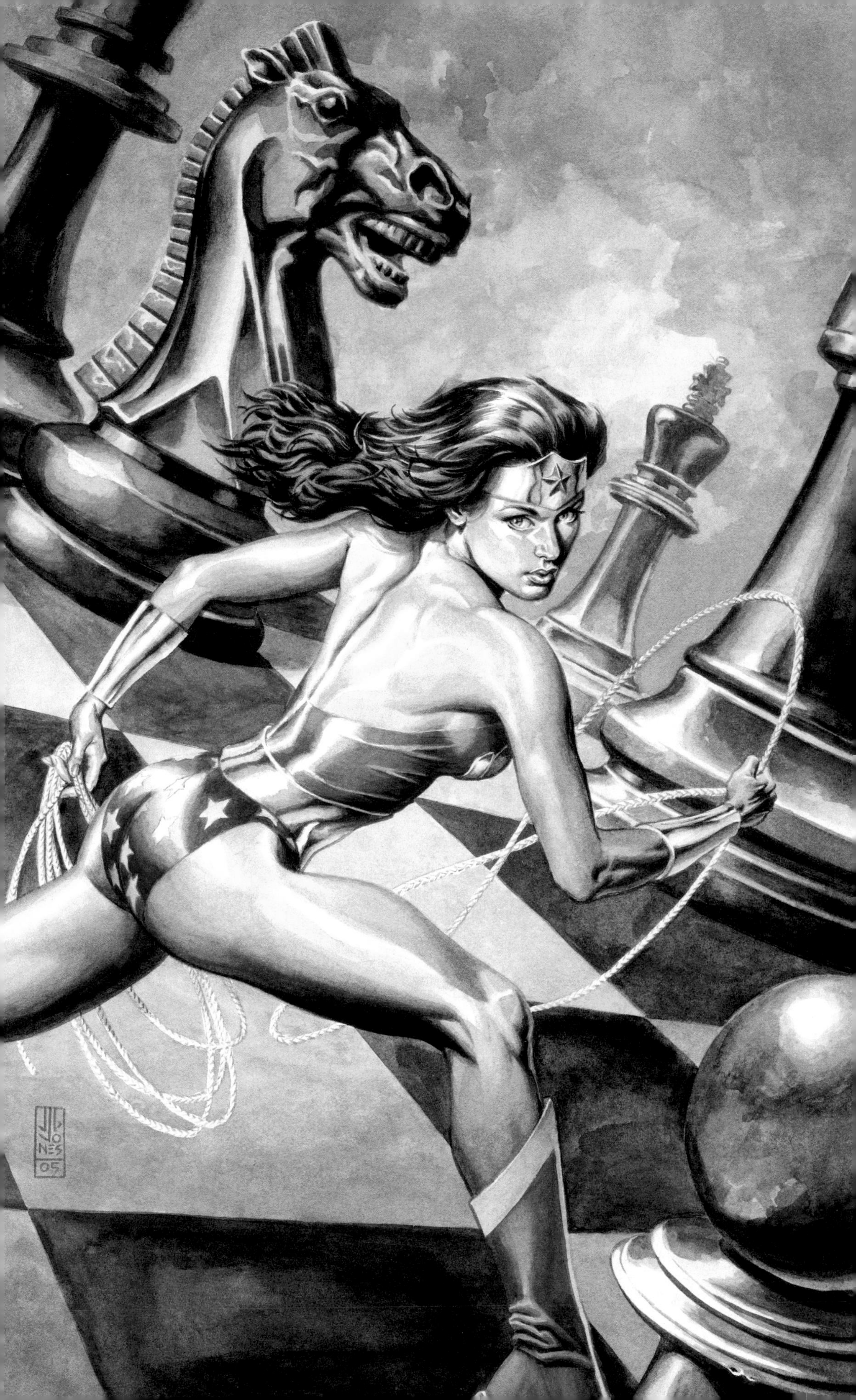

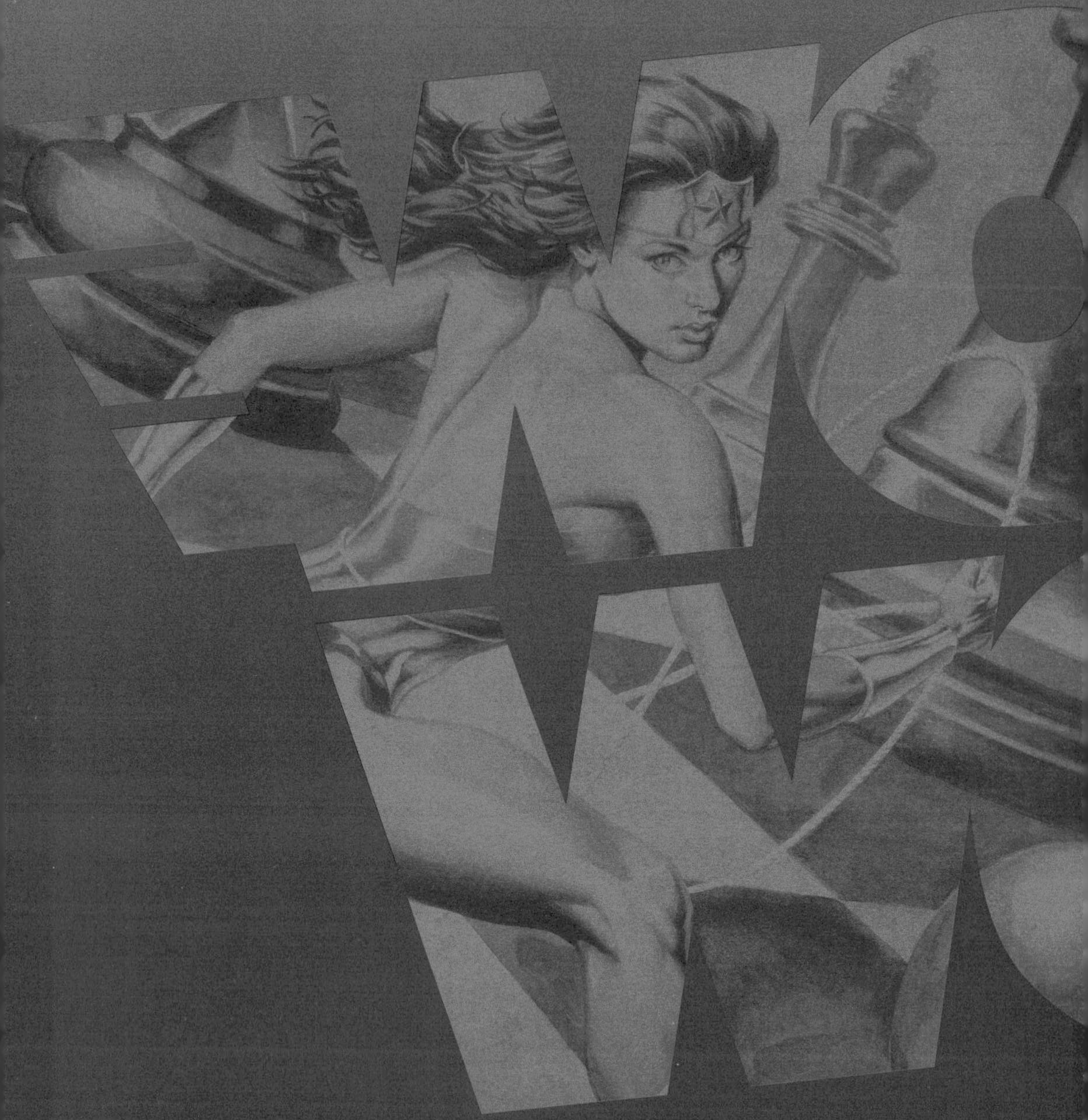

“THE CALM”

Greg Rucka – *writer*
Ron Randall – *pencils*
Ray Snyder and **Ron Randall** – *inks*
Richard and **Tanya Horie** – *colors*
Todd Klein – *letters*
J.G. Jones – *cover*

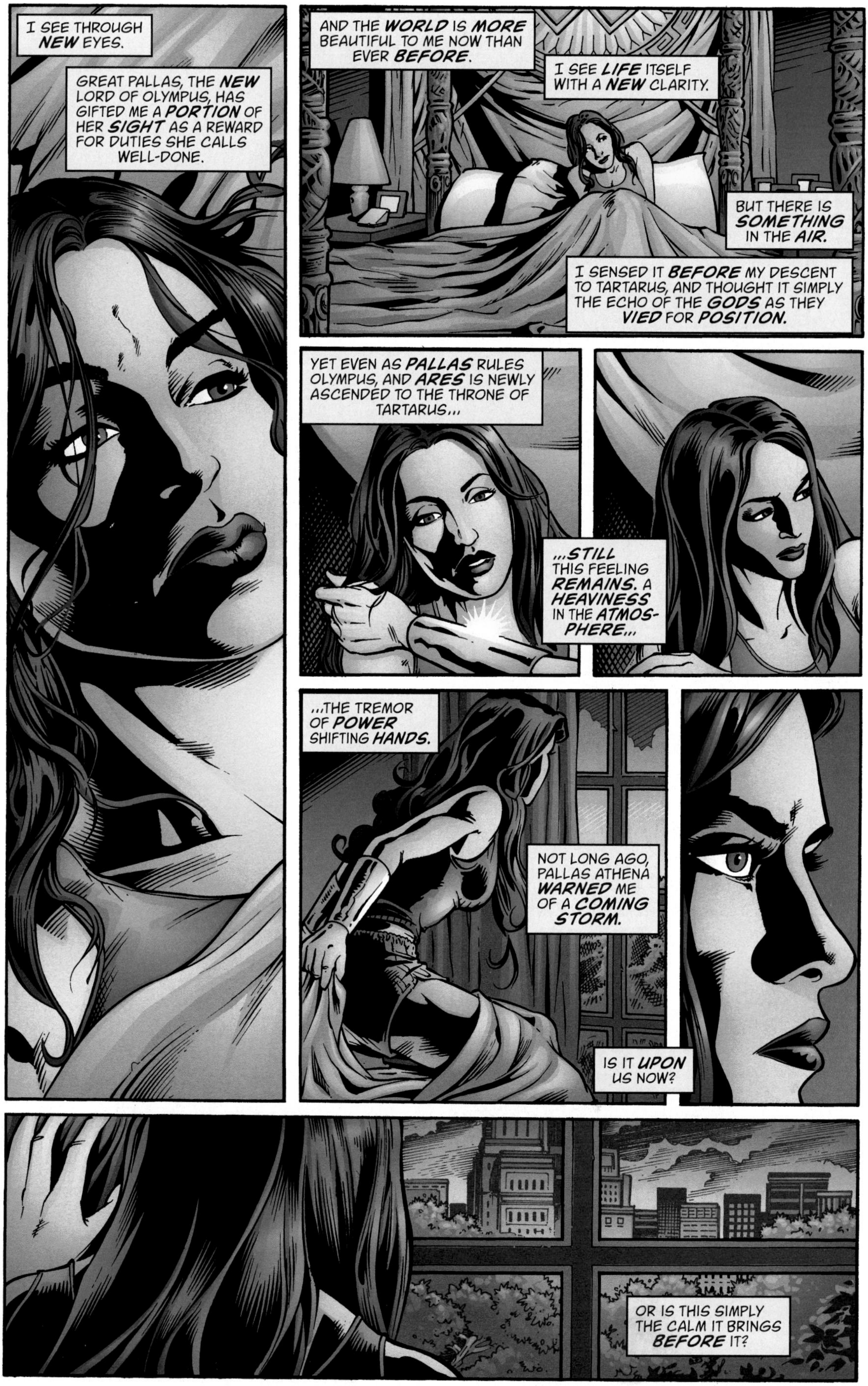
I SEE THROUGH NEW EYES.
GREAT PALLAS, THE NEW LORD OF OLYMPUS, HAS GIFTED ME A PORTION OF HER SIGHT AS A REWARD FOR DUTIES SHE CALLS WELL-DONE.
AND THE WORLD IS MORE BEAUTIFUL TO ME NOW THAN EVER BEFORE.
I SEE LIFE ITSELF WITH A NEW CLARITY.
BUT THERE IS SOMETHING IN THE AIR.
I SENSED IT BEFORE MY DESCENT TO TARTARUS, AND THOUGHT IT SIMPLY THE ECHO OF THE GODS AS THEY VIED FOR POSITION.
YET EVEN AS PALLAS RULES OLYMPUS, AND ARES IS NEWLY ASCENDED TO THE THRONE OF TARTARUS...
...STILL THIS FEELING REMAINS. A HEAVINESS IN THE ATMOSPHERE...
...THE TREMOR OF POWER SHIFTING HANDS.
NOT LONG AGO, PALLAS ATHENA WARNED ME OF A COMING STORM.
IS IT UPON US NOW?
OR IS THIS SIMPLY THE CALM IT BRINGS BEFORE IT?

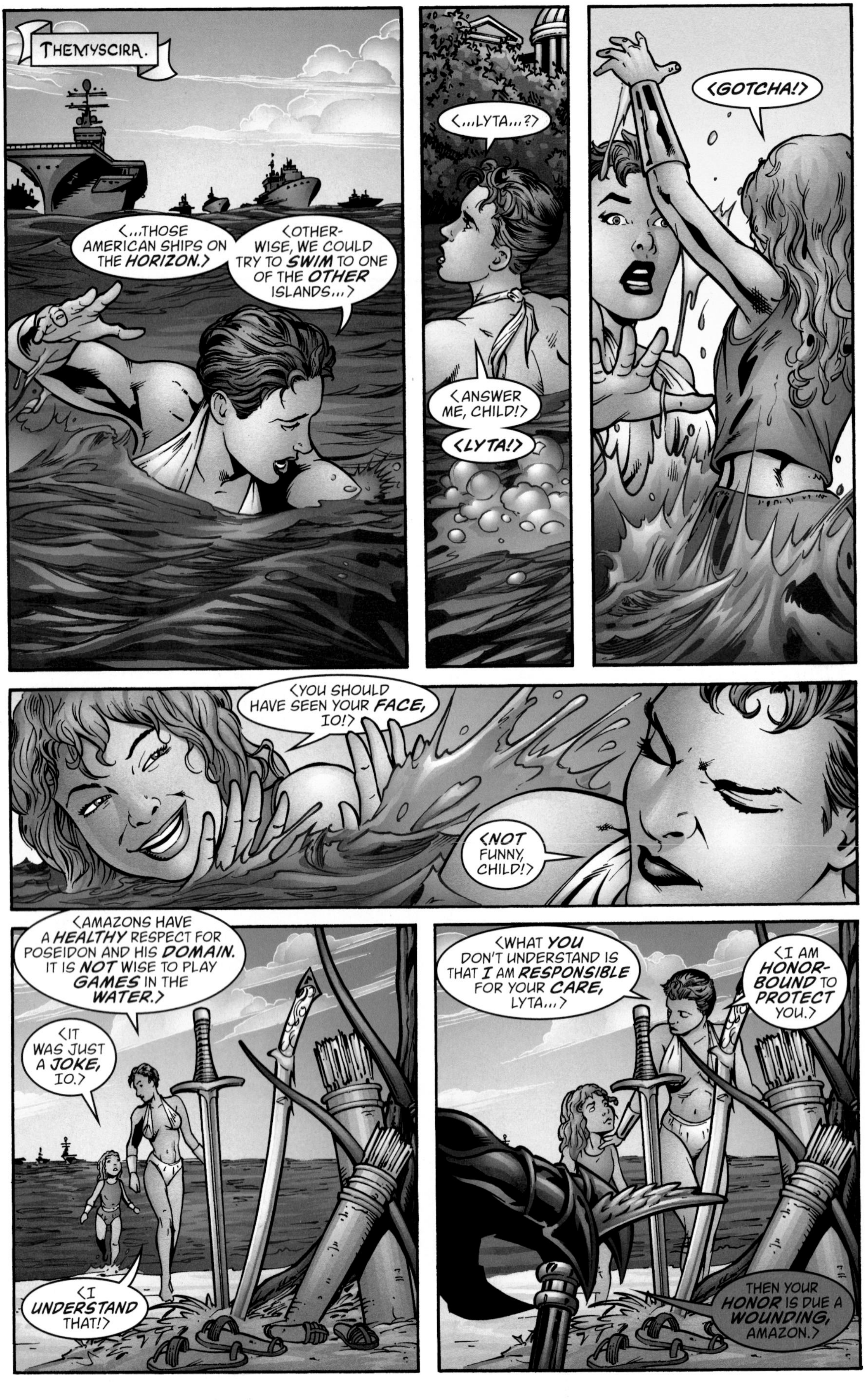
THEMYSCIRA.
<...THOSE AMERICAN SHIPS ON THE HORIZON.>
<OTHER-WISE, WE COULD TRY TO SWIM TO ONE OF THE OTHER ISLANDS...>
<...LYTA...?>
<ANSWER ME, CHILD!>
<LYTA!>
<GOTCHA!>
<YOU SHOULD HAVE SEEN YOUR FACE, IO!>
<NOT FUNNY, CHILD!>
<AMAZONS HAVE A HEALTHY RESPECT FOR POSEIDON AND HIS DOMAIN. IT IS NOT WISE TO PLAY GAMES IN THE WATER.>
<IT WAS JUST A JOKE, IO.>
<I UNDERSTAND THAT!>
<WHAT YOU DON'T UNDERSTAND IS THAT I AM RESPONSIBLE FOR YOUR CARE, LYTA...>
<I AM HONOR-BOUND TO PROTECT YOU.>
THEN YOUR HONOR IS DUE A WOUNDING, AMAZON.>

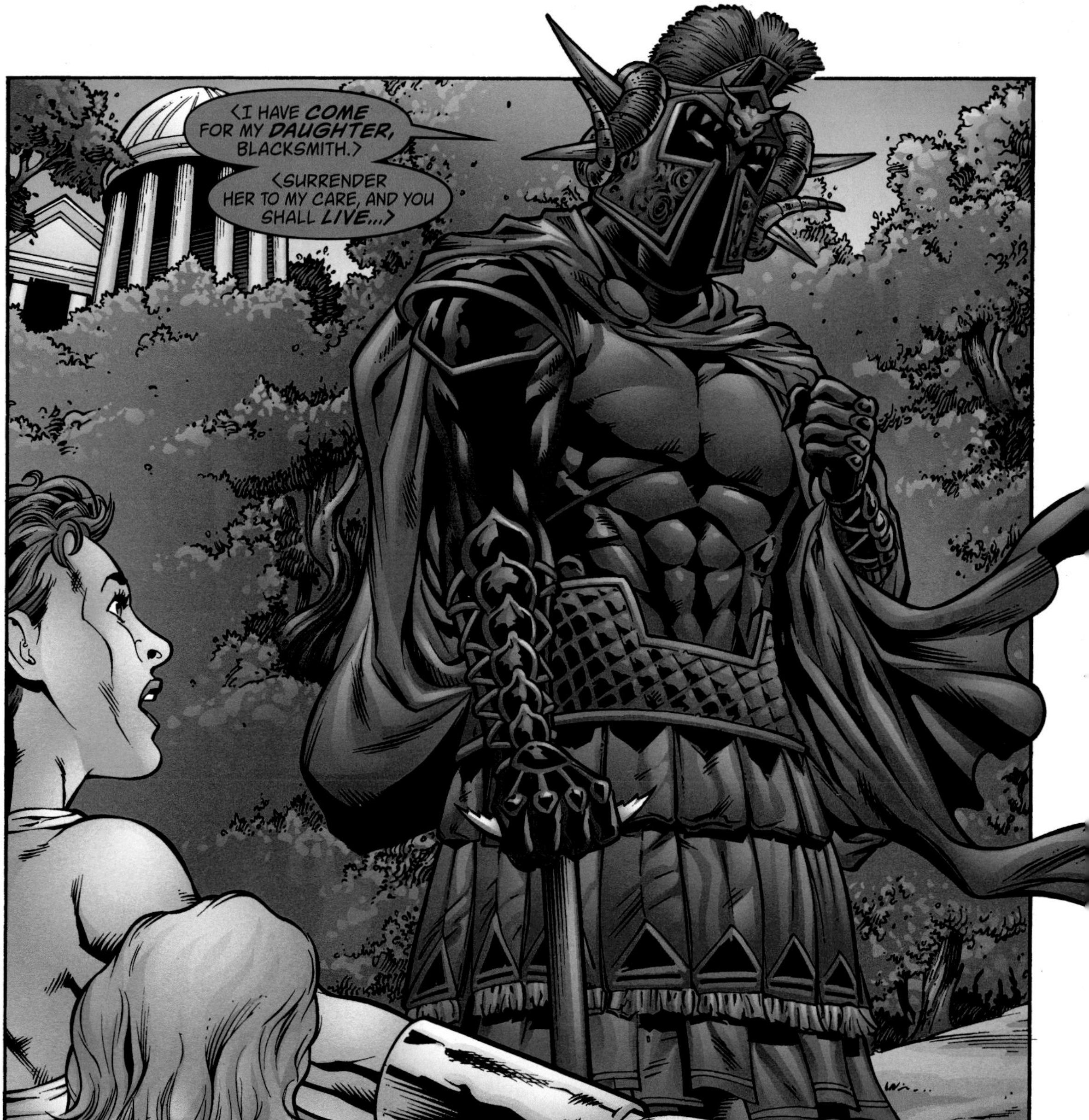
<I HAVE COME FOR MY DAUGHTER, BLACKSMITH.>
<SURRENDER HER TO MY CARE, AND YOU SHALL LIVE...>

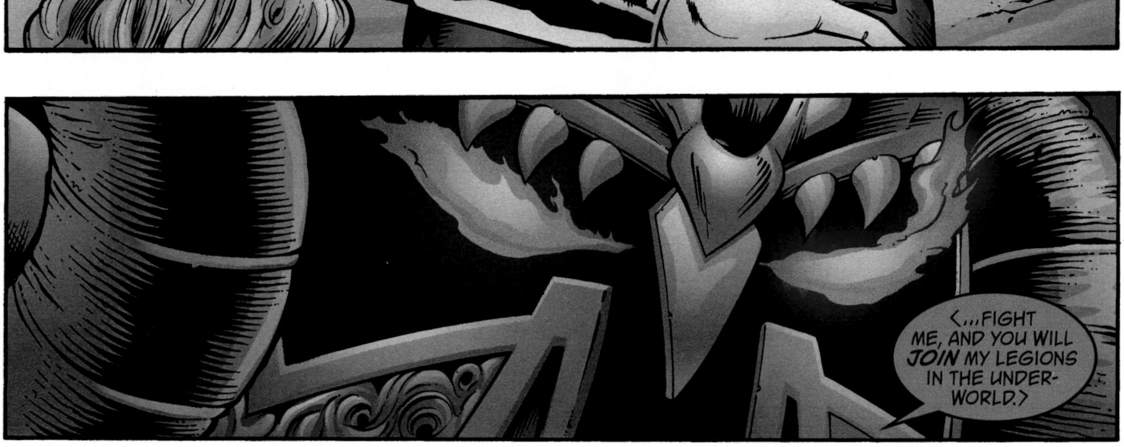
<...FIGHT ME, AND YOU WILL JOIN MY LEGIONS IN THE UNDER-WORLD.>

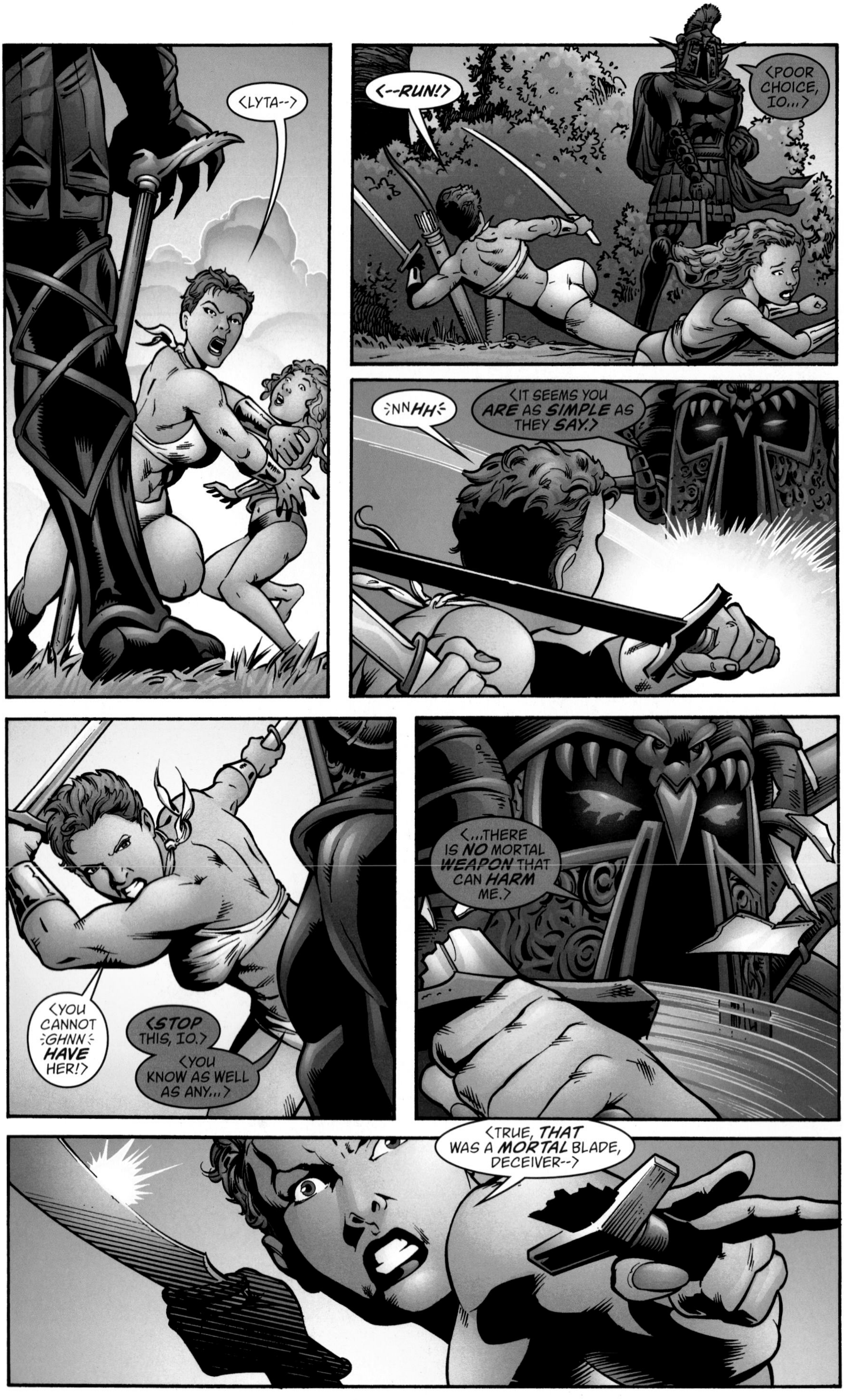
<LYTA-->
<--RUN!>
<POOR CHOICE, IO...>
NNHH
<IT SEEMS YOU ARE AS SIMPLE AS THEY SAY.>
<YOU CANNOT GHNN HAVE HER!>
<STOP THIS, IO.>
<YOU KNOW AS WELL AS ANY...>
<...THERE IS NO MORTAL WEAPON THAT CAN HARM ME.>
<TRUE, THAT WAS A MORTAL BLADE, DECEIVER-->

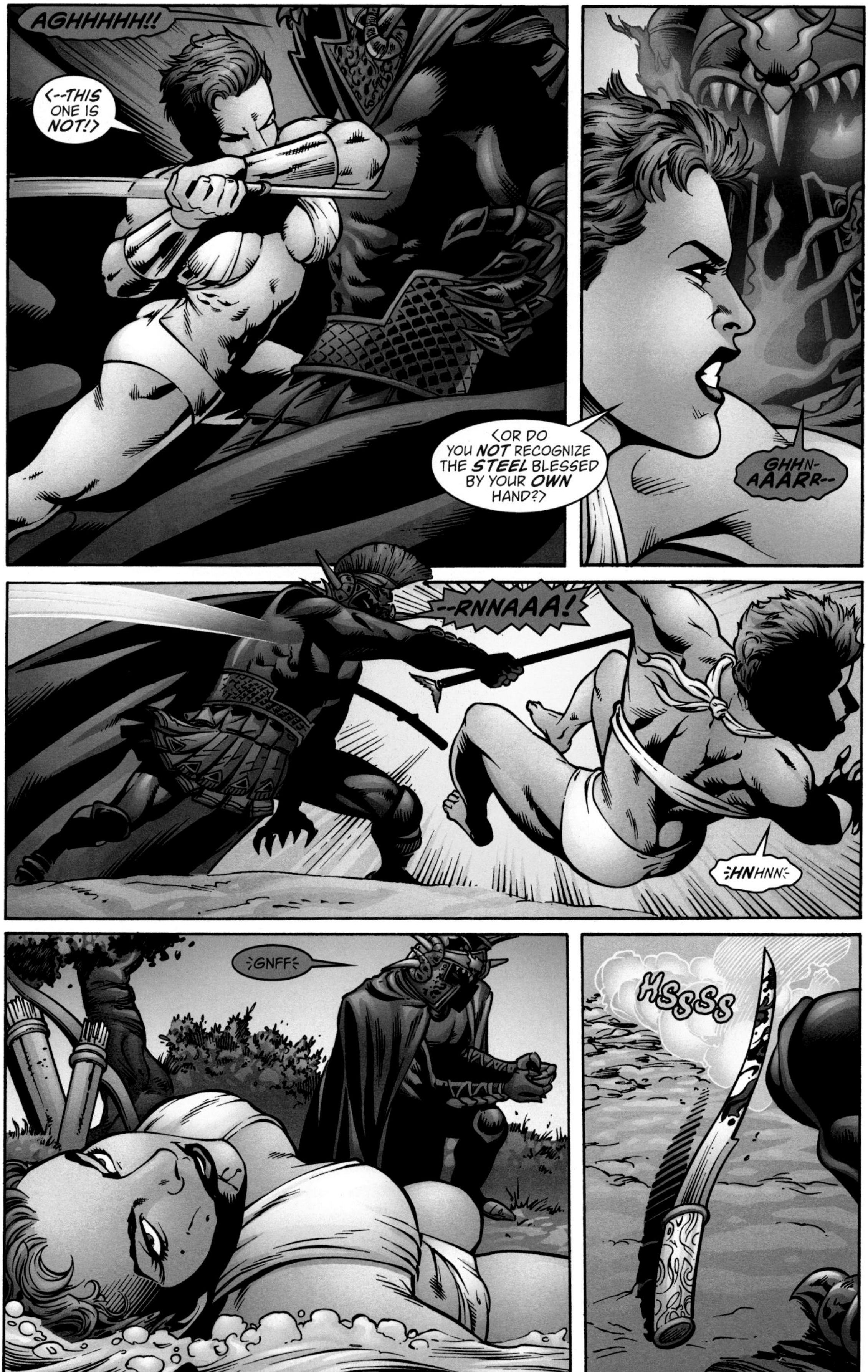
AGHHHHH!!
<--THIS ONE IS NOT!>
<OR DO YOU NOT RECOGNIZE THE STEEL BLESSED BY YOUR OWN HAND?>
GHHN-AAARR--
--RNNAAA!
HNHNN
GNFF
HSSSS

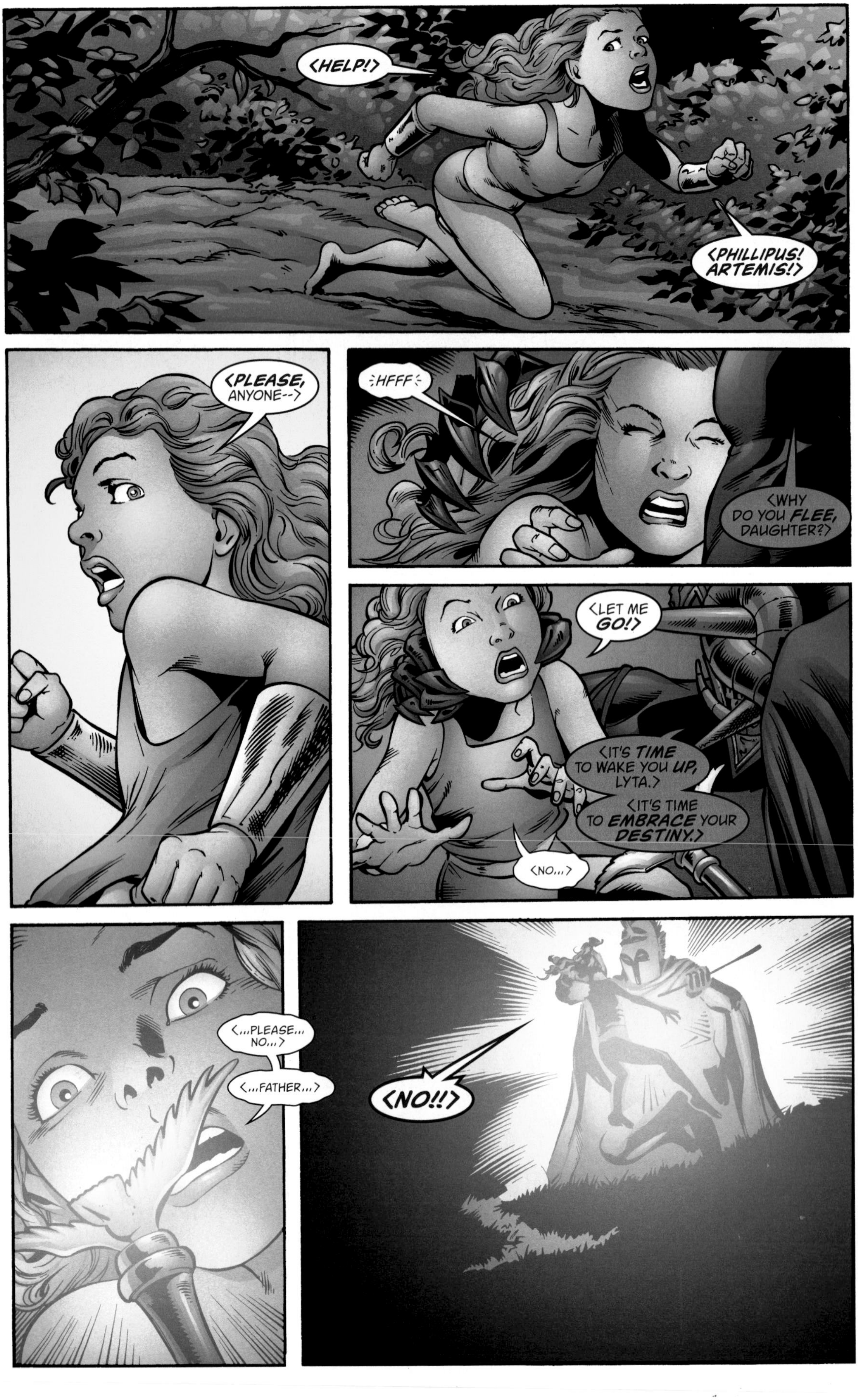

<HELP!>
<PHILLIPUS! ARTEMIS!>
<PLEASE, ANYONE-->
HFFF
<WHY DO YOU FLEE, DAUGHTER?>
<LET ME GO!>
<IT'S TIME TO WAKE YOU UP, LYTA.>
<IT'S TIME TO EMBRACE YOUR DESTINY.>
<NO...>
<...PLEASE... NO...>
<...FATHER...>
<NO!!>

ALL OF US WHO MADE THE *JOURNEY* TO THE UNDERWORLD WERE GIVEN *REWARDS* ON OUR *RETURN*...

--THAT SHE *DIDN'T* TELL ME! *ALL* THIS *TIME*, AND MY *MOTHER* DIDN'T EVEN *TELL* ME, NOT EVEN WHEN I *ASKED!*

AND DIANA *KNEW*, TOO, SHE KNEW *ZEUS* WAS MY *FATHER* AND SHE *NEVER* SAID *ANYTHING!*

This issue takes place before TEEN TITANS #24! --Ivan

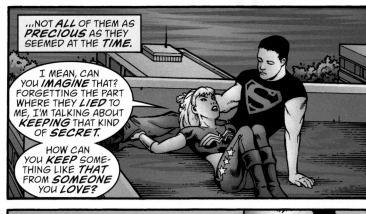

...NOT *ALL* OF THEM AS *PRECIOUS* AS THEY SEEMED AT THE *TIME.*

I MEAN, CAN YOU *IMAGINE* THAT? FORGETTING THE PART WHERE THEY *LIED* TO ME, I'M TALKING ABOUT *KEEPING* THAT KIND OF *SECRET.*

HOW CAN YOU *KEEP* SOMETHING LIKE *THAT* FROM *SOMEONE* YOU *LOVE?*

FOR CASSANDRA, IT WAS THE *REVELATION* THAT ZEUS IS HER *FATHER.*

MAYBE THEY WERE *AFRAID* OF WHAT YOU'D *THINK.*

IT WAS KNOWLEDGE SHE *DESIRED.*

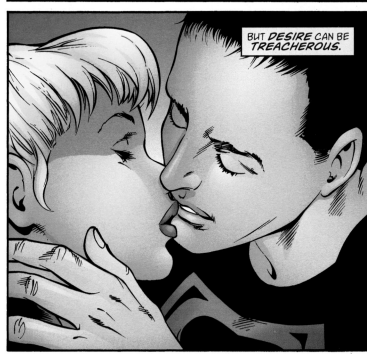

BUT *DESIRE* CAN BE *TREACHEROUS.*

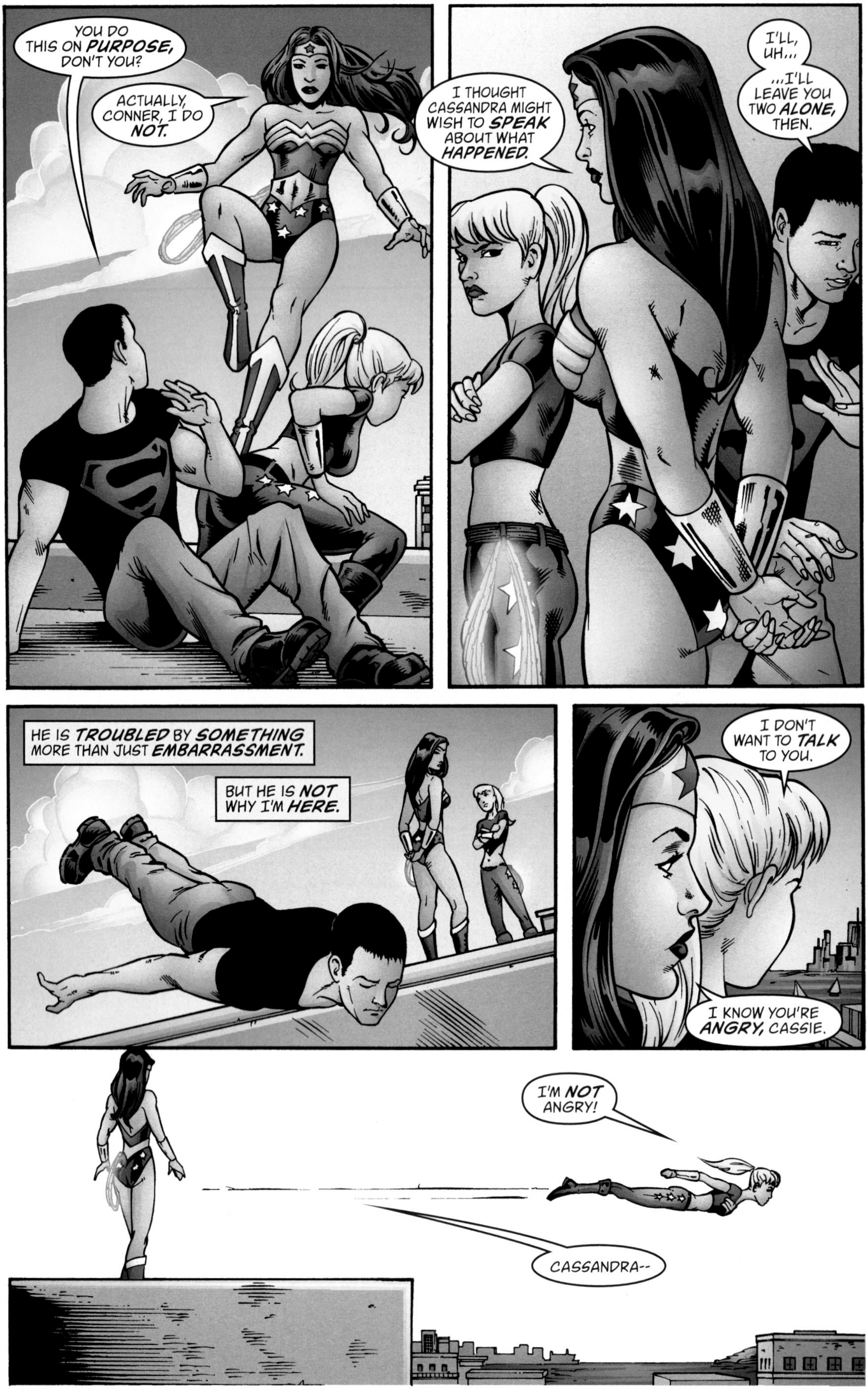

YOU DO THIS ON PURPOSE, DON'T YOU?
ACTUALLY, CONNER, I DO NOT.
I THOUGHT CASSANDRA MIGHT WISH TO SPEAK ABOUT WHAT HAPPENED.
I'LL, UH...
...I'LL LEAVE YOU TWO ALONE, THEN.
HE IS TROUBLED BY SOMETHING MORE THAN JUST EMBARRASSMENT.
BUT HE IS NOT WHY I'M HERE.
I DON'T WANT TO TALK TO YOU.
I KNOW YOU'RE ANGRY, CASSIE.
I'M NOT ANGRY!
CASSANDRA--

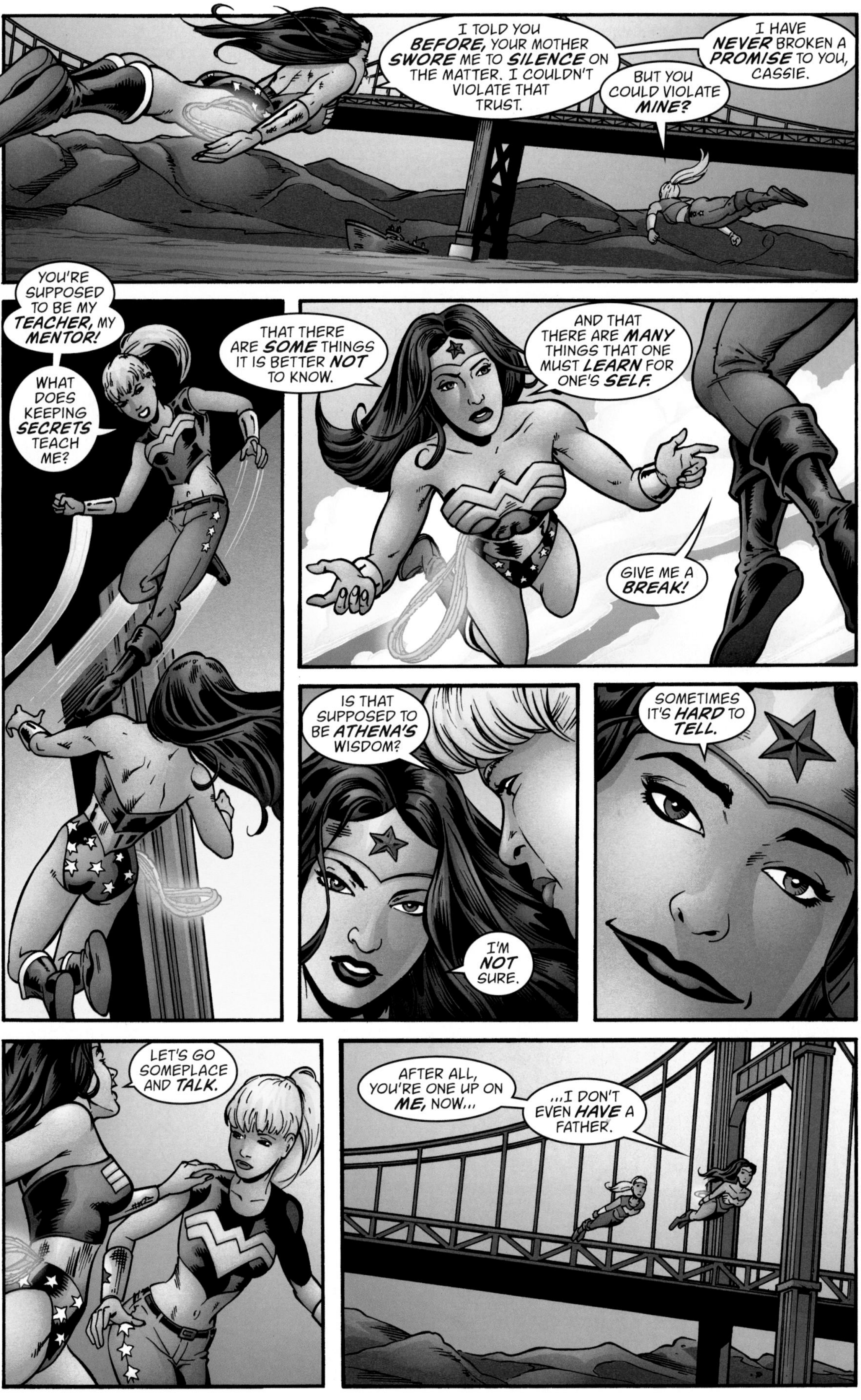
I TOLD YOU BEFORE, YOUR MOTHER SWORE ME TO SILENCE ON THE MATTER. I COULDN'T VIOLATE THAT TRUST.
I HAVE NEVER BROKEN A PROMISE TO YOU, CASSIE.
BUT YOU COULD VIOLATE MINE?
YOU'RE SUPPOSED TO BE MY TEACHER, MY MENTOR!
WHAT DOES KEEPING SECRETS TEACH ME?
THAT THERE ARE SOME THINGS IT IS BETTER NOT TO KNOW.
AND THAT THERE ARE MANY THINGS THAT ONE MUST LEARN FOR ONE'S SELF.
GIVE ME A BREAK!
IS THAT SUPPOSED TO BE ATHENA'S WISDOM?
I'M NOT SURE.
SOMETIMES IT'S HARD TO TELL.
LET'S GO SOMEPLACE AND TALK.
AFTER ALL, YOU'RE ONE UP ON ME, NOW...
...I DON'T EVEN HAVE A FATHER.

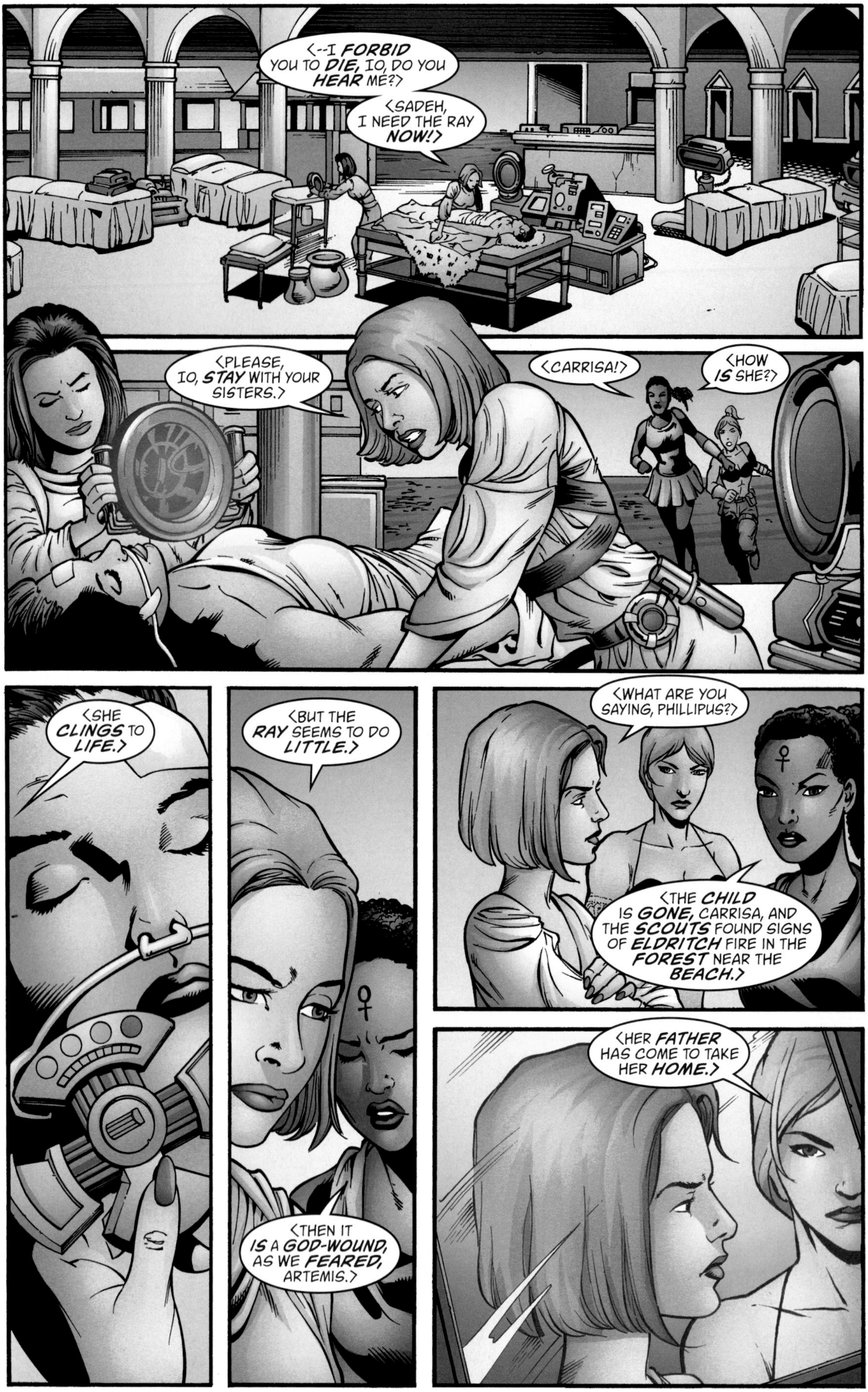
<--I FORBID YOU TO DIE, IO, DO YOU HEAR ME?>
<SADEH, I NEED THE RAY NOW!>
<PLEASE, IO, STAY WITH YOUR SISTERS.>
<CARRISA!>
<HOW IS SHE?>
<SHE CLINGS TO LIFE.>
<BUT THE RAY SEEMS TO DO LITTLE.>
<THEN IT IS A GOD-WOUND, AS WE FEARED, ARTEMIS.>
<WHAT ARE YOU SAYING, PHILLIPUS?>
<THE CHILD IS GONE, CARRISA, AND THE SCOUTS FOUND SIGNS OF ELDRITCH FIRE IN THE FOREST NEAR THE BEACH.>
<HER FATHER HAS COME TO TAKE HER HOME.>

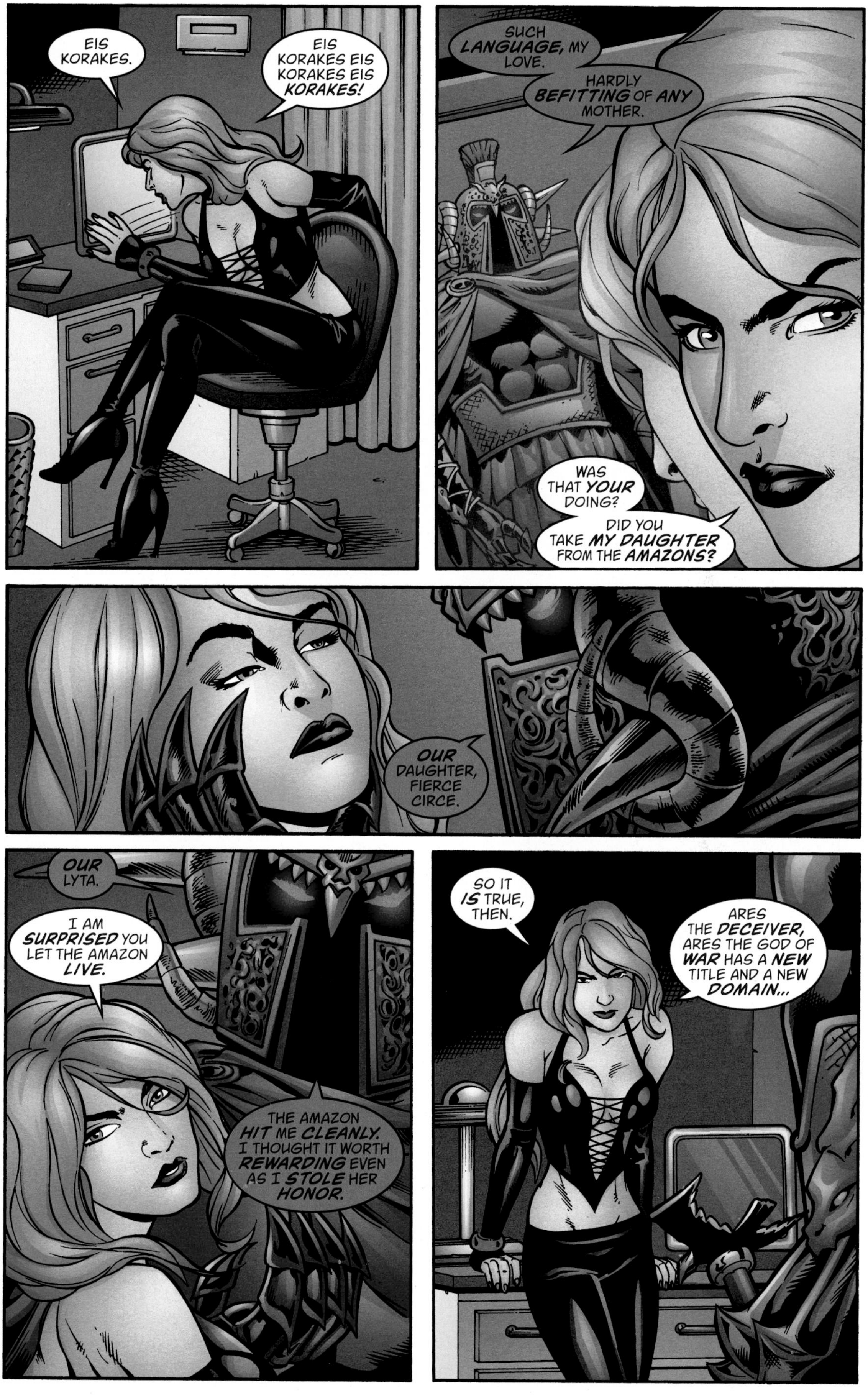
EIS KORAKES.
EIS KORAKES EIS KORAKES EIS KORAKES!
SUCH LANGUAGE, MY LOVE.
HARDLY BEFITTING OF ANY MOTHER.
WAS THAT YOUR DOING?
DID YOU TAKE MY DAUGHTER FROM THE AMAZONS?
OUR DAUGHTER, FIERCE CIRCE.
OUR LYTA.
I AM SURPRISED YOU LET THE AMAZON LIVE.
THE AMAZON HIT ME CLEANLY. I THOUGHT IT WORTH REWARDING EVEN AS I STOLE HER HONOR.
SO IT IS TRUE, THEN.
ARES THE DECEIVER, ARES THE GOD OF WAR HAS A NEW TITLE AND A NEW DOMAIN...

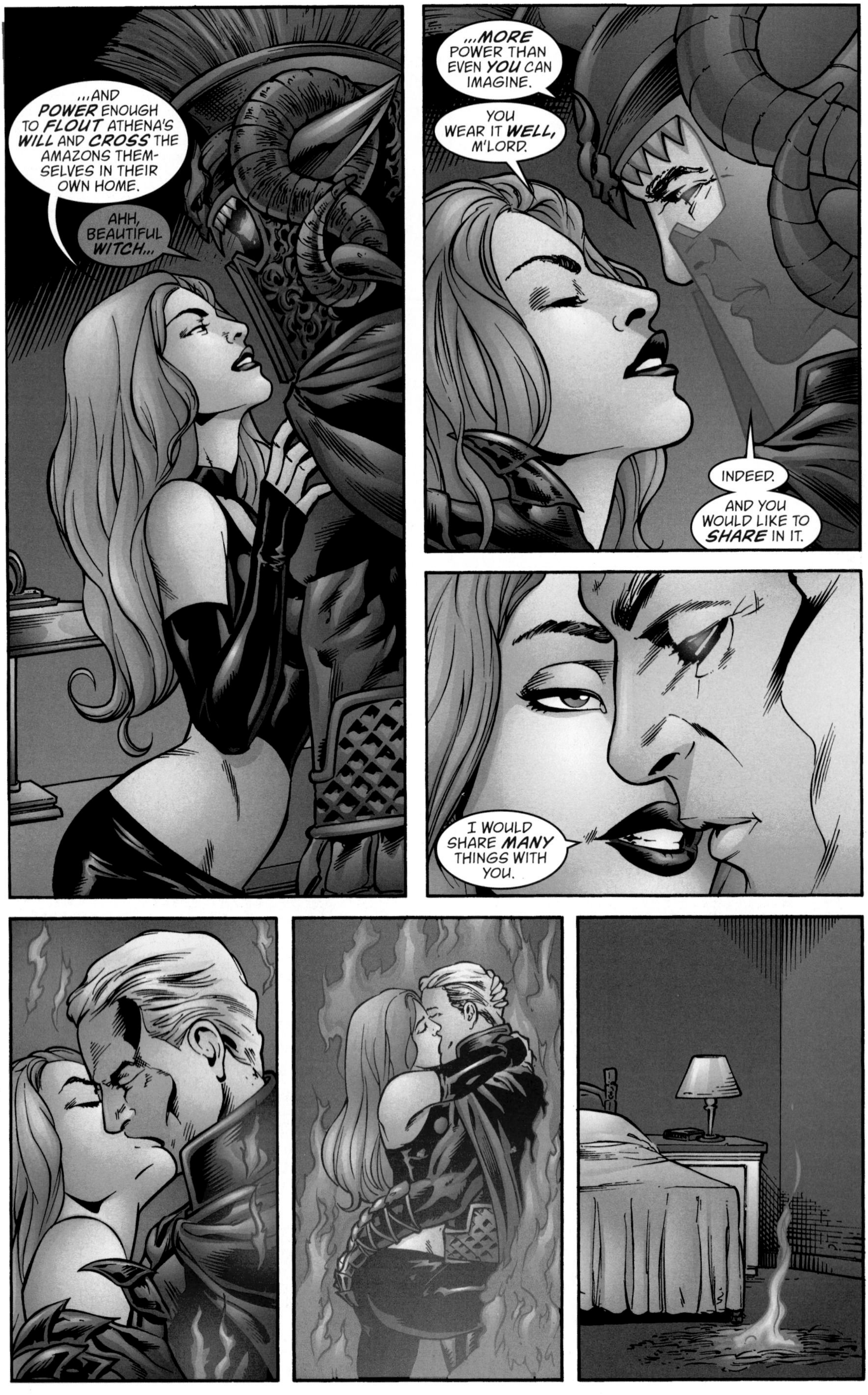
...AND POWER ENOUGH TO FLOUT ATHENA'S WILL AND CROSS THE AMAZONS THEM-SELVES IN THEIR OWN HOME.
AHH, BEAUTIFUL WITCH...
...MORE POWER THAN EVEN YOU CAN IMAGINE.
YOU WEAR IT WELL, M'LORD.
INDEED.
AND YOU WOULD LIKE TO SHARE IN IT.
I WOULD SHARE MANY THINGS WITH YOU.

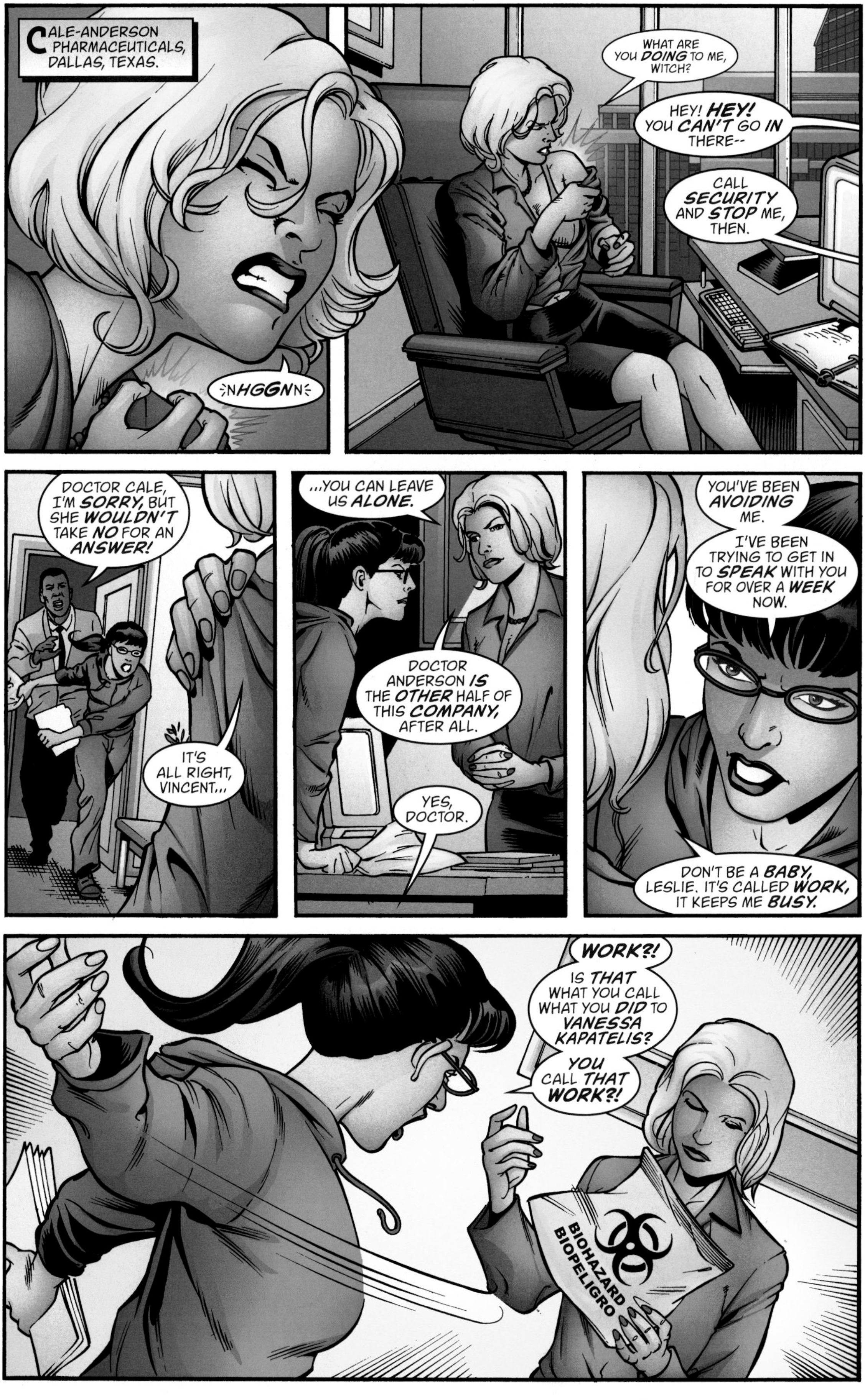
CALE-ANDERSON PHARMACEUTICALS, DALLAS, TEXAS.
NHGGNN
WHAT ARE YOU DOING TO ME, WITCH?
HEY! HEY! YOU CAN'T GO IN THERE--
CALL SECURITY AND STOP ME, THEN.
DOCTOR CALE, I'M SORRY, BUT SHE WOULDN'T TAKE NO FOR AN ANSWER!
IT'S ALL RIGHT, VINCENT...
...YOU CAN LEAVE US ALONE.
DOCTOR ANDERSON IS THE OTHER HALF OF THIS COMPANY, AFTER ALL.
YES, DOCTOR.
YOU'VE BEEN AVOIDING ME.
I'VE BEEN TRYING TO GET IN TO SPEAK WITH YOU FOR OVER A WEEK NOW.
DON'T BE A BABY, LESLIE. IT'S CALLED WORK, IT KEEPS ME BUSY.
WORK?!
IS THAT WHAT YOU CALL WHAT YOU DID TO VANESSA KAPATELIS?
YOU CALL THAT WORK?!
BIOHAZARD
BIOPELIGRO

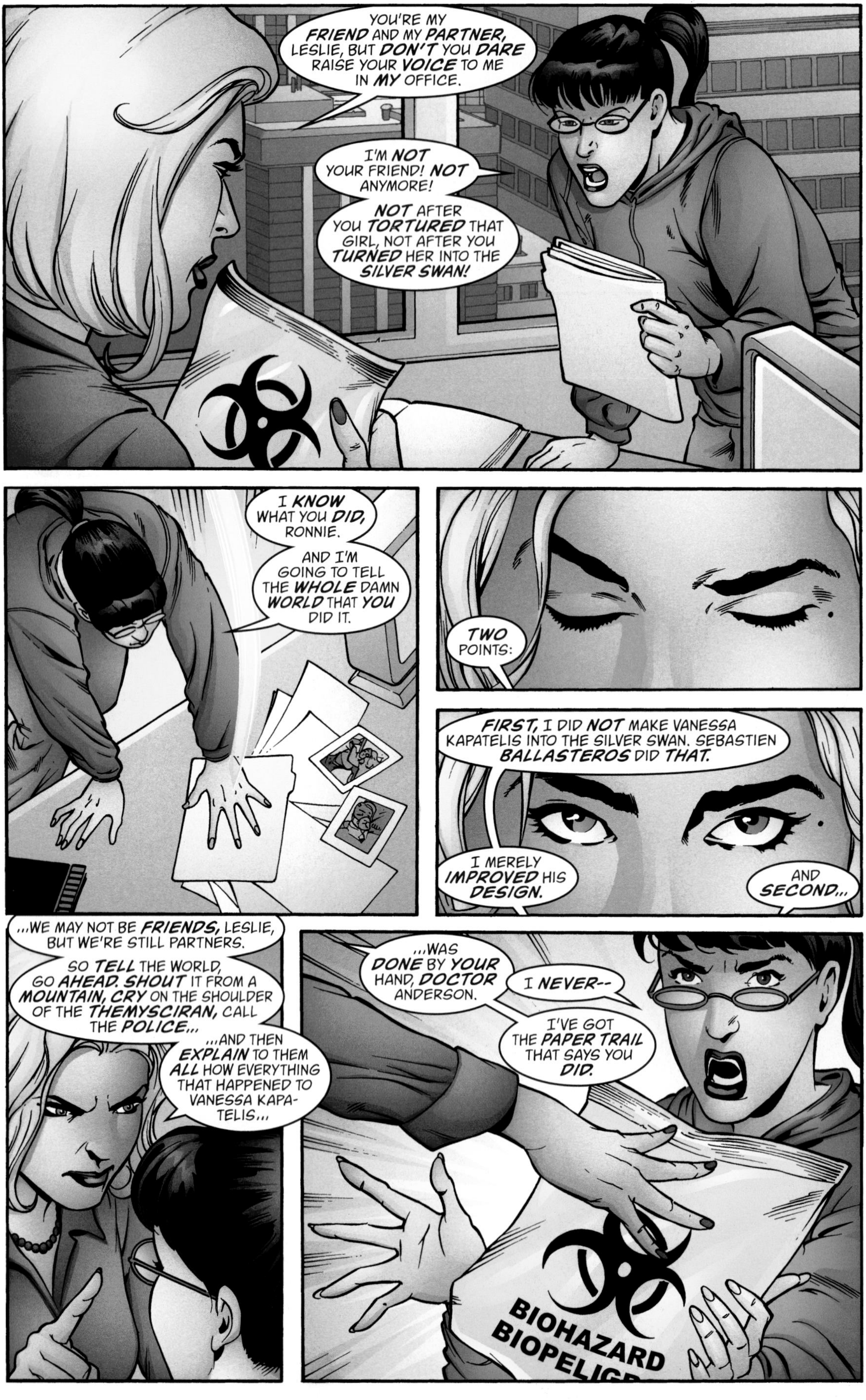
YOU'RE MY FRIEND AND MY PARTNER, LESLIE, BUT DON'T YOU DARE RAISE YOUR VOICE TO ME IN MY OFFICE.
I'M NOT YOUR FRIEND! NOT ANYMORE!
NOT AFTER YOU TORTURED THAT GIRL, NOT AFTER YOU TURNED HER INTO THE SILVER SWAN!
I KNOW WHAT YOU DID, RONNIE.
AND I'M GOING TO TELL THE WHOLE DAMN WORLD THAT YOU DID IT.
TWO POINTS:
FIRST, I DID NOT MAKE VANESSA KAPATELIS INTO THE SILVER SWAN. SEBASTIEN BALLASTEROS DID THAT.
I MERELY IMPROVED HIS DESIGN.
AND SECOND...
...WE MAY NOT BE FRIENDS, LESLIE, BUT WE'RE STILL PARTNERS.
SO TELL THE WORLD, GO AHEAD. SHOUT IT FROM A MOUNTAIN, CRY ON THE SHOULDER OF THE THEMYSCIRAN, CALL THE POLICE...
...AND THEN EXPLAIN TO THEM ALL HOW EVERYTHING THAT HAPPENED TO VANESSA KAPATELIS...
...WAS DONE BY YOUR HAND, DOCTOR ANDERSON.
I NEVER--
I'VE GOT THE PAPER TRAIL THAT SAYS YOU DID.
BIOHAZARD
BIOPELIGR

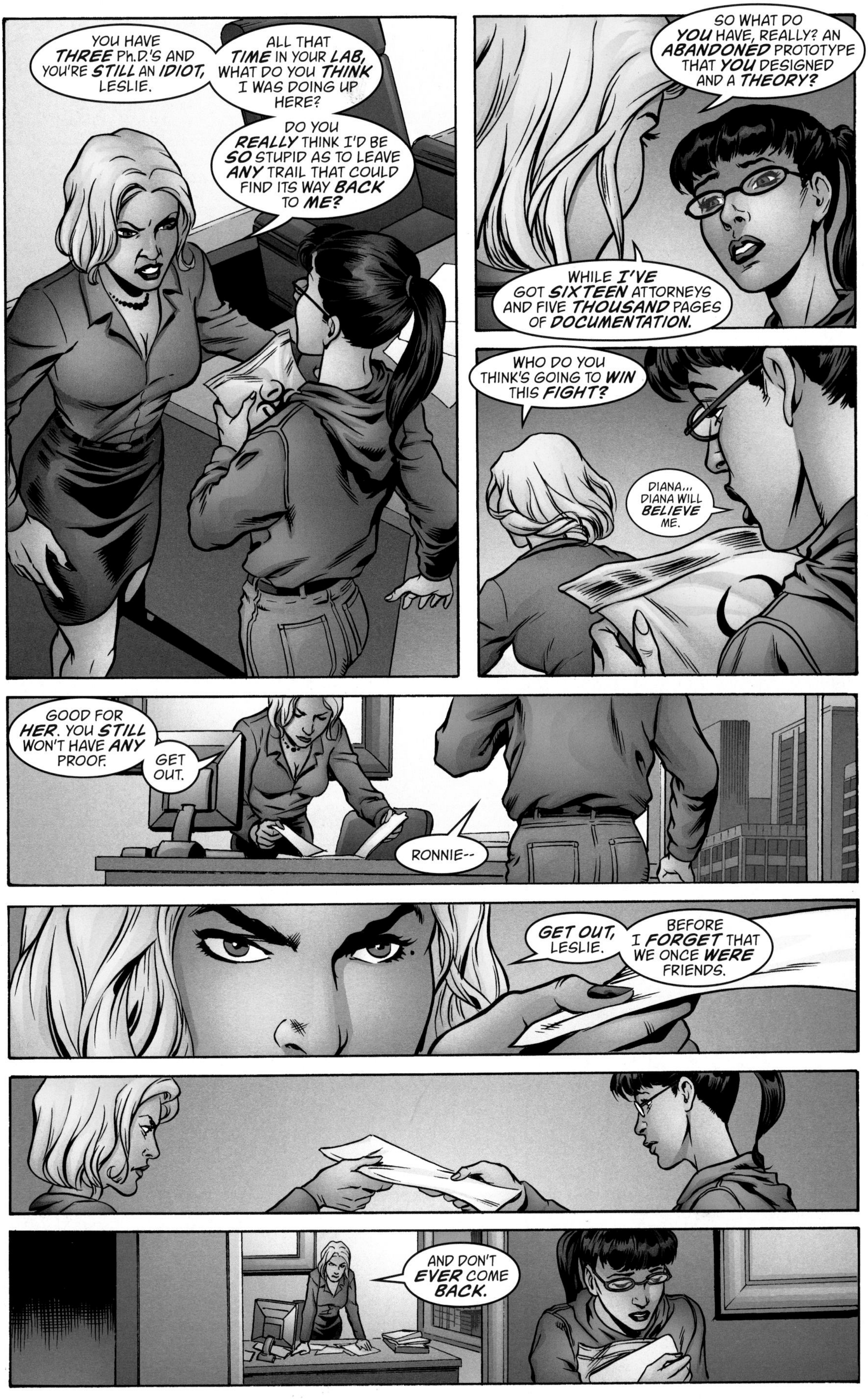
YOU HAVE THREE Ph.D.'S AND YOU'RE STILL AN IDIOT, LESLIE.
ALL THAT TIME IN YOUR LAB, WHAT DO YOU THINK I WAS DOING UP HERE?
DO YOU REALLY THINK I'D BE SO STUPID AS TO LEAVE ANY TRAIL THAT COULD FIND ITS WAY BACK TO ME?
SO WHAT DO YOU HAVE, REALLY? AN ABANDONED PROTOTYPE THAT YOU DESIGNED AND A THEORY?
WHILE I'VE GOT SIXTEEN ATTORNEYS AND FIVE THOUSAND PAGES OF DOCUMENTATION.
WHO DO YOU THINK'S GOING TO WIN THIS FIGHT?
DIANA... DIANA WILL BELIEVE ME.
GOOD FOR HER. YOU STILL WON'T HAVE ANY PROOF.
GET OUT.
RONNIE--
GET OUT, LESLIE.
BEFORE I FORGET THAT WE ONCE WERE FRIENDS.
AND DON'T EVER COME BACK.

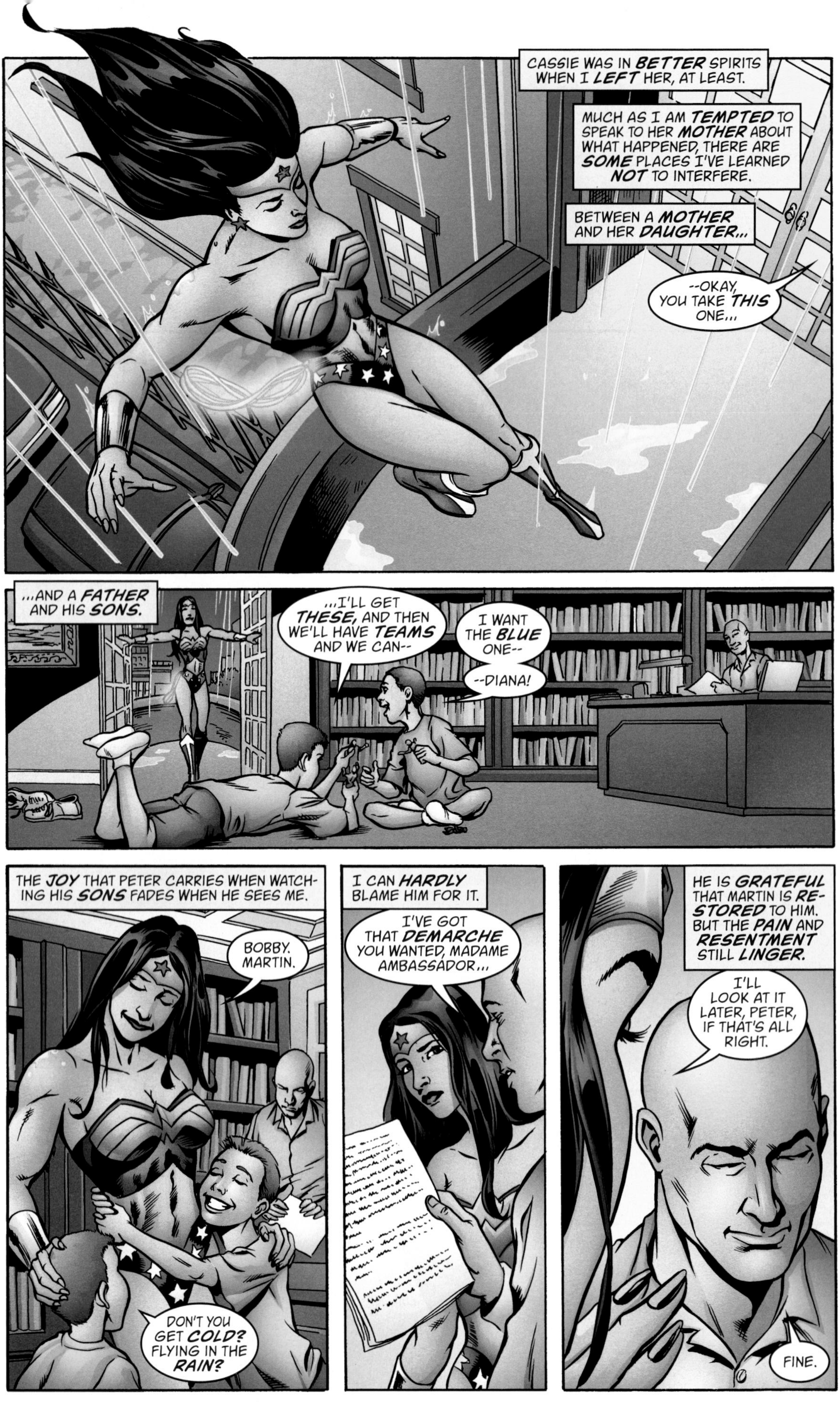
CASSIE WAS IN BETTER SPIRITS WHEN I LEFT HER, AT LEAST.
MUCH AS I AM TEMPTED TO SPEAK TO HER MOTHER ABOUT WHAT HAPPENED, THERE ARE SOME PLACES I'VE LEARNED NOT TO INTERFERE.
BETWEEN A MOTHER AND HER DAUGHTER...
--OKAY, YOU TAKE THIS ONE...
...AND A FATHER AND HIS SONS.
...I'LL GET THESE, AND THEN WE'LL HAVE TEAMS AND WE CAN--
I WANT THE BLUE ONE--
--DIANA!
THE JOY THAT PETER CARRIES WHEN WATCHING HIS SONS FADES WHEN HE SEES ME.
BOBBY. MARTIN.
DON'T YOU GET COLD? FLYING IN THE RAIN?
I CAN HARDLY BLAME HIM FOR IT.
I'VE GOT THAT DEMARCHE YOU WANTED, MADAME AMBASSADOR...
HE IS GRATEFUL THAT MARTIN IS RESTORED TO HIM. BUT THE PAIN AND RESENTMENT STILL LINGER.
I'LL LOOK AT IT LATER, PETER, IF THAT'S ALL RIGHT.
FINE.

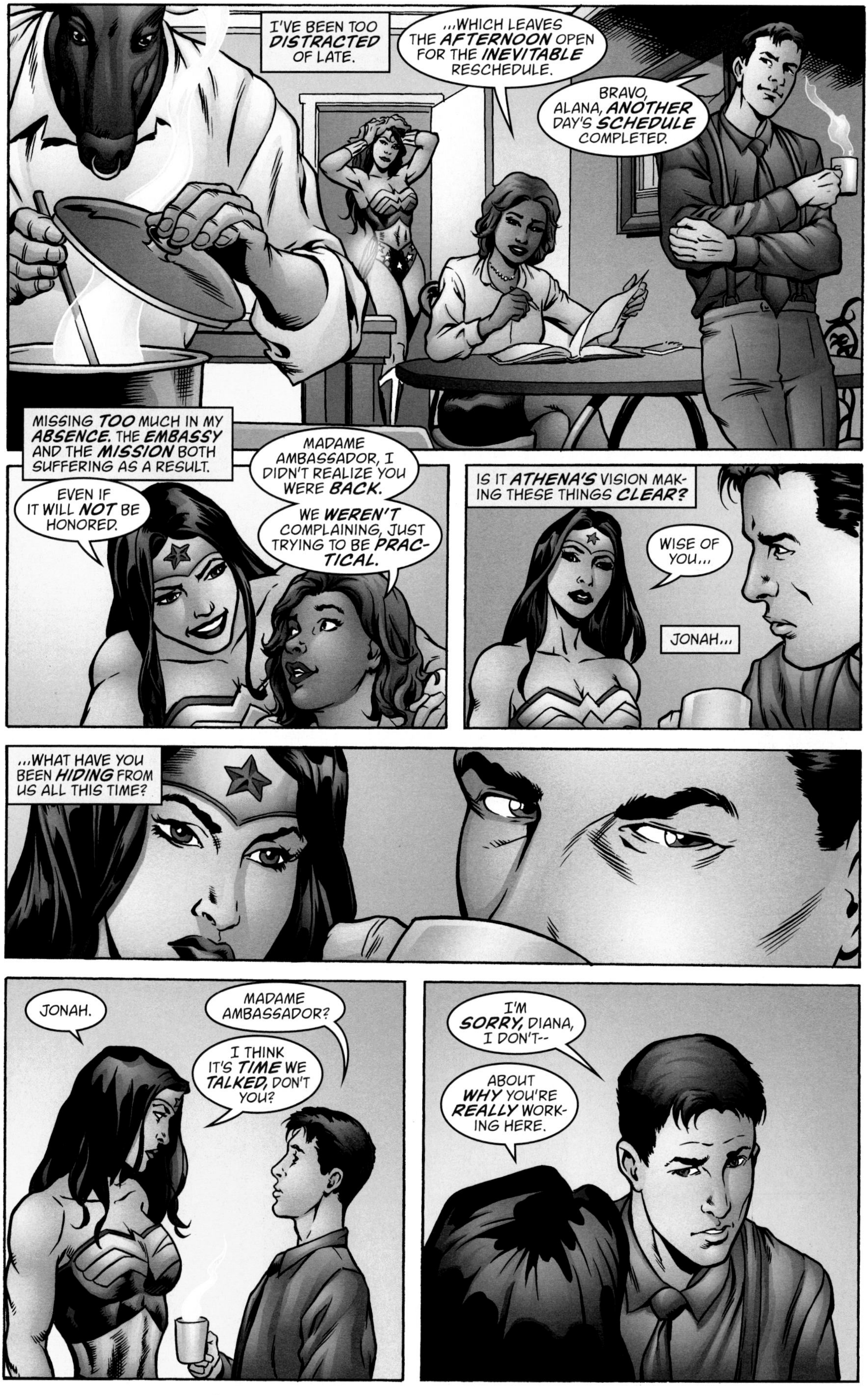
I'VE BEEN TOO DISTRACTED OF LATE.
...WHICH LEAVES THE AFTERNOON OPEN FOR THE INEVITABLE RESCHEDULE.
BRAVO, ALANA, ANOTHER DAY'S SCHEDULE COMPLETED.
MISSING TOO MUCH IN MY ABSENCE. THE EMBASSY AND THE MISSION BOTH SUFFERING AS A RESULT.
EVEN IF IT WILL NOT BE HONORED.
MADAME AMBASSADOR, I DIDN'T REALIZE YOU WERE BACK.
WE WEREN'T COMPLAINING, JUST TRYING TO BE PRACTICAL.
IS IT ATHENA'S VISION MAKING THESE THINGS CLEAR?
WISE OF YOU...
JONAH...
...WHAT HAVE YOU BEEN HIDING FROM US ALL THIS TIME?
JONAH.
MADAME AMBASSADOR?
I THINK IT'S TIME WE TALKED, DON'T YOU?
I'M SORRY, DIANA, I DON'T--
ABOUT WHY YOU'RE REALLY WORKING HERE.

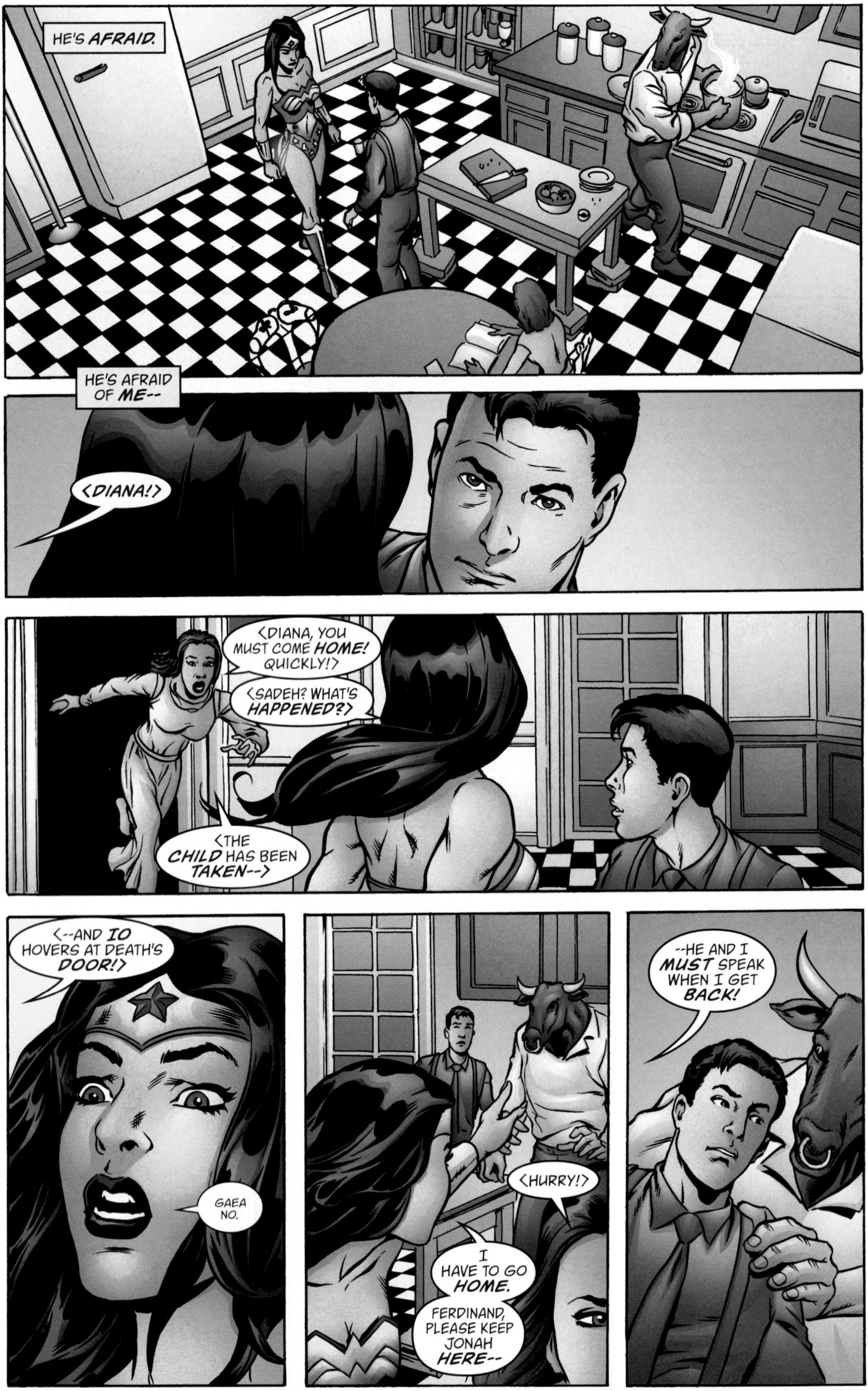

HE'S AFRAID.
HE'S AFRAID OF ME--
<DIANA!>
<DIANA, YOU MUST COME HOME! QUICKLY!>
<SADEH? WHAT'S HAPPENED?>
<THE CHILD HAS BEEN TAKEN-->
<--AND IO HOVERS AT DEATH'S DOOR!>
GAEA NO.
<HURRY!>
I HAVE TO GO HOME.
FERDINAND, PLEASE KEEP JONAH HERE--
--HE AND I MUST SPEAK WHEN I GET BACK!

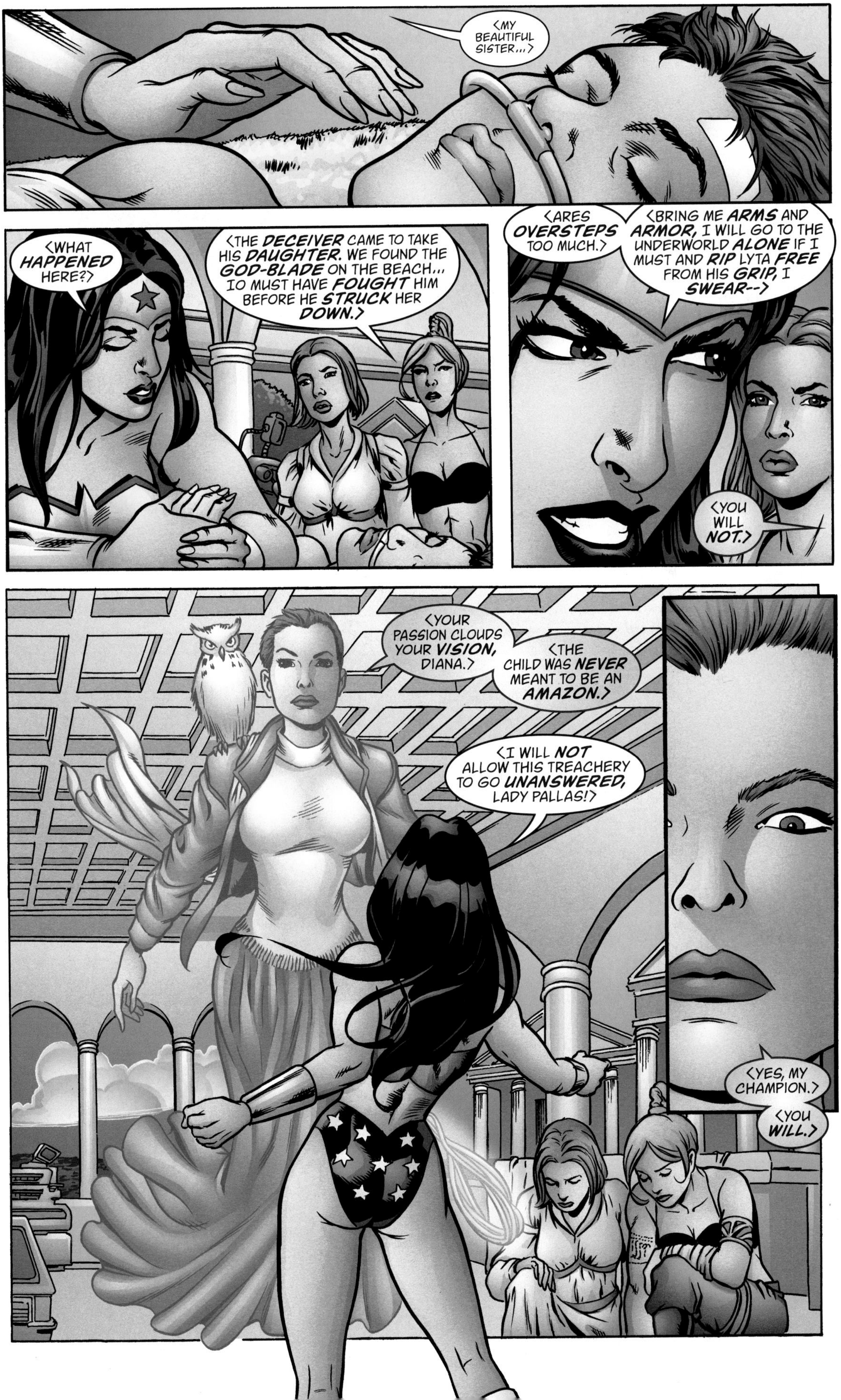
<MY BEAUTIFUL SISTER...>
<WHAT HAPPENED HERE?>
<THE DECEIVER CAME TO TAKE HIS DAUGHTER. WE FOUND THE GOD-BLADE ON THE BEACH... IO MUST HAVE FOUGHT HIM BEFORE HE STRUCK HER DOWN.>
<ARES OVERSTEPS TOO MUCH.>
<BRING ME ARMS AND ARMOR, I WILL GO TO THE UNDERWORLD ALONE IF I MUST AND RIP LYTA FREE FROM HIS GRIP, I SWEAR-->
<YOU WILL NOT.>
<YOUR PASSION CLOUDS YOUR VISION, DIANA.>
<THE CHILD WAS NEVER MEANT TO BE AN AMAZON.>
<I WILL NOT ALLOW THIS TREACHERY TO GO UNANSWERED, LADY PALLAS!>
<YES, MY CHAMPION.>
<YOU WILL.>

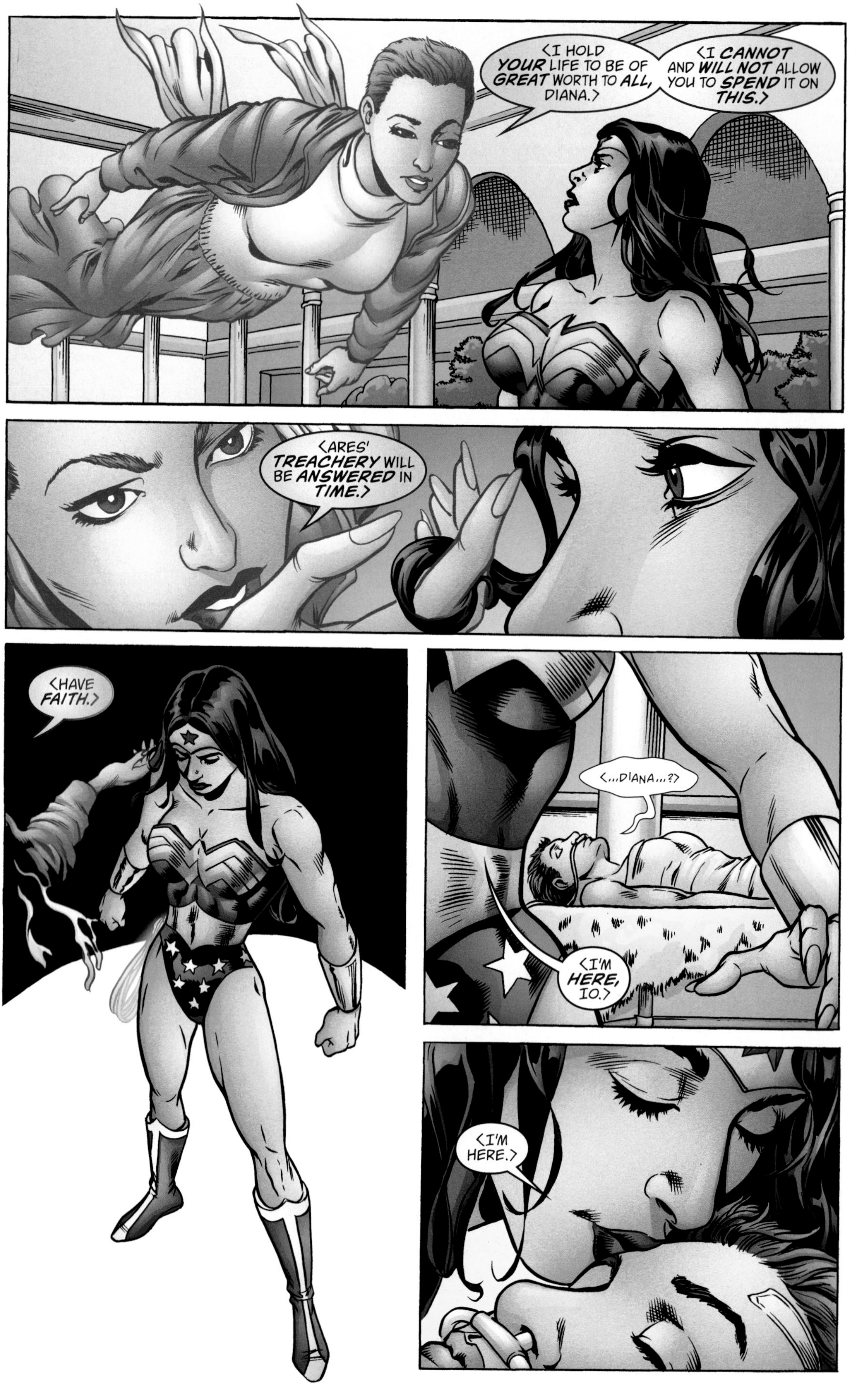
<I HOLD YOUR LIFE TO BE OF GREAT WORTH TO ALL, DIANA.>
<I CANNOT AND WILL NOT ALLOW YOU TO SPEND IT ON THIS.>
<ARES' TREACHERY WILL BE ANSWERED IN TIME.>
<HAVE FAITH.>
<...DIANA...?>
<I'M HERE, IO.>
<I'M HERE.>

YOU *HUNGRY?*

ARE YOU *KIDDING* ME?

HEY, EVERYBODY'S GONE *HOME,* IT'S JUST YOU AND ME, HERE.

DIANA SAID TO *KEEP* YOU *HERE,* SHE DIDN'T SAY TO *STARVE* YOU--

--WHERE DO YOU THINK YOU'RE *GOING?*

I'M *LEAVING.*

NO, YOU'RE NOT.

YES, I *AM.*

SON, *DON'T* MAKE ME *STOP* YOU.

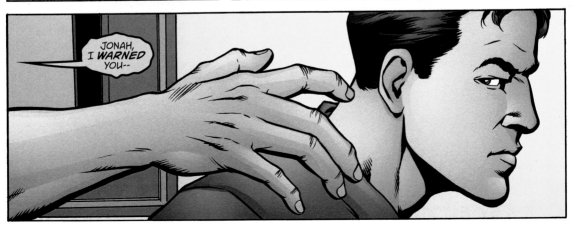

JONAH, I *WARNED* YOU--

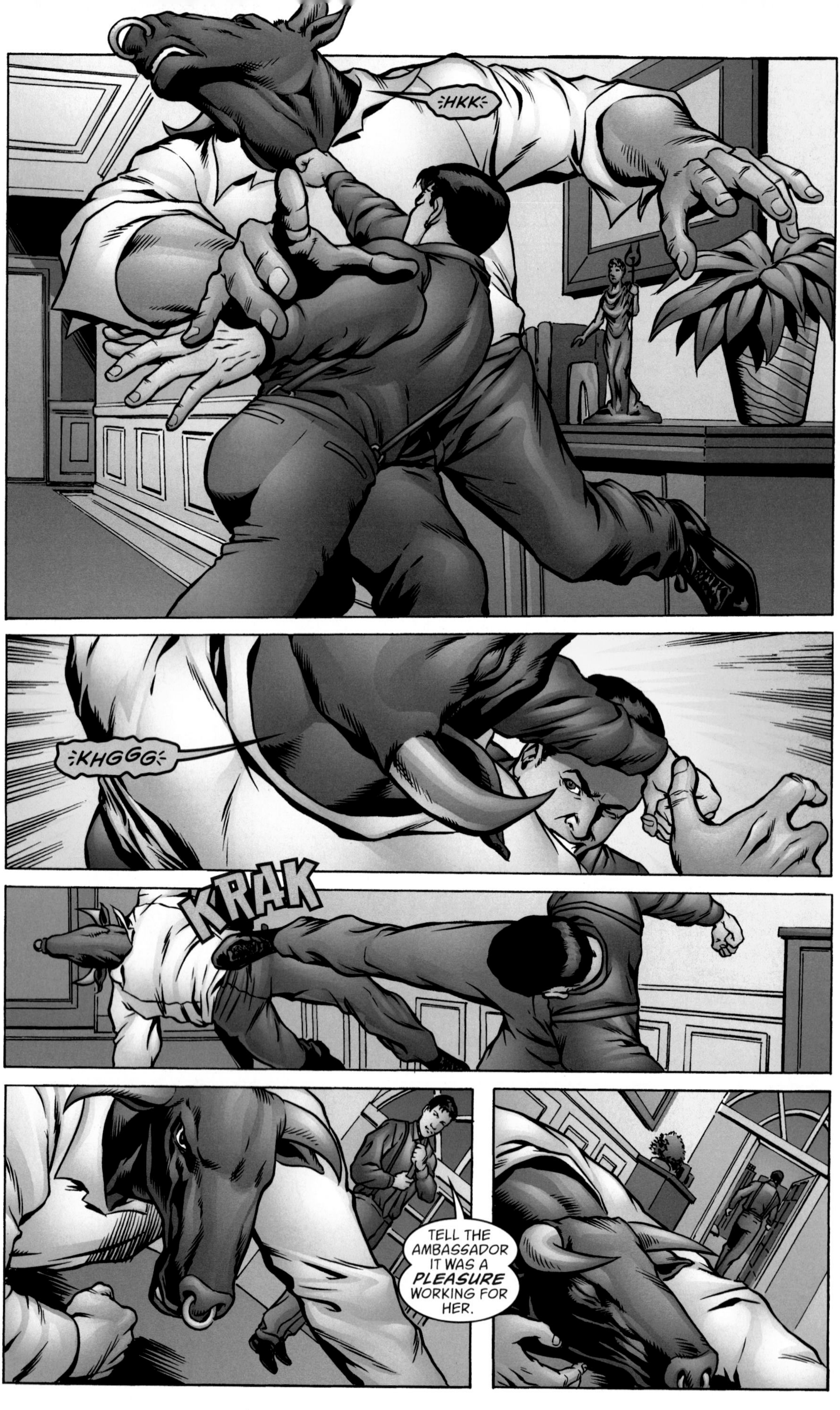
HKK
KHGGG
KRAK
TELL THE AMBASSADOR IT WAS A PLEASURE WORKING FOR HER.

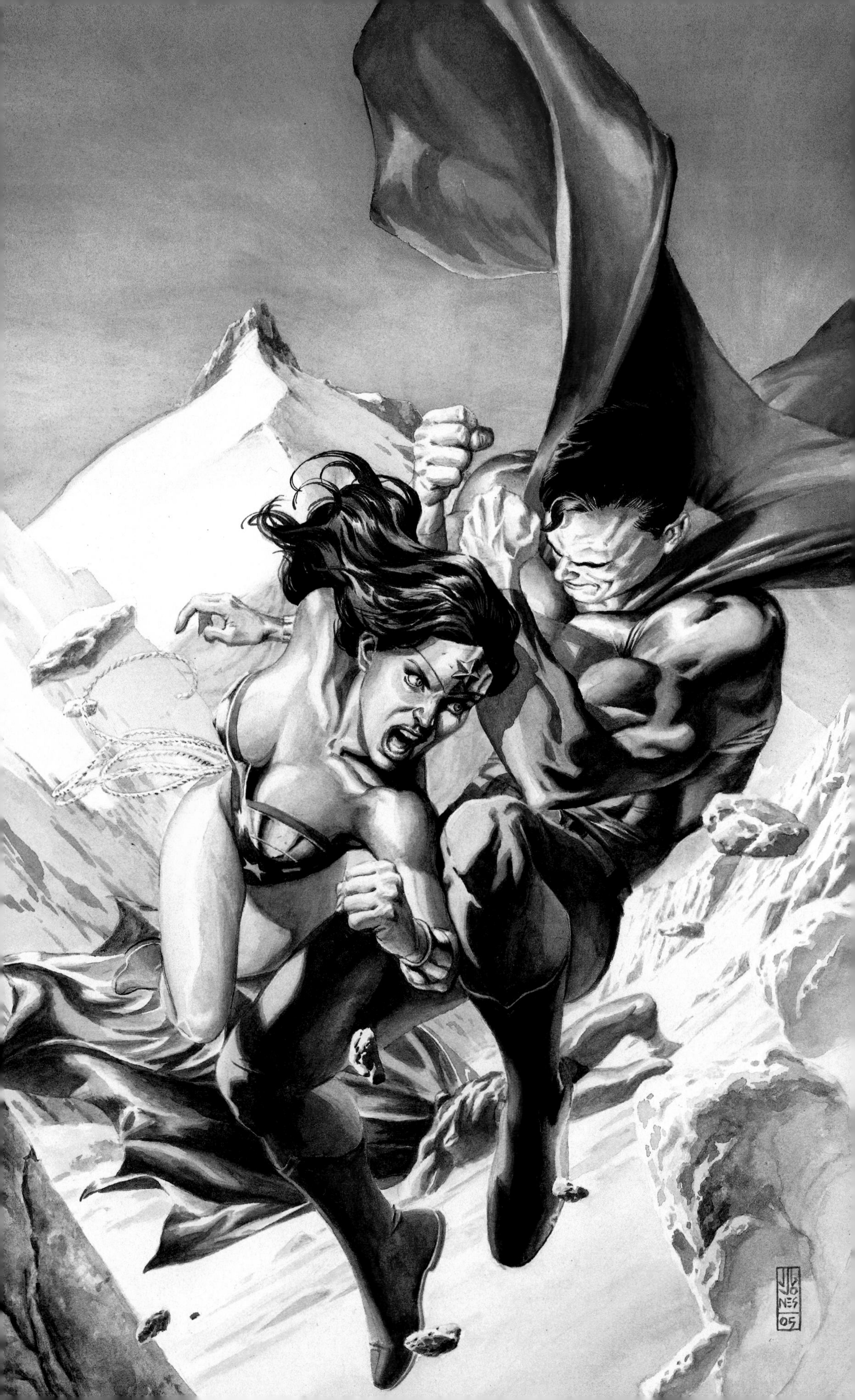
JG JONES
05

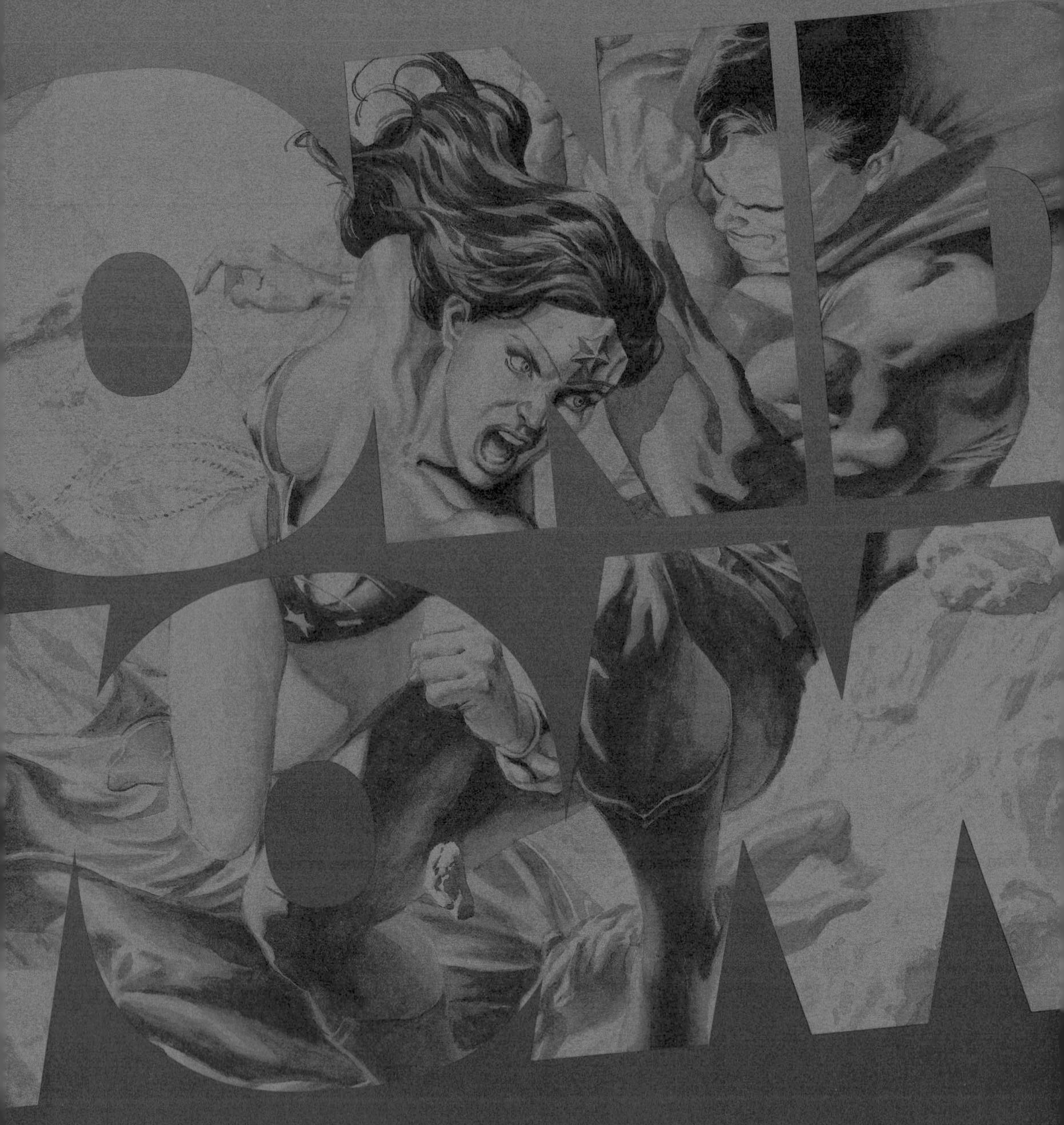

"SACRIFICE: PART 4"

Greg Rucka – *writer*
Rags Morales, David Lopez, Tom Derenick, Georges Jeanty and **Karl Kerschl** – *pencils*
Mark Propst, Bit, Dexter Vines, Bob Petrecca and **Nelson** – *inks*
Richard and **Tanya Horie** – *colors*
Todd Klein – *letters*
J.G. Jones – *cover*

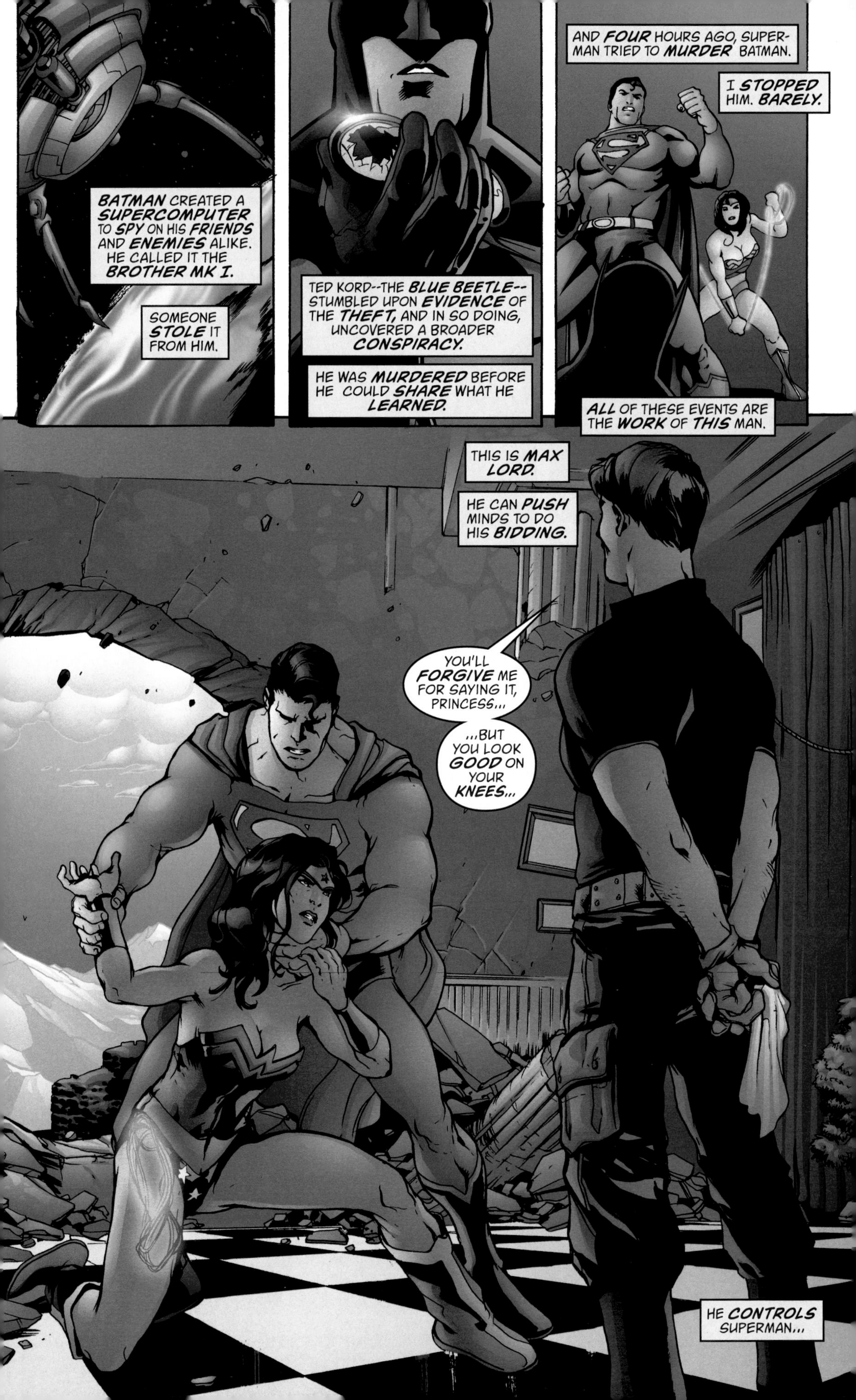
BATMAN CREATED A SUPERCOMPUTER TO SPY ON HIS FRIENDS AND ENEMIES ALIKE. HE CALLED IT THE BROTHER MK I.
SOMEONE STOLE IT FROM HIM.
TED KORD--THE BLUE BEETLE--STUMBLED UPON EVIDENCE OF THE THEFT, AND IN SO DOING, UNCOVERED A BROADER CONSPIRACY.
HE WAS MURDERED BEFORE HE COULD SHARE WHAT HE LEARNED.
AND FOUR HOURS AGO, SUPER-MAN TRIED TO MURDER BATMAN.
I STOPPED HIM. BARELY.
ALL OF THESE EVENTS ARE THE WORK OF THIS MAN.
THIS IS MAX LORD.
HE CAN PUSH MINDS TO DO HIS BIDDING.
YOU'LL FORGIVE ME FOR SAYING IT, PRINCESS...
...BUT YOU LOOK GOOD ON YOUR KNEES...
HE CONTROLS SUPERMAN...

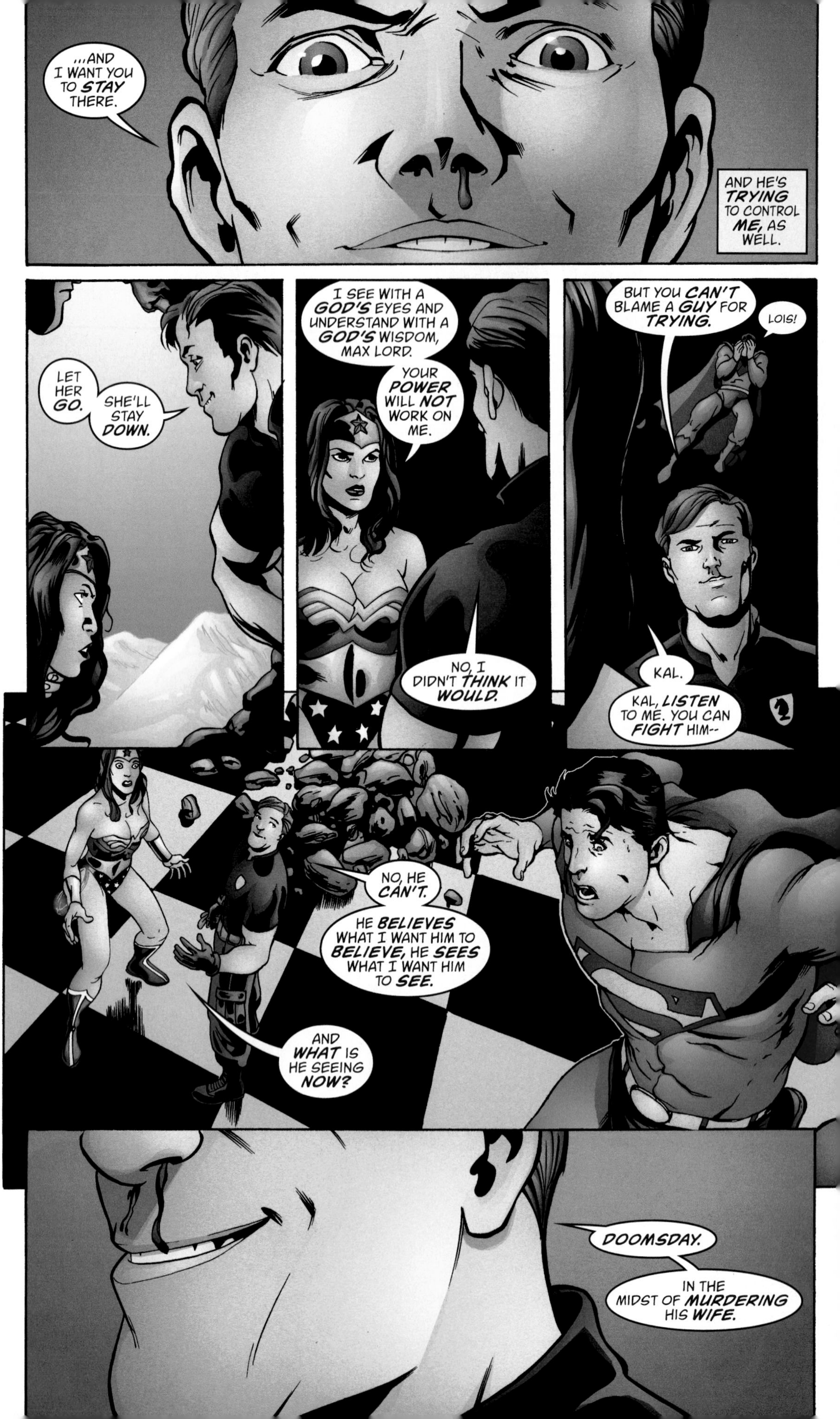
...AND I WANT YOU TO STAY THERE.
AND HE'S TRYING TO CONTROL ME, AS WELL.
LET HER GO.
SHE'LL STAY DOWN.
I SEE WITH A GOD'S EYES AND UNDERSTAND WITH A GOD'S WISDOM, MAX LORD.
YOUR POWER WILL NOT WORK ON ME.
NO, I DIDN'T THINK IT WOULD.
BUT YOU CAN'T BLAME A GUY FOR TRYING.
LOIS!
KAL.
KAL, LISTEN TO ME. YOU CAN FIGHT HIM--
NO, HE CAN'T.
HE BELIEVES WHAT I WANT HIM TO BELIEVE, HE SEES WHAT I WANT HIM TO SEE.
AND WHAT IS HE SEEING NOW?
DOOMSDAY.
IN THE MIDST OF MURDERING HIS WIFE.

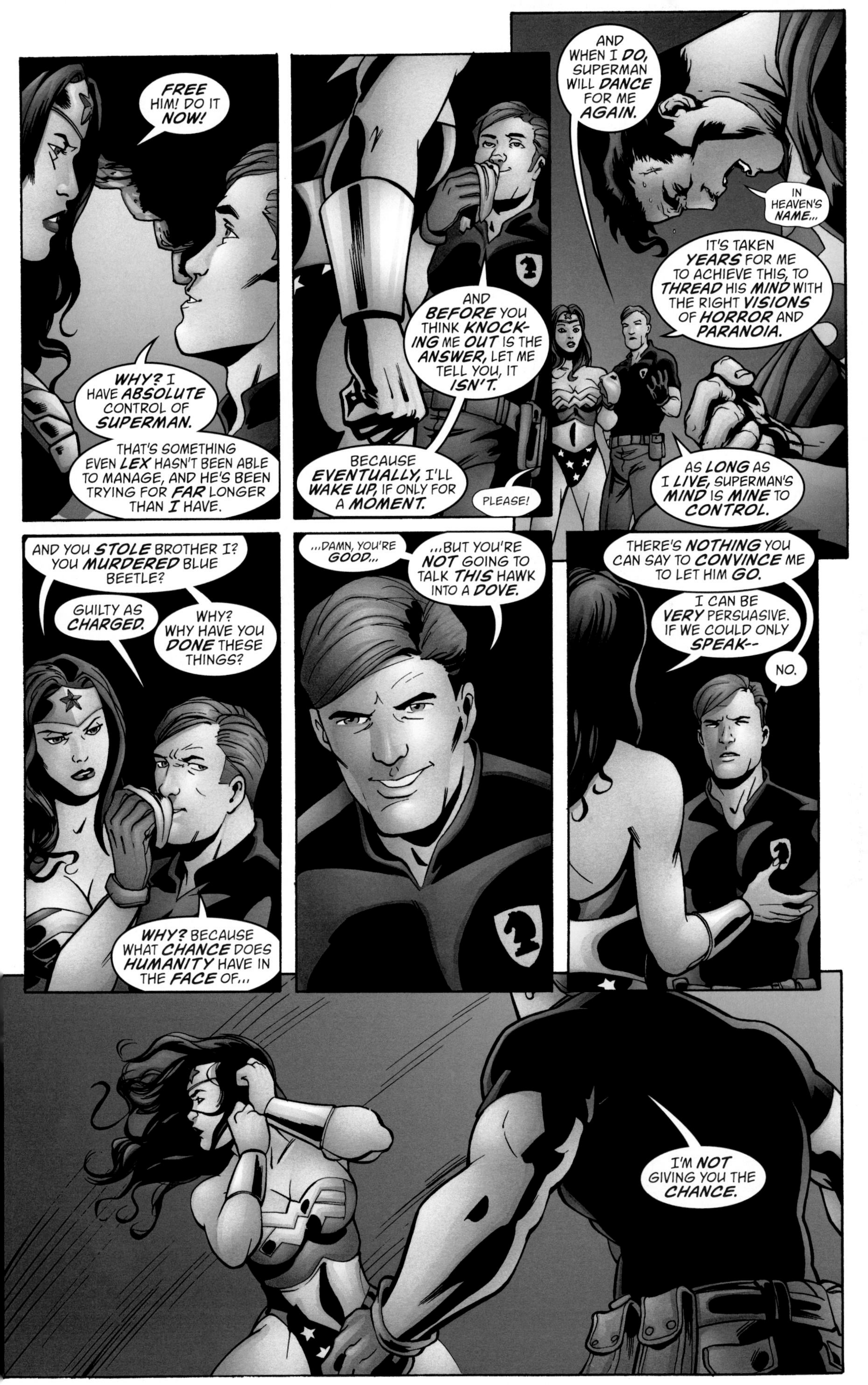
FREE HIM! DO IT NOW!
WHY? I HAVE ABSOLUTE CONTROL OF SUPERMAN.
THAT'S SOMETHING EVEN LEX HASN'T BEEN ABLE TO MANAGE, AND HE'S BEEN TRYING FOR FAR LONGER THAN I HAVE.
AND BEFORE YOU THINK KNOCKING ME OUT IS THE ANSWER, LET ME TELL YOU, IT ISN'T.
BECAUSE EVENTUALLY, I'LL WAKE UP, IF ONLY FOR A MOMENT.
PLEASE!
AND WHEN I DO, SUPERMAN WILL DANCE FOR ME AGAIN.
IN HEAVEN'S NAME...
IT'S TAKEN YEARS FOR ME TO ACHIEVE THIS, TO THREAD HIS MIND WITH THE RIGHT VISIONS OF HORROR AND PARANOIA.
AS LONG AS I LIVE, SUPERMAN'S MIND IS MINE TO CONTROL.
AND YOU STOLE BROTHER I? YOU MURDERED BLUE BEETLE?
GUILTY AS CHARGED.
WHY? WHY HAVE YOU DONE THESE THINGS?
WHY? BECAUSE WHAT CHANCE DOES HUMANITY HAVE IN THE FACE OF...
...DAMN, YOU'RE GOOD...
...BUT YOU'RE NOT GOING TO TALK THIS HAWK INTO A DOVE.
THERE'S NOTHING YOU CAN SAY TO CONVINCE ME TO LET HIM GO.
I CAN BE VERY PERSUASIVE. IF WE COULD ONLY SPEAK--
NO.
I'M NOT GIVING YOU THE CHANCE.

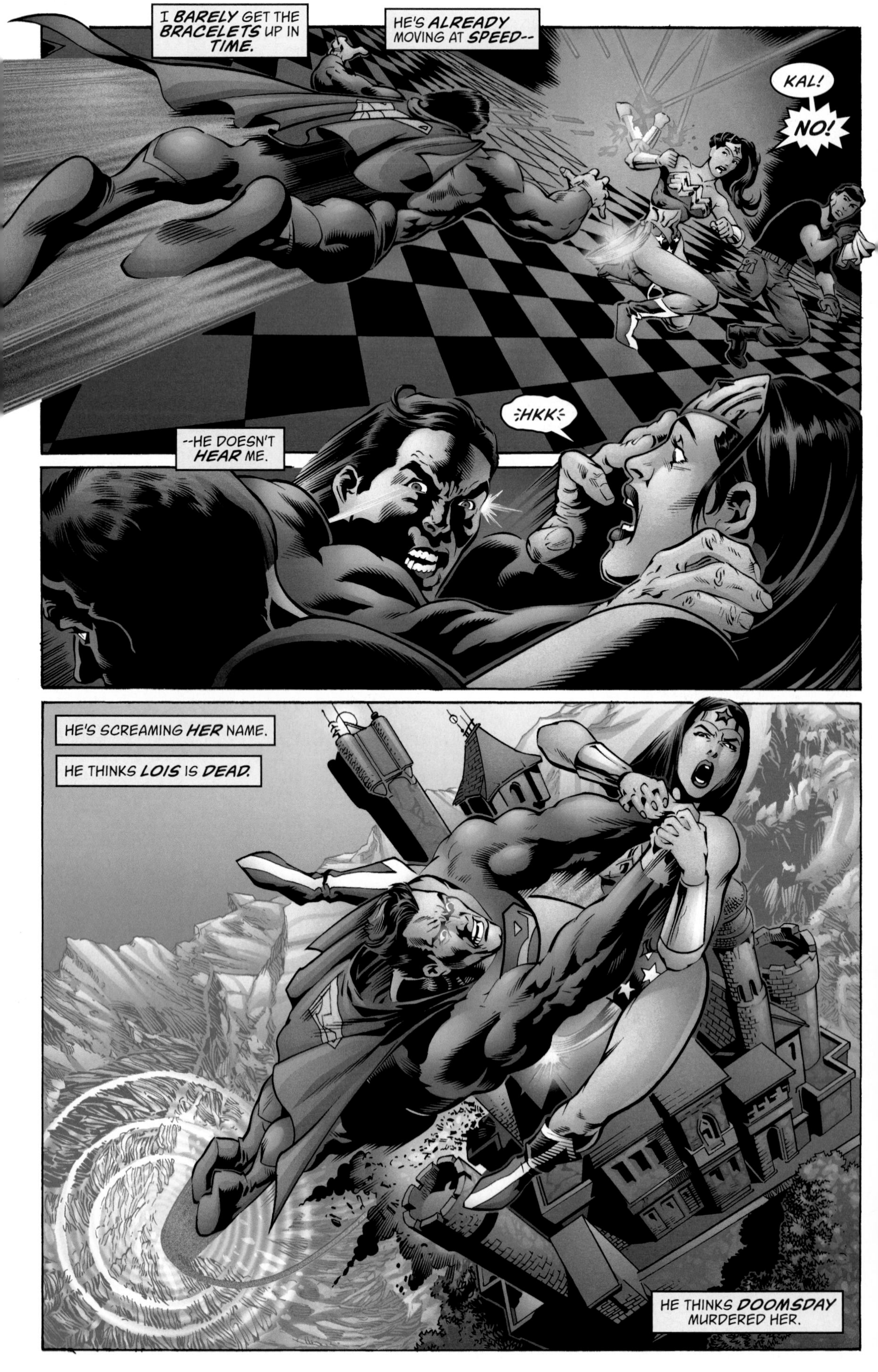
I BARELY GET THE BRACELETS UP IN TIME.
HE'S ALREADY MOVING AT SPEED--
KAL!
NO!
--HE DOESN'T HEAR ME.
HKK
HE'S SCREAMING HER NAME.
HE THINKS LOIS IS DEAD.
HE THINKS DOOMSDAY MURDERED HER.

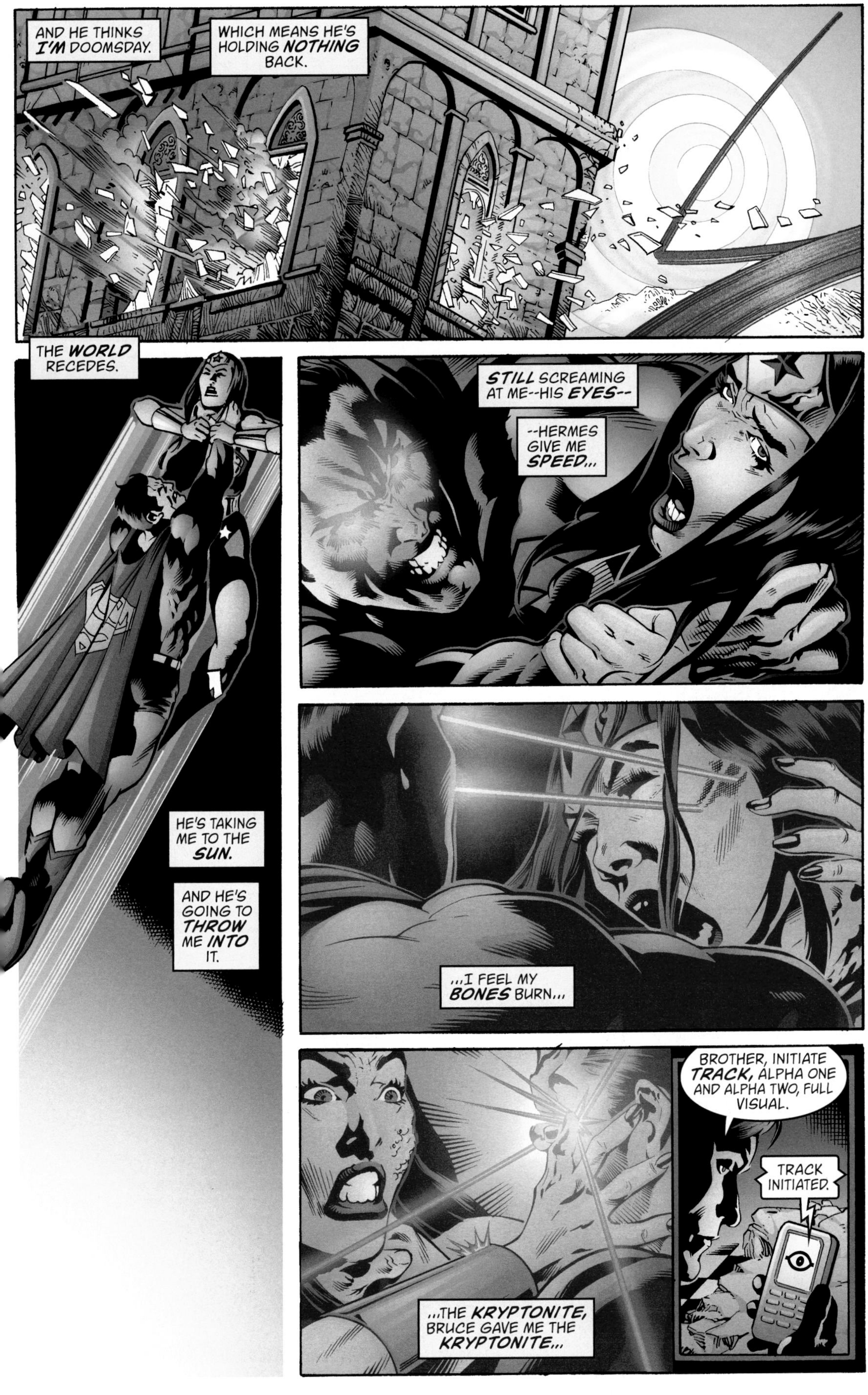
AND HE THINKS I'M DOOMSDAY.
WHICH MEANS HE'S HOLDING NOTHING BACK.
THE WORLD RECEDES.
HE'S TAKING ME TO THE SUN.
AND HE'S GOING TO THROW ME INTO IT.
STILL SCREAMING AT ME--HIS EYES--
--HERMES GIVE ME SPEED...
...I FEEL MY BONES BURN...
...THE KRYPTONITE, BRUCE GAVE ME THE KRYPTONITE...
BROTHER, INITIATE TRACK, ALPHA ONE AND ALPHA TWO, FULL VISUAL.
TRACK INITIATED.

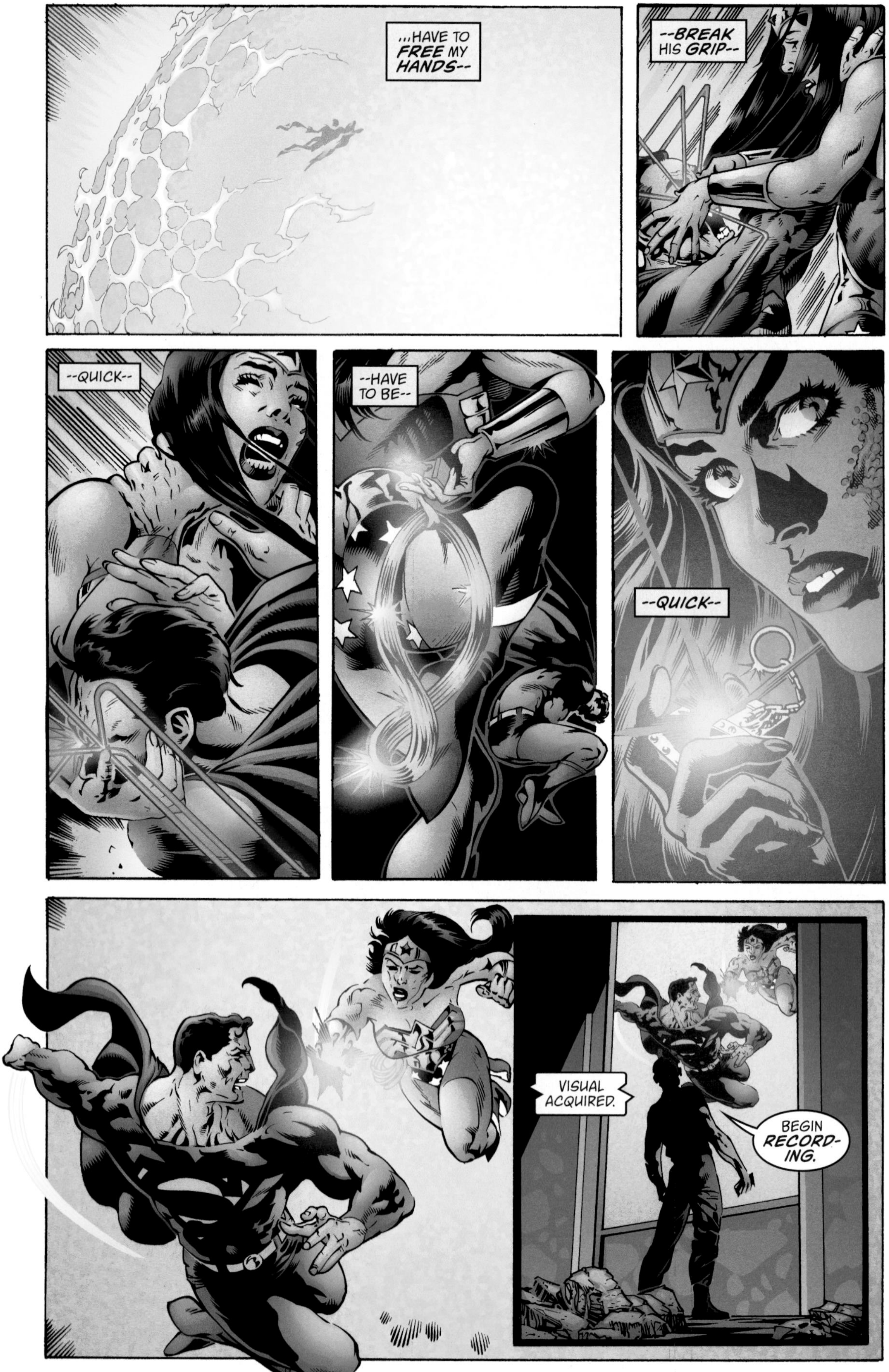
...HAVE TO FREE MY HANDS--
--BREAK HIS GRIP--
--QUICK--
--HAVE TO BE--
--QUICK--
VISUAL ACQUIRED.
BEGIN RECORD-ING.

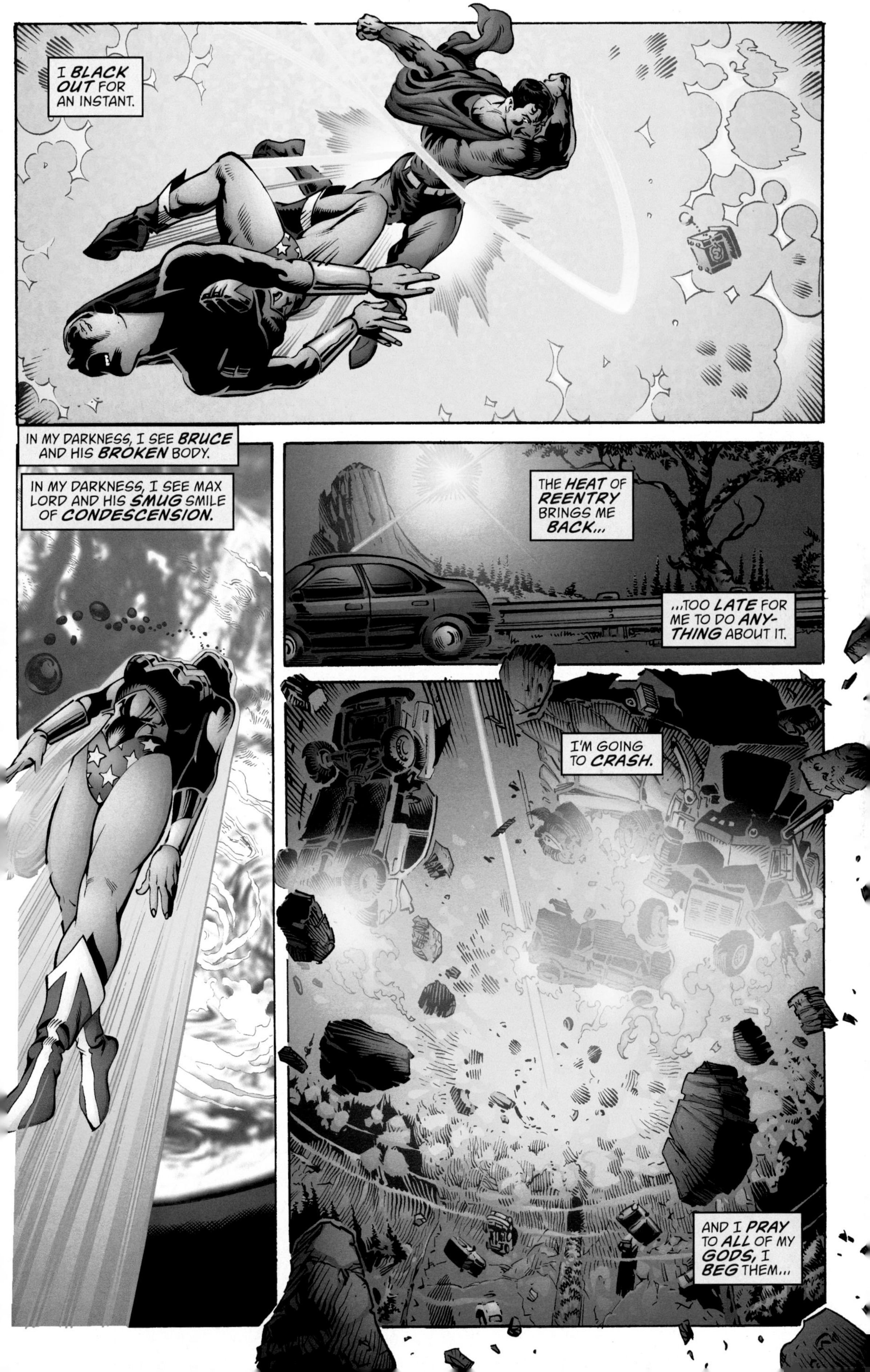
I BLACK OUT FOR AN INSTANT.
IN MY DARKNESS, I SEE BRUCE AND HIS BROKEN BODY.
IN MY DARKNESS, I SEE MAX LORD AND HIS SMUG SMILE OF CONDESCENSION.
THE HEAT OF REENTRY BRINGS ME BACK...
...TOO LATE FOR ME TO DO ANY-THING ABOUT IT.
I'M GOING TO CRASH.
AND I PRAY TO ALL OF MY GODS, I BEG THEM...

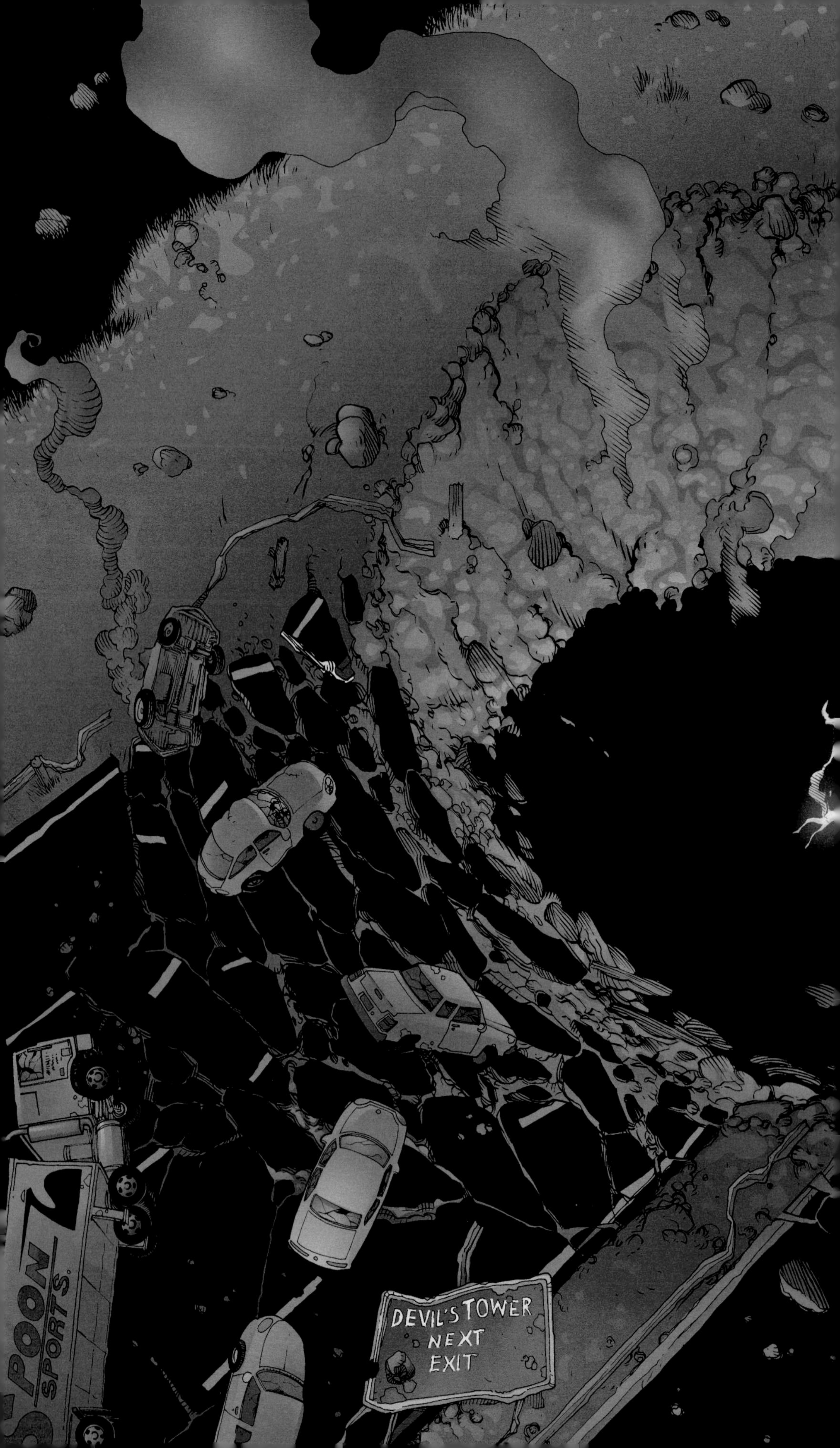
DEVIL'S TOWER
NEXT
EXIT
S'POON
SPORTS.

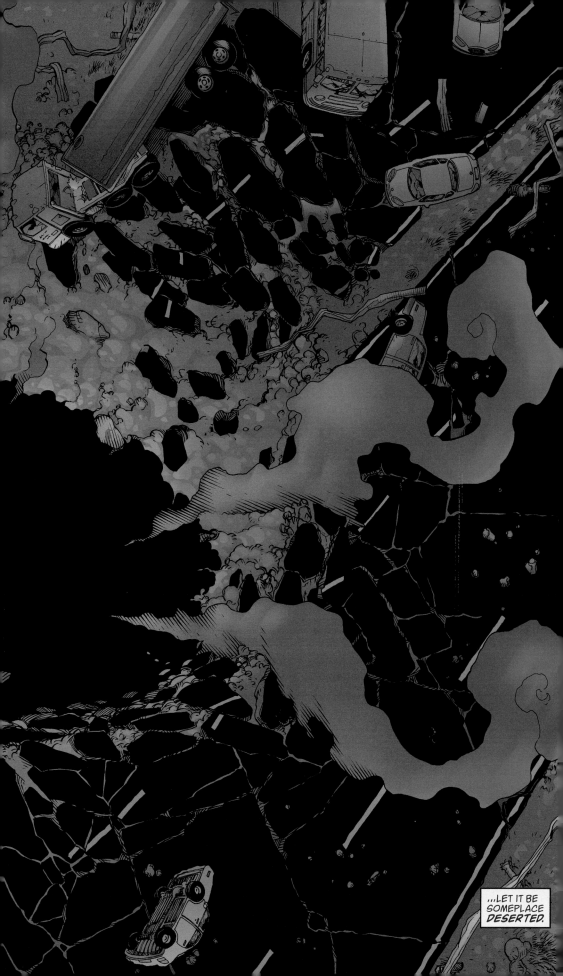

...LET IT BE
SOMEPLACE
DESERTED.

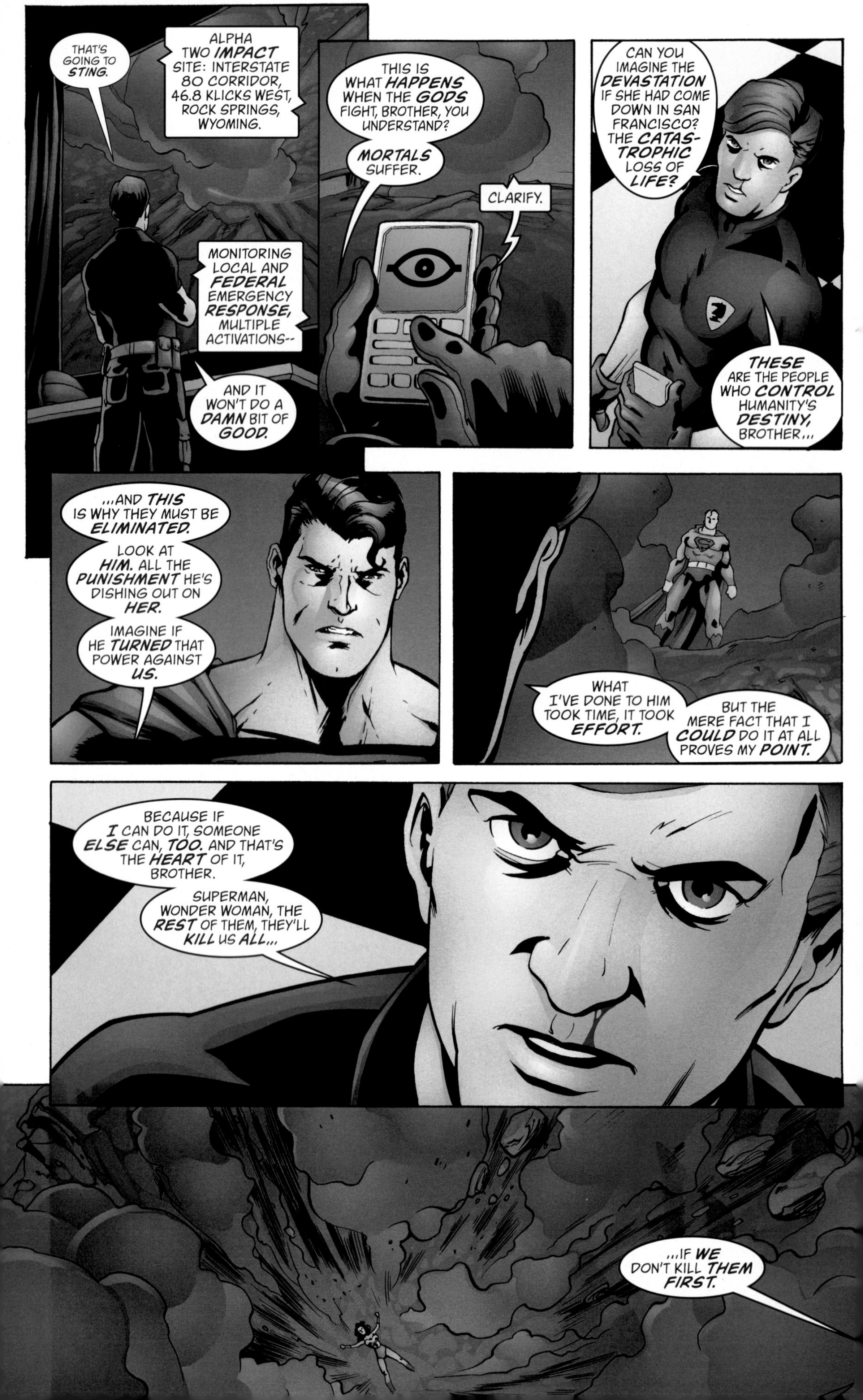
THAT'S GOING TO STING.
ALPHA TWO IMPACT SITE: INTERSTATE 80 CORRIDOR, 46.8 KLICKS WEST, ROCK SPRINGS, WYOMING.
MONITORING LOCAL AND FEDERAL EMERGENCY RESPONSE, MULTIPLE ACTIVATIONS--
AND IT WON'T DO A DAMN BIT OF GOOD.
THIS IS WHAT HAPPENS WHEN THE GODS FIGHT, BROTHER, YOU UNDERSTAND?
MORTALS SUFFER.
CLARIFY.
CAN YOU IMAGINE THE DEVASTATION IF SHE HAD COME DOWN IN SAN FRANCISCO? THE CATAS-TROPHIC LOSS OF LIFE?
THESE ARE THE PEOPLE WHO CONTROL HUMANITY'S DESTINY, BROTHER...
...AND THIS IS WHY THEY MUST BE ELIMINATED.
LOOK AT HIM. ALL THE PUNISHMENT HE'S DISHING OUT ON HER.
IMAGINE IF HE TURNED THAT POWER AGAINST US.
WHAT I'VE DONE TO HIM TOOK TIME, IT TOOK EFFORT.
BUT THE MERE FACT THAT I COULD DO IT AT ALL PROVES MY POINT.
BECAUSE IF I CAN DO IT, SOMEONE ELSE CAN, TOO. AND THAT'S THE HEART OF IT, BROTHER.
SUPERMAN, WONDER WOMAN, THE REST OF THEM, THEY'LL KILL US ALL...
...IF WE DON'T KILL THEM FIRST.

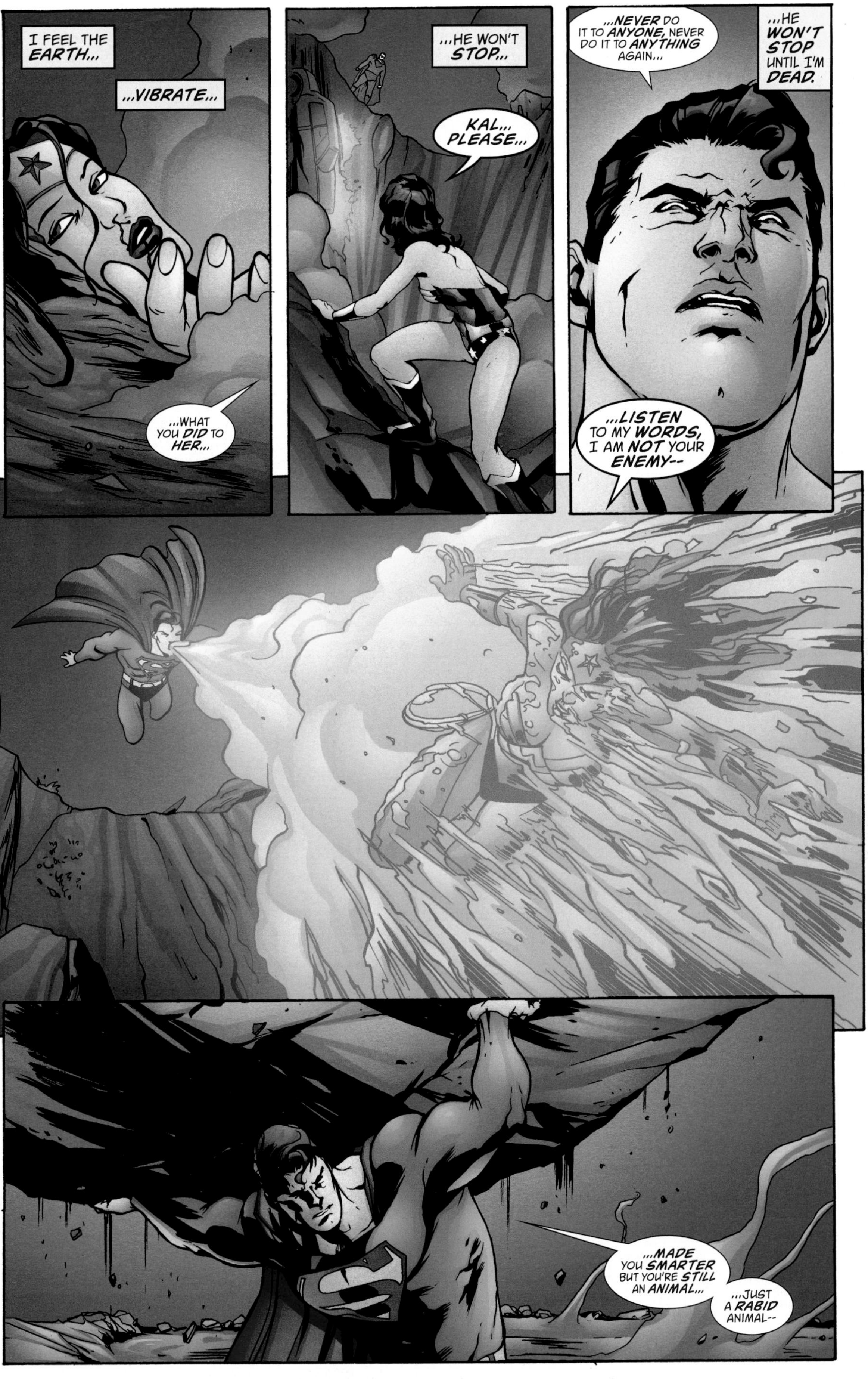
I FEEL THE EARTH...
...VIBRATE...
...WHAT YOU DID TO HER...
...HE WON'T STOP...
KAL... PLEASE...
...NEVER DO IT TO ANYONE, NEVER DO IT TO ANYTHING AGAIN...
...HE WON'T STOP UNTIL I'M DEAD.
...LISTEN TO MY WORDS, I AM NOT YOUR ENEMY--
...MADE YOU SMARTER BUT YOU'RE STILL AN ANIMAL...
...JUST A RABID ANIMAL--

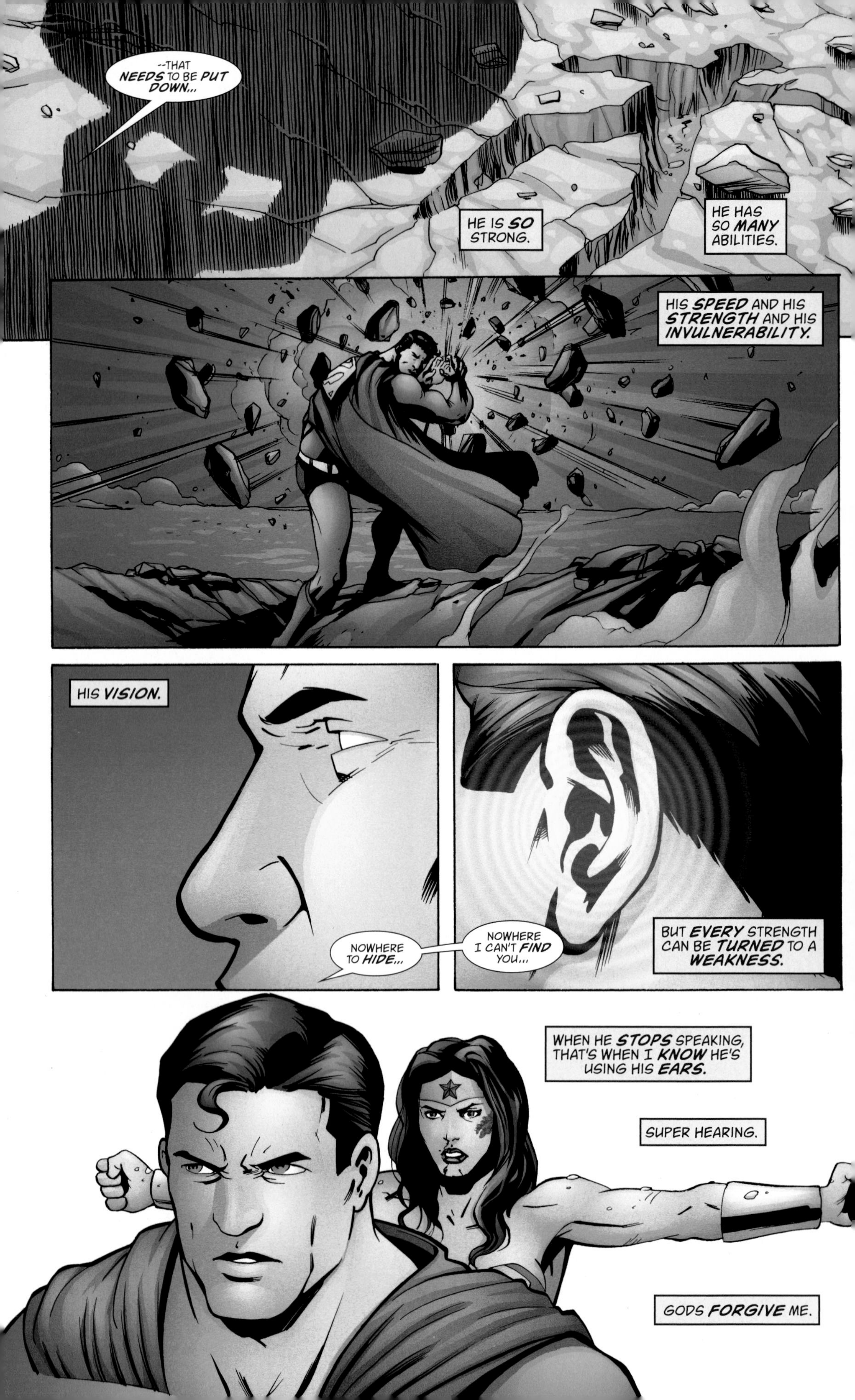
--THAT NEEDS TO BE PUT DOWN...
HE IS SO STRONG.
HE HAS SO MANY ABILITIES.
HIS SPEED AND HIS STRENGTH AND HIS INVULNERABILITY.
HIS VISION.
NOWHERE TO HIDE...
NOWHERE I CAN'T FIND YOU...
BUT EVERY STRENGTH CAN BE TURNED TO A WEAKNESS.
WHEN HE STOPS SPEAKING, THAT'S WHEN I KNOW HE'S USING HIS EARS.
SUPER HEARING.
GODS FORGIVE ME.

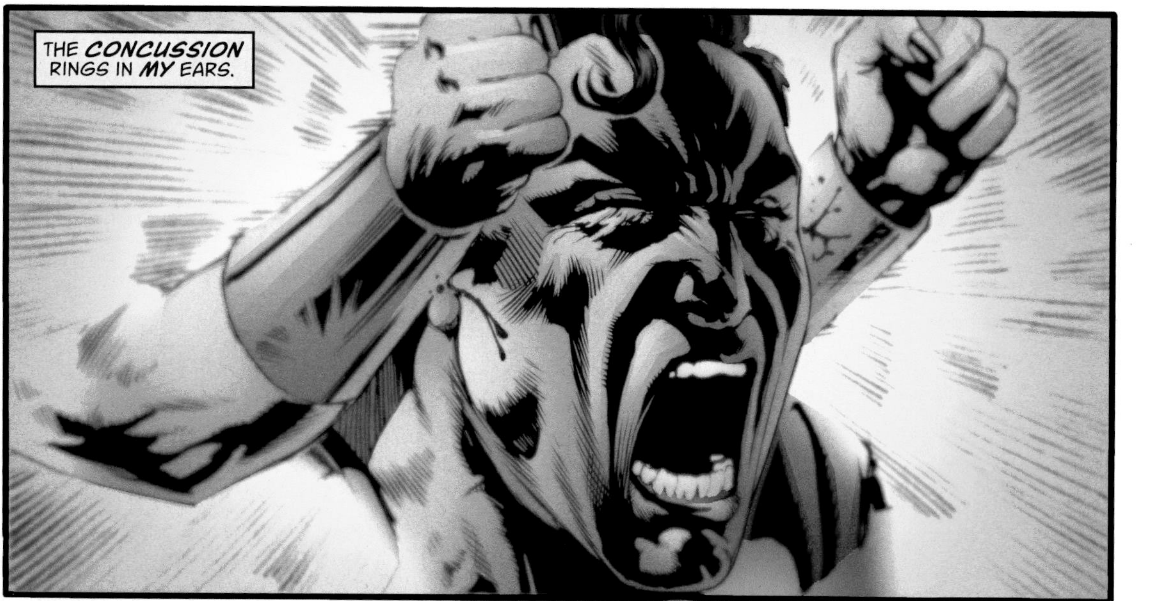
THE CONCUSSION RINGS IN MY EARS.

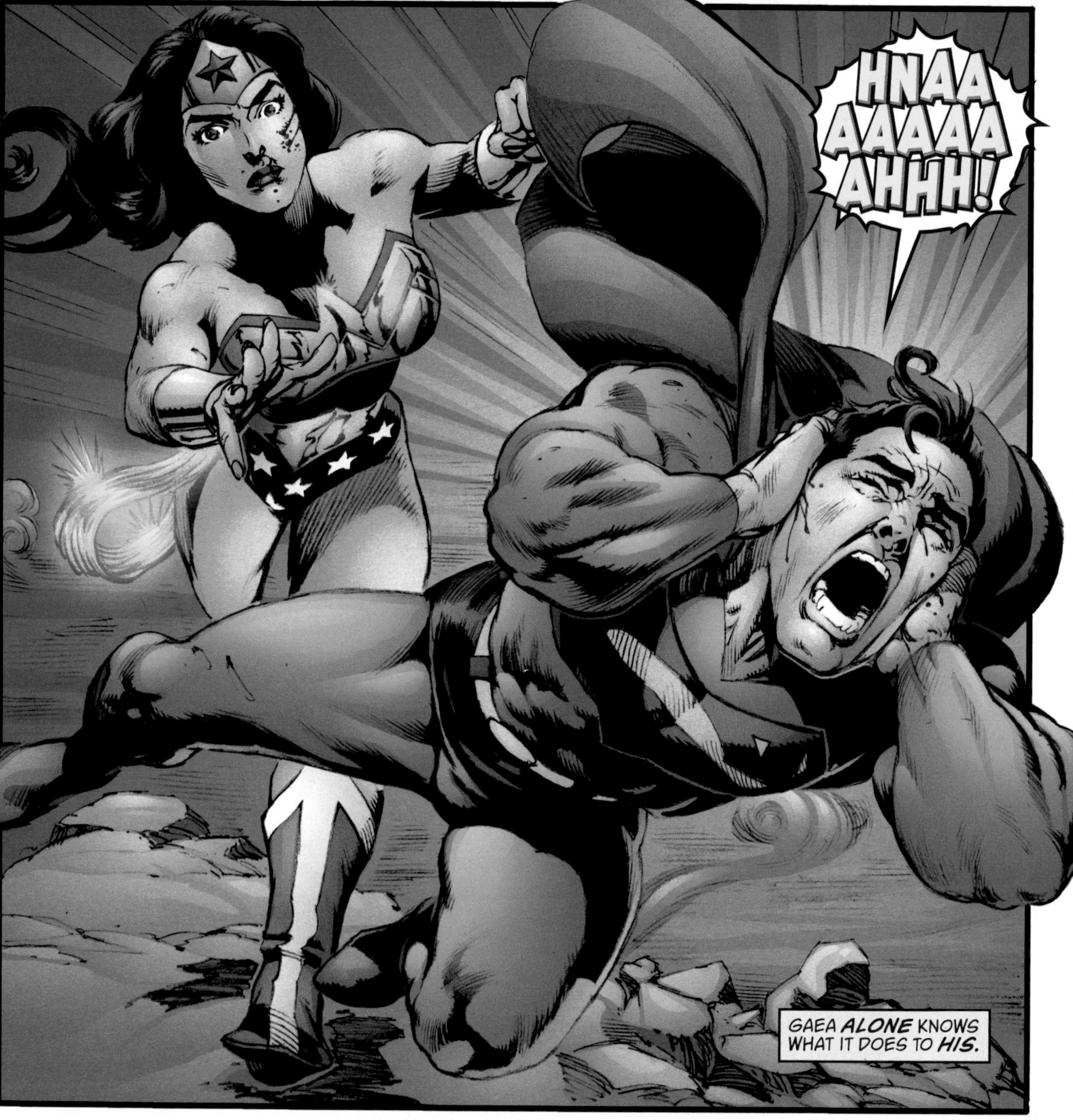
HNAA AAAAA AHHH!
GAEA ALONE KNOWS WHAT IT DOES TO HIS.

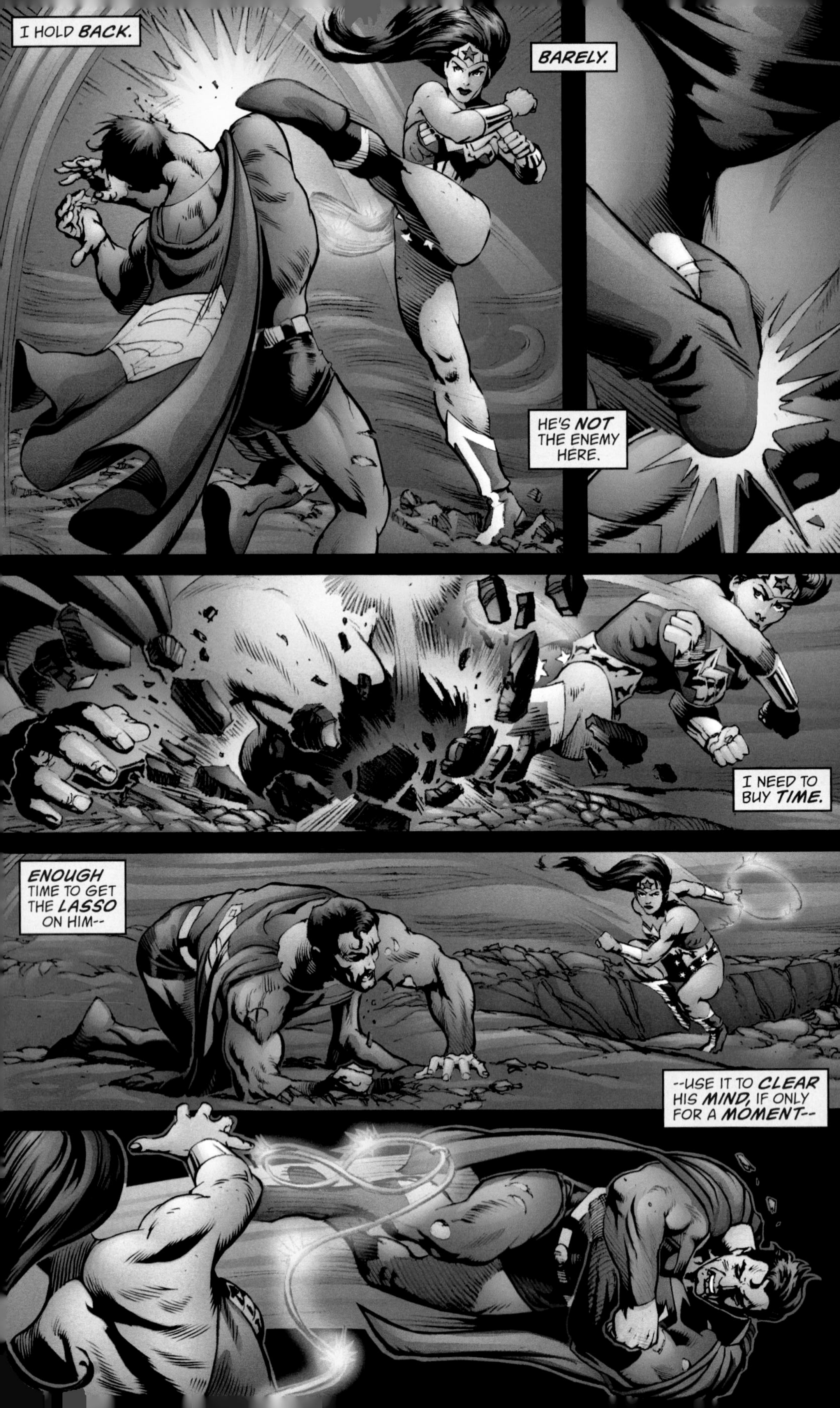
I HOLD BACK.
BARELY.
HE'S NOT THE ENEMY HERE.
I NEED TO BUY TIME.
ENOUGH TIME TO GET THE LASSO ON HIM--
--USE IT TO CLEAR HIS MIND, IF ONLY FOR A MOMENT--

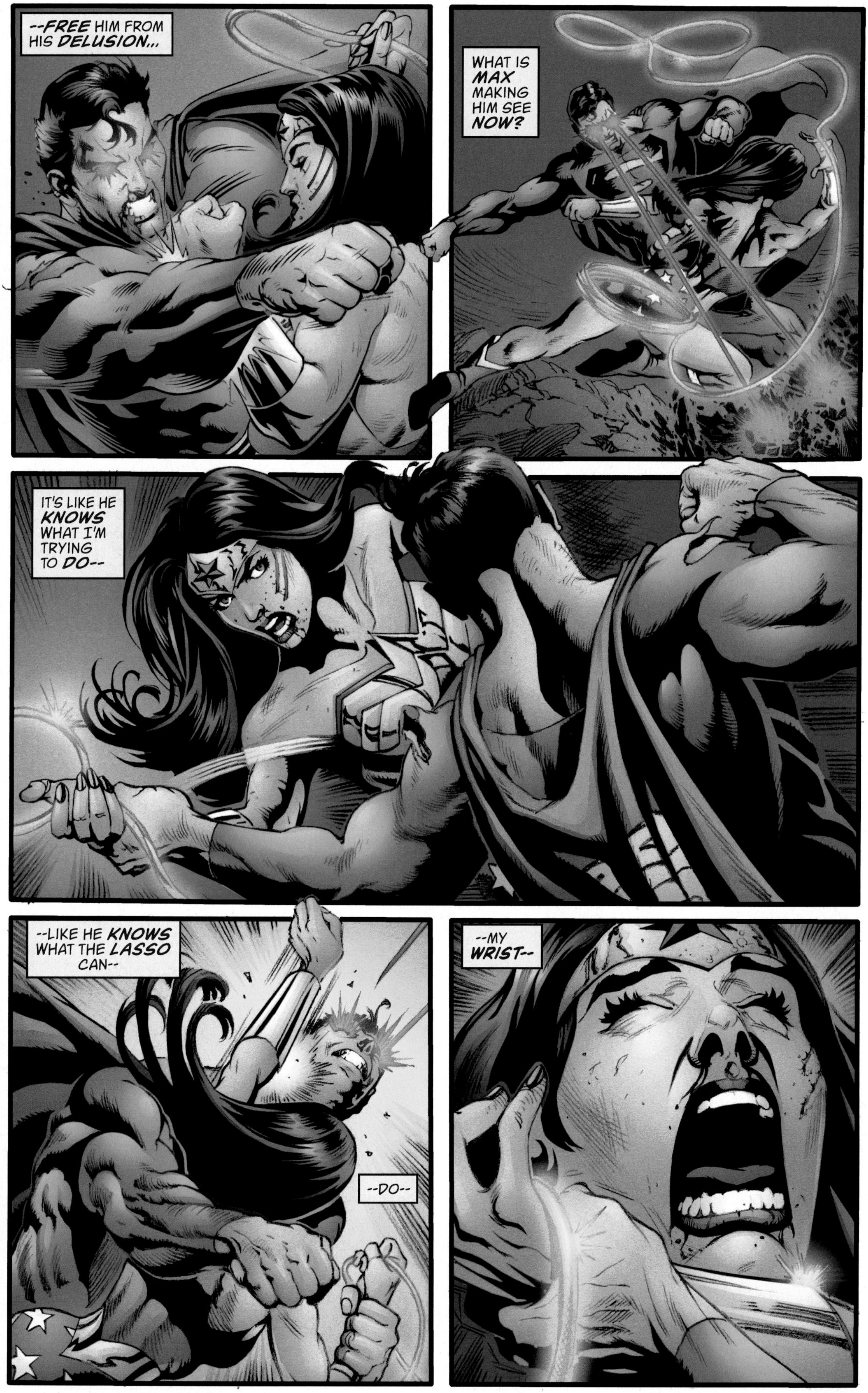
--FREE HIM FROM HIS DELUSION...
WHAT IS MAX MAKING HIM SEE NOW?
IT'S LIKE HE KNOWS WHAT I'M TRYING TO DO--
--LIKE HE KNOWS WHAT THE LASSO CAN--
--DO--
--MY WRIST--

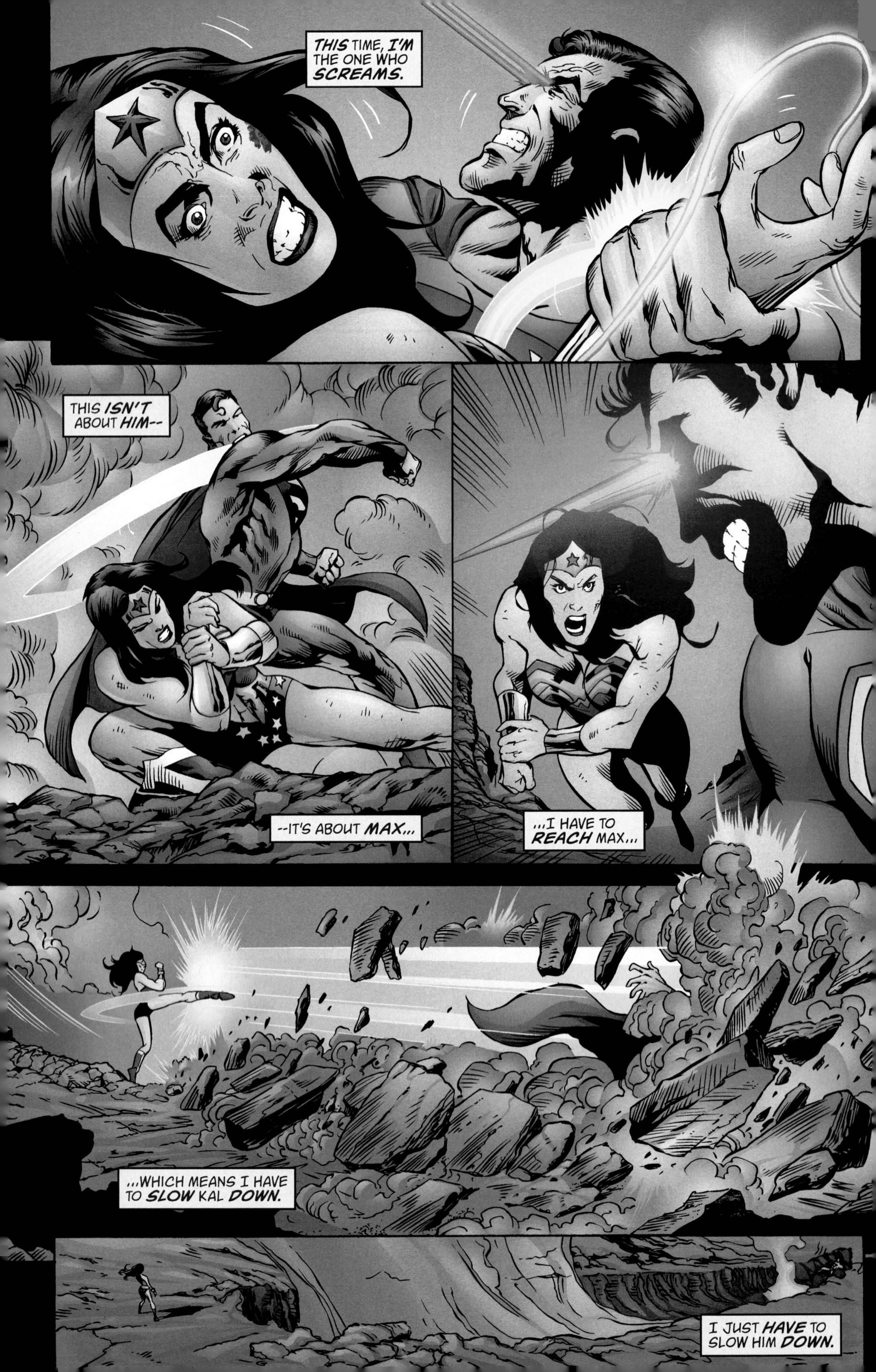
THIS TIME, I'M THE ONE WHO SCREAMS.
THIS ISN'T ABOUT HIM--
--IT'S ABOUT MAX...
...I HAVE TO REACH MAX...
...WHICH MEANS I HAVE TO SLOW KAL DOWN.
I JUST HAVE TO SLOW HIM DOWN.

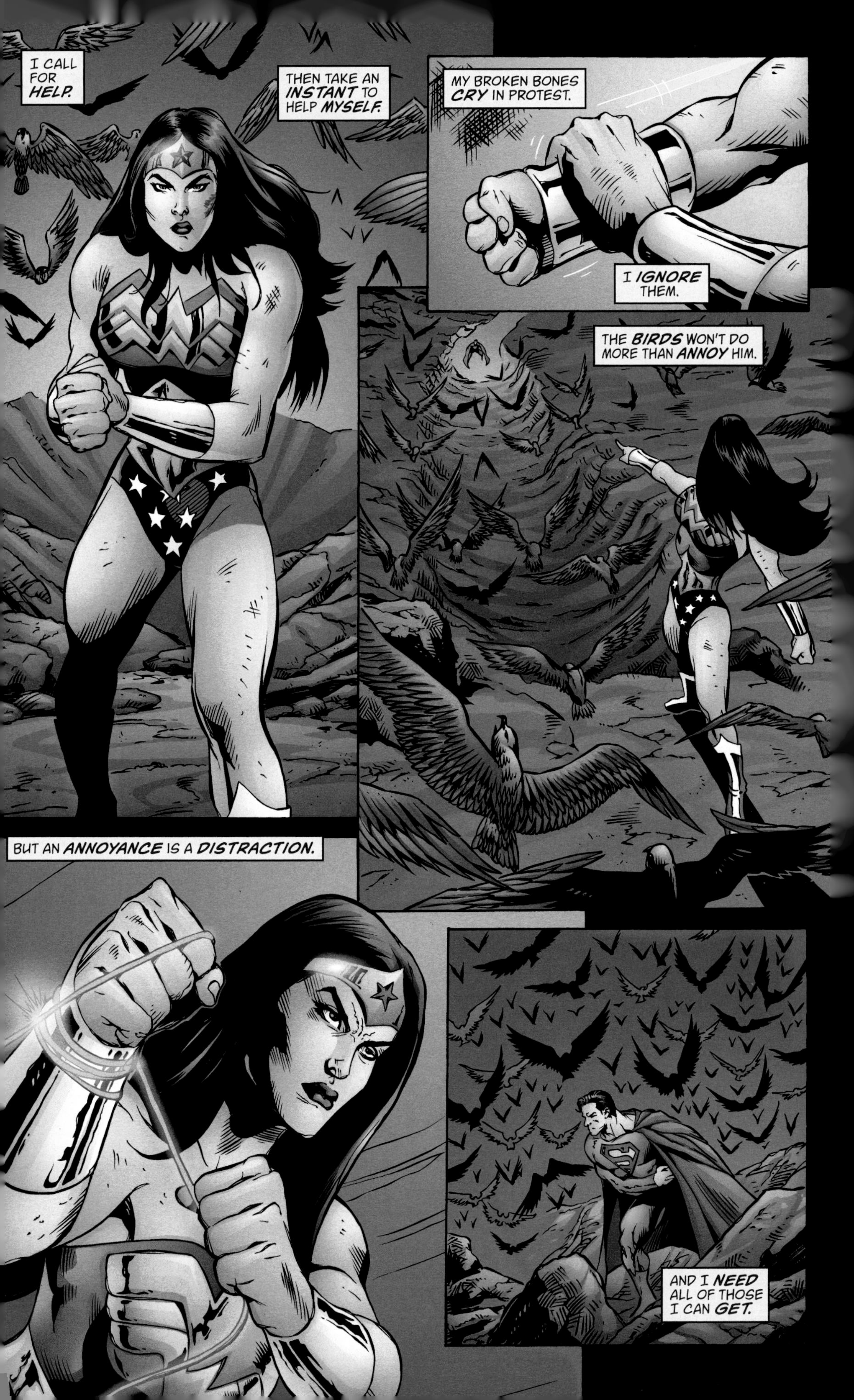
I CALL FOR HELP.
THEN TAKE AN INSTANT TO HELP MYSELF.
MY BROKEN BONES CRY IN PROTEST.
I IGNORE THEM.
THE BIRDS WON'T DO MORE THAN ANNOY HIM.
BUT AN ANNOYANCE IS A DISTRACTION.
AND I NEED ALL OF THOSE I CAN GET.

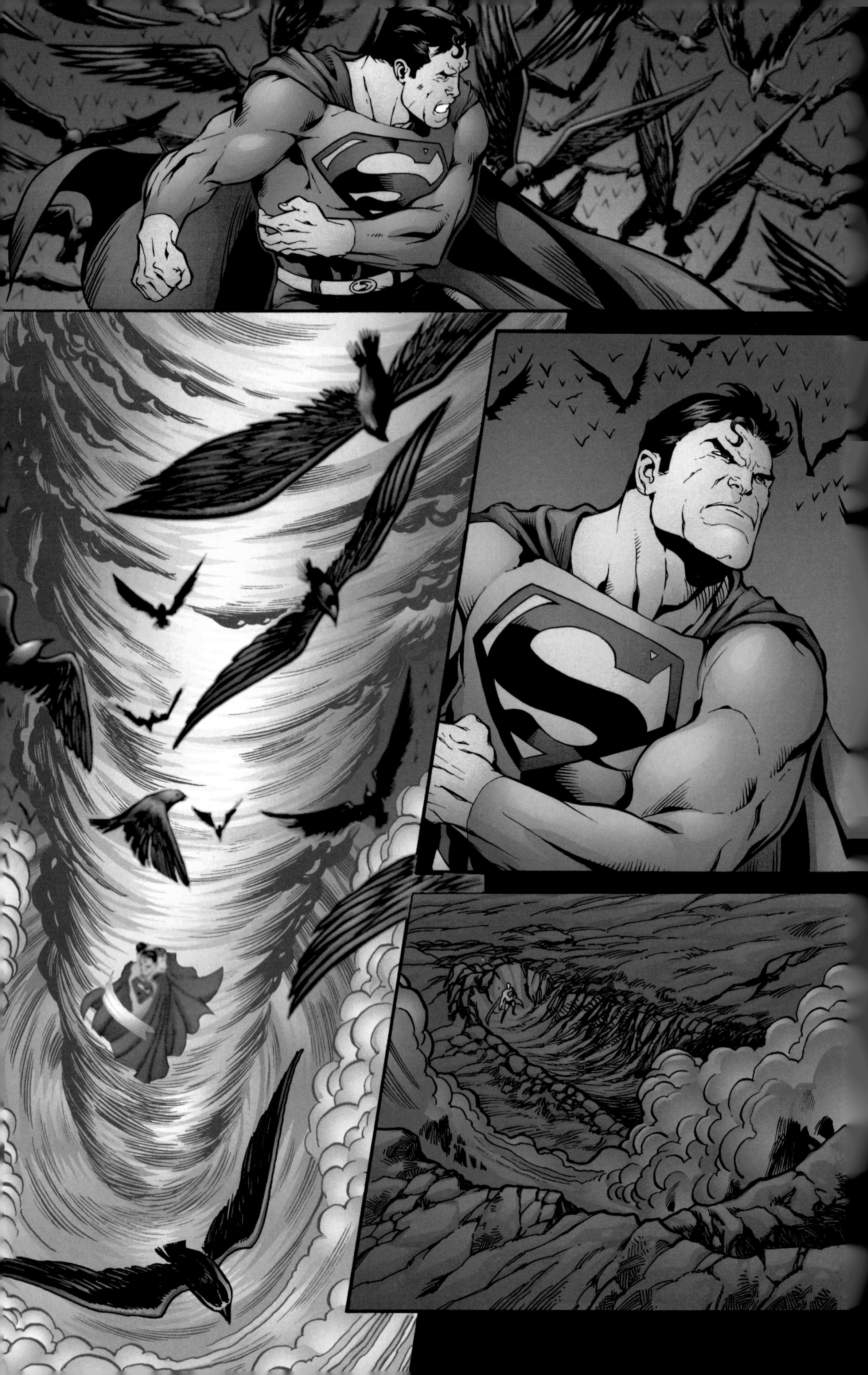

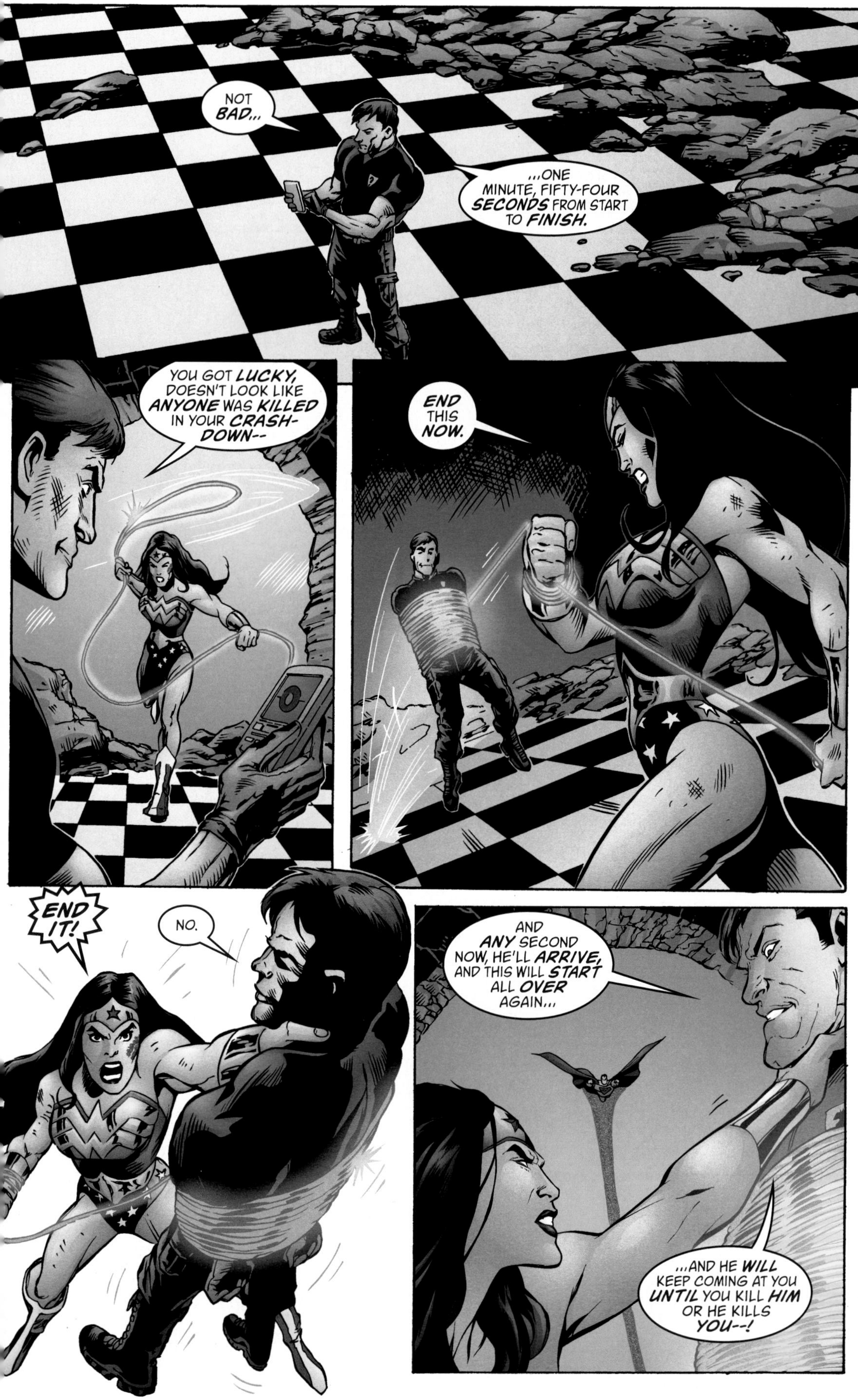
NOT BAD...
...ONE MINUTE, FIFTY-FOUR SECONDS FROM START TO FINISH.
YOU GOT LUCKY, DOESN'T LOOK LIKE ANYONE WAS KILLED IN YOUR CRASH-DOWN--
END THIS NOW.
END IT!
NO.
AND ANY SECOND NOW, HE'LL ARRIVE, AND THIS WILL START ALL OVER AGAIN...
...AND HE WILL KEEP COMING AT YOU UNTIL YOU KILL HIM OR HE KILLS YOU--!

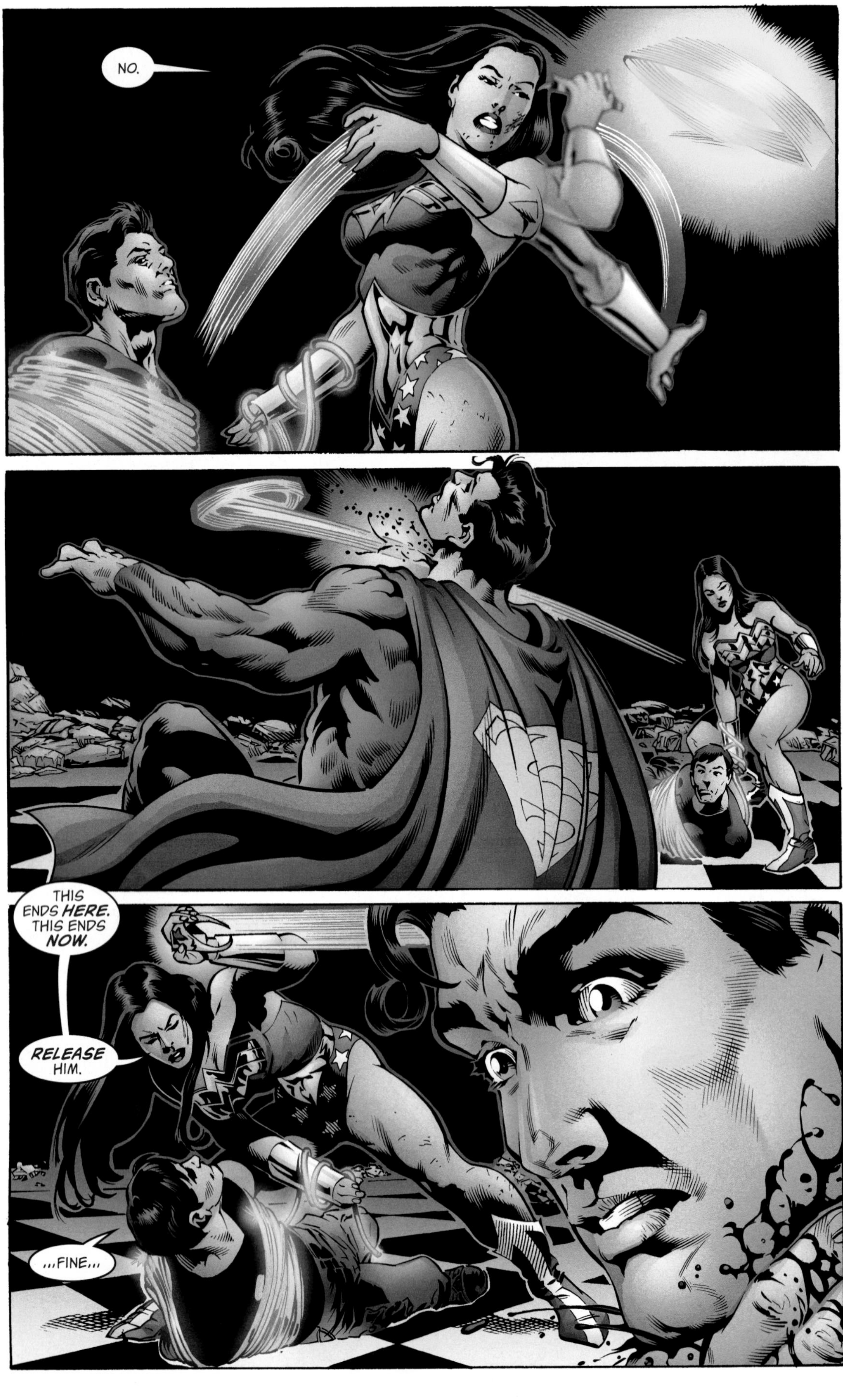
NO.
THIS ENDS *HERE.* THIS ENDS *NOW.*
RELEASE HIM.
...FINE...

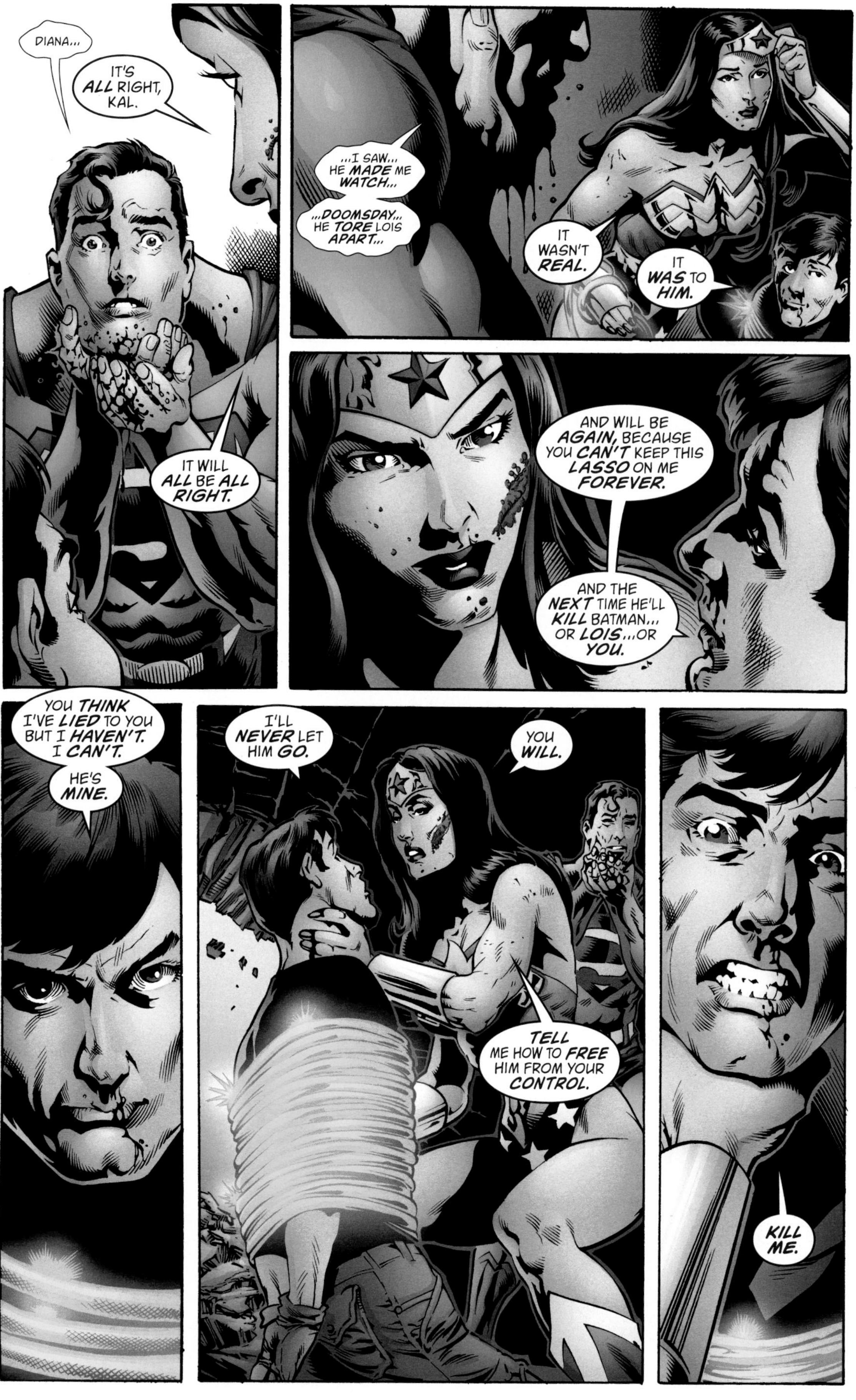

DIANA...
IT'S ALL RIGHT, KAL.
IT WILL ALL BE ALL RIGHT.
...I SAW... HE MADE ME WATCH...
...DOOMSDAY... HE TORE LOIS APART...
IT WASN'T REAL.
IT WAS TO HIM.
AND WILL BE AGAIN, BECAUSE YOU CAN'T KEEP THIS LASSO ON ME FOREVER.
AND THE NEXT TIME HE'LL KILL BATMAN... OR LOIS...OR YOU.
YOU THINK I'VE LIED TO YOU BUT I HAVEN'T. I CAN'T.
HE'S MINE.
I'LL NEVER LET HIM GO.
YOU WILL.
TELL ME HOW TO FREE HIM FROM YOUR CONTROL.
KILL ME.

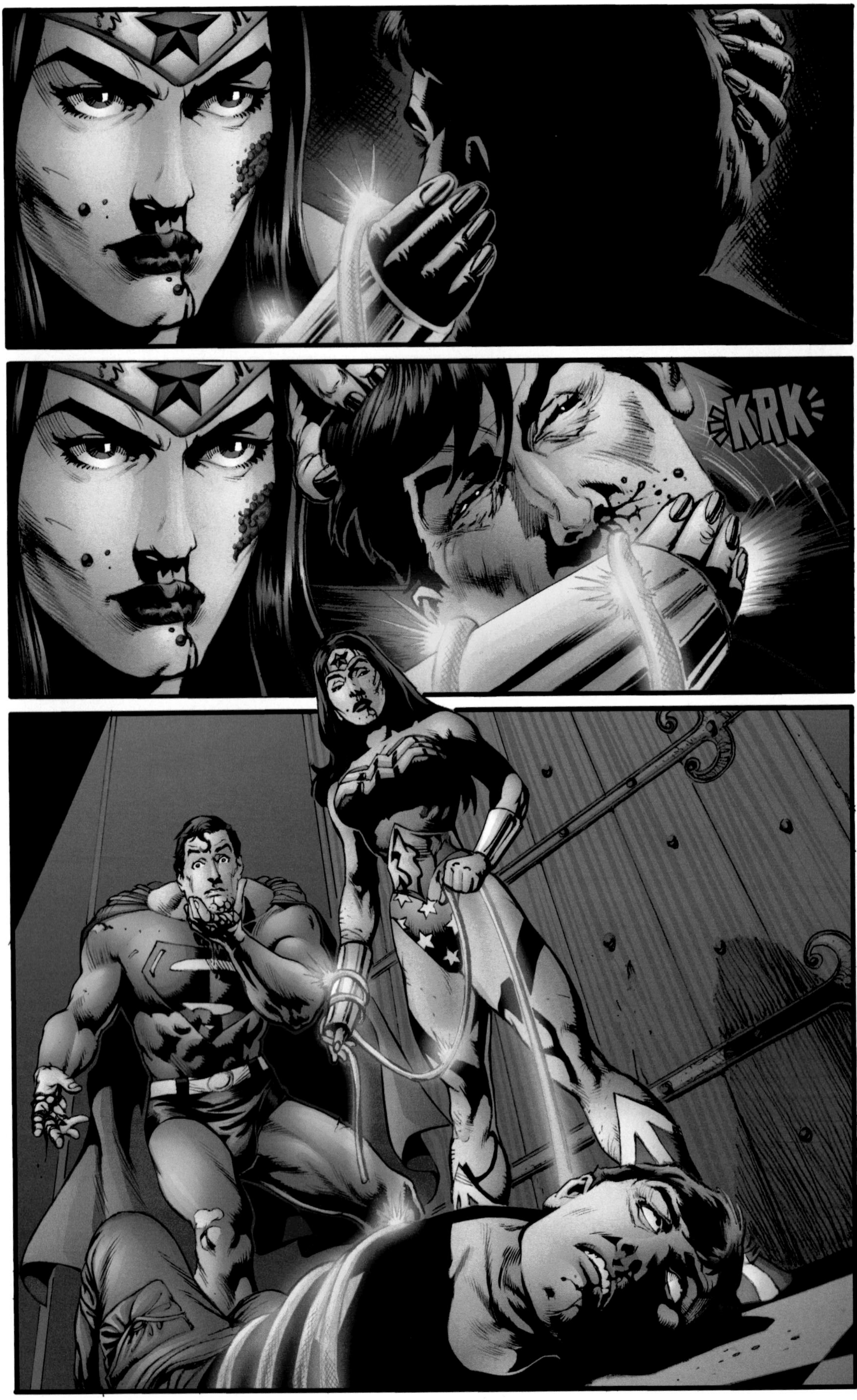
KRK

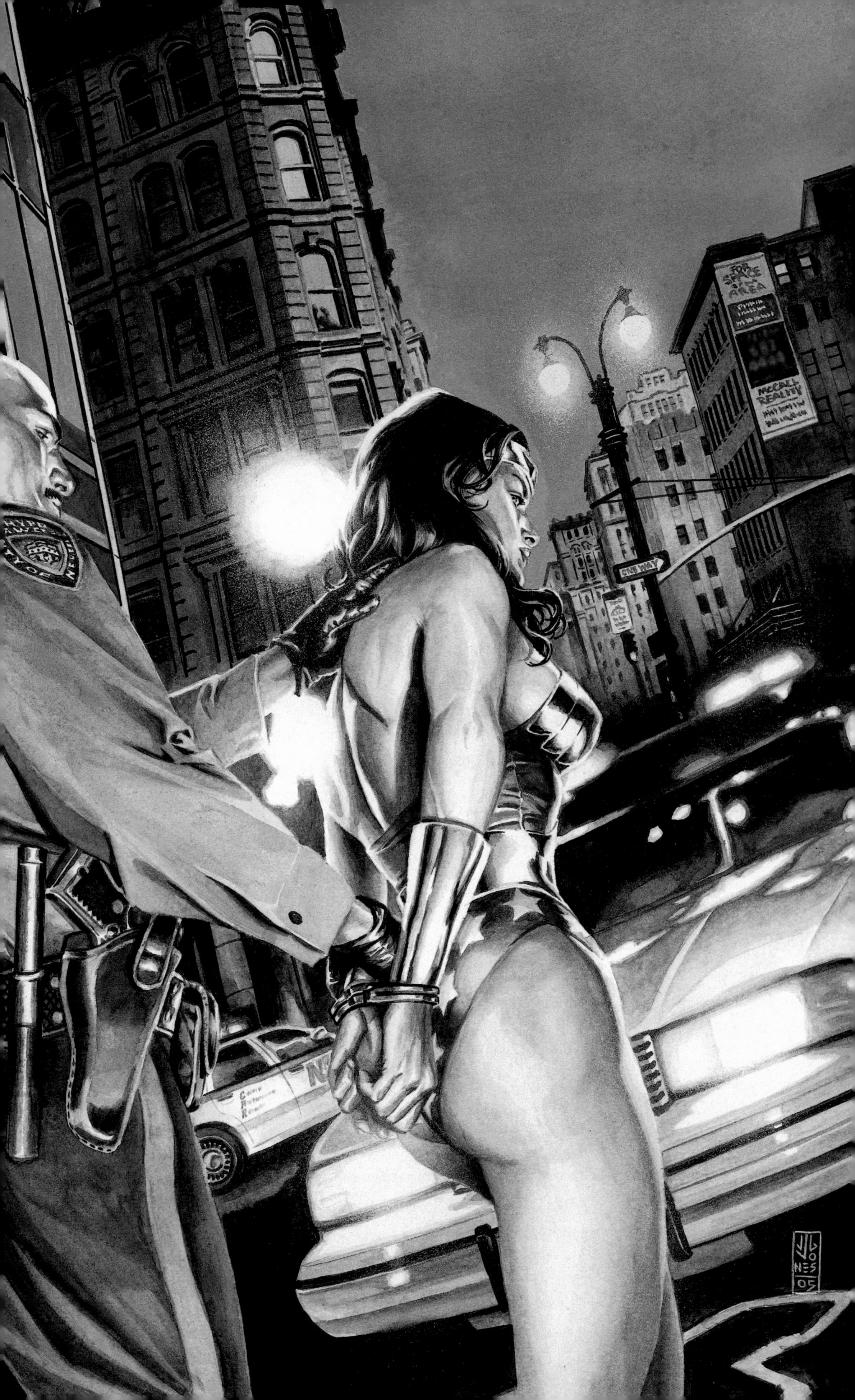
FOR SPACE
AREA
MCCALL REALTY
ONE WAY
JG JONES 05

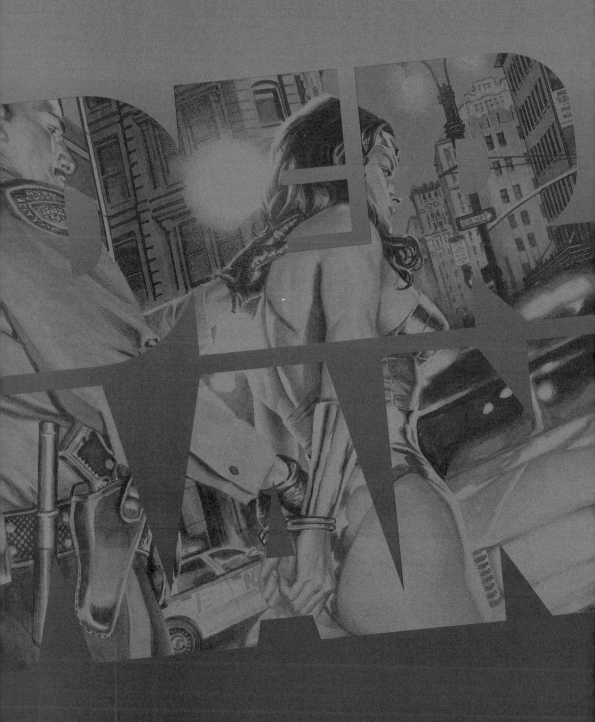

"AFFIRMATIVE DEFENSE"

Greg Rucka - *writer*

David Lopez - *pencils*

Bit - *inks*

WildStorm - *colors*

Todd Klein - *letters*

J.G. Jones - *cover*

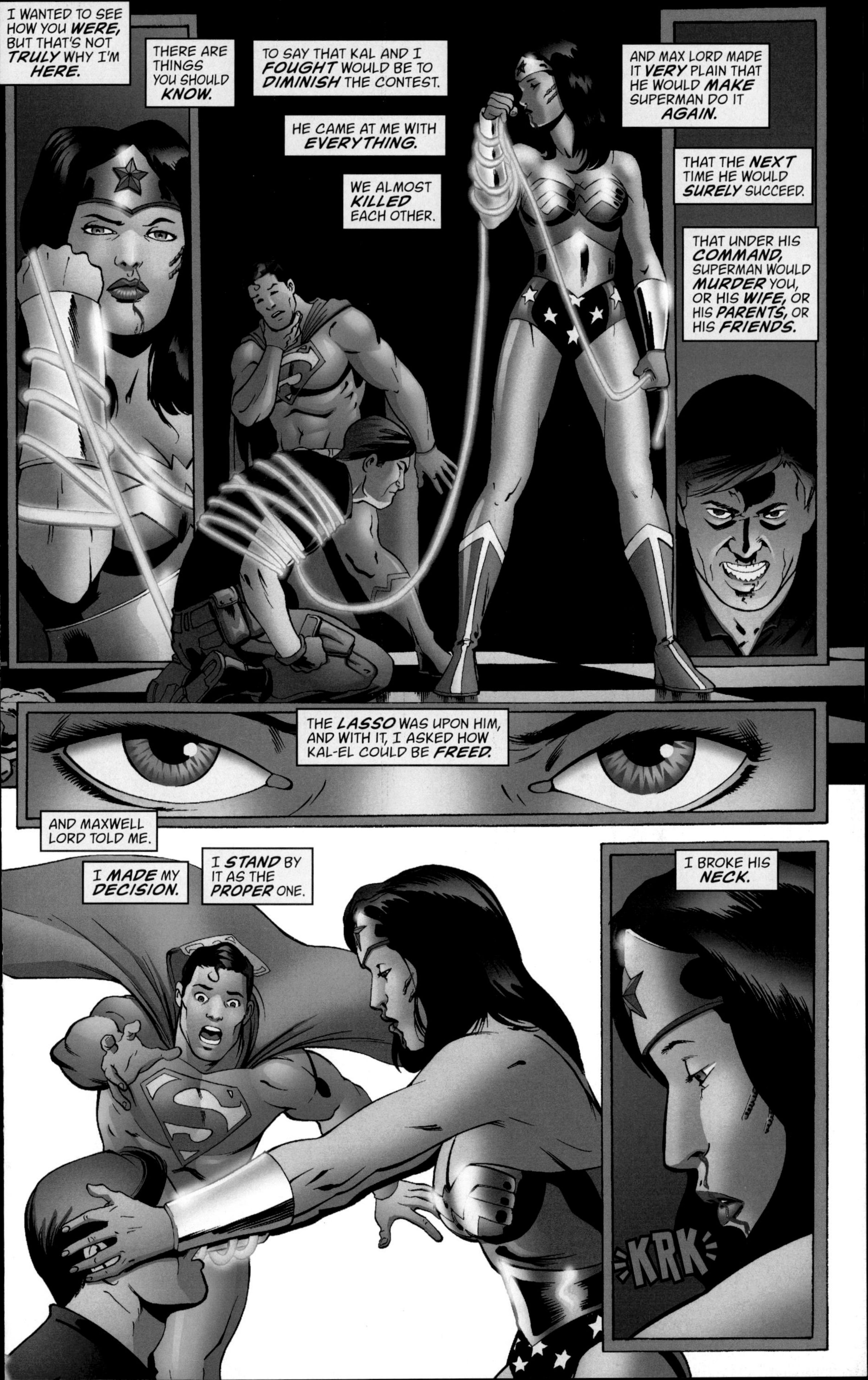

I WANTED TO SEE HOW YOU WERE, BUT THAT'S NOT TRULY WHY I'M HERE.
THERE ARE THINGS YOU SHOULD KNOW.
TO SAY THAT KAL AND I FOUGHT WOULD BE TO DIMINISH THE CONTEST.
HE CAME AT ME WITH EVERYTHING.
WE ALMOST KILLED EACH OTHER.
AND MAX LORD MADE IT VERY PLAIN THAT HE WOULD MAKE SUPERMAN DO IT AGAIN.
THAT THE NEXT TIME HE WOULD SURELY SUCCEED.
THAT UNDER HIS COMMAND, SUPERMAN WOULD MURDER YOU, OR HIS WIFE, OR HIS PARENTS, OR HIS FRIENDS.
THE LASSO WAS UPON HIM, AND WITH IT, I ASKED HOW KAL-EL COULD BE FREED.
AND MAXWELL LORD TOLD ME.
I MADE MY DECISION.
I STAND BY IT AS THE PROPER ONE.
I BROKE HIS NECK.
KRK

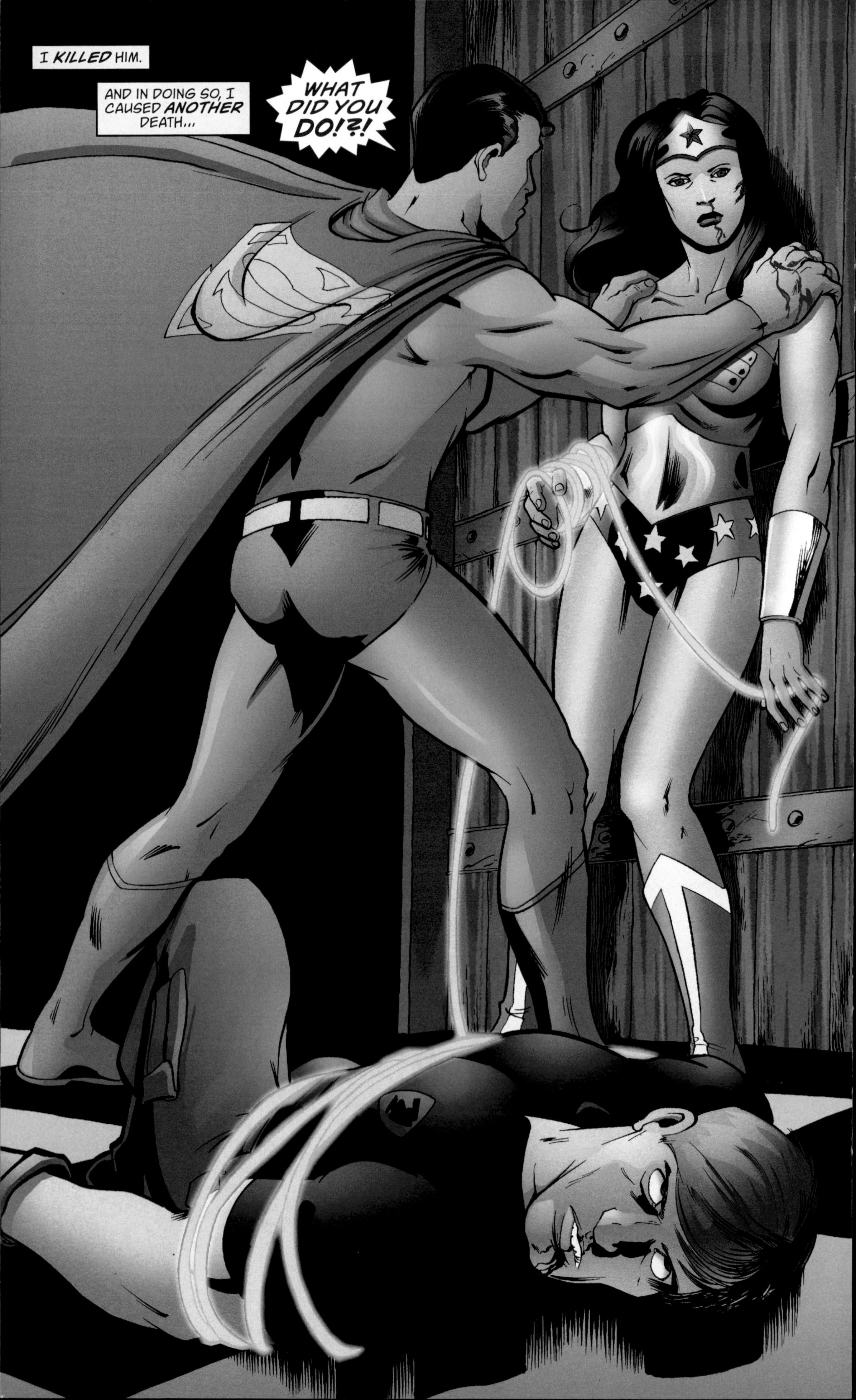
I KILLED HIM.
AND IN DOING SO, I CAUSED ANOTHER DEATH...
WHAT DID YOU DO!?!

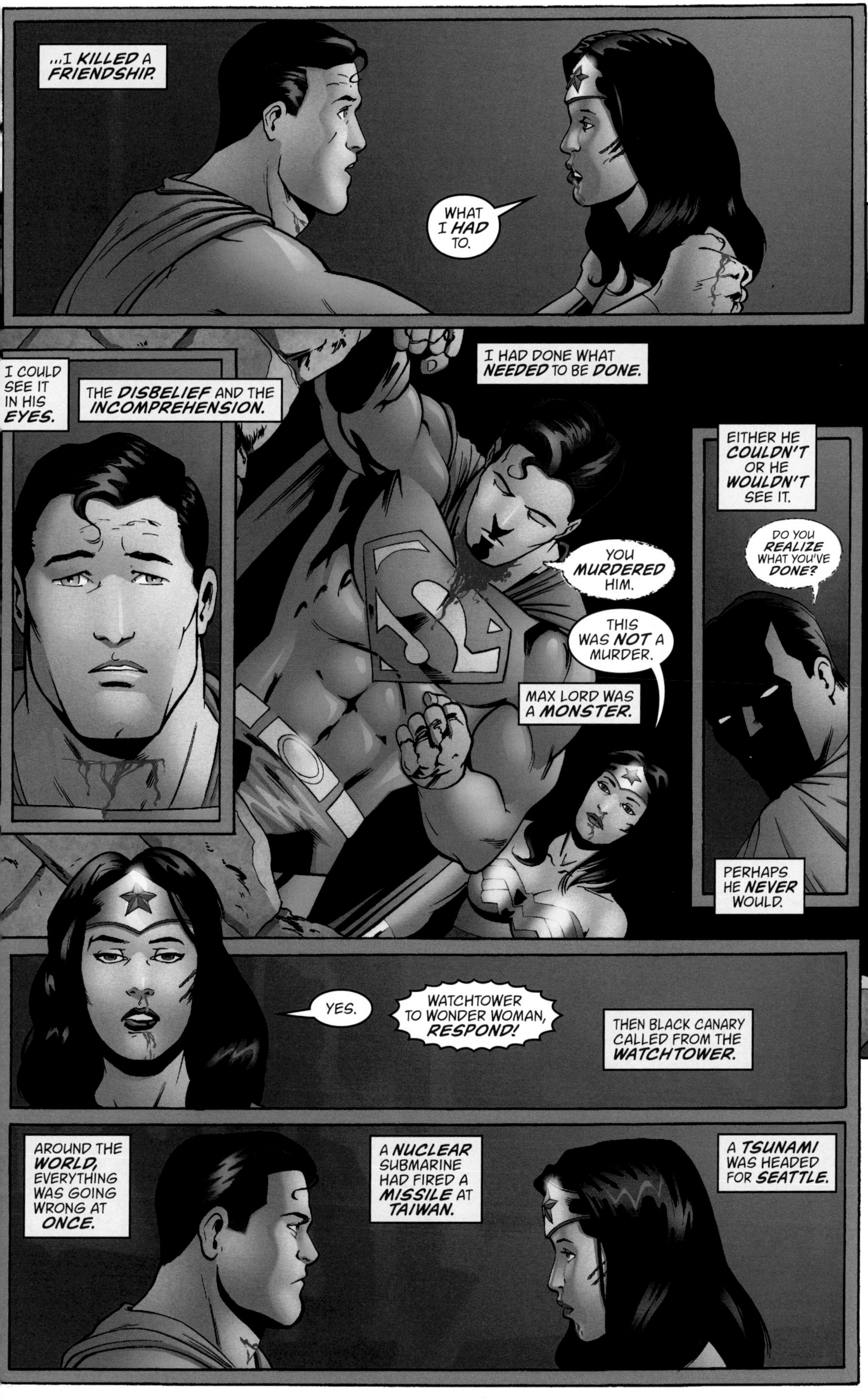
...I KILLED A FRIENDSHIP.
WHAT I HAD TO.
I COULD SEE IT IN HIS EYES.
THE DISBELIEF AND THE INCOMPREHENSION.
I HAD DONE WHAT NEEDED TO BE DONE.
YOU MURDERED HIM.
THIS WAS NOT A MURDER.
MAX LORD WAS A MONSTER.
EITHER HE COULDN'T OR HE WOULDN'T SEE IT.
DO YOU REALIZE WHAT YOU'VE DONE?
PERHAPS HE NEVER WOULD.
YES.
WATCHTOWER TO WONDER WOMAN, RESPOND!
THEN BLACK CANARY CALLED FROM THE WATCHTOWER.
AROUND THE WORLD, EVERYTHING WAS GOING WRONG AT ONCE.
A NUCLEAR SUBMARINE HAD FIRED A MISSILE AT TAIWAN.
A TSUNAMI WAS HEADED FOR SEATTLE.

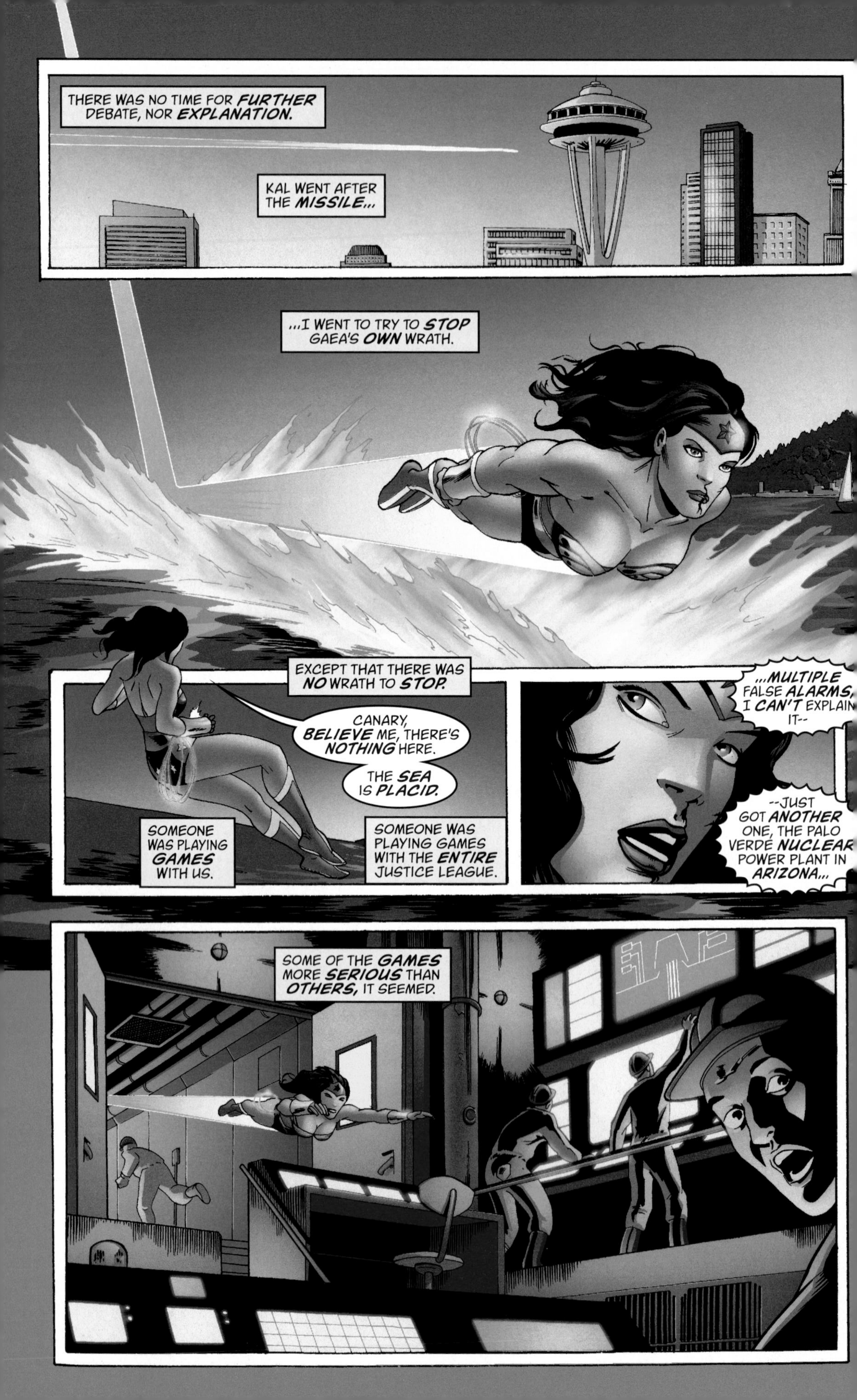
THERE WAS NO TIME FOR FURTHER DEBATE, NOR EXPLANATION.
KAL WENT AFTER THE MISSILE...
...I WENT TO TRY TO STOP GAEA'S OWN WRATH.
EXCEPT THAT THERE WAS NO WRATH TO STOP.
CANARY, BELIEVE ME, THERE'S NOTHING HERE.
THE SEA IS PLACID.
SOMEONE WAS PLAYING GAMES WITH US.
SOMEONE WAS PLAYING GAMES WITH THE ENTIRE JUSTICE LEAGUE.
...MULTIPLE FALSE ALARMS, I CAN'T EXPLAIN IT--
--JUST GOT ANOTHER ONE, THE PALO VERDE NUCLEAR POWER PLANT IN ARIZONA...
SOME OF THE GAMES MORE SERIOUS THAN OTHERS, IT SEEMED.

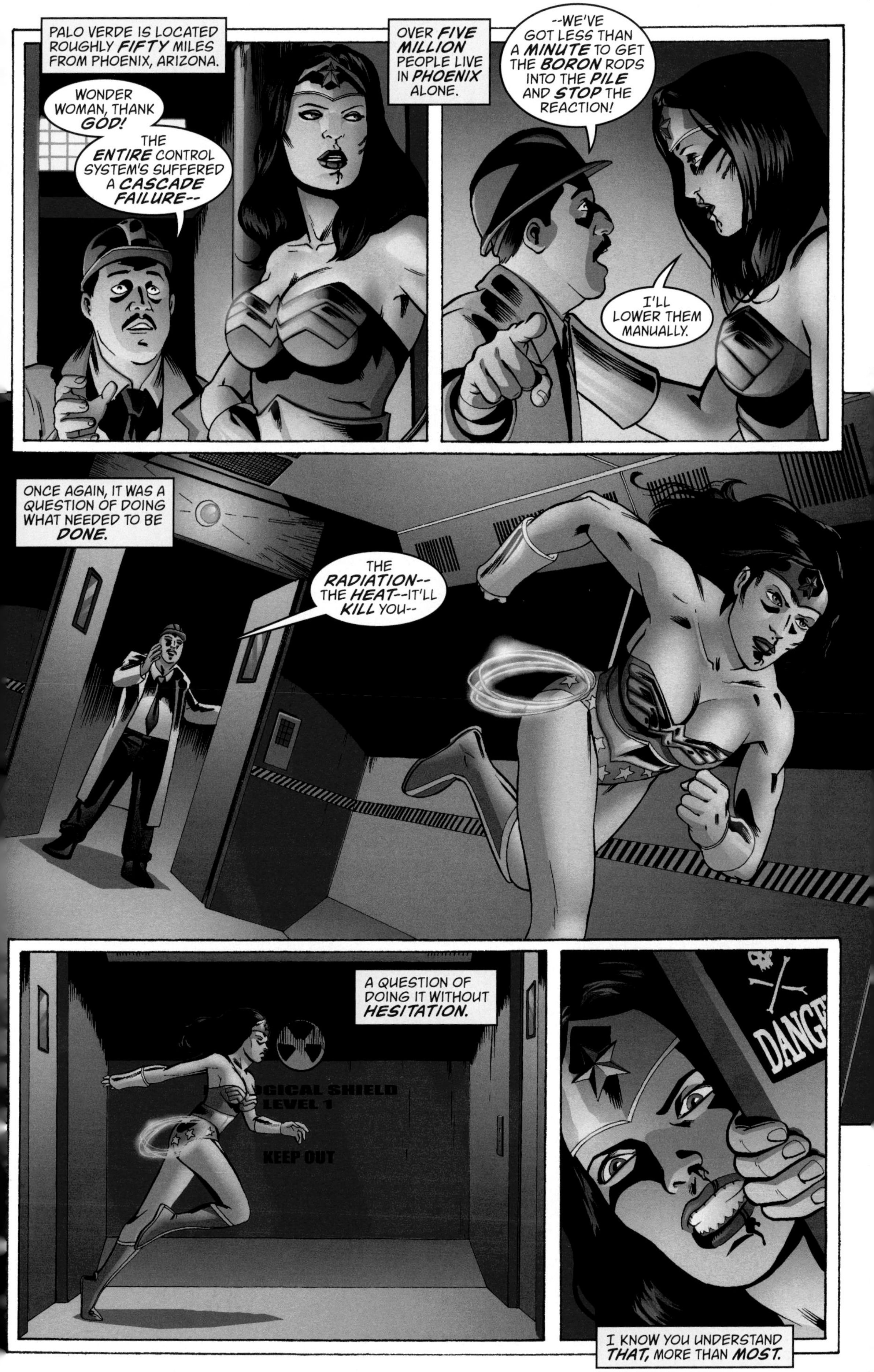

PALO VERDE IS LOCATED ROUGHLY FIFTY MILES FROM PHOENIX, ARIZONA.
WONDER WOMAN, THANK GOD!
THE ENTIRE CONTROL SYSTEM'S SUFFERED A CASCADE FAILURE--
OVER FIVE MILLION PEOPLE LIVE IN PHOENIX ALONE.
--WE'VE GOT LESS THAN A MINUTE TO GET THE BORON RODS INTO THE PILE AND STOP THE REACTION!
I'LL LOWER THEM MANUALLY.
ONCE AGAIN, IT WAS A QUESTION OF DOING WHAT NEEDED TO BE DONE.
THE RADIATION-- THE HEAT--IT'LL KILL YOU--
A QUESTION OF DOING IT WITHOUT HESITATION.
LEVEL 1
KEEP OUT
I KNOW YOU UNDERSTAND THAT, MORE THAN MOST.

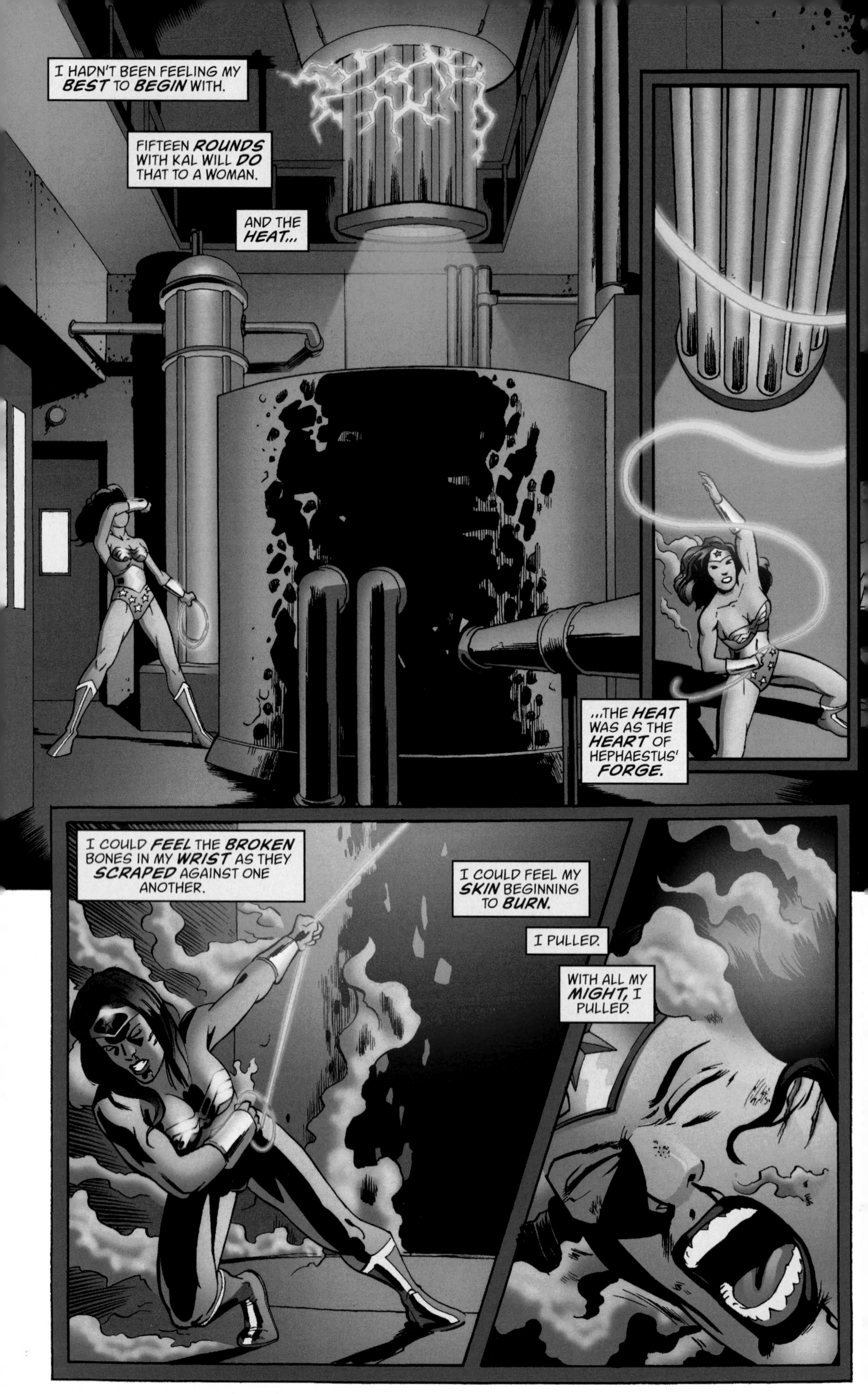
I HADN'T BEEN FEELING MY BEST TO BEGIN WITH.
FIFTEEN ROUNDS WITH KAL WILL DO THAT TO A WOMAN.
AND THE HEAT...
...THE HEAT WAS AS THE HEART OF HEPHAESTUS' FORGE.
I COULD FEEL THE BROKEN BONES IN MY WRIST AS THEY SCRAPED AGAINST ONE ANOTHER.
I COULD FEEL MY SKIN BEGINNING TO BURN.
I PULLED.
WITH ALL MY MIGHT, I PULLED.

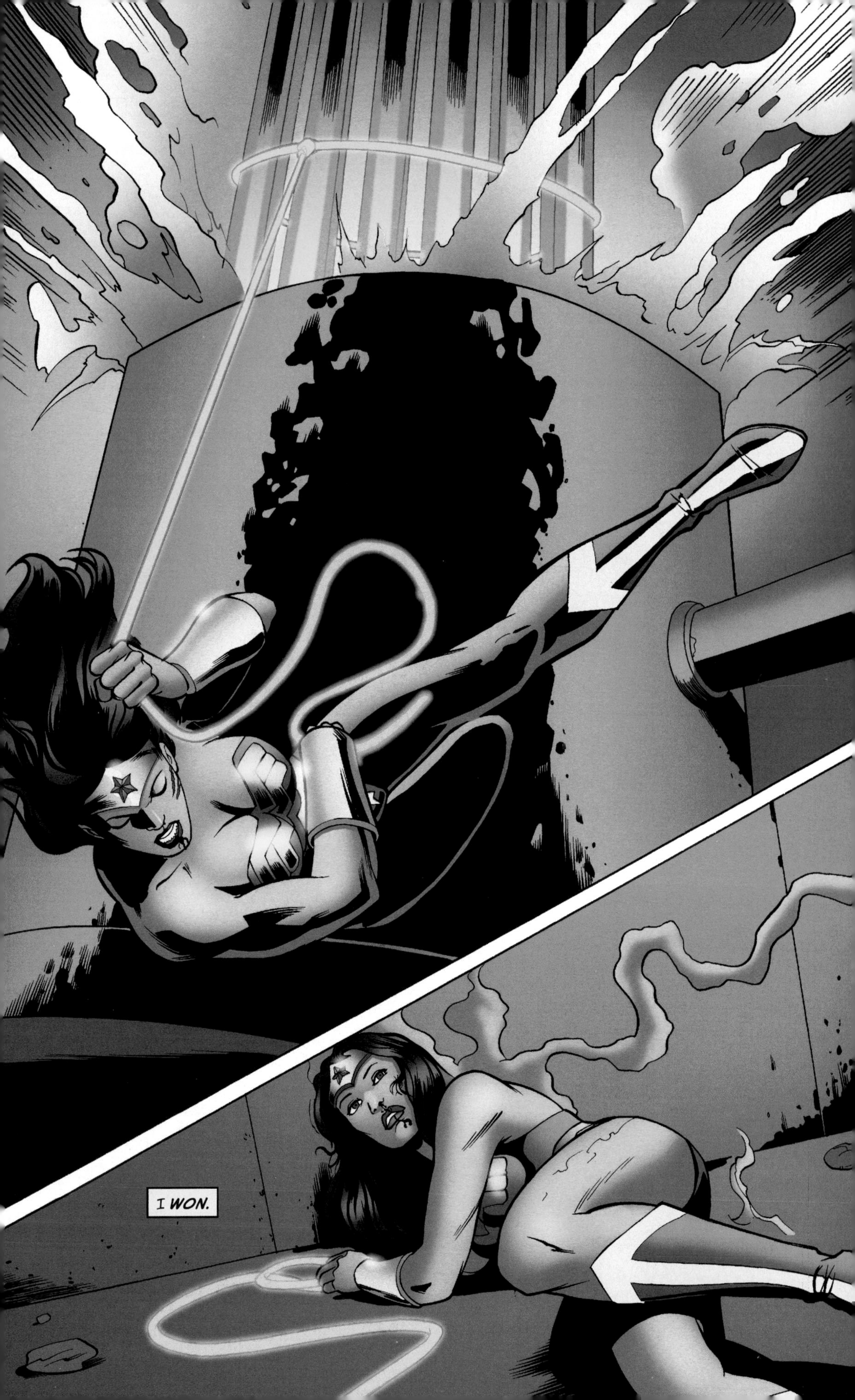
I WON.

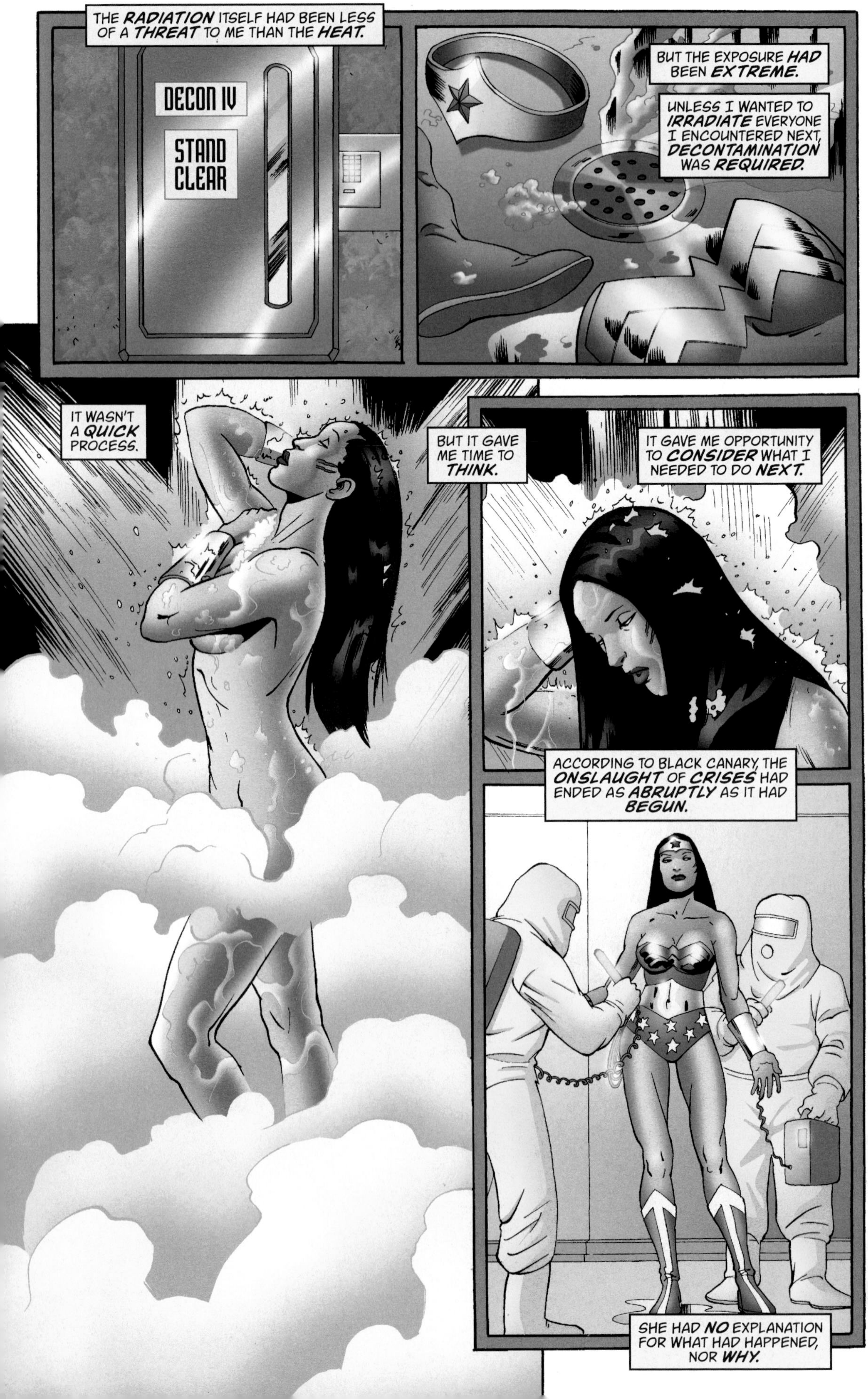
THE RADIATION ITSELF HAD BEEN LESS OF A THREAT TO ME THAN THE HEAT.
DECON IV
STAND CLEAR
BUT THE EXPOSURE HAD BEEN EXTREME.
UNLESS I WANTED TO IRRADIATE EVERYONE I ENCOUNTERED NEXT, DECONTAMINATION WAS REQUIRED.
IT WASN'T A QUICK PROCESS.
BUT IT GAVE ME TIME TO THINK.
IT GAVE ME OPPORTUNITY TO CONSIDER WHAT I NEEDED TO DO NEXT.
ACCORDING TO BLACK CANARY, THE ONSLAUGHT OF CRISES HAD ENDED AS ABRUPTLY AS IT HAD BEGUN.
SHE HAD NO EXPLANATION FOR WHAT HAD HAPPENED, NOR WHY.

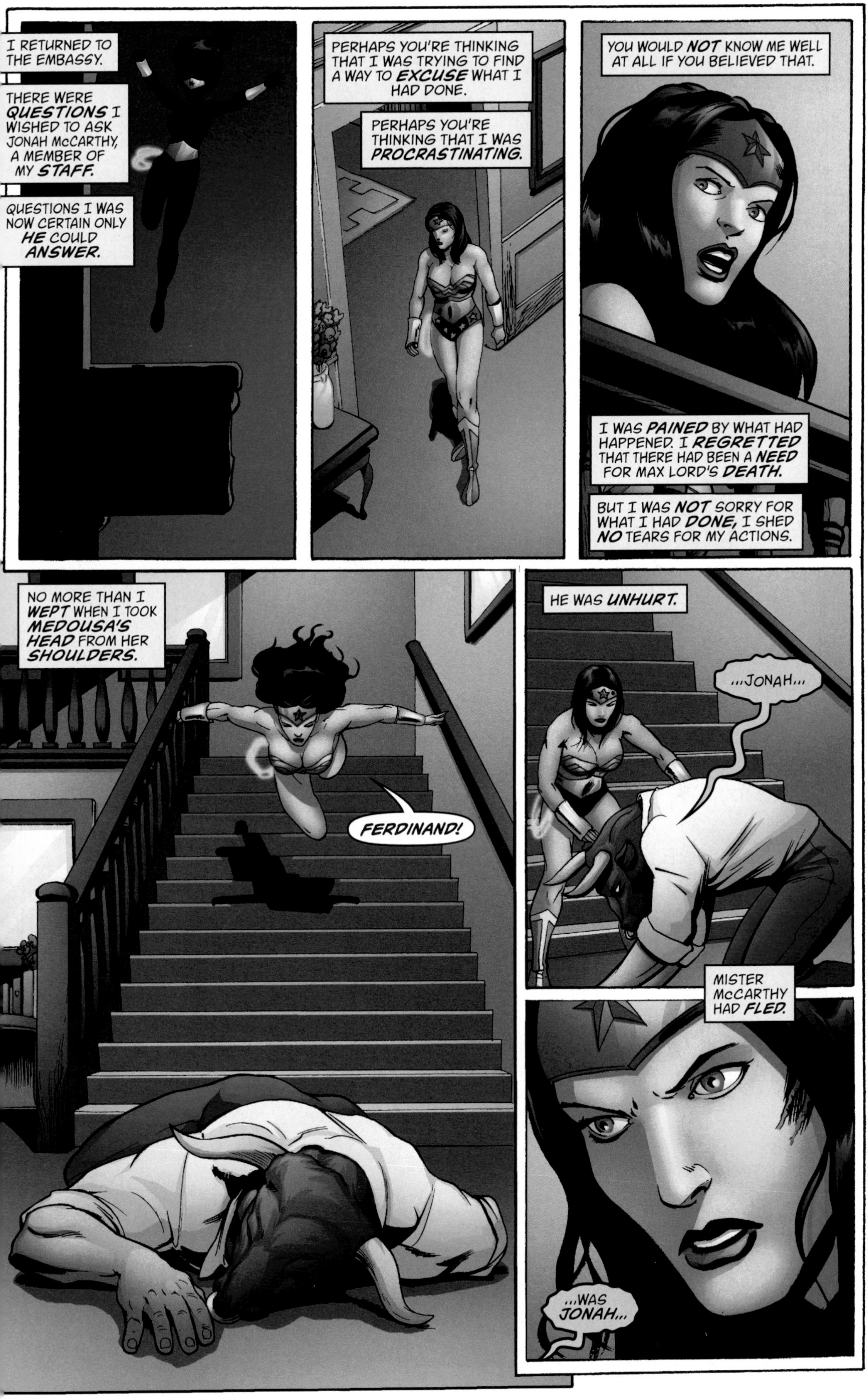
I RETURNED TO THE EMBASSY.
THERE WERE QUESTIONS I WISHED TO ASK JONAH McCARTHY, A MEMBER OF MY STAFF.
QUESTIONS I WAS NOW CERTAIN ONLY HE COULD ANSWER.
PERHAPS YOU'RE THINKING THAT I WAS TRYING TO FIND A WAY TO EXCUSE WHAT I HAD DONE.
PERHAPS YOU'RE THINKING THAT I WAS PROCRASTINATING.
YOU WOULD NOT KNOW ME WELL AT ALL IF YOU BELIEVED THAT.
I WAS PAINED BY WHAT HAD HAPPENED. I REGRETTED THAT THERE HAD BEEN A NEED FOR MAX LORD'S DEATH.
BUT I WAS NOT SORRY FOR WHAT I HAD DONE, I SHED NO TEARS FOR MY ACTIONS.
NO MORE THAN I WEPT WHEN I TOOK MEDOUSA'S HEAD FROM HER SHOULDERS.
FERDINAND!
HE WAS UNHURT.
...JONAH...
MISTER McCARTHY HAD FLED.
...WAS JONAH...

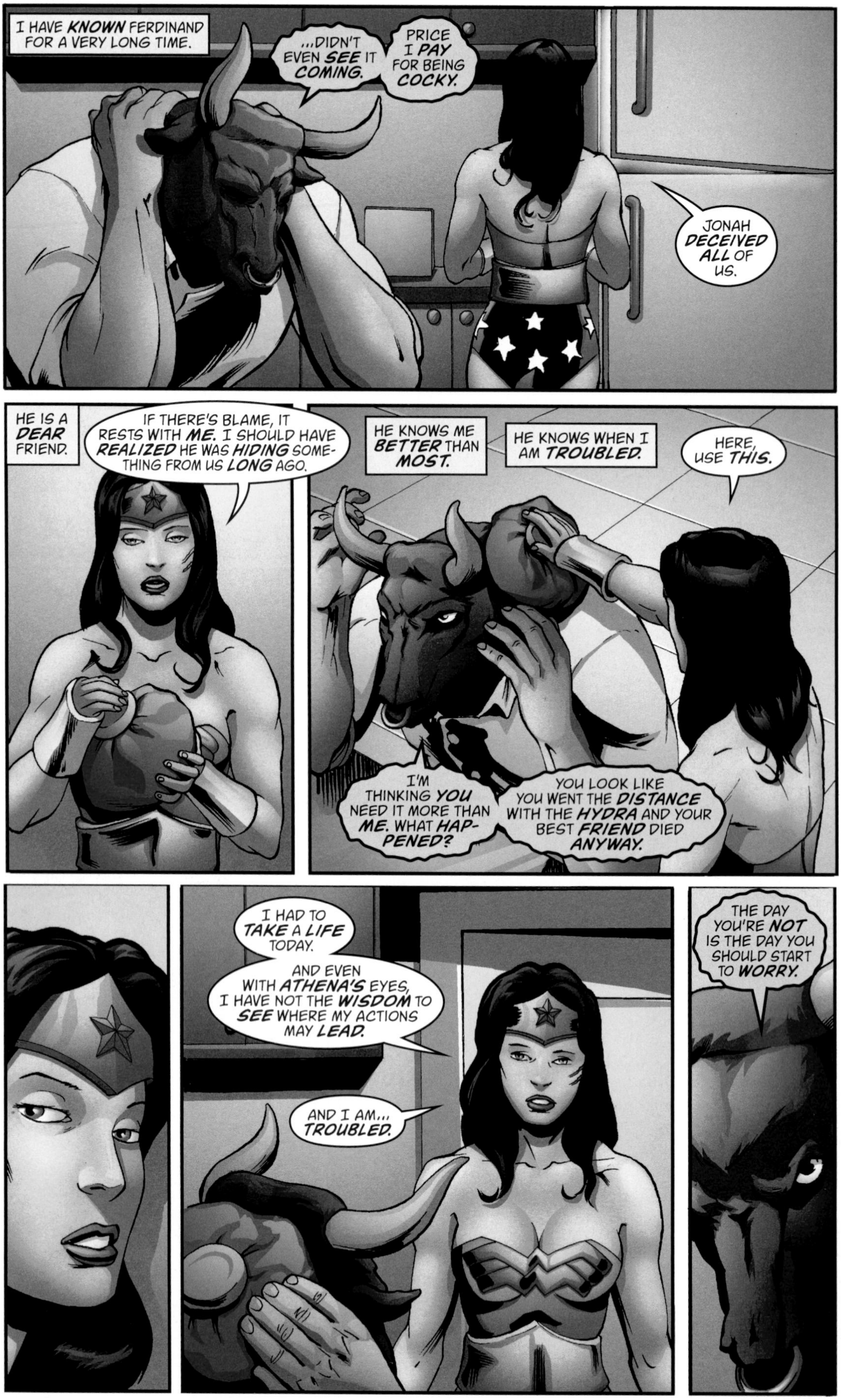
I HAVE KNOWN FERDINAND FOR A VERY LONG TIME.
...DIDN'T EVEN SEE IT COMING.
PRICE I PAY FOR BEING COCKY.
JONAH DECEIVED ALL OF US.
HE IS A DEAR FRIEND.
IF THERE'S BLAME, IT RESTS WITH ME. I SHOULD HAVE REALIZED HE WAS HIDING SOMETHING FROM US LONG AGO.
HE KNOWS ME BETTER THAN MOST.
HE KNOWS WHEN I AM TROUBLED.
HERE, USE THIS.
I'M THINKING YOU NEED IT MORE THAN ME. WHAT HAPPENED?
YOU LOOK LIKE YOU WENT THE DISTANCE WITH THE HYDRA AND YOUR BEST FRIEND DIED ANYWAY.
I HAD TO TAKE A LIFE TODAY.
AND EVEN WITH ATHENA'S EYES, I HAVE NOT THE WISDOM TO SEE WHERE MY ACTIONS MAY LEAD.
AND I AM... TROUBLED.
THE DAY YOU'RE NOT IS THE DAY YOU SHOULD START TO WORRY.

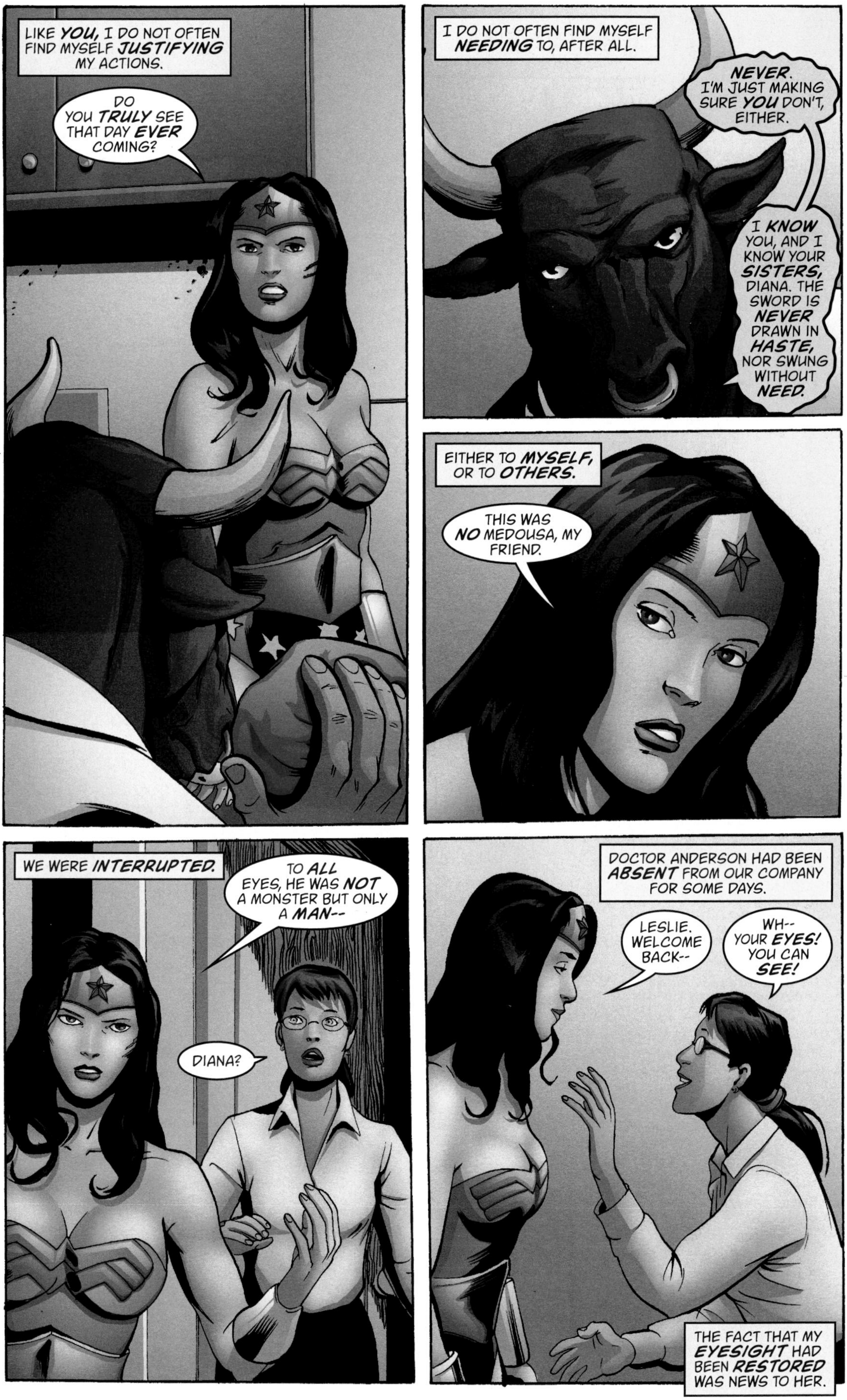
LIKE YOU, I DO NOT OFTEN FIND MYSELF JUSTIFYING MY ACTIONS.
DO YOU TRULY SEE THAT DAY EVER COMING?
I DO NOT OFTEN FIND MYSELF NEEDING TO, AFTER ALL.
NEVER. I'M JUST MAKING SURE YOU DON'T, EITHER.
I KNOW YOU, AND I KNOW YOUR SISTERS, DIANA. THE SWORD IS NEVER DRAWN IN HASTE, NOR SWUNG WITHOUT NEED.
EITHER TO MYSELF, OR TO OTHERS.
THIS WAS NO MEDOUSA, MY FRIEND.
WE WERE INTERRUPTED.
TO ALL EYES, HE WAS NOT A MONSTER BUT ONLY A MAN--
DIANA?
DOCTOR ANDERSON HAD BEEN ABSENT FROM OUR COMPANY FOR SOME DAYS.
LESLIE. WELCOME BACK--
WH-- YOUR EYES! YOU CAN SEE!
THE FACT THAT MY EYESIGHT HAD BEEN RESTORED WAS NEWS TO HER.

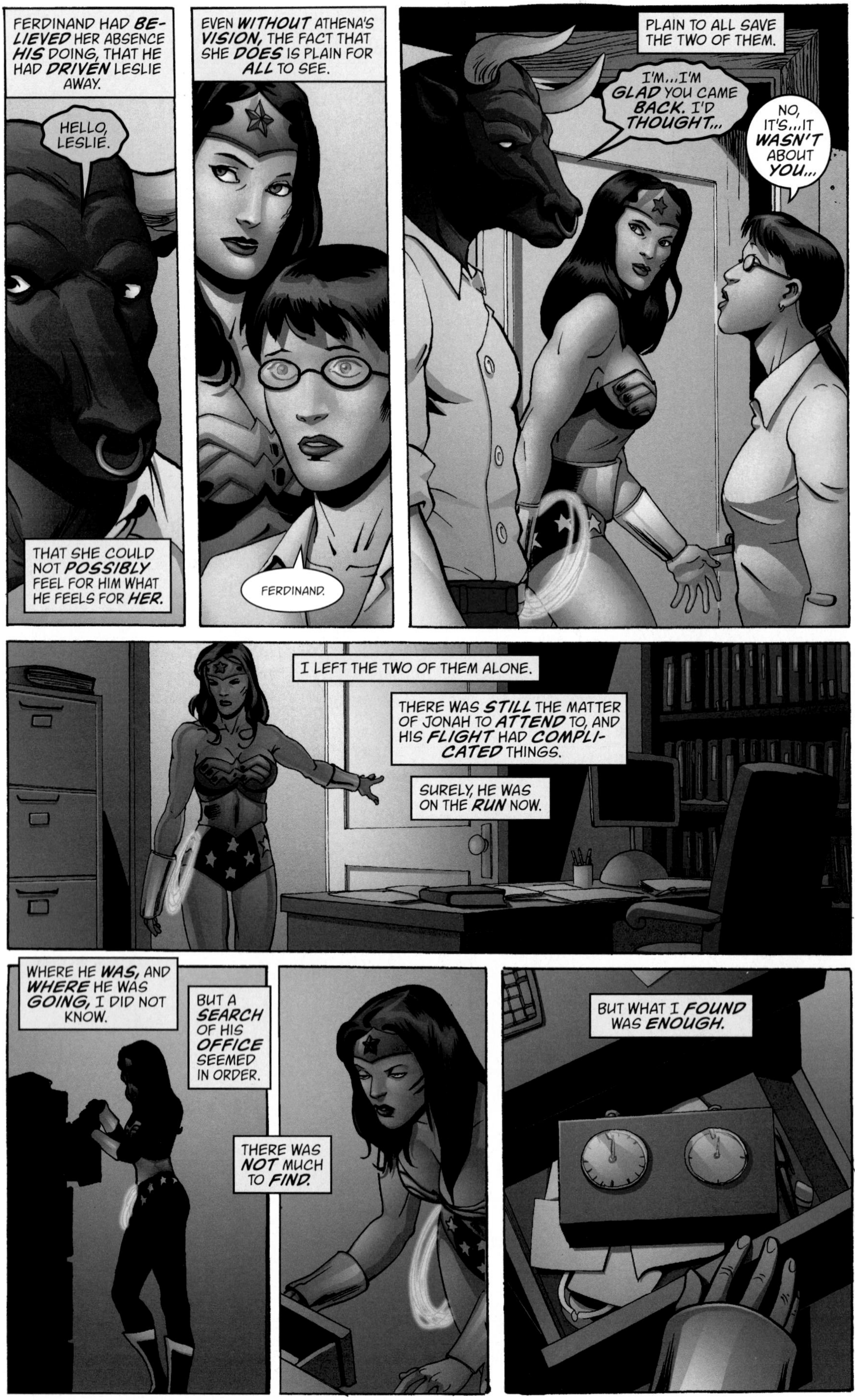

FERDINAND HAD BE-LIEVED HER ABSENCE HIS DOING, THAT HE HAD DRIVEN LESLIE AWAY.
HELLO, LESLIE.
THAT SHE COULD NOT POSSIBLY FEEL FOR HIM WHAT HE FEELS FOR HER.
EVEN WITHOUT ATHENA'S VISION, THE FACT THAT SHE DOES IS PLAIN FOR ALL TO SEE.
FERDINAND.
PLAIN TO ALL SAVE THE TWO OF THEM.
I'M...I'M GLAD YOU CAME BACK. I'D THOUGHT...
NO, IT'S...IT WASN'T ABOUT YOU...
I LEFT THE TWO OF THEM ALONE.
THERE WAS STILL THE MATTER OF JONAH TO ATTEND TO, AND HIS FLIGHT HAD COMPLI-CATED THINGS.
SURELY, HE WAS ON THE RUN NOW.
WHERE HE WAS, AND WHERE HE WAS GOING, I DID NOT KNOW.
BUT A SEARCH OF HIS OFFICE SEEMED IN ORDER.
THERE WAS NOT MUCH TO FIND.
BUT WHAT I FOUND WAS ENOUGH.

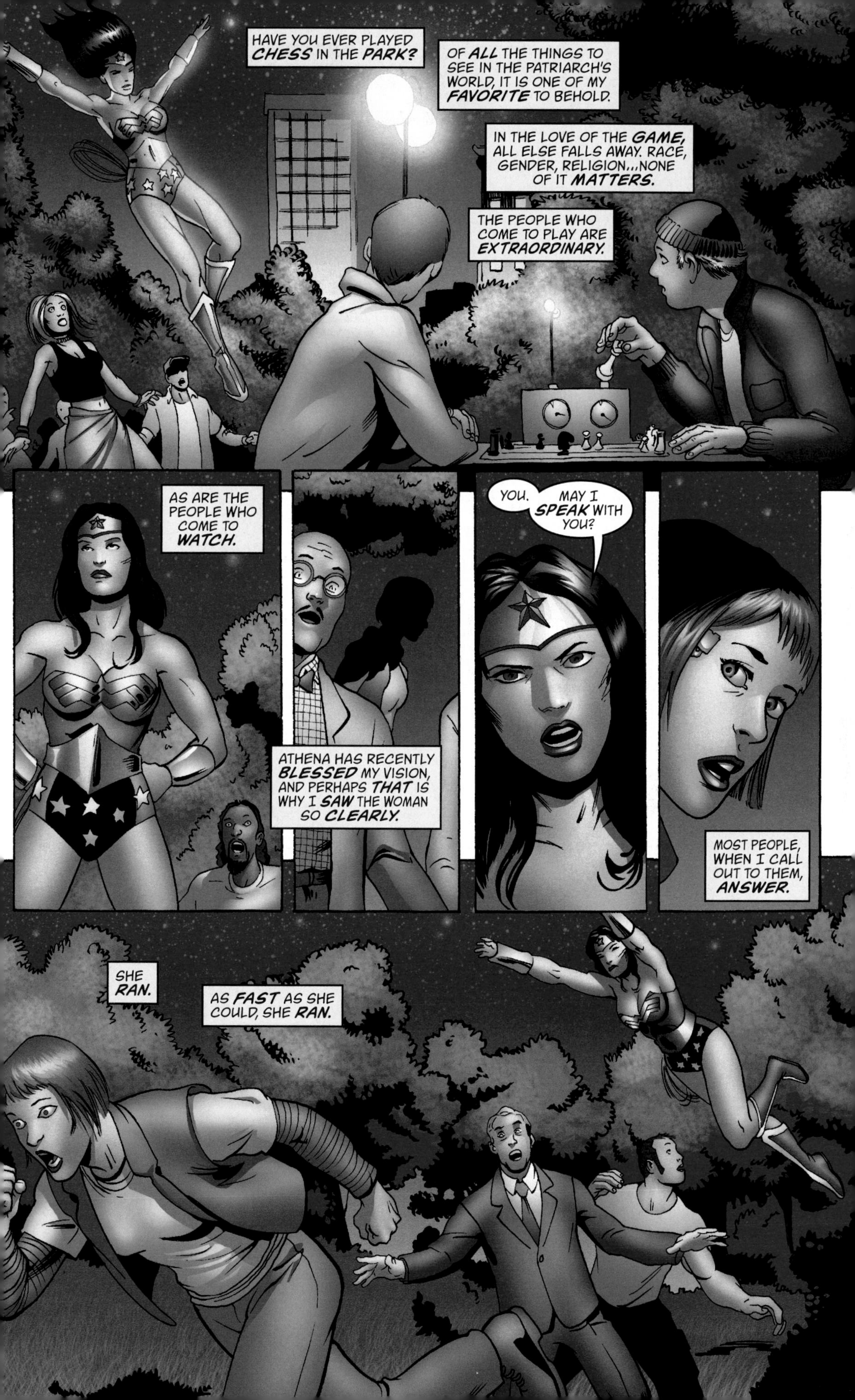
HAVE YOU EVER PLAYED CHESS IN THE PARK?
OF ALL THE THINGS TO SEE IN THE PATRIARCH'S WORLD, IT IS ONE OF MY FAVORITE TO BEHOLD.
IN THE LOVE OF THE GAME, ALL ELSE FALLS AWAY. RACE, GENDER, RELIGION...NONE OF IT MATTERS.
THE PEOPLE WHO COME TO PLAY ARE EXTRAORDINARY.
AS ARE THE PEOPLE WHO COME TO WATCH.
ATHENA HAS RECENTLY BLESSED MY VISION, AND PERHAPS THAT IS WHY I SAW THE WOMAN SO CLEARLY.
YOU.
MAY I SPEAK WITH YOU?
MOST PEOPLE, WHEN I CALL OUT TO THEM, ANSWER.
SHE RAN.
AS FAST AS SHE COULD, SHE RAN.

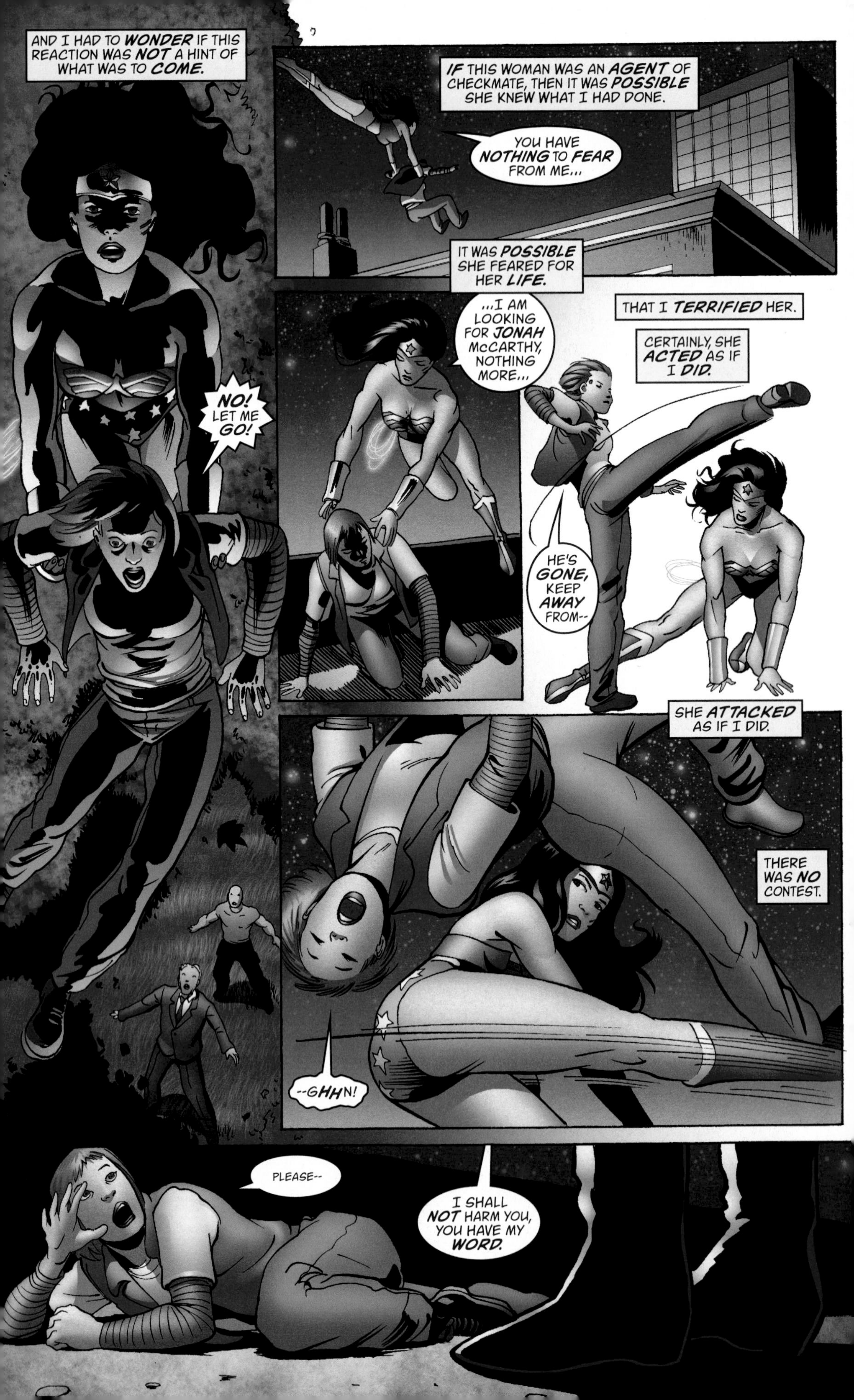
AND I HAD TO WONDER IF THIS REACTION WAS NOT A HINT OF WHAT WAS TO COME.
NO! LET ME GO!
IF THIS WOMAN WAS AN AGENT OF CHECKMATE, THEN IT WAS POSSIBLE SHE KNEW WHAT I HAD DONE.
YOU HAVE NOTHING TO FEAR FROM ME...
IT WAS POSSIBLE SHE FEARED FOR HER LIFE.
...I AM LOOKING FOR JONAH McCARTHY, NOTHING MORE...
THAT I TERRIFIED HER.
CERTAINLY, SHE ACTED AS IF I DID.
HE'S GONE, KEEP AWAY FROM--
SHE ATTACKED AS IF I DID.
THERE WAS NO CONTEST.
--GHHN!
PLEASE--
I SHALL NOT HARM YOU, YOU HAVE MY WORD.

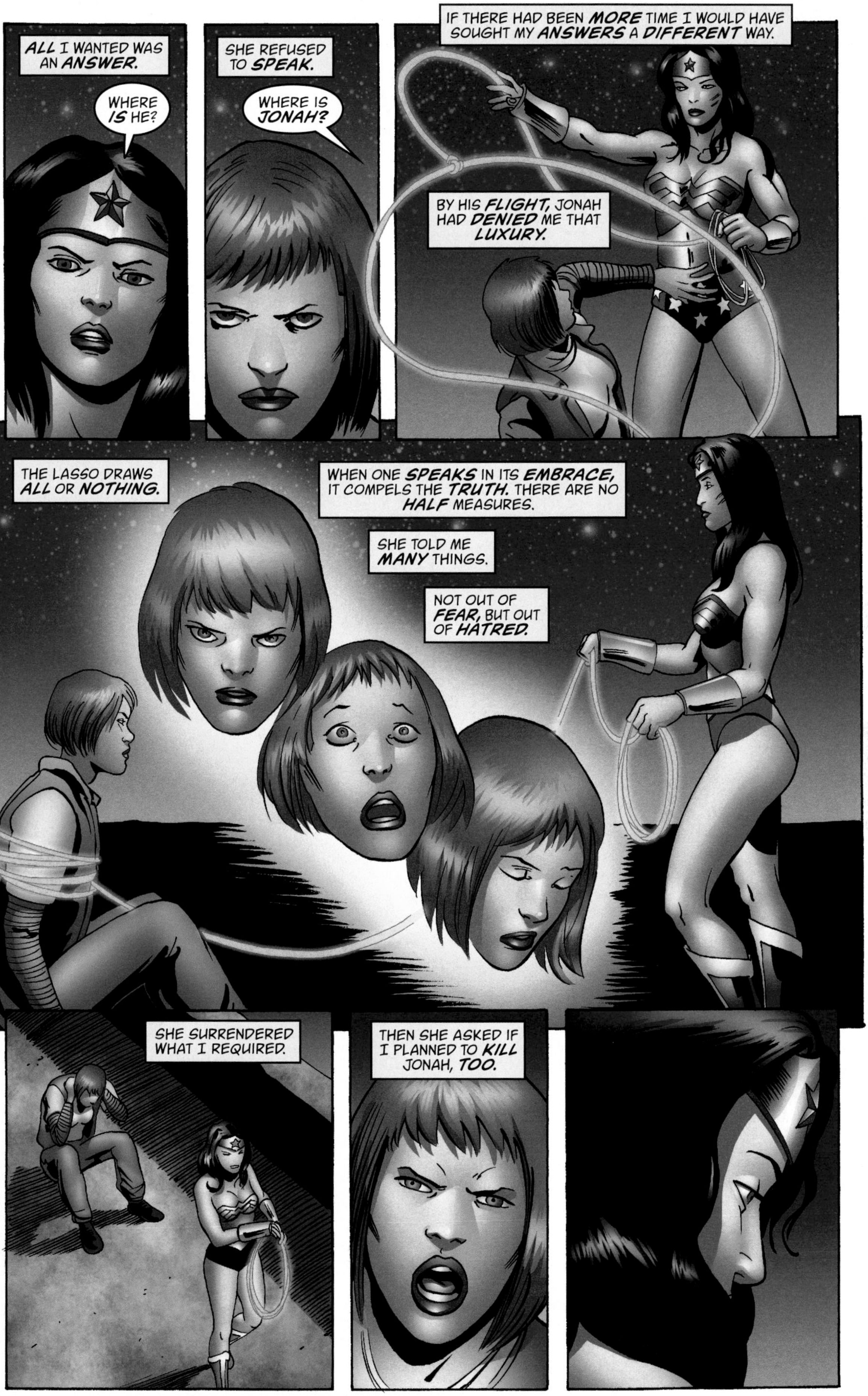
ALL I WANTED WAS AN ANSWER.
WHERE IS HE?
SHE REFUSED TO SPEAK.
WHERE IS JONAH?
IF THERE HAD BEEN MORE TIME I WOULD HAVE SOUGHT MY ANSWERS A DIFFERENT WAY.
BY HIS FLIGHT, JONAH HAD DENIED ME THAT LUXURY.
THE LASSO DRAWS ALL OR NOTHING.
WHEN ONE SPEAKS IN ITS EMBRACE, IT COMPELS THE TRUTH. THERE ARE NO HALF MEASURES.
SHE TOLD ME MANY THINGS.
NOT OUT OF FEAR, BUT OUT OF HATRED.
SHE SURRENDERED WHAT I REQUIRED.
THEN SHE ASKED IF I PLANNED TO KILL JONAH, TOO.

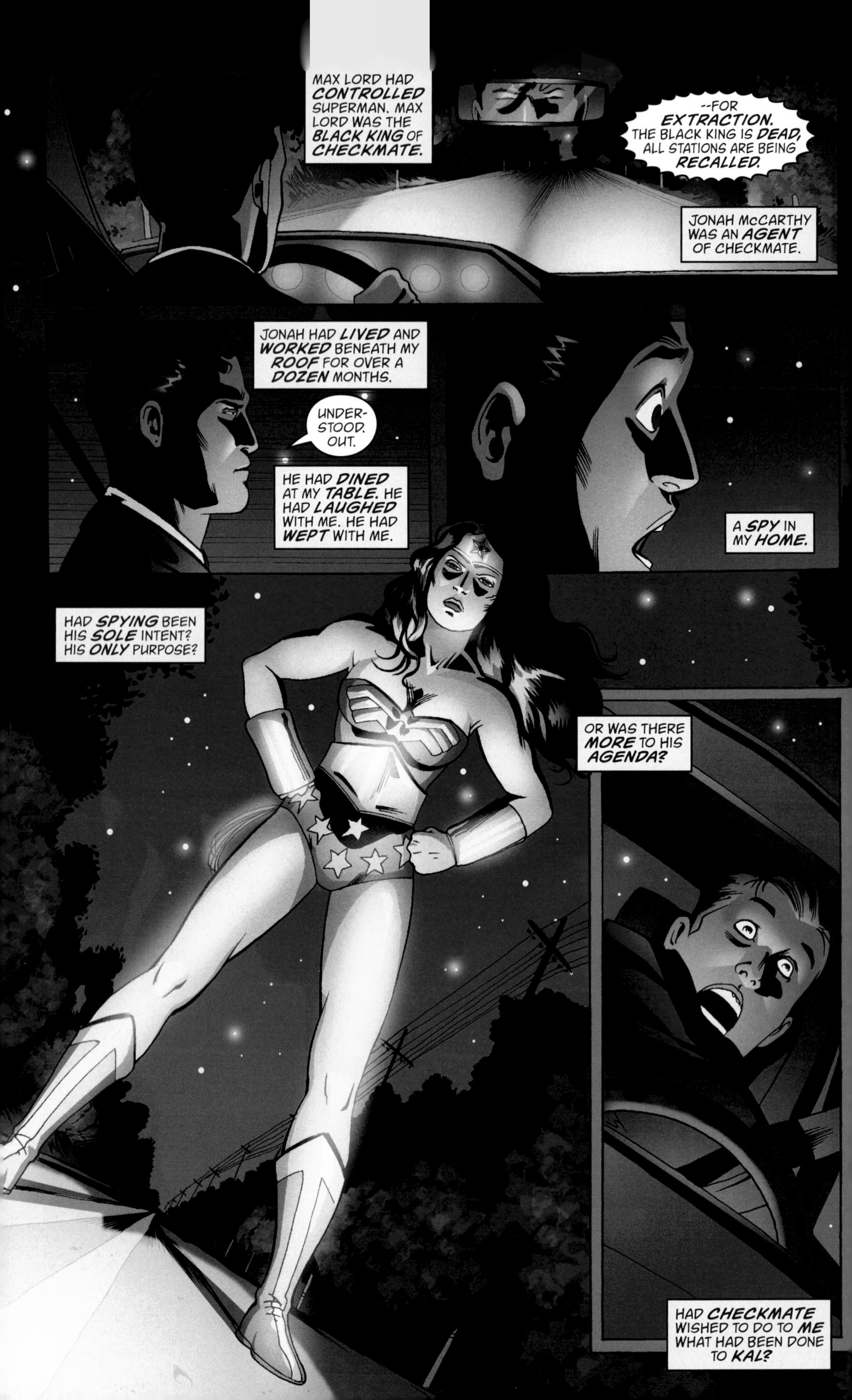
MAX LORD HAD CONTROLLED SUPERMAN. MAX LORD WAS THE BLACK KING OF CHECKMATE.
--FOR EXTRACTION. THE BLACK KING IS DEAD, ALL STATIONS ARE BEING RECALLED.
JONAH McCARTHY WAS AN AGENT OF CHECKMATE.
JONAH HAD LIVED AND WORKED BENEATH MY ROOF FOR OVER A DOZEN MONTHS.
UNDER-STOOD. OUT.
HE HAD DINED AT MY TABLE. HE HAD LAUGHED WITH ME. HE HAD WEPT WITH ME.
A SPY IN MY HOME.
HAD SPYING BEEN HIS SOLE INTENT? HIS ONLY PURPOSE?
OR WAS THERE MORE TO HIS AGENDA?
HAD CHECKMATE WISHED TO DO TO ME WHAT HAD BEEN DONE TO KAL?

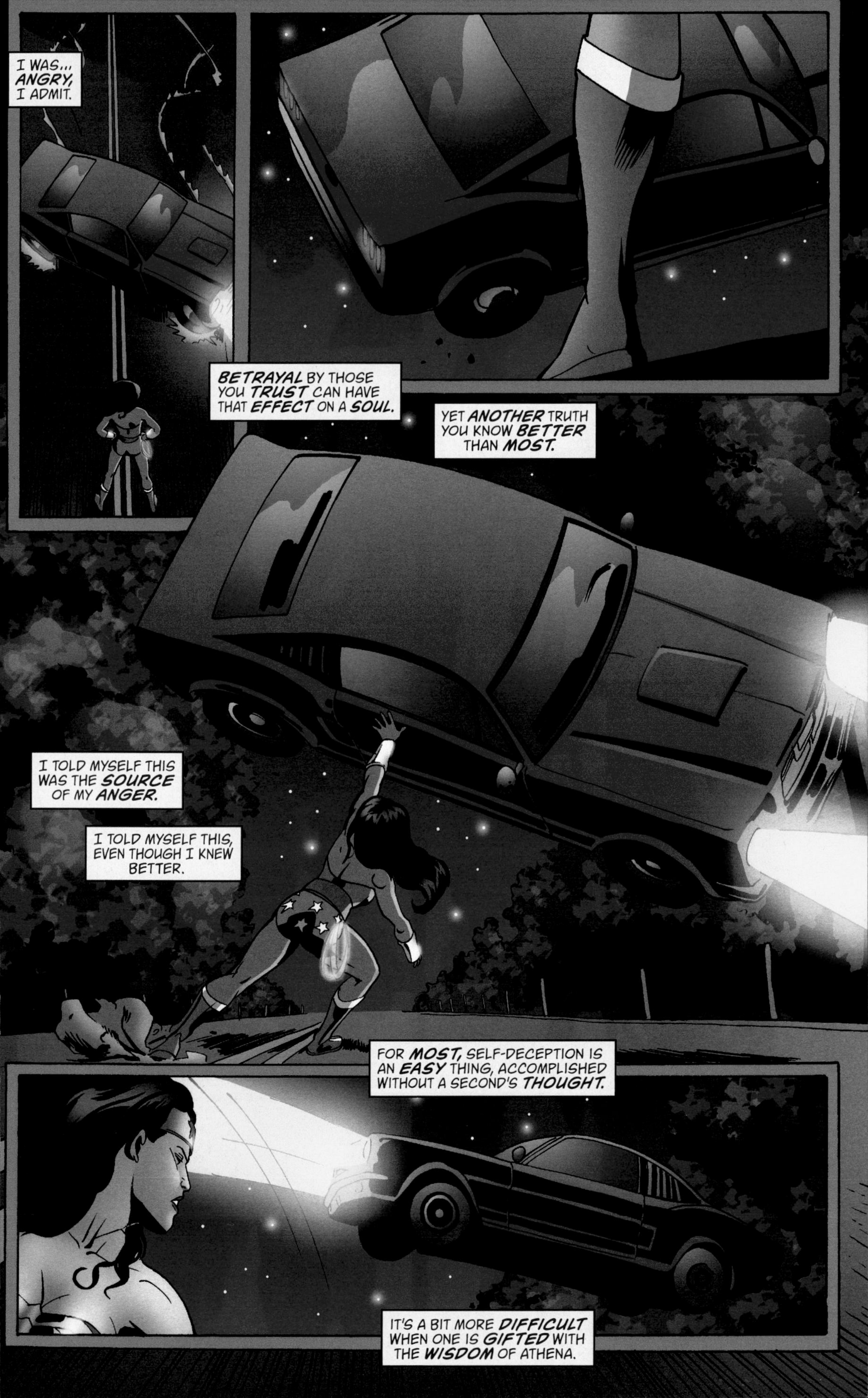
I WAS... ANGRY, I ADMIT.
BETRAYAL BY THOSE YOU TRUST CAN HAVE THAT EFFECT ON A SOUL.
YET ANOTHER TRUTH YOU KNOW BETTER THAN MOST.
I TOLD MYSELF THIS WAS THE SOURCE OF MY ANGER.
I TOLD MYSELF THIS, EVEN THOUGH I KNEW BETTER.
FOR MOST, SELF-DECEPTION IS AN EASY THING, ACCOMPLISHED WITHOUT A SECOND'S THOUGHT.
IT'S A BIT MORE DIFFICULT WHEN ONE IS GIFTED WITH THE WISDOM OF ATHENA.

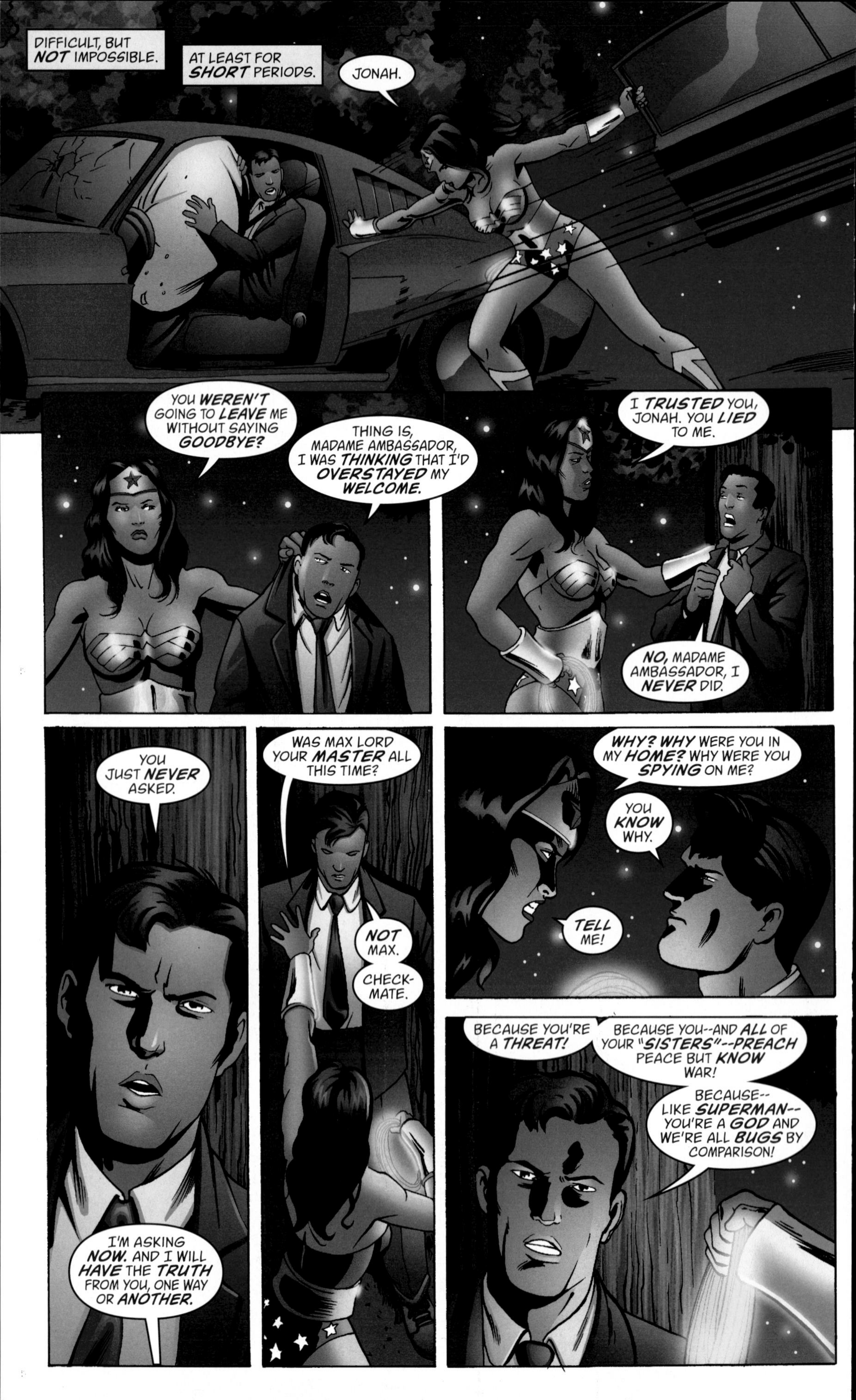
DIFFICULT, BUT NOT IMPOSSIBLE.
AT LEAST FOR SHORT PERIODS.
JONAH.
YOU WEREN'T GOING TO LEAVE ME WITHOUT SAYING GOODBYE?
THING IS, MADAME AMBASSADOR, I WAS THINKING THAT I'D OVERSTAYED MY WELCOME.
I TRUSTED YOU, JONAH. YOU LIED TO ME.
NO, MADAME AMBASSADOR, I NEVER DID.
YOU JUST NEVER ASKED.
I'M ASKING NOW. AND I WILL HAVE THE TRUTH FROM YOU, ONE WAY OR ANOTHER.
WAS MAX LORD YOUR MASTER ALL THIS TIME?
NOT MAX.
CHECK-MATE.
WHY? WHY WERE YOU IN MY HOME? WHY WERE YOU SPYING ON ME?
YOU KNOW WHY.
TELL ME!
BECAUSE YOU'RE A THREAT!
BECAUSE YOU--AND ALL OF YOUR "SISTERS"--PREACH PEACE BUT KNOW WAR!
BECAUSE--LIKE SUPERMAN--YOU'RE A GOD AND WE'RE ALL BUGS BY COMPARISON!

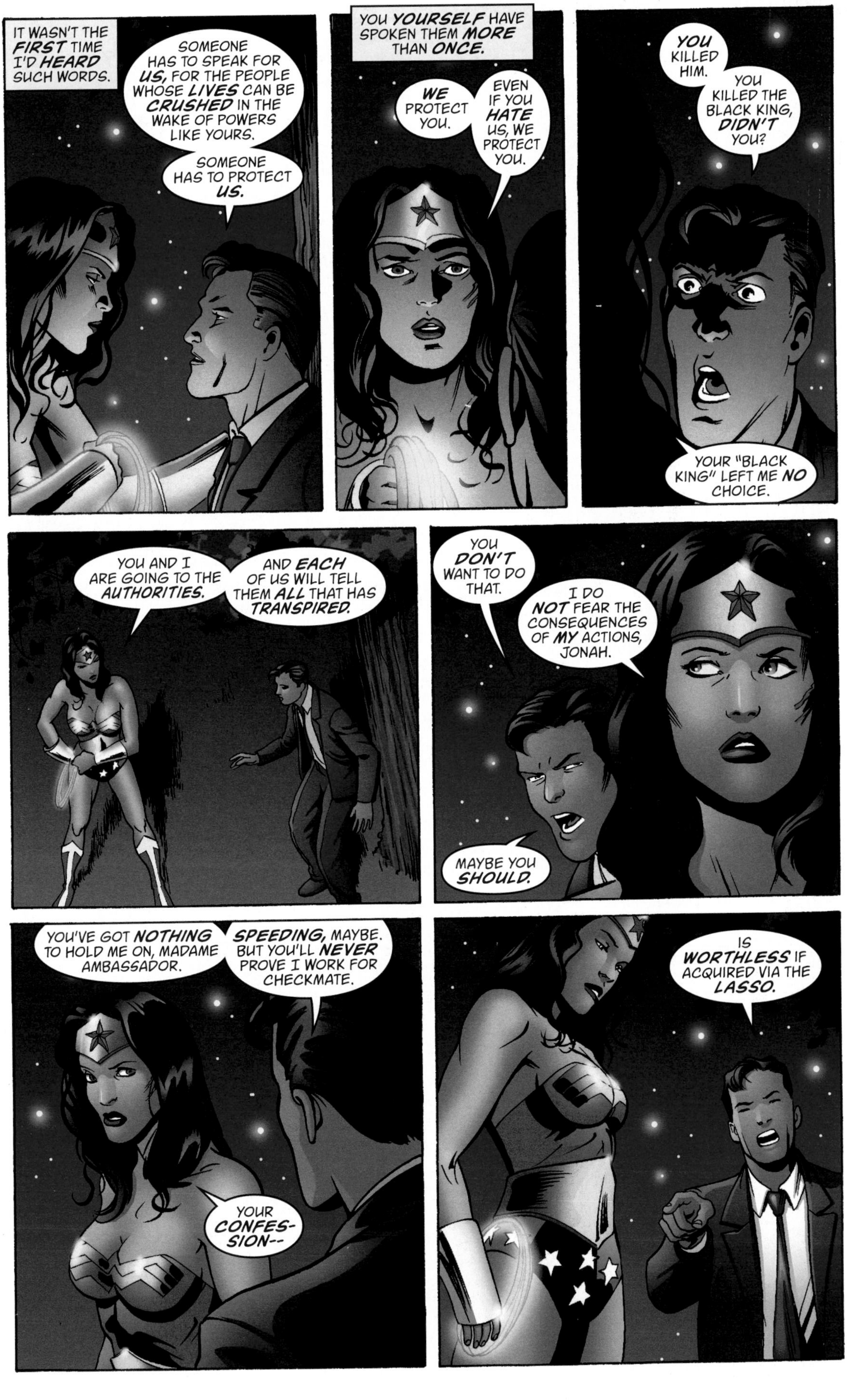
IT WASN'T THE FIRST TIME I'D HEARD SUCH WORDS.
SOMEONE HAS TO SPEAK FOR US, FOR THE PEOPLE WHOSE LIVES CAN BE CRUSHED IN THE WAKE OF POWERS LIKE YOURS.
SOMEONE HAS TO PROTECT US.
YOU YOURSELF HAVE SPOKEN THEM MORE THAN ONCE.
WE PROTECT YOU.
EVEN IF YOU HATE US, WE PROTECT YOU.
YOU KILLED HIM.
YOU KILLED THE BLACK KING, DIDN'T YOU?
YOUR "BLACK KING" LEFT ME NO CHOICE.
YOU AND I ARE GOING TO THE AUTHORITIES.
AND EACH OF US WILL TELL THEM ALL THAT HAS TRANSPIRED.
YOU DON'T WANT TO DO THAT.
I DO NOT FEAR THE CONSEQUENCES OF MY ACTIONS, JONAH.
MAYBE YOU SHOULD.
YOU'VE GOT NOTHING TO HOLD ME ON, MADAME AMBASSADOR.
SPEEDING, MAYBE. BUT YOU'LL NEVER PROVE I WORK FOR CHECKMATE.
YOUR CONFES- SION--
IS WORTHLESS IF ACQUIRED VIA THE LASSO.

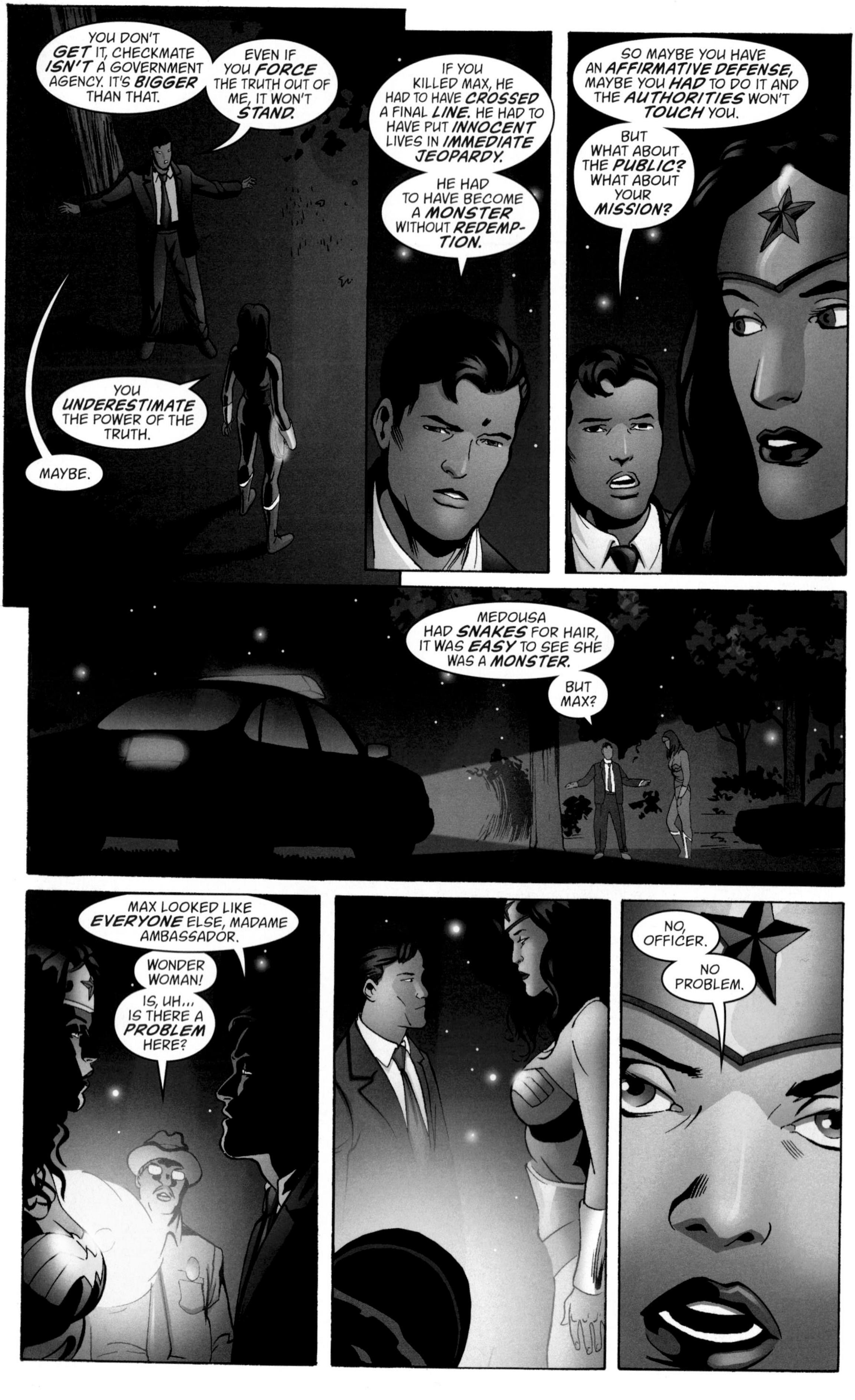
YOU DON'T GET IT, CHECKMATE ISN'T A GOVERNMENT AGENCY. IT'S BIGGER THAN THAT.
EVEN IF YOU FORCE THE TRUTH OUT OF ME, IT WON'T STAND.
YOU UNDERESTIMATE THE POWER OF THE TRUTH.
MAYBE.
IF YOU KILLED MAX, HE HAD TO HAVE CROSSED A FINAL LINE. HE HAD TO HAVE PUT INNOCENT LIVES IN IMMEDIATE JEOPARDY.
HE HAD TO HAVE BECOME A MONSTER WITHOUT REDEMP-TION.
SO MAYBE YOU HAVE AN AFFIRMATIVE DEFENSE, MAYBE YOU HAD TO DO IT AND THE AUTHORITIES WON'T TOUCH YOU.
BUT WHAT ABOUT THE PUBLIC? WHAT ABOUT YOUR MISSION?
MEDOUSA HAD SNAKES FOR HAIR, IT WAS EASY TO SEE SHE WAS A MONSTER.
BUT MAX?
MAX LOOKED LIKE EVERYONE ELSE, MADAME AMBASSADOR.
WONDER WOMAN!
IS, UH... IS THERE A PROBLEM HERE?
NO, OFFICER.
NO PROBLEM.

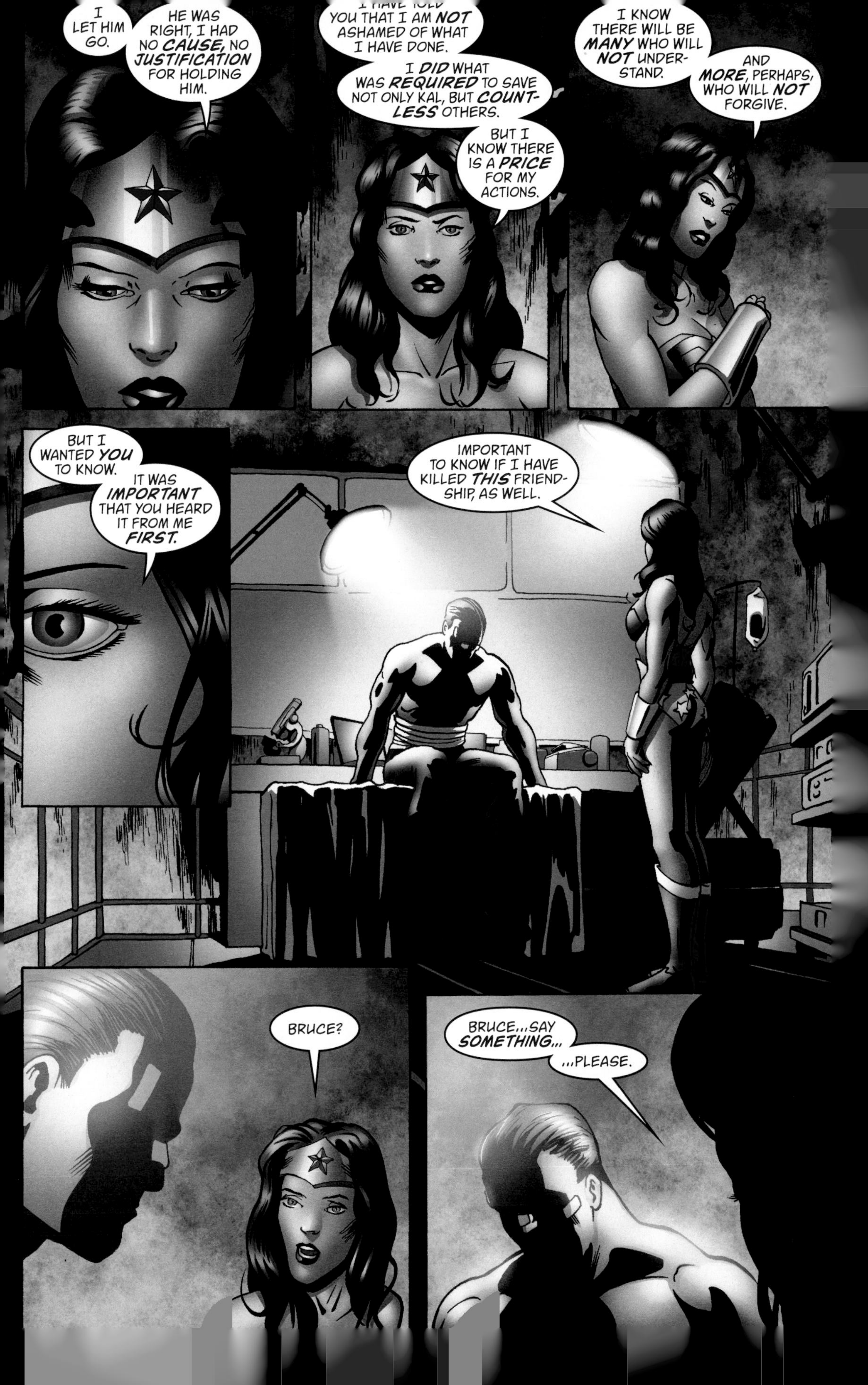
I LET HIM GO.
HE WAS RIGHT, I HAD NO CAUSE, NO JUSTIFICATION FOR HOLDING HIM.
YOU THAT I AM NOT ASHAMED OF WHAT I HAVE DONE.
I DID WHAT WAS REQUIRED TO SAVE NOT ONLY KAL, BUT COUNTLESS OTHERS.
BUT I KNOW THERE IS A PRICE FOR MY ACTIONS.
I KNOW THERE WILL BE MANY WHO WILL NOT UNDERSTAND.
AND MORE, PERHAPS, WHO WILL NOT FORGIVE.
BUT I WANTED YOU TO KNOW.
IT WAS IMPORTANT THAT YOU HEARD IT FROM ME FIRST.
IMPORTANT TO KNOW IF I HAVE KILLED THIS FRIENDSHIP, AS WELL.
BRUCE?
BRUCE...SAY SOMETHING...
...PLEASE.

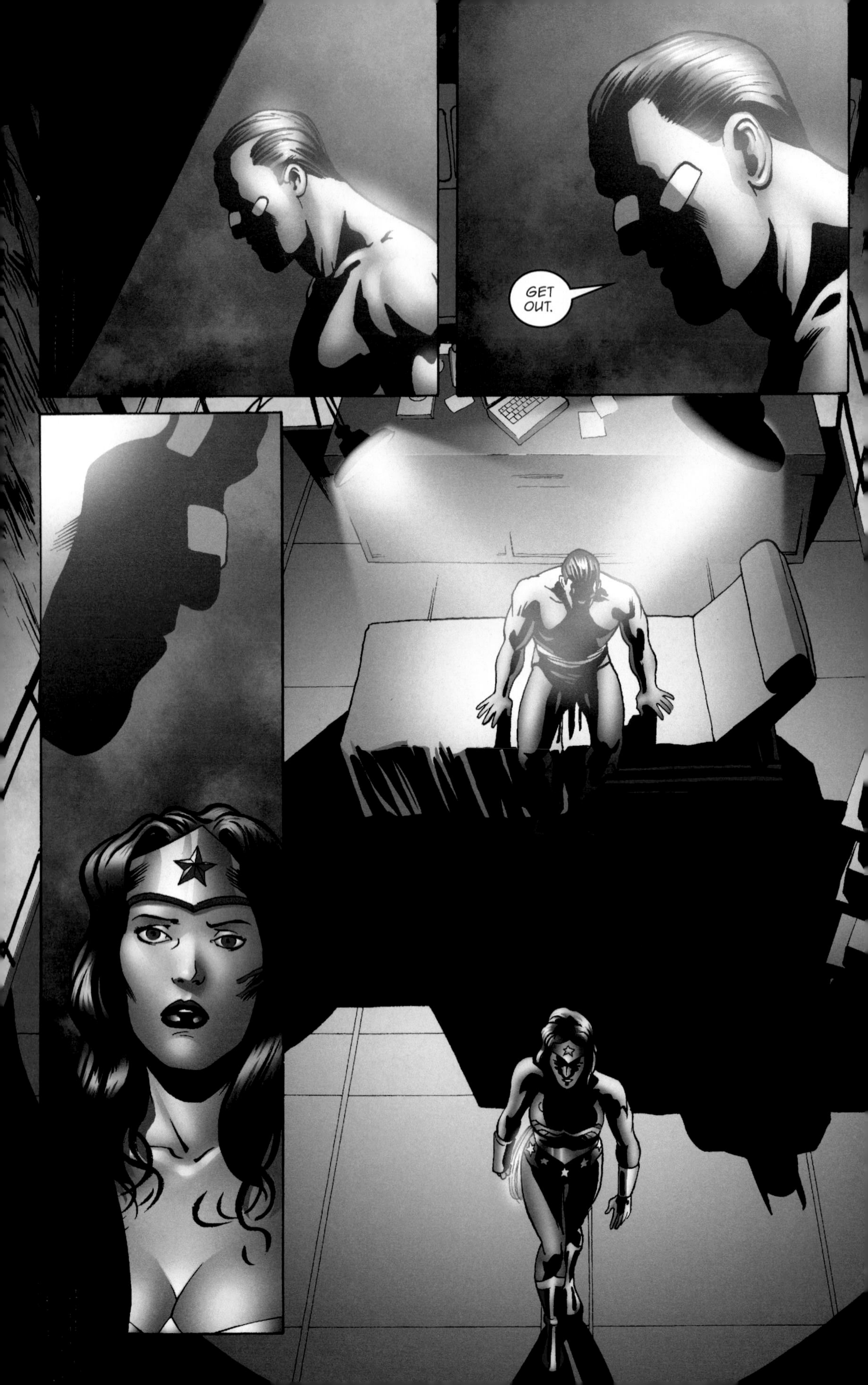
GET OUT.

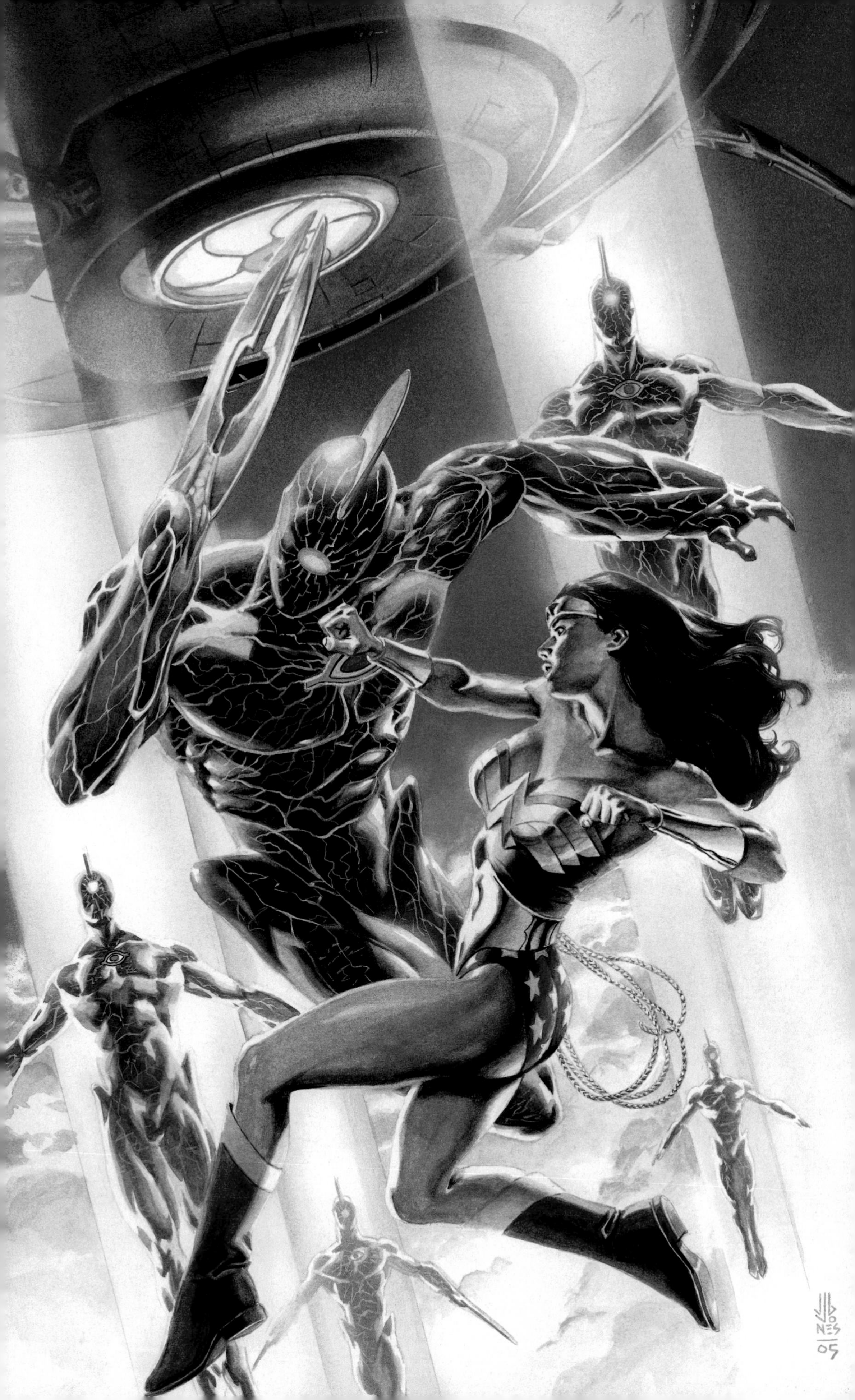

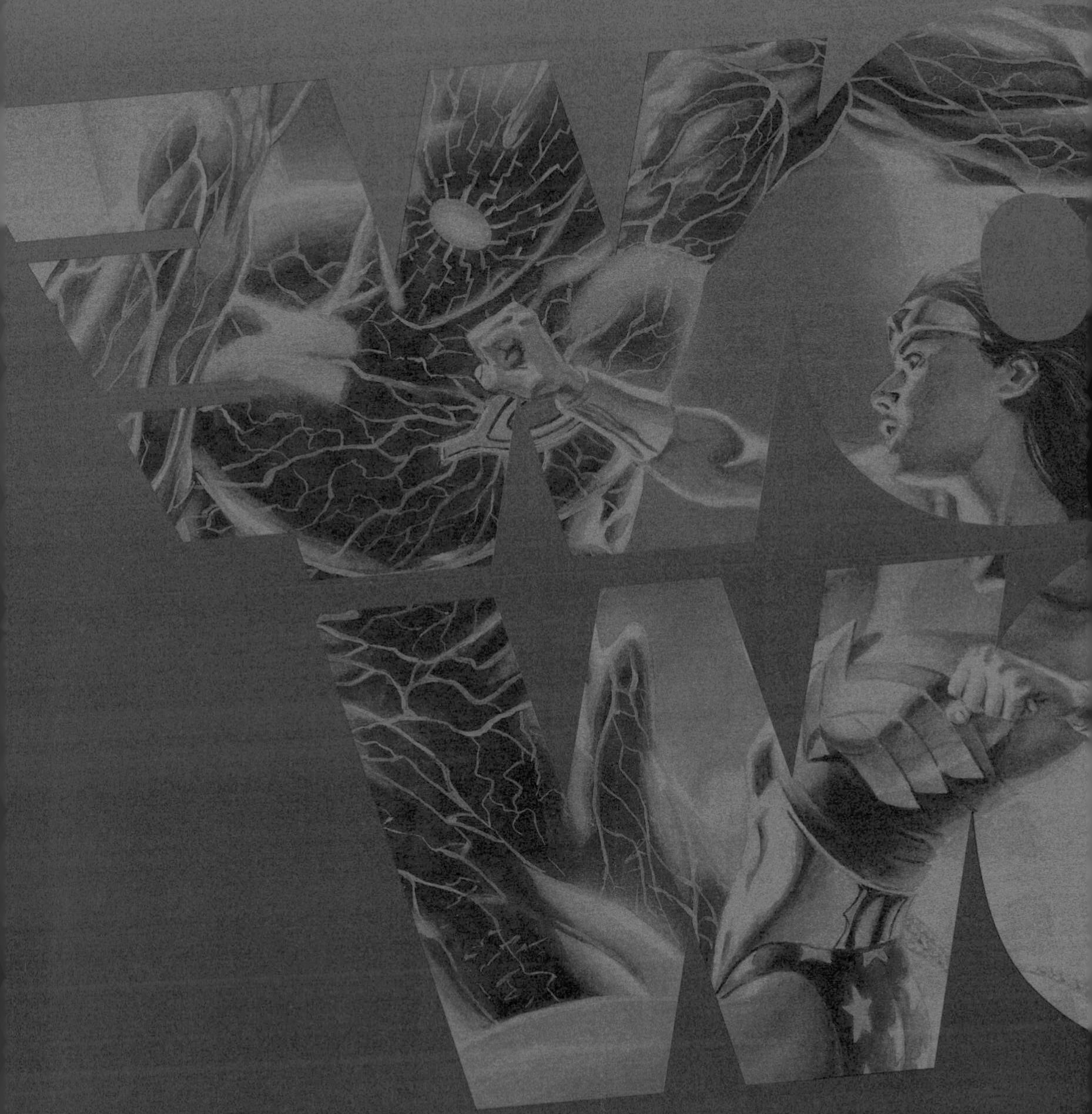

"PRIDE OF THE AMAZONS"

Greg Rucka – *writer*
Rags Morales and **Cliff Richards** – *pencils*
Michael Bair, Ray Snyder and **Mark Propst** – *inks*
Richard and **Tanya Horie** – *colors*
Todd Klein – *letters*
J.G. Jones – *cover*

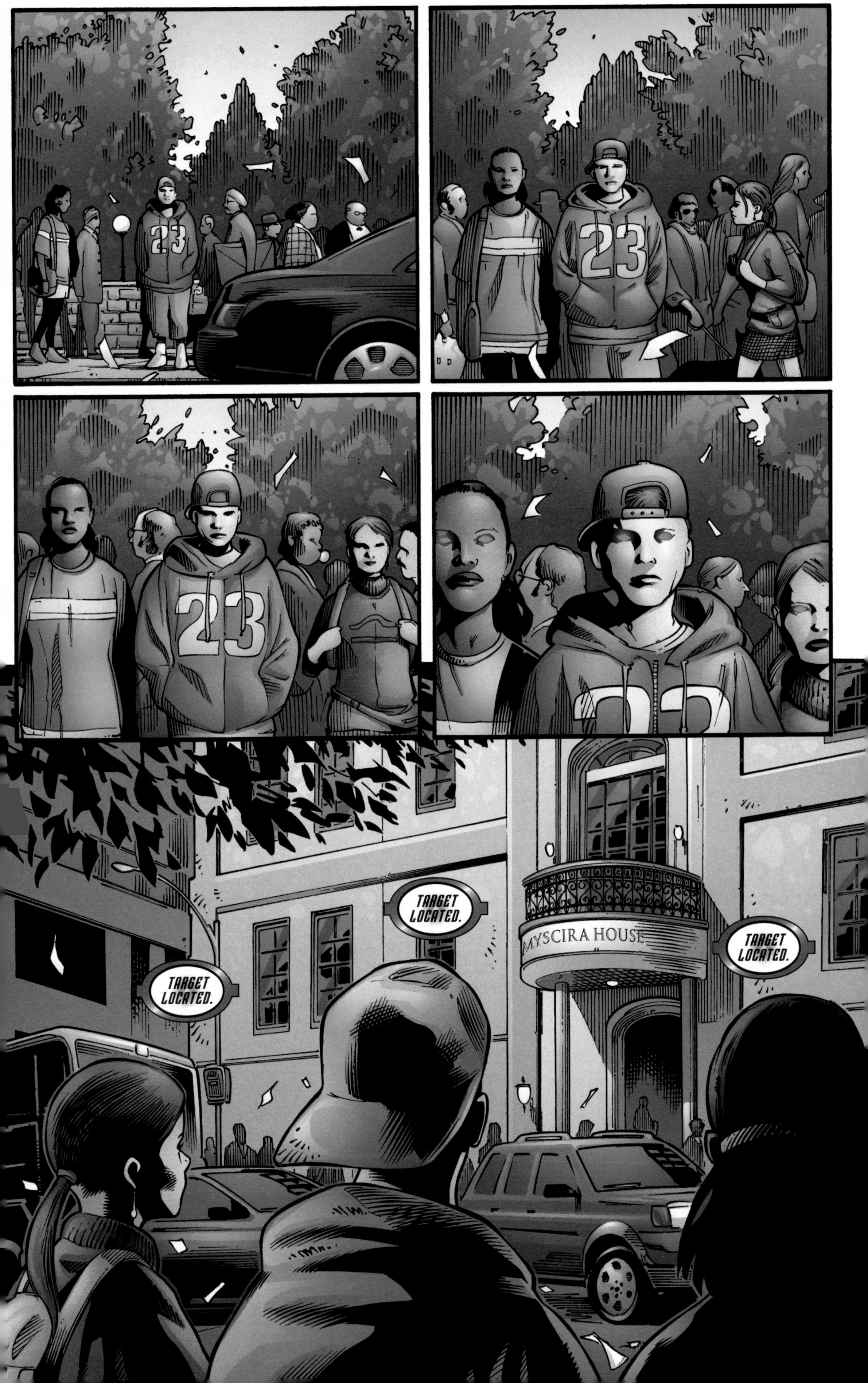

23
23
23
MYSCIRA HOUSE
TARGET LOCATED.
TARGET LOCATED.
TARGET LOCATED.

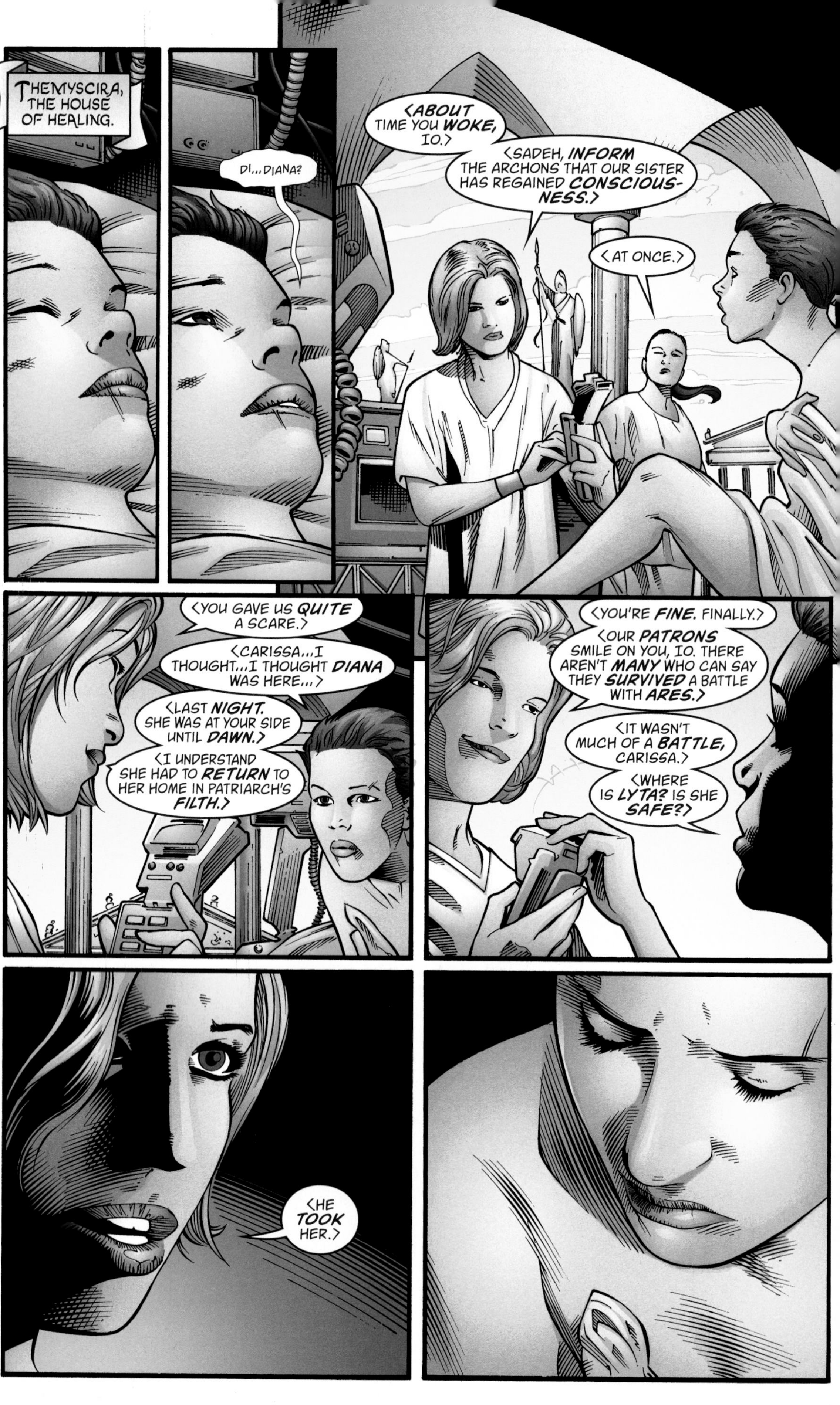
THEMYSCIRA, THE HOUSE OF HEALING.
DI...DIANA?
<ABOUT TIME YOU WOKE, IO.>
<SADEH, INFORM THE ARCHONS THAT OUR SISTER HAS REGAINED CONSCIOUSNESS.>
<AT ONCE.>
<YOU GAVE US QUITE A SCARE.>
<CARISSA...I THOUGHT...I THOUGHT DIANA WAS HERE...>
<LAST NIGHT. SHE WAS AT YOUR SIDE UNTIL DAWN.>
<I UNDERSTAND SHE HAD TO RETURN TO HER HOME IN PATRIARCH'S FILTH.>
<YOU'RE FINE. FINALLY.>
<OUR PATRONS SMILE ON YOU, IO. THERE AREN'T MANY WHO CAN SAY THEY SURVIVED A BATTLE WITH ARES.>
<IT WASN'T MUCH OF A BATTLE, CARISSA.>
<WHERE IS LYTA? IS SHE SAFE?>
<HE TOOK HER.>

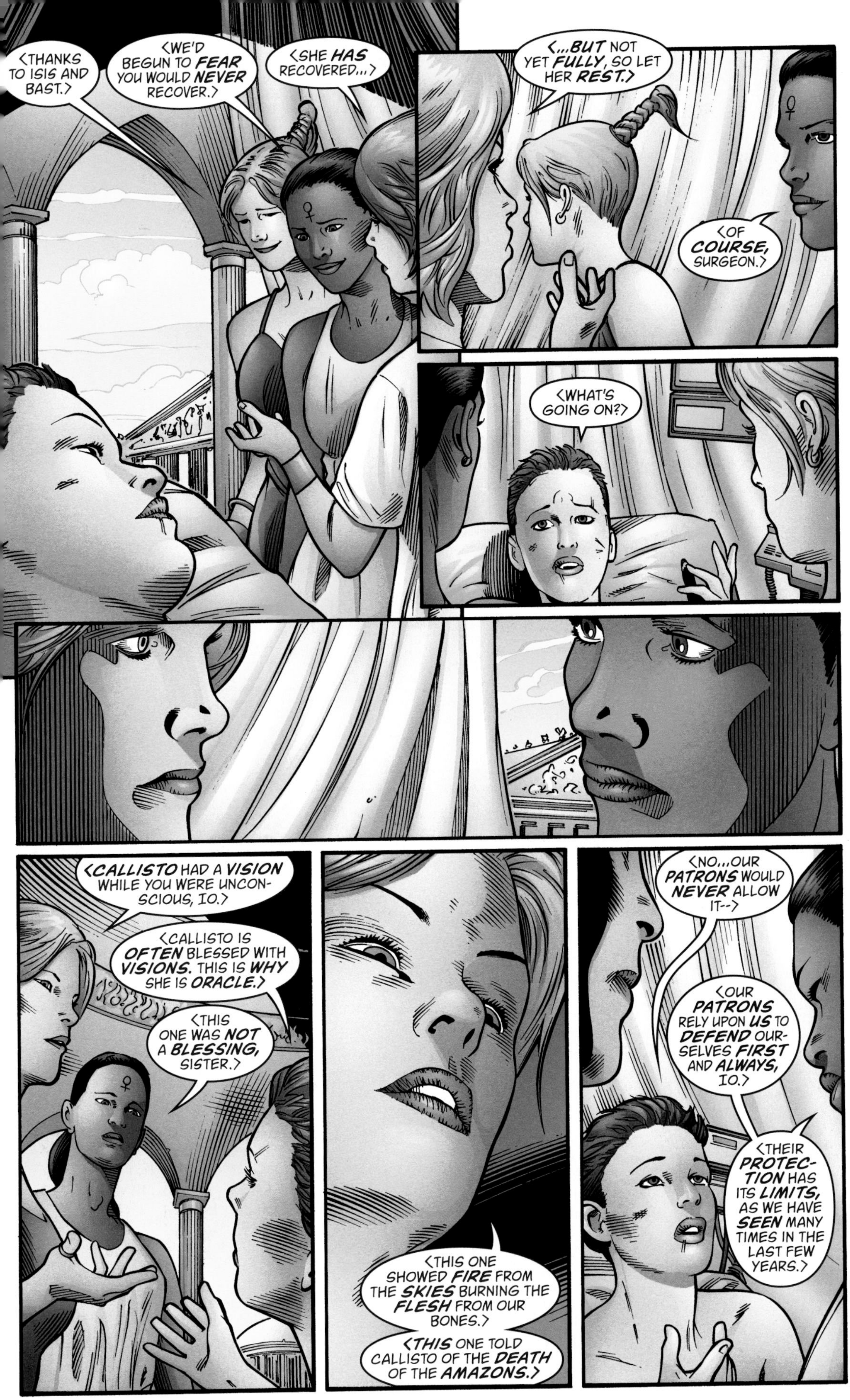

<THANKS TO ISIS AND BAST.>
<WE'D BEGUN TO FEAR YOU WOULD NEVER RECOVER.>
<SHE HAS RECOVERED...>
<...BUT NOT YET FULLY, SO LET HER REST.>
<OF COURSE, SURGEON.>
<WHAT'S GOING ON?>
<CALLISTO HAD A VISION WHILE YOU WERE UNCON-SCIOUS, IO.>
<CALLISTO IS OFTEN BLESSED WITH VISIONS. THIS IS WHY SHE IS ORACLE.>
<THIS ONE WAS NOT A BLESSING, SISTER.>
<THIS ONE SHOWED FIRE FROM THE SKIES BURNING THE FLESH FROM OUR BONES.>
<THIS ONE TOLD CALLISTO OF THE DEATH OF THE AMAZONS.>
<NO...OUR PATRONS WOULD NEVER ALLOW IT-->
<OUR PATRONS RELY UPON US TO DEFEND OUR-SELVES FIRST AND ALWAYS, IO.>
<THEIR PROTEC-TION HAS ITS LIMITS, AS WE HAVE SEEN MANY TIMES IN THE LAST FEW YEARS.>

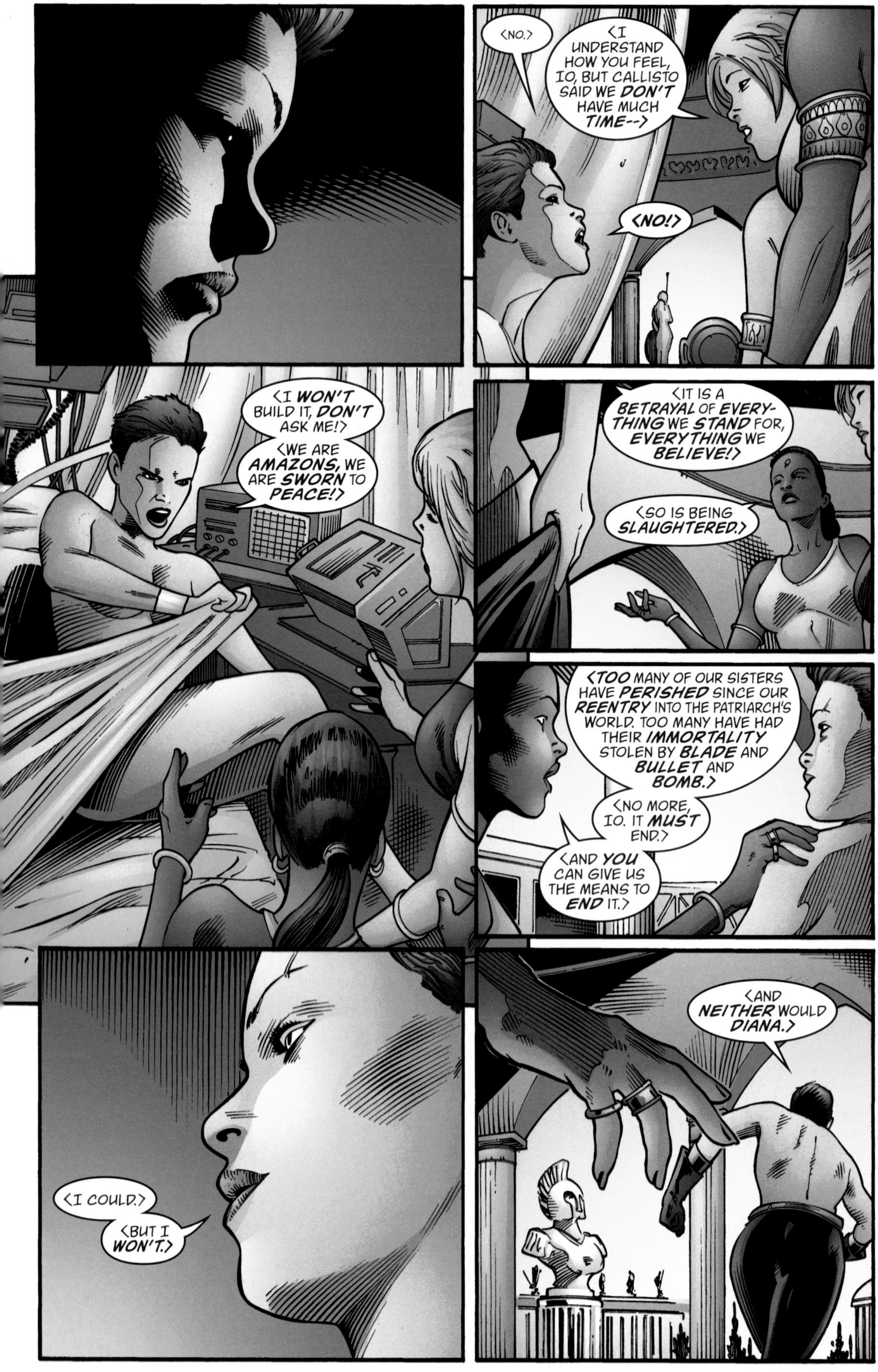

<NO.>
<I UNDERSTAND HOW YOU FEEL, IO, BUT CALLISTO SAID WE DON'T HAVE MUCH TIME-->
<NO!>
<I WON'T BUILD IT, DON'T ASK ME!>
<WE ARE AMAZONS, WE ARE SWORN TO PEACE!>
<IT IS A BETRAYAL OF EVERYTHING WE STAND FOR, EVERYTHING WE BELIEVE!>
<SO IS BEING SLAUGHTERED.>
<TOO MANY OF OUR SISTERS HAVE PERISHED SINCE OUR REENTRY INTO THE PATRIARCH'S WORLD. TOO MANY HAVE HAD THEIR IMMORTALITY STOLEN BY BLADE AND BULLET AND BOMB.>
<NO MORE, IO. IT MUST END.>
<AND YOU CAN GIVE US THE MEANS TO END IT.>
<I COULD.>
<BUT I WON'T.>
<AND NEITHER WOULD DIANA.>

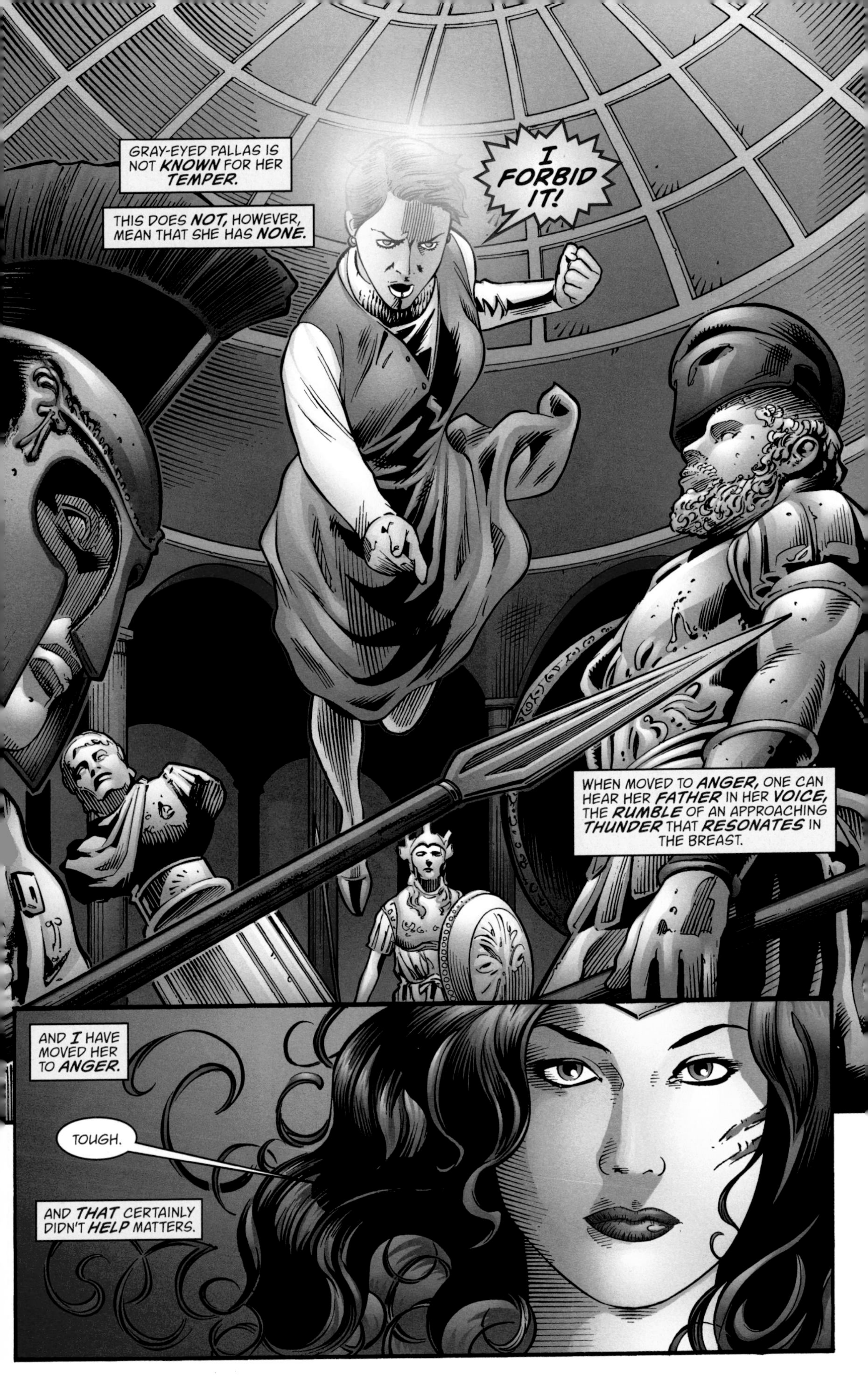
GRAY-EYED PALLAS IS NOT KNOWN FOR HER TEMPER.
THIS DOES NOT, HOWEVER, MEAN THAT SHE HAS NONE.
I FORBID IT!
WHEN MOVED TO ANGER, ONE CAN HEAR HER FATHER IN HER VOICE, THE RUMBLE OF AN APPROACHING THUNDER THAT RESONATES IN THE BREAST.
AND I HAVE MOVED HER TO ANGER.
TOUGH.
AND THAT CERTAINLY DIDN'T HELP MATTERS.

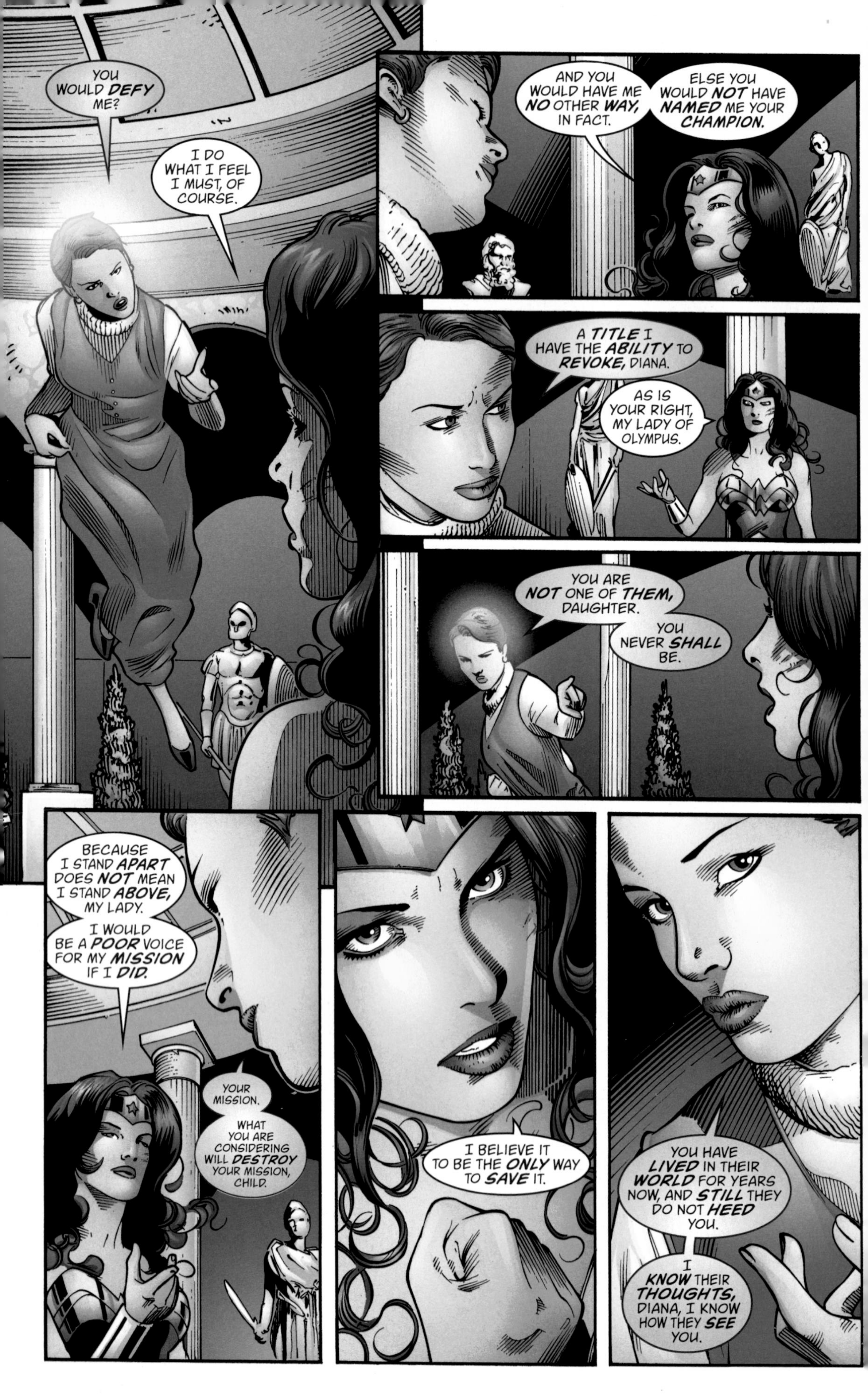
YOU WOULD DEFY ME?
I DO WHAT I FEEL I MUST, OF COURSE.
AND YOU WOULD HAVE ME NO OTHER WAY, IN FACT.
ELSE YOU WOULD NOT HAVE NAMED ME YOUR CHAMPION.
A TITLE I HAVE THE ABILITY TO REVOKE, DIANA.
AS IS YOUR RIGHT, MY LADY OF OLYMPUS.
YOU ARE NOT ONE OF THEM, DAUGHTER.
YOU NEVER SHALL BE.
BECAUSE I STAND APART DOES NOT MEAN I STAND ABOVE, MY LADY.
I WOULD BE A POOR VOICE FOR MY MISSION IF I DID.
YOUR MISSION.
WHAT YOU ARE CONSIDERING WILL DESTROY YOUR MISSION, CHILD.
I BELIEVE IT TO BE THE ONLY WAY TO SAVE IT.
YOU HAVE LIVED IN THEIR WORLD FOR YEARS NOW, AND STILL THEY DO NOT HEED YOU.
I KNOW THEIR THOUGHTS, DIANA, I KNOW HOW THEY SEE YOU.

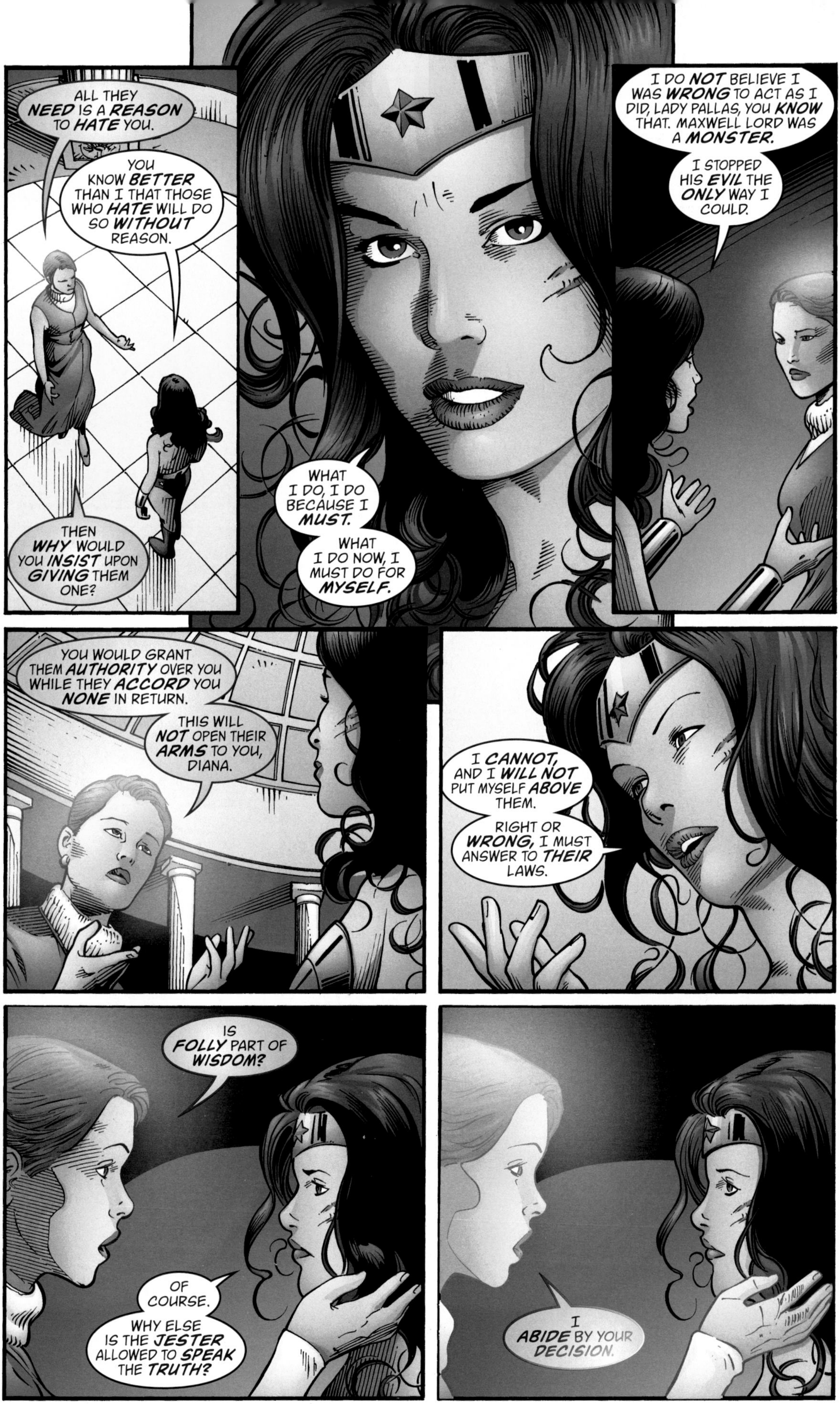
ALL THEY NEED IS A REASON TO HATE YOU.
YOU KNOW BETTER THAN I THAT THOSE WHO HATE WILL DO SO WITHOUT REASON.
THEN WHY WOULD YOU INSIST UPON GIVING THEM ONE?
WHAT I DO, I DO BECAUSE I MUST.
WHAT I DO NOW, I MUST DO FOR MYSELF.
I DO NOT BELIEVE I WAS WRONG TO ACT AS I DID, LADY PALLAS, YOU KNOW THAT. MAXWELL LORD WAS A MONSTER.
I STOPPED HIS EVIL THE ONLY WAY I COULD.
YOU WOULD GRANT THEM AUTHORITY OVER YOU WHILE THEY ACCORD YOU NONE IN RETURN.
THIS WILL NOT OPEN THEIR ARMS TO YOU, DIANA.
I CANNOT, AND I WILL NOT PUT MYSELF ABOVE THEM.
RIGHT OR WRONG, I MUST ANSWER TO THEIR LAWS.
IS FOLLY PART OF WISDOM?
OF COURSE.
WHY ELSE IS THE JESTER ALLOWED TO SPEAK THE TRUTH?
I ABIDE BY YOUR DECISION.

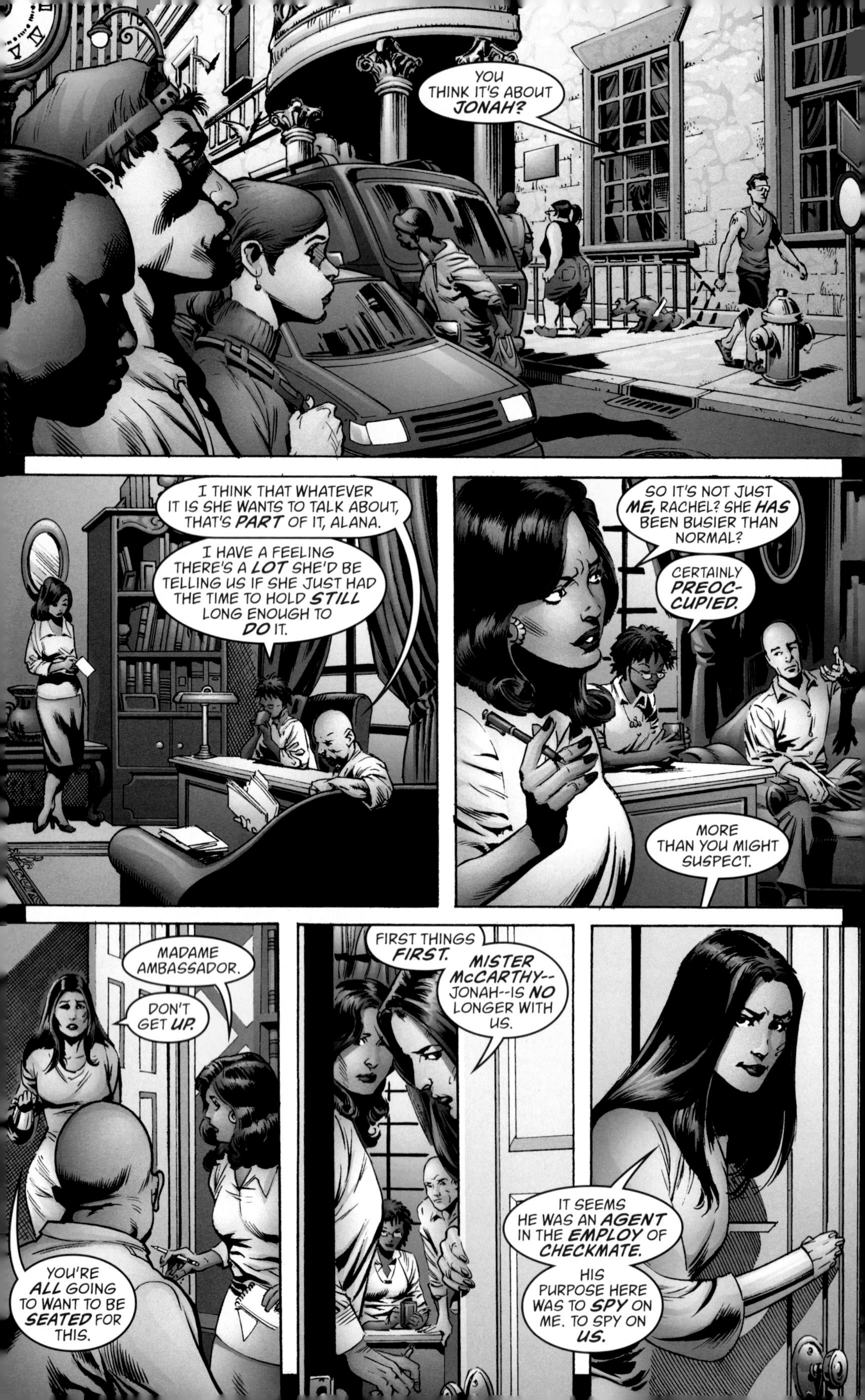

YOU THINK IT'S ABOUT JONAH?
I THINK THAT WHATEVER IT IS SHE WANTS TO TALK ABOUT, THAT'S PART OF IT, ALANA.
I HAVE A FEELING THERE'S A LOT SHE'D BE TELLING US IF SHE JUST HAD THE TIME TO HOLD STILL LONG ENOUGH TO DO IT.
SO IT'S NOT JUST ME, RACHEL? SHE HAS BEEN BUSIER THAN NORMAL?
CERTAINLY PREOC-CUPIED.
MORE THAN YOU MIGHT SUSPECT.
MADAME AMBASSADOR.
DON'T GET UP.
YOU'RE ALL GOING TO WANT TO BE SEATED FOR THIS.
FIRST THINGS FIRST.
MISTER McCARTHY--JONAH--IS NO LONGER WITH US.
IT SEEMS HE WAS AN AGENT IN THE EMPLOY OF CHECKMATE.
HIS PURPOSE HERE WAS TO SPY ON ME. TO SPY ON US.

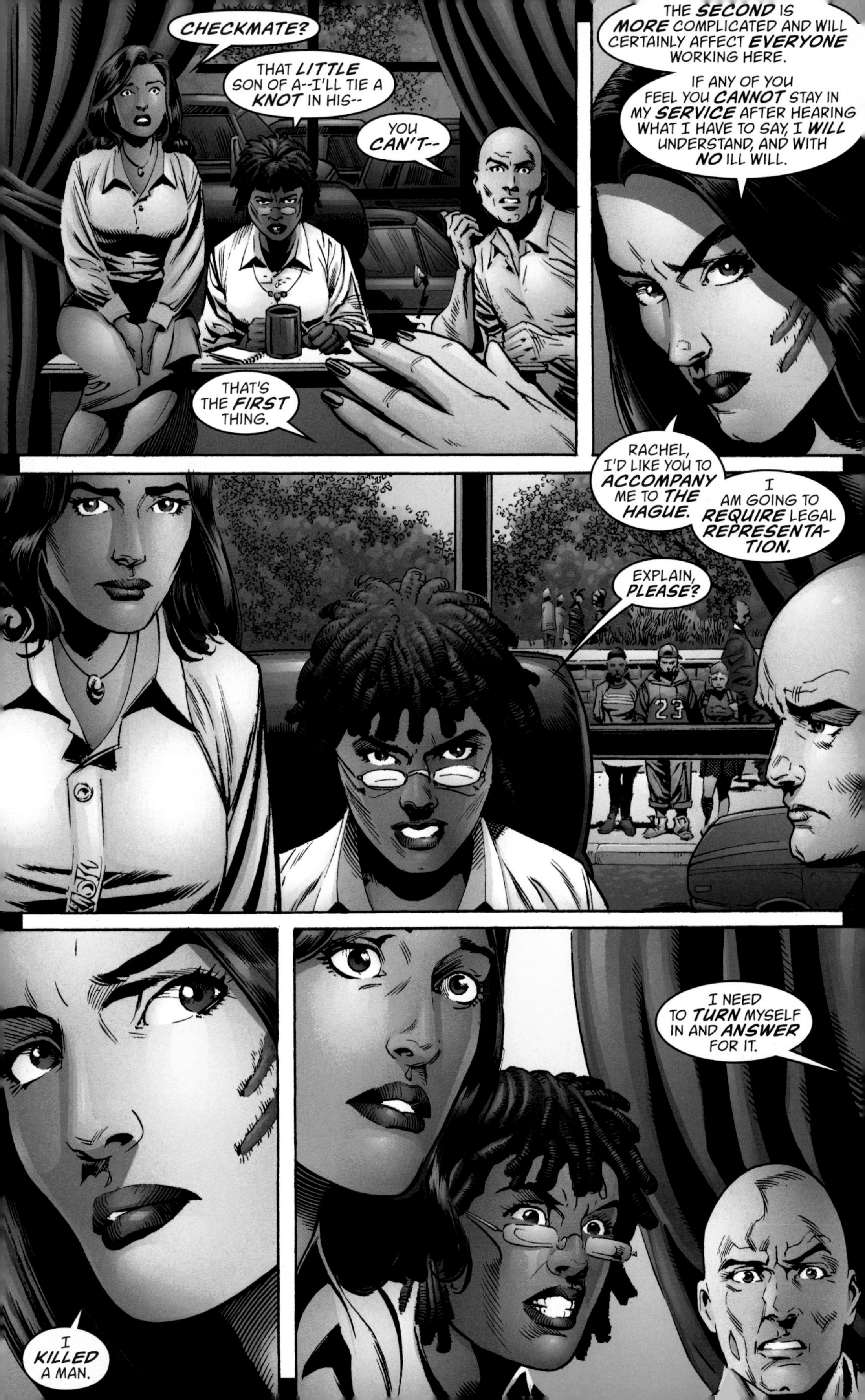
CHECKMATE?
THAT LITTLE SON OF A--I'LL TIE A KNOT IN HIS--
YOU CAN'T--
THAT'S THE FIRST THING.
THE SECOND IS MORE COMPLICATED AND WILL CERTAINLY AFFECT EVERYONE WORKING HERE.
IF ANY OF YOU FEEL YOU CANNOT STAY IN MY SERVICE AFTER HEARING WHAT I HAVE TO SAY, I WILL UNDERSTAND, AND WITH NO ILL WILL.
RACHEL, I'D LIKE YOU TO ACCOMPANY ME TO THE HAGUE.
I AM GOING TO REQUIRE LEGAL REPRESENTATION.
EXPLAIN, PLEASE?
I KILLED A MAN.
I NEED TO TURN MYSELF IN AND ANSWER FOR IT.

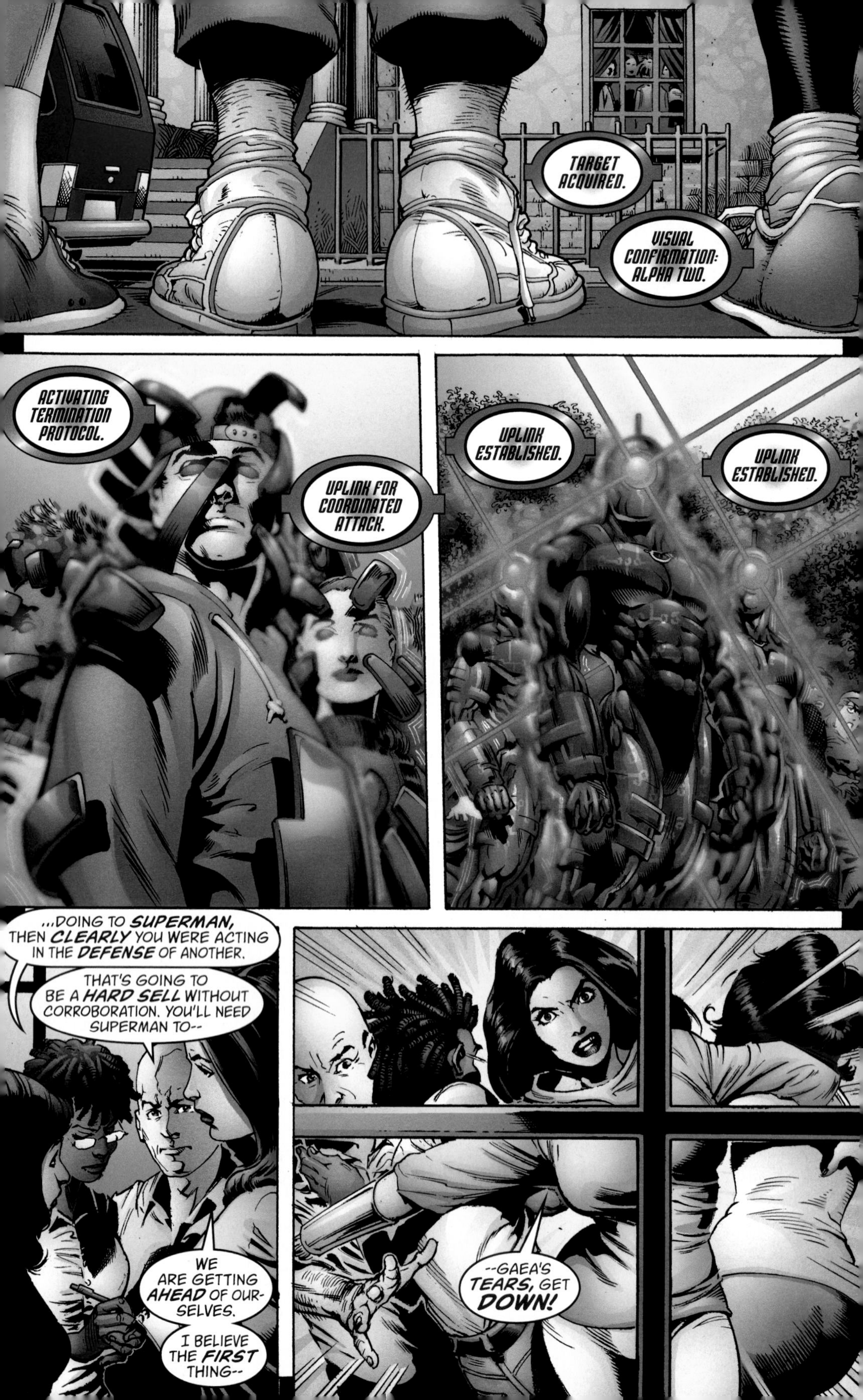

TARGET ACQUIRED.
VISUAL CONFIRMATION: ALPHA TWO.
ACTIVATING TERMINATION PROTOCOL.
UPLINK FOR COORDINATED ATTACK.
UPLINK ESTABLISHED.
UPLINK ESTABLISHED.
...DOING TO SUPERMAN, THEN CLEARLY YOU WERE ACTING IN THE DEFENSE OF ANOTHER.
THAT'S GOING TO BE A HARD SELL WITHOUT CORROBORATION. YOU'LL NEED SUPERMAN TO--
WE ARE GETTING AHEAD OF OURSELVES.
I BELIEVE THE FIRST THING--
--GAEA'S TEARS, GET DOWN!

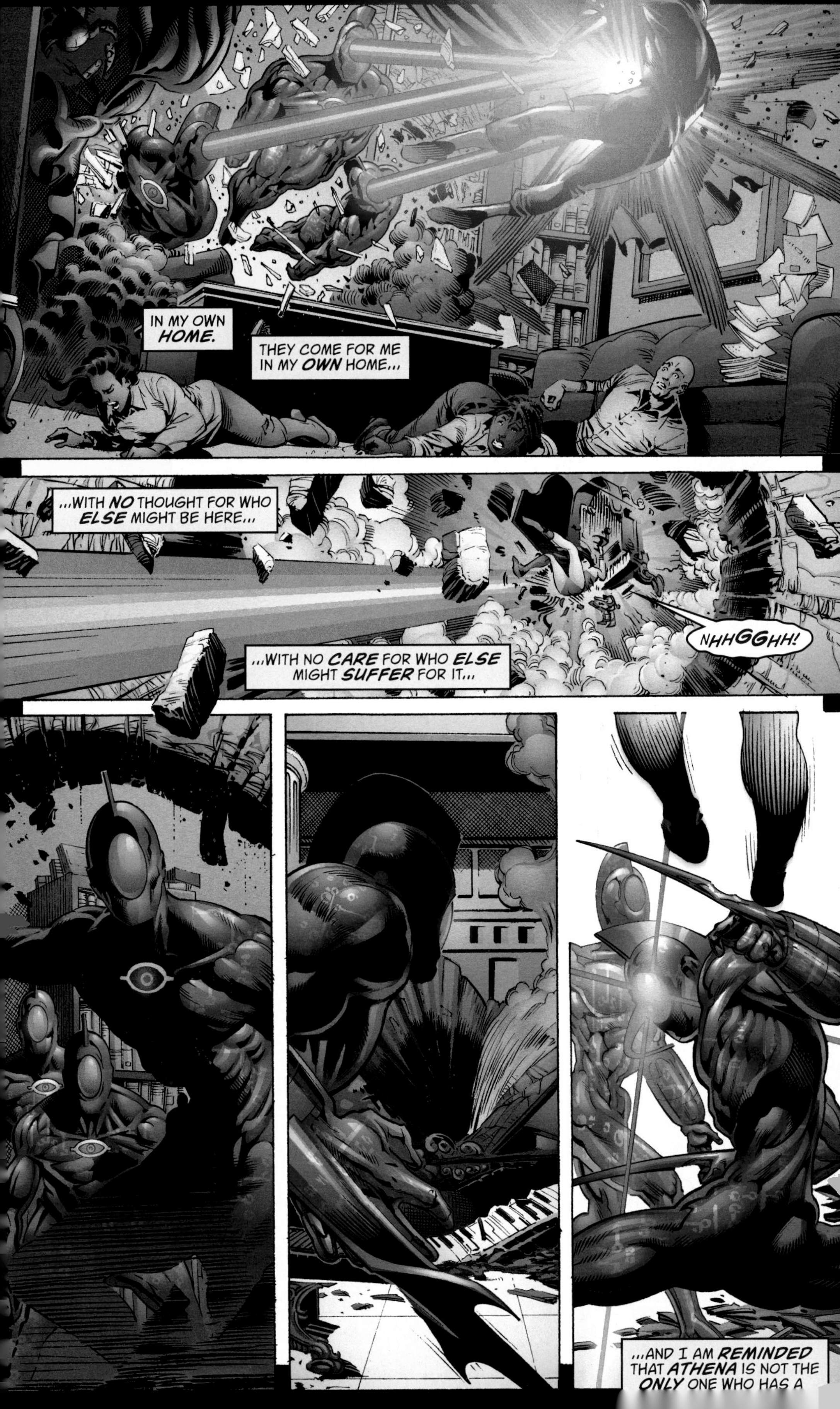

IN MY OWN HOME.
THEY COME FOR ME IN MY OWN HOME...
...WITH NO THOUGHT FOR WHO ELSE MIGHT BE HERE...
NHHGGHH!
...WITH NO CARE FOR WHO ELSE MIGHT SUFFER FOR IT...
...AND I AM REMINDED THAT ATHENA IS NOT THE ONLY ONE WHO HAS A

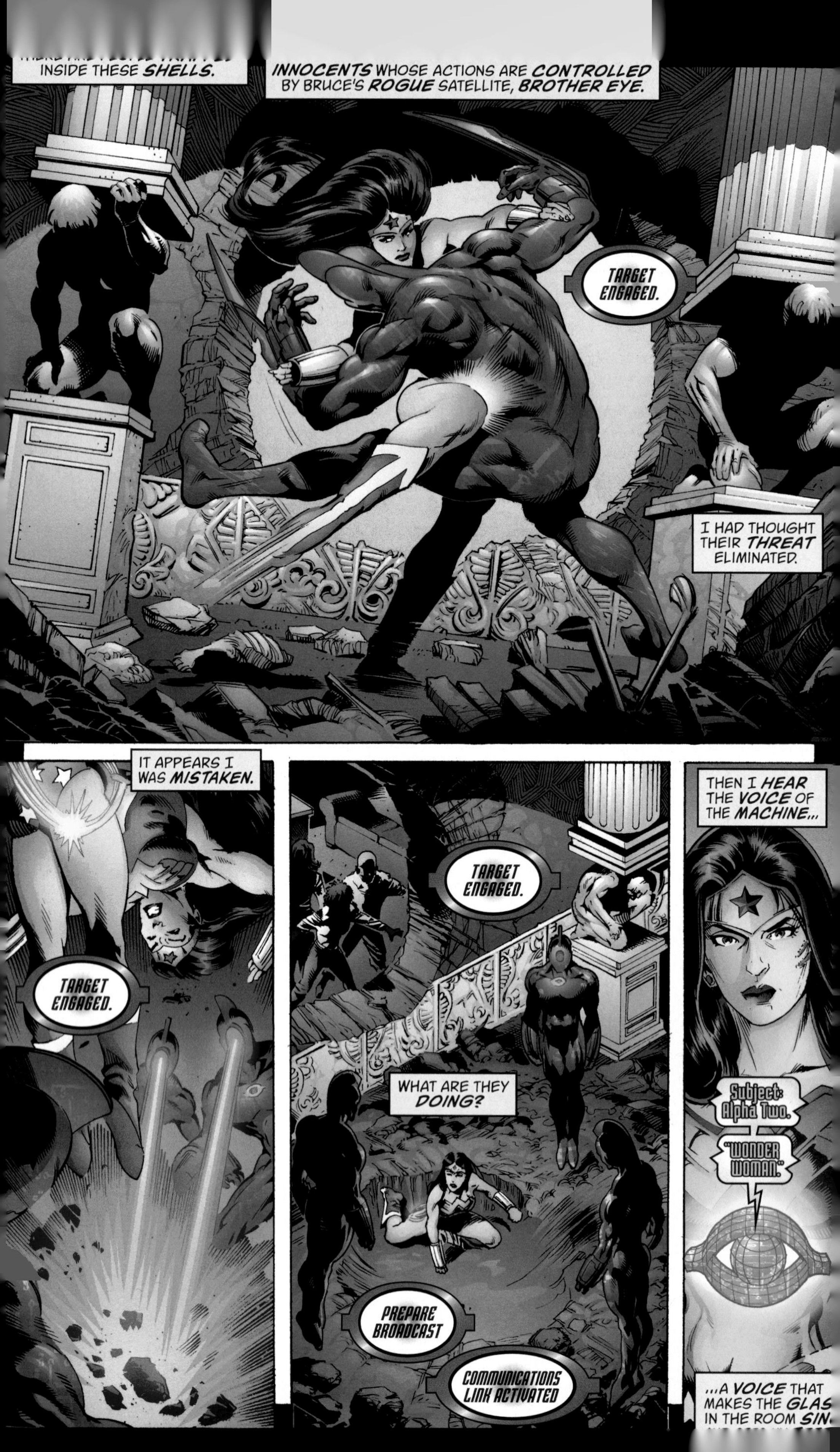
INSIDE THESE SHELLS.
INNOCENTS WHOSE ACTIONS ARE CONTROLLED BY BRUCE'S ROGUE SATELLITE, BROTHER EYE.
TARGET ENGAGED.
I HAD THOUGHT THEIR THREAT ELIMINATED.
IT APPEARS I WAS MISTAKEN.
TARGET ENGAGED.
TARGET ENGAGED.
WHAT ARE THEY DOING?
PREPARE BROADCAST
COMMUNICATIONS LINK ACTIVATED
THEN I HEAR THE VOICE OF THE MACHINE...
Subject: Alpha Two.
"WONDER WOMAN."
...A VOICE THAT MAKES THE GLAS IN THE ROOM SIN

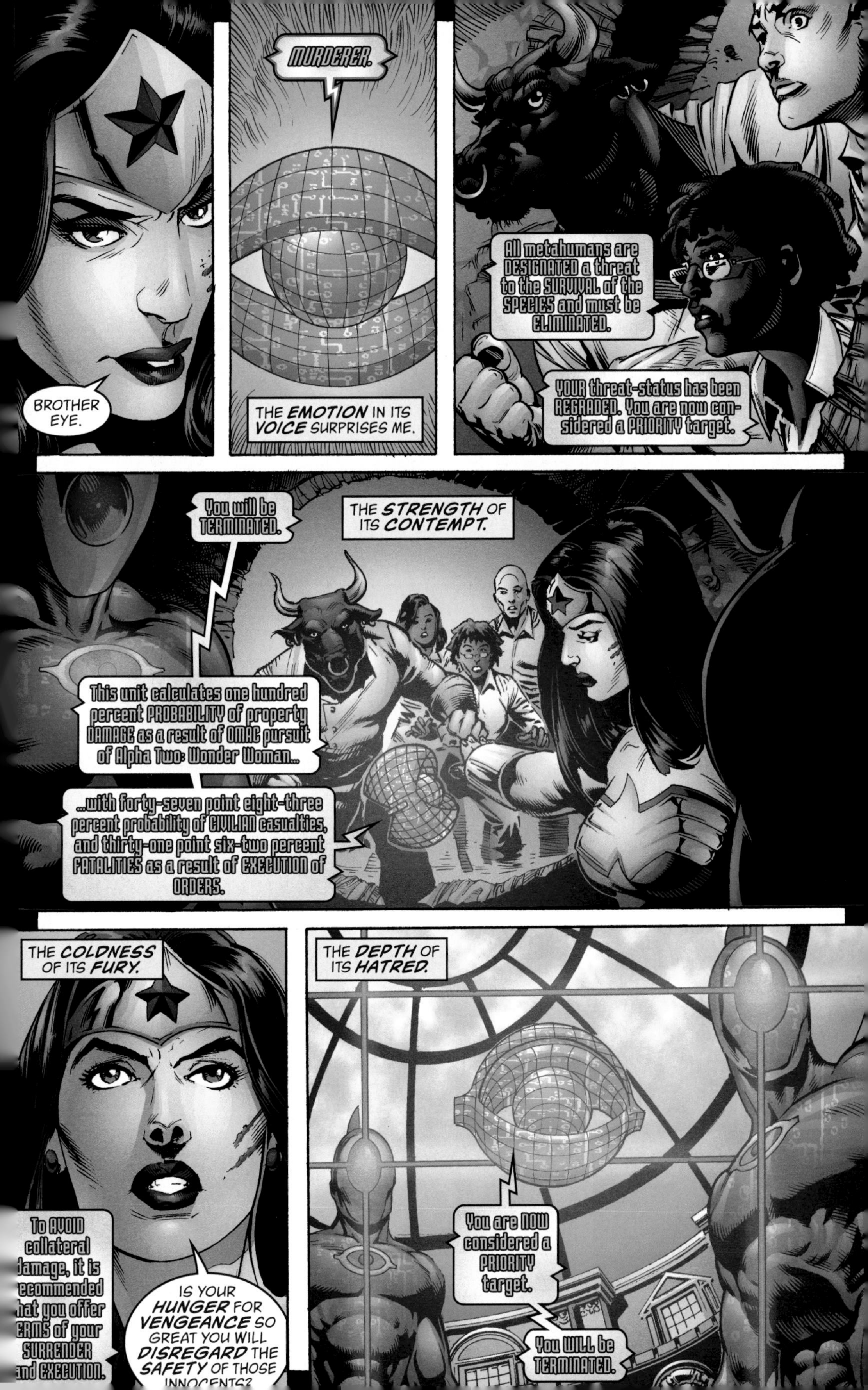

BROTHER EYE.
MURDERER.
THE EMOTION IN ITS VOICE SURPRISES ME.
All metahumans are DESIGNATED a threat to the SURVIVAL of the SPECIES and must be ELIMINATED.
YOUR threat-status has been REGRADED. You are now considered a PRIORITY target.
You will be TERMINATED.
THE STRENGTH OF ITS CONTEMPT.
This unit calculates one hundred percent PROBABILITY of property DAMAGE as a result of OMAC pursuit of Alpha Two: Wonder Woman...
...with forty-seven point eight-three percent probability of CIVILIAN casualties, and thirty-one point six-two percent FATALITIES as a result of EXECUTION of ORDERS.
THE COLDNESS OF ITS FURY.
To AVOID collateral damage, it is ecommended hat you offer ERMS of your SURRENDER and EXECUTION.
IS YOUR HUNGER FOR VENGEANCE SO GREAT YOU WILL DISREGARD THE SAFETY OF THOSE INNOCENTS?
THE DEPTH OF ITS HATRED.
You are NOW considered a PRIORITY target.
You WILL be TERMINATED.

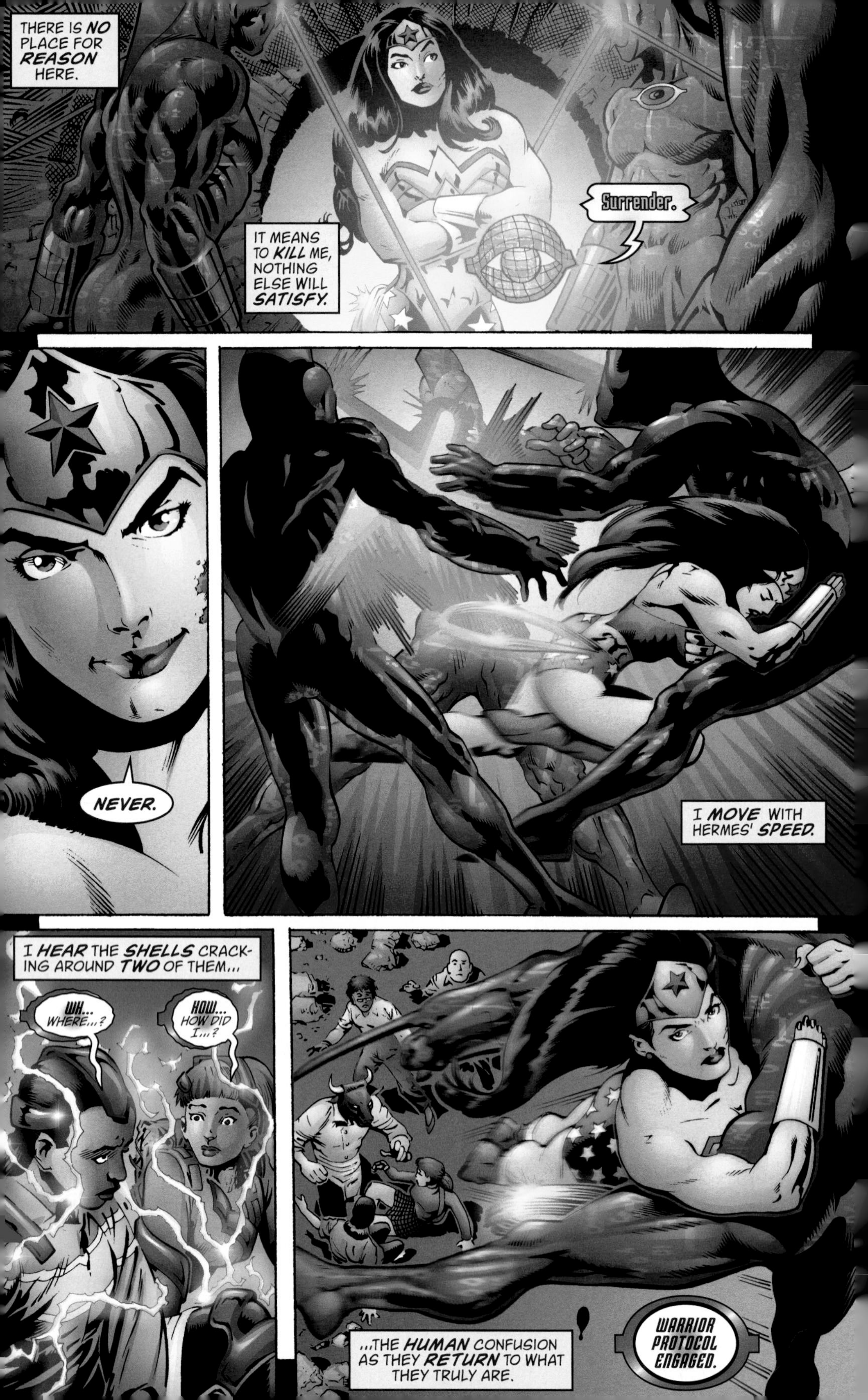
THERE IS NO PLACE FOR REASON HERE.
IT MEANS TO KILL ME, NOTHING ELSE WILL SATISFY.
Surrender.
NEVER.
I MOVE WITH HERMES' SPEED.
I HEAR THE SHELLS CRACKING AROUND TWO OF THEM...
WH... WHERE...?
HOW... HOW DID I...?
...THE HUMAN CONFUSION AS THEY RETURN TO WHAT THEY TRULY ARE.
WARRIOR PROTOCOL ENGAGED.

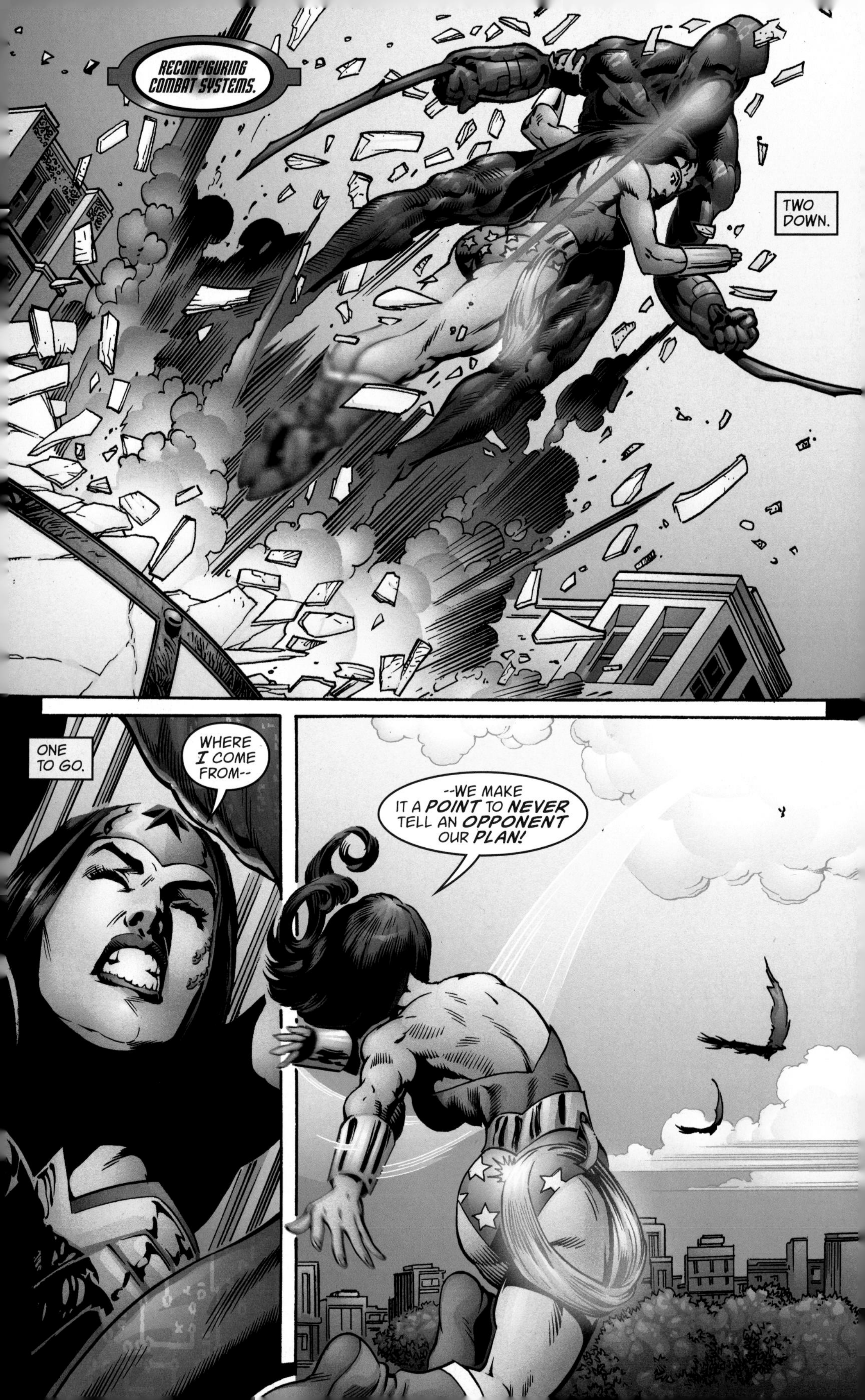
RECONFIGURING COMBAT SYSTEMS.
TWO DOWN.
ONE TO GO.
WHERE I COME FROM--
--WE MAKE IT A POINT TO NEVER TELL AN OPPONENT OUR PLAN!

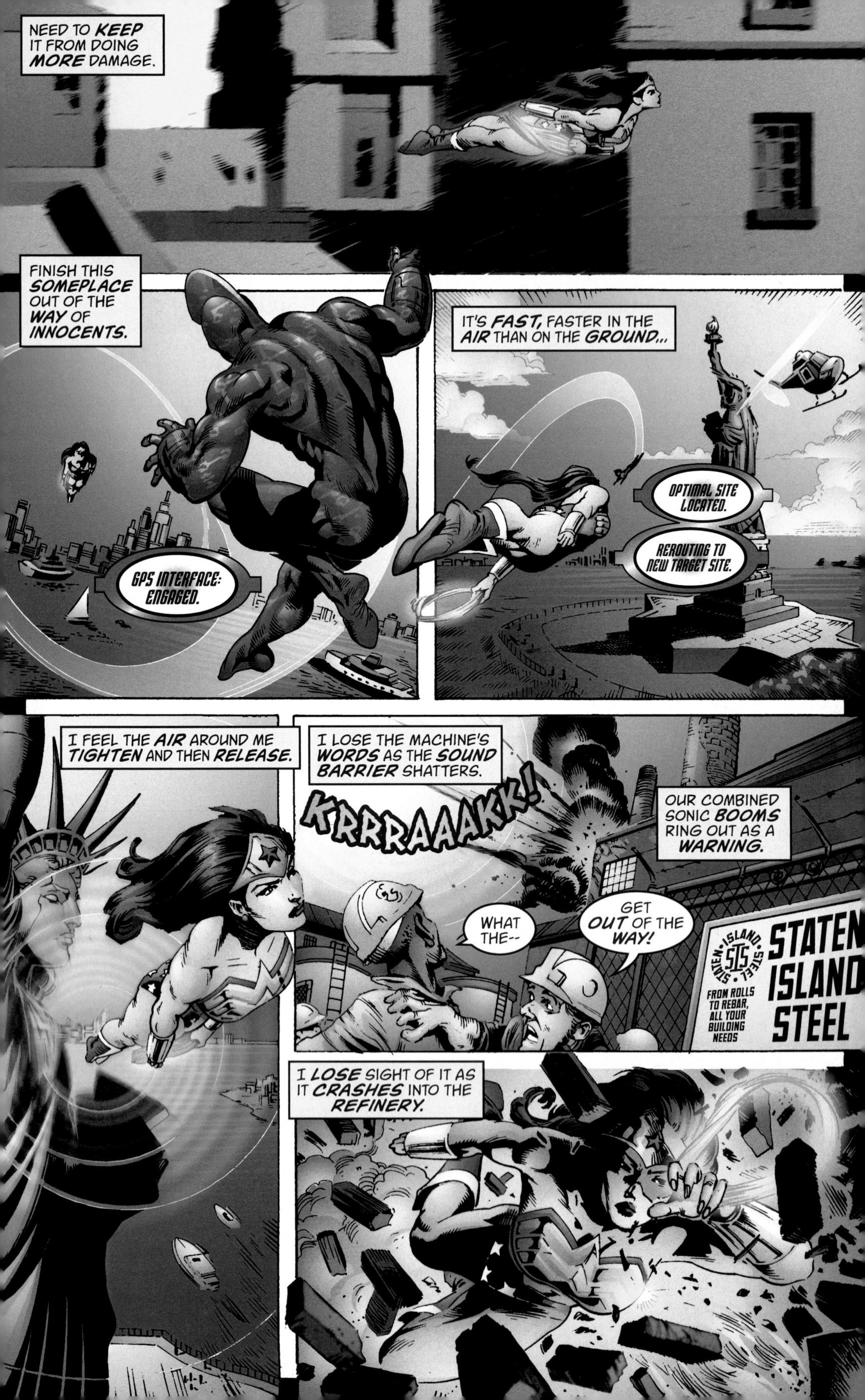
NEED TO KEEP IT FROM DOING MORE DAMAGE.
FINISH THIS SOMEPLACE OUT OF THE WAY OF INNOCENTS.
GPS INTERFACE: ENGAGED.
IT'S FAST, FASTER IN THE AIR THAN ON THE GROUND...
OPTIMAL SITE LOCATED.
REROUTING TO NEW TARGET SITE.
I FEEL THE AIR AROUND ME TIGHTEN AND THEN RELEASE.
I LOSE THE MACHINE'S WORDS AS THE SOUND BARRIER SHATTERS.
KRRRAAAKK!
OUR COMBINED SONIC BOOMS RING OUT AS A WARNING.
WHAT THE--
GET OUT OF THE WAY!
STATEN ISLAND STEEL
STS
FROM ROLLS TO REBAR, ALL YOUR BUILDING NEEDS
STATEN ISLAND STEEL
I LOSE SIGHT OF IT AS IT CRASHES INTO THE REFINERY.

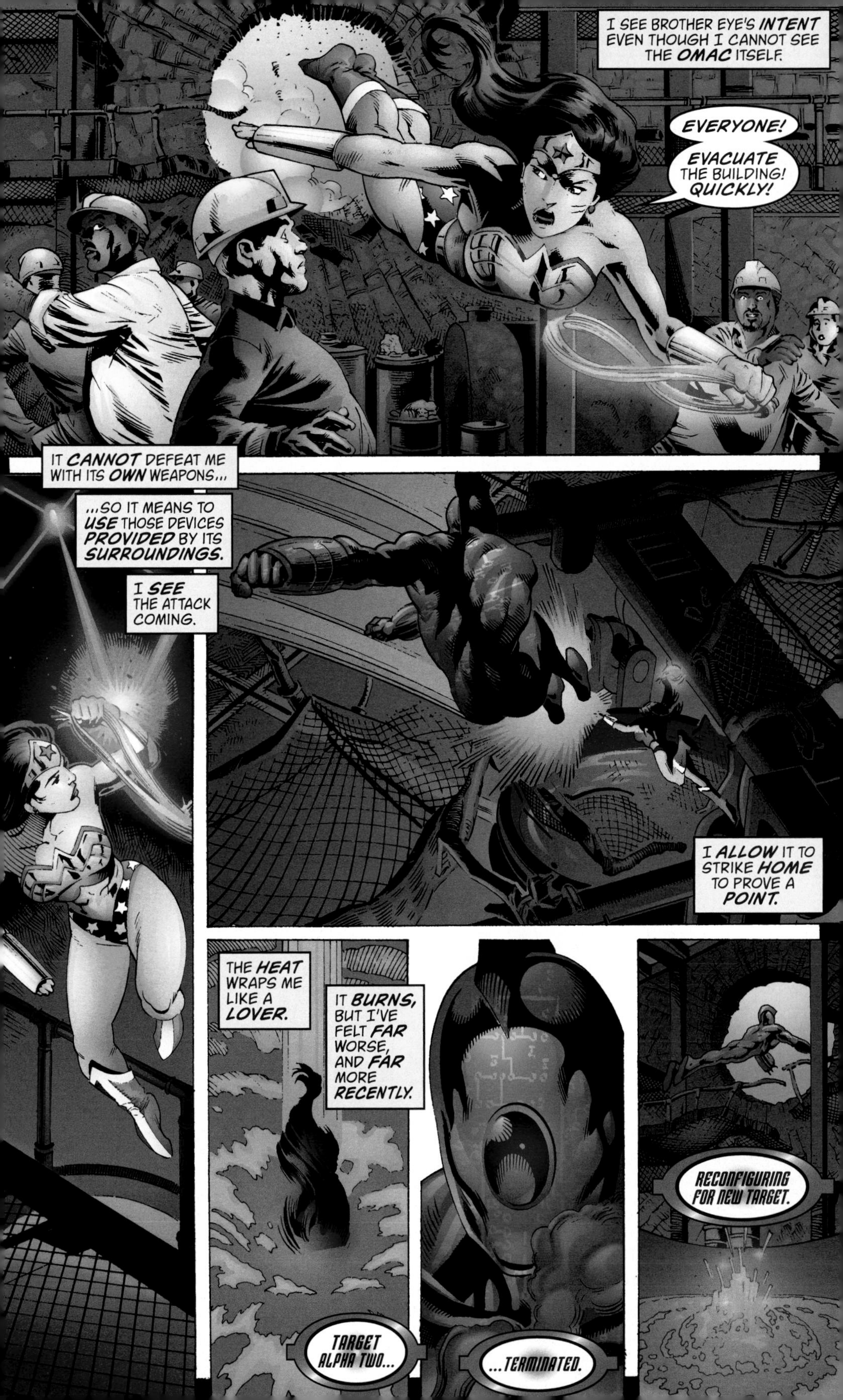

I SEE BROTHER EYE'S INTENT EVEN THOUGH I CANNOT SEE THE OMAC ITSELF.
EVERYONE!
EVACUATE THE BUILDING! QUICKLY!
IT CANNOT DEFEAT ME WITH ITS OWN WEAPONS...
...SO IT MEANS TO USE THOSE DEVICES PROVIDED BY ITS SURROUNDINGS.
I SEE THE ATTACK COMING.
I ALLOW IT TO STRIKE HOME TO PROVE A POINT.
THE HEAT WRAPS ME LIKE A LOVER.
IT BURNS, BUT I'VE FELT FAR WORSE, AND FAR MORE RECENTLY.
TARGET ALPHA TWO...
...TERMINATED.
RECONFIGURING FOR NEW TARGET.

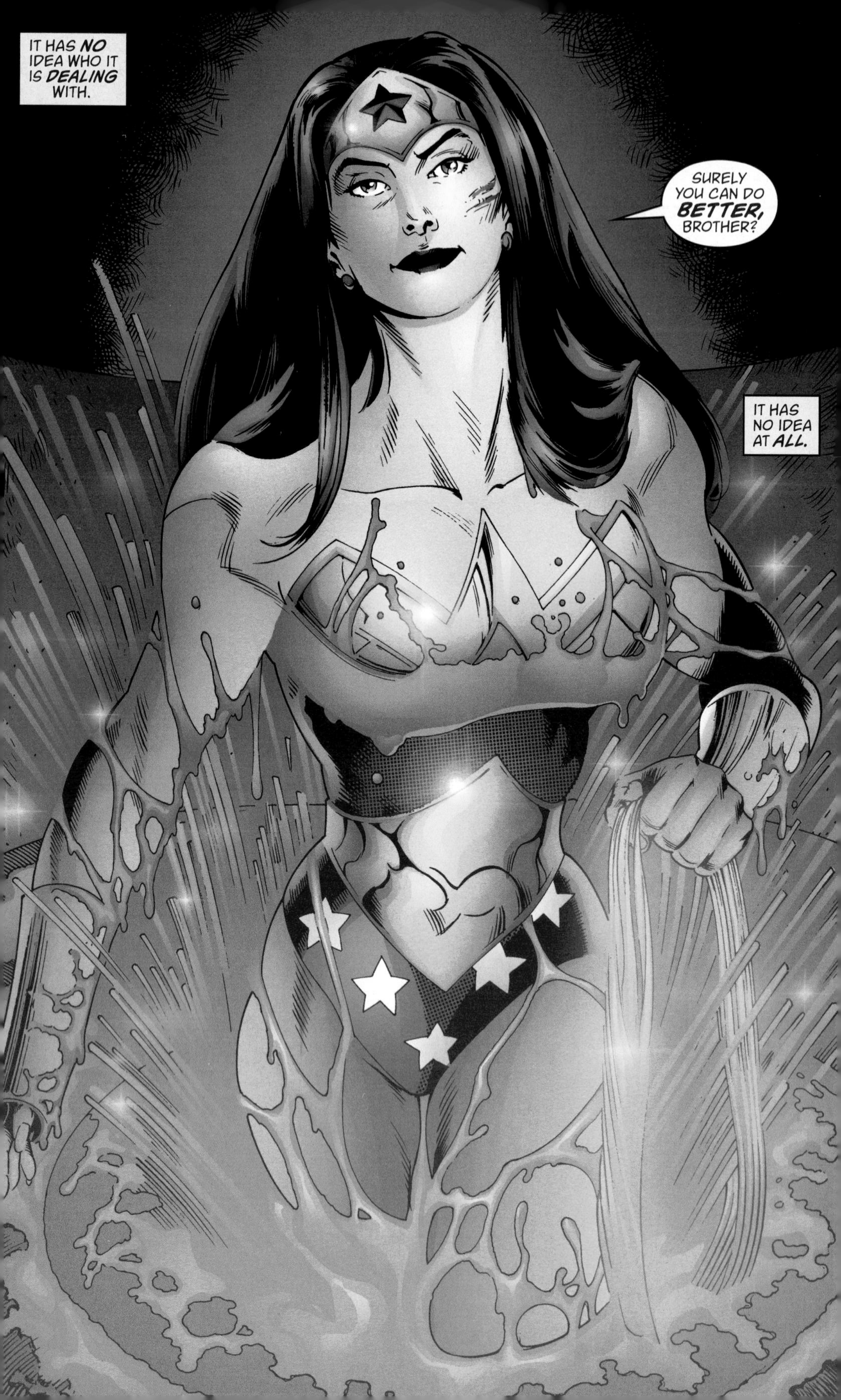
IT HAS NO IDEA WHO IT IS DEALING WITH.
SURELY YOU CAN DO BETTER, BROTHER?
IT HAS NO IDEA AT ALL.

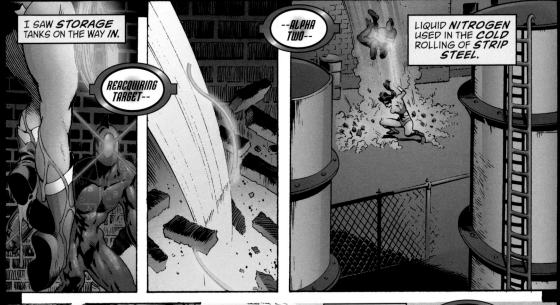

I SAW *STORAGE* TANKS ON THE WAY *IN.*

REACQUIRING TARGET--

--ALPHA TWO--

LIQUID *NITROGEN* USED IN THE *COLD* ROLLING OF *STRIP STEEL.*

IT USED *HEAT.*

--COUNTER-MEASURES--

I USE *COLD.*

77 DEGREES *KELVIN,* IF I REMEMBER CORRECTLY.

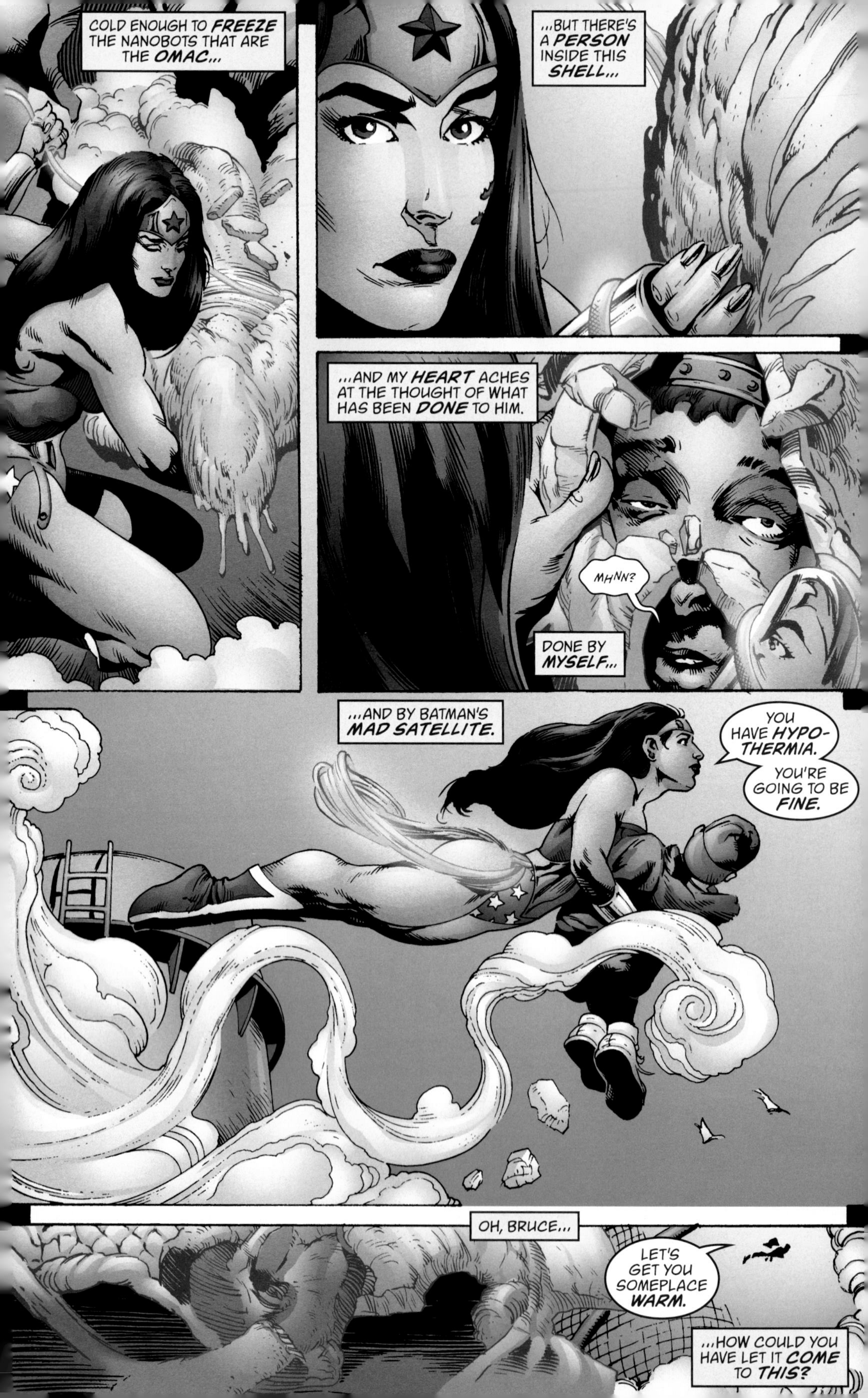
COLD ENOUGH TO FREEZE THE NANOBOTS THAT ARE THE OMAC...
...BUT THERE'S A PERSON INSIDE THIS SHELL...
...AND MY HEART ACHES AT THE THOUGHT OF WHAT HAS BEEN DONE TO HIM.
MHNN?
DONE BY MYSELF...
...AND BY BATMAN'S MAD SATELLITE.
YOU HAVE HYPOTHERMIA. YOU'RE GOING TO BE FINE.
OH, BRUCE...
LET'S GET YOU SOMEPLACE WARM.
...HOW COULD YOU HAVE LET IT COME TO THIS?

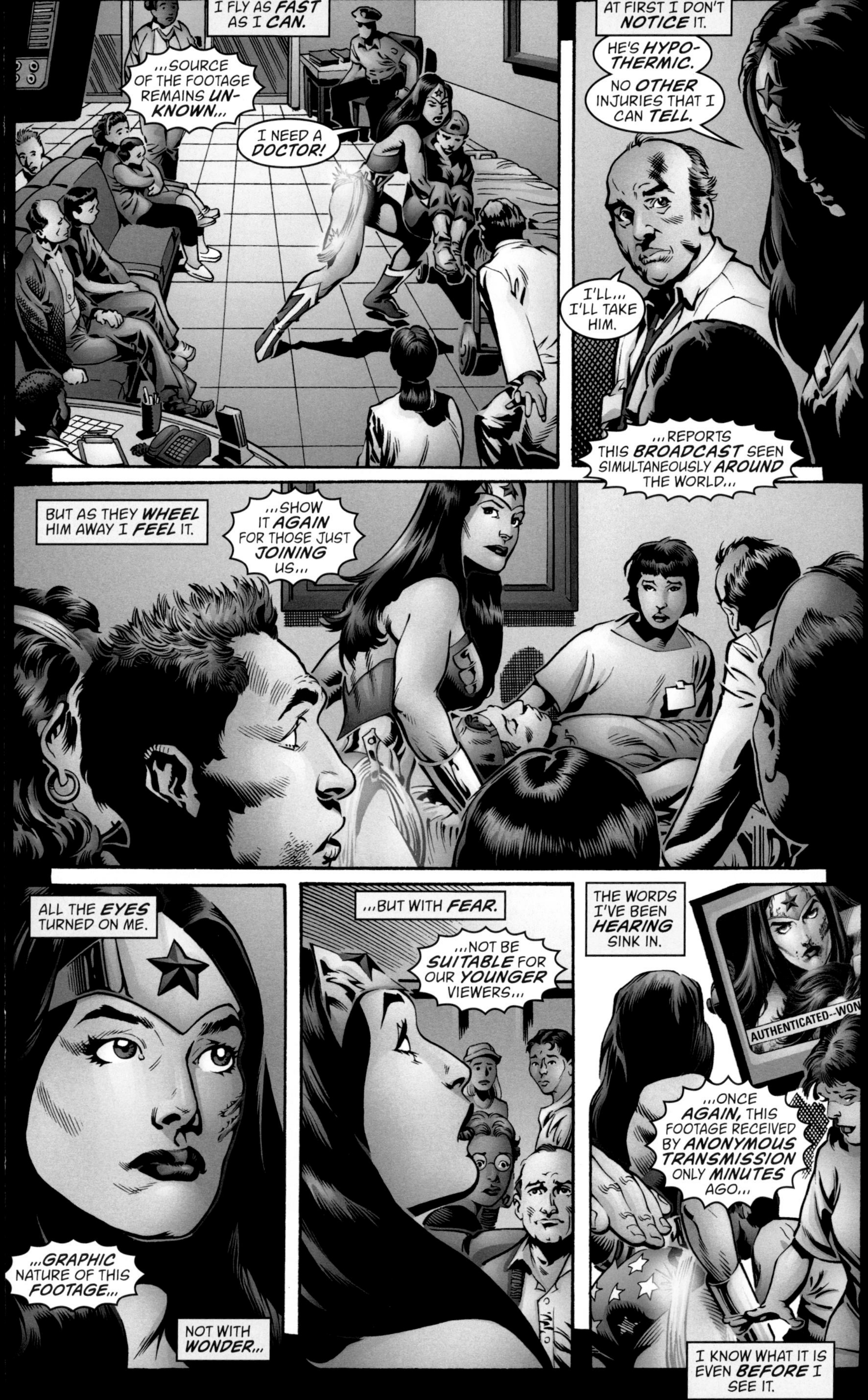
I FLY AS FAST AS I CAN.
...SOURCE OF THE FOOTAGE REMAINS UN-KNOWN...
I NEED A DOCTOR!
AT FIRST I DON'T NOTICE IT.
HE'S HYPO-THERMIC.
NO OTHER INJURIES THAT I CAN TELL.
I'LL... I'LL TAKE HIM.
...REPORTS THIS BROADCAST SEEN SIMULTANEOUSLY AROUND THE WORLD...
BUT AS THEY WHEEL HIM AWAY I FEEL IT.
...SHOW IT AGAIN FOR THOSE JUST JOINING US...
ALL THE EYES TURNED ON ME.
...GRAPHIC NATURE OF THIS FOOTAGE...
NOT WITH WONDER...
...BUT WITH FEAR.
...NOT BE SUITABLE FOR OUR YOUNGER VIEWERS...
THE WORDS I'VE BEEN HEARING SINK IN.
AUTHENTICATED--WON
...ONCE AGAIN, THIS FOOTAGE RECEIVED BY ANONYMOUS TRANSMISSION ONLY MINUTES AGO...
I KNOW WHAT IT IS EVEN BEFORE I SEE IT.

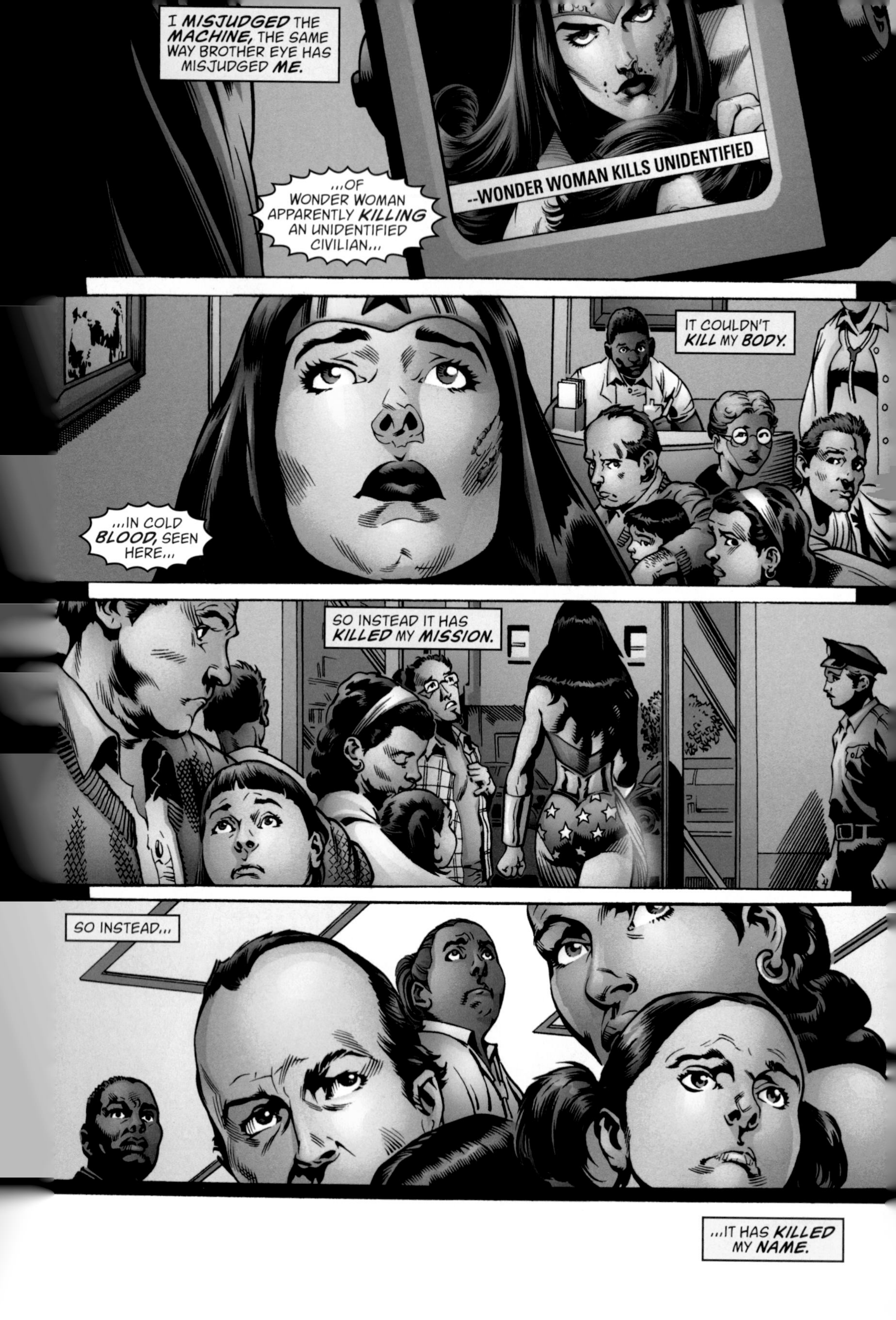
I MISJUDGED THE MACHINE, THE SAME WAY BROTHER EYE HAS MISJUDGED ME.
--WONDER WOMAN KILLS UNIDENTIFIED
...OF WONDER WOMAN APPARENTLY KILLING AN UNIDENTIFIED CIVILIAN...
IT COULDN'T KILL MY BODY.
...IN COLD BLOOD, SEEN HERE...
SO INSTEAD IT HAS KILLED MY MISSION.
SO INSTEAD...
...IT HAS KILLED MY NAME.

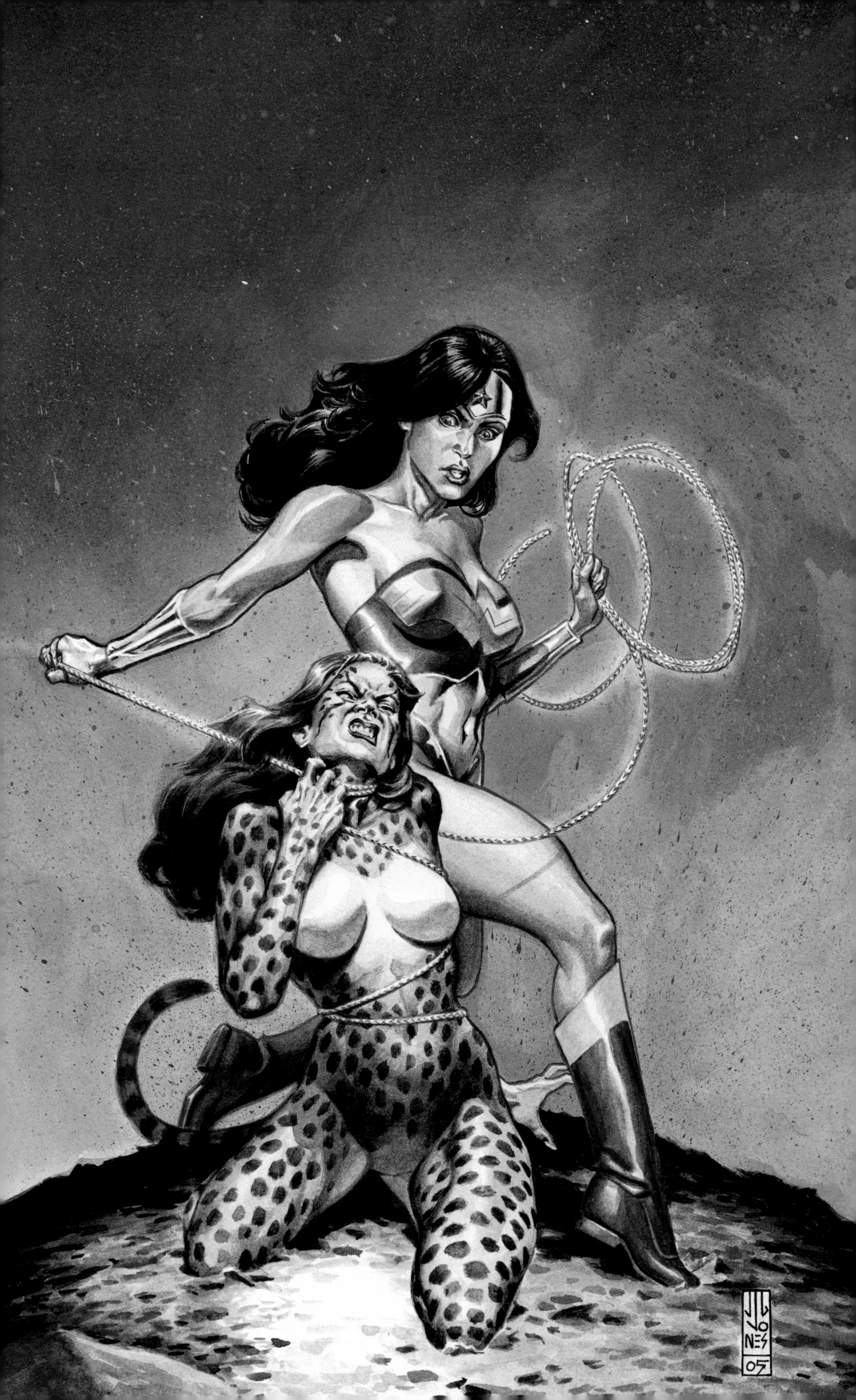

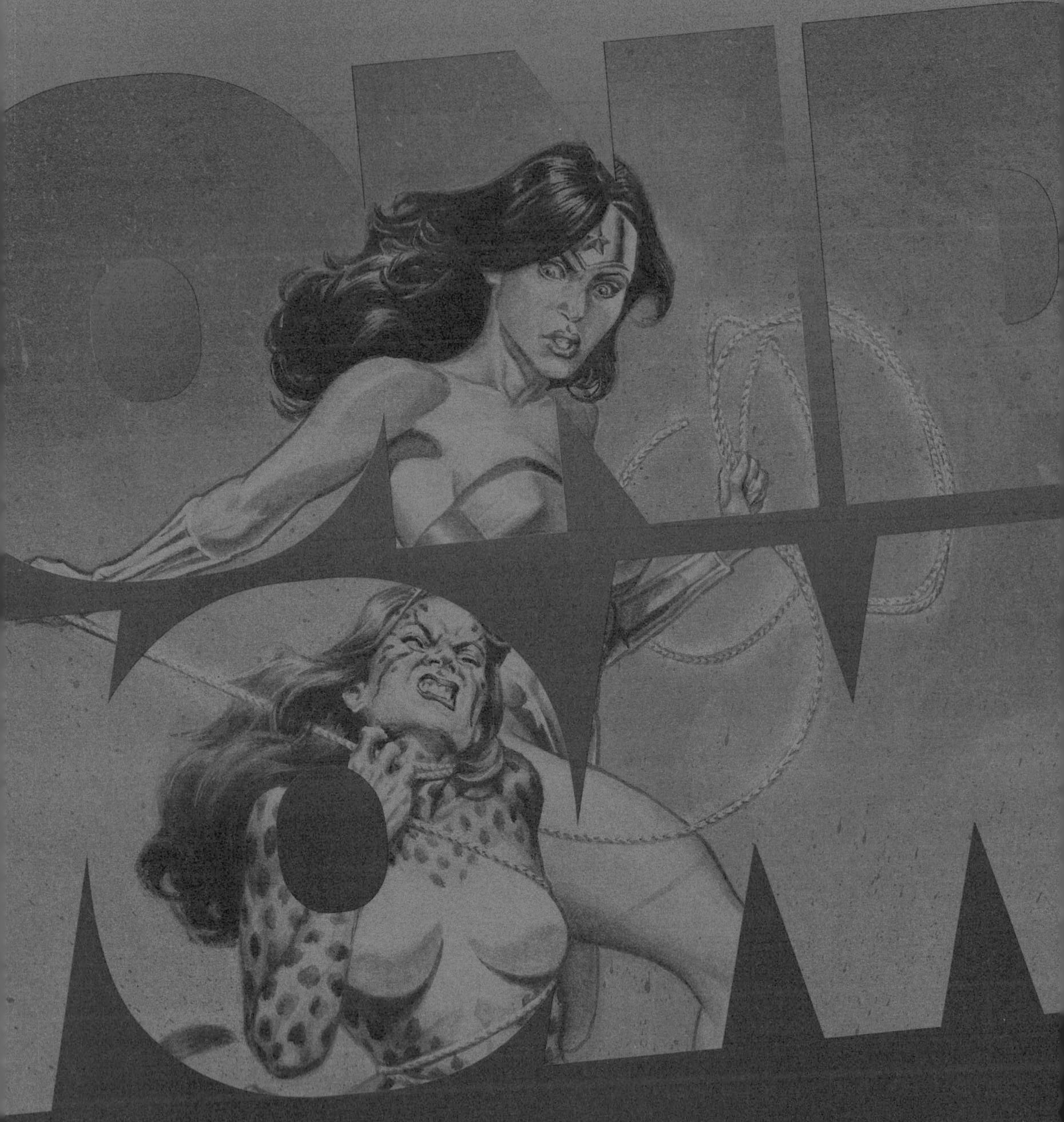

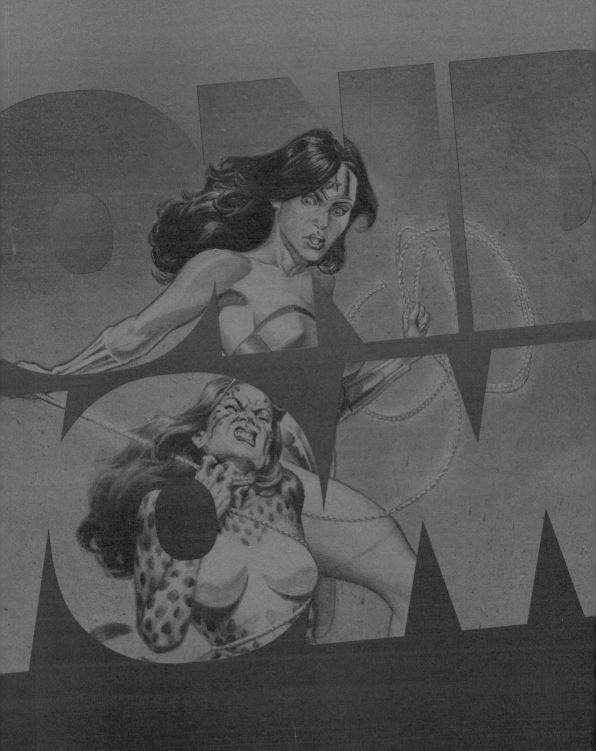

"BLOOD DEBT"

Greg Rucka – *writer*
Cliff Richards – *pencils*
Ray Snyder – *inks*
Richard and **Tanya Horie** – *colors*
Todd Klein – *letters*
J.G. Jones – *cover*

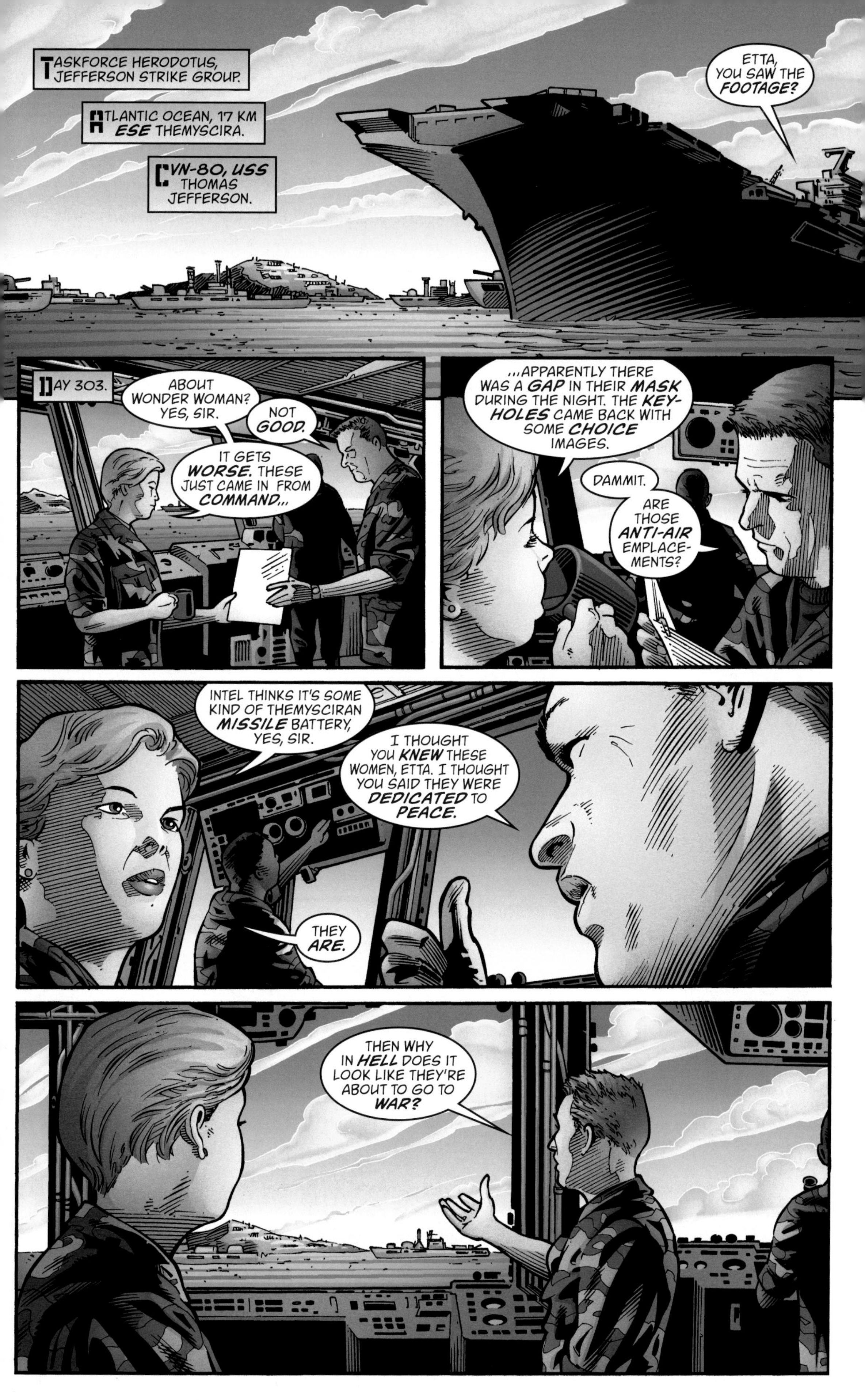
TASKFORCE HERODOTUS, JEFFERSON STRIKE GROUP.
ATLANTIC OCEAN, 17 KM ESE THEMYSCIRA.
CVN-80, USS THOMAS JEFFERSON.
ETTA, YOU SAW THE FOOTAGE?
DAY 303.
ABOUT WONDER WOMAN? YES, SIR.
NOT GOOD.
IT GETS WORSE. THESE JUST CAME IN FROM COMMAND...
...APPARENTLY THERE WAS A GAP IN THEIR MASK DURING THE NIGHT. THE KEY-HOLES CAME BACK WITH SOME CHOICE IMAGES.
DAMMIT.
ARE THOSE ANTI-AIR EMPLACE-MENTS?
INTEL THINKS IT'S SOME KIND OF THEMYSCIRAN MISSILE BATTERY, YES, SIR.
I THOUGHT YOU KNEW THESE WOMEN, ETTA. I THOUGHT YOU SAID THEY WERE DEDICATED TO PEACE.
THEY ARE.
THEN WHY IN HELL DOES IT LOOK LIKE THEY'RE ABOUT TO GO TO WAR?

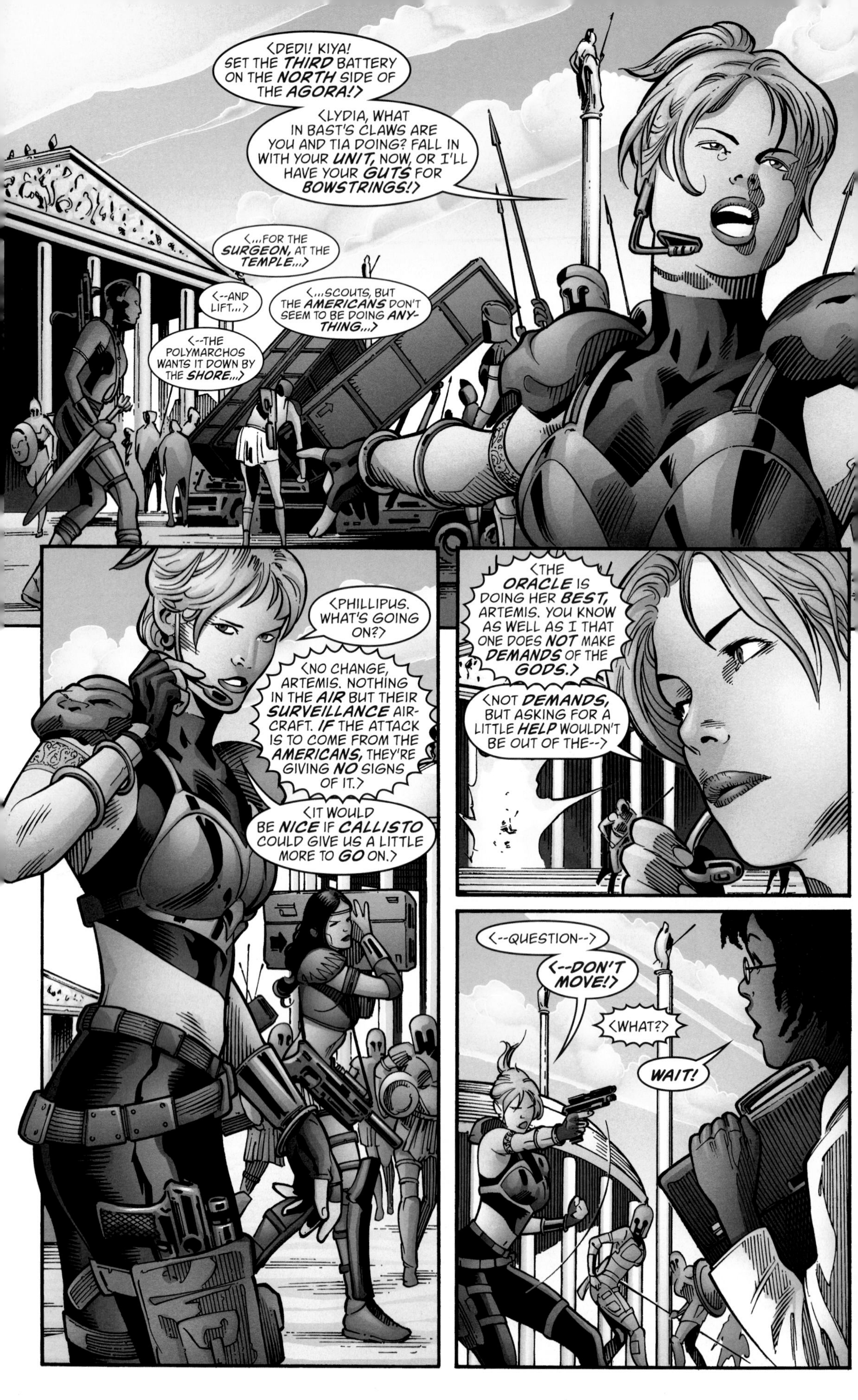
<DEDI! KIYA! SET THE THIRD BATTERY ON THE NORTH SIDE OF THE AGORA!>
<LYDIA, WHAT IN BAST'S CLAWS ARE YOU AND TIA DOING? FALL IN WITH YOUR UNIT, NOW, OR I'LL HAVE YOUR GUTS FOR BOWSTRINGS!>
<...FOR THE SURGEON, AT THE TEMPLE...>
<--AND LIFT...>
<...SCOUTS, BUT THE AMERICANS DON'T SEEM TO BE DOING ANYTHING...>
<--THE POLYMARCHOS WANTS IT DOWN BY THE SHORE...>
<PHILLIPUS. WHAT'S GOING ON?>
<NO CHANGE, ARTEMIS. NOTHING IN THE AIR BUT THEIR SURVEILLANCE AIRCRAFT. IF THE ATTACK IS TO COME FROM THE AMERICANS, THEY'RE GIVING NO SIGNS OF IT.>
<IT WOULD BE NICE IF CALLISTO COULD GIVE US A LITTLE MORE TO GO ON.>
<THE ORACLE IS DOING HER BEST, ARTEMIS. YOU KNOW AS WELL AS I THAT ONE DOES NOT MAKE DEMANDS OF THE GODS.>
<NOT DEMANDS, BUT ASKING FOR A LITTLE HELP WOULDN'T BE OUT OF THE-->
<--QUESTION-->
<--DON'T MOVE!>
<WHAT?>
WAIT!

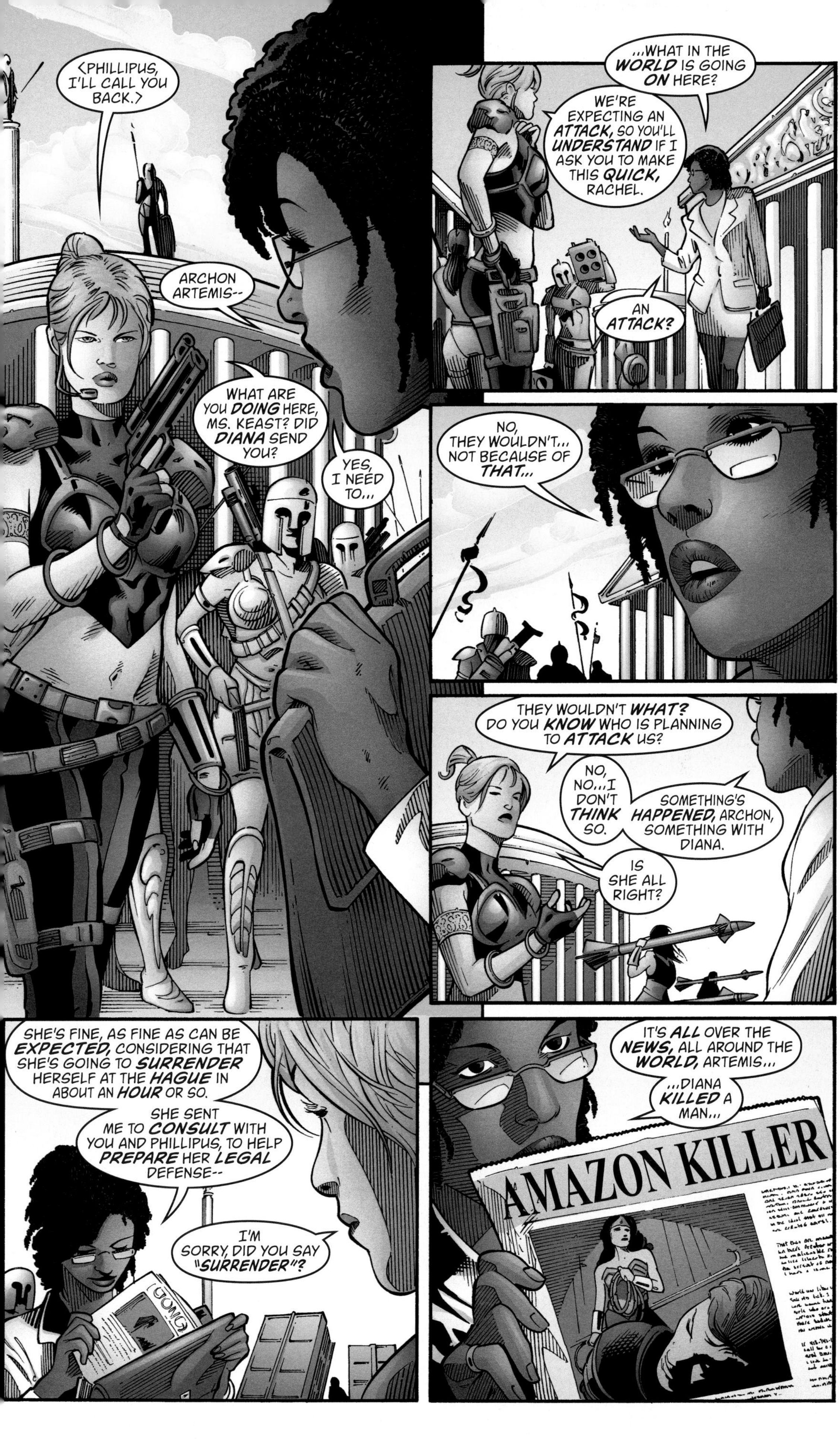
<PHILLIPUS, I'LL CALL YOU BACK.>
ARCHON ARTEMIS--
WHAT ARE YOU DOING HERE, MS. KEAST? DID DIANA SEND YOU?
YES, I NEED TO...
...WHAT IN THE WORLD IS GOING ON HERE?
WE'RE EXPECTING AN ATTACK, SO YOU'LL UNDERSTAND IF I ASK YOU TO MAKE THIS QUICK, RACHEL.
AN ATTACK?
NO, THEY WOULDN'T... NOT BECAUSE OF THAT...
THEY WOULDN'T WHAT? DO YOU KNOW WHO IS PLANNING TO ATTACK US?
NO, NO...I DON'T THINK SO.
SOMETHING'S HAPPENED, ARCHON, SOMETHING WITH DIANA.
IS SHE ALL RIGHT?
SHE'S FINE, AS FINE AS CAN BE EXPECTED, CONSIDERING THAT SHE'S GOING TO SURRENDER HERSELF AT THE HAGUE IN ABOUT AN HOUR OR SO.
SHE SENT ME TO CONSULT WITH YOU AND PHILLIPUS, TO HELP PREPARE HER LEGAL DEFENSE--
I'M SORRY, DID YOU SAY "SURRENDER"?
IT'S ALL OVER THE NEWS, ALL AROUND THE WORLD, ARTEMIS...
...DIANA KILLED A MAN...
AMAZON KILLER

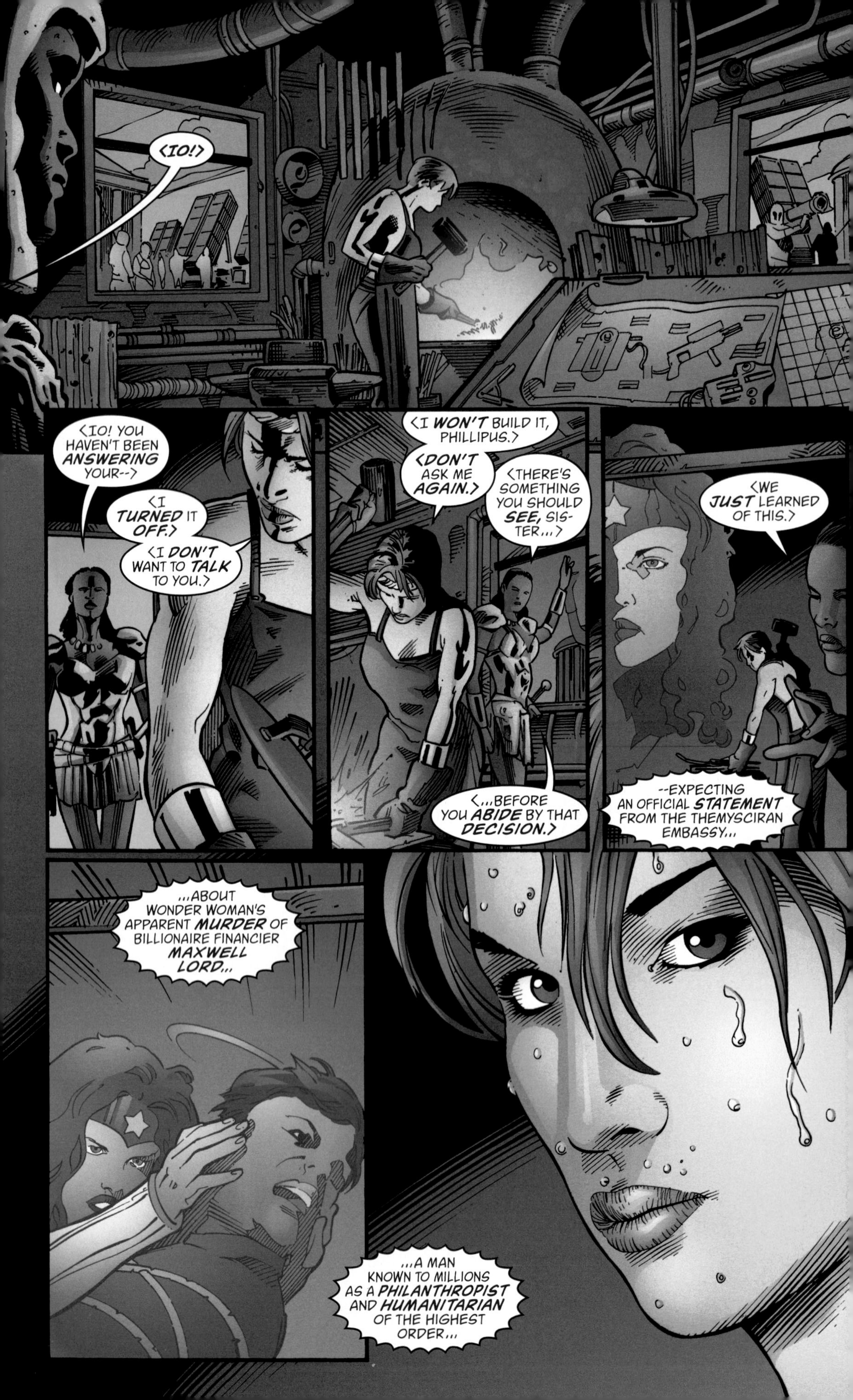
<IO!>
<IO! YOU HAVEN'T BEEN ANSWERING YOUR-->
<I TURNED IT OFF.>
<I DON'T WANT TO TALK TO YOU.>
<I WON'T BUILD IT, PHILLIPUS.>
<DON'T ASK ME AGAIN.>
<THERE'S SOMETHING YOU SHOULD SEE, SISTER...>
<...BEFORE YOU ABIDE BY THAT DECISION.>
<WE JUST LEARNED OF THIS.>
--EXPECTING AN OFFICIAL STATEMENT FROM THE THEMYSCIRAN EMBASSY...
...ABOUT WONDER WOMAN'S APPARENT MURDER OF BILLIONAIRE FINANCIER MAXWELL LORD...
...A MAN KNOWN TO MILLIONS AS A PHILANTHROPIST AND HUMANITARIAN OF THE HIGHEST ORDER...

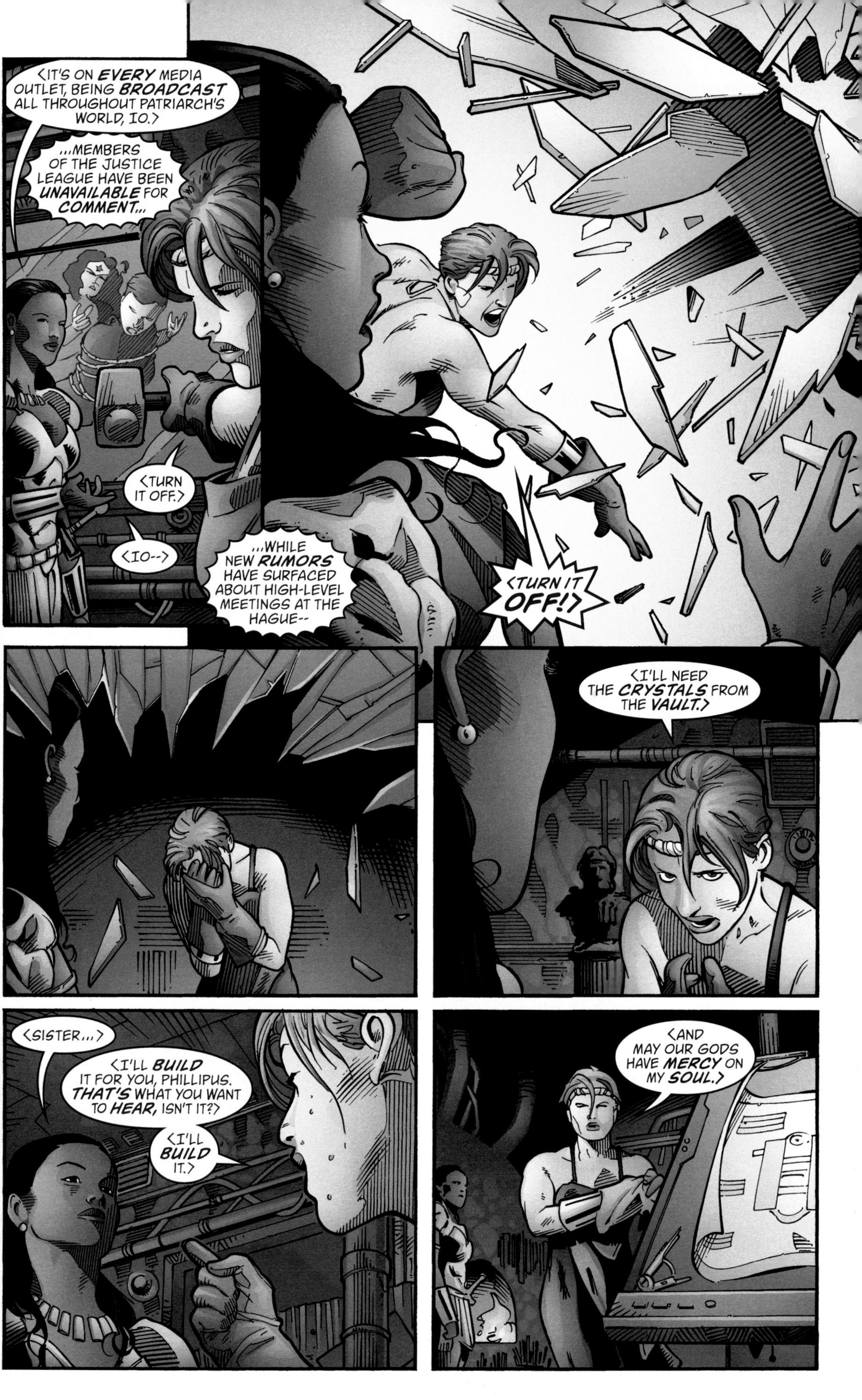

<IT'S ON EVERY MEDIA OUTLET, BEING BROADCAST ALL THROUGHOUT PATRIARCH'S WORLD, IO.>
...MEMBERS OF THE JUSTICE LEAGUE HAVE BEEN UNAVAILABLE FOR COMMENT...
<TURN IT OFF.>
<IO-->
...WHILE NEW RUMORS HAVE SURFACED ABOUT HIGH-LEVEL MEETINGS AT THE HAGUE--
<TURN IT OFF!>
<I'LL NEED THE CRYSTALS FROM THE VAULT.>
<SISTER...>
<I'LL BUILD IT FOR YOU, PHILLIPUS. THAT'S WHAT YOU WANT TO HEAR, ISN'T IT?>
<I'LL BUILD IT.>
<AND MAY OUR GODS HAVE MERCY ON MY SOUL.>

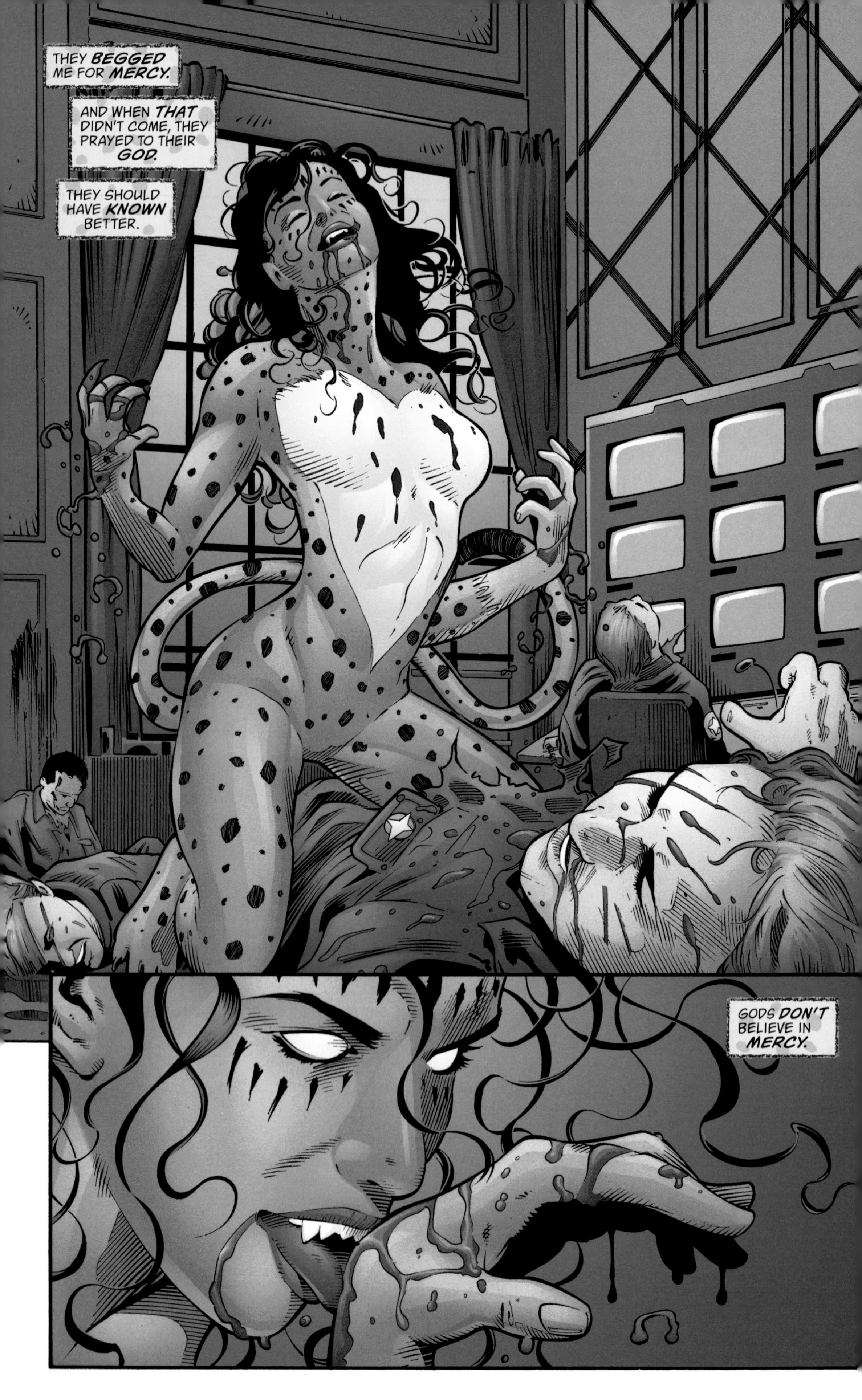
THEY BEGGED ME FOR MERCY.
AND WHEN THAT DIDN'T COME, THEY PRAYED TO THEIR GOD.
THEY SHOULD HAVE KNOWN BETTER.
GODS DON'T BELIEVE IN MERCY.

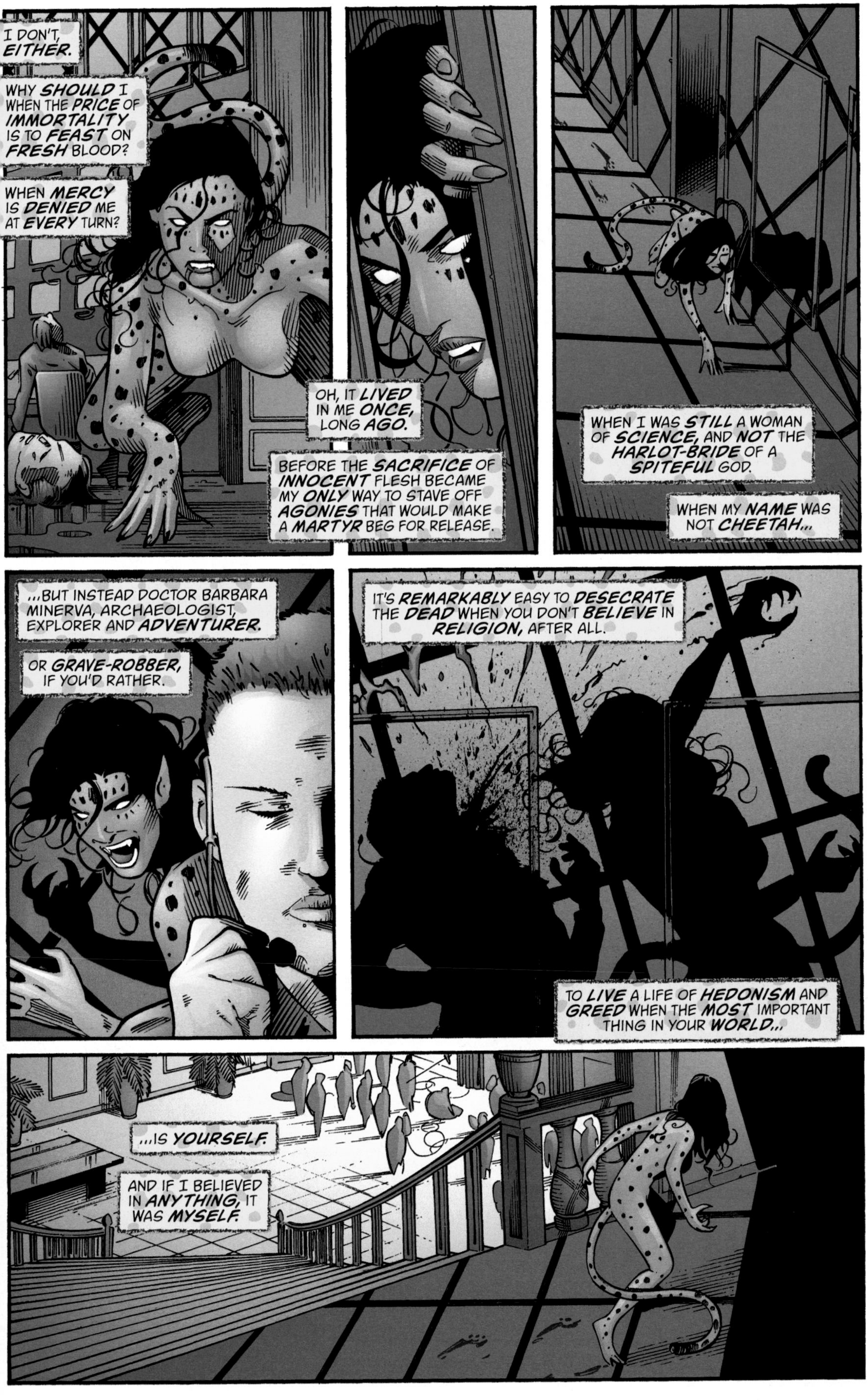
I DON'T, EITHER.
WHY SHOULD I WHEN THE PRICE OF IMMORTALITY IS TO FEAST ON FRESH BLOOD?
WHEN MERCY IS DENIED ME AT EVERY TURN?
OH, IT LIVED IN ME ONCE, LONG AGO.
BEFORE THE SACRIFICE OF INNOCENT FLESH BECAME MY ONLY WAY TO STAVE OFF AGONIES THAT WOULD MAKE A MARTYR BEG FOR RELEASE.
WHEN I WAS STILL A WOMAN OF SCIENCE, AND NOT THE HARLOT-BRIDE OF A SPITEFUL GOD.
WHEN MY NAME WAS NOT CHEETAH...
...BUT INSTEAD DOCTOR BARBARA MINERVA, ARCHAEOLOGIST, EXPLORER AND ADVENTURER.
OR GRAVE-ROBBER, IF YOU'D RATHER.
IT'S REMARKABLY EASY TO DESECRATE THE DEAD WHEN YOU DON'T BELIEVE IN RELIGION, AFTER ALL.
TO LIVE A LIFE OF HEDONISM AND GREED WHEN THE MOST IMPORTANT THING IN YOUR WORLD...
...IS YOURSELF.
AND IF I BELIEVED IN ANYTHING, IT WAS MYSELF.

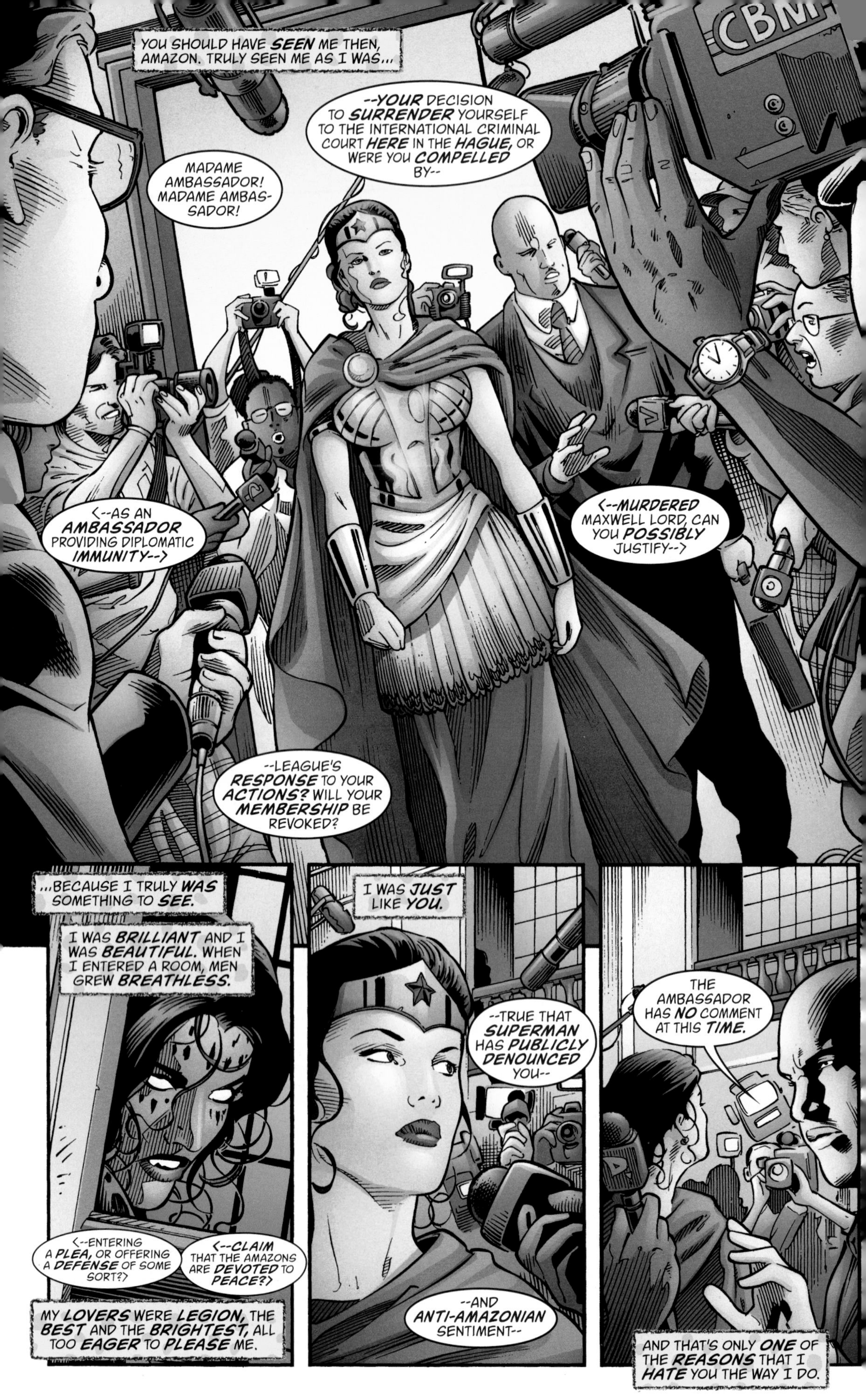

YOU SHOULD HAVE SEEN ME THEN, AMAZON. TRULY SEEN ME AS I WAS...
MADAME AMBASSADOR! MADAME AMBASSADOR!
--YOUR DECISION TO SURRENDER YOURSELF TO THE INTERNATIONAL CRIMINAL COURT HERE IN THE HAGUE, OR WERE YOU COMPELLED BY--
CBM
<--AS AN AMBASSADOR PROVIDING DIPLOMATIC IMMUNITY-->
<--MURDERED MAXWELL LORD, CAN YOU POSSIBLY JUSTIFY-->
--LEAGUE'S RESPONSE TO YOUR ACTIONS? WILL YOUR MEMBERSHIP BE REVOKED?
...BECAUSE I TRULY WAS SOMETHING TO SEE.
I WAS BRILLIANT AND I WAS BEAUTIFUL. WHEN I ENTERED A ROOM, MEN GREW BREATHLESS.
<--ENTERING A PLEA, OR OFFERING A DEFENSE OF SOME SORT?>
<--CLAIM THAT THE AMAZONS ARE DEVOTED TO PEACE?>
MY LOVERS WERE LEGION, THE BEST AND THE BRIGHTEST, ALL TOO EAGER TO PLEASE ME.
I WAS JUST LIKE YOU.
--TRUE THAT SUPERMAN HAS PUBLICLY DENOUNCED YOU--
--AND ANTI-AMAZONIAN SENTIMENT--
THE AMBASSADOR HAS NO COMMENT AT THIS TIME.
AND THAT'S ONLY ONE OF THE REASONS THAT I HATE YOU THE WAY I DO.

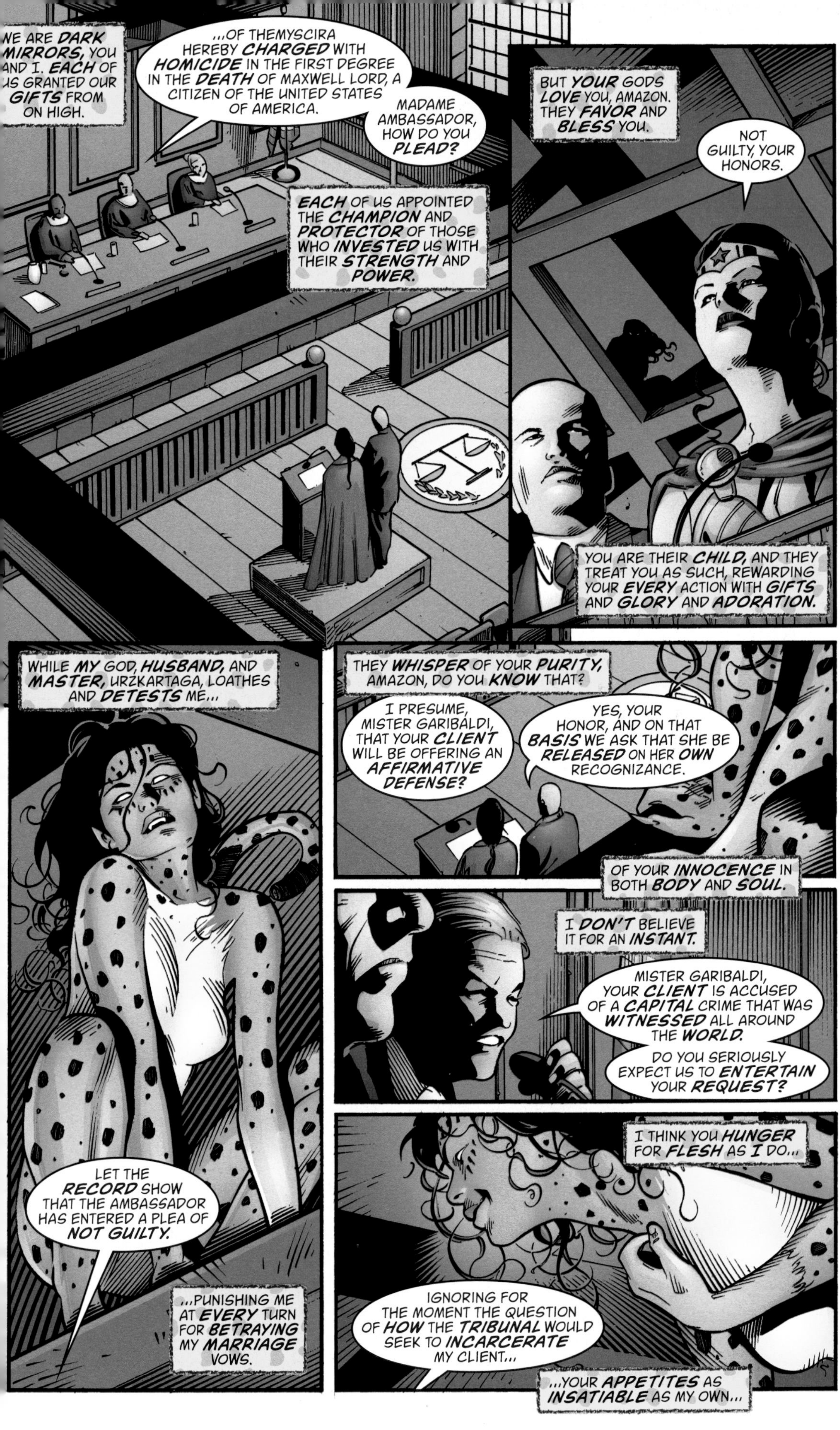

WE ARE DARK MIRRORS, YOU AND I. EACH OF US GRANTED OUR GIFTS FROM ON HIGH.
...OF THEMYSCIRA HEREBY CHARGED WITH HOMICIDE IN THE FIRST DEGREE IN THE DEATH OF MAXWELL LORD, A CITIZEN OF THE UNITED STATES OF AMERICA.
MADAME AMBASSADOR, HOW DO YOU PLEAD?
EACH OF US APPOINTED THE CHAMPION AND PROTECTOR OF THOSE WHO INVESTED US WITH THEIR STRENGTH AND POWER.
BUT YOUR GODS LOVE YOU, AMAZON. THEY FAVOR AND BLESS YOU.
NOT GUILTY, YOUR HONORS.
YOU ARE THEIR CHILD, AND THEY TREAT YOU AS SUCH, REWARDING YOUR EVERY ACTION WITH GIFTS AND GLORY AND ADORATION.
WHILE MY GOD, HUSBAND, AND MASTER, URZKARTAGA, LOATHES AND DETESTS ME...
LET THE RECORD SHOW THAT THE AMBASSADOR HAS ENTERED A PLEA OF NOT GUILTY.
...PUNISHING ME AT EVERY TURN FOR BETRAYING MY MARRIAGE VOWS.
THEY WHISPER OF YOUR PURITY, AMAZON, DO YOU KNOW THAT?
I PRESUME, MISTER GARIBALDI, THAT YOUR CLIENT WILL BE OFFERING AN AFFIRMATIVE DEFENSE?
YES, YOUR HONOR, AND ON THAT BASIS WE ASK THAT SHE BE RELEASED ON HER OWN RECOGNIZANCE.
OF YOUR INNOCENCE IN BOTH BODY AND SOUL.
I DON'T BELIEVE IT FOR AN INSTANT.
MISTER GARIBALDI, YOUR CLIENT IS ACCUSED OF A CAPITAL CRIME THAT WAS WITNESSED ALL AROUND THE WORLD.
DO YOU SERIOUSLY EXPECT US TO ENTERTAIN YOUR REQUEST?
I THINK YOU HUNGER FOR FLESH AS I DO...
IGNORING FOR THE MOMENT THE QUESTION OF HOW THE TRIBUNAL WOULD SEEK TO INCARCERATE MY CLIENT...
...YOUR APPETITES AS INSATIABLE AS MY OWN...

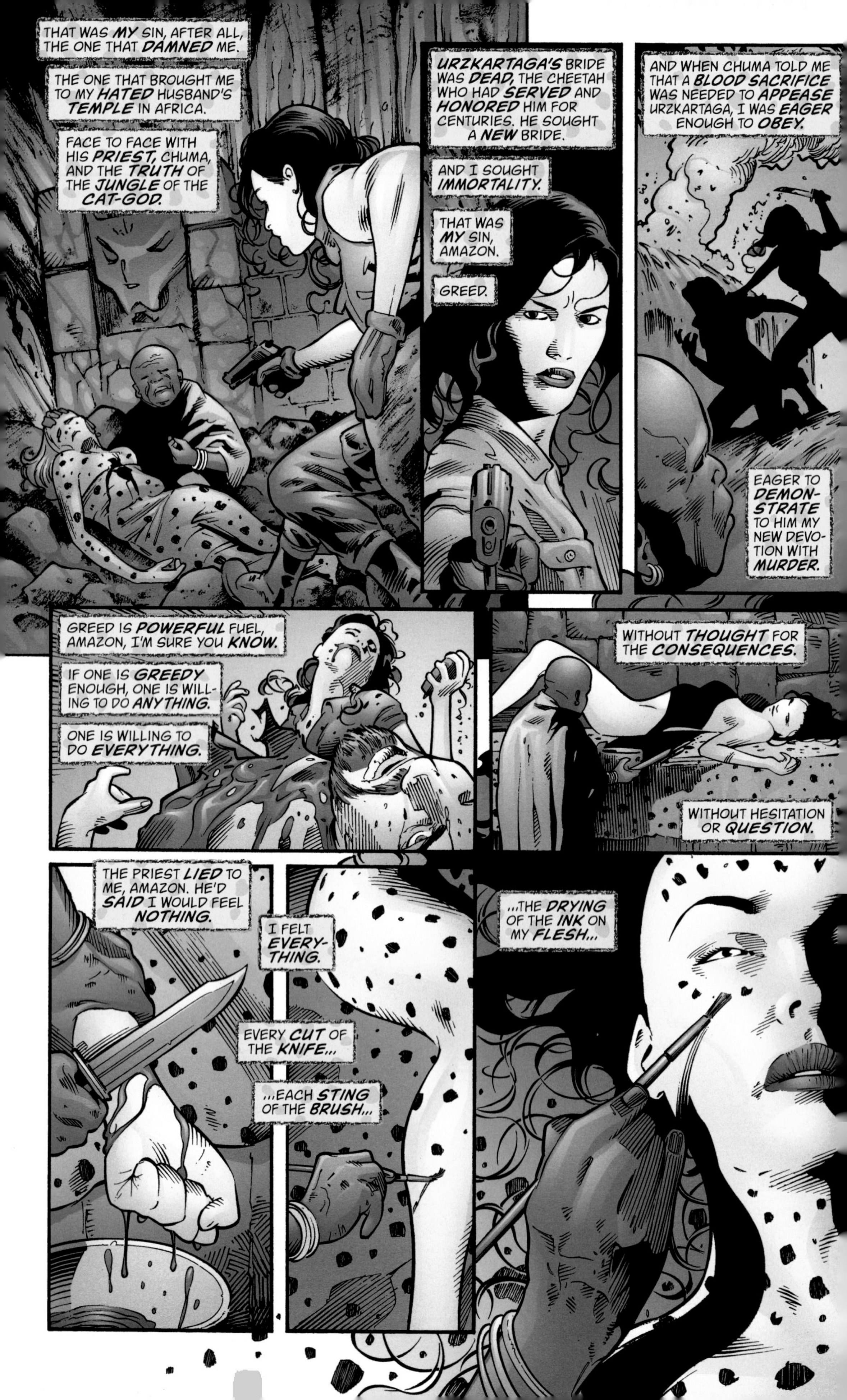
THAT WAS MY SIN, AFTER ALL, THE ONE THAT DAMNED ME.
THE ONE THAT BROUGHT ME TO MY HATED HUSBAND'S TEMPLE IN AFRICA.
FACE TO FACE WITH HIS PRIEST, CHUMA, AND THE TRUTH OF THE JUNGLE OF THE CAT-GOD.
URZKARTAGA'S BRIDE WAS DEAD, THE CHEETAH WHO HAD SERVED AND HONORED HIM FOR CENTURIES. HE SOUGHT A NEW BRIDE.
AND I SOUGHT IMMORTALITY.
THAT WAS MY SIN, AMAZON.
GREED.
AND WHEN CHUMA TOLD ME THAT A BLOOD SACRIFICE WAS NEEDED TO APPEASE URZKARTAGA, I WAS EAGER ENOUGH TO OBEY.
EAGER TO DEMON-STRATE TO HIM MY NEW DEVO-TION WITH MURDER.
GREED IS POWERFUL FUEL, AMAZON, I'M SURE YOU KNOW.
IF ONE IS GREEDY ENOUGH, ONE IS WILL-ING TO DO ANYTHING.
ONE IS WILLING TO DO EVERYTHING.
WITHOUT THOUGHT FOR THE CONSEQUENCES.
WITHOUT HESITATION OR QUESTION.
THE PRIEST LIED TO ME, AMAZON. HE'D SAID I WOULD FEEL NOTHING.
I FELT EVERY-THING.
EVERY CUT OF THE KNIFE...
...EACH STING OF THE BRUSH...
...THE DRYING OF THE INK ON MY FLESH...

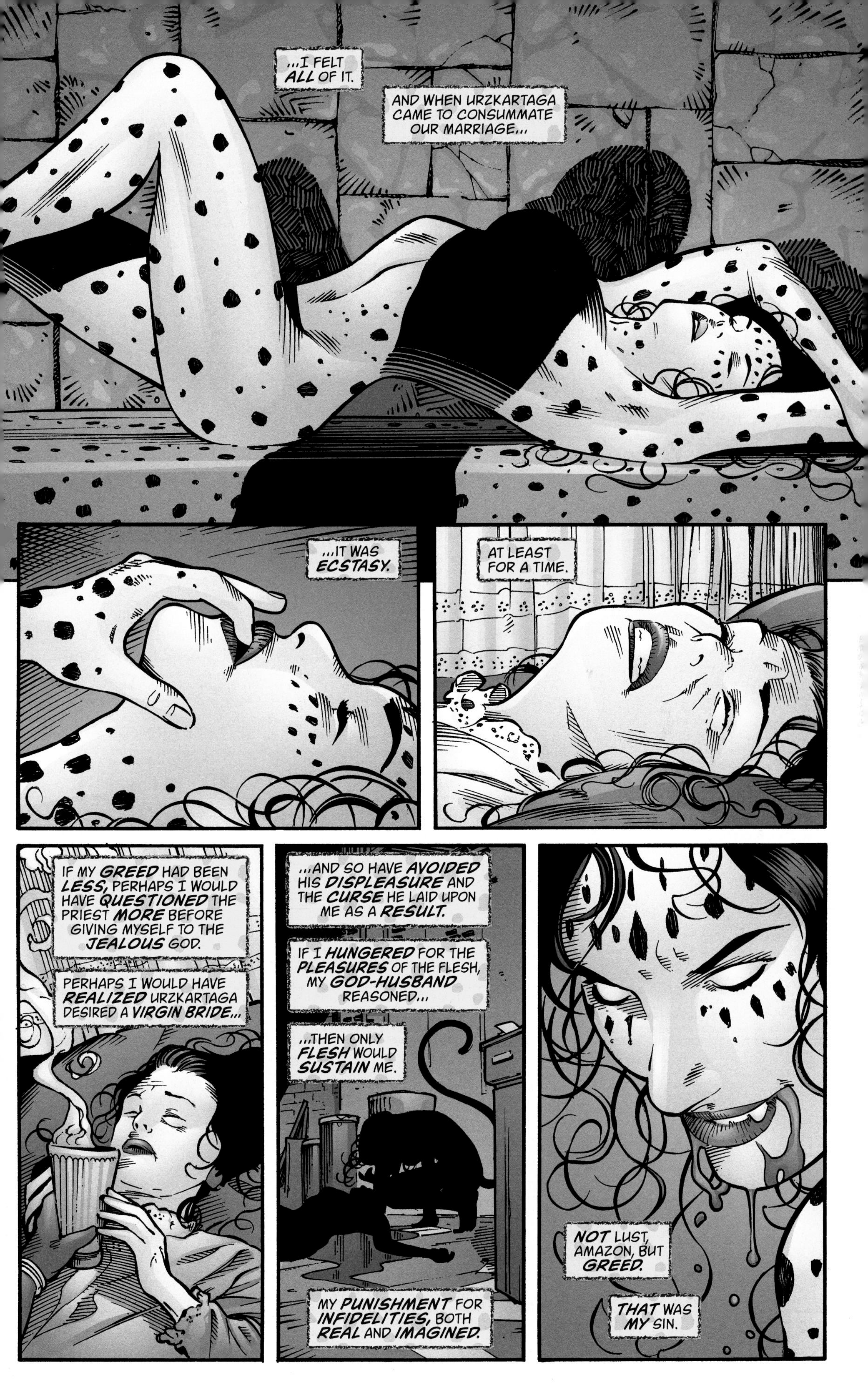
...I FELT ALL OF IT.
AND WHEN URZKARTAGA CAME TO CONSUMMATE OUR MARRIAGE...
...IT WAS ECSTASY.
AT LEAST FOR A TIME.
IF MY GREED HAD BEEN LESS, PERHAPS I WOULD HAVE QUESTIONED THE PRIEST MORE BEFORE GIVING MYSELF TO THE JEALOUS GOD.
PERHAPS I WOULD HAVE REALIZED URZKARTAGA DESIRED A VIRGIN BRIDE...
...AND SO HAVE AVOIDED HIS DISPLEASURE AND THE CURSE HE LAID UPON ME AS A RESULT.
IF I HUNGERED FOR THE PLEASURES OF THE FLESH, MY GOD-HUSBAND REASONED...
...THEN ONLY FLESH WOULD SUSTAIN ME.
MY PUNISHMENT FOR INFIDELITIES, BOTH REAL AND IMAGINED.
NOT LUST, AMAZON, BUT GREED.
THAT WAS MY SIN.

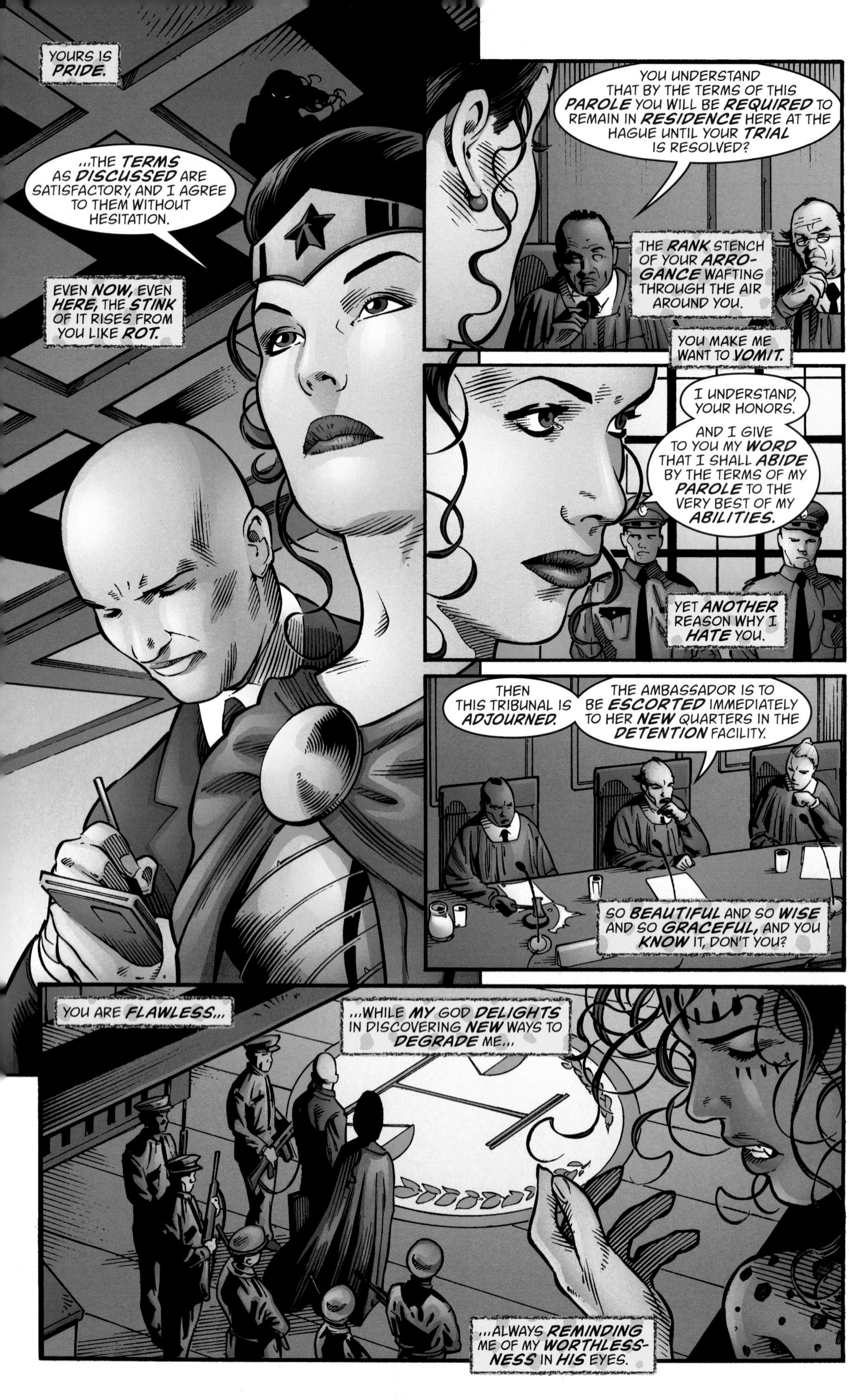
YOURS IS PRIDE.
...THE TERMS AS DISCUSSED ARE SATISFACTORY, AND I AGREE TO THEM WITHOUT HESITATION.
EVEN NOW, EVEN HERE, THE STINK OF IT RISES FROM YOU LIKE ROT.
YOU UNDERSTAND THAT BY THE TERMS OF THIS PAROLE YOU WILL BE REQUIRED TO REMAIN IN RESIDENCE HERE AT THE HAGUE UNTIL YOUR TRIAL IS RESOLVED?
THE RANK STENCH OF YOUR ARROGANCE WAFTING THROUGH THE AIR AROUND YOU.
YOU MAKE ME WANT TO VOMIT.
I UNDERSTAND, YOUR HONORS.
AND I GIVE TO YOU MY WORD THAT I SHALL ABIDE BY THE TERMS OF MY PAROLE TO THE VERY BEST OF MY ABILITIES.
YET ANOTHER REASON WHY I HATE YOU.
THEN THIS TRIBUNAL IS ADJOURNED.
THE AMBASSADOR IS TO BE ESCORTED IMMEDIATELY TO HER NEW QUARTERS IN THE DETENTION FACILITY.
SO BEAUTIFUL AND SO WISE AND SO GRACEFUL, AND YOU KNOW IT, DON'T YOU?
YOU ARE FLAWLESS...
...WHILE MY GOD DELIGHTS IN DISCOVERING NEW WAYS TO DEGRADE ME...
...ALWAYS REMINDING ME OF MY WORTHLESSNESS IN HIS EYES.

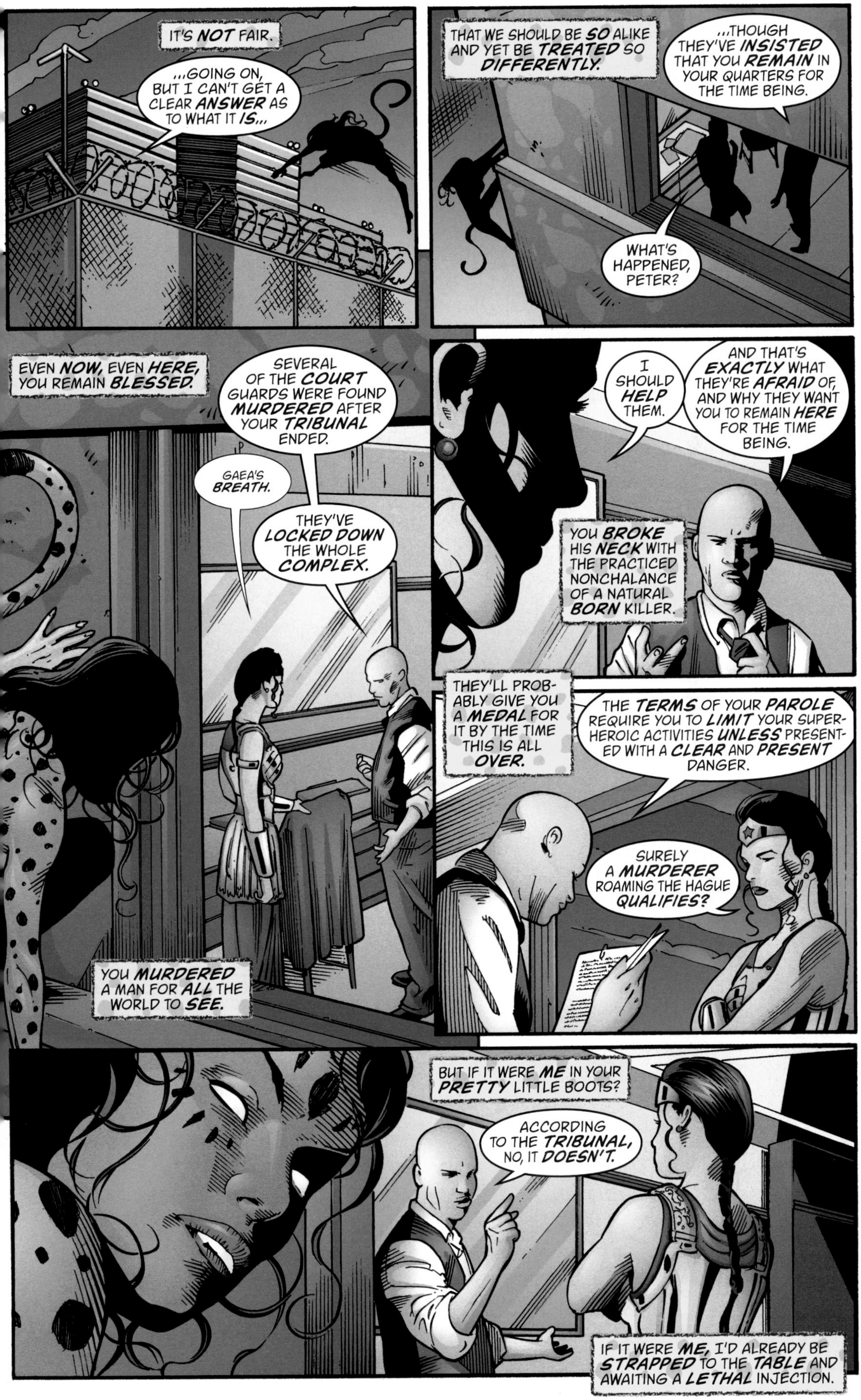
IT'S NOT FAIR.
...GOING ON, BUT I CAN'T GET A CLEAR ANSWER AS TO WHAT IT IS...
THAT WE SHOULD BE SO ALIKE AND YET BE TREATED SO DIFFERENTLY.
...THOUGH THEY'VE INSISTED THAT YOU REMAIN IN YOUR QUARTERS FOR THE TIME BEING.
WHAT'S HAPPENED, PETER?
EVEN NOW, EVEN HERE, YOU REMAIN BLESSED.
SEVERAL OF THE COURT GUARDS WERE FOUND MURDERED AFTER YOUR TRIBUNAL ENDED.
GAEA'S BREATH.
THEY'VE LOCKED DOWN THE WHOLE COMPLEX.
YOU MURDERED A MAN FOR ALL THE WORLD TO SEE.
I SHOULD HELP THEM.
AND THAT'S EXACTLY WHAT THEY'RE AFRAID OF, AND WHY THEY WANT YOU TO REMAIN HERE FOR THE TIME BEING.
YOU BROKE HIS NECK WITH THE PRACTICED NONCHALANCE OF A NATURAL BORN KILLER.
THEY'LL PROBABLY GIVE YOU A MEDAL FOR IT BY THE TIME THIS IS ALL OVER.
THE TERMS OF YOUR PAROLE REQUIRE YOU TO LIMIT YOUR SUPERHEROIC ACTIVITIES UNLESS PRESENTED WITH A CLEAR AND PRESENT DANGER.
SURELY A MURDERER ROAMING THE HAGUE QUALIFIES?
BUT IF IT WERE ME IN YOUR PRETTY LITTLE BOOTS?
ACCORDING TO THE TRIBUNAL, NO, IT DOESN'T.
IF IT WERE ME, I'D ALREADY BE STRAPPED TO THE TABLE AND AWAITING A LETHAL INJECTION.

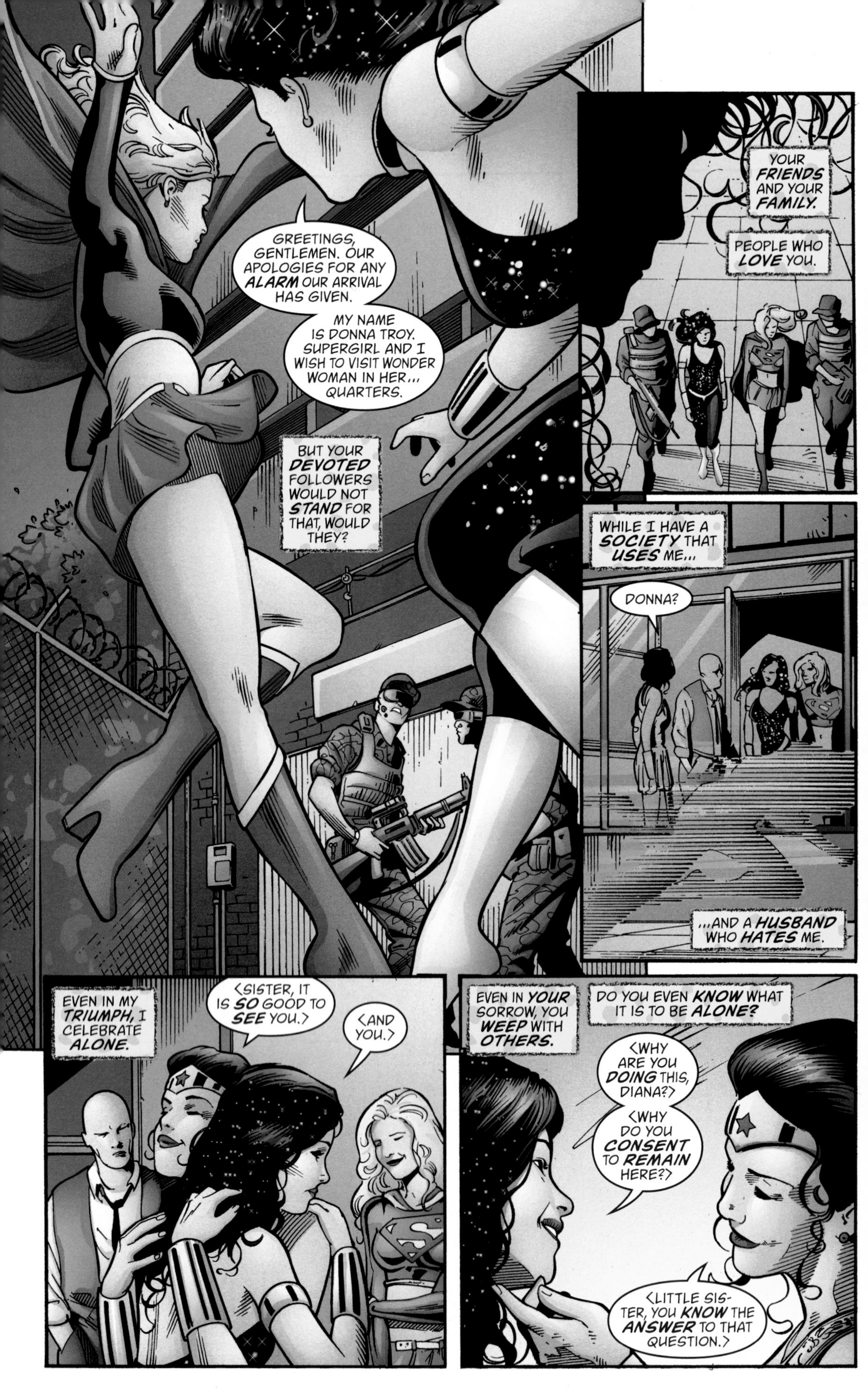
GREETINGS, GENTLEMEN. OUR APOLOGIES FOR ANY ALARM OUR ARRIVAL HAS GIVEN.
MY NAME IS DONNA TROY. SUPERGIRL AND I WISH TO VISIT WONDER WOMAN IN HER... QUARTERS.
BUT YOUR DEVOTED FOLLOWERS WOULD NOT STAND FOR THAT, WOULD THEY?
YOUR FRIENDS AND YOUR FAMILY.
PEOPLE WHO LOVE YOU.
WHILE I HAVE A SOCIETY THAT USES ME...
DONNA?
...AND A HUSBAND WHO HATES ME.
EVEN IN MY TRIUMPH, I CELEBRATE ALONE.
<SISTER, IT IS SO GOOD TO SEE YOU.>
<AND YOU.>
EVEN IN YOUR SORROW, YOU WEEP WITH OTHERS.
DO YOU EVEN KNOW WHAT IT IS TO BE ALONE?
<WHY ARE YOU DOING THIS, DIANA?>
<WHY DO YOU CONSENT TO REMAIN HERE?>
<LITTLE SISTER, YOU KNOW THE ANSWER TO THAT QUESTION.>

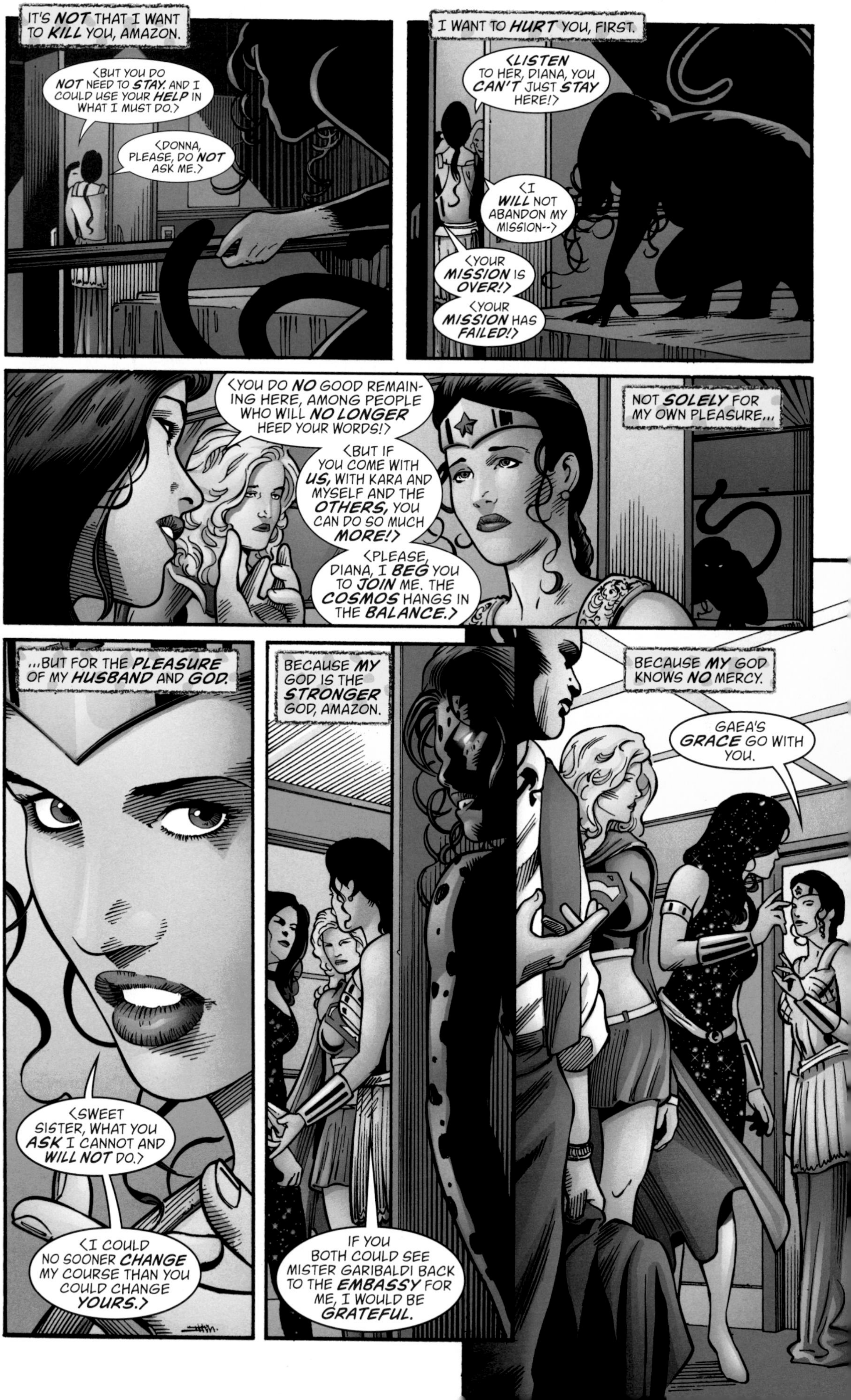
IT'S NOT THAT I WANT TO KILL YOU, AMAZON.
<BUT YOU DO NOT NEED TO STAY. AND I COULD USE YOUR HELP IN WHAT I MUST DO.>
<DONNA, PLEASE, DO NOT ASK ME.>
I WANT TO HURT YOU, FIRST.
<LISTEN TO HER, DIANA, YOU CAN'T JUST STAY HERE!>
<I WILL NOT ABANDON MY MISSION-->
<YOUR MISSION IS OVER!>
<YOUR MISSION HAS FAILED!>
<YOU DO NO GOOD REMAINING HERE, AMONG PEOPLE WHO WILL NO LONGER HEED YOUR WORDS!>
<BUT IF YOU COME WITH US, WITH KARA AND MYSELF AND THE OTHERS, YOU CAN DO SO MUCH MORE!>
<PLEASE, DIANA, I BEG YOU TO JOIN ME. THE COSMOS HANGS IN THE BALANCE.>
NOT SOLELY FOR MY OWN PLEASURE...
...BUT FOR THE PLEASURE OF MY HUSBAND AND GOD.
<SWEET SISTER, WHAT YOU ASK I CANNOT AND WILL NOT DO.>
<I COULD NO SOONER CHANGE MY COURSE THAN YOU COULD CHANGE YOURS.>
BECAUSE MY GOD IS THE STRONGER GOD, AMAZON.
IF YOU BOTH COULD SEE MISTER GARIBALDI BACK TO THE EMBASSY FOR ME, I WOULD BE GRATEFUL.
BECAUSE MY GOD KNOWS NO MERCY.
GAEA'S GRACE GO WITH YOU.

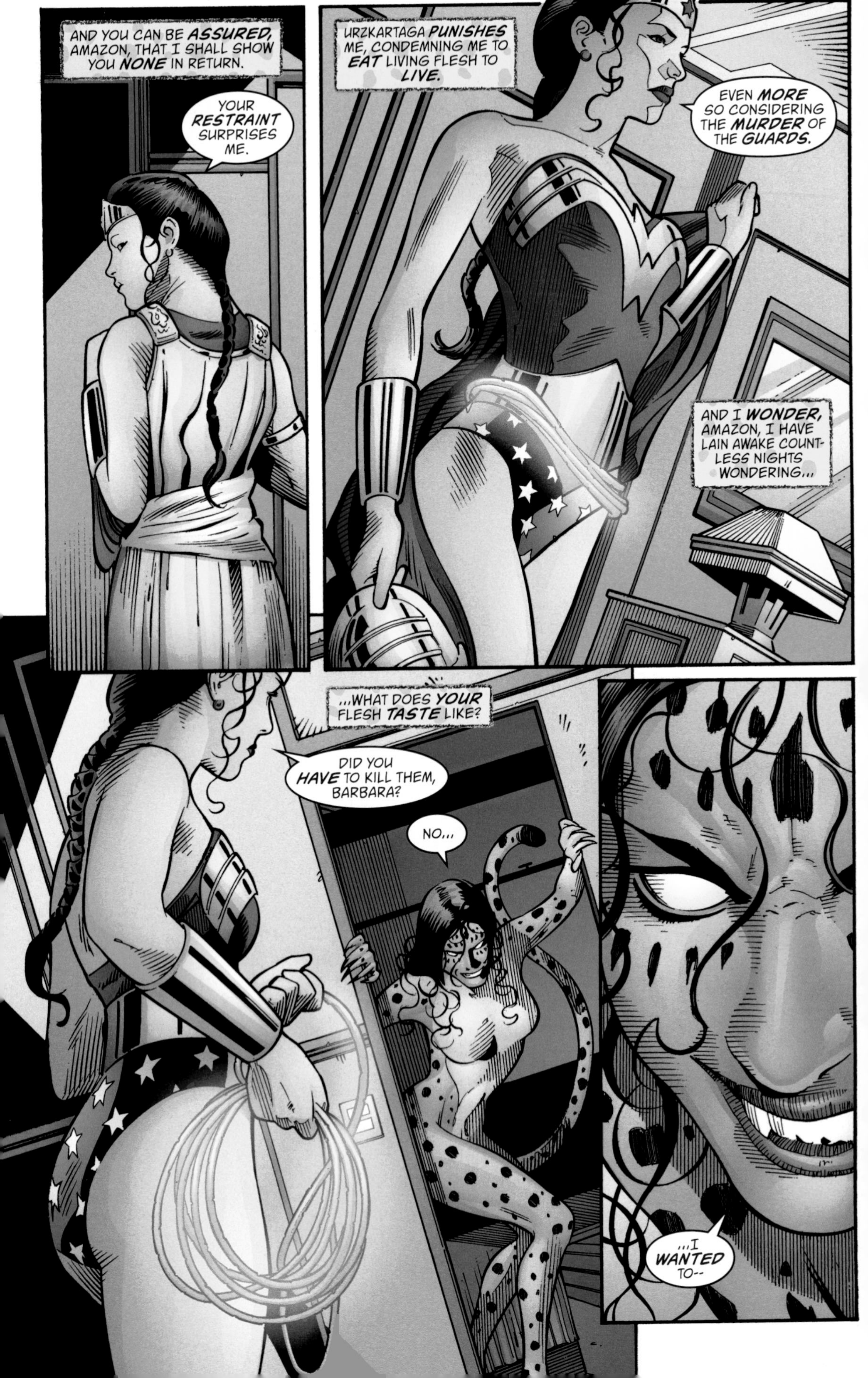
AND YOU CAN BE ASSURED, AMAZON, THAT I SHALL SHOW YOU NONE IN RETURN.
YOUR RESTRAINT SURPRISES ME.
URZKARTAGA PUNISHES ME, CONDEMNING ME TO EAT LIVING FLESH TO LIVE.
EVEN MORE SO CONSIDERING THE MURDER OF THE GUARDS.
AND I WONDER, AMAZON, I HAVE LAIN AWAKE COUNTLESS NIGHTS WONDERING...
...WHAT DOES YOUR FLESH TASTE LIKE?
DID YOU HAVE TO KILL THEM, BARBARA?
NO...
...I WANTED TO--

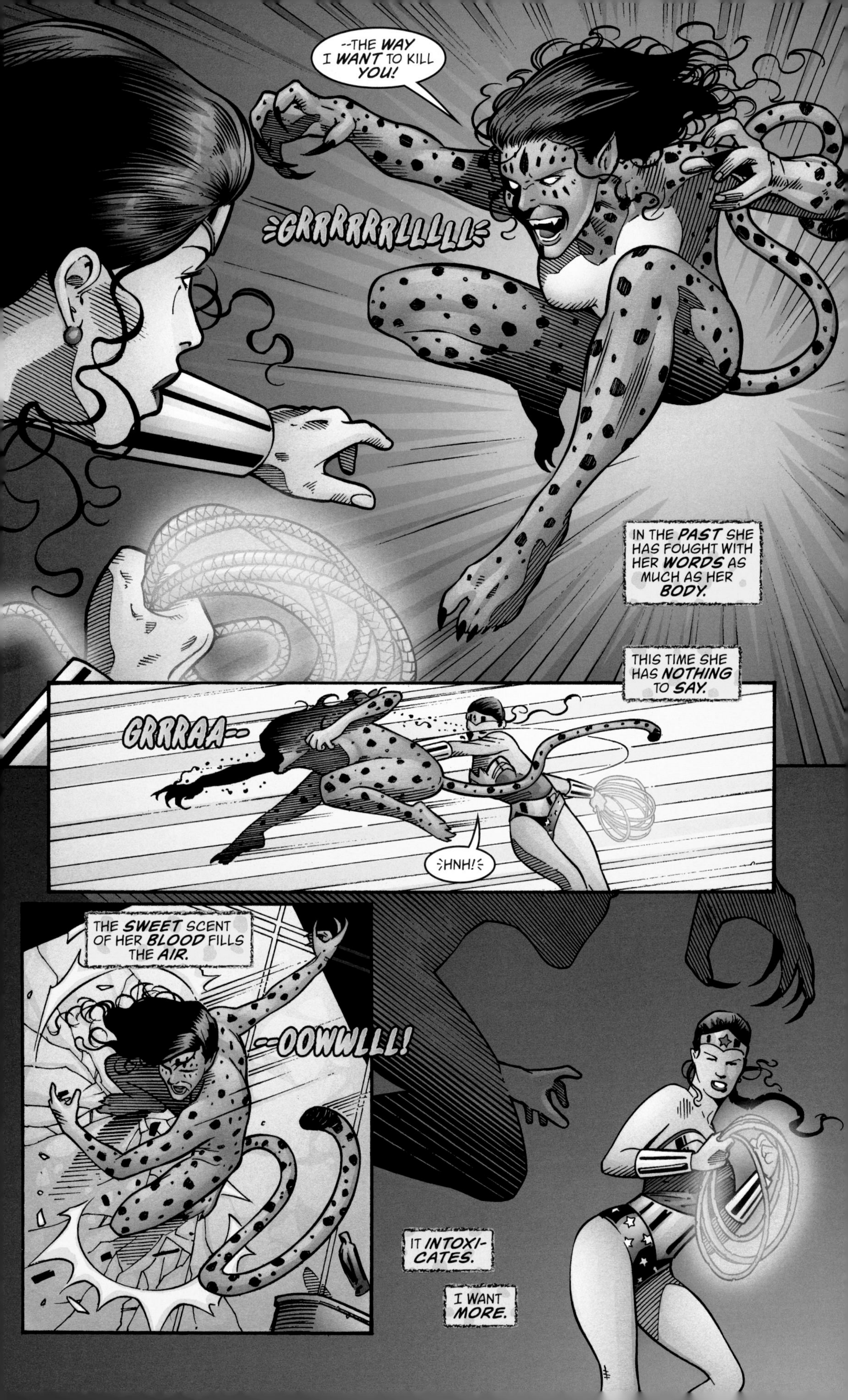
--THE WAY I WANT TO KILL YOU!
GRRRRRRLLLLLL
IN THE PAST SHE HAS FOUGHT WITH HER WORDS AS MUCH AS HER BODY.
THIS TIME SHE HAS NOTHING TO SAY.
GRRRAA--
HNH!
THE SWEET SCENT OF HER BLOOD FILLS THE AIR.
--OOWWLLL!
IT INTOXI- CATES.
I WANT MORE.

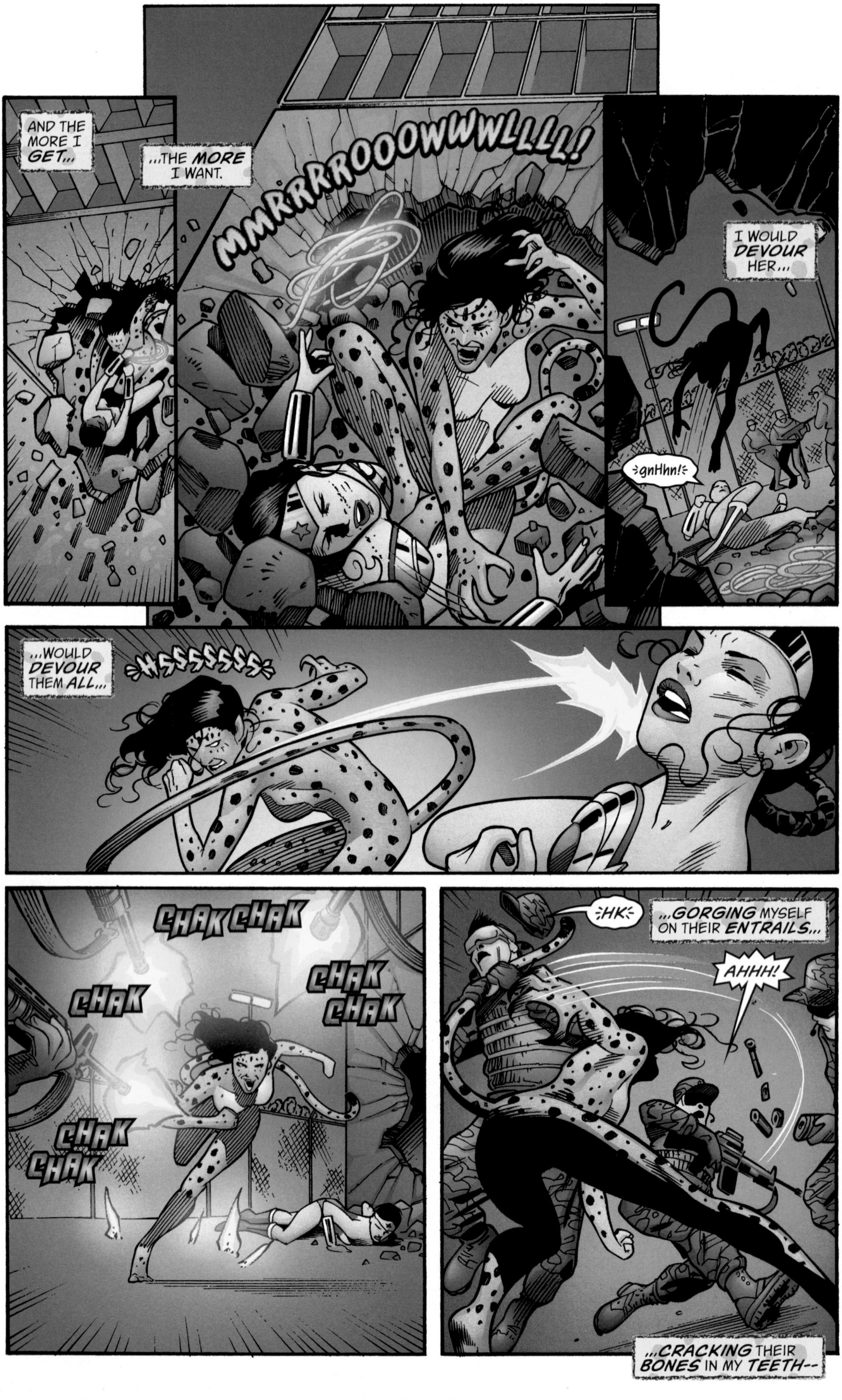
AND THE MORE I GET...
...THE MORE I WANT.
MMRRRROOOWWWLLLL!
I WOULD DEVOUR HER...
gnHhn!
...WOULD DEVOUR THEM ALL...
HSSSSSSS
CHAK CHAK
CHAK
CHAK CHAK
CHAK CHAK
HK
...GORGING MYSELF ON THEIR ENTRAILS...
AHHH!
...CRACKING THEIR BONES IN MY TEETH--

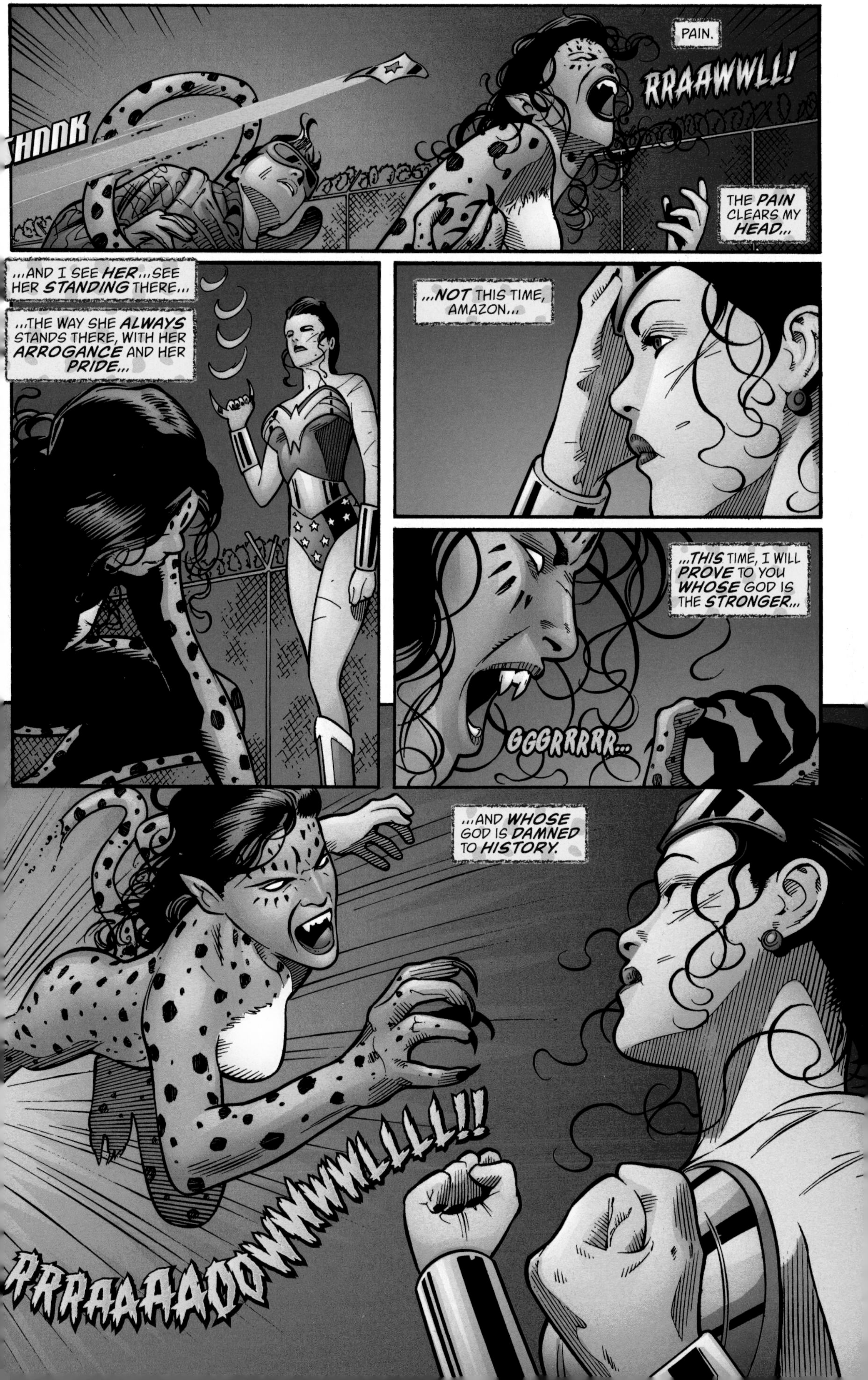
SHNNK
PAIN.
RRAAWLL!
THE PAIN CLEARS MY HEAD...
...AND I SEE HER...SEE HER STANDING THERE...
...THE WAY SHE ALWAYS STANDS THERE, WITH HER ARROGANCE AND HER PRIDE...
...NOT THIS TIME, AMAZON...
...THIS TIME, I WILL PROVE TO YOU WHOSE GOD IS THE STRONGER...
GGGRRRRR...
...AND WHOSE GOD IS DAMNED TO HISTORY.
RRRAAAAAOOWWWWWLLLLL!!

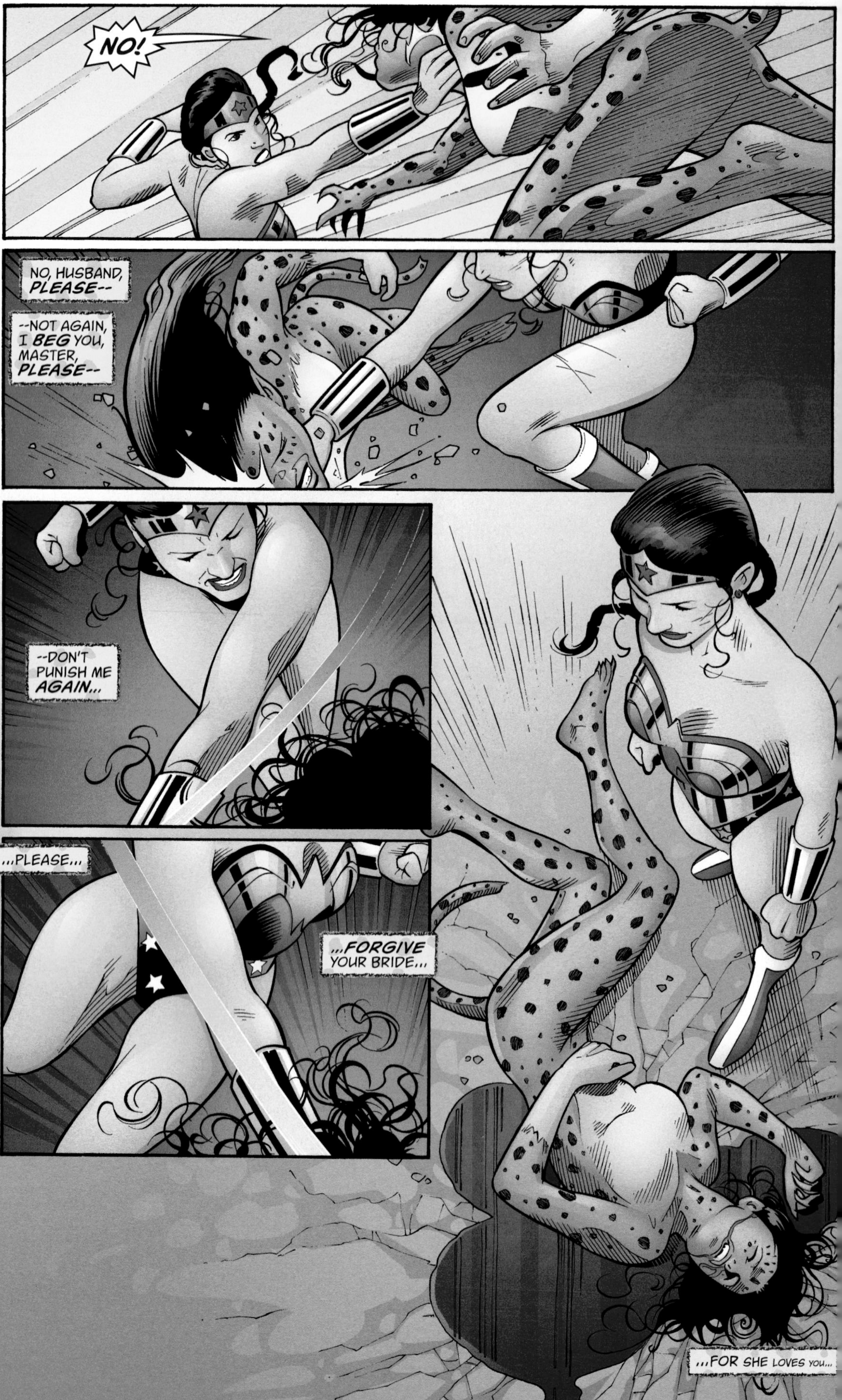
NO!
NO, HUSBAND, PLEASE--
--NOT AGAIN, I BEG YOU, MASTER, PLEASE--
--DON'T PUNISH ME AGAIN...
...PLEASE...
...FORGIVE YOUR BRIDE...
...FOR SHE LOVES YOU...

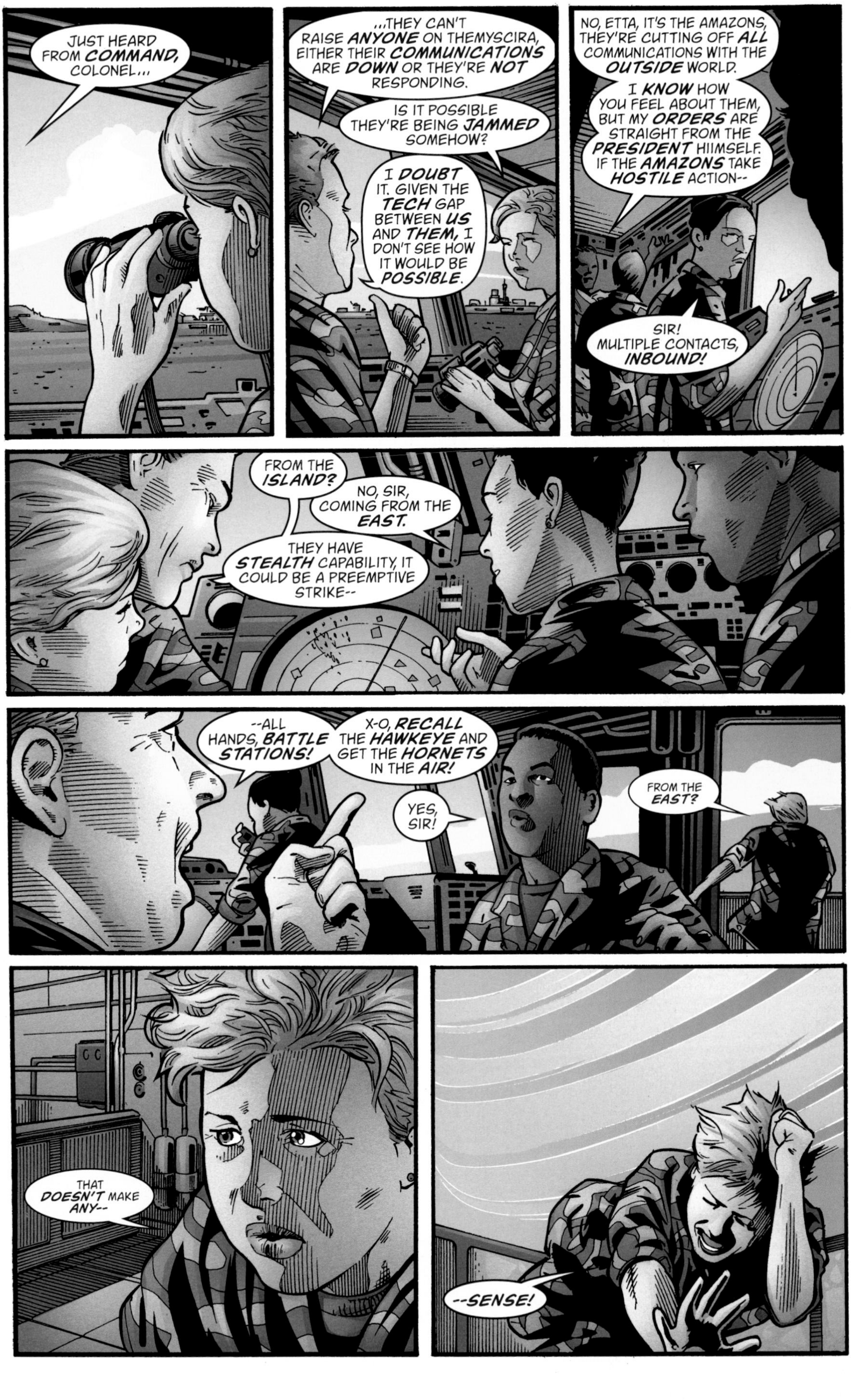
JUST HEARD FROM COMMAND, COLONEL...
...THEY CAN'T RAISE ANYONE ON THEMYSCIRA, EITHER THEIR COMMUNICATIONS ARE DOWN OR THEY'RE NOT RESPONDING.
IS IT POSSIBLE THEY'RE BEING JAMMED SOMEHOW?
I DOUBT IT. GIVEN THE TECH GAP BETWEEN US AND THEM, I DON'T SEE HOW IT WOULD BE POSSIBLE.
NO, ETTA, IT'S THE AMAZONS, THEY'RE CUTTING OFF ALL COMMUNICATIONS WITH THE OUTSIDE WORLD.
I KNOW HOW YOU FEEL ABOUT THEM, BUT MY ORDERS ARE STRAIGHT FROM THE PRESIDENT HIIMSELF. IF THE AMAZONS TAKE HOSTILE ACTION--
SIR! MULTIPLE CONTACTS, INBOUND!
FROM THE ISLAND?
NO, SIR, COMING FROM THE EAST.
THEY HAVE STEALTH CAPABILITY, IT COULD BE A PREEMPTIVE STRIKE--
--ALL HANDS, BATTLE STATIONS!
X-O, RECALL THE HAWKEYE AND GET THE HORNETS IN THE AIR!
YES, SIR!
FROM THE EAST?
THAT DOESN'T MAKE ANY--
--SENSE!

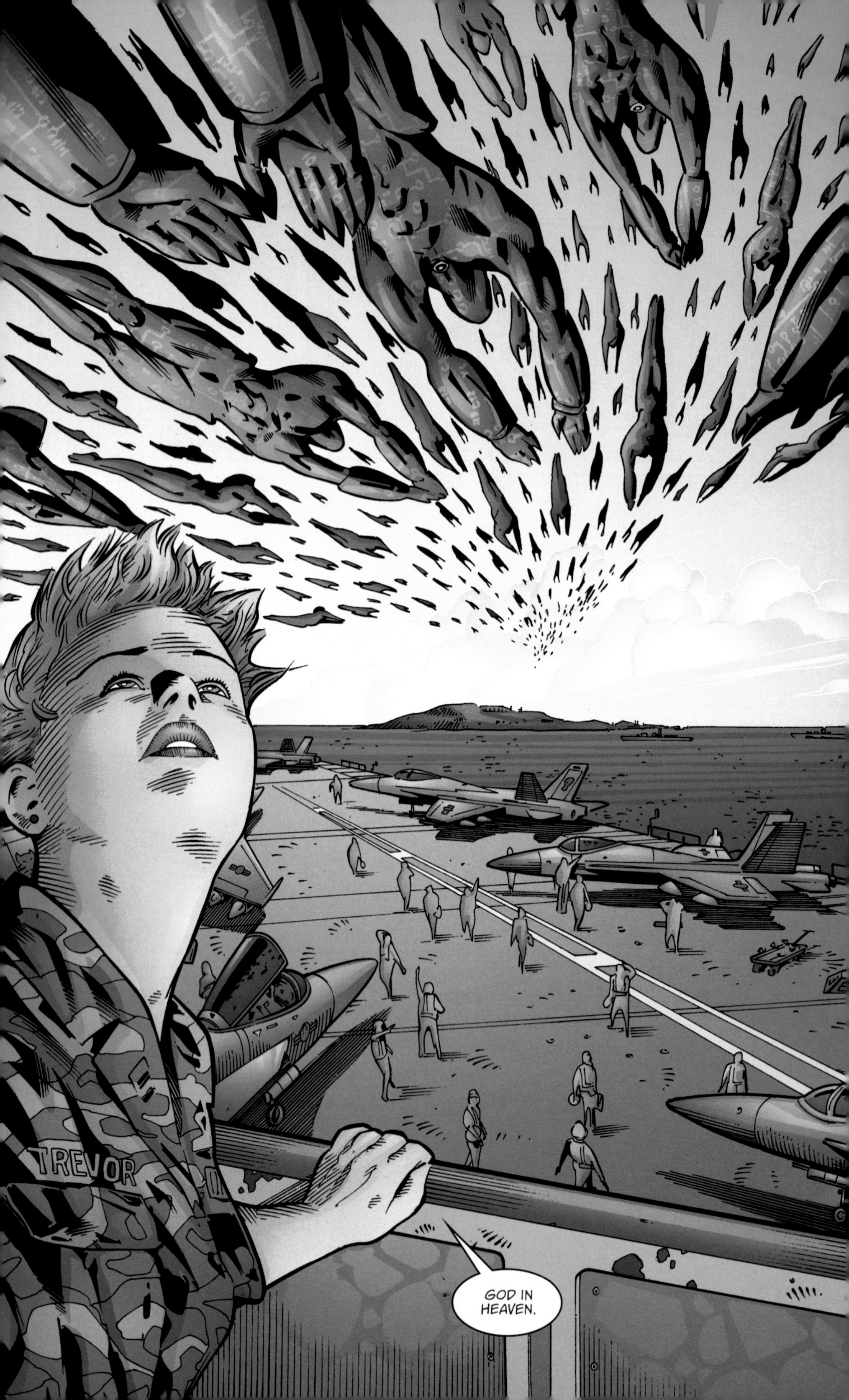
TREVOR
GOD IN HEAVEN.

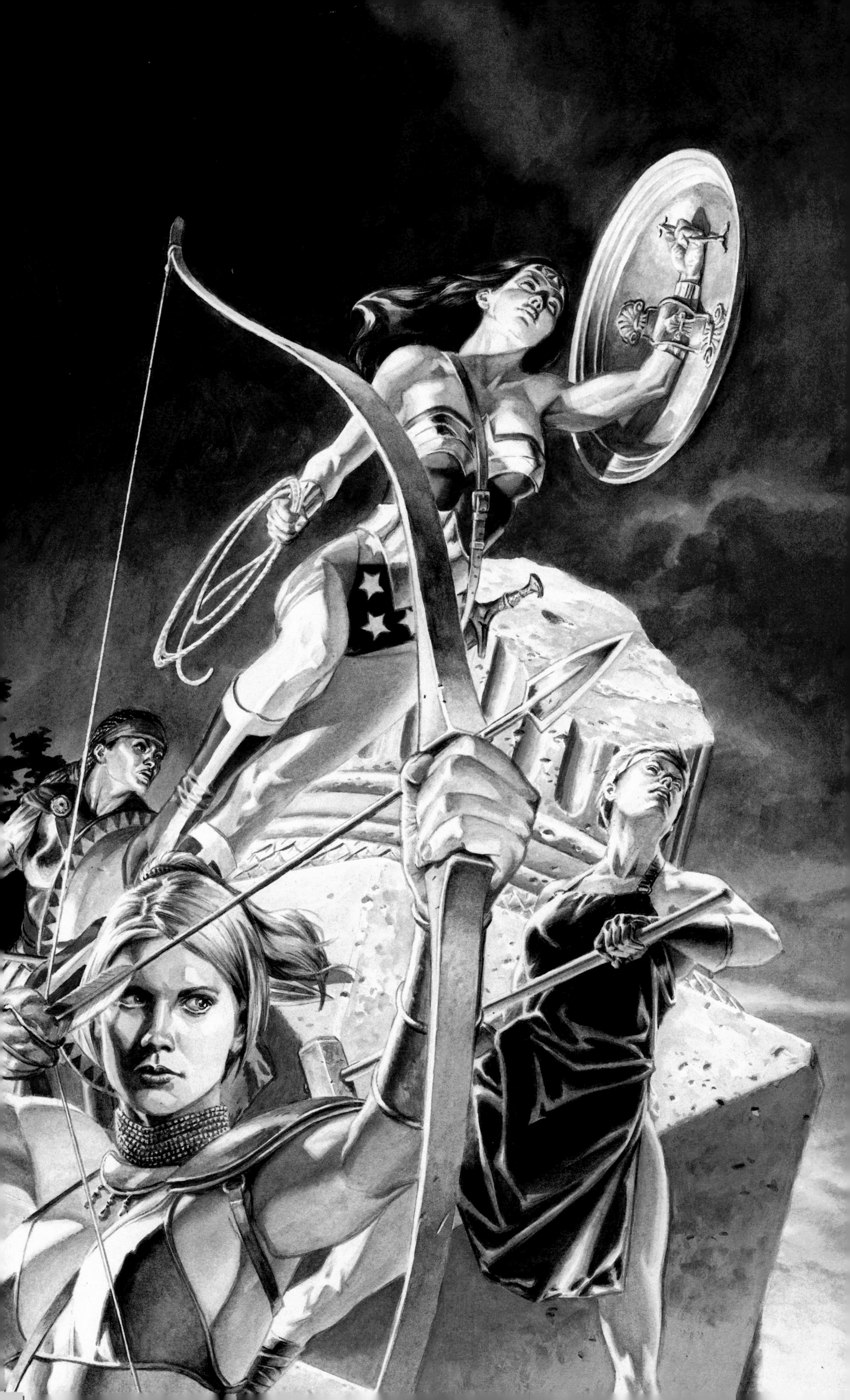

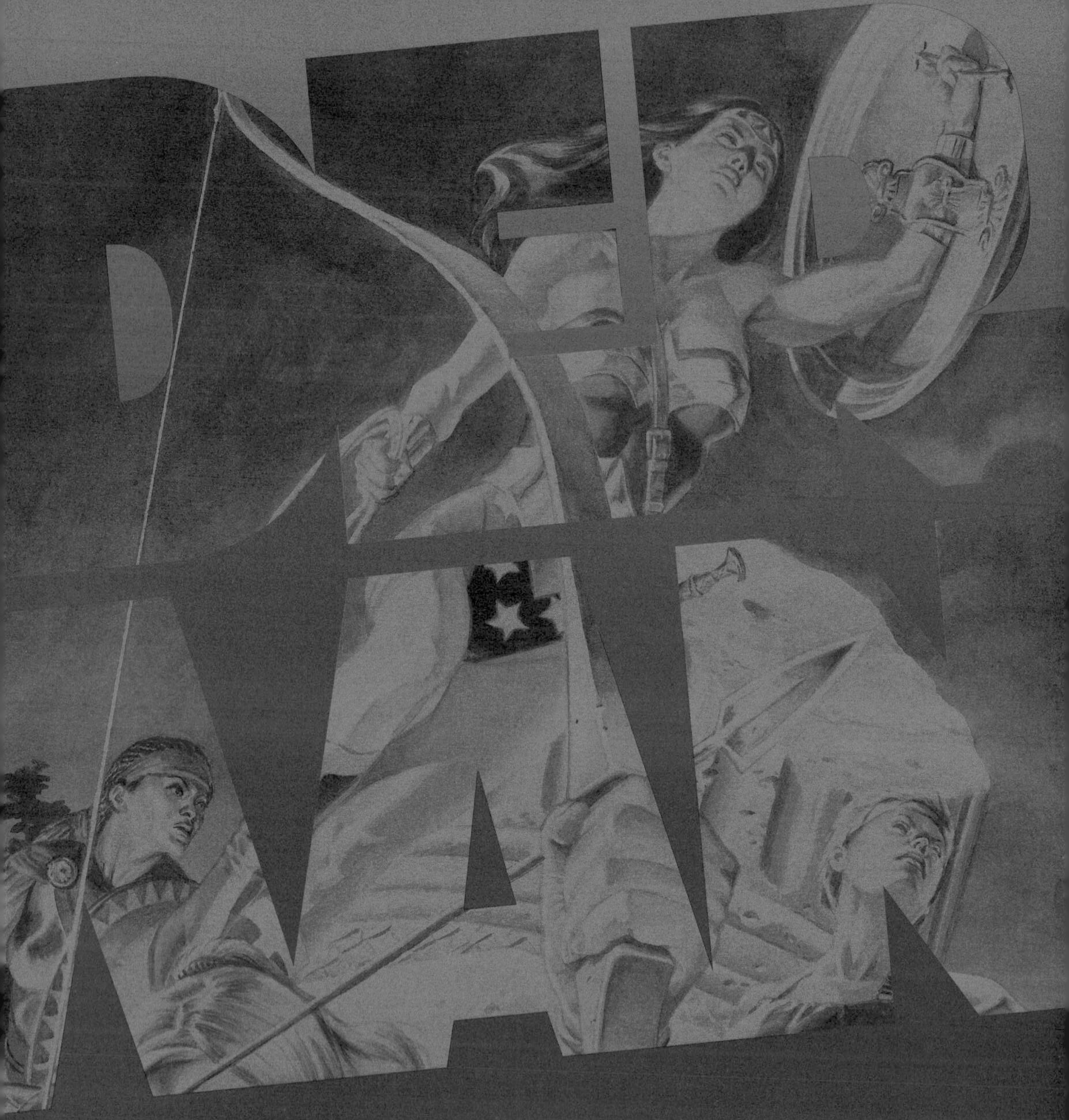

"MARATHON: PART ONE"

Greg Rucka – *writer*
Rags Morales – *pencils, pages 1-5*
Cliff Richards – *pencils, pages 6-22*
Michael Bair – *inks, page 1*
Ray Snyder – *inks, pages 2-22*
Richard and **Tanya Horie** – *colors*
Todd Klein – *letters*
J.G. Jones – *cover*

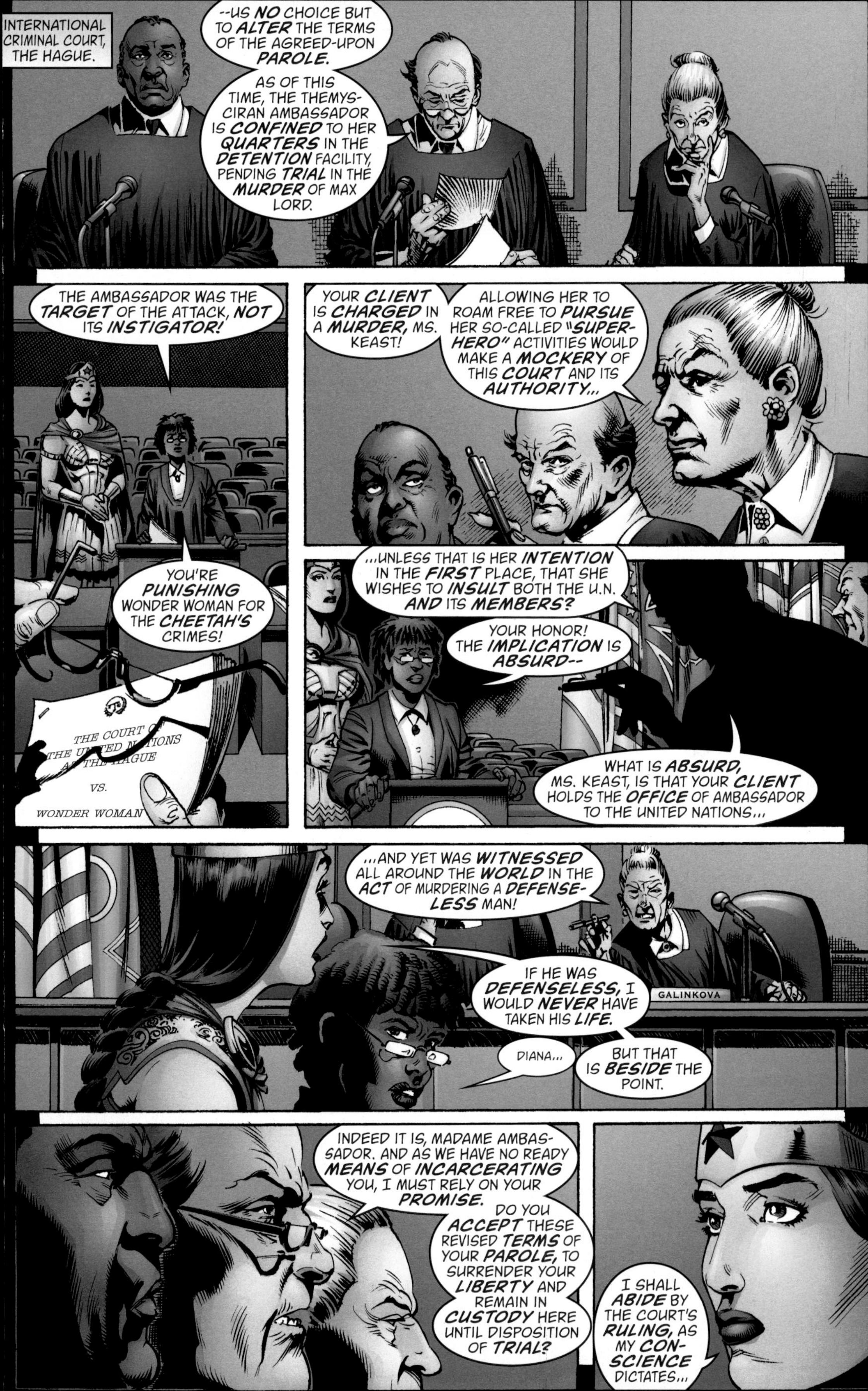

INTERNATIONAL CRIMINAL COURT, THE HAGUE.
--US NO CHOICE BUT TO ALTER THE TERMS OF THE AGREED-UPON PAROLE.
AS OF THIS TIME, THE THEMYSCIRAN AMBASSADOR IS CONFINED TO HER QUARTERS IN THE DETENTION FACILITY, PENDING TRIAL IN THE MURDER OF MAX LORD.
THE AMBASSADOR WAS THE TARGET OF THE ATTACK, NOT ITS INSTIGATOR!
YOU'RE PUNISHING WONDER WOMAN FOR THE CHEETAH'S CRIMES!
THE COURT OF THE UNITED NATIONS AT THE HAGUE
VS.
WONDER WOMAN
YOUR CLIENT IS CHARGED IN A MURDER, MS. KEAST!
ALLOWING HER TO ROAM FREE TO PURSUE HER SO-CALLED "SUPER-HERO" ACTIVITIES WOULD MAKE A MOCKERY OF THIS COURT AND ITS AUTHORITY...
...UNLESS THAT IS HER INTENTION IN THE FIRST PLACE, THAT SHE WISHES TO INSULT BOTH THE U.N. AND ITS MEMBERS?
YOUR HONOR! THE IMPLICATION IS ABSURD--
WHAT IS ABSURD, MS. KEAST, IS THAT YOUR CLIENT HOLDS THE OFFICE OF AMBASSADOR TO THE UNITED NATIONS...
...AND YET WAS WITNESSED ALL AROUND THE WORLD IN THE ACT OF MURDERING A DEFENSELESS MAN!
GALINKOVA
IF HE WAS DEFENSELESS, I WOULD NEVER HAVE TAKEN HIS LIFE.
DIANA...
BUT THAT IS BESIDE THE POINT.
INDEED IT IS, MADAME AMBASSADOR. AND AS WE HAVE NO READY MEANS OF INCARCERATING YOU, I MUST RELY ON YOUR PROMISE.
DO YOU ACCEPT THESE REVISED TERMS OF YOUR PAROLE, TO SURRENDER YOUR LIBERTY AND REMAIN IN CUSTODY HERE UNTIL DISPOSITION OF TRIAL?
I SHALL ABIDE BY THE COURT'S RULING, AS MY CONSCIENCE DICTATES...

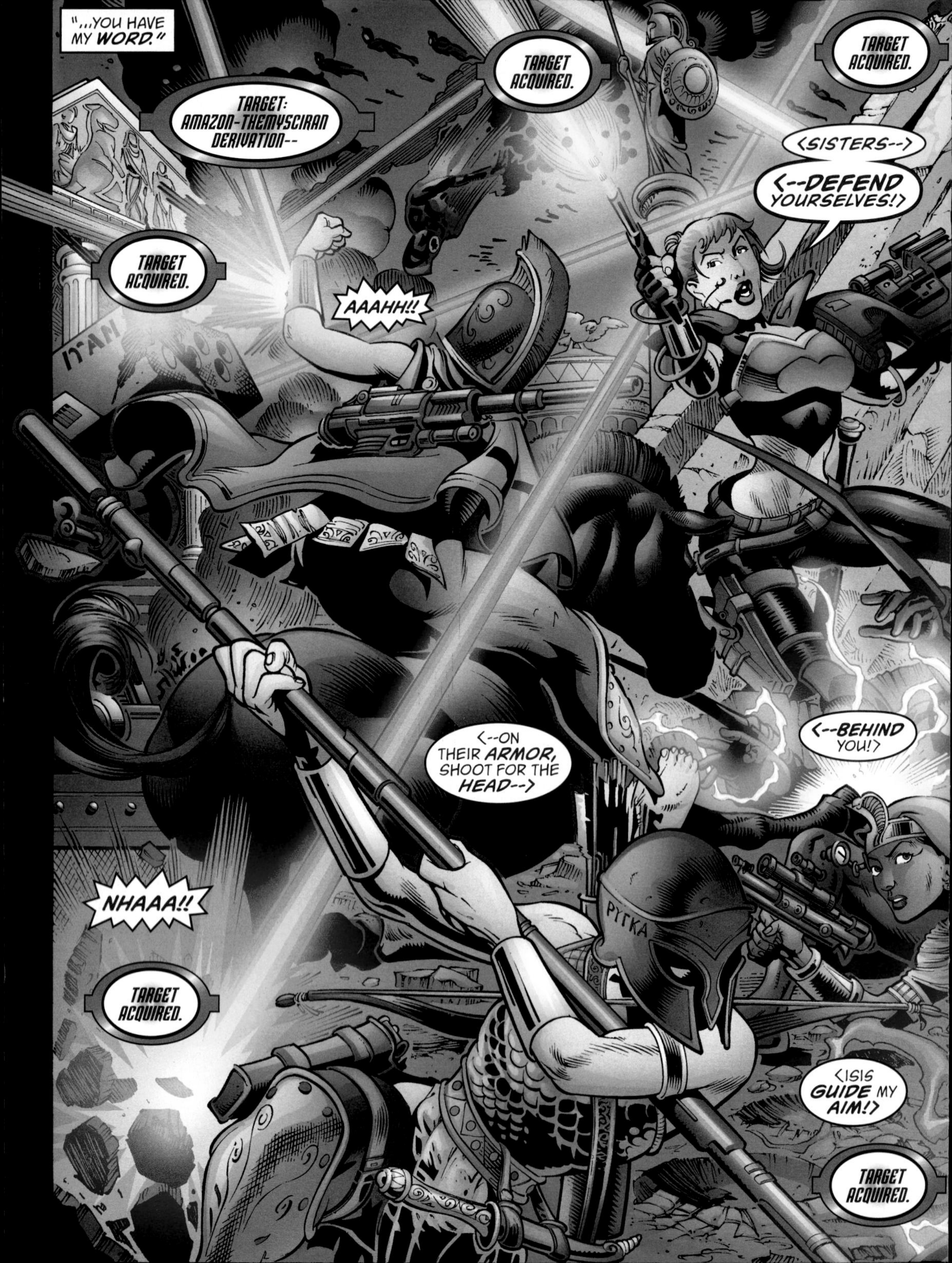
"...YOU HAVE MY WORD."
TARGET: AMAZON-THEMYSCIRAN DERIVATION--
TARGET ACQUIRED.
TARGET ACQUIRED.
<SISTERS-->
<--DEFEND YOURSELVES!>
TARGET ACQUIRED.
AAAHH!!
<--ON THEIR ARMOR, SHOOT FOR THE HEAD-->
<--BEHIND YOU!>
NHAAA!!
TARGET ACQUIRED.
<ISIS GUIDE MY AIM!>
TARGET ACQUIRED.

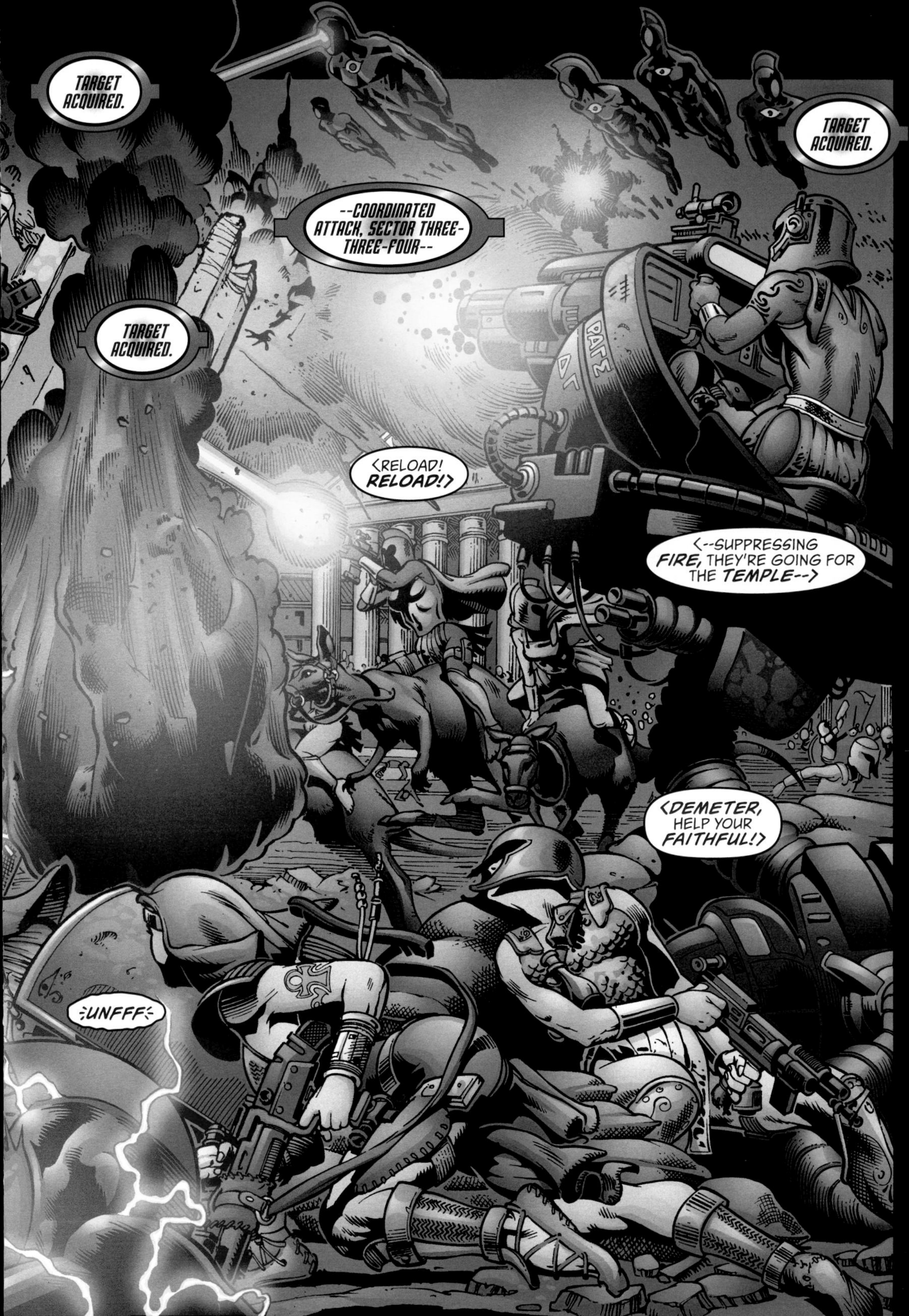

TARGET ACQUIRED.
TARGET ACQUIRED.
--COORDINATED ATTACK, SECTOR THREE-THREE-FOUR--
TARGET ACQUIRED.
<RELOAD! RELOAD!>
<--SUPPRESSING FIRE, THEY'RE GOING FOR THE TEMPLE-->
<DEMETER, HELP YOUR FAITHFUL!>
UNFFF

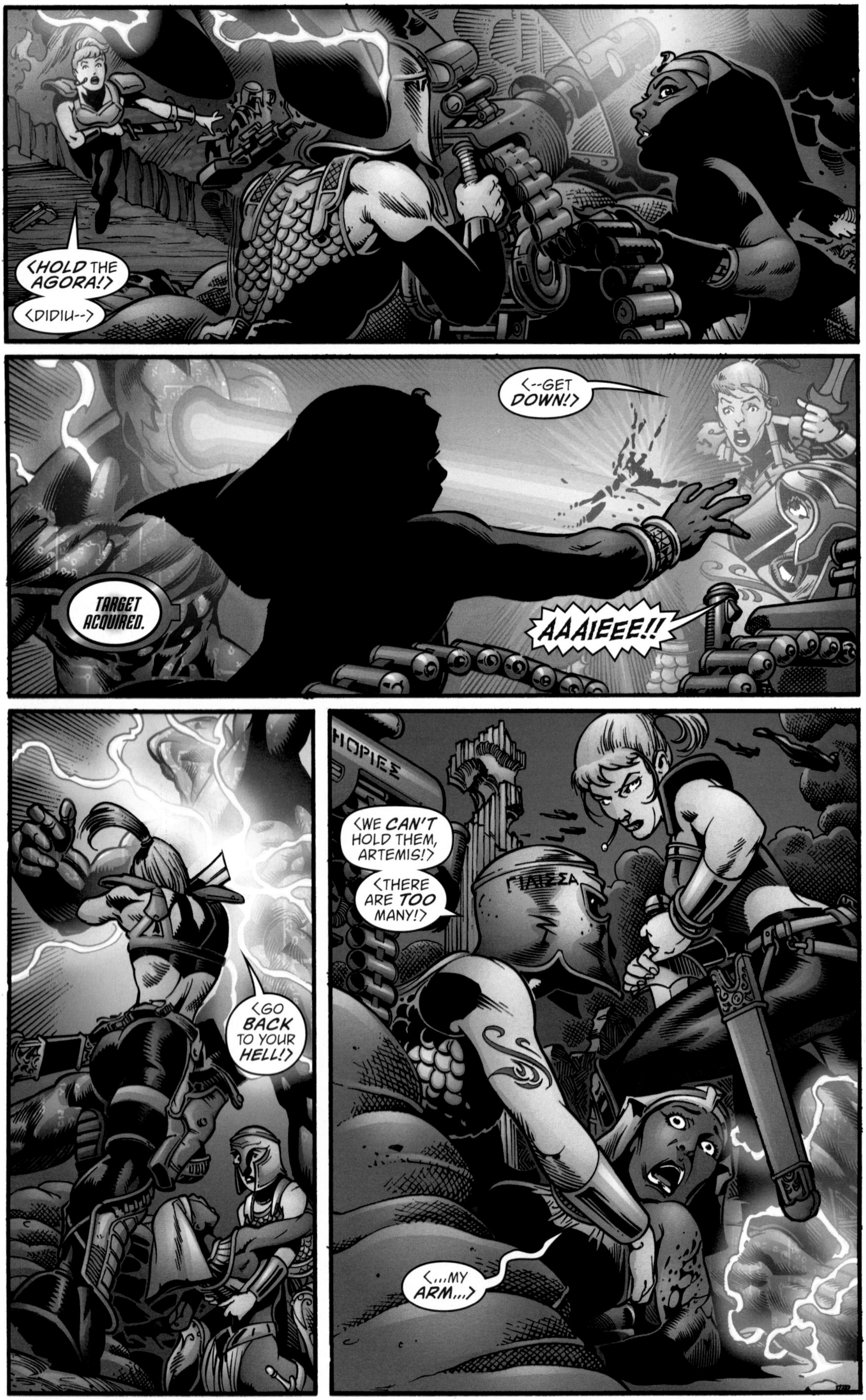

<HOLD THE AGORA!>
<DIDIU-->
<--GET DOWN!>
TARGET ACQUIRED.
AAAIEEE!!
<GO BACK TO YOUR HELL!>
<WE CAN'T HOLD THEM, ARTEMIS!>
<THERE ARE TOO MANY!>
<...MY ARM...>

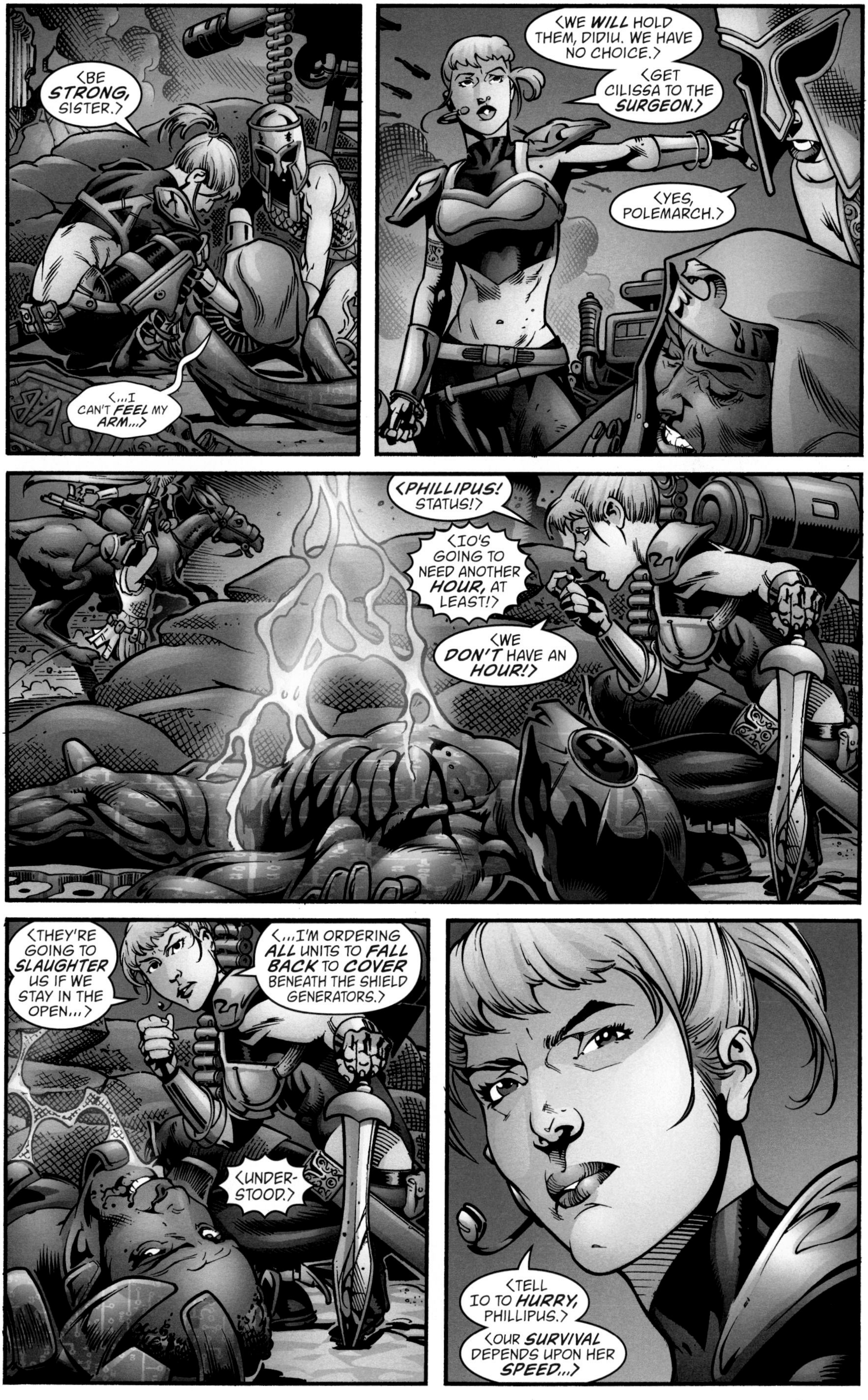
<BE STRONG, SISTER.>
<...I CAN'T FEEL MY ARM...>
<WE WILL HOLD THEM, DIDIU. WE HAVE NO CHOICE.>
<GET CILISSA TO THE SURGEON.>
<YES, POLEMARCH.>
<PHILLIPUS! STATUS!>
<IO'S GOING TO NEED ANOTHER HOUR, AT LEAST!>
<WE DON'T HAVE AN HOUR!>
<THEY'RE GOING TO SLAUGHTER US IF WE STAY IN THE OPEN...>
<...I'M ORDERING ALL UNITS TO FALL BACK TO COVER BENEATH THE SHIELD GENERATORS.>
<UNDER-STOOD.>
<TELL IO TO HURRY, PHILLIPUS.>
<OUR SURVIVAL DEPENDS UPON HER SPEED...>

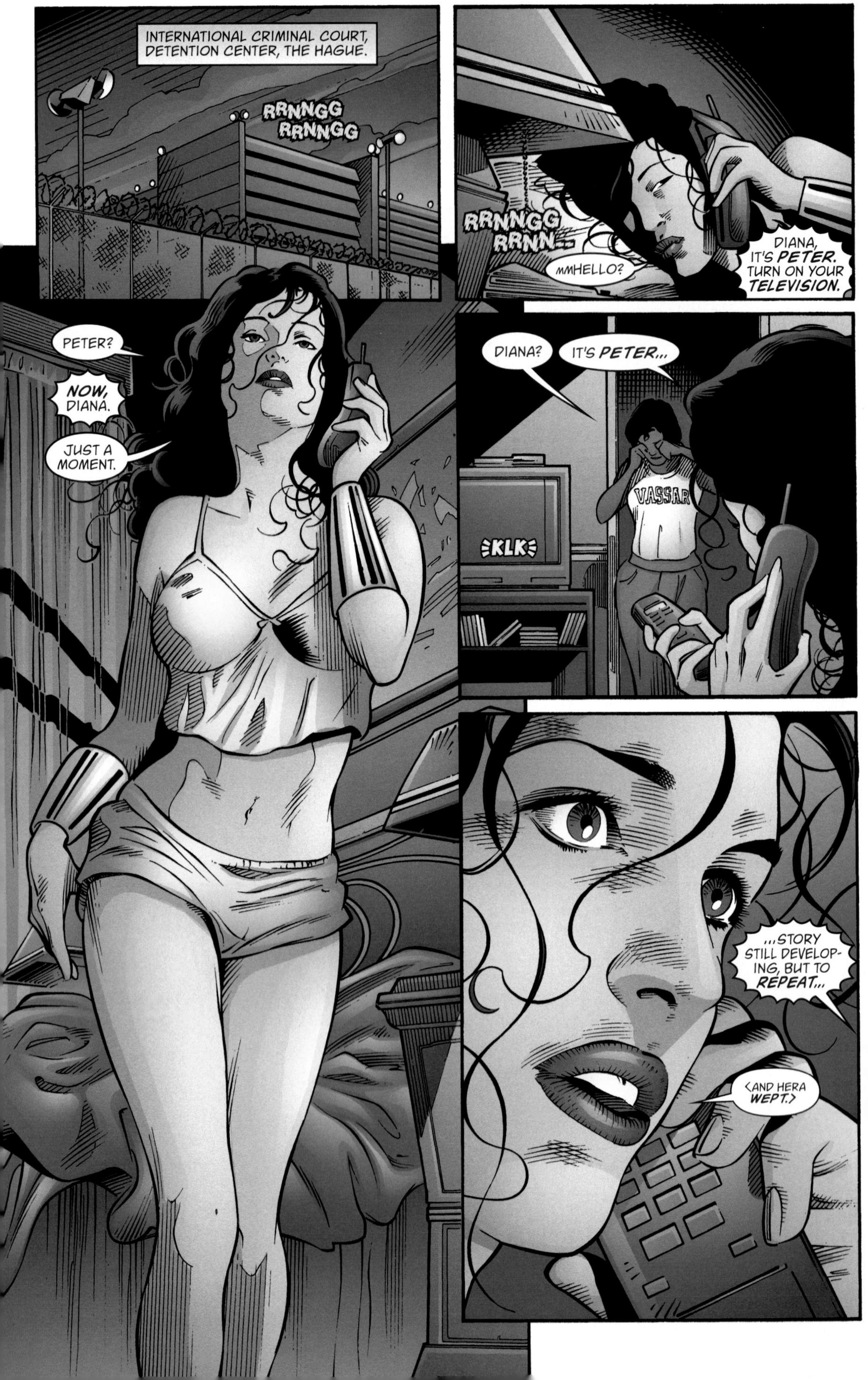

INTERNATIONAL CRIMINAL COURT, DETENTION CENTER, THE HAGUE.
RRNNGG RRNNGG
RRNNGG RRNN...
MMHELLO?
DIANA, IT'S PETER. TURN ON YOUR TELEVISION.
PETER?
NOW, DIANA.
JUST A MOMENT.
DIANA?
IT'S PETER...
KLK
VASSAR
...STORY STILL DEVELOPING, BUT TO REPEAT...
<AND HERA WEPT.>

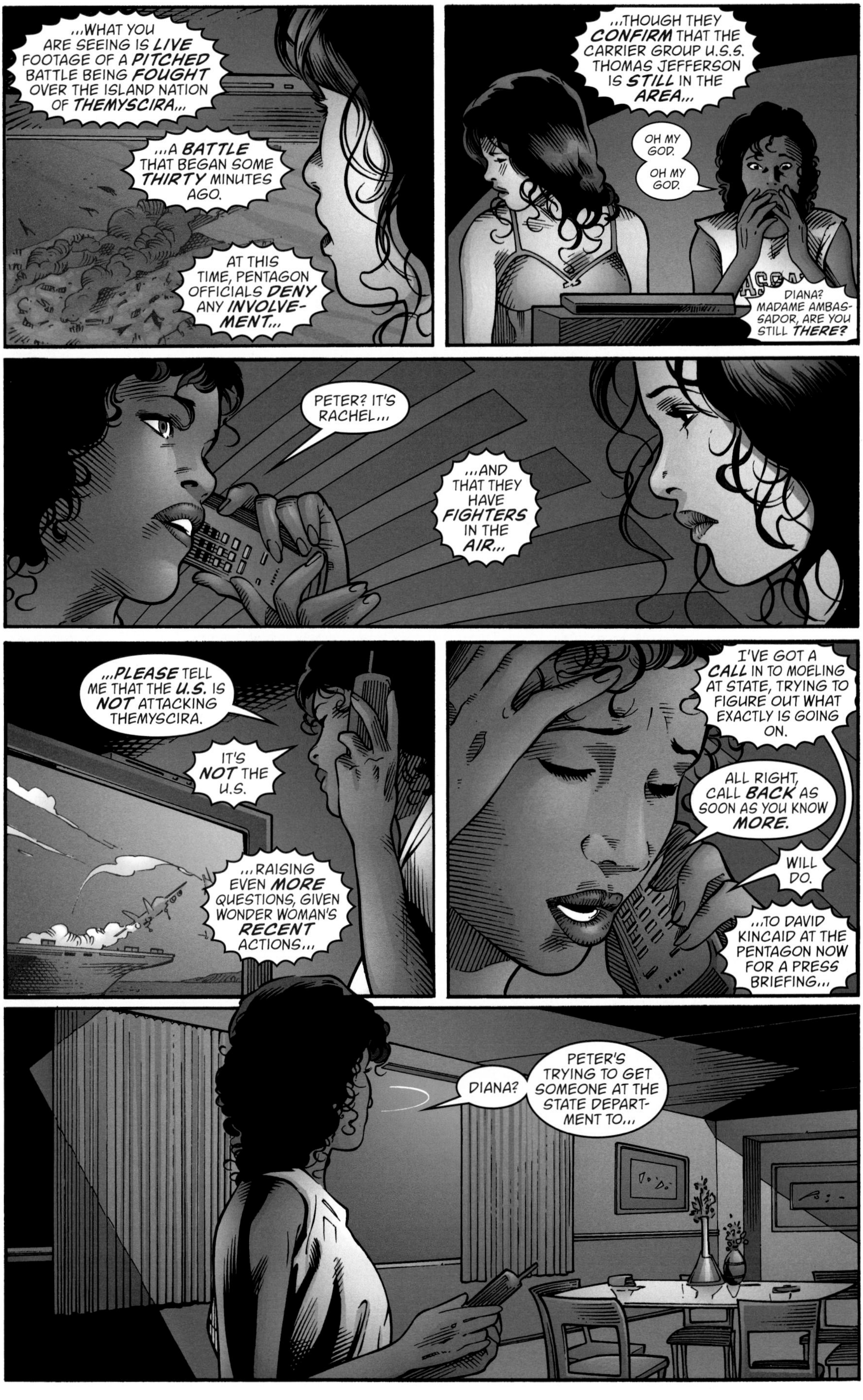
...WHAT YOU ARE SEEING IS LIVE FOOTAGE OF A PITCHED BATTLE BEING FOUGHT OVER THE ISLAND NATION OF THEMYSCIRA...
...A BATTLE THAT BEGAN SOME THIRTY MINUTES AGO.
AT THIS TIME, PENTAGON OFFICIALS DENY ANY INVOLVEMENT...
...THOUGH THEY CONFIRM THAT THE CARRIER GROUP U.S.S. THOMAS JEFFERSON IS STILL IN THE AREA...
OH MY GOD.
OH MY GOD.
DIANA? MADAME AMBASSADOR, ARE YOU STILL THERE?
PETER? IT'S RACHEL...
...AND THAT THEY HAVE FIGHTERS IN THE AIR...
...PLEASE TELL ME THAT THE U.S. IS NOT ATTACKING THEMYSCIRA.
IT'S NOT THE U.S.
...RAISING EVEN MORE QUESTIONS, GIVEN WONDER WOMAN'S RECENT ACTIONS...
I'VE GOT A CALL IN TO MOELING AT STATE, TRYING TO FIGURE OUT WHAT EXACTLY IS GOING ON.
ALL RIGHT, CALL BACK AS SOON AS YOU KNOW MORE.
WILL DO.
...TO DAVID KINCAID AT THE PENTAGON NOW FOR A PRESS BRIEFING...
DIANA?
PETER'S TRYING TO GET SOMEONE AT THE STATE DEPARTMENT TO...

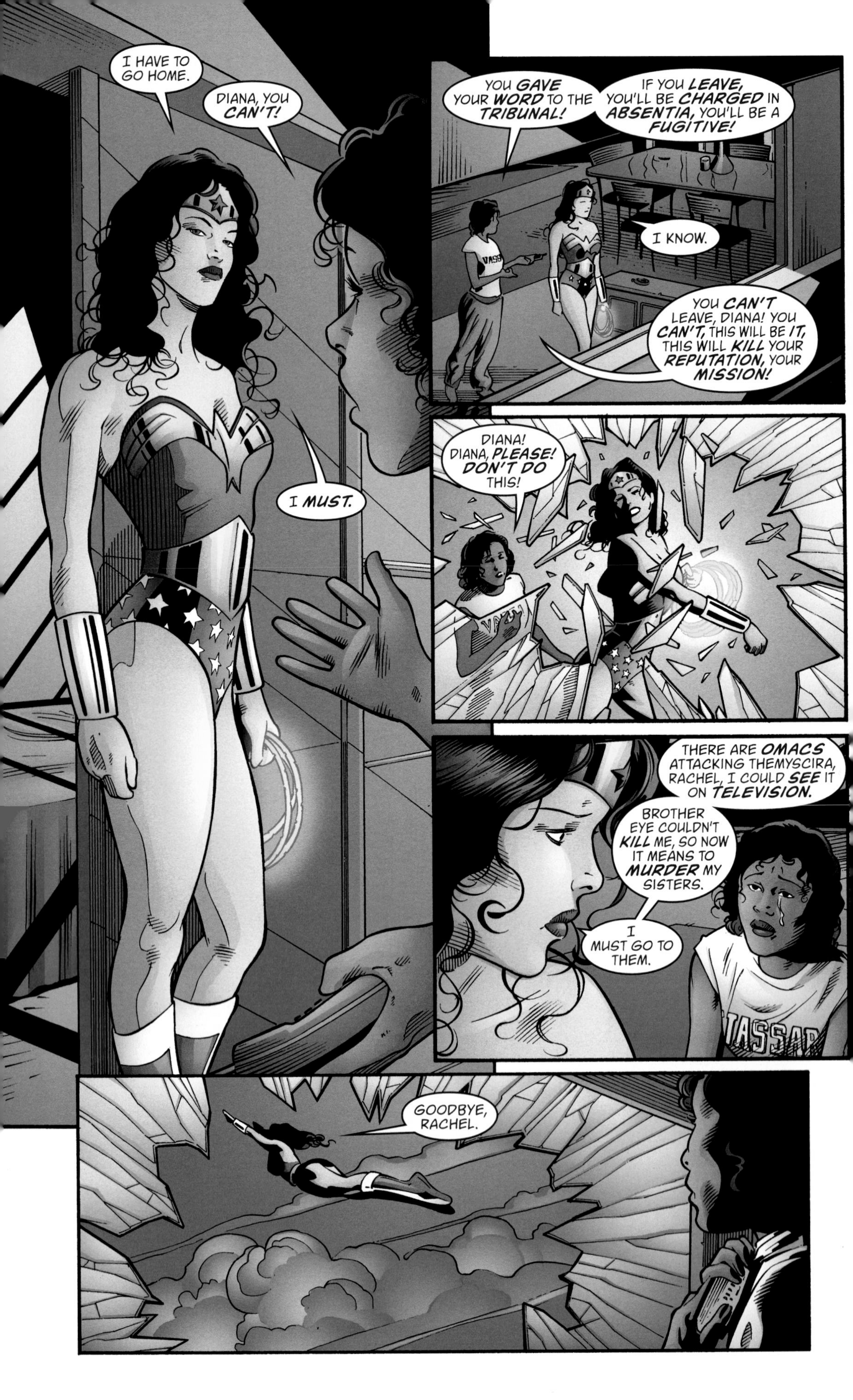
I HAVE TO GO HOME.
DIANA, YOU CAN'T!
I MUST.
YOU GAVE YOUR WORD TO THE TRIBUNAL!
IF YOU LEAVE, YOU'LL BE CHARGED IN ABSENTIA, YOU'LL BE A FUGITIVE!
I KNOW.
YOU CAN'T LEAVE, DIANA! YOU CAN'T, THIS WILL BE IT, THIS WILL KILL YOUR REPUTATION, YOUR MISSION!
DIANA! DIANA, PLEASE! DON'T DO THIS!
THERE ARE OMACS ATTACKING THEMYSCIRA, RACHEL, I COULD SEE IT ON TELEVISION.
BROTHER EYE COULDN'T KILL ME, SO NOW IT MEANS TO MURDER MY SISTERS.
I MUST GO TO THEM.
GOODBYE, RACHEL.

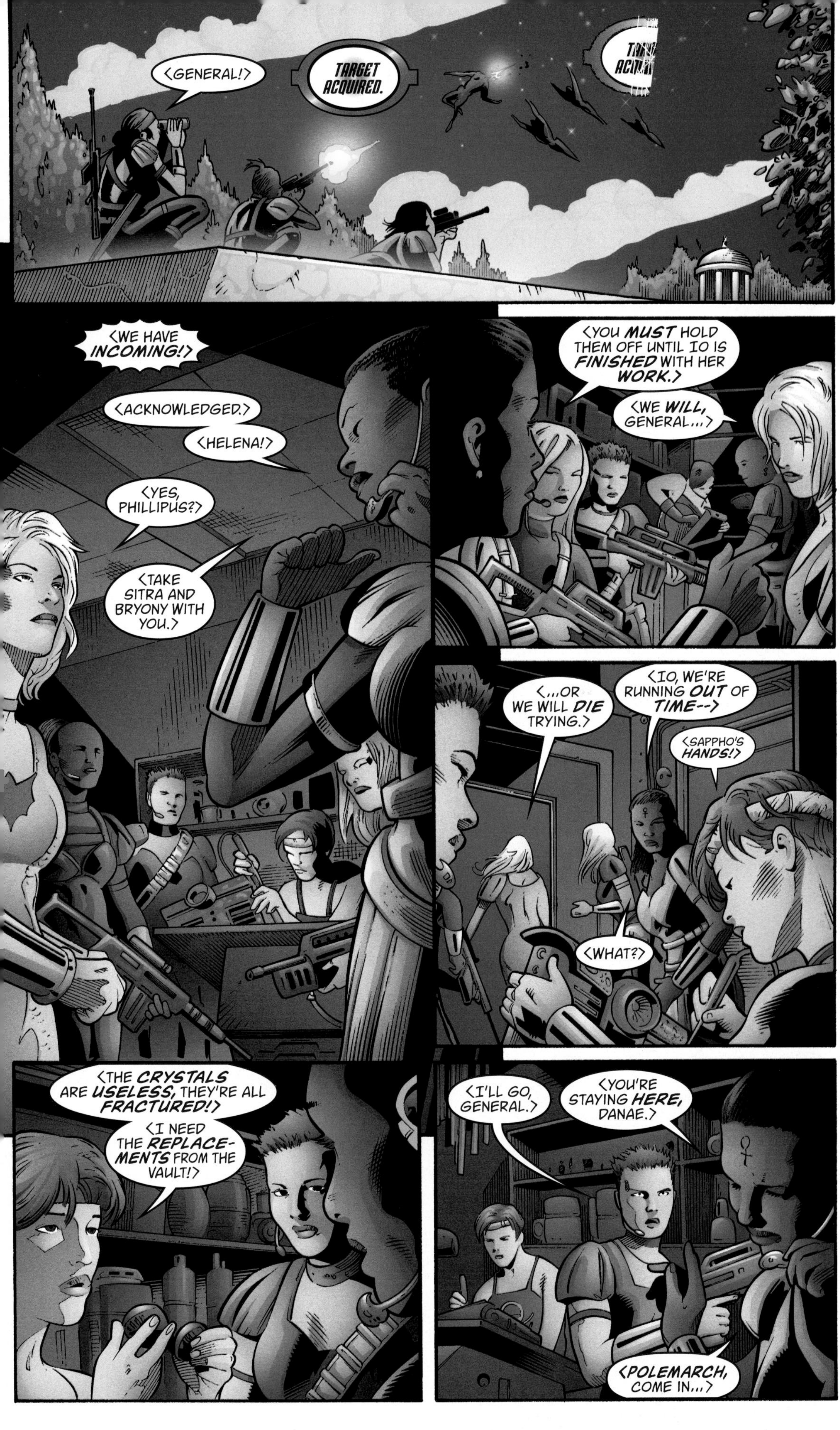
<GENERAL!>
TARGET ACQUIRED.
TARGET ACQUIRED
<WE HAVE INCOMING!>
<ACKNOWLEDGED.>
<HELENA!>
<YES, PHILLIPUS?>
<TAKE SITRA AND BRYONY WITH YOU.>
<YOU MUST HOLD THEM OFF UNTIL IO IS FINISHED WITH HER WORK.>
<WE WILL, GENERAL...>
<...OR WE WILL DIE TRYING.>
<IO, WE'RE RUNNING OUT OF TIME-->
<SAPPHO'S HANDS!>
<WHAT?>
<THE CRYSTALS ARE USELESS, THEY'RE ALL FRACTURED!>
<I NEED THE REPLACEMENTS FROM THE VAULT!>
<I'LL GO, GENERAL.>
<YOU'RE STAYING HERE, DANAE.>
<POLEMARCH, COME IN...>

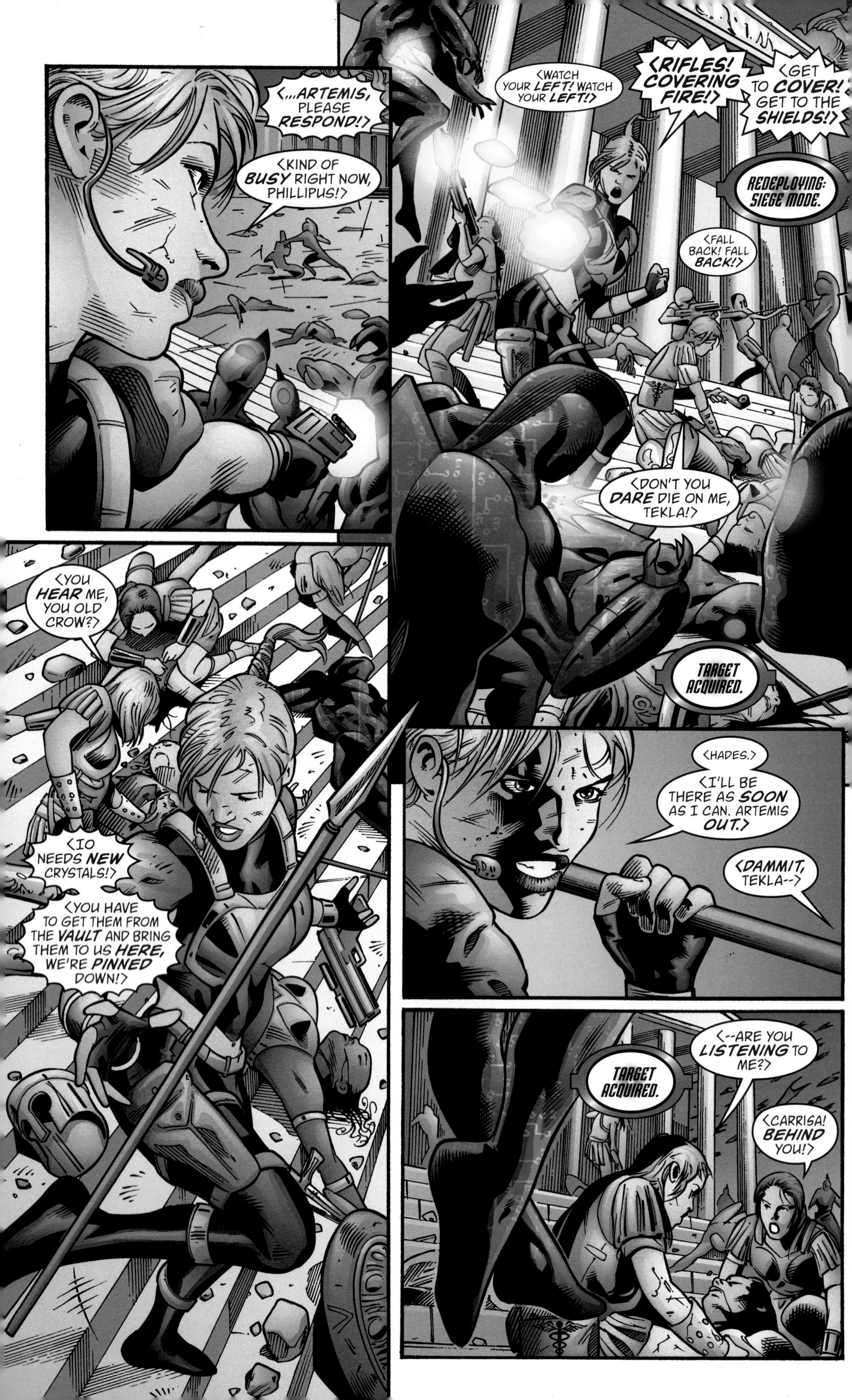

<...ARTEMIS, PLEASE RESPOND!>
<KIND OF BUSY RIGHT NOW, PHILLIPUS!>
<WATCH YOUR LEFT! WATCH YOUR LEFT!>
<RIFLES! COVERING FIRE!>
<GET TO COVER! GET TO THE SHIELDS!>
REDEPLOYING: SIEGE MODE.
<FALL BACK! FALL BACK!>
<DON'T YOU DARE DIE ON ME, TEKLA!>
TARGET ACQUIRED.
<YOU HEAR ME, YOU OLD CROW?>
<IO NEEDS NEW CRYSTALS!>
<YOU HAVE TO GET THEM FROM THE VAULT AND BRING THEM TO US HERE, WE'RE PINNED DOWN!>
<HADES.>
<I'LL BE THERE AS SOON AS I CAN. ARTEMIS OUT.>
<DAMMIT, TEKLA-->
<--ARE YOU LISTENING TO ME?>
TARGET ACQUIRED.
<CARRISA! BEHIND YOU!>

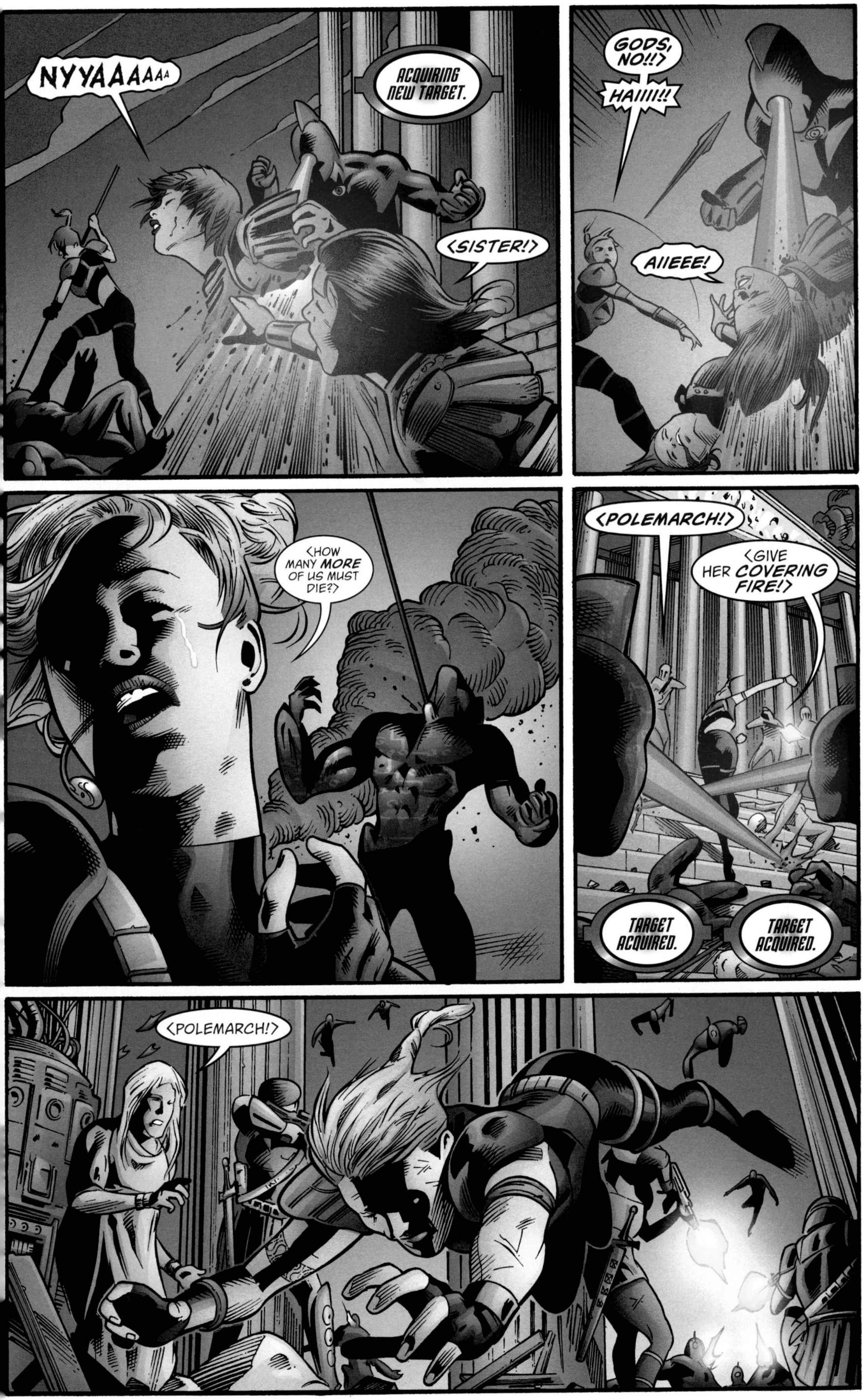
NYYAAAAAA
ACQUIRING NEW TARGET.
<SISTER!>
GODS, NO!!>
HAIIII!!
AIIEEE!
<HOW MANY MORE OF US MUST DIE?>
<POLEMARCH!>
<GIVE HER COVERING FIRE!>
TARGET ACQUIRED.
TARGET ACQUIRED.
<POLEMARCH!>

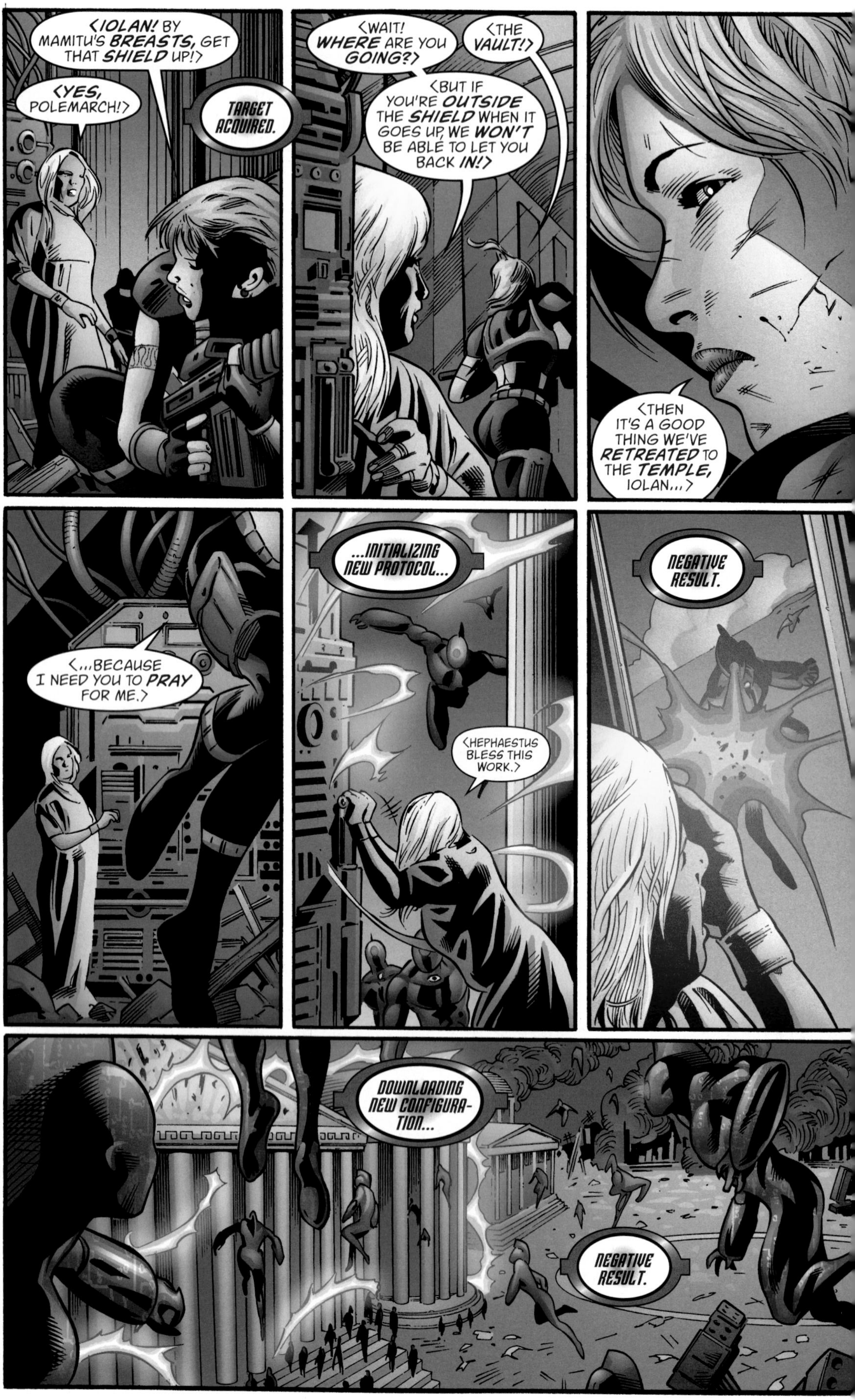

<IOLAN! BY MAMITU'S BREASTS, GET THAT SHIELD UP!>
<YES, POLEMARCH!>
TARGET ACQUIRED.
<WAIT! WHERE ARE YOU GOING?>
<THE VAULT!>
<BUT IF YOU'RE OUTSIDE THE SHIELD WHEN IT GOES UP, WE WON'T BE ABLE TO LET YOU BACK IN!>
<THEN IT'S A GOOD THING WE'VE RETREATED TO THE TEMPLE, IOLAN...>
<...BECAUSE I NEED YOU TO PRAY FOR ME.>
...INITIALIZING NEW PROTOCOL...
<HEPHAESTUS BLESS THIS WORK.>
NEGATIVE RESULT.
DOWNLOADING NEW CONFIGURA-TION...
NEGATIVE RESULT.

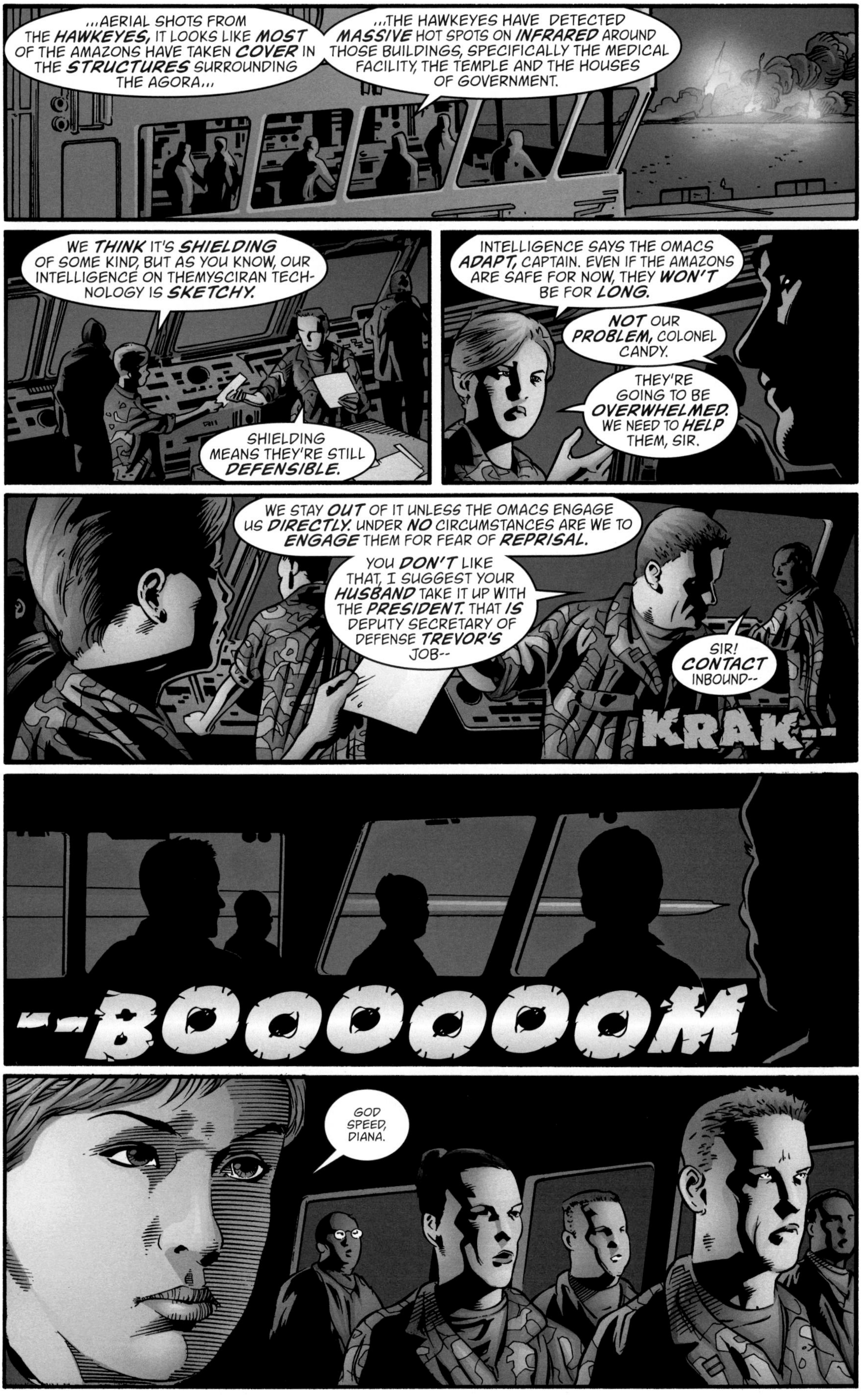
...AERIAL SHOTS FROM THE HAWKEYES, IT LOOKS LIKE MOST OF THE AMAZONS HAVE TAKEN COVER IN THE STRUCTURES SURROUNDING THE AGORA...
...THE HAWKEYES HAVE DETECTED MASSIVE HOT SPOTS ON INFRARED AROUND THOSE BUILDINGS, SPECIFICALLY THE MEDICAL FACILITY, THE TEMPLE AND THE HOUSES OF GOVERNMENT.
WE THINK IT'S SHIELDING OF SOME KIND, BUT AS YOU KNOW, OUR INTELLIGENCE ON THEMYSCIRAN TECHNOLOGY IS SKETCHY.
SHIELDING MEANS THEY'RE STILL DEFENSIBLE.
INTELLIGENCE SAYS THE OMACS ADAPT, CAPTAIN. EVEN IF THE AMAZONS ARE SAFE FOR NOW, THEY WON'T BE FOR LONG.
NOT OUR PROBLEM, COLONEL CANDY.
THEY'RE GOING TO BE OVERWHELMED. WE NEED TO HELP THEM, SIR.
WE STAY OUT OF IT UNLESS THE OMACS ENGAGE US DIRECTLY. UNDER NO CIRCUMSTANCES ARE WE TO ENGAGE THEM FOR FEAR OF REPRISAL.
YOU DON'T LIKE THAT, I SUGGEST YOUR HUSBAND TAKE IT UP WITH THE PRESIDENT. THAT IS DEPUTY SECRETARY OF DEFENSE TREVOR'S JOB--
SIR! CONTACT INBOUND--
KRAK--
--BOOOOOOM
GOD SPEED, DIANA.

<PRAISE TO GODS.>

TARGET--

--ACQUIRED.

GNH!

PARTIAL RESULT. ASSESSING...

...POSIT: PERSONAL DEFENSE SHIELD EMPLOYED.

MODULATING PRIMARY WEAPON SPECTRUM FOR OPTIMAL SHIELD PENETRATION.

<OH, SHUT UP AND DO IT ALREADY.>

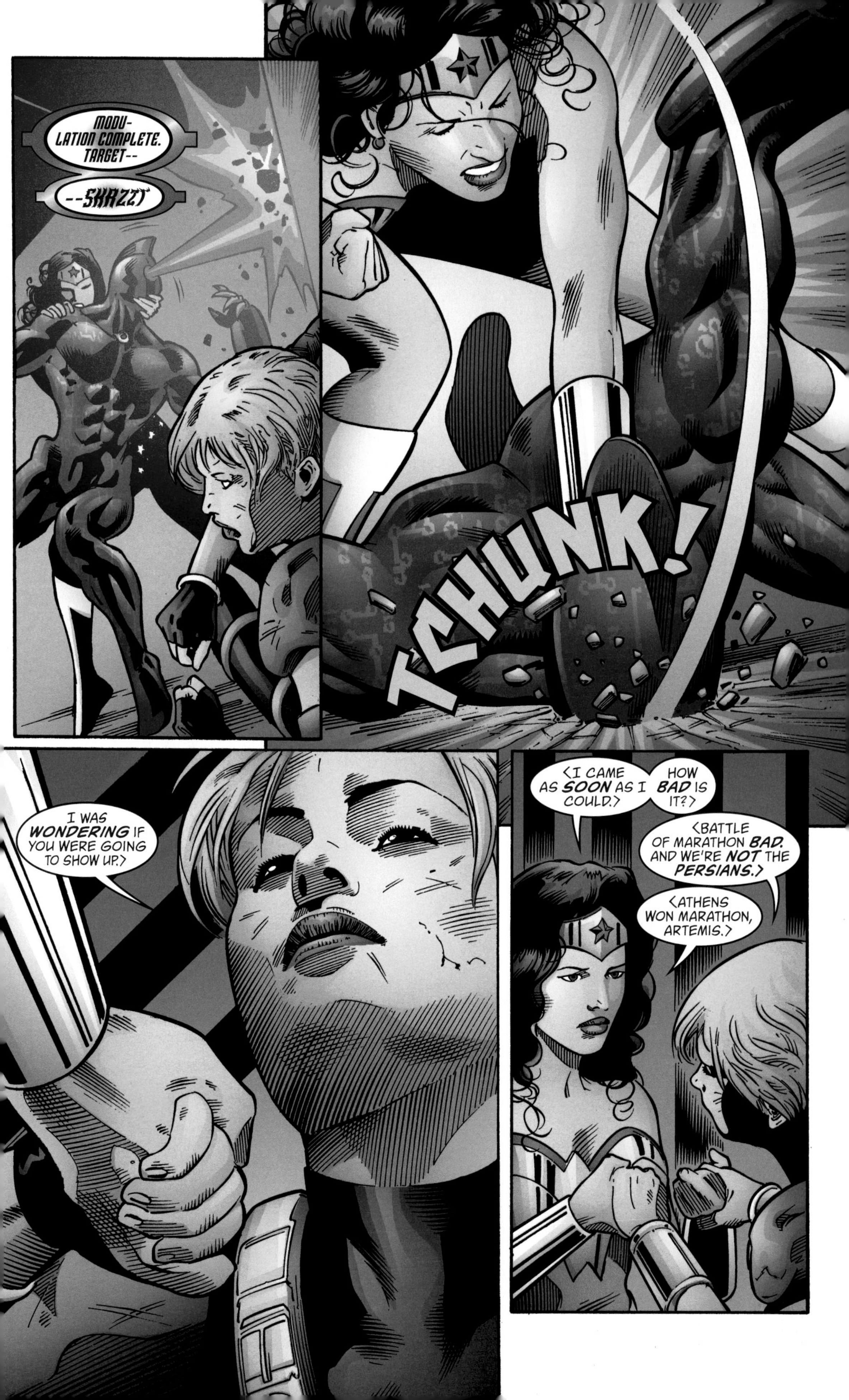
MODU-LATION COMPLETE. TARGET--
--SKRZZT
TCHUNK!
<I WAS WONDERING IF YOU WERE GOING TO SHOW UP.>
<I CAME AS SOON AS I COULD.>
HOW BAD IS IT?>
<BATTLE OF MARATHON BAD. AND WE'RE NOT THE PERSIANS.>
<ATHENS WON MARATHON, ARTEMIS.>

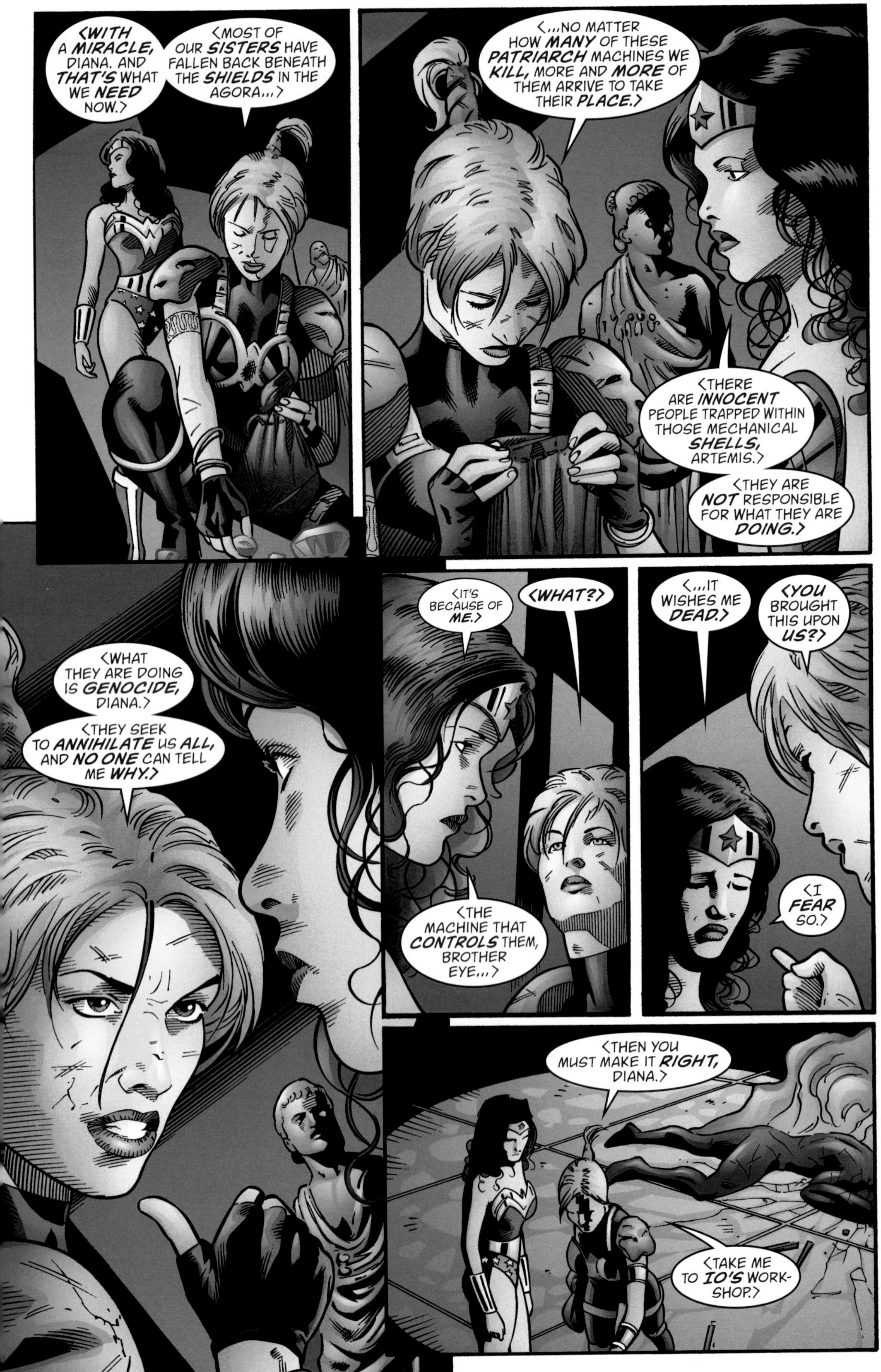

<WITH A MIRACLE, DIANA. AND THAT'S WHAT WE NEED NOW.>
<MOST OF OUR SISTERS HAVE FALLEN BACK BENEATH THE SHIELDS IN THE AGORA...>
<...NO MATTER HOW MANY OF THESE PATRIARCH MACHINES WE KILL, MORE AND MORE OF THEM ARRIVE TO TAKE THEIR PLACE.>
<THERE ARE INNOCENT PEOPLE TRAPPED WITHIN THOSE MECHANICAL SHELLS, ARTEMIS.>
<THEY ARE NOT RESPONSIBLE FOR WHAT THEY ARE DOING.>
<WHAT THEY ARE DOING IS GENOCIDE, DIANA.>
<THEY SEEK TO ANNIHILATE US ALL, AND NO ONE CAN TELL ME WHY.>
<IT'S BECAUSE OF ME.>
<WHAT?>
<THE MACHINE THAT CONTROLS THEM, BROTHER EYE...>
<...IT WISHES ME DEAD.>
<YOU BROUGHT THIS UPON US?>
<I FEAR SO.>
<THEN YOU MUST MAKE IT RIGHT, DIANA.>
<TAKE ME TO IO'S WORK-SHOP.>

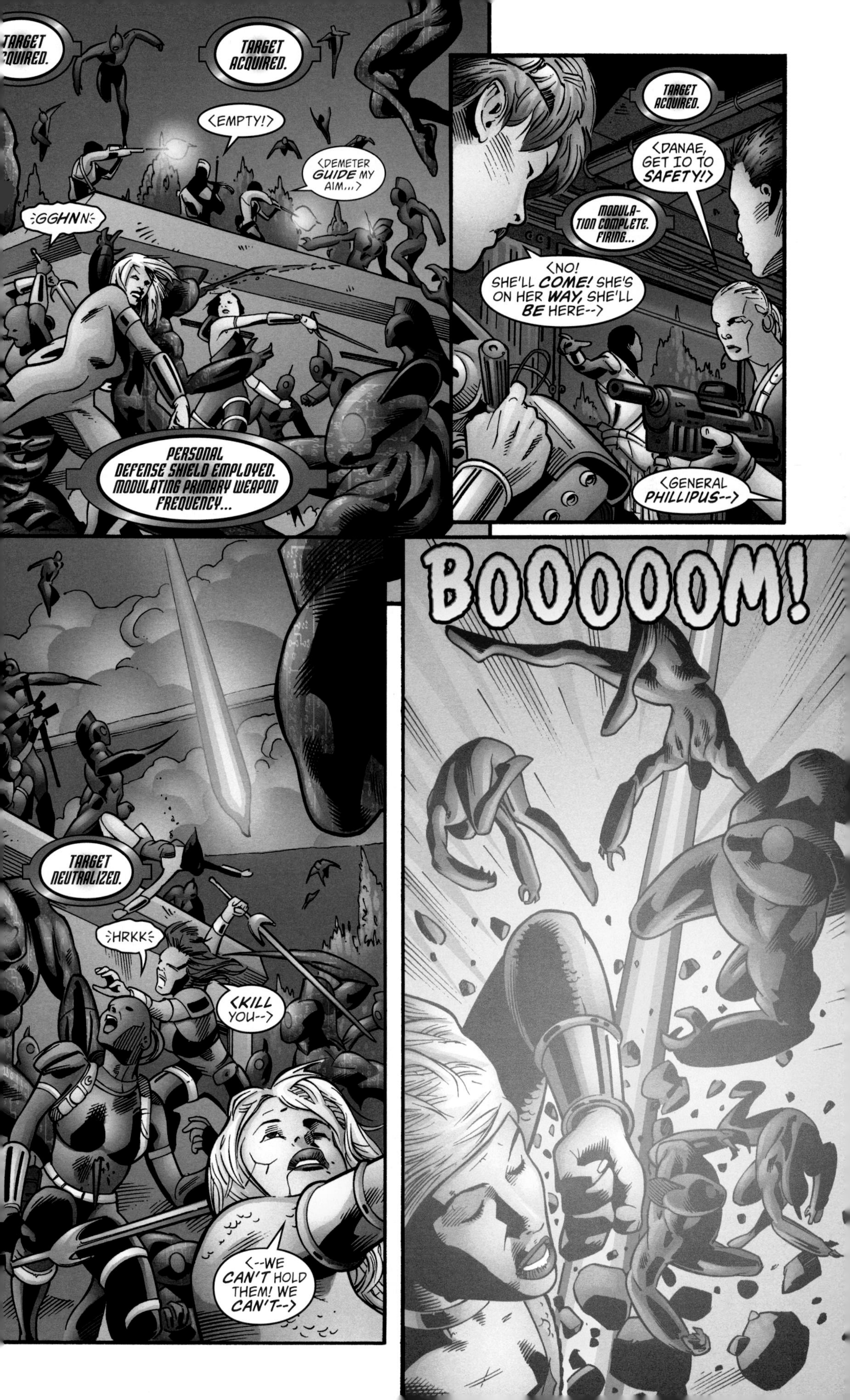

TARGET ACQUIRED.
TARGET ACQUIRED.
<EMPTY!>
<DEMETER GUIDE MY AIM...>
GGHNN
PERSONAL DEFENSE SHIELD EMPLOYED. MODULATING PRIMARY WEAPON FREQUENCY...
TARGET ACQUIRED.
<DANAE, GET IO TO SAFETY!>
MODULATION COMPLETE. FIRING...
<NO! SHE'LL COME! SHE'S ON HER WAY, SHE'LL BE HERE-->
<GENERAL PHILLIPUS-->
TARGET NEUTRALIZED.
HRKK
<KILL YOU-->
<--WE CAN'T HOLD THEM! WE CAN'T-->
BOOOOOM!

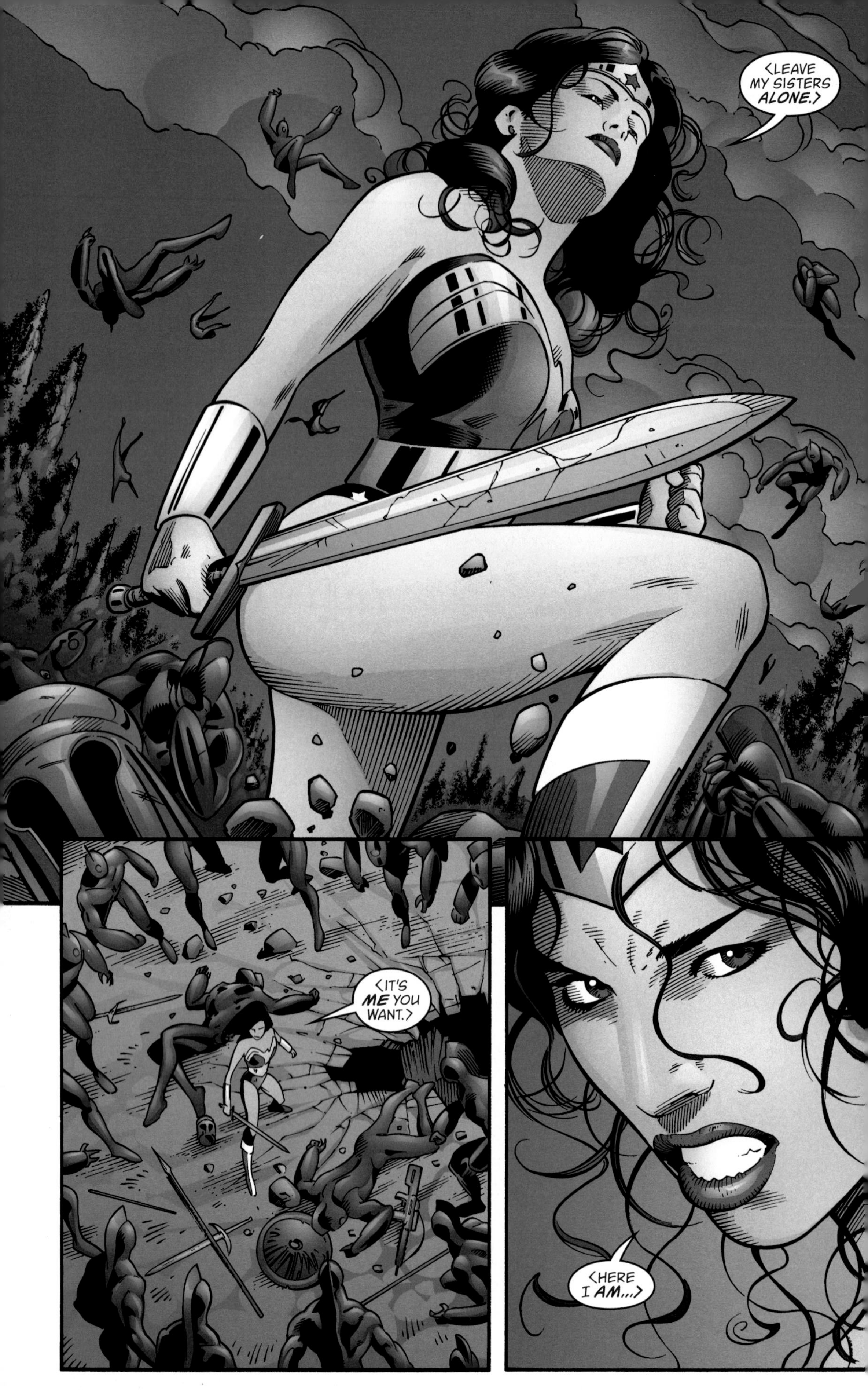
<LEAVE MY SISTERS ALONE.>
<IT'S ME YOU WANT.>
<HERE I AM...>

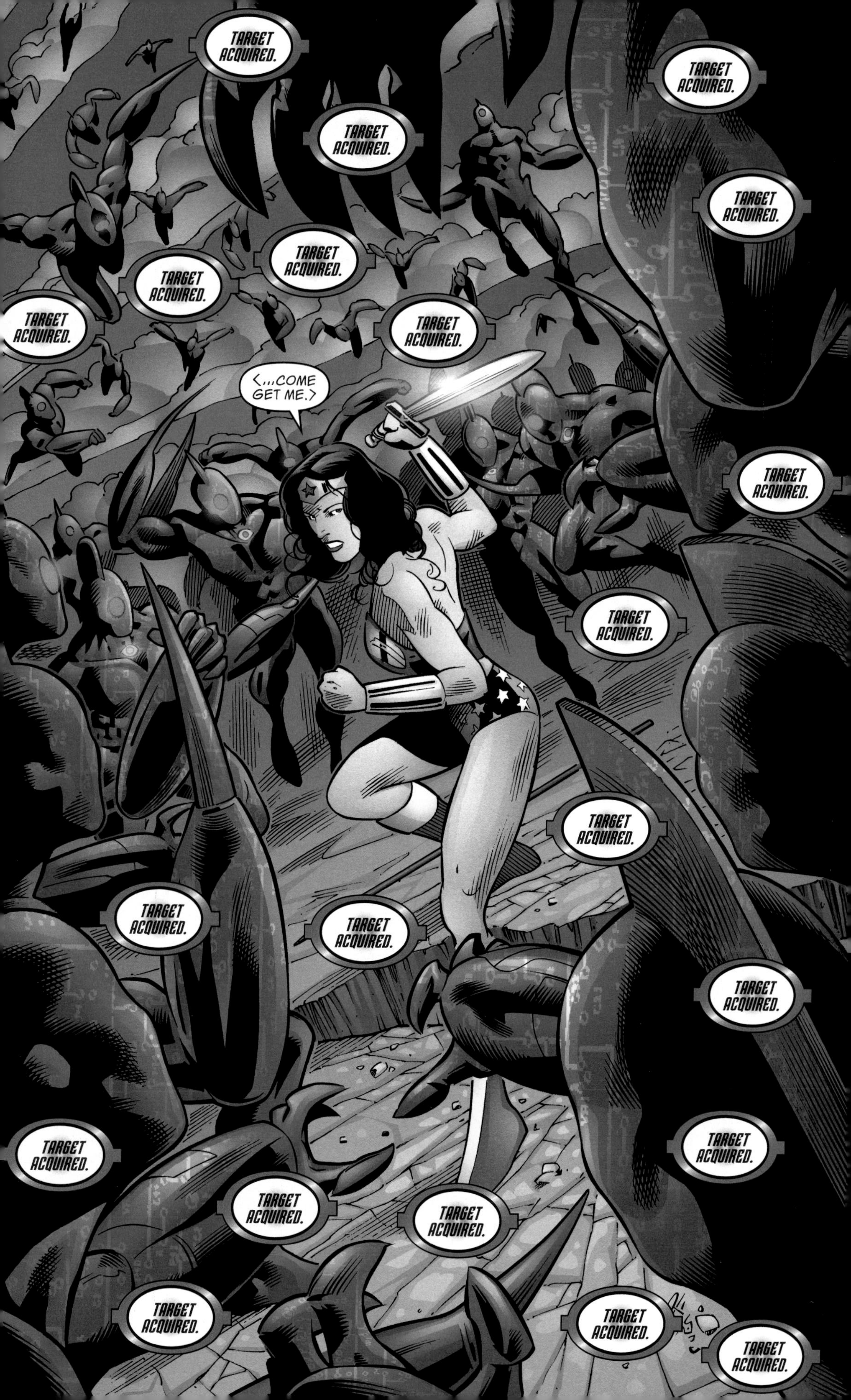

TARGET ACQUIRED.
TARGET ACQUIRED.
TARGET ACQUIRED.
TARGET ACQUIRED.
TARGET ACQUIRED.
TARGET ACQUIRED.
TARGET ACQUIRED.
TARGET ACQUIRED.
<...COME GET ME.>
TARGET ACQUIRED.
TARGET ACQUIRED.
TARGET ACQUIRED.
TARGET ACQUIRED.
TARGET ACQUIRED.
TARGET ACQUIRED.
TARGET ACQUIRED.
TARGET ACQUIRED.
TARGET ACQUIRED.
TARGET ACQUIRED.
TARGET ACQUIRED.
TARGET ACQUIRED.
TARGET ACQUIRED.

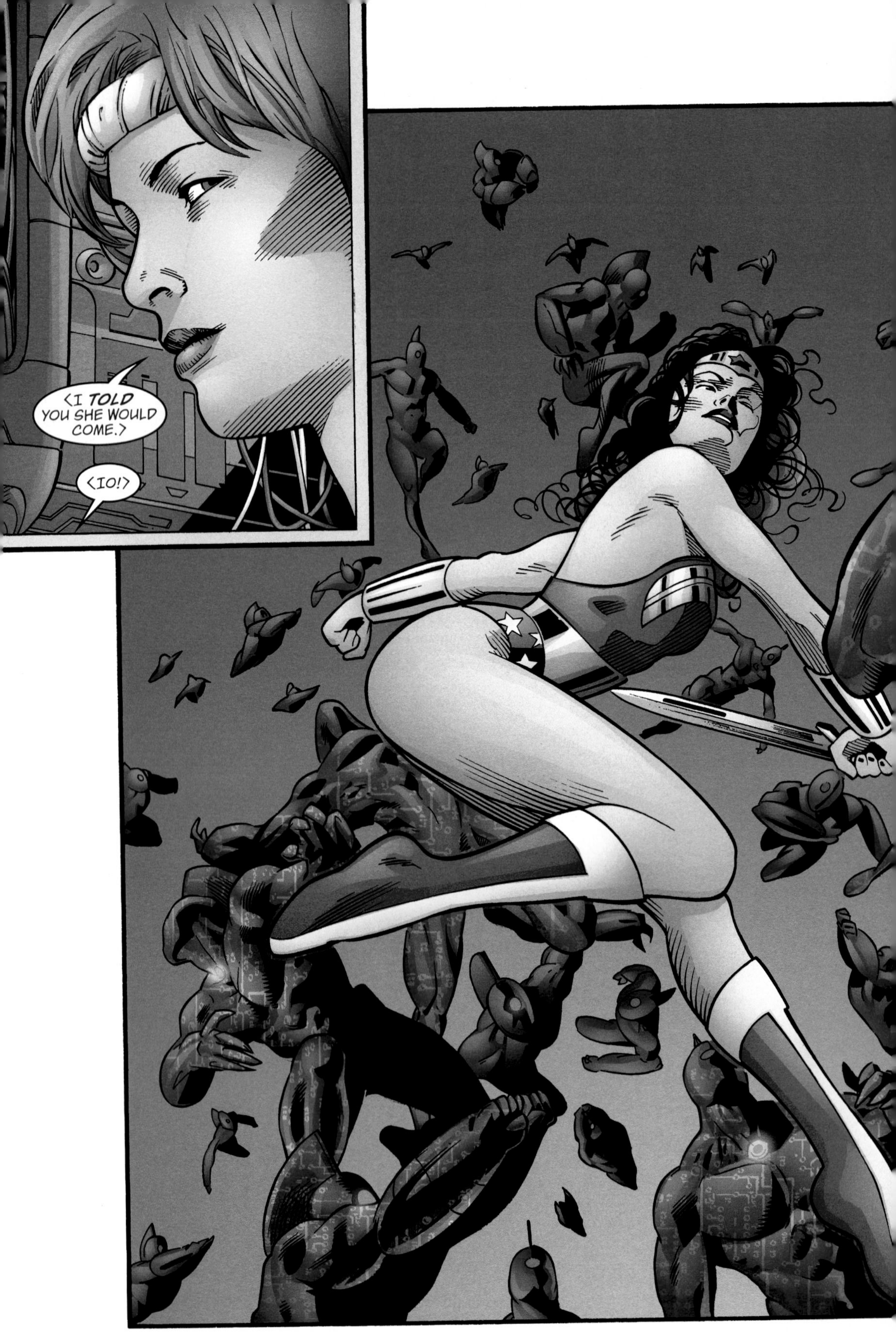

<I TOLD YOU SHE WOULD COME.>
<IO!>

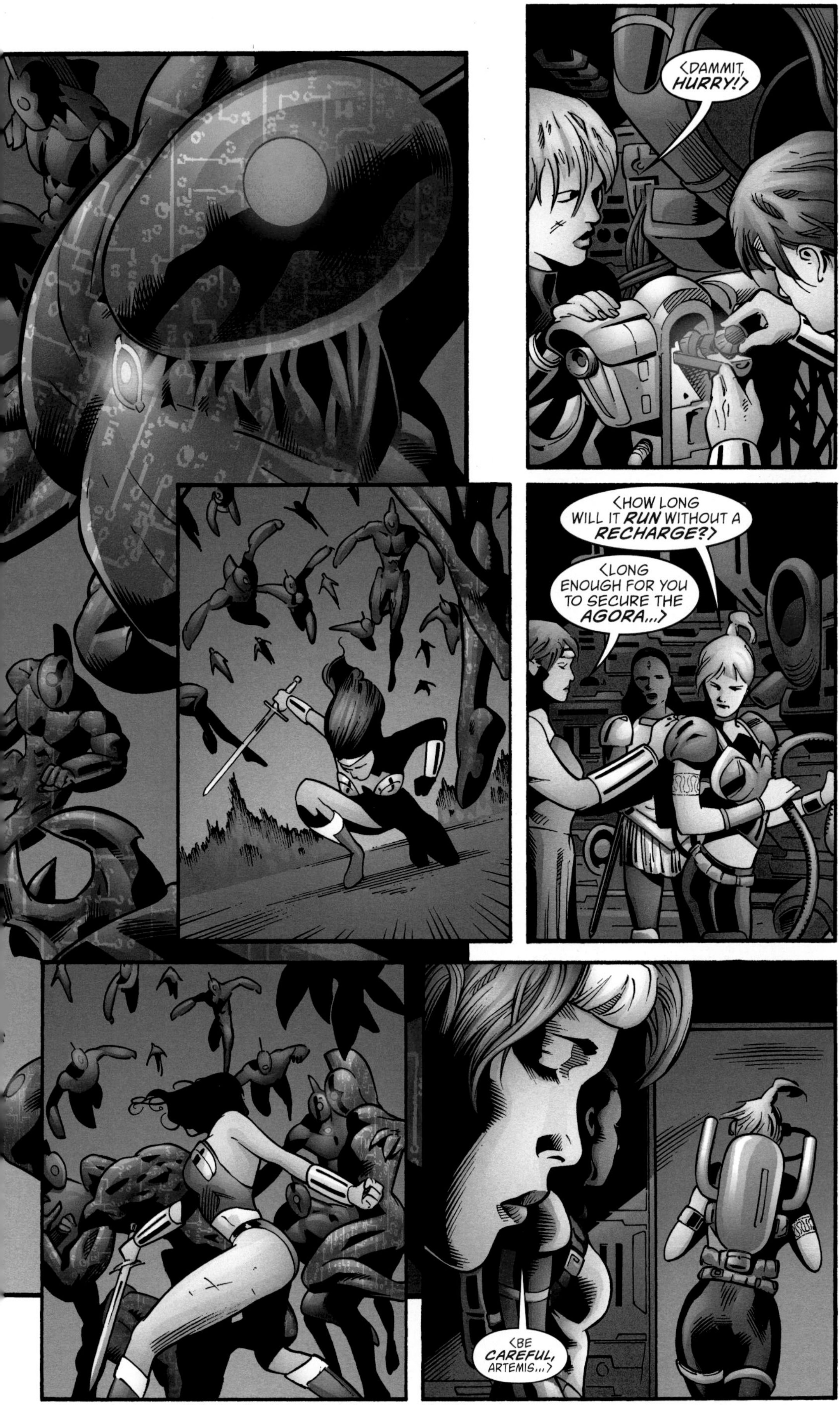
<DAMMIT, HURRY!>
<HOW LONG WILL IT RUN WITHOUT A RECHARGE?>
<LONG ENOUGH FOR YOU TO SECURE THE AGORA...>
<BE CAREFUL, ARTEMIS...>

"<...YOU CARRY DOOM ON YOUR *BACK*...>

"<...DOOM FOR OUR *ENEMIES*...>

"<...AND, DIANA *FORGIVE* ME...>

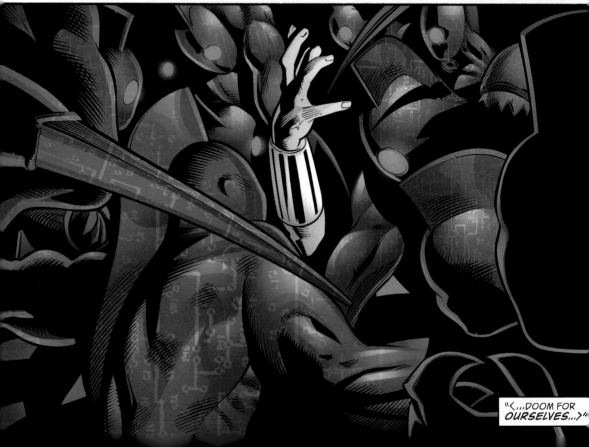

"<...DOOM FOR *OURSELVES*...>"

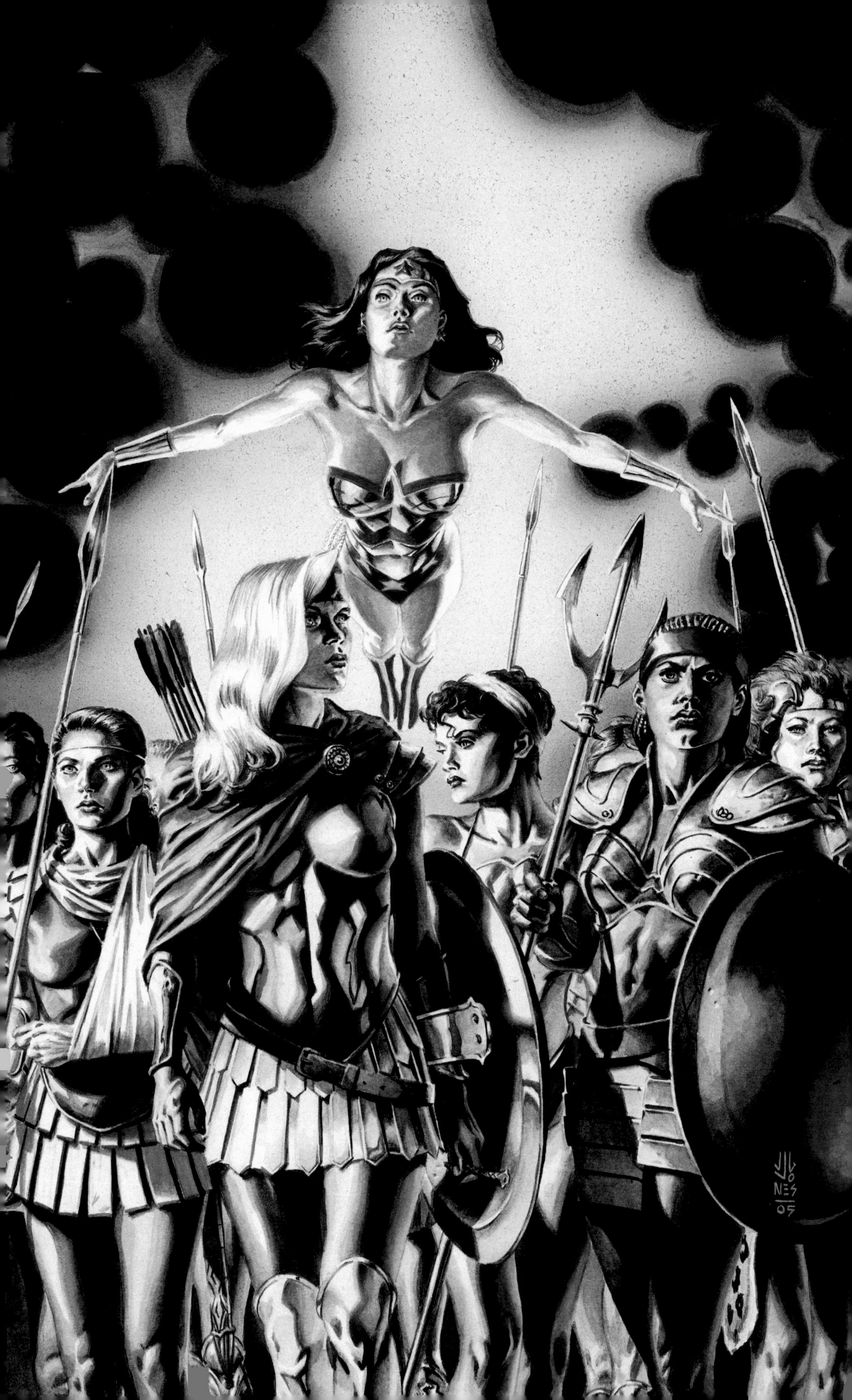

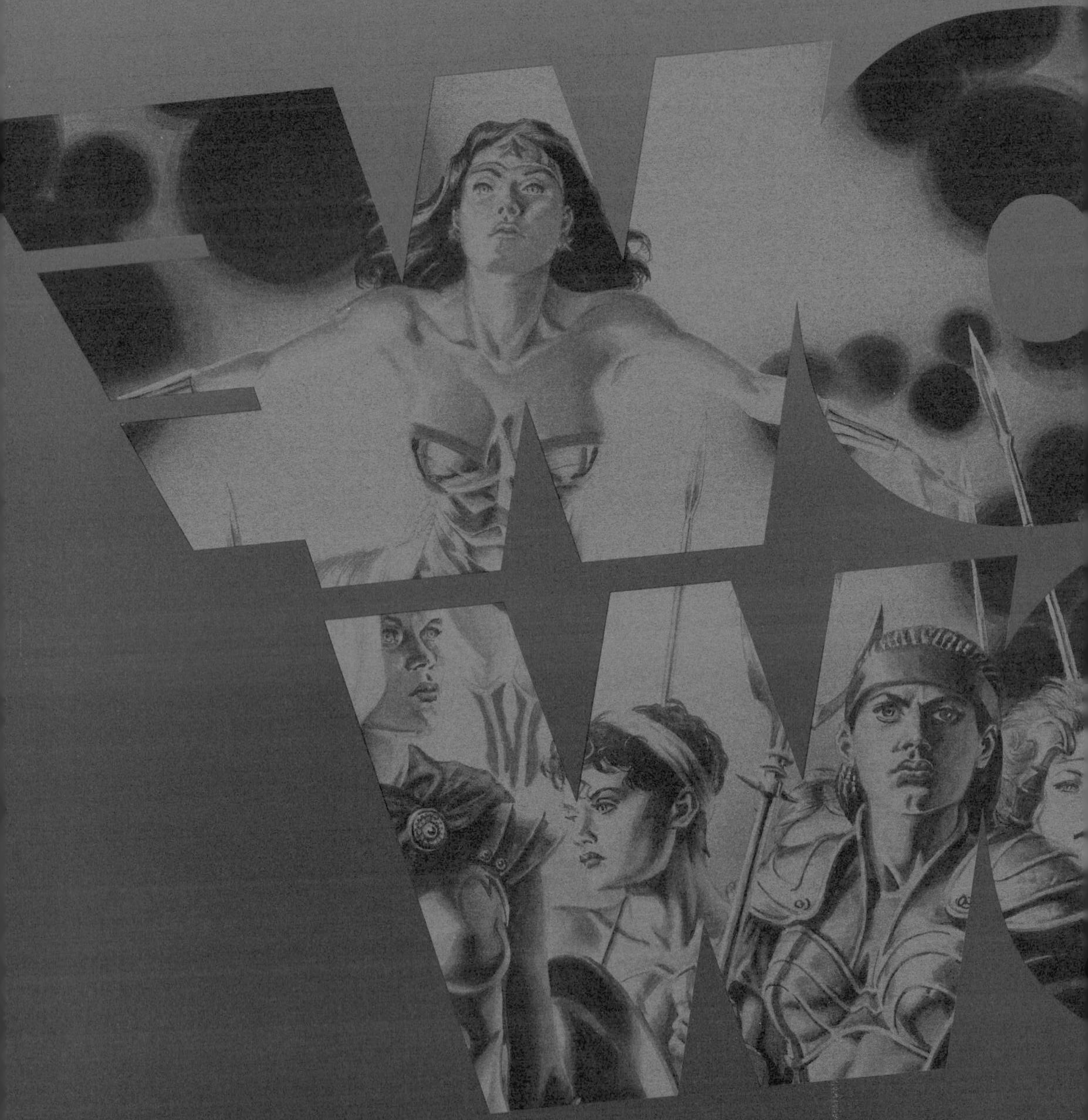

"MARATHON: PART TWO"

Greg Rucka – *writer*
Cliff Richards – *pencils*
Ray Snyder – *inks*
Richard and **Tanya Horie** – *colors*
Todd Klein – *letters*
J.G. Jones – *cover*

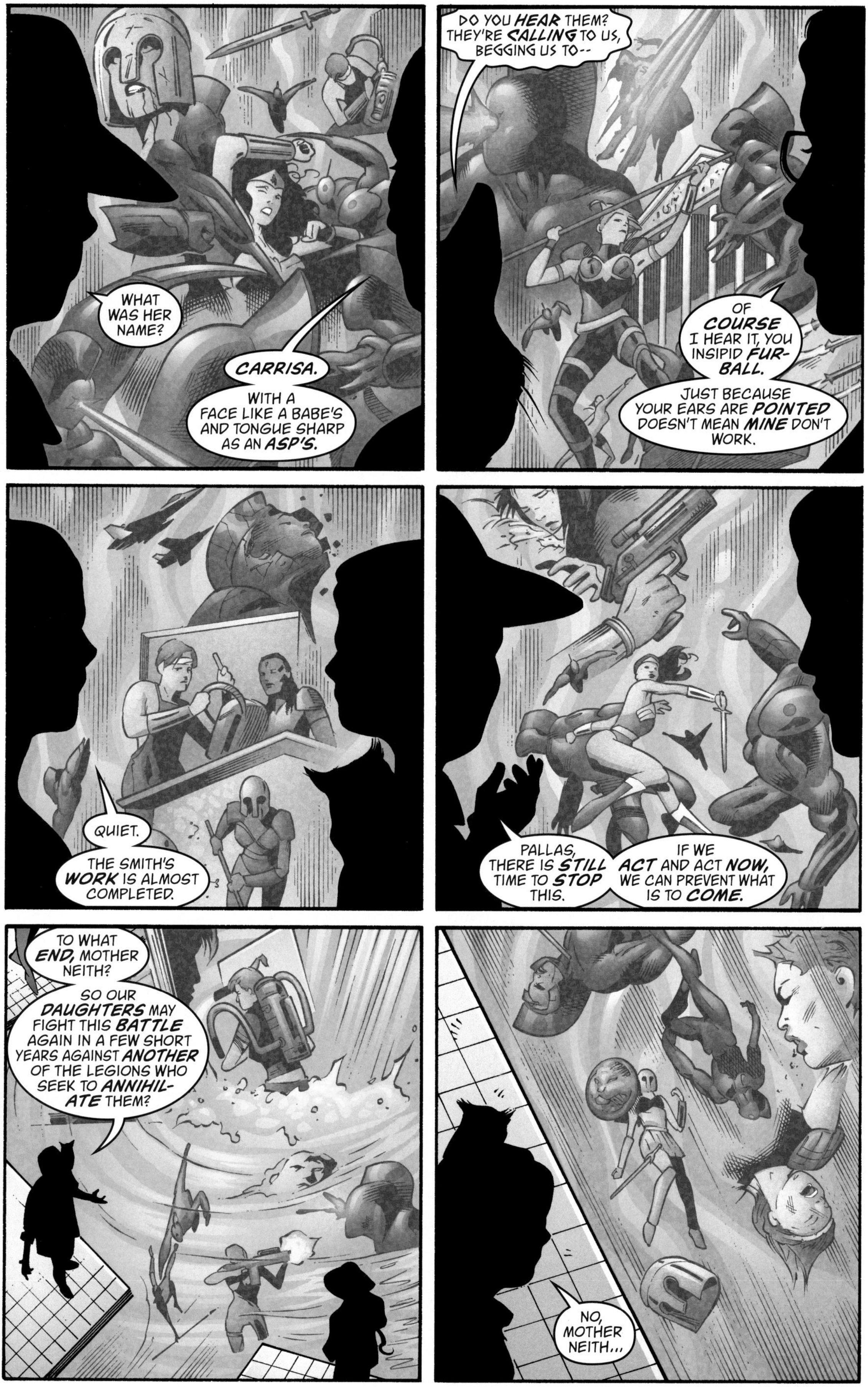
WHAT WAS HER NAME?
CARRISA.
WITH A FACE LIKE A BABE'S AND TONGUE SHARP AS AN ASP'S.
DO YOU HEAR THEM? THEY'RE CALLING TO US, BEGGING US TO--
OF COURSE I HEAR IT, YOU INSIPID FUR-BALL.
JUST BECAUSE YOUR EARS ARE POINTED DOESN'T MEAN MINE DON'T WORK.
QUIET.
THE SMITH'S WORK IS ALMOST COMPLETED.
PALLAS, THERE IS STILL TIME TO STOP THIS.
IF WE ACT AND ACT NOW, WE CAN PREVENT WHAT IS TO COME.
TO WHAT END, MOTHER NEITH?
SO OUR DAUGHTERS MAY FIGHT THIS BATTLE AGAIN IN A FEW SHORT YEARS AGAINST ANOTHER OF THE LEGIONS WHO SEEK TO ANNIHIL-ATE THEM?
NO, MOTHER NEITH...

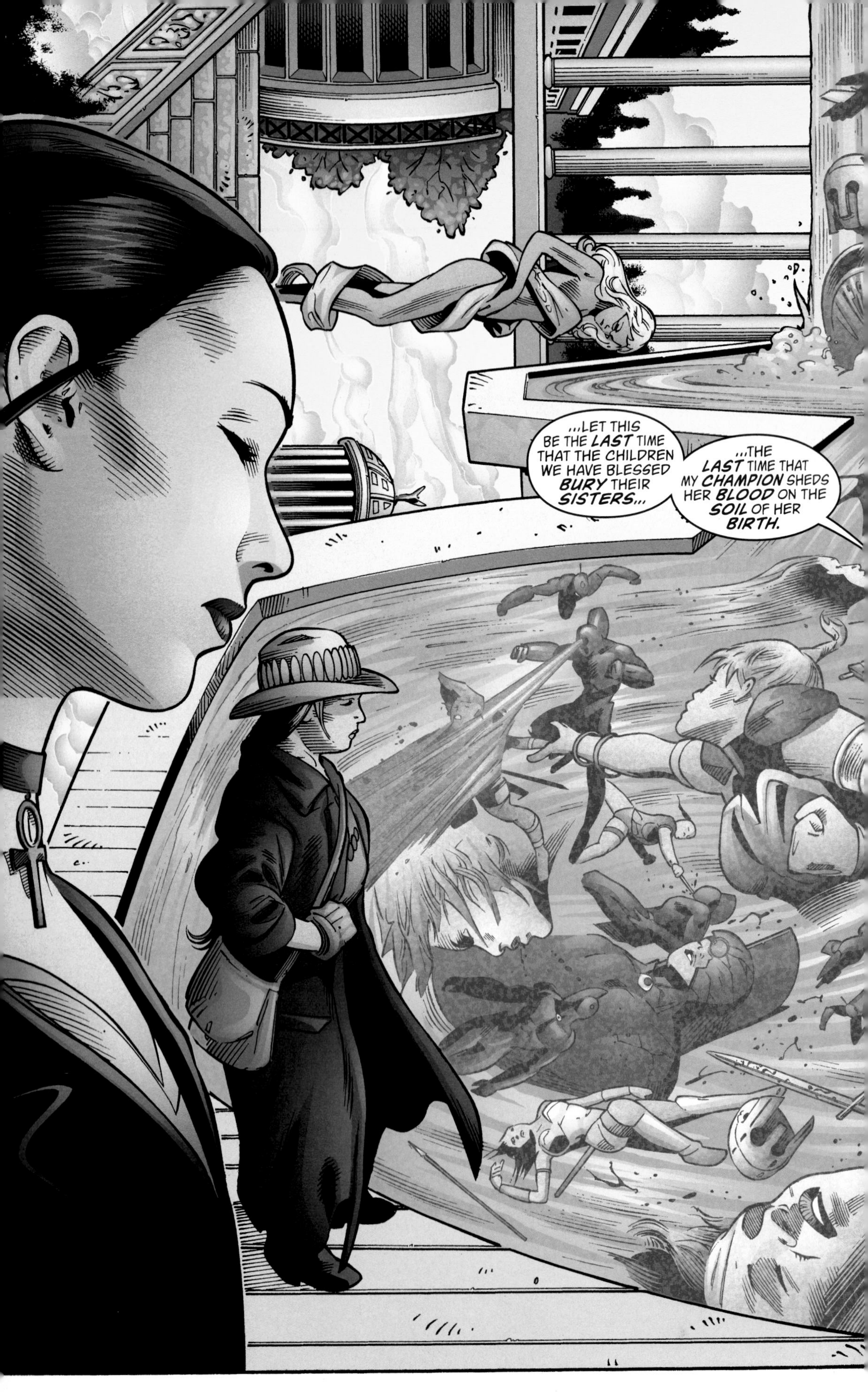
...LET THIS BE THE LAST TIME THAT THE CHILDREN WE HAVE BLESSED BURY THEIR SISTERS...
...THE LAST TIME THAT MY CHAMPION SHEDS HER BLOOD ON THE SOIL OF HER BIRTH.

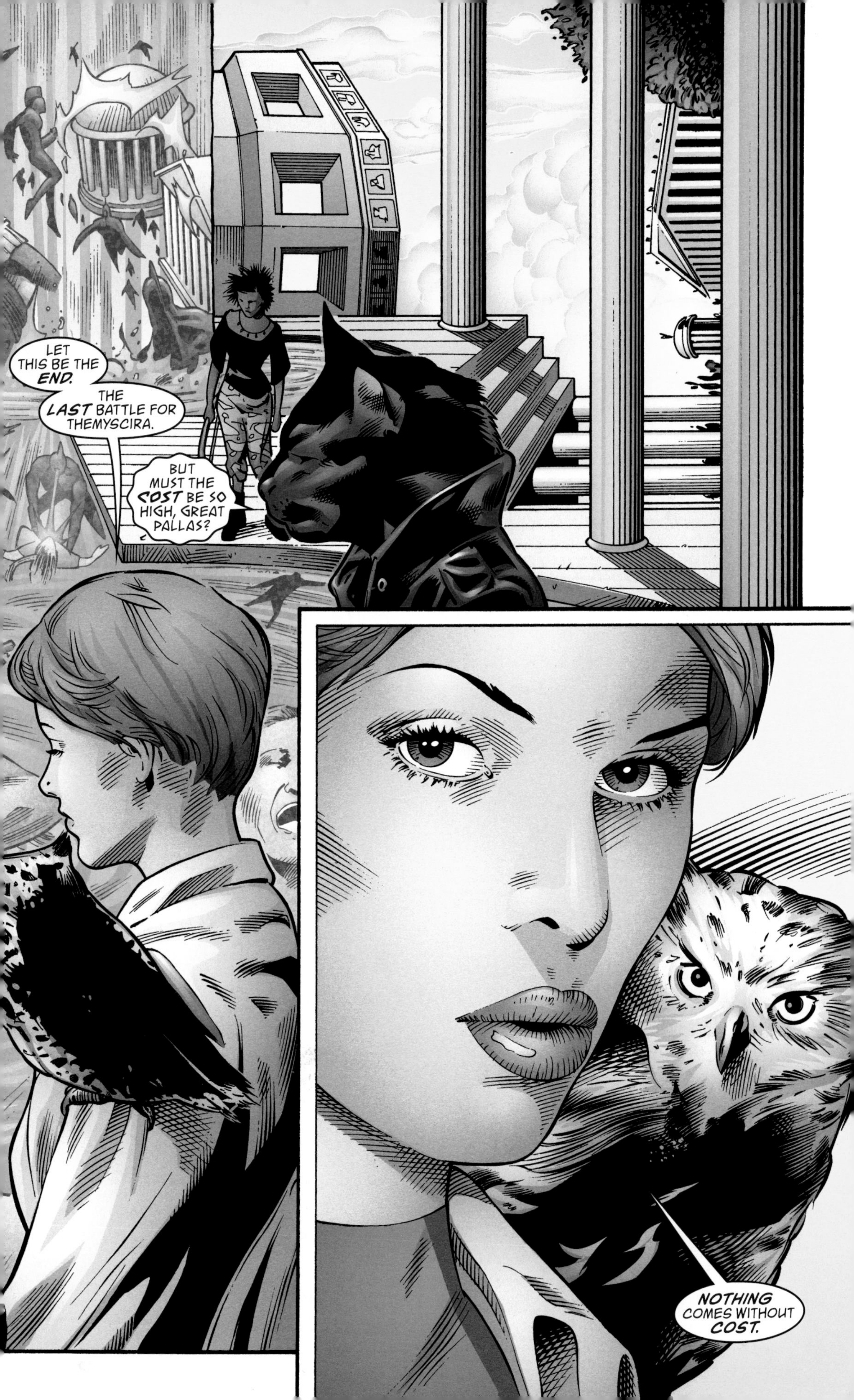
LET THIS BE THE END.
THE LAST BATTLE FOR THEMYSCIRA.
BUT MUST THE COST BE SO HIGH, GREAT PALLAS?
NOTHING COMES WITHOUT COST.

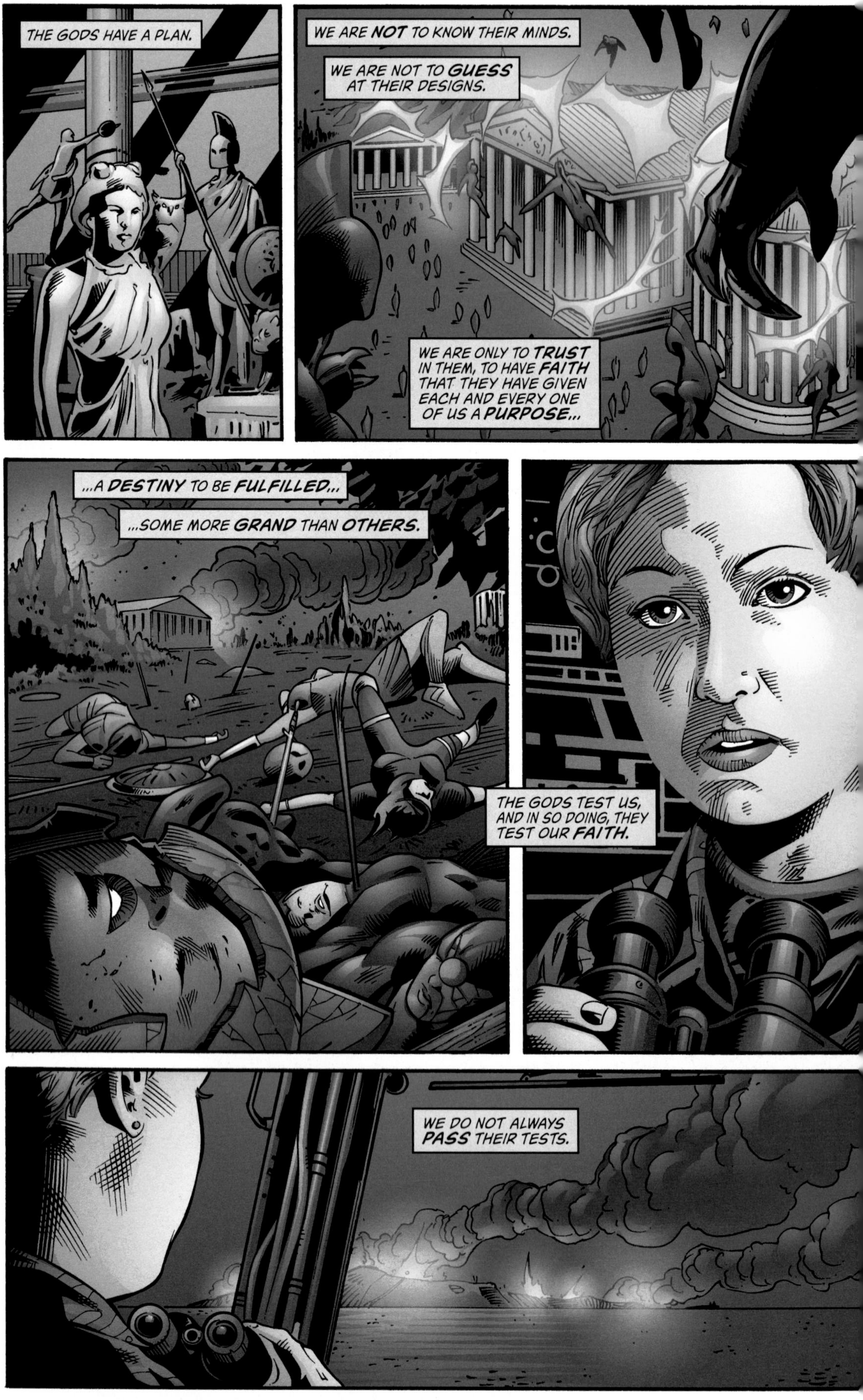
THE GODS HAVE A PLAN.
WE ARE NOT TO KNOW THEIR MINDS.
WE ARE NOT TO GUESS AT THEIR DESIGNS.
WE ARE ONLY TO TRUST IN THEM, TO HAVE FAITH THAT THEY HAVE GIVEN EACH AND EVERY ONE OF US A PURPOSE...
...A DESTINY TO BE FULFILLED...
...SOME MORE GRAND THAN OTHERS.
THE GODS TEST US, AND IN SO DOING, THEY TEST OUR FAITH.
WE DO NOT ALWAYS PASS THEIR TESTS.

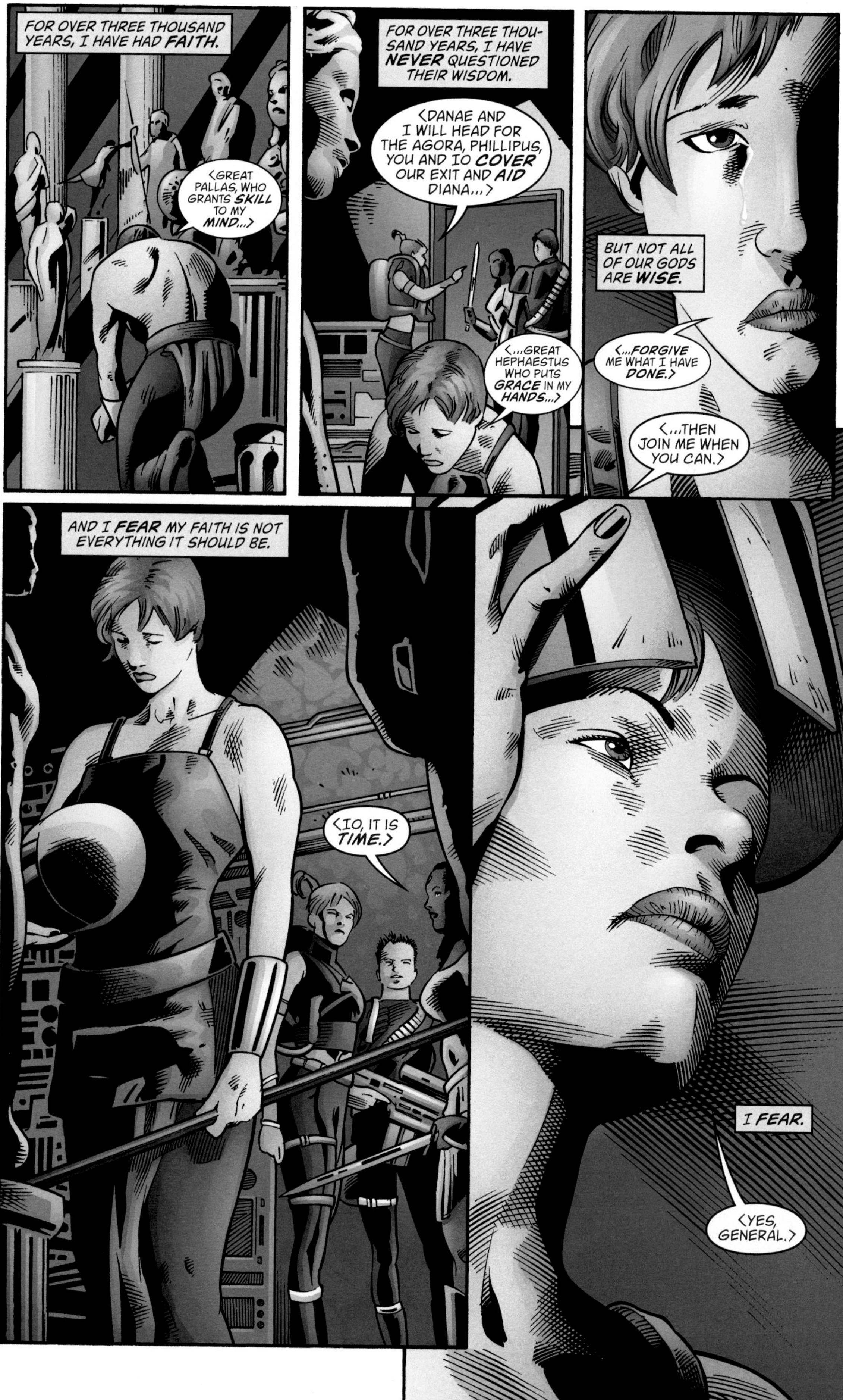
FOR OVER THREE THOUSAND YEARS, I HAVE HAD FAITH.
<GREAT PALLAS, WHO GRANTS SKILL TO MY MIND...>
FOR OVER THREE THOUSAND YEARS, I HAVE NEVER QUESTIONED THEIR WISDOM.
<DANAE AND I WILL HEAD FOR THE AGORA, PHILLIPUS, YOU AND IO COVER OUR EXIT AND AID DIANA...>
<...GREAT HEPHAESTUS WHO PUTS GRACE IN MY HANDS...>
BUT NOT ALL OF OUR GODS ARE WISE.
<...FORGIVE ME WHAT I HAVE DONE.>
<...THEN JOIN ME WHEN YOU CAN.>
AND I FEAR MY FAITH IS NOT EVERYTHING IT SHOULD BE.
<IO, IT IS TIME.>
I FEAR.
<YES, GENERAL.>

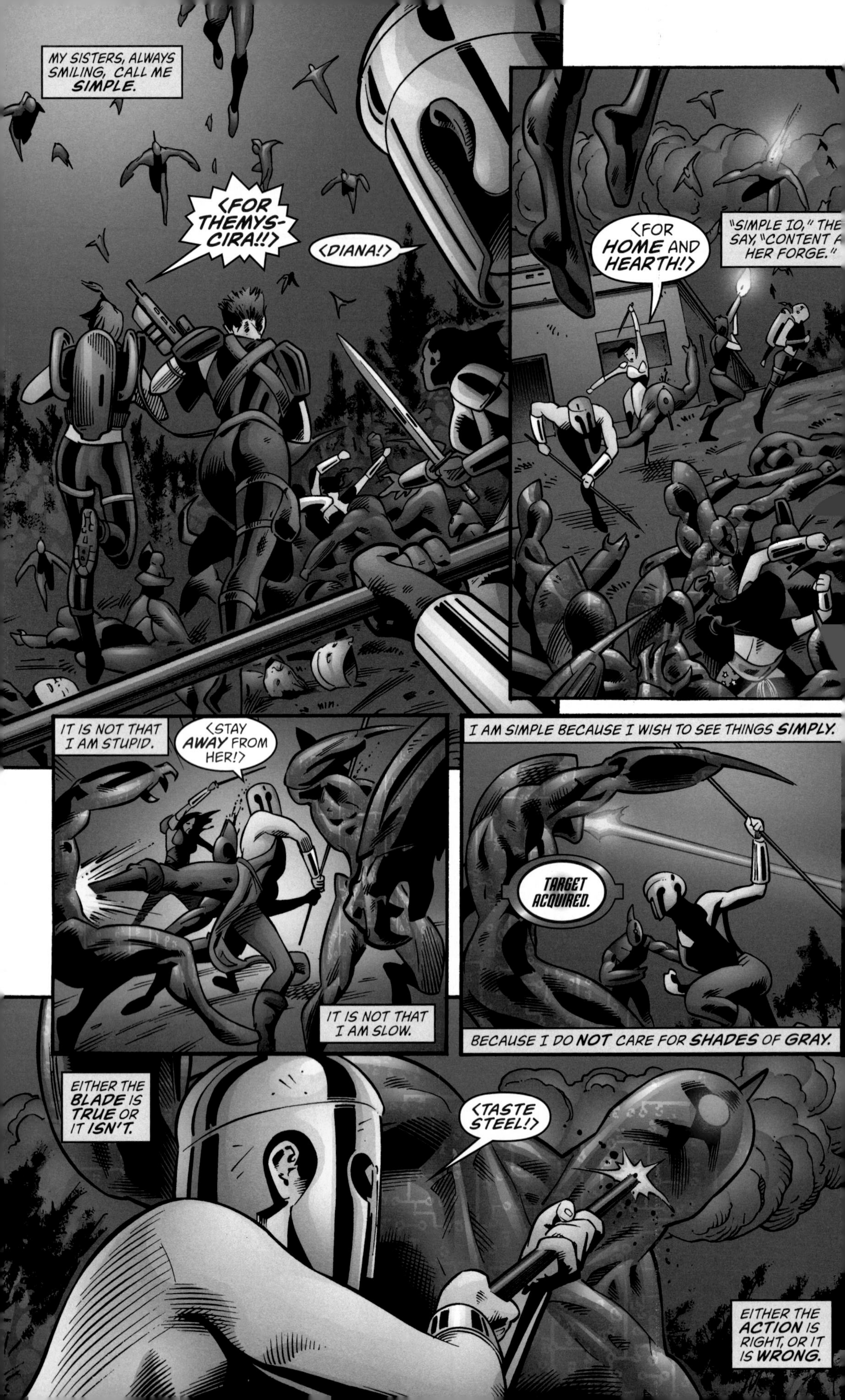

MY SISTERS, ALWAYS SMILING, CALL ME SIMPLE.
<FOR THEMYSCIRA!!>
<DIANA!>
<FOR HOME AND HEARTH!>
"SIMPLE IO," THEY SAY, "CONTENT AT HER FORGE."
IT IS NOT THAT I AM STUPID.
<STAY AWAY FROM HER!>
IT IS NOT THAT I AM SLOW.
I AM SIMPLE BECAUSE I WISH TO SEE THINGS SIMPLY.
TARGET ACQUIRED.
BECAUSE I DO NOT CARE FOR SHADES OF GRAY.
EITHER THE BLADE IS TRUE OR IT ISN'T.
<TASTE STEEL!>
EITHER THE ACTION IS RIGHT, OR IT IS WRONG.

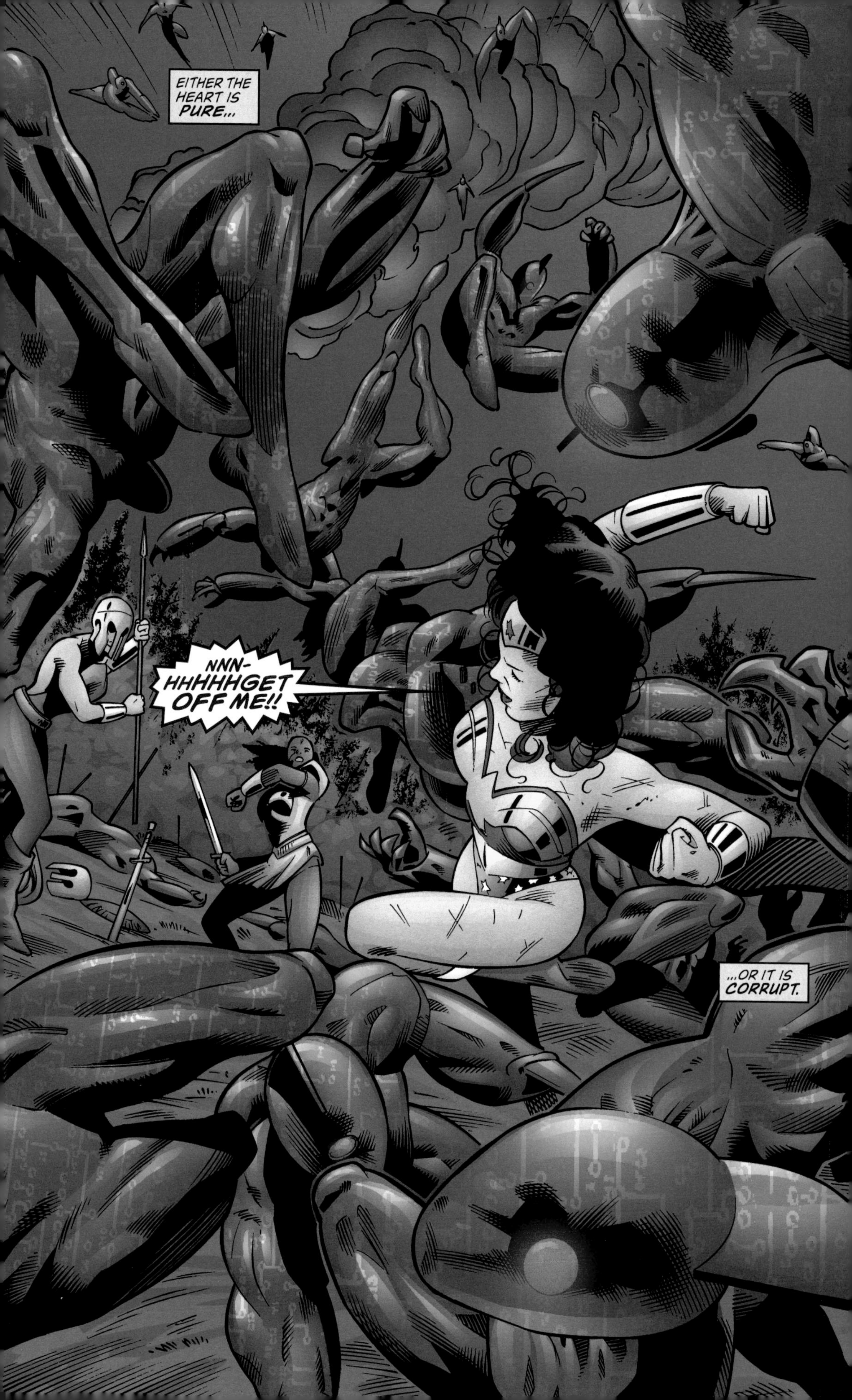
EITHER THE HEART IS PURE...
NNN-HHHHHGET OFF ME!!
...OR IT IS CORRUPT.

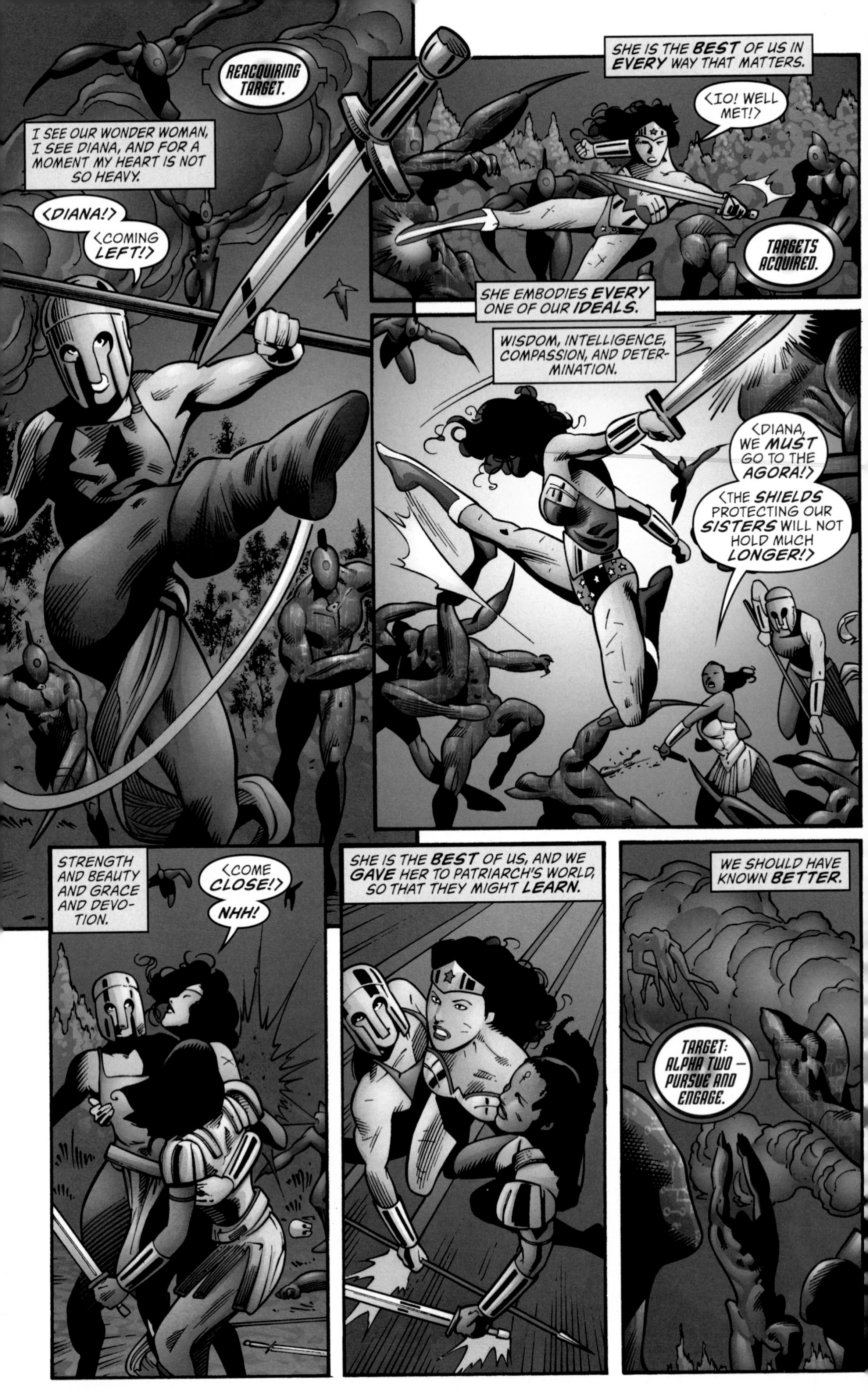
REACQUIRING TARGET.
I SEE OUR WONDER WOMAN, I SEE DIANA, AND FOR A MOMENT MY HEART IS NOT SO HEAVY.
<DIANA!>
<COMING LEFT!>
SHE IS THE BEST OF US IN EVERY WAY THAT MATTERS.
<IO! WELL MET!>
TARGETS ACQUIRED.
SHE EMBODIES EVERY ONE OF OUR IDEALS.
WISDOM, INTELLIGENCE, COMPASSION, AND DETERMINATION.
<DIANA, WE MUST GO TO THE AGORA!>
<THE SHIELDS PROTECTING OUR SISTERS WILL NOT HOLD MUCH LONGER!>
STRENGTH AND BEAUTY AND GRACE AND DEVOTION.
<COME CLOSE!>
NHH!
SHE IS THE BEST OF US, AND WE GAVE HER TO PATRIARCH'S WORLD, SO THAT THEY MIGHT LEARN.
WE SHOULD HAVE KNOWN BETTER.
TARGET: ALPHA TWO — PURSUE AND ENGAGE.

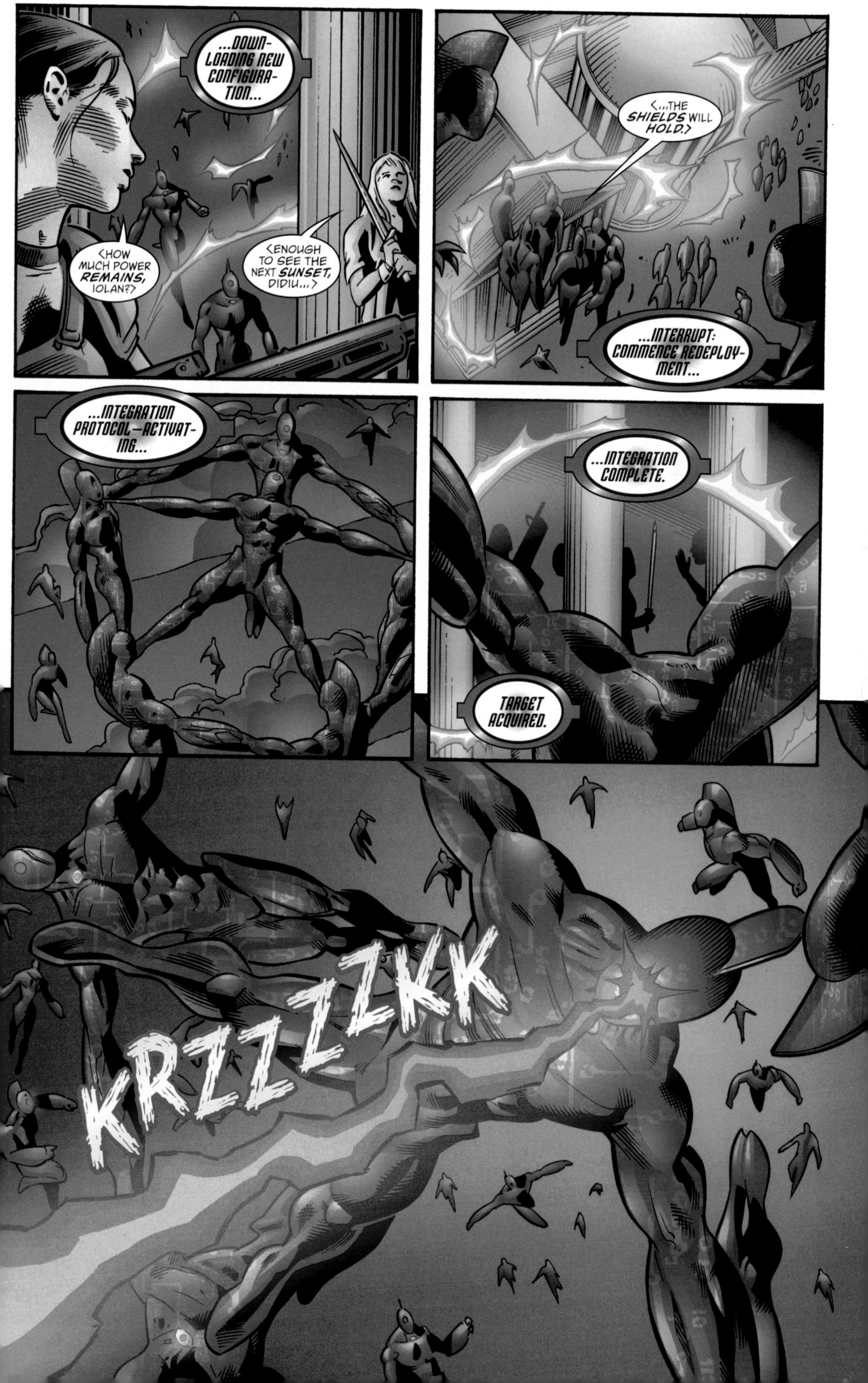
...DOWN-LOADING NEW CONFIGURA-TION...
<HOW MUCH POWER REMAINS, IOLAN?>
<ENOUGH TO SEE THE NEXT SUNSET, DIDIU...>
<...THE SHIELDS WILL HOLD.>
...INTERRUPT: COMMENCE REDEPLOY-MENT...
...INTEGRATION PROTOCOL—ACTIVAT-ING...
...INTEGRATION COMPLETE.
TARGET ACQUIRED.
KRZZZZKK

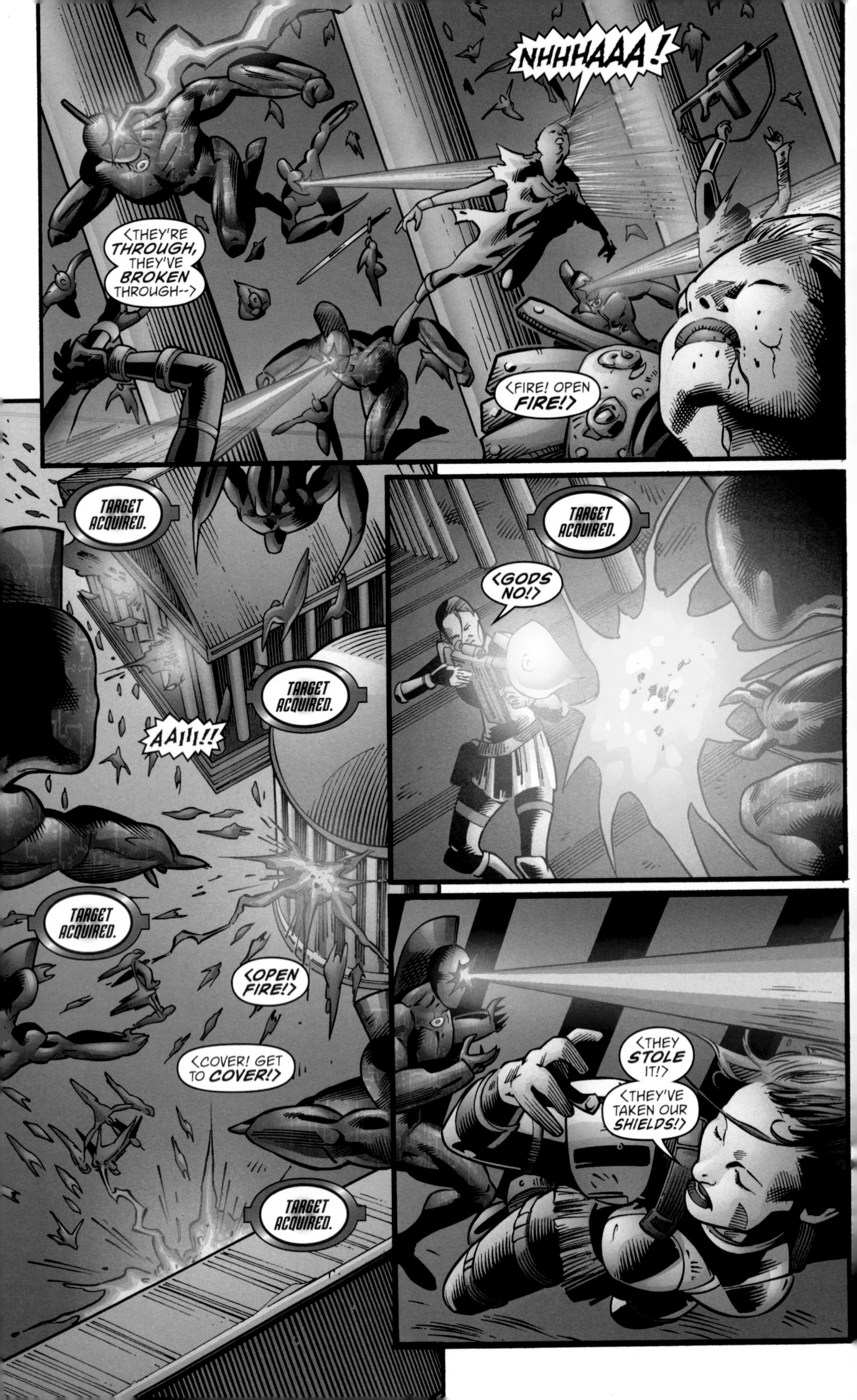
NHHHAAA!
<THEY'RE THROUGH, THEY'VE BROKEN THROUGH-->
<FIRE! OPEN FIRE!>
TARGET ACQUIRED.
TARGET ACQUIRED.
AAIII!!
TARGET ACQUIRED.
<OPEN FIRE!>
<COVER! GET TO COVER!>
TARGET ACQUIRED.
TARGET ACQUIRED.
<GODS NO!>
<THEY STOLE IT!>
<THEY'VE TAKEN OUR SHIELDS!>

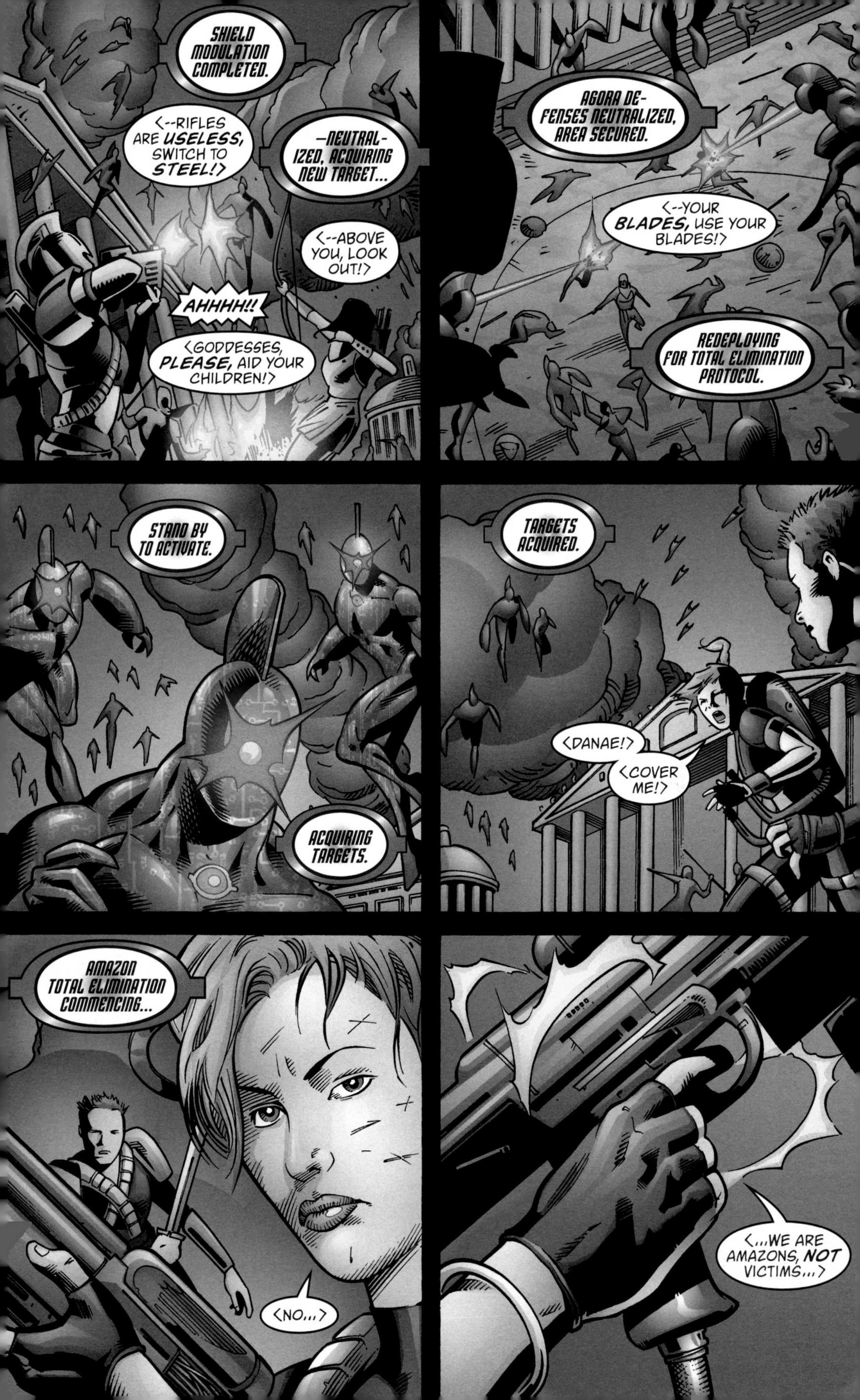
SHIELD MODULATION COMPLETED.
<--RIFLES ARE USELESS, SWITCH TO STEEL!>
—NEUTRAL-IZED, ACQUIRING NEW TARGET...
<--ABOVE YOU, LOOK OUT!>
AHHHH!!
<GODDESSES, PLEASE, AID YOUR CHILDREN!>
AGORA DE-FENSES NEUTRALIZED, AREA SECURED.
<--YOUR BLADES, USE YOUR BLADES!>
REDEPLOYING FOR TOTAL ELIMINATION PROTOCOL.
STAND BY TO ACTIVATE.
ACQUIRING TARGETS.
TARGETS ACQUIRED.
<DANAE!>
<COVER ME!>
AMAZON TOTAL ELIMINATION COMMENCING...
<NO...>
<...WE ARE AMAZONS, NOT VICTIMS...>

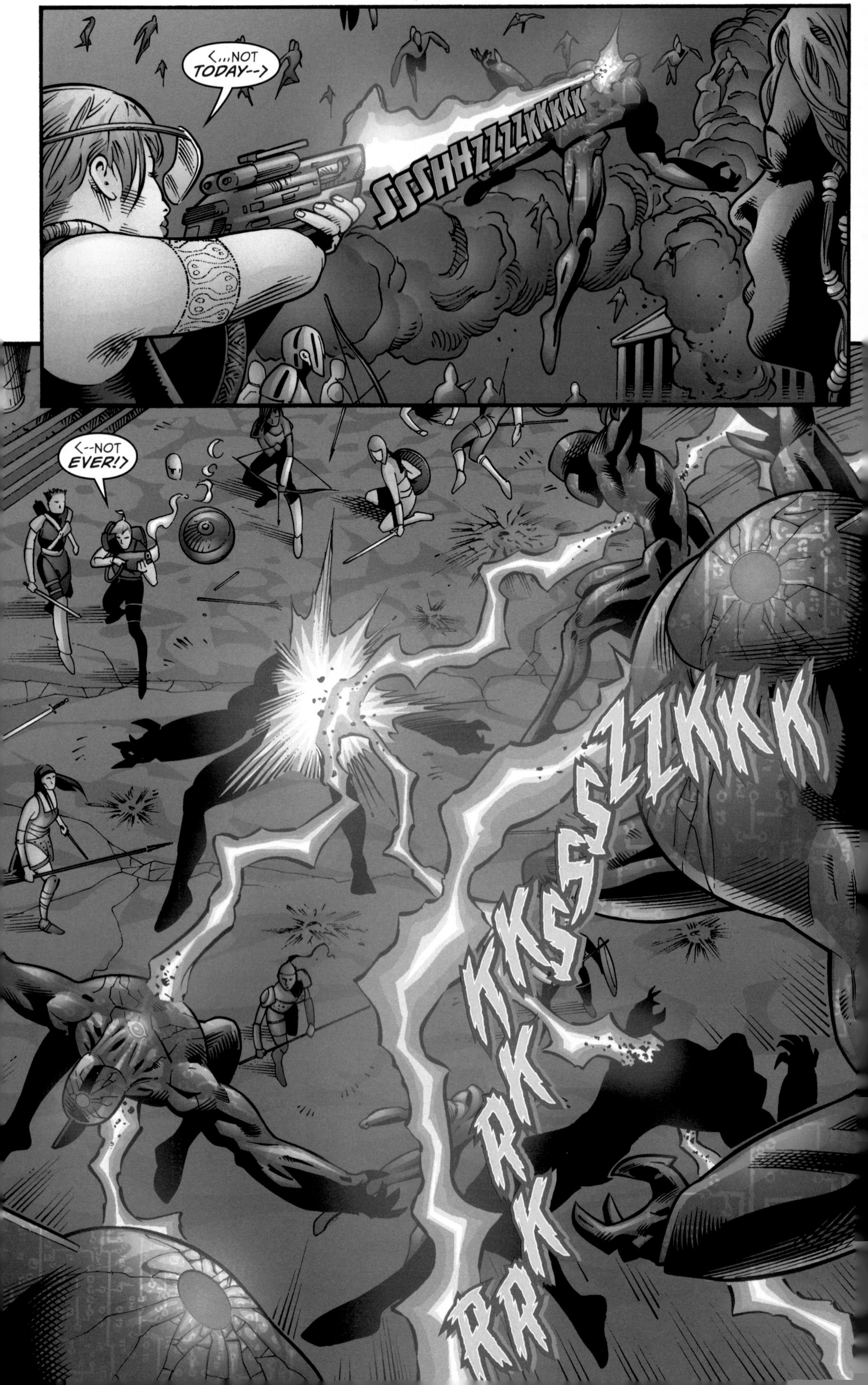

<...NOT TODAY-->
SSSHHZZZKKKKK
<--NOT EVER!>
RRAKKSSZZKKKK

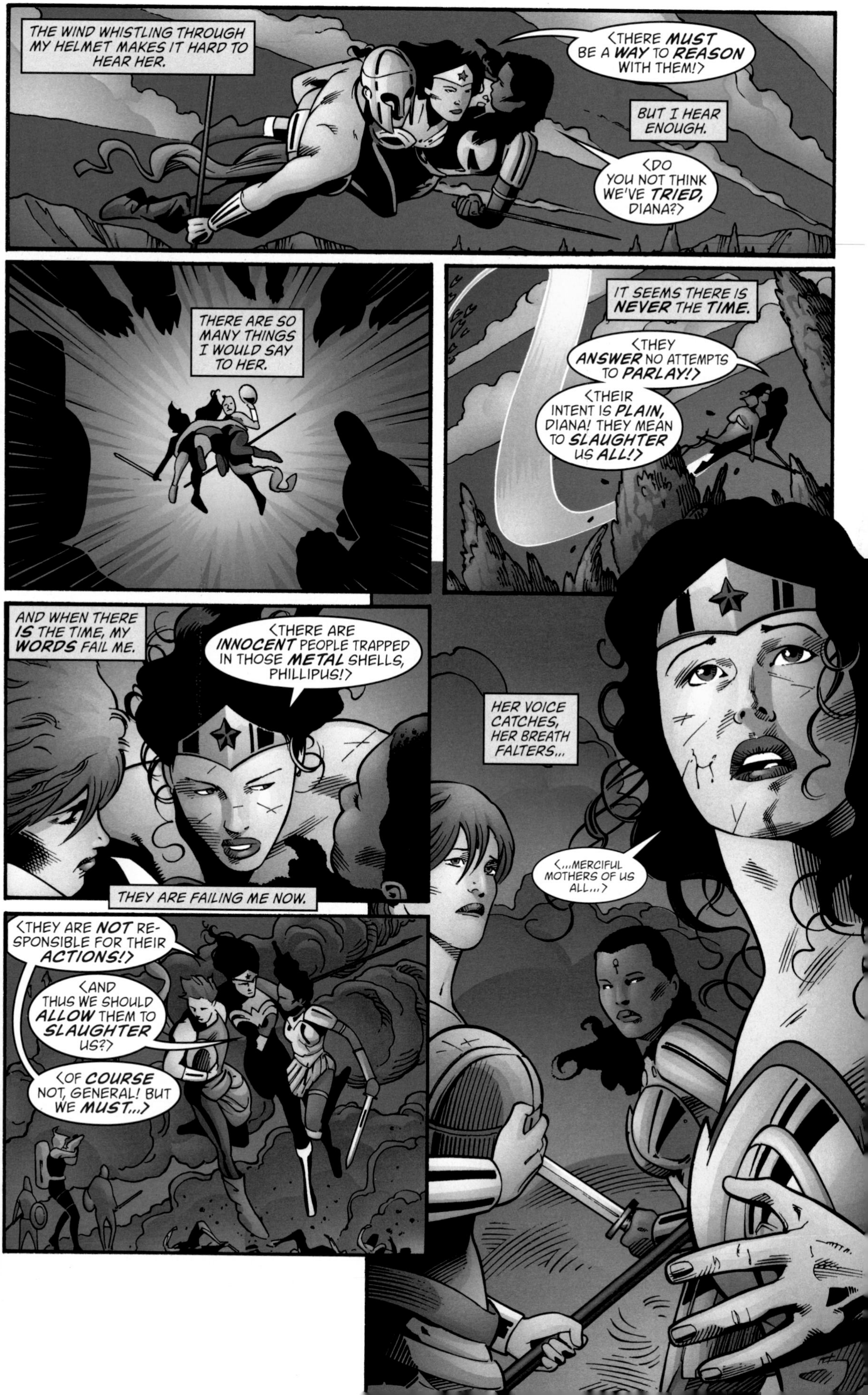
THE WIND WHISTLING THROUGH MY HELMET MAKES IT HARD TO HEAR HER.
<THERE MUST BE A WAY TO REASON WITH THEM!>
BUT I HEAR ENOUGH.
<DO YOU NOT THINK WE'VE TRIED, DIANA?>
THERE ARE SO MANY THINGS I WOULD SAY TO HER.
IT SEEMS THERE IS NEVER THE TIME.
<THEY ANSWER NO ATTEMPTS TO PARLAY!>
<THEIR INTENT IS PLAIN, DIANA! THEY MEAN TO SLAUGHTER US ALL!>
AND WHEN THERE IS THE TIME, MY WORDS FAIL ME.
<THERE ARE INNOCENT PEOPLE TRAPPED IN THOSE METAL SHELLS, PHILLIPUS!>
THEY ARE FAILING ME NOW.
<THEY ARE NOT RESPONSIBLE FOR THEIR ACTIONS!>
<AND THUS WE SHOULD ALLOW THEM TO SLAUGHTER US?>
<OF COURSE NOT, GENERAL! BUT WE MUST...>
HER VOICE CATCHES, HER BREATH FALTERS...
<...MERCIFUL MOTHERS OF US ALL...>

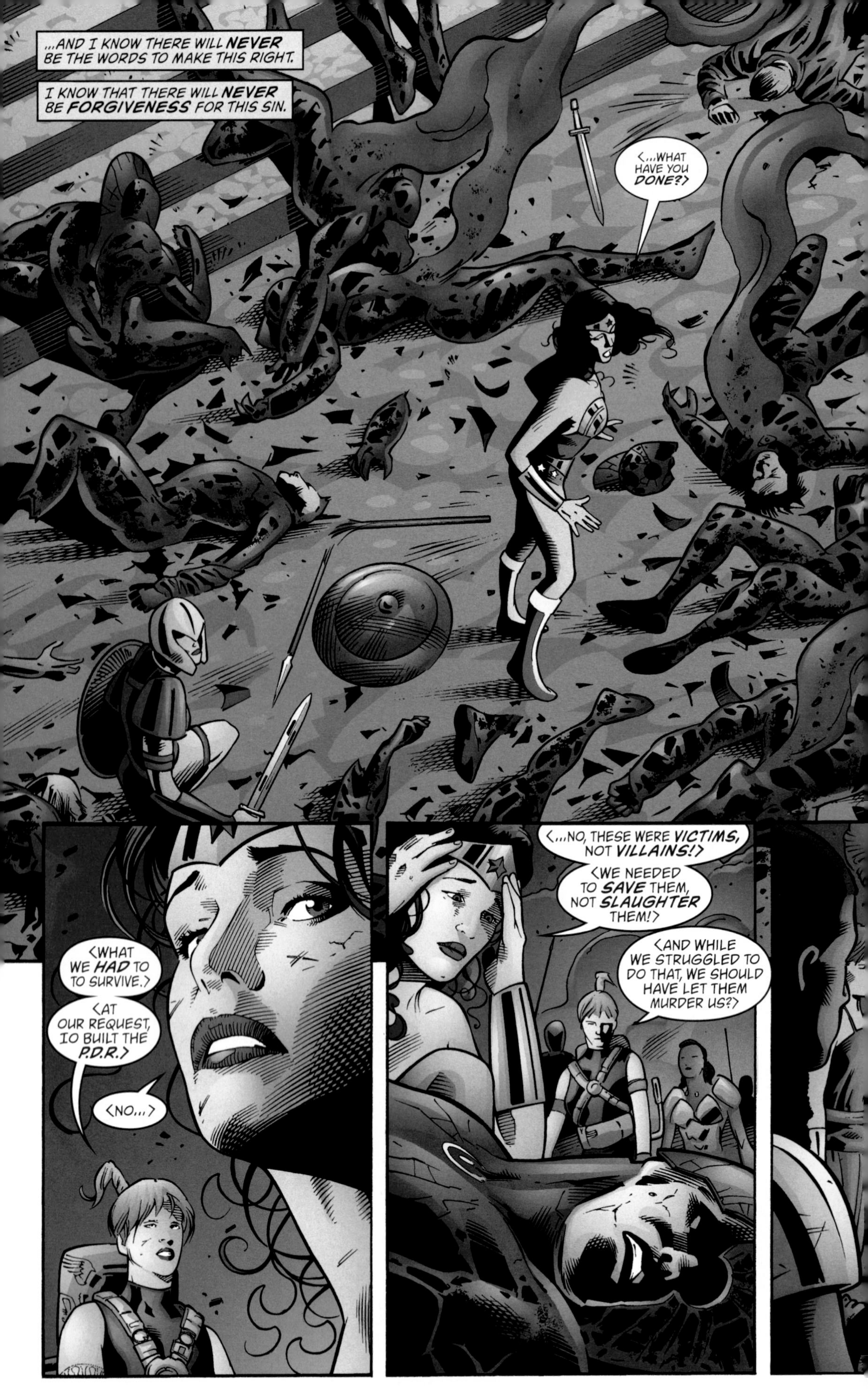

...AND I KNOW THERE WILL NEVER BE THE WORDS TO MAKE THIS RIGHT.
I KNOW THAT THERE WILL NEVER BE FORGIVENESS FOR THIS SIN.
<...WHAT HAVE YOU DONE?>
<WHAT WE HAD TO TO SURVIVE.>
<AT OUR REQUEST, IO BUILT THE P.D.R.>
<NO...>
<...NO, THESE WERE VICTIMS, NOT VILLAINS!>
<WE NEEDED TO SAVE THEM, NOT SLAUGHTER THEM!>
<AND WHILE WE STRUGGLED TO DO THAT, WE SHOULD HAVE LET THEM MURDER US?>

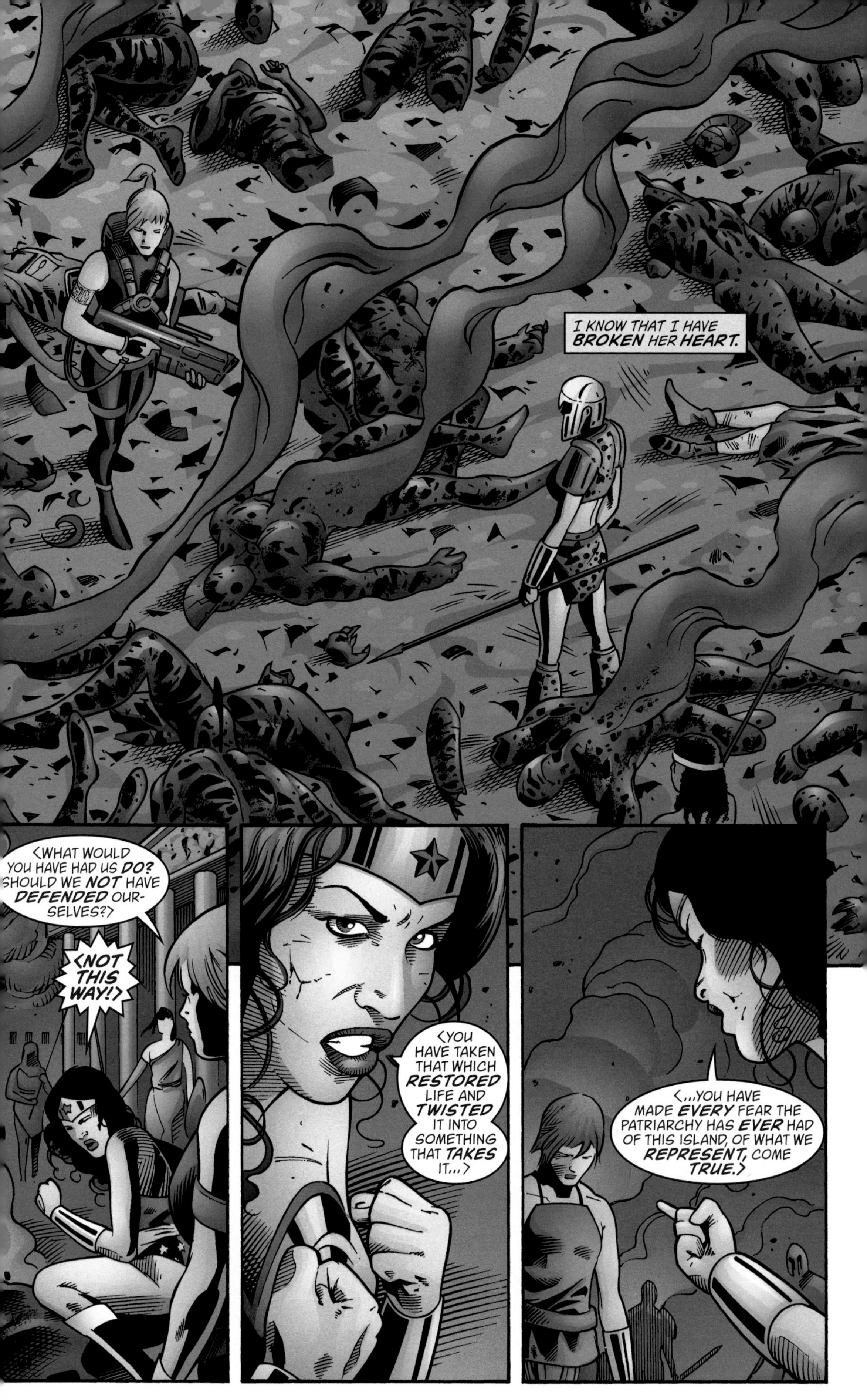
I KNOW THAT I HAVE BROKEN HER HEART.
<WHAT WOULD YOU HAVE HAD US DO? SHOULD WE NOT HAVE DEFENDED OUR-SELVES?>
<NOT THIS WAY!>
<YOU HAVE TAKEN THAT WHICH RESTORED LIFE AND TWISTED IT INTO SOMETHING THAT TAKES IT...>
<...YOU HAVE MADE EVERY FEAR THE PATRIARCHY HAS EVER HAD OF THIS ISLAND, OF WHAT WE REPRESENT, COME TRUE.>

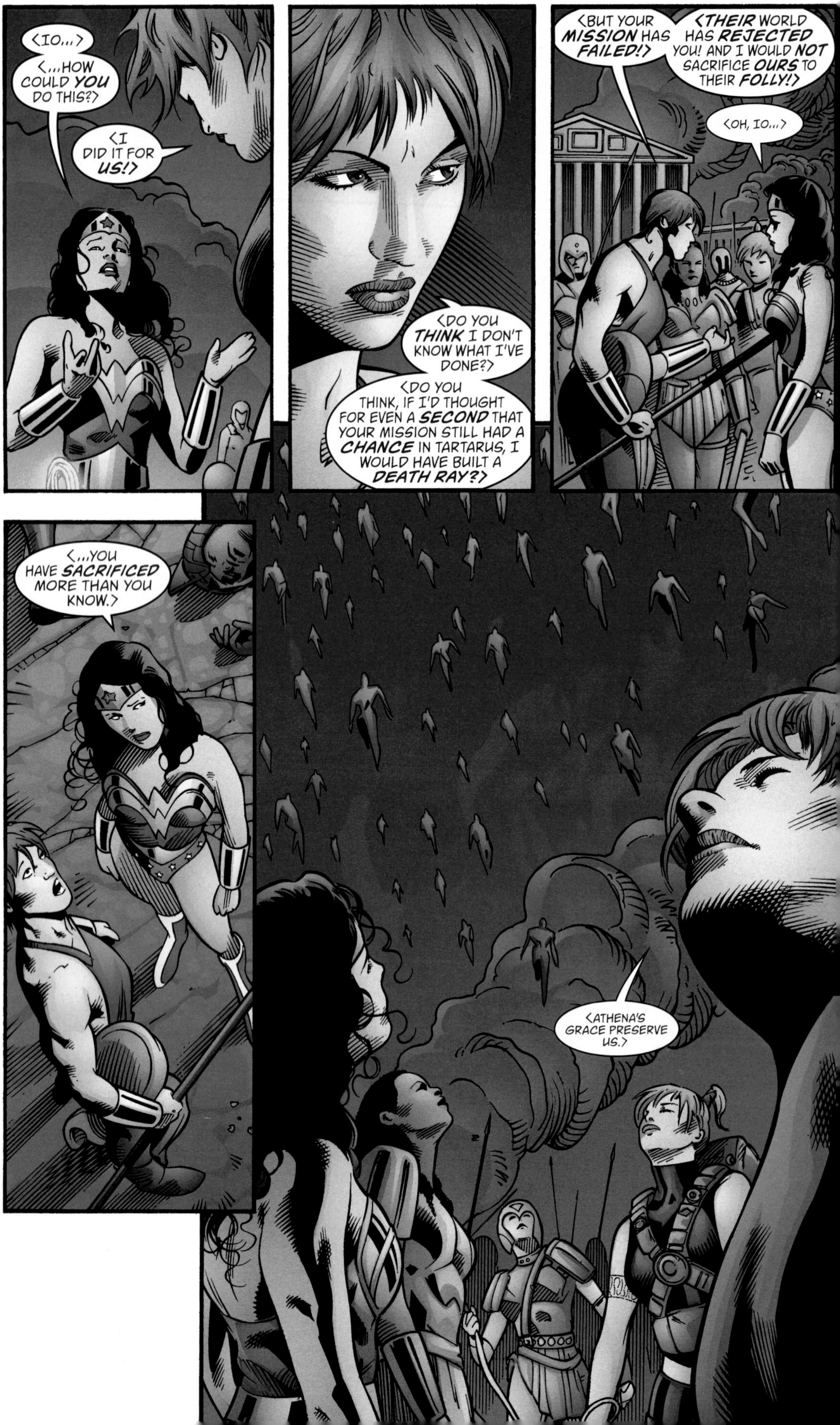

<IO...>
<...HOW COULD YOU DO THIS?>
<I DID IT FOR US!>
<DO YOU THINK I DON'T KNOW WHAT I'VE DONE?>
<DO YOU THINK, IF I'D THOUGHT FOR EVEN A SECOND THAT YOUR MISSION STILL HAD A CHANCE IN TARTARUS, I WOULD HAVE BUILT A DEATH RAY?>
<BUT YOUR MISSION HAS FAILED!>
<THEIR WORLD HAS REJECTED YOU! AND I WOULD NOT SACRIFICE OURS TO THEIR FOLLY!>
<OH, IO...>
<...YOU HAVE SACRIFICED MORE THAN YOU KNOW.>
<ATHENA'S GRACE PRESERVE US.>

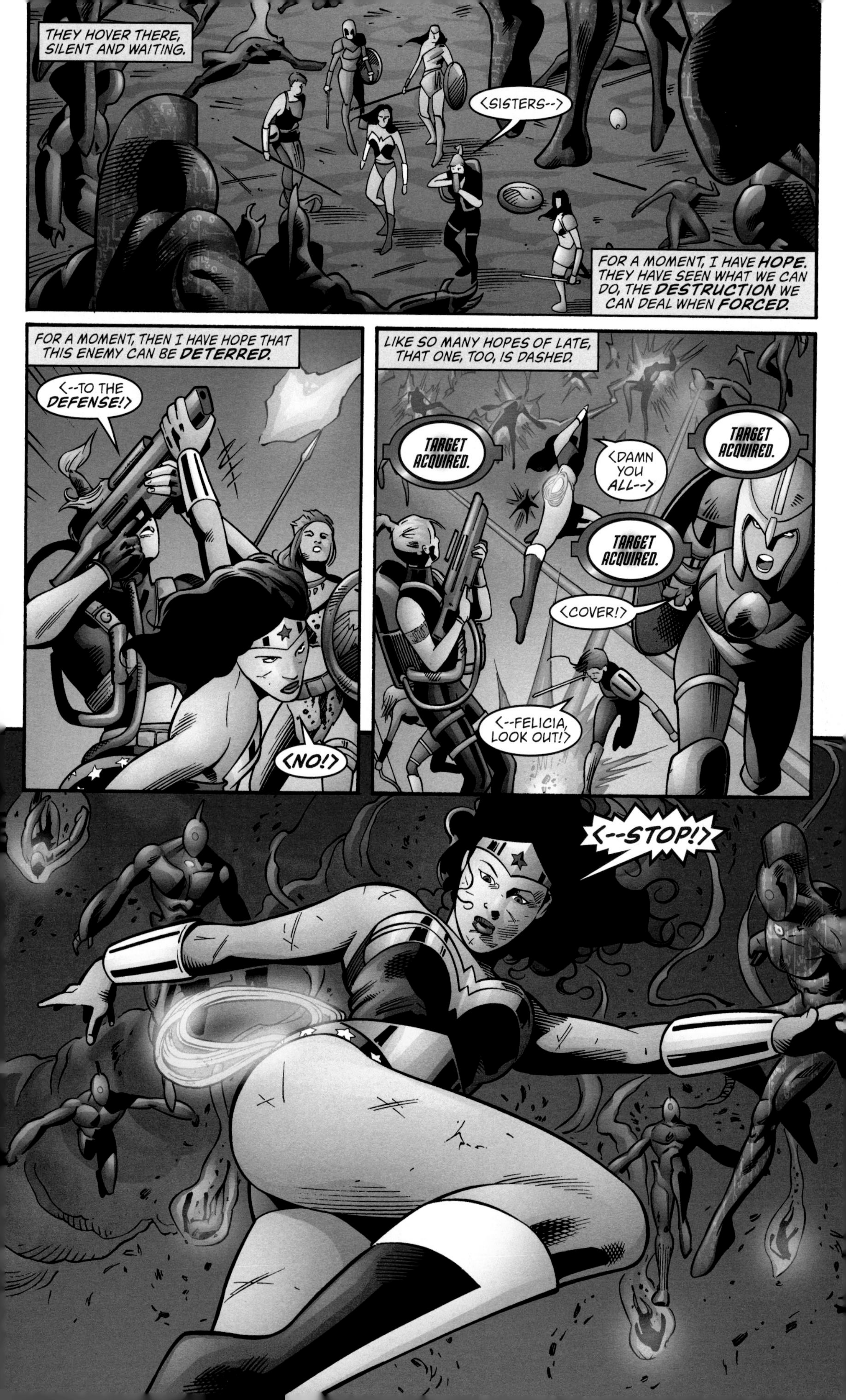

THEY HOVER THERE, SILENT AND WAITING.
<SISTERS-->
FOR A MOMENT, I HAVE **HOPE.** THEY HAVE SEEN WHAT WE CAN DO, THE **DESTRUCTION** WE CAN DEAL WHEN **FORCED.**
FOR A MOMENT, THEN I HAVE HOPE THAT THIS ENEMY CAN BE **DETERRED.**
<--TO THE **DEFENSE!**>
<NO!>
LIKE SO MANY HOPES OF LATE, THAT ONE, TOO, IS DASHED.
TARGET ACQUIRED.
<DAMN YOU **ALL**-->
TARGET ACQUIRED.
TARGET ACQUIRED.
<COVER!>
<--FELICIA, LOOK OUT!>
<--STOP!>

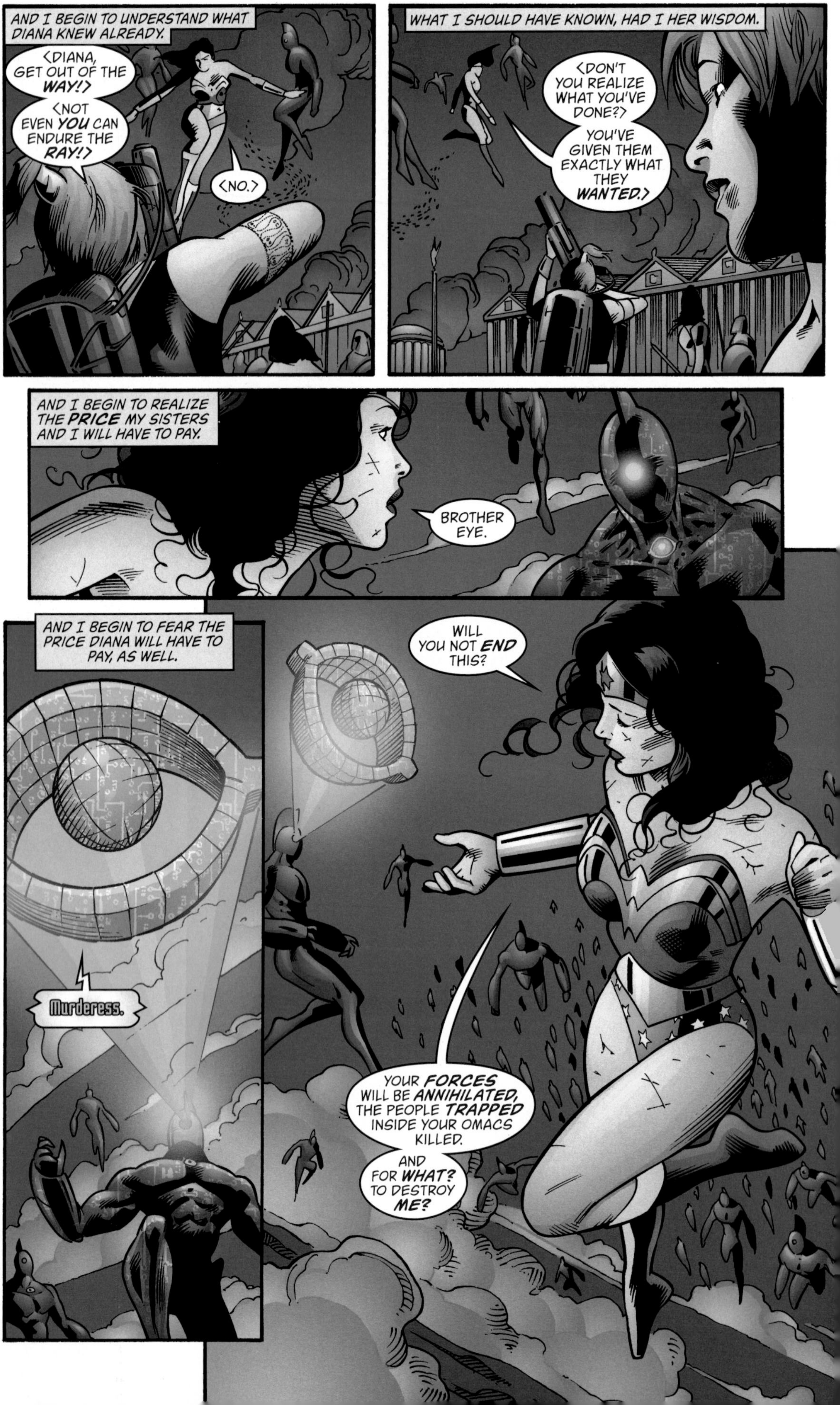
AND I BEGIN TO UNDERSTAND WHAT DIANA KNEW ALREADY.
<DIANA, GET OUT OF THE WAY!>
<NOT EVEN YOU CAN ENDURE THE RAY!>
<NO.>
WHAT I SHOULD HAVE KNOWN, HAD I HER WISDOM.
<DON'T YOU REALIZE WHAT YOU'VE DONE?>
YOU'VE GIVEN THEM EXACTLY WHAT THEY WANTED.>
AND I BEGIN TO REALIZE THE PRICE MY SISTERS AND I WILL HAVE TO PAY.
BROTHER EYE.
AND I BEGIN TO FEAR THE PRICE DIANA WILL HAVE TO PAY, AS WELL.
Murderess.
WILL YOU NOT END THIS?
YOUR FORCES WILL BE ANNIHILATED, THE PEOPLE TRAPPED INSIDE YOUR OMACS KILLED.
AND FOR WHAT? TO DESTROY ME?

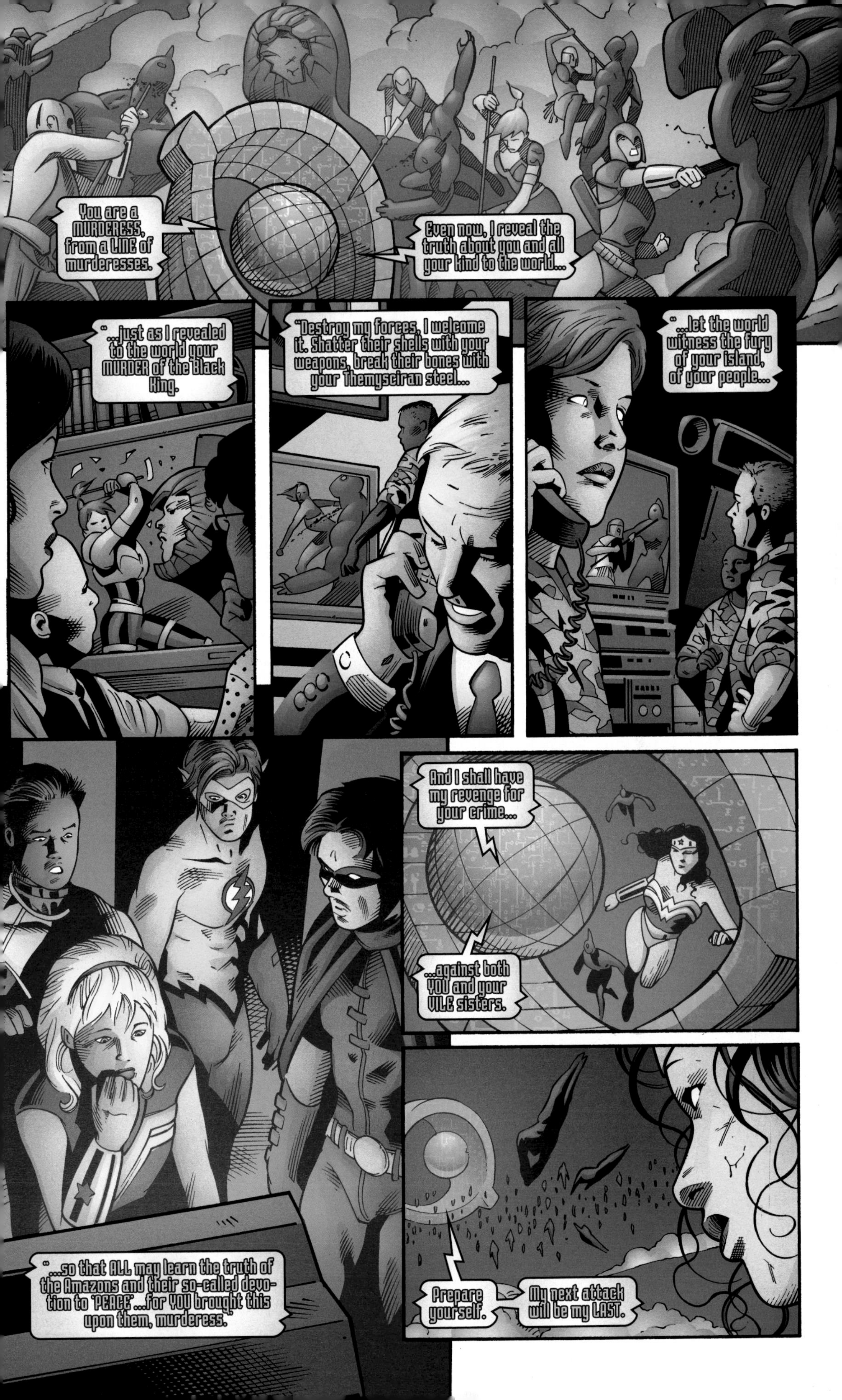

You are a MURDERESS, from a LINE of murderesses.
Even now, I reveal the truth about you and all your kind to the world...
"...just as I revealed to the world your MURDER of the Black King.
"Destroy my forces, I welcome it. Shatter their shells with your weapons, break their bones with your Themysciran steel...
"...let the world witness the fury of your island, of your people...
"...so that ALL may learn the truth of the Amazons and their so-called devotion to 'PEACE'...for YOU brought this upon them, murderess."
And I shall have my revenge for your crime...
...against both YOU and your VILE sisters.
Prepare yourself.
My next attack will be my LAST.

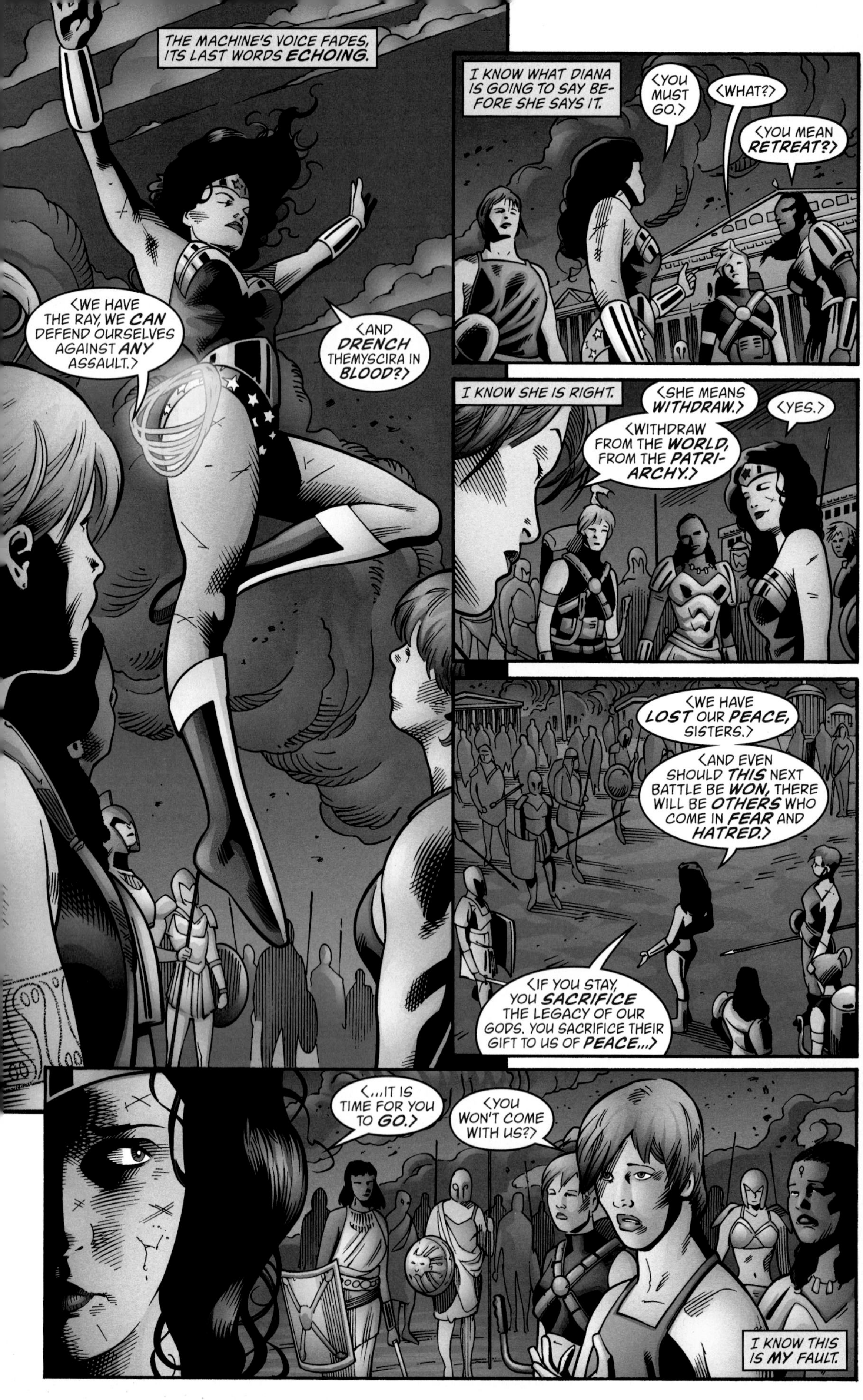
THE MACHINE'S VOICE FADES, ITS LAST WORDS ECHOING.
<WE HAVE THE RAY, WE CAN DEFEND OURSELVES AGAINST ANY ASSAULT.>
<AND DRENCH THEMYSCIRA IN BLOOD?>
I KNOW WHAT DIANA IS GOING TO SAY BEFORE SHE SAYS IT.
<YOU MUST GO.>
<WHAT?>
<YOU MEAN RETREAT?>
I KNOW SHE IS RIGHT.
<SHE MEANS WITHDRAW.>
<WITHDRAW FROM THE WORLD, FROM THE PATRIARCHY.>
<YES.>
<WE HAVE LOST OUR PEACE, SISTERS.>
<AND EVEN SHOULD THIS NEXT BATTLE BE WON, THERE WILL BE OTHERS WHO COME IN FEAR AND HATRED.>
<IF YOU STAY, YOU SACRIFICE THE LEGACY OF OUR GODS. YOU SACRIFICE THEIR GIFT TO US OF PEACE...>
<...IT IS TIME FOR YOU TO GO.>
<YOU WON'T COME WITH US?>
I KNOW THIS IS MY FAULT.

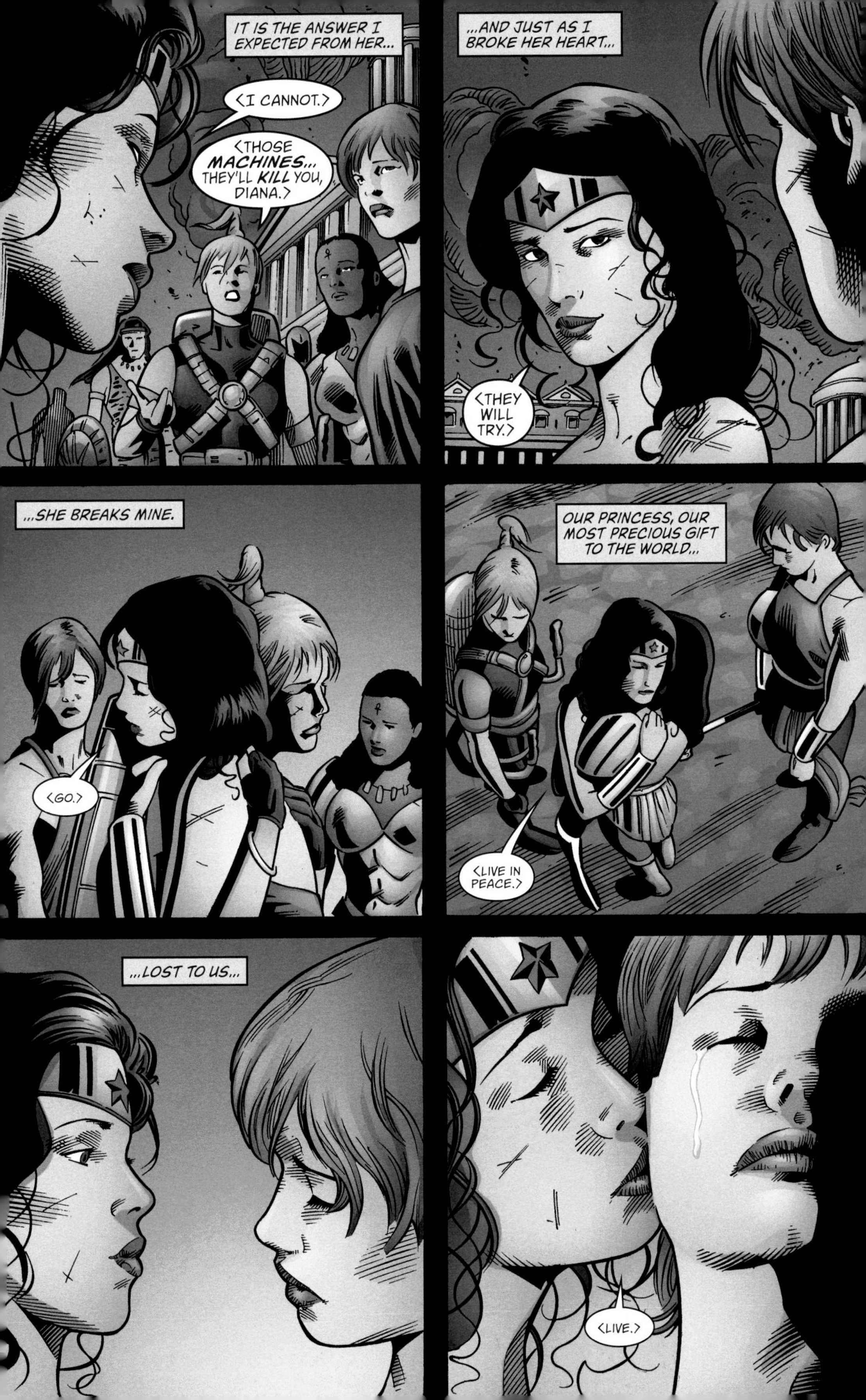

IT IS THE ANSWER I EXPECTED FROM HER...
<I CANNOT.>
<THOSE MACHINES... THEY'LL KILL YOU, DIANA.>
...AND JUST AS I BROKE HER HEART...
<THEY WILL TRY.>
...SHE BREAKS MINE.
<GO.>
OUR PRINCESS, OUR MOST PRECIOUS GIFT TO THE WORLD...
<LIVE IN PEACE.>
...LOST TO US...
<LIVE.>

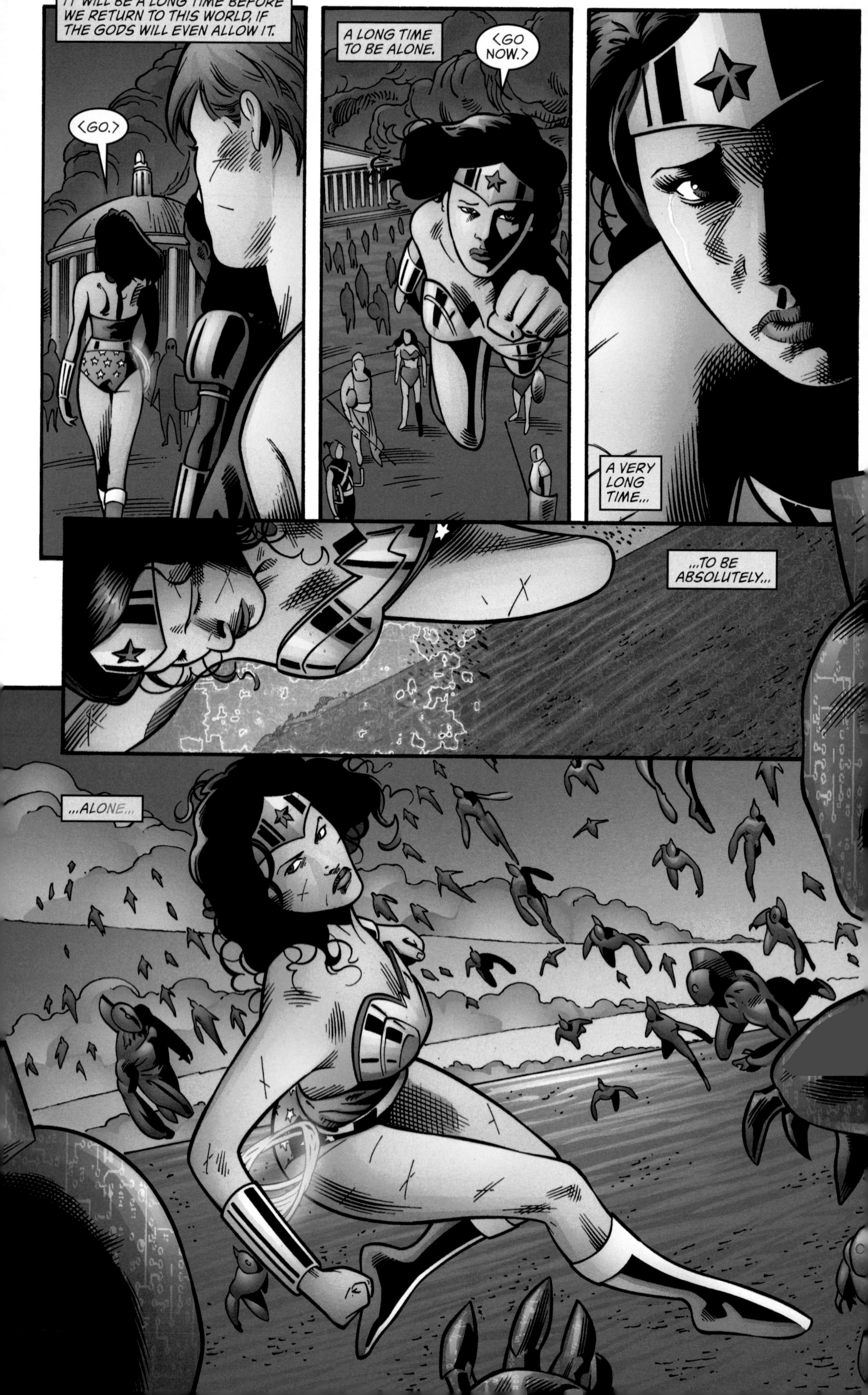
IT WILL BE A LONG TIME BEFORE WE RETURN TO THIS WORLD, IF THE GODS WILL EVEN ALLOW IT.
<GO.>
A LONG TIME TO BE ALONE.
<GO NOW.>
A VERY LONG TIME...
...TO BE ABSOLUTELY...
...ALONE...

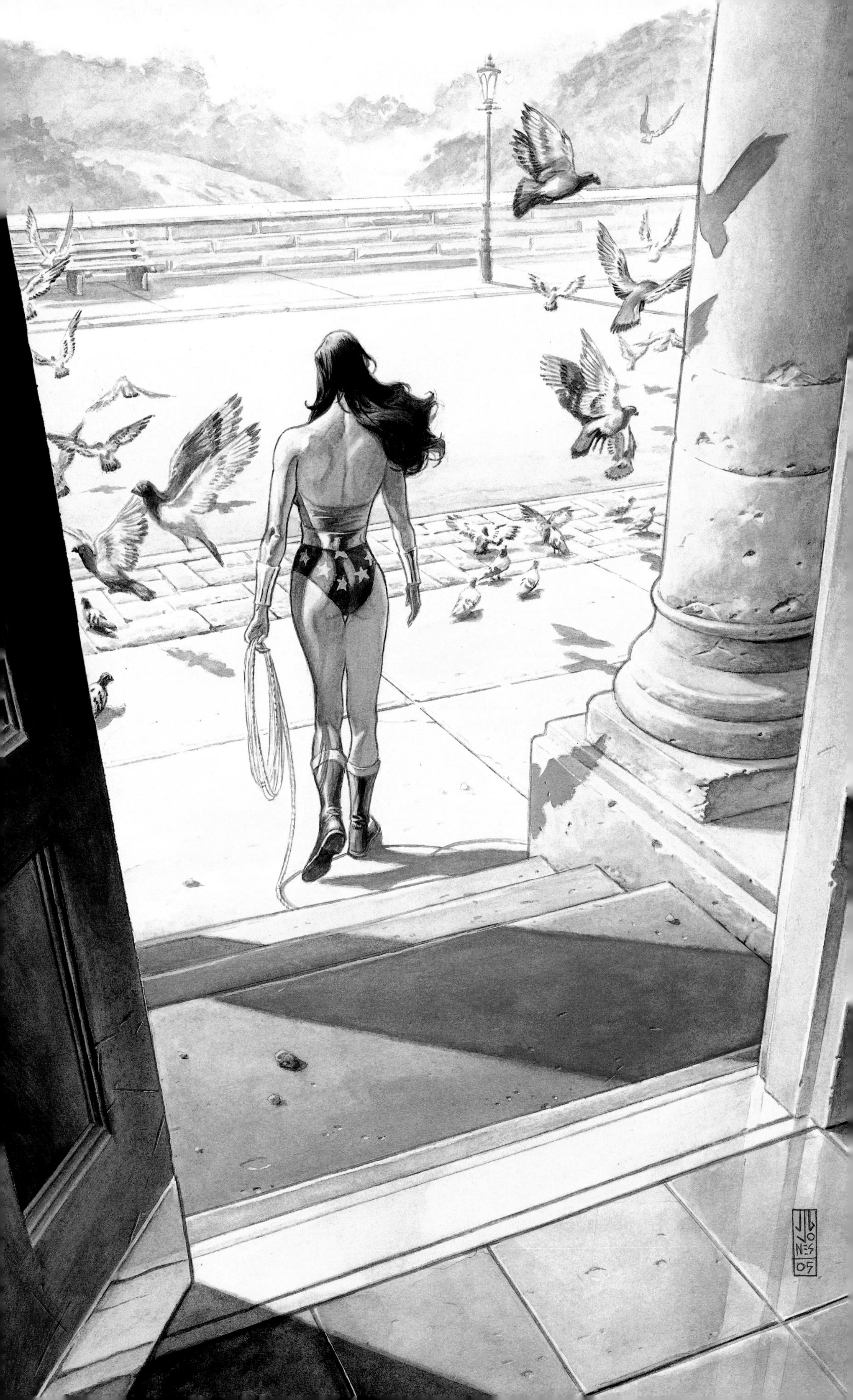

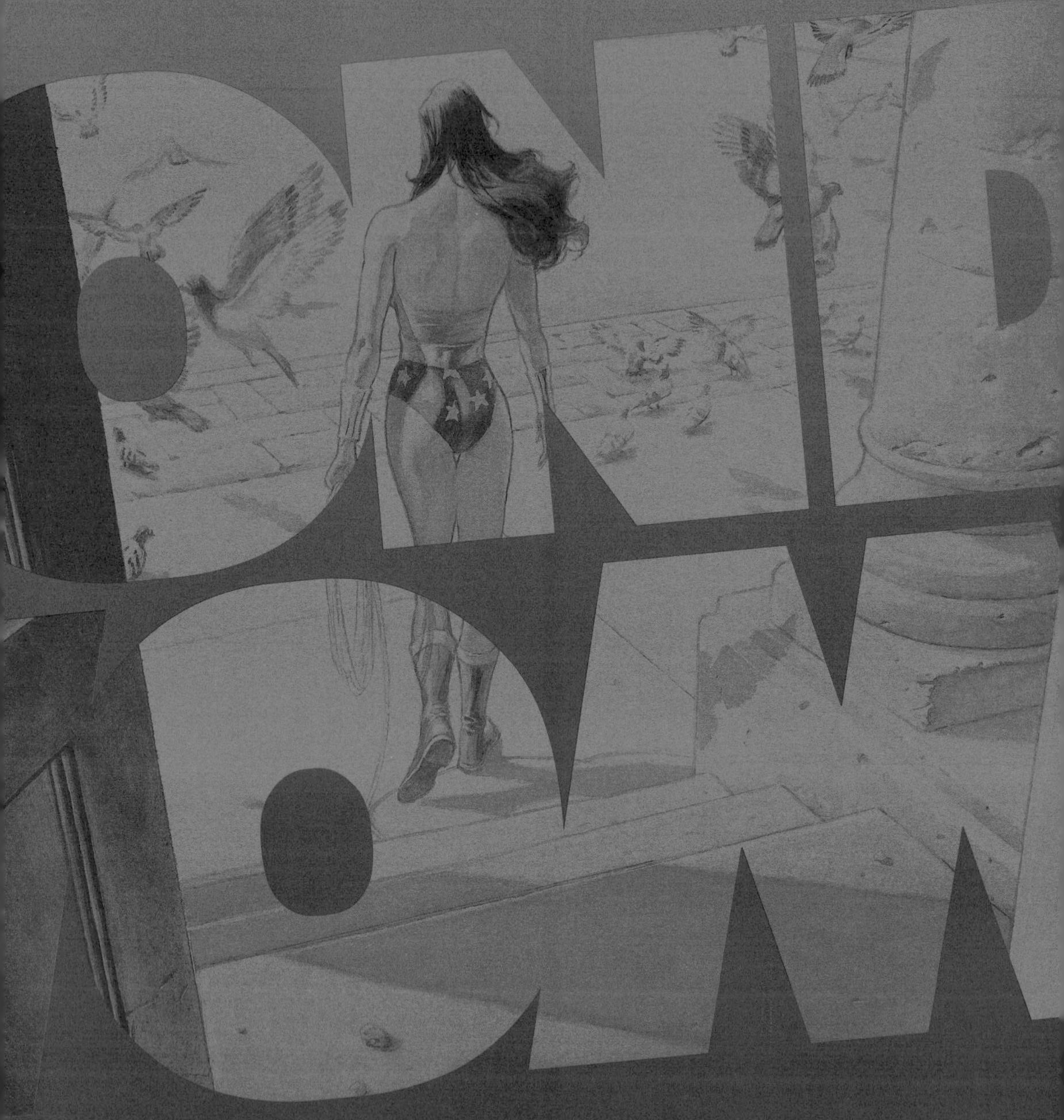

"NOTHING FINISHED, ONLY ABANDONED"

Greg Rucka – *writer*
Cliff Richards – *pencils*
Ray Snyder – *inks*
Richard and **Tanya Horie** – *colors*
Todd Klein – *letters*
J.G. Jones – *cover*

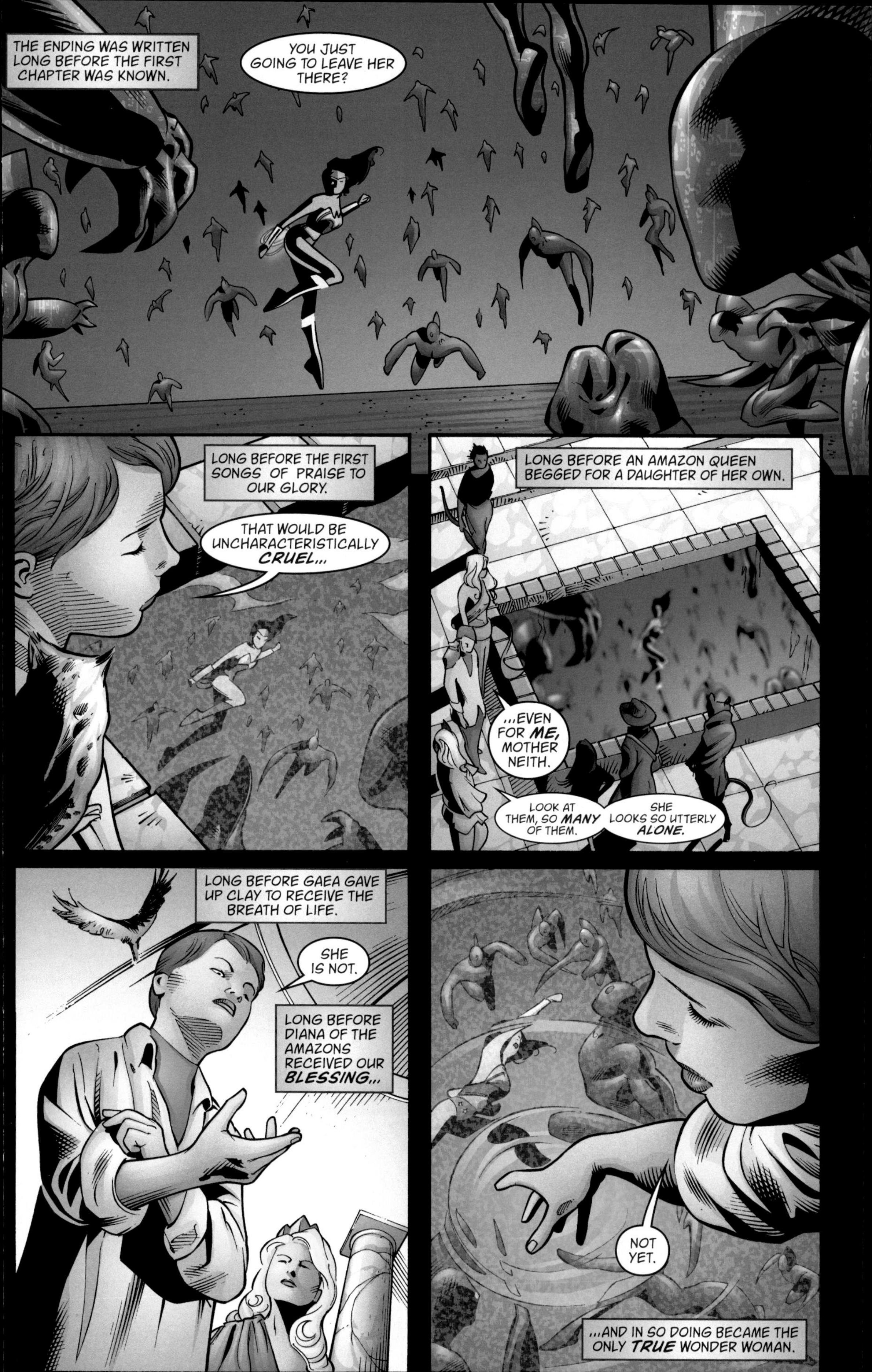
THE ENDING WAS WRITTEN LONG BEFORE THE FIRST CHAPTER WAS KNOWN.
YOU JUST GOING TO LEAVE HER THERE?
LONG BEFORE THE FIRST SONGS OF PRAISE TO OUR GLORY.
THAT WOULD BE UNCHARACTERISTICALLY CRUEL...
LONG BEFORE AN AMAZON QUEEN BEGGED FOR A DAUGHTER OF HER OWN.
...EVEN FOR ME, MOTHER NEITH.
LOOK AT THEM, SO MANY OF THEM.
SHE LOOKS SO UTTERLY ALONE.
LONG BEFORE GAEA GAVE UP CLAY TO RECEIVE THE BREATH OF LIFE.
SHE IS NOT.
LONG BEFORE DIANA OF THE AMAZONS RECEIVED OUR BLESSING...
NOT YET.
...AND IN SO DOING BECAME THE ONLY TRUE WONDER WOMAN.

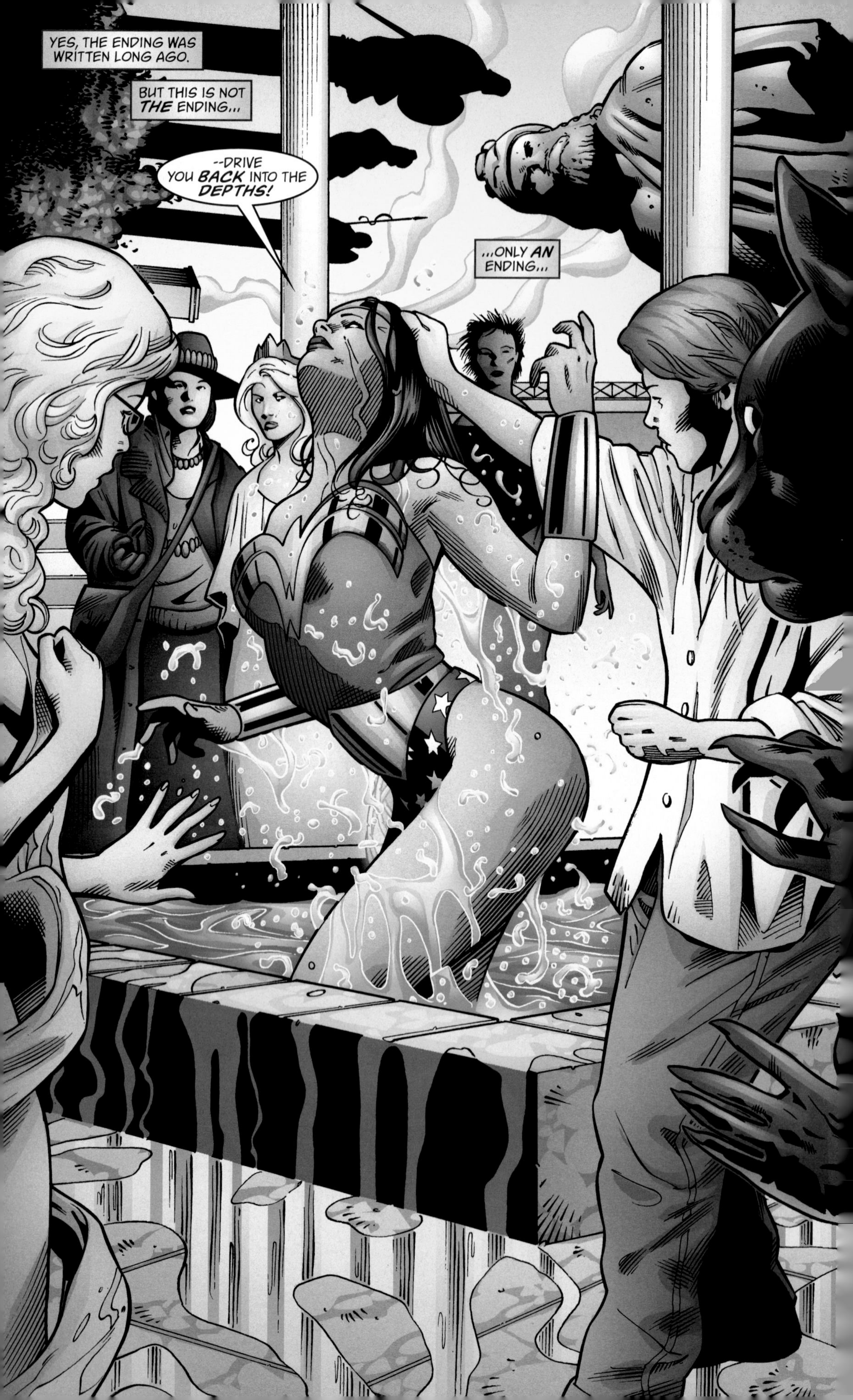
YES, THE ENDING WAS WRITTEN LONG AGO.
BUT THIS IS NOT THE ENDING...
--DRIVE YOU BACK INTO THE DEPTHS!
...ONLY AN ENDING...

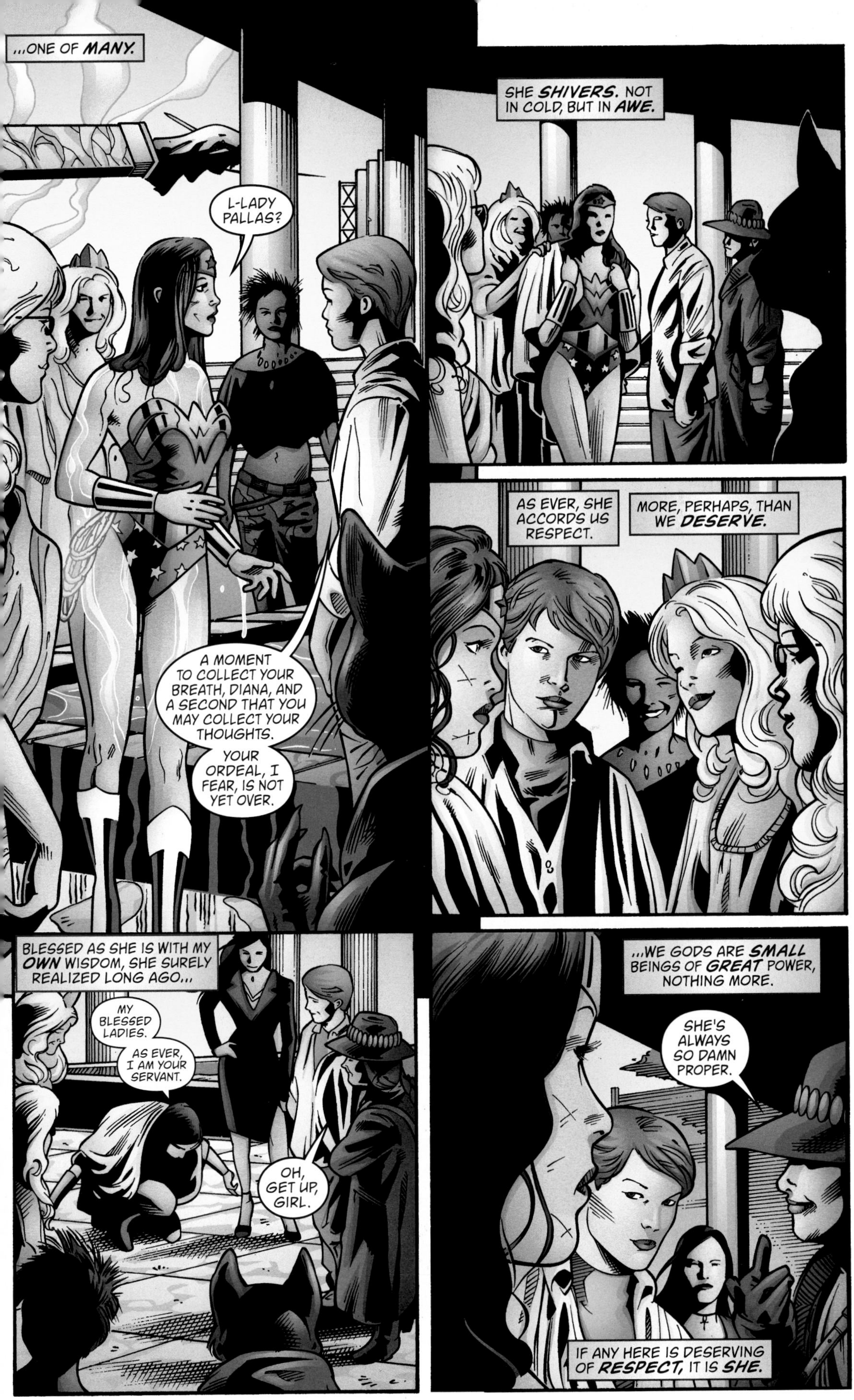
...ONE OF MANY.
L-LADY PALLAS?
A MOMENT TO COLLECT YOUR BREATH, DIANA, AND A SECOND THAT YOU MAY COLLECT YOUR THOUGHTS.
YOUR ORDEAL, I FEAR, IS NOT YET OVER.
SHE SHIVERS. NOT IN COLD, BUT IN AWE.
AS EVER, SHE ACCORDS US RESPECT.
MORE, PERHAPS, THAN WE DESERVE.
BLESSED AS SHE IS WITH MY OWN WISDOM, SHE SURELY REALIZED LONG AGO...
MY BLESSED LADIES.
AS EVER, I AM YOUR SERVANT.
OH, GET UP, GIRL.
...WE GODS ARE SMALL BEINGS OF GREAT POWER, NOTHING MORE.
SHE'S ALWAYS SO DAMN PROPER.
IF ANY HERE IS DESERVING OF RESPECT, IT IS SHE.

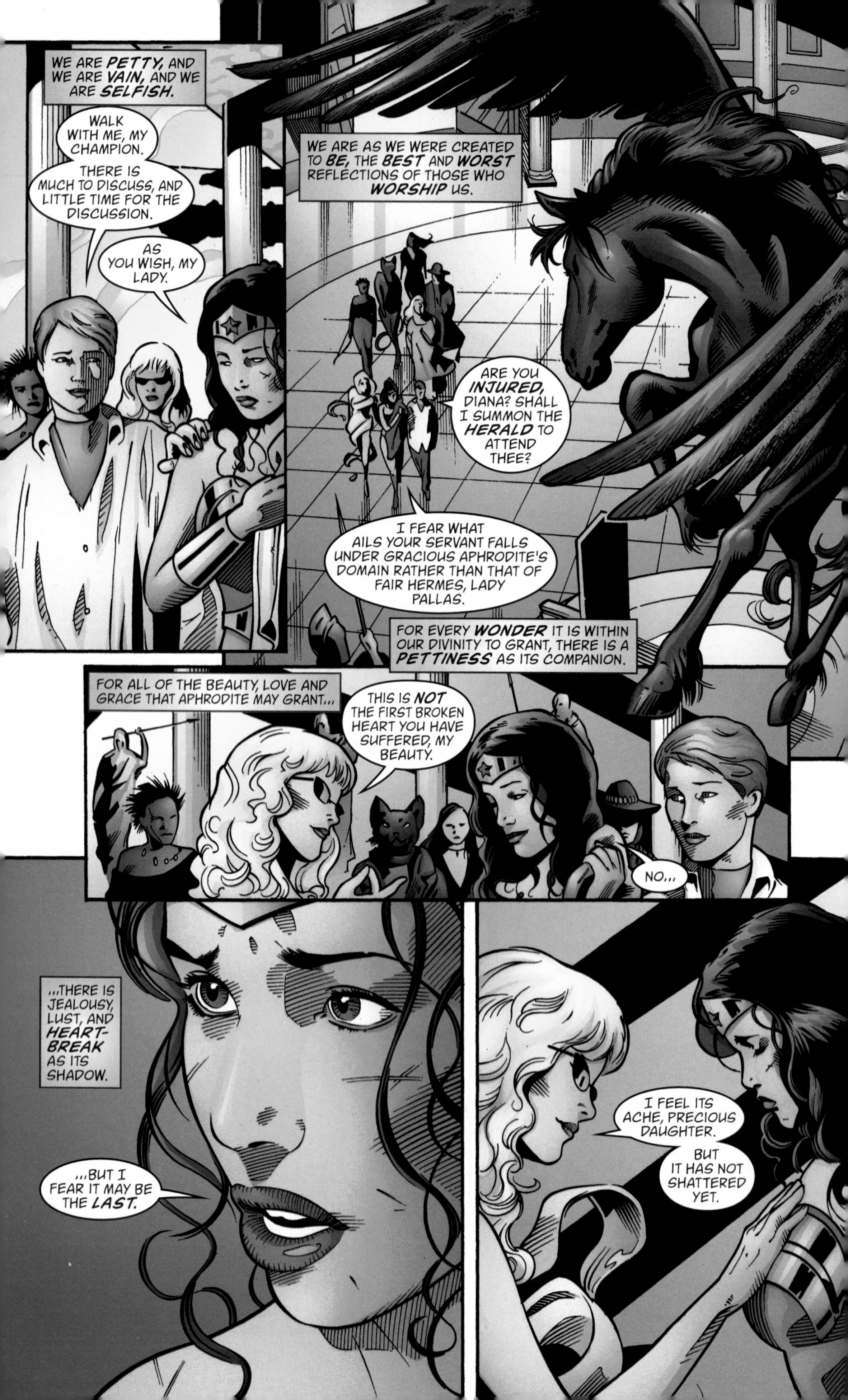

WE ARE PETTY, AND WE ARE VAIN, AND WE ARE SELFISH.
WALK WITH ME, MY CHAMPION.
THERE IS MUCH TO DISCUSS, AND LITTLE TIME FOR THE DISCUSSION.
AS YOU WISH, MY LADY.
WE ARE AS WE WERE CREATED TO BE, THE BEST AND WORST REFLECTIONS OF THOSE WHO WORSHIP US.
ARE YOU INJURED, DIANA? SHALL I SUMMON THE HERALD TO ATTEND THEE?
I FEAR WHAT AILS YOUR SERVANT FALLS UNDER GRACIOUS APHRODITE'S DOMAIN RATHER THAN THAT OF FAIR HERMES, LADY PALLAS.
FOR EVERY WONDER IT IS WITHIN OUR DIVINITY TO GRANT, THERE IS A PETTINESS AS ITS COMPANION.
FOR ALL OF THE BEAUTY, LOVE AND GRACE THAT APHRODITE MAY GRANT...
THIS IS NOT THE FIRST BROKEN HEART YOU HAVE SUFFERED, MY BEAUTY.
NO...
...THERE IS JEALOUSY, LUST, AND HEART-BREAK AS ITS SHADOW.
...BUT I FEAR IT MAY BE THE LAST.
I FEEL ITS ACHE, PRECIOUS DAUGHTER.
BUT IT HAS NOT SHATTERED YET.

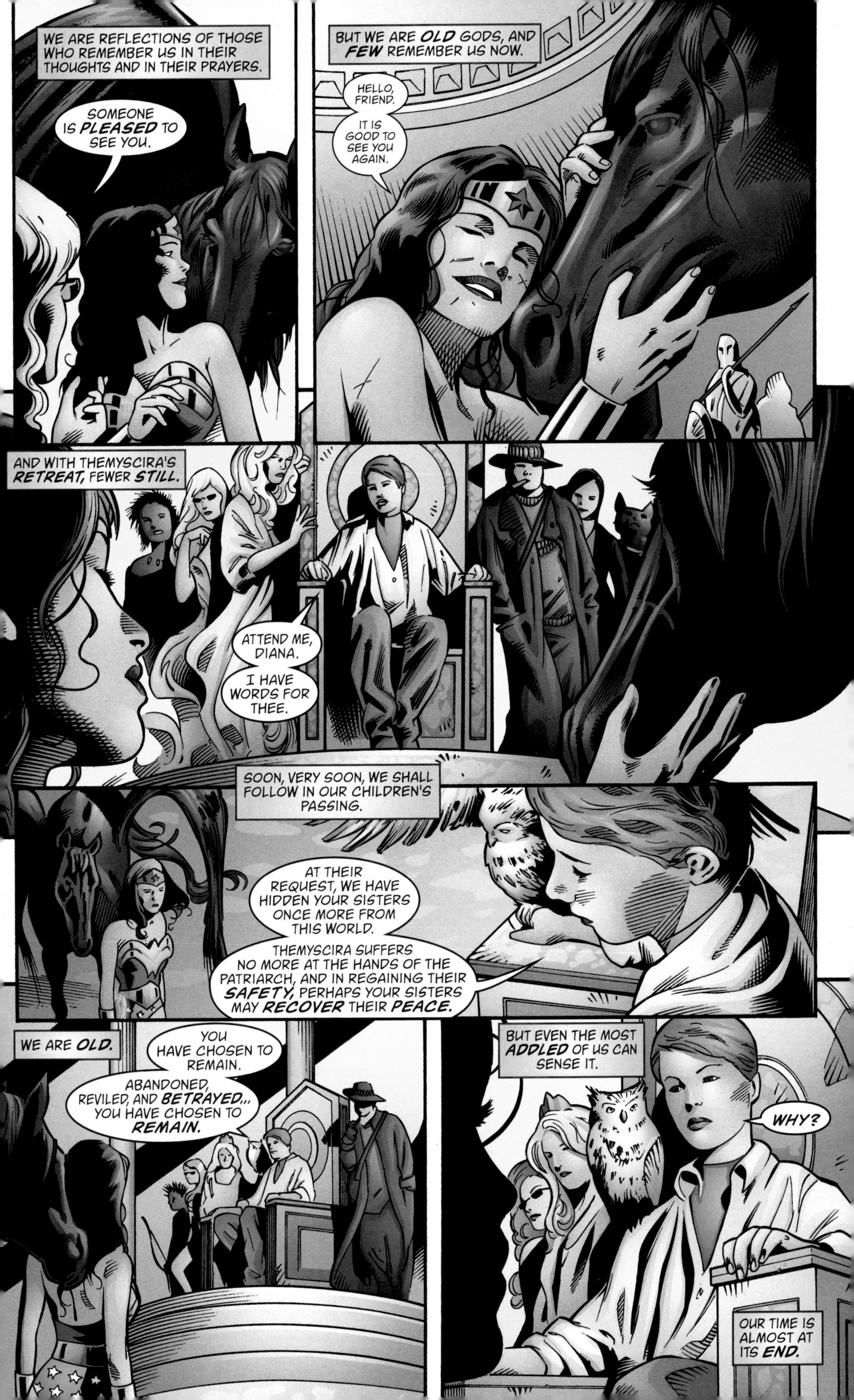
WE ARE REFLECTIONS OF THOSE WHO REMEMBER US IN THEIR THOUGHTS AND IN THEIR PRAYERS.
SOMEONE IS PLEASED TO SEE YOU.
BUT WE ARE OLD GODS, AND FEW REMEMBER US NOW.
HELLO, FRIEND.
IT IS GOOD TO SEE YOU AGAIN.
AND WITH THEMYSCIRA'S RETREAT, FEWER STILL.
ATTEND ME, DIANA.
I HAVE WORDS FOR THEE.
SOON, VERY SOON, WE SHALL FOLLOW IN OUR CHILDREN'S PASSING.
AT THEIR REQUEST, WE HAVE HIDDEN YOUR SISTERS ONCE MORE FROM THIS WORLD.
THEMYSCIRA SUFFERS NO MORE AT THE HANDS OF THE PATRIARCH, AND IN REGAINING THEIR SAFETY, PERHAPS YOUR SISTERS MAY RECOVER THEIR PEACE.
WE ARE OLD.
YOU HAVE CHOSEN TO REMAIN.
ABANDONED, REVILED, AND BETRAYED... YOU HAVE CHOSEN TO REMAIN.
BUT EVEN THE MOST ADDLED OF US CAN SENSE IT.
WHY?
OUR TIME IS ALMOST AT ITS END.

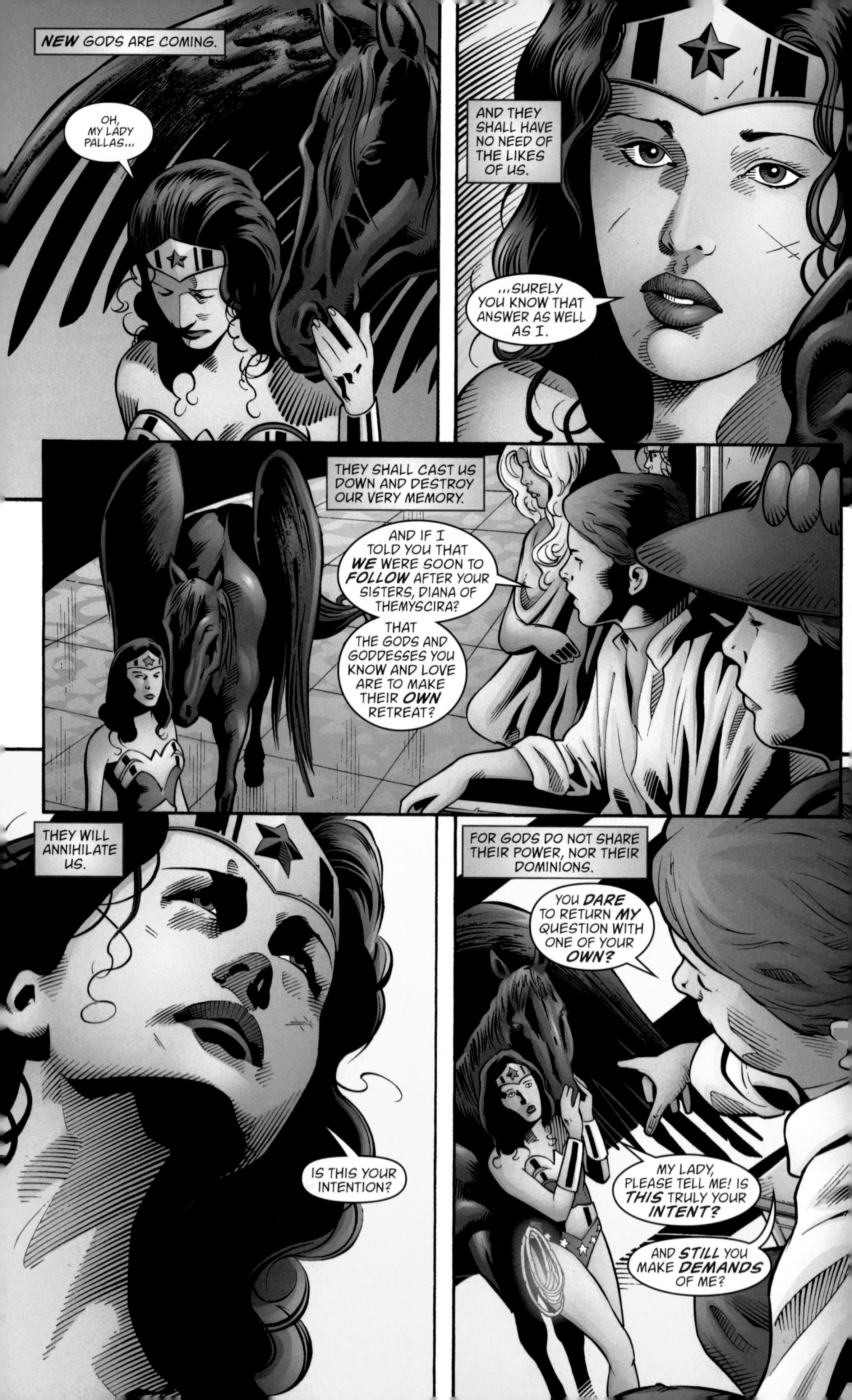
NEW GODS ARE COMING.
OH, MY LADY PALLAS...
AND THEY SHALL HAVE NO NEED OF THE LIKES OF US.
...SURELY YOU KNOW THAT ANSWER AS WELL AS I.
THEY SHALL CAST US DOWN AND DESTROY OUR VERY MEMORY.
AND IF I TOLD YOU THAT WE WERE SOON TO FOLLOW AFTER YOUR SISTERS, DIANA OF THEMYSCIRA?
THAT THE GODS AND GODDESSES YOU KNOW AND LOVE ARE TO MAKE THEIR OWN RETREAT?
THEY WILL ANNIHILATE US.
IS THIS YOUR INTENTION?
FOR GODS DO NOT SHARE THEIR POWER, NOR THEIR DOMINIONS.
YOU DARE TO RETURN MY QUESTION WITH ONE OF YOUR OWN?
MY LADY, PLEASE TELL ME! IS THIS TRULY YOUR INTENT?
AND STILL YOU MAKE DEMANDS OF ME?

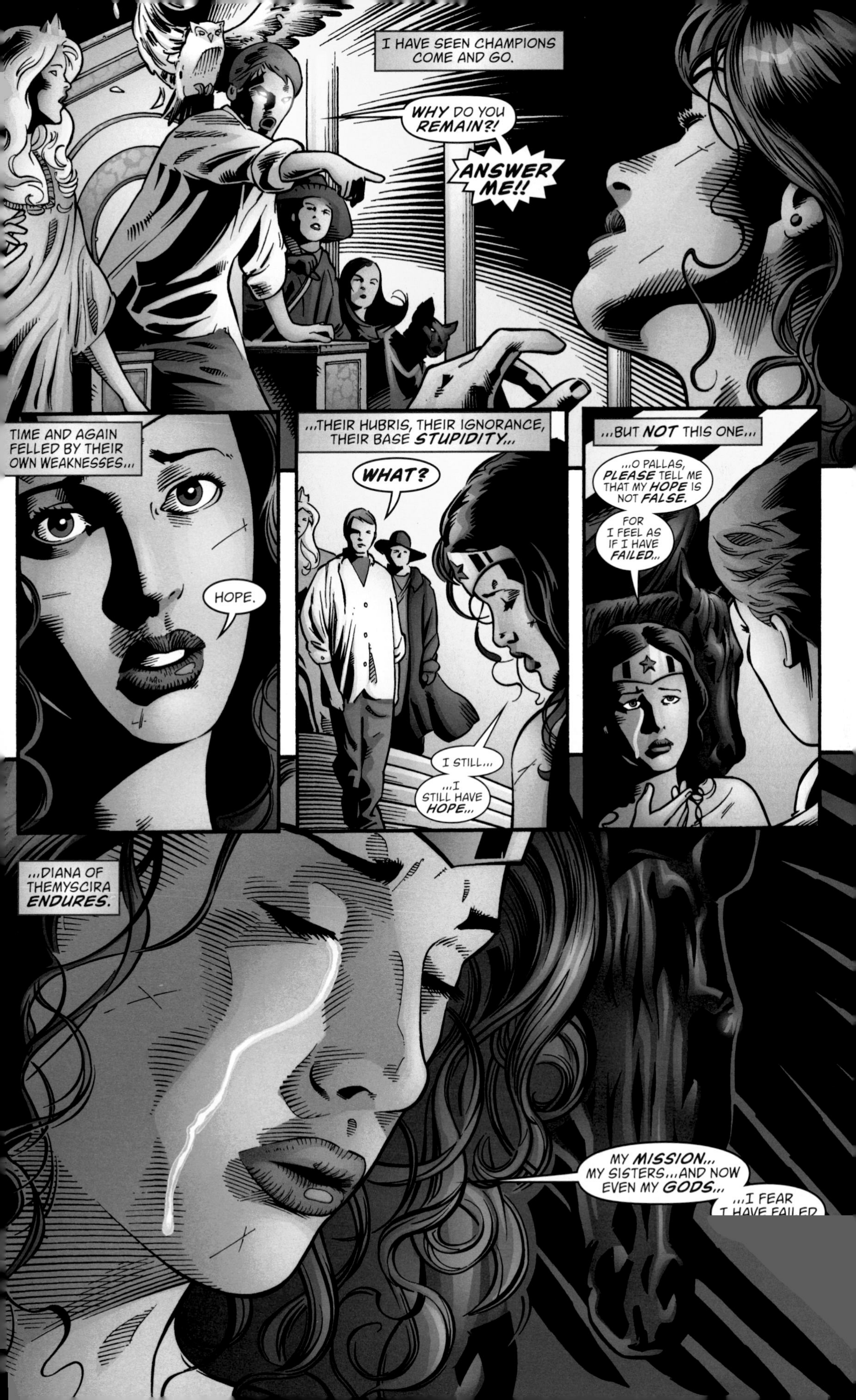
I HAVE SEEN CHAMPIONS COME AND GO.
WHY DO YOU REMAIN?!
ANSWER ME!!
TIME AND AGAIN FELLED BY THEIR OWN WEAKNESSES...
HOPE.
...THEIR HUBRIS, THEIR IGNORANCE, THEIR BASE STUPIDITY...
WHAT?
I STILL...
...I STILL HAVE HOPE...
...BUT NOT THIS ONE...
...O PALLAS, PLEASE TELL ME THAT MY HOPE IS NOT FALSE.
FOR I FEEL AS IF I HAVE FAILED...
...DIANA OF THEMYSCIRA ENDURES.
MY MISSION... MY SISTERS... AND NOW EVEN MY GODS...
...I FEAR

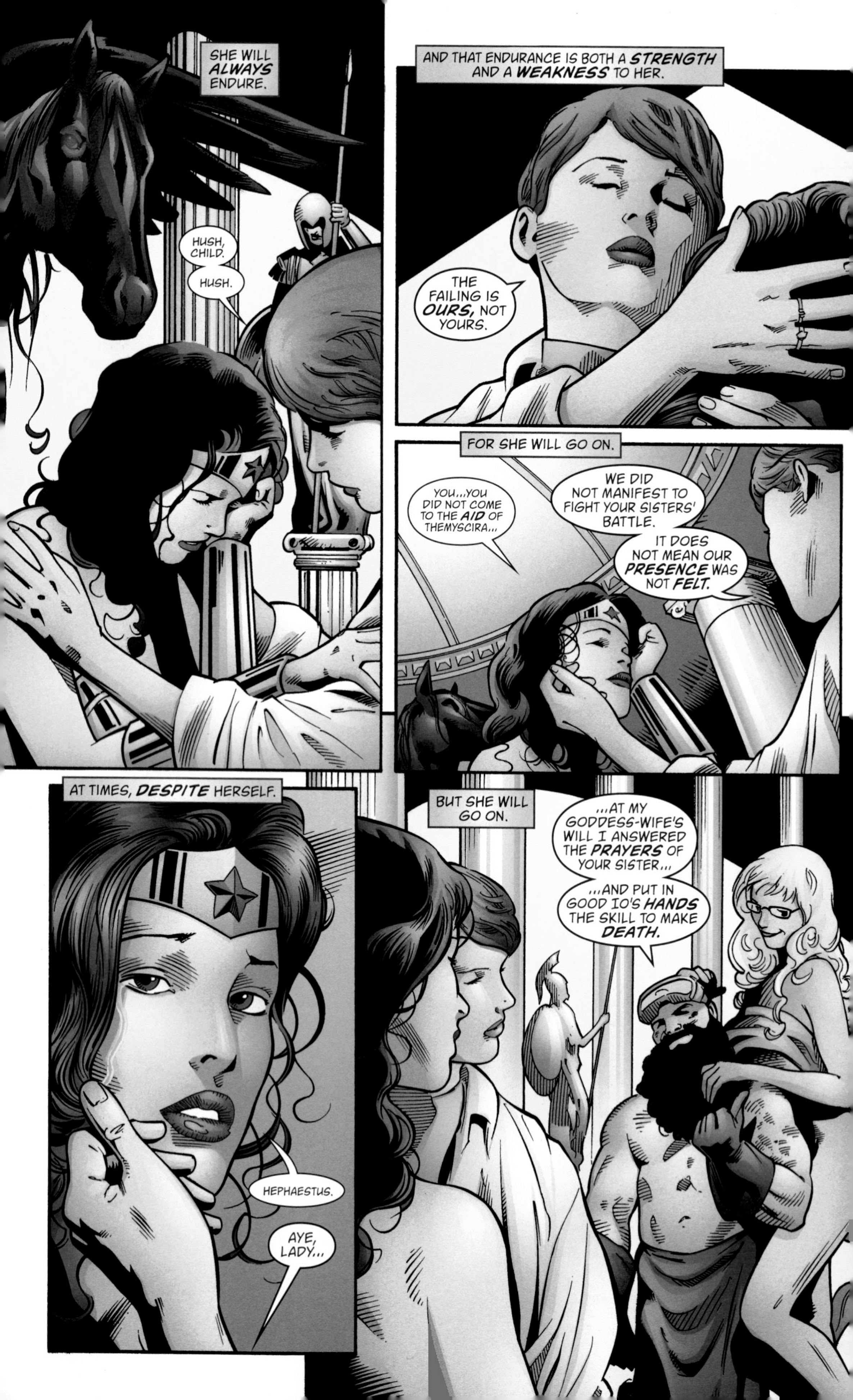
SHE WILL ALWAYS ENDURE.
HUSH, CHILD.
HUSH.
AND THAT ENDURANCE IS BOTH A STRENGTH AND A WEAKNESS TO HER.
THE FAILING IS OURS, NOT YOURS.
FOR SHE WILL GO ON.
YOU...YOU DID NOT COME TO THE AID OF THEMYSCIRA...
WE DID NOT MANIFEST TO FIGHT YOUR SISTERS' BATTLE.
IT DOES NOT MEAN OUR PRESENCE WAS NOT FELT.
AT TIMES, DESPITE HERSELF.
HEPHAESTUS.
AYE, LADY...
BUT SHE WILL GO ON.
...AT MY GODDESS-WIFE'S WILL I ANSWERED THE PRAYERS OF YOUR SISTER...
...AND PUT IN GOOD IO'S HANDS THE SKILL TO MAKE DEATH.

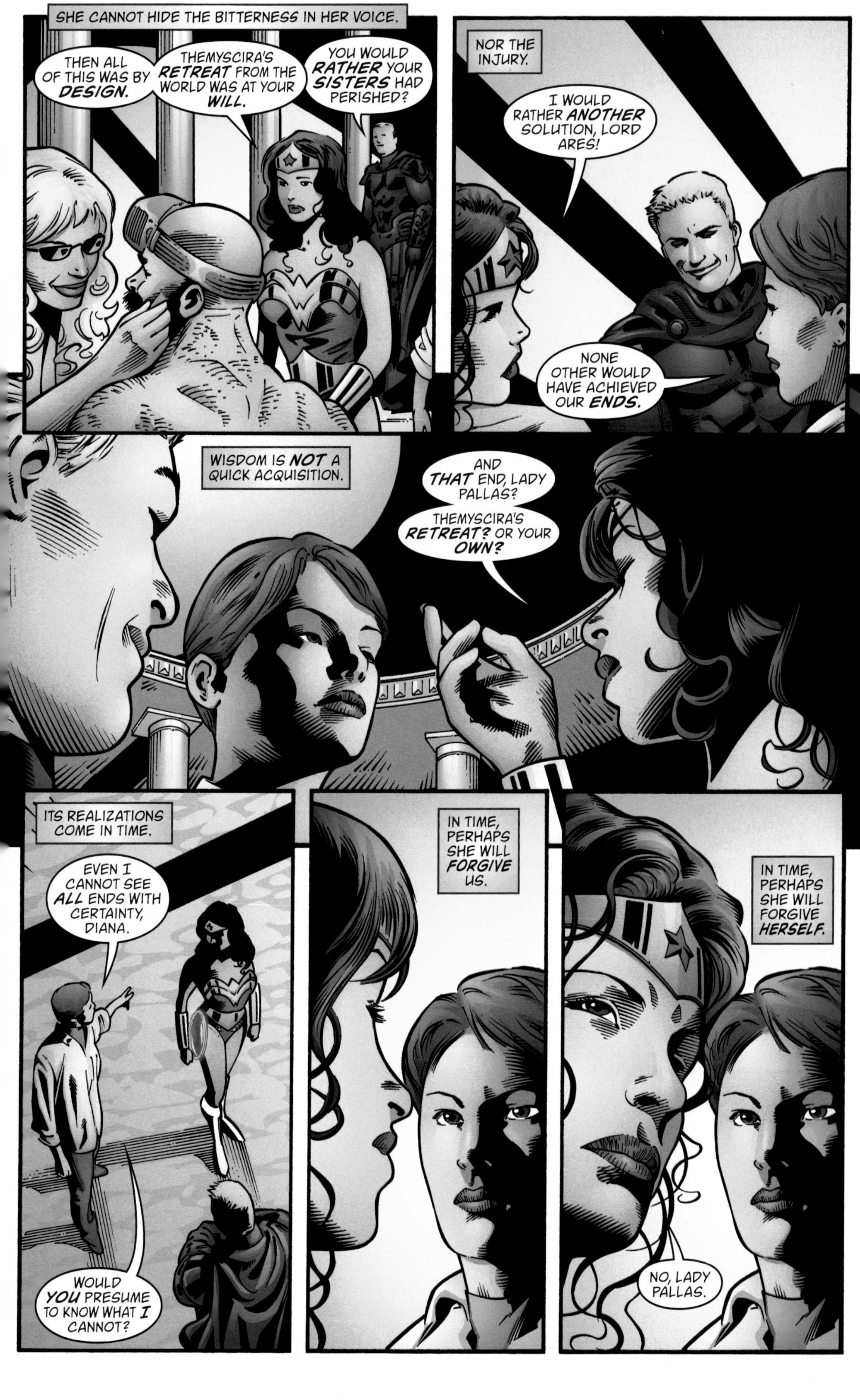
SHE CANNOT HIDE THE BITTERNESS IN HER VOICE.
THEN ALL OF THIS WAS BY DESIGN.
THEMYSCIRA'S RETREAT FROM THE WORLD WAS AT YOUR WILL.
YOU WOULD RATHER YOUR SISTERS HAD PERISHED?
NOR THE INJURY.
I WOULD RATHER ANOTHER SOLUTION, LORD ARES!
NONE OTHER WOULD HAVE ACHIEVED OUR ENDS.
WISDOM IS NOT A QUICK ACQUISITION.
AND THAT END, LADY PALLAS?
THEMYSCIRA'S RETREAT? OR YOUR OWN?
ITS REALIZATIONS COME IN TIME.
EVEN I CANNOT SEE ALL ENDS WITH CERTAINTY, DIANA.
WOULD YOU PRESUME TO KNOW WHAT I CANNOT?
IN TIME, PERHAPS SHE WILL FORGIVE US.
IN TIME, PERHAPS SHE WILL FORGIVE HERSELF.
NO, LADY PALLAS.

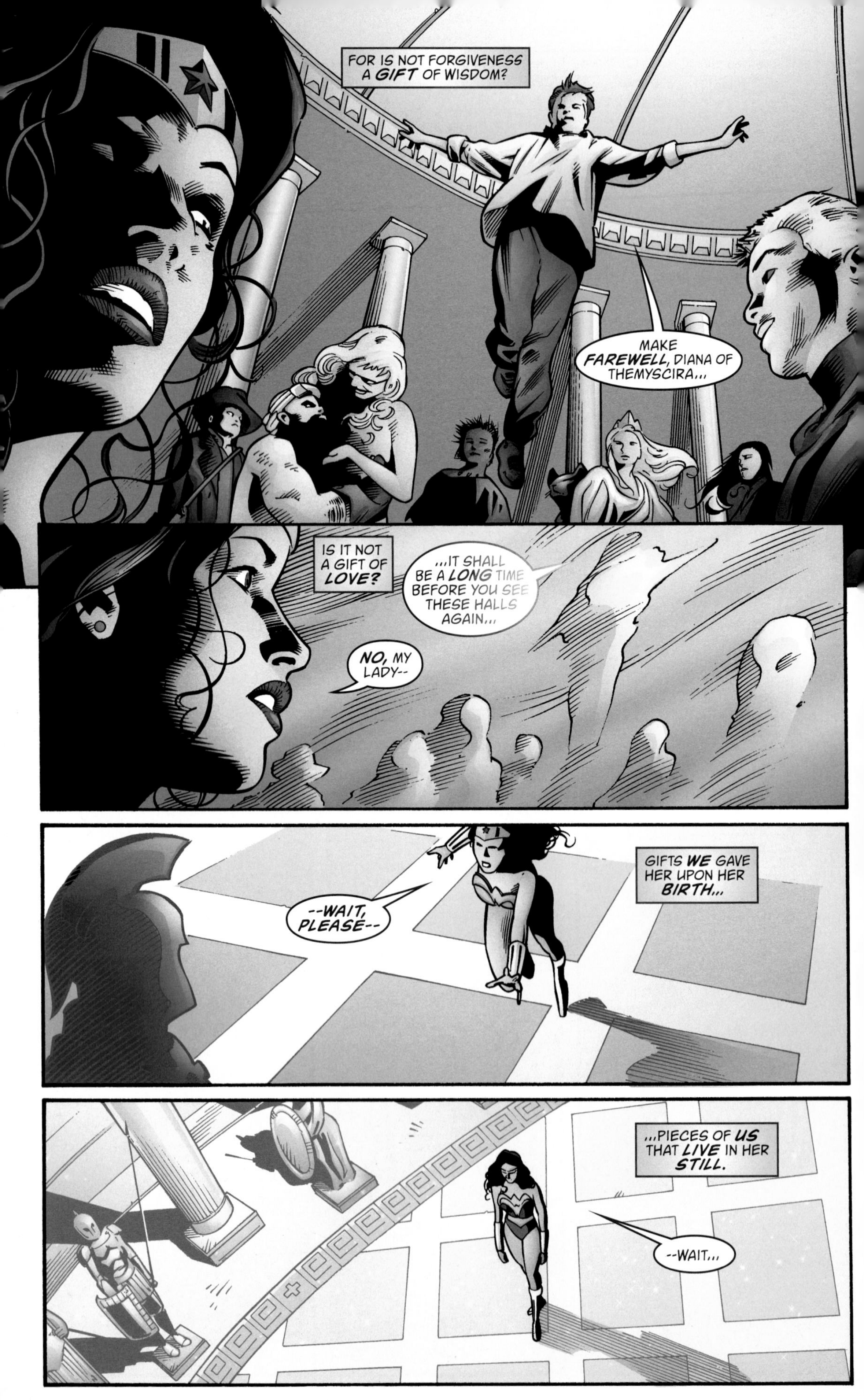
FOR IS NOT FORGIVENESS A GIFT OF WISDOM?
MAKE FAREWELL, DIANA OF THEMYSCIRA...
IS IT NOT A GIFT OF LOVE?
...IT SHALL BE A LONG TIME BEFORE YOU SEE THESE HALLS AGAIN...
NO, MY LADY--
GIFTS WE GAVE HER UPON HER BIRTH...
--WAIT, PLEASE--
...PIECES OF US THAT LIVE IN HER STILL.
--WAIT...

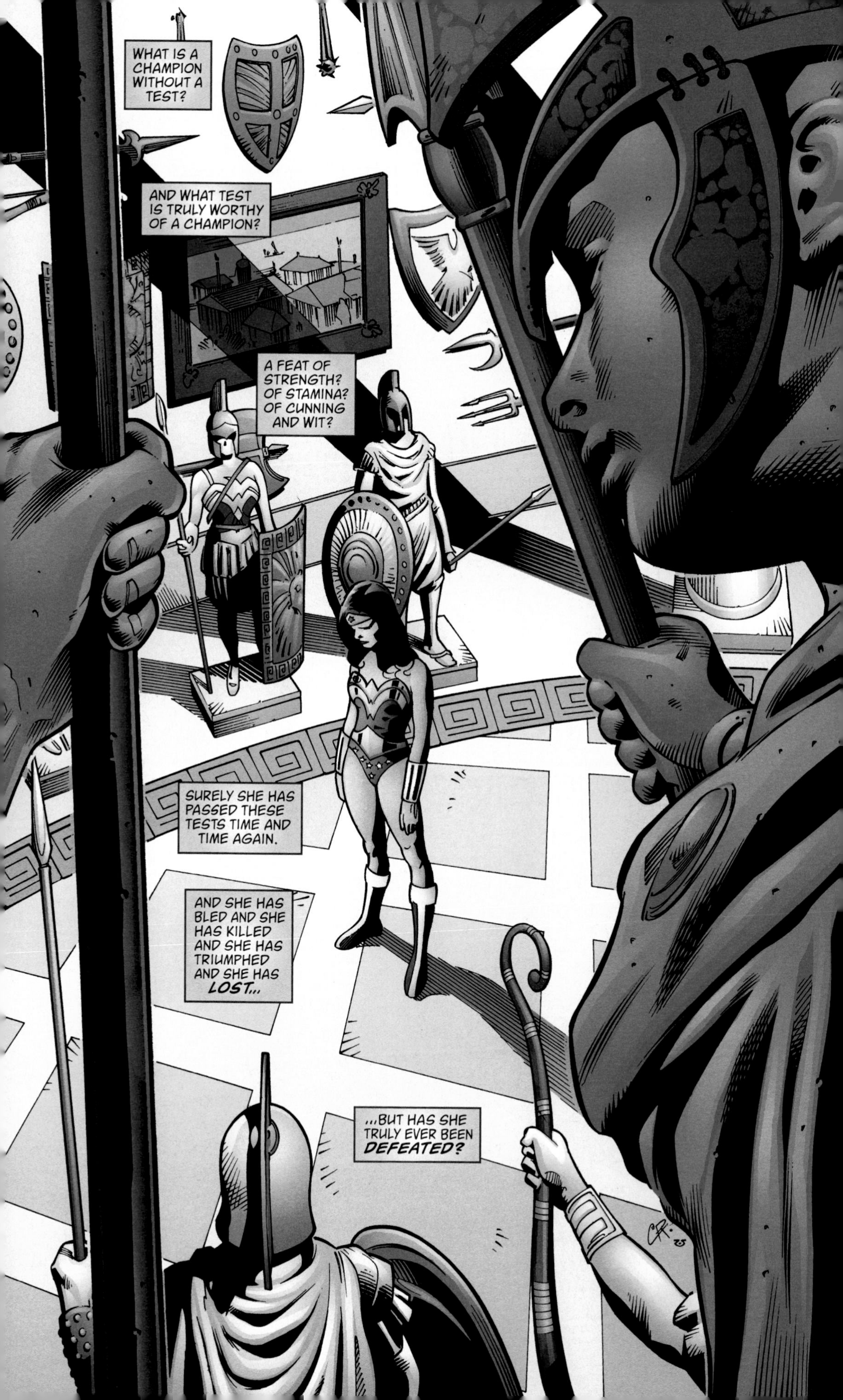
WHAT IS A CHAMPION WITHOUT A TEST?
AND WHAT TEST IS TRULY WORTHY OF A CHAMPION?
A FEAT OF STRENGTH? OF STAMINA? OF CUNNING AND WIT?
SURELY SHE HAS PASSED THESE TESTS TIME AND TIME AGAIN.
AND SHE HAS BLED AND SHE HAS KILLED AND SHE HAS TRIUMPHED AND SHE HAS LOST...
...BUT HAS SHE TRULY EVER BEEN DEFEATED?

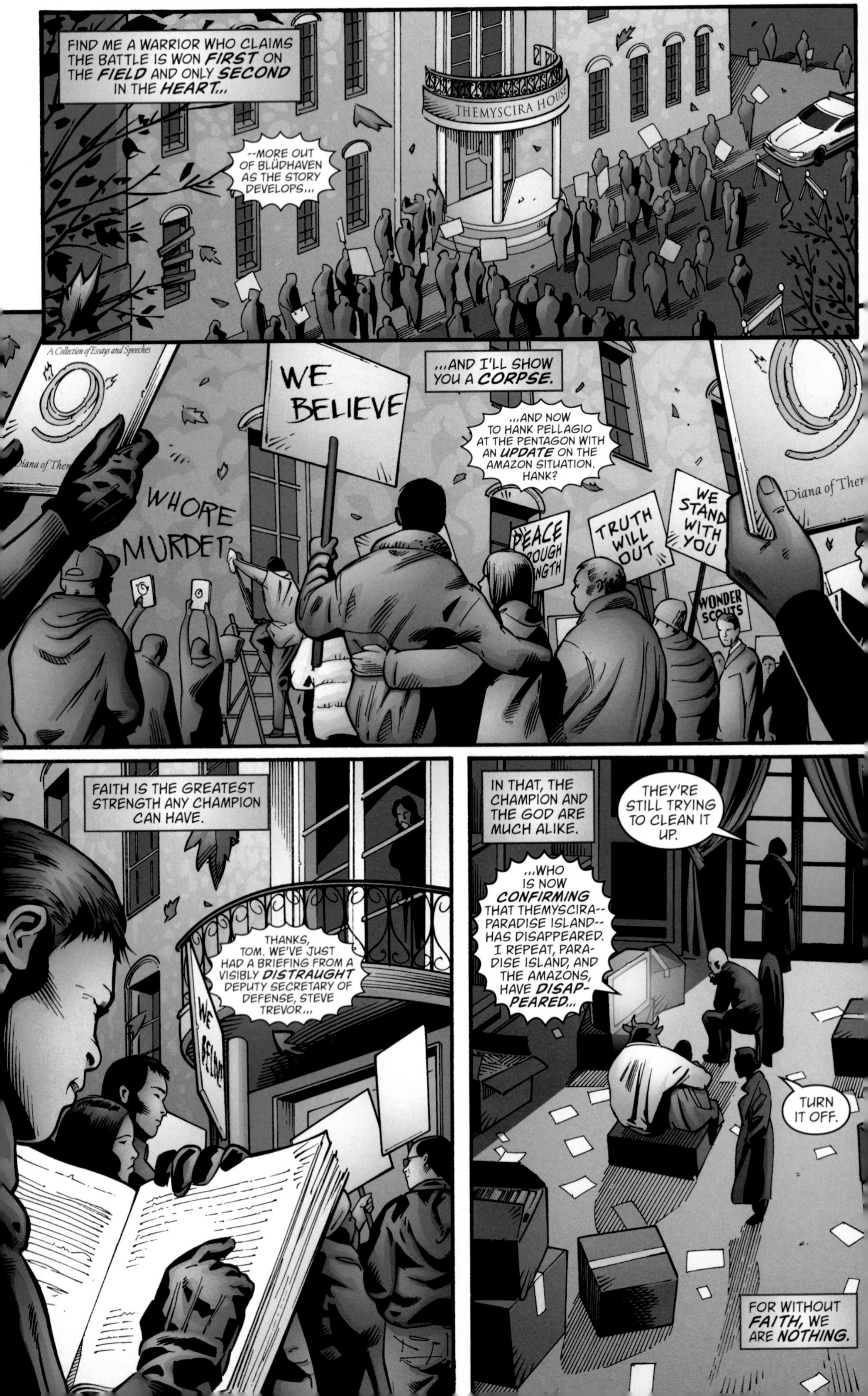
FIND ME A WARRIOR WHO CLAIMS THE BATTLE IS WON FIRST ON THE FIELD AND ONLY SECOND IN THE HEART...
THEMYSCIRA HOUSE
--MORE OUT OF BLÜDHAVEN AS THE STORY DEVELOPS...
A Collection of Essays and Speeches
Diana of Ther
WE BELIEVE
...AND I'LL SHOW YOU A CORPSE.
...AND NOW TO HANK PELLAGIO AT THE PENTAGON WITH AN UPDATE ON THE AMAZON SITUATION. HANK?
WHORE
MURDER
PEACE ROUGH NGTH
TRUTH WILL OUT
WE STAND WITH YOU
Diana of Ther
WONDER SCOUTS
FAITH IS THE GREATEST STRENGTH ANY CHAMPION CAN HAVE.
THANKS, TOM. WE'VE JUST HAD A BRIEFING FROM A VISIBLY DISTRAUGHT DEPUTY SECRETARY OF DEFENSE, STEVE TREVOR...
IN THAT, THE CHAMPION AND THE GOD ARE MUCH ALIKE.
THEY'RE STILL TRYING TO CLEAN IT UP.
...WHO IS NOW CONFIRMING THAT THEMYSCIRA--PARADISE ISLAND--HAS DISAPPEARED. I REPEAT, PARADISE ISLAND, AND THE AMAZONS, HAVE DISAPPEARED...
TURN IT OFF.
FOR WITHOUT FAITH, WE ARE NOTHING.

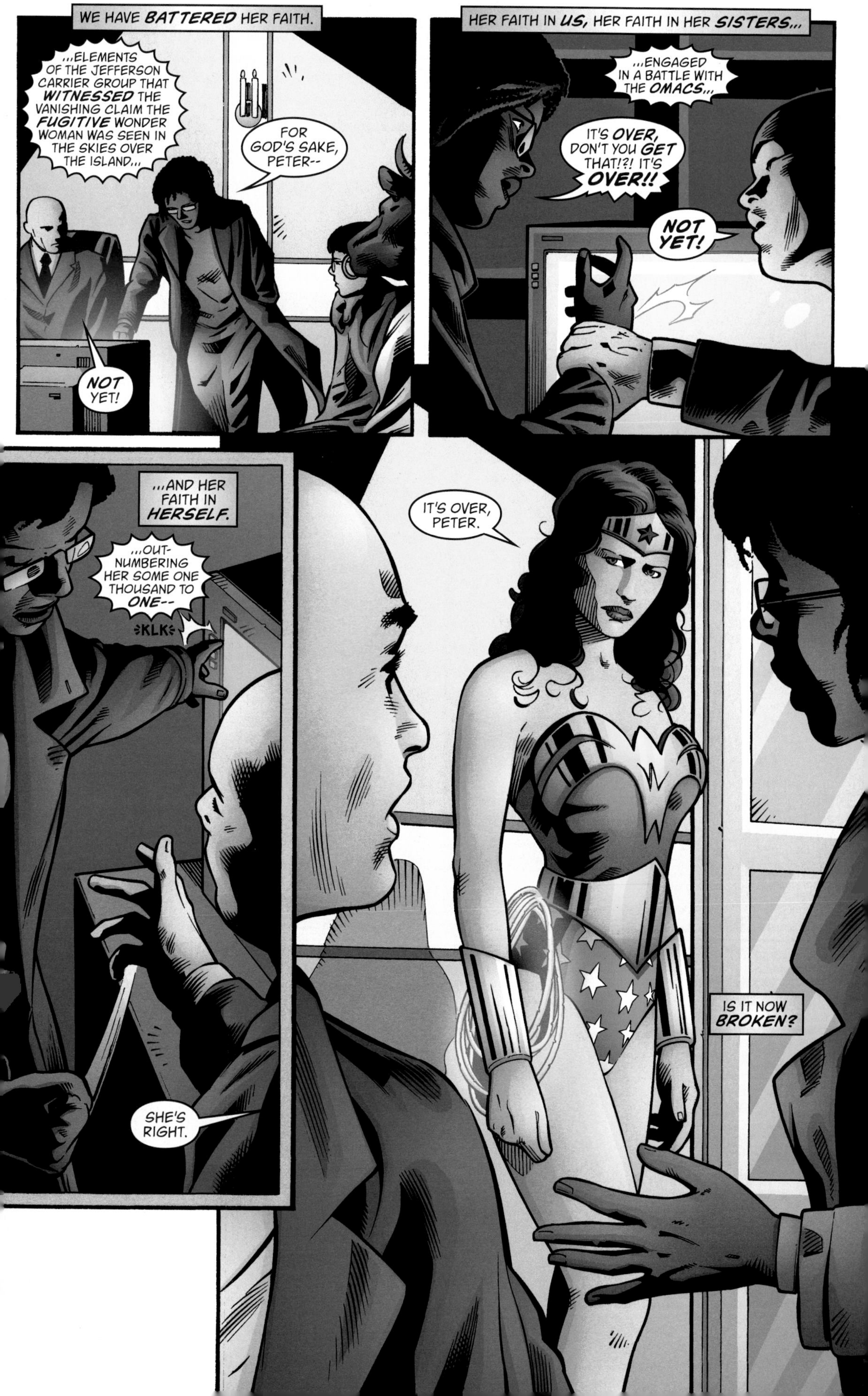

WE HAVE BATTERED HER FAITH.
...ELEMENTS OF THE JEFFERSON CARRIER GROUP THAT WITNESSED THE VANISHING CLAIM THE FUGITIVE WONDER WOMAN WAS SEEN IN THE SKIES OVER THE ISLAND...
FOR GOD'S SAKE, PETER--
NOT YET!
HER FAITH IN US, HER FAITH IN HER SISTERS...
...ENGAGED IN A BATTLE WITH THE OMACS...
IT'S OVER, DON'T YOU GET THAT!?! IT'S OVER!!
NOT YET!
...AND HER FAITH IN HERSELF.
...OUT-NUMBERING HER SOME ONE THOUSAND TO ONE--
KLK
SHE'S RIGHT.
IT'S OVER, PETER.
IS IT NOW BROKEN?

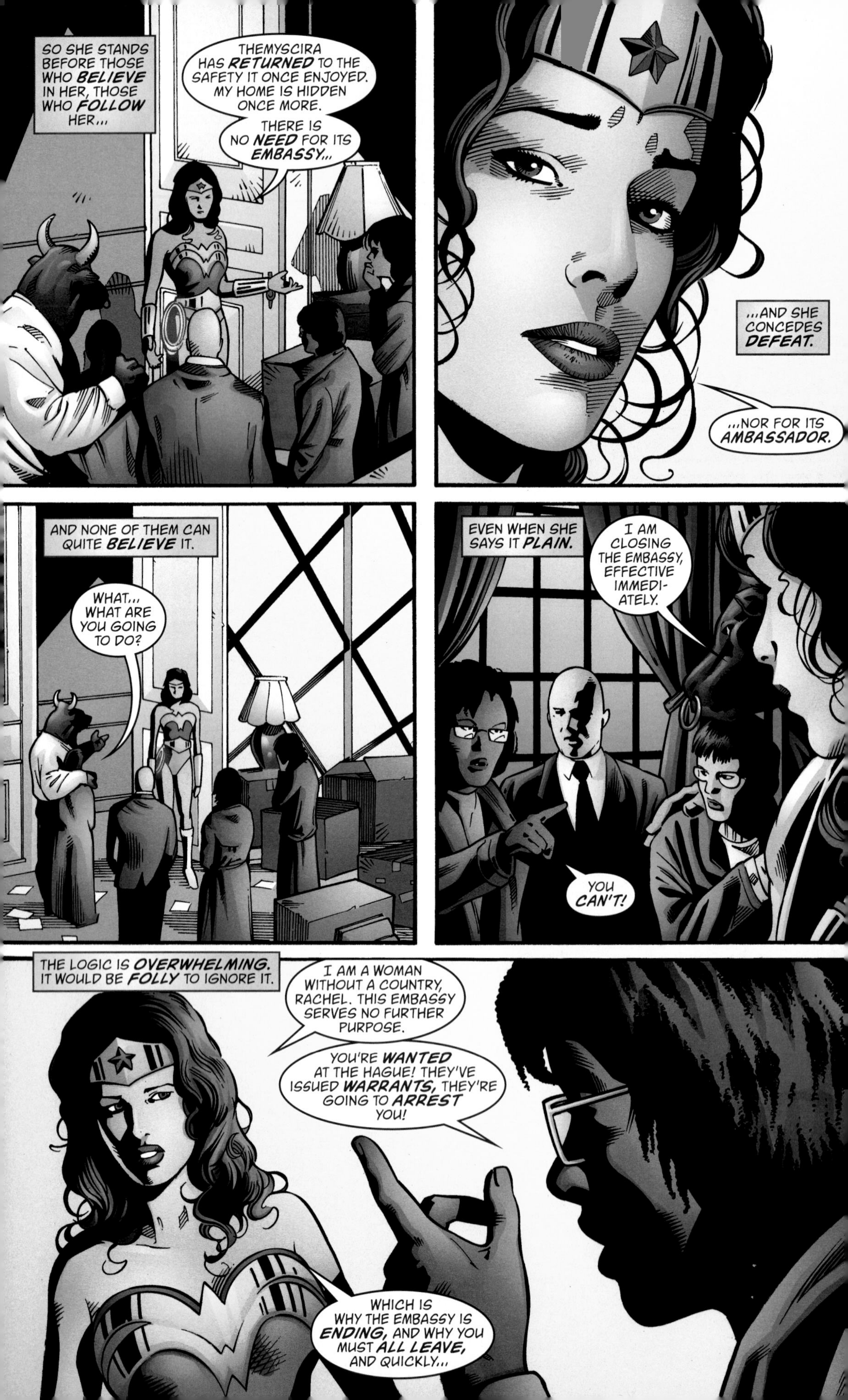
SO SHE STANDS BEFORE THOSE WHO BELIEVE IN HER, THOSE WHO FOLLOW HER...
THEMYSCIRA HAS RETURNED TO THE SAFETY IT ONCE ENJOYED. MY HOME IS HIDDEN ONCE MORE.
THERE IS NO NEED FOR ITS EMBASSY...
...AND SHE CONCEDES DEFEAT.
...NOR FOR ITS AMBASSADOR.
AND NONE OF THEM CAN QUITE BELIEVE IT.
WHAT... WHAT ARE YOU GOING TO DO?
EVEN WHEN SHE SAYS IT PLAIN.
I AM CLOSING THE EMBASSY, EFFECTIVE IMMEDI-ATELY.
YOU CAN'T!
THE LOGIC IS OVERWHELMING. IT WOULD BE FOLLY TO IGNORE IT.
I AM A WOMAN WITHOUT A COUNTRY, RACHEL. THIS EMBASSY SERVES NO FURTHER PURPOSE.
YOU'RE WANTED AT THE HAGUE! THEY'VE ISSUED WARRANTS, THEY'RE GOING TO ARREST YOU!
WHICH IS WHY THE EMBASSY IS ENDING, AND WHY YOU MUST ALL LEAVE, AND QUICKLY...

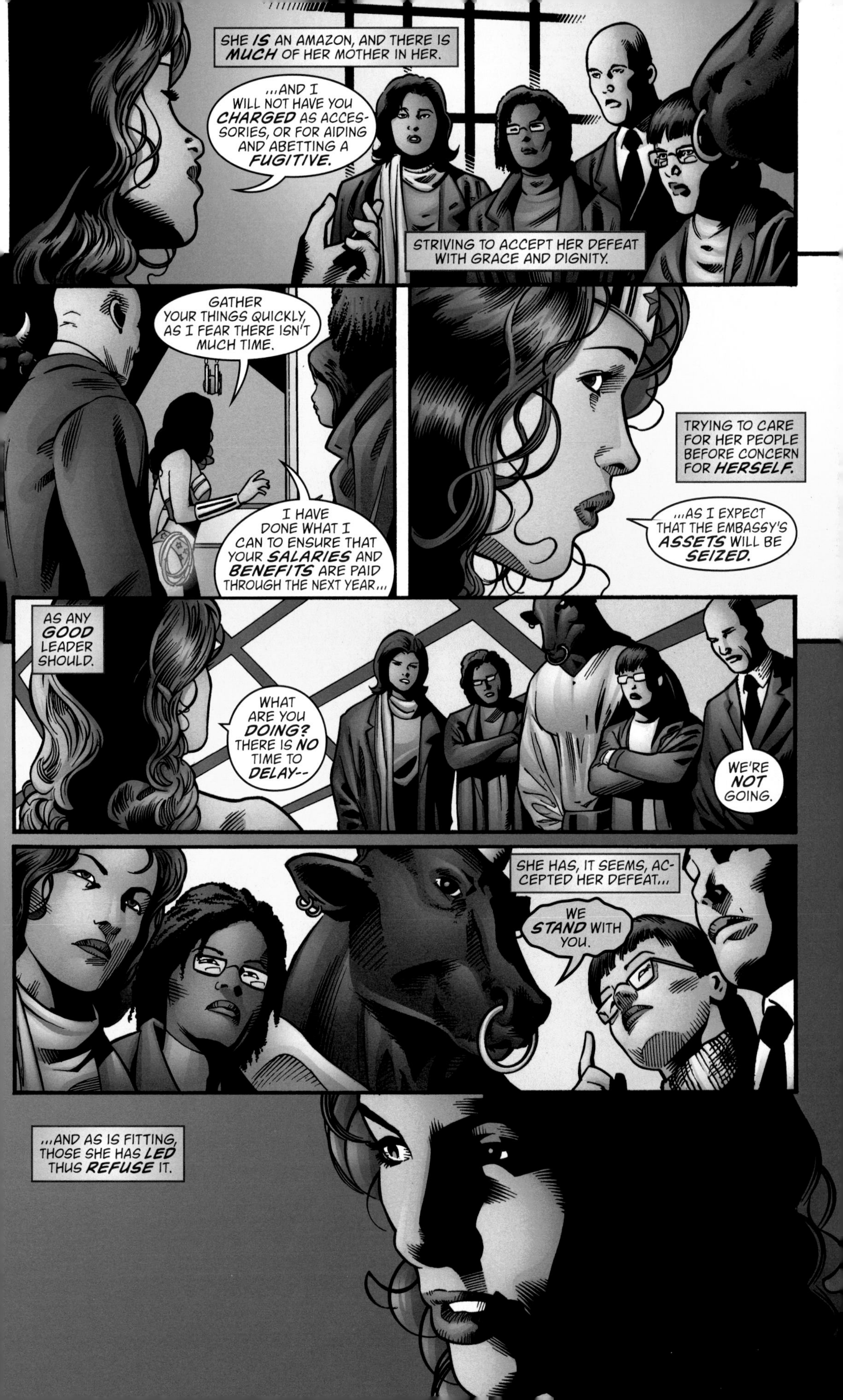
SHE IS AN AMAZON, AND THERE IS MUCH OF HER MOTHER IN HER.
...AND I WILL NOT HAVE YOU CHARGED AS ACCESSORIES, OR FOR AIDING AND ABETTING A FUGITIVE.
STRIVING TO ACCEPT HER DEFEAT WITH GRACE AND DIGNITY.
GATHER YOUR THINGS QUICKLY, AS I FEAR THERE ISN'T MUCH TIME.
I HAVE DONE WHAT I CAN TO ENSURE THAT YOUR SALARIES AND BENEFITS ARE PAID THROUGH THE NEXT YEAR...
TRYING TO CARE FOR HER PEOPLE BEFORE CONCERN FOR HERSELF.
...AS I EXPECT THAT THE EMBASSY'S ASSETS WILL BE SEIZED.
AS ANY GOOD LEADER SHOULD.
WHAT ARE YOU DOING? THERE IS NO TIME TO DELAY--
WE'RE NOT GOING.
SHE HAS, IT SEEMS, ACCEPTED HER DEFEAT...
WE STAND WITH YOU.
...AND AS IS FITTING, THOSE SHE HAS LED THUS REFUSE IT.

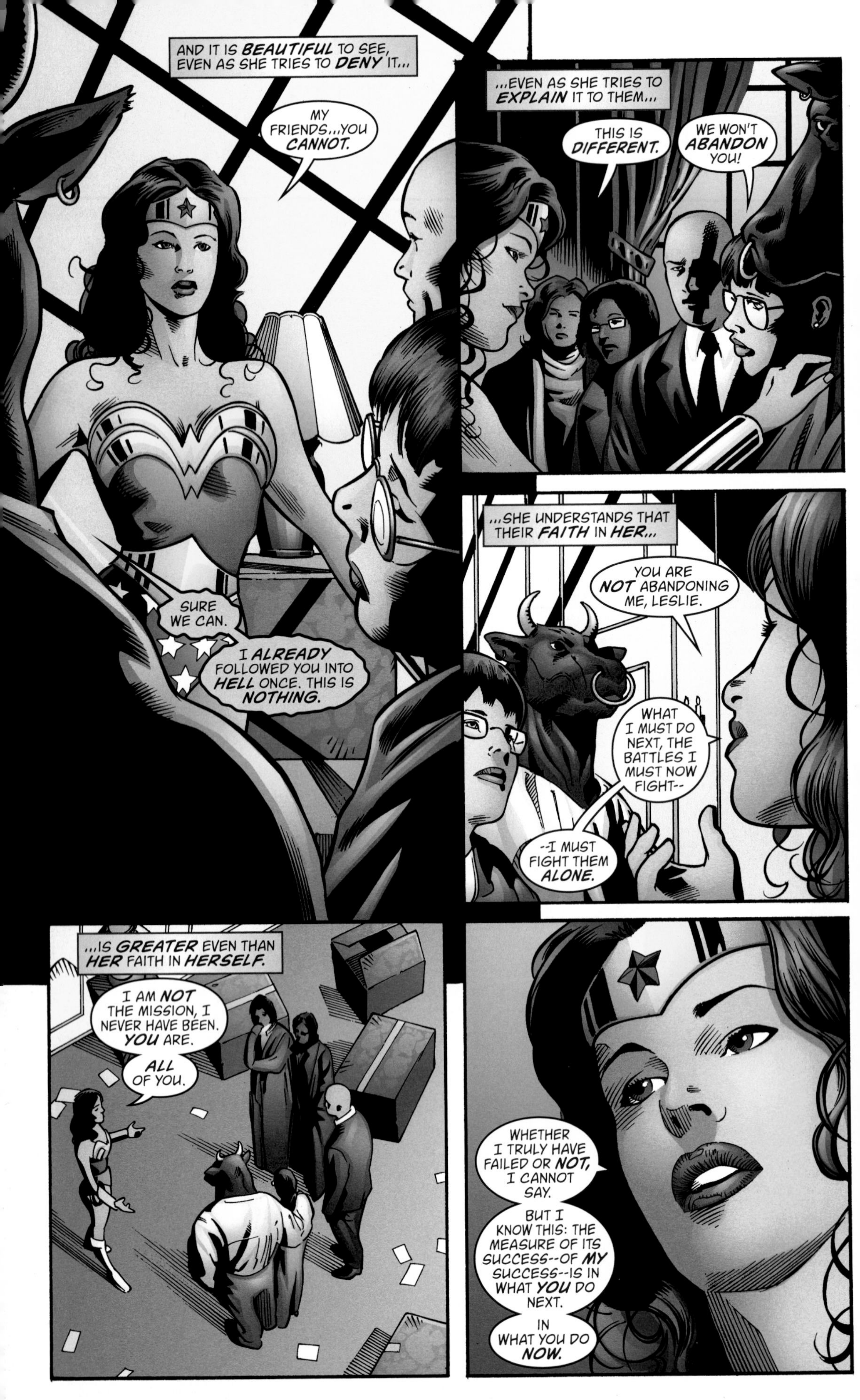
AND IT IS BEAUTIFUL TO SEE, EVEN AS SHE TRIES TO DENY IT...
MY FRIENDS...YOU CANNOT.
SURE WE CAN.
I ALREADY FOLLOWED YOU INTO HELL ONCE. THIS IS NOTHING.
...EVEN AS SHE TRIES TO EXPLAIN IT TO THEM...
THIS IS DIFFERENT.
WE WON'T ABANDON YOU!
...SHE UNDERSTANDS THAT THEIR FAITH IN HER...
YOU ARE NOT ABANDONING ME, LESLIE.
WHAT I MUST DO NEXT, THE BATTLES I MUST NOW FIGHT--
--I MUST FIGHT THEM ALONE.
...IS GREATER EVEN THAN HER FAITH IN HERSELF.
I AM NOT THE MISSION, I NEVER HAVE BEEN. YOU ARE.
ALL OF YOU.
WHETHER I TRULY HAVE FAILED OR NOT, I CANNOT SAY.
BUT I KNOW THIS: THE MEASURE OF ITS SUCCESS--OF MY SUCCESS--IS IN WHAT YOU DO NEXT.
IN WHAT YOU DO NOW.

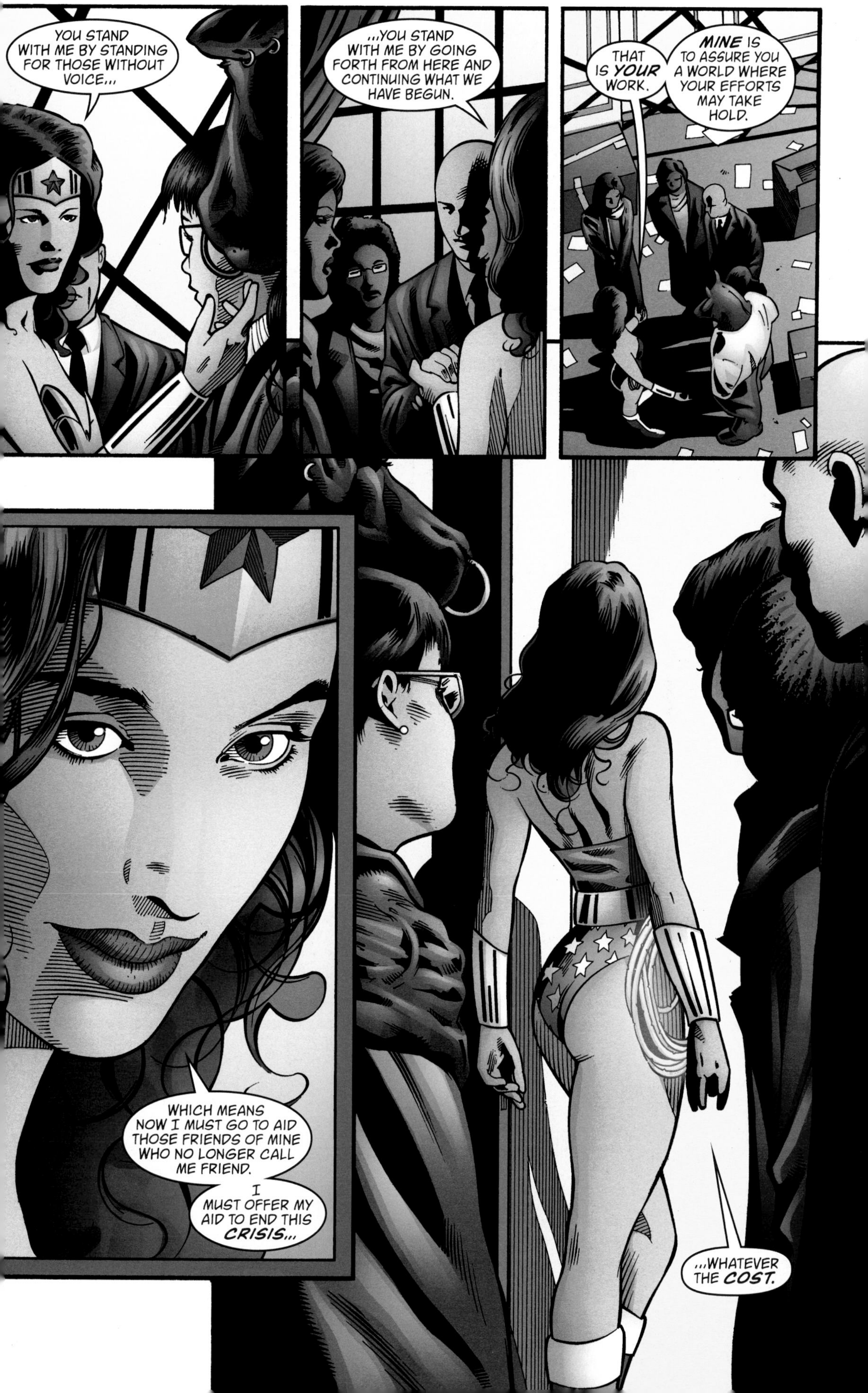
YOU STAND WITH ME BY STANDING FOR THOSE WITHOUT VOICE...
...YOU STAND WITH ME BY GOING FORTH FROM HERE AND CONTINUING WHAT WE HAVE BEGUN.
THAT IS YOUR WORK.
MINE IS TO ASSURE YOU A WORLD WHERE YOUR EFFORTS MAY TAKE HOLD.
WHICH MEANS NOW I MUST GO TO AID THOSE FRIENDS OF MINE WHO NO LONGER CALL ME FRIEND.
I MUST OFFER MY AID TO END THIS CRISIS...
...WHATEVER THE COST.

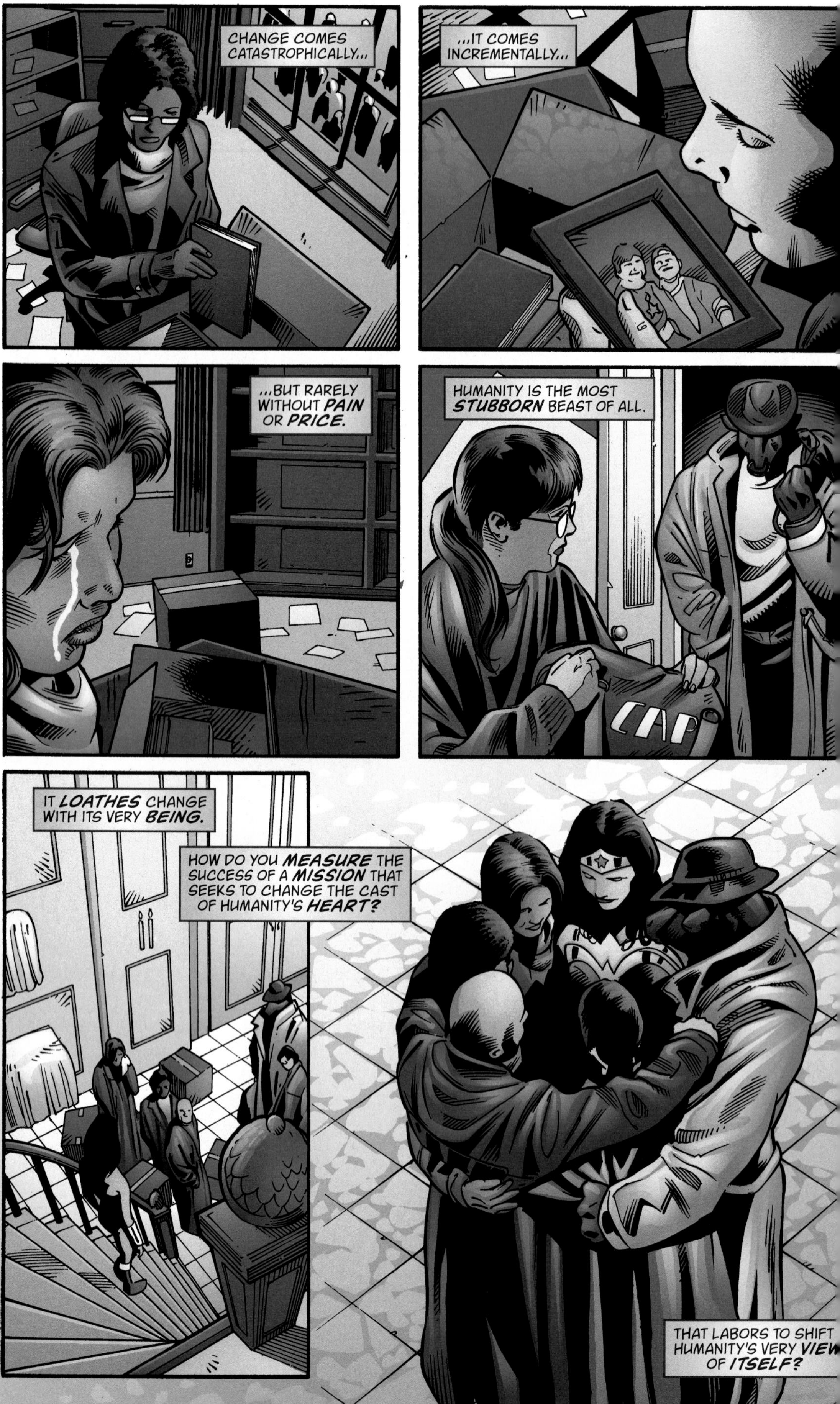
CHANGE COMES CATASTROPHICALLY...
...IT COMES INCREMENTALLY...
...BUT RARELY WITHOUT PAIN OR PRICE.
HUMANITY IS THE MOST STUBBORN BEAST OF ALL.
CAP
IT LOATHES CHANGE WITH ITS VERY BEING.
HOW DO YOU MEASURE THE SUCCESS OF A MISSION THAT SEEKS TO CHANGE THE CAST OF HUMANITY'S HEART?
THAT LABORS TO SHIFT HUMANITY'S VERY VIEW OF ITSELF?

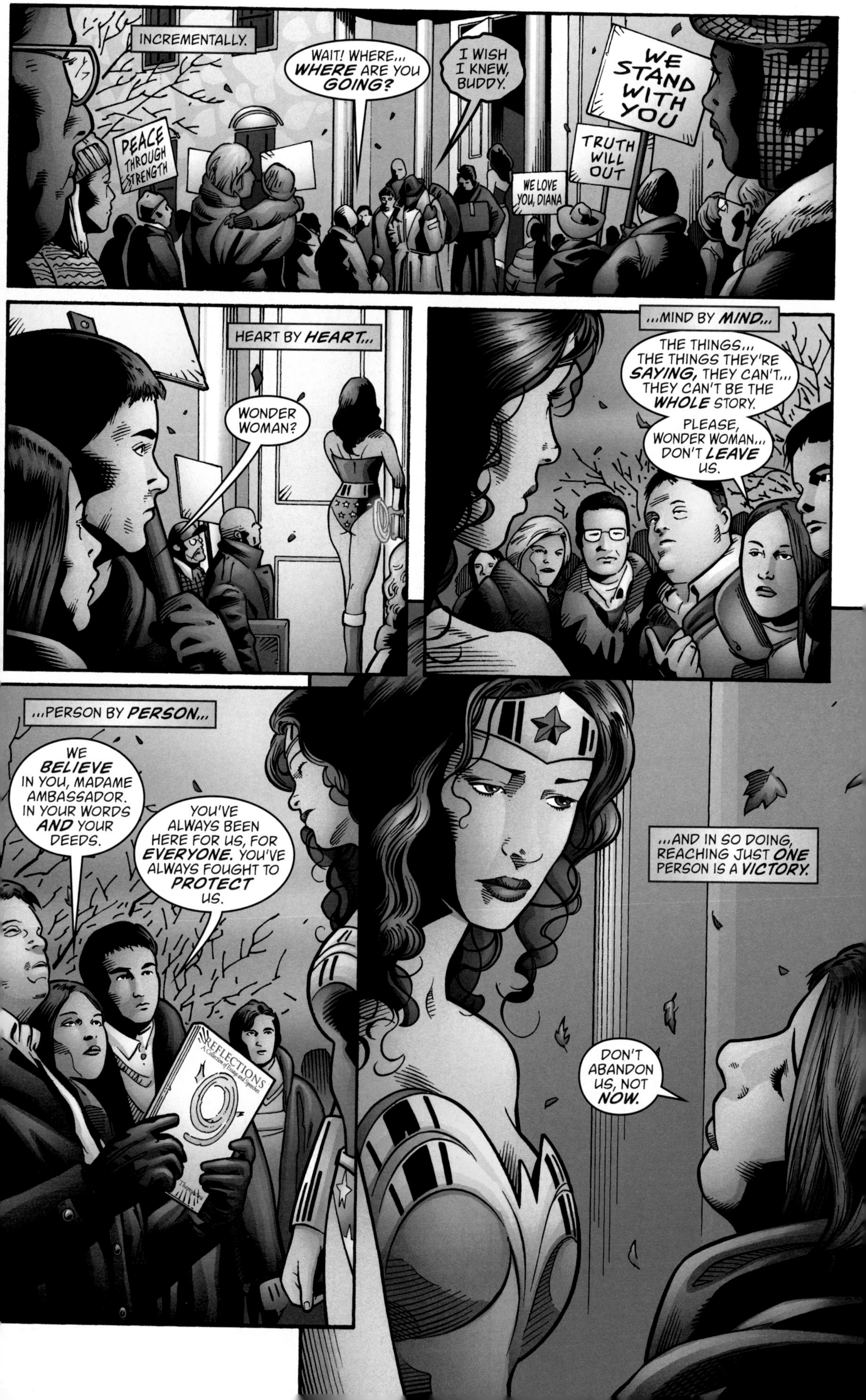

INCREMENTALLY.
WAIT! WHERE... WHERE ARE YOU GOING?
I WISH I KNEW, BUDDY.
PEACE THROUGH STRENGTH
WE STAND WITH YOU
TRUTH WILL OUT
WE LOVE YOU, DIANA
HEART BY HEART...
WONDER WOMAN?
...MIND BY MIND...
THE THINGS... THE THINGS THEY'RE SAYING, THEY CAN'T... THEY CAN'T BE THE WHOLE STORY.
PLEASE, WONDER WOMAN... DON'T LEAVE US.
...PERSON BY PERSON...
WE BELIEVE IN YOU, MADAME AMBASSADOR. IN YOUR WORDS AND YOUR DEEDS.
YOU'VE ALWAYS BEEN HERE FOR US, FOR EVERYONE. YOU'VE ALWAYS FOUGHT TO PROTECT US.
REFLECTIONS
A Collection of Essays and Speeches
...AND IN SO DOING, REACHING JUST ONE PERSON IS A VICTORY.
DON'T ABANDON US, NOT NOW.

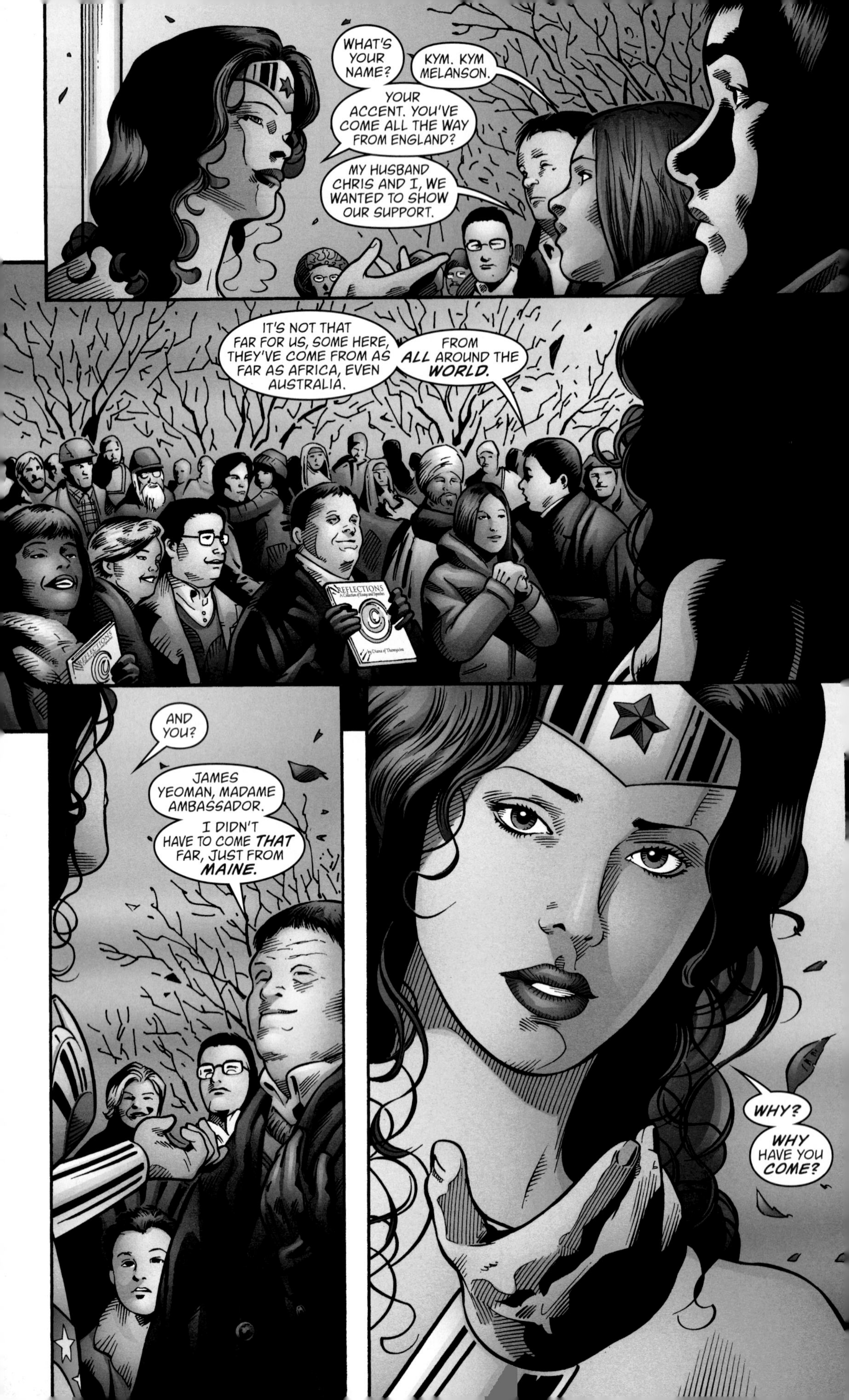
WHAT'S YOUR NAME?
KYM. KYM MELANSON.
YOUR ACCENT. YOU'VE COME ALL THE WAY FROM ENGLAND?
MY HUSBAND CHRIS AND I, WE WANTED TO SHOW OUR SUPPORT.
IT'S NOT THAT FAR FOR US, SOME HERE, THEY'VE COME FROM AS FAR AS AFRICA, EVEN AUSTRALIA.
FROM ALL AROUND THE WORLD.
REFLECTIONS
AND YOU?
JAMES YEOMAN, MADAME AMBASSADOR.
I DIDN'T HAVE TO COME THAT FAR, JUST FROM MAINE.
WHY?
WHY HAVE YOU COME?

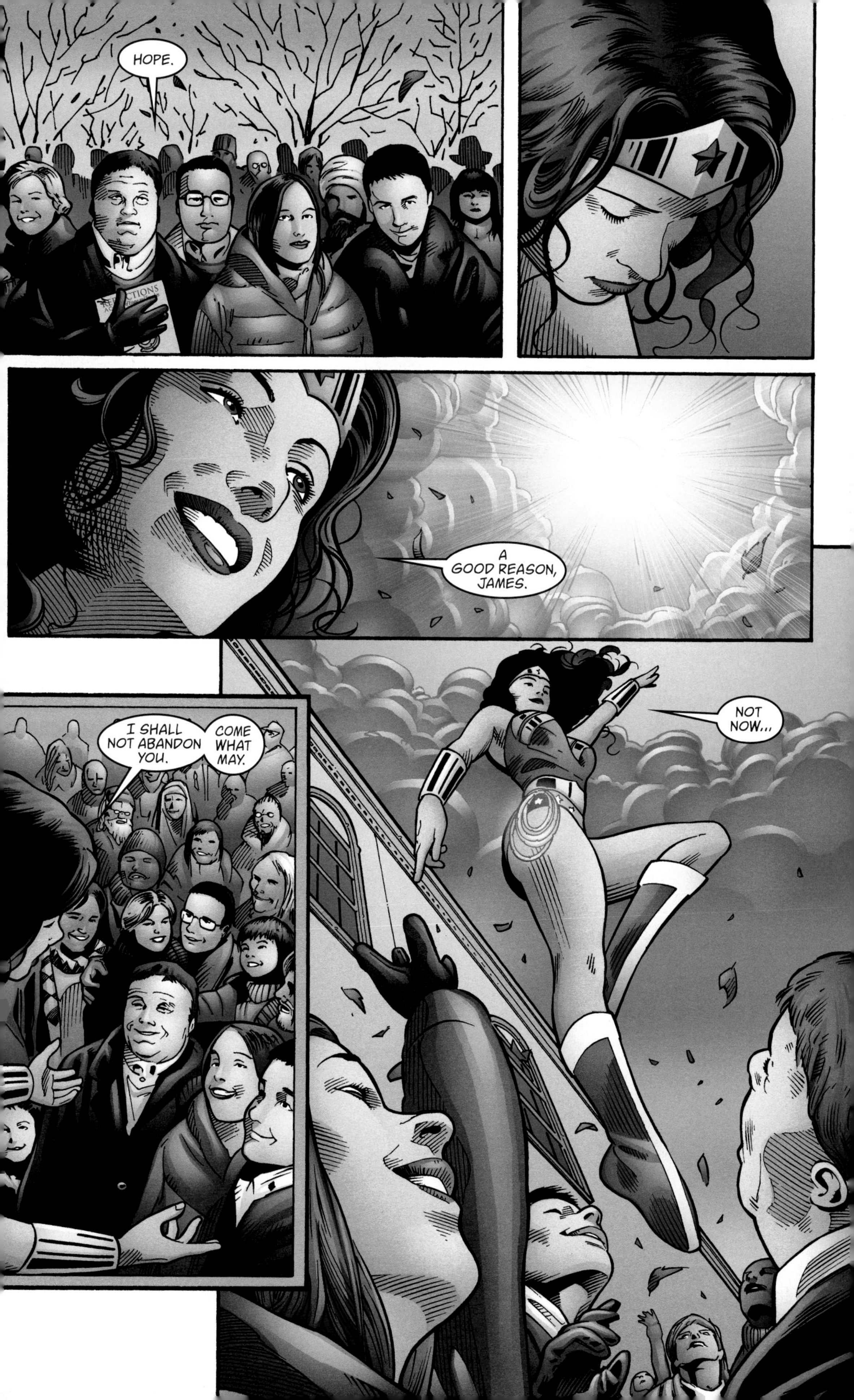
HOPE.
A GOOD REASON, JAMES.
NOT NOW...
I SHALL NOT ABANDON YOU.
COME WHAT MAY.

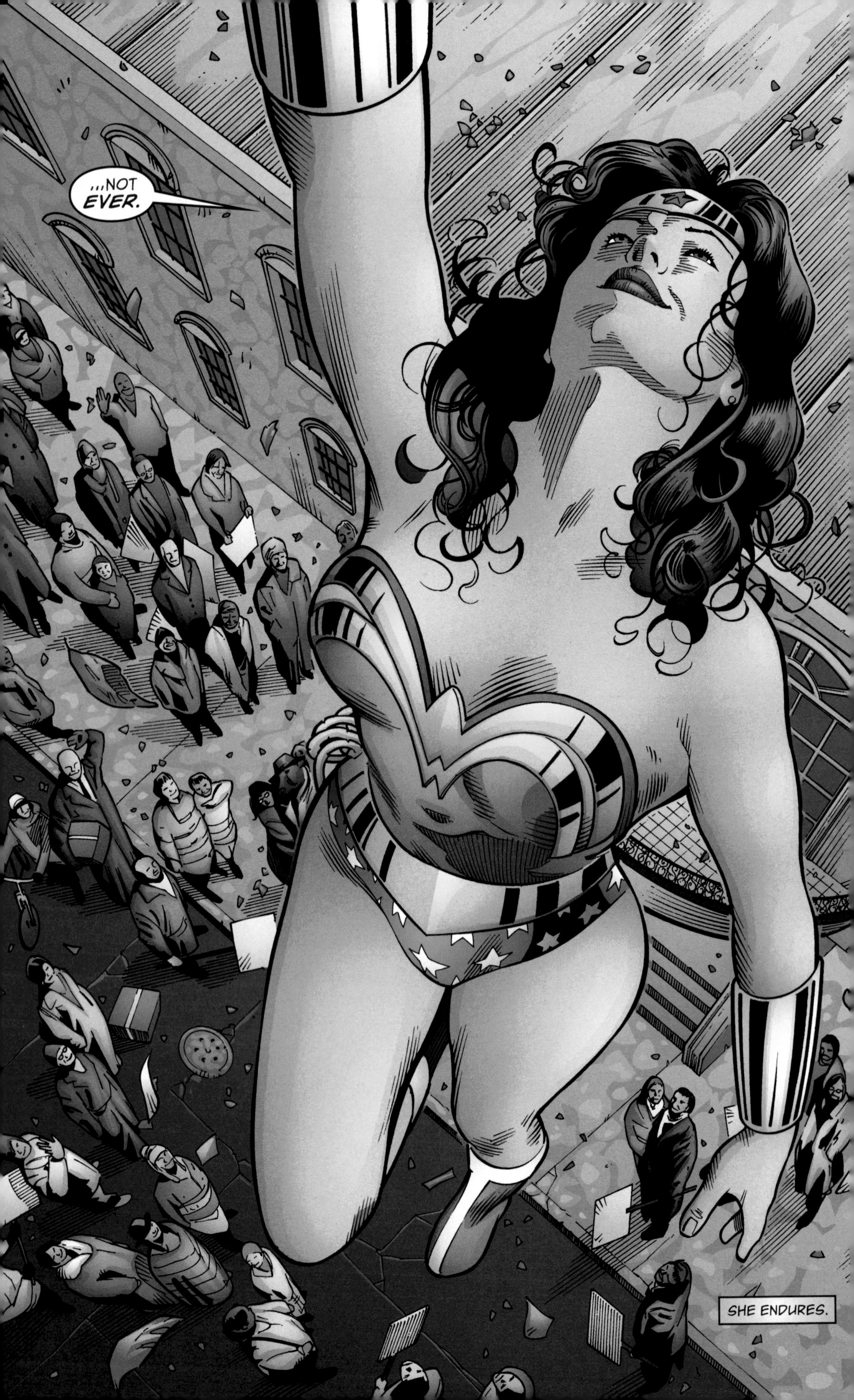
...NOT EVER.
SHE ENDURES.

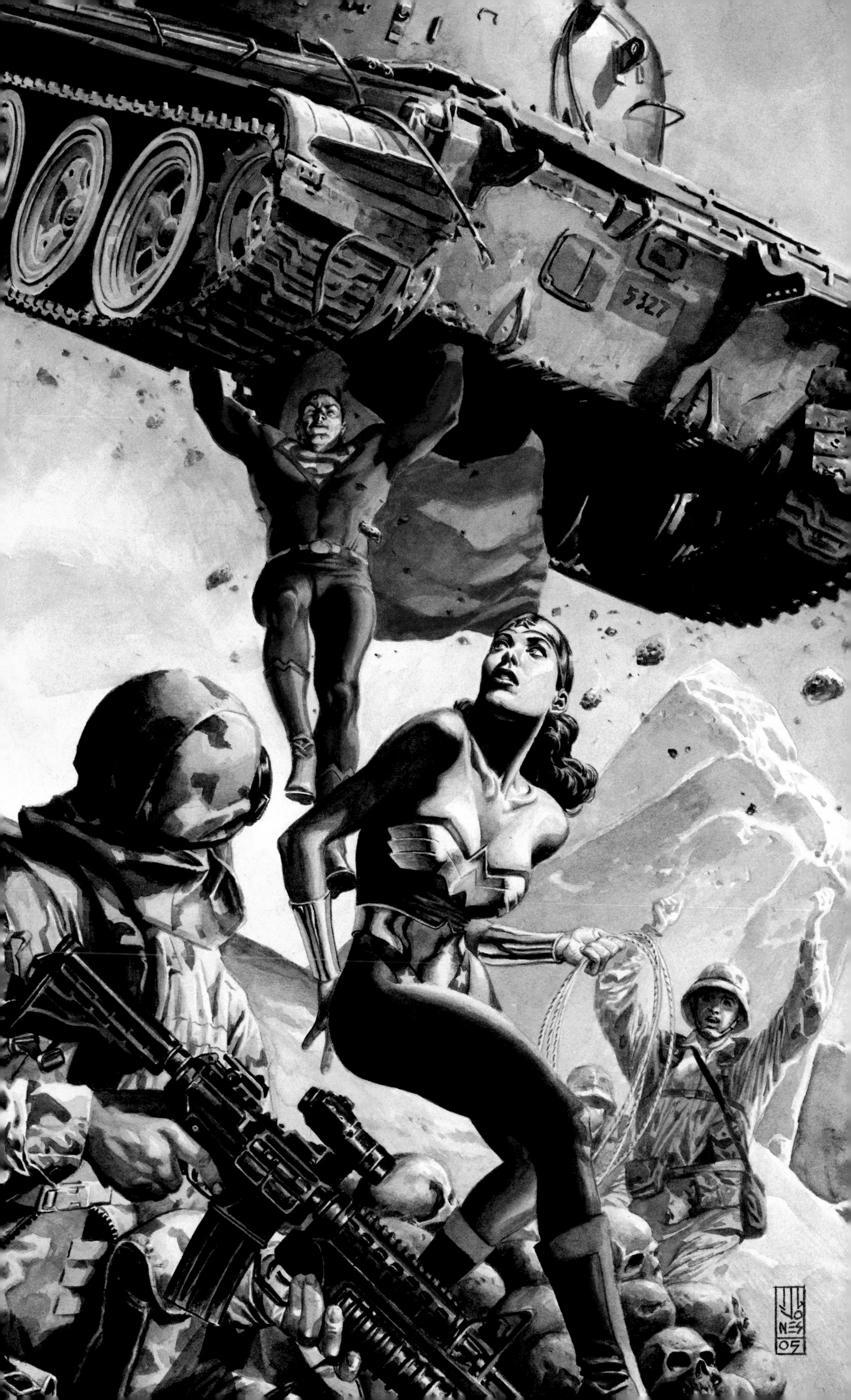
5327

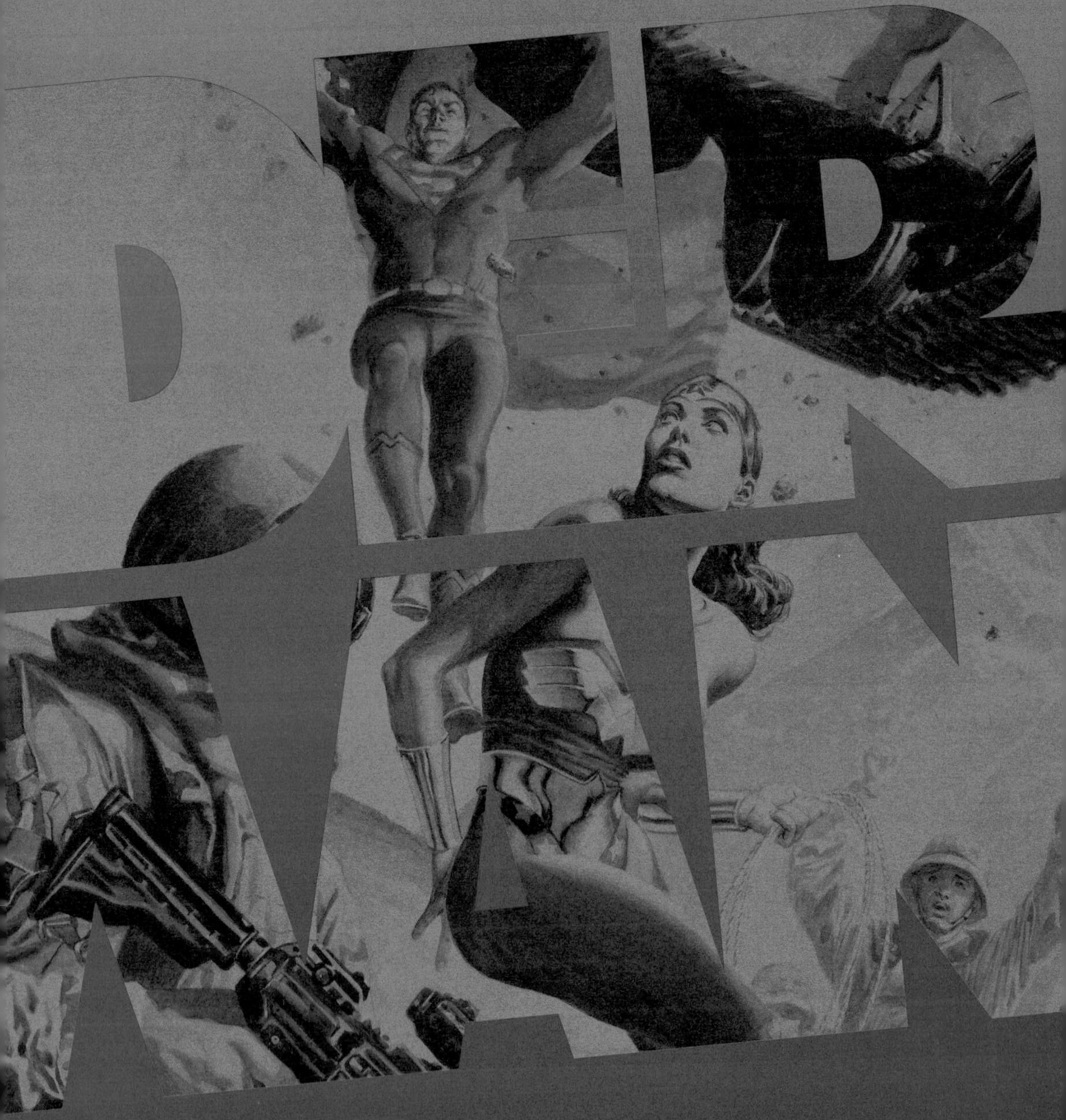

"COVER DATE"

Greg Rucka – *writer*
Cliff Richards – *pencils*
Ray Snyder – *inks*
Richard and **Tanya Horie** – *colors*
Todd Klein – *letters*
J.G. Jones – *cover*

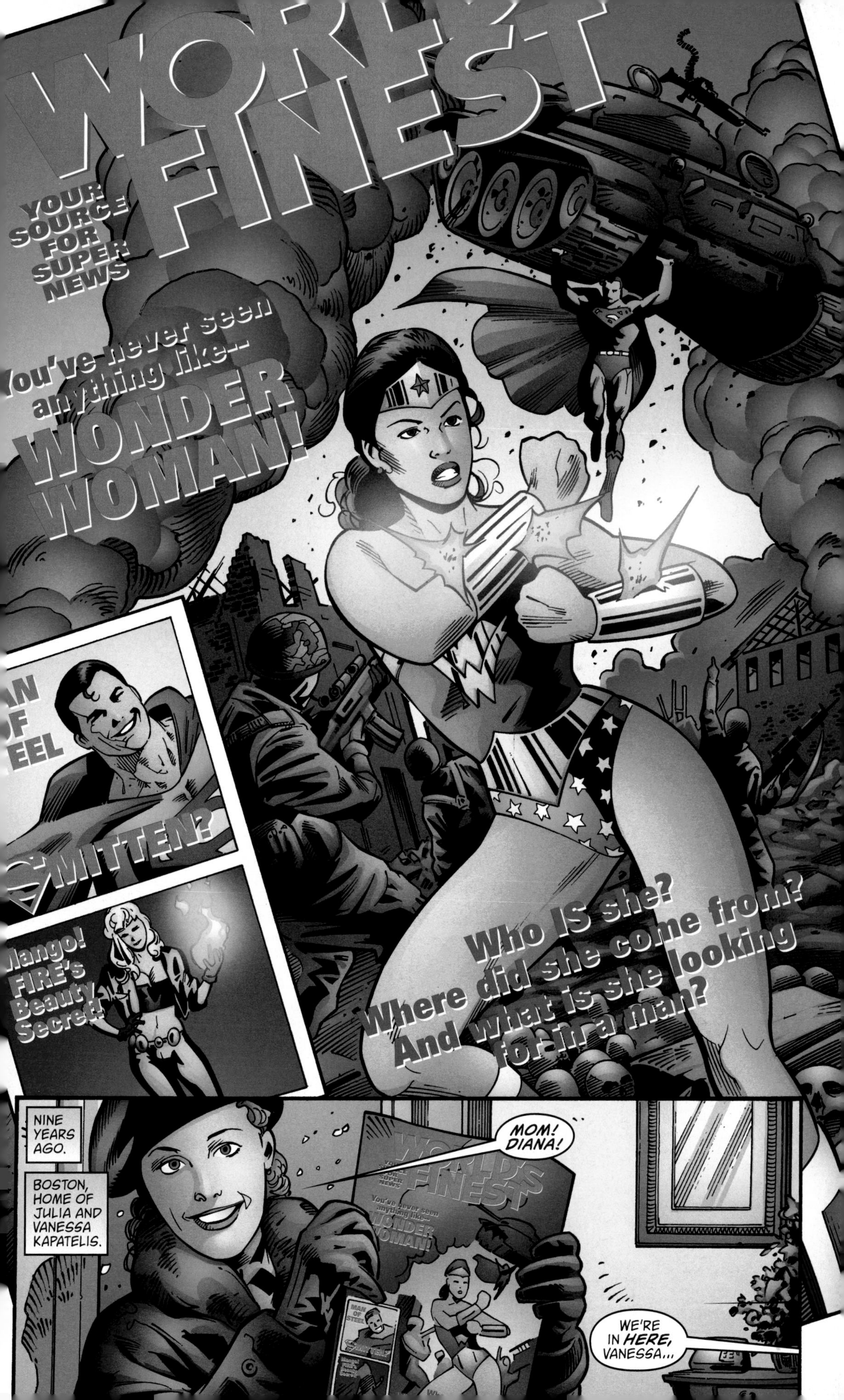

FINEST
YOUR SOURCE FOR SUPER NEWS
You've never seen anything like-- WONDER WOMAN!
Who IS she? Where did she come from? And what is she looking for in a man?
NINE YEARS AGO.
BOSTON, HOME OF JULIA AND VANESSA KAPATELIS.
MOM! DIANA!
WE'RE IN HERE, VANESSA...

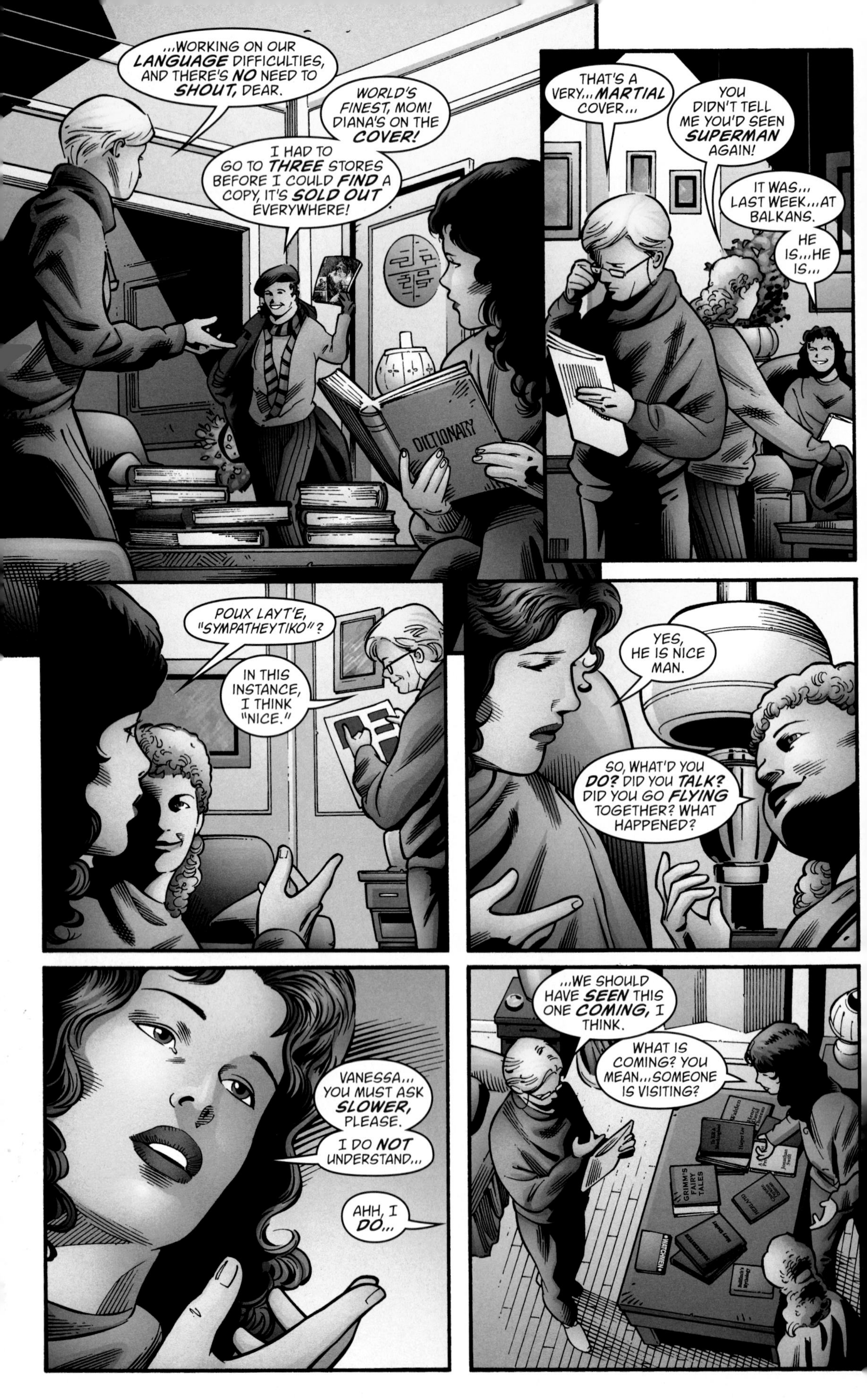
...WORKING ON OUR LANGUAGE DIFFICULTIES, AND THERE'S NO NEED TO SHOUT, DEAR.
WORLD'S FINEST, MOM! DIANA'S ON THE COVER!
I HAD TO GO TO THREE STORES BEFORE I COULD FIND A COPY, IT'S SOLD OUT EVERYWHERE!
DICTIONARY
THAT'S A VERY... MARTIAL COVER...
YOU DIDN'T TELL ME YOU'D SEEN SUPERMAN AGAIN!
IT WAS... LAST WEEK... AT BALKANS.
HE IS... HE IS...
POUX LAYT'E, "SYMPATHEYTIKO"?
IN THIS INSTANCE, I THINK "NICE."
YES, HE IS NICE MAN.
SO, WHAT'D YOU DO? DID YOU TALK? DID YOU GO FLYING TOGETHER? WHAT HAPPENED?
VANESSA... YOU MUST ASK SLOWER, PLEASE.
I DO NOT UNDERSTAND...
AHH, I DO...
...WE SHOULD HAVE SEEN THIS ONE COMING, I THINK.
WHAT IS COMING? YOU MEAN... SOMEONE IS VISITING?
GRIMM'S FAIRY TALES
WATCHMEN

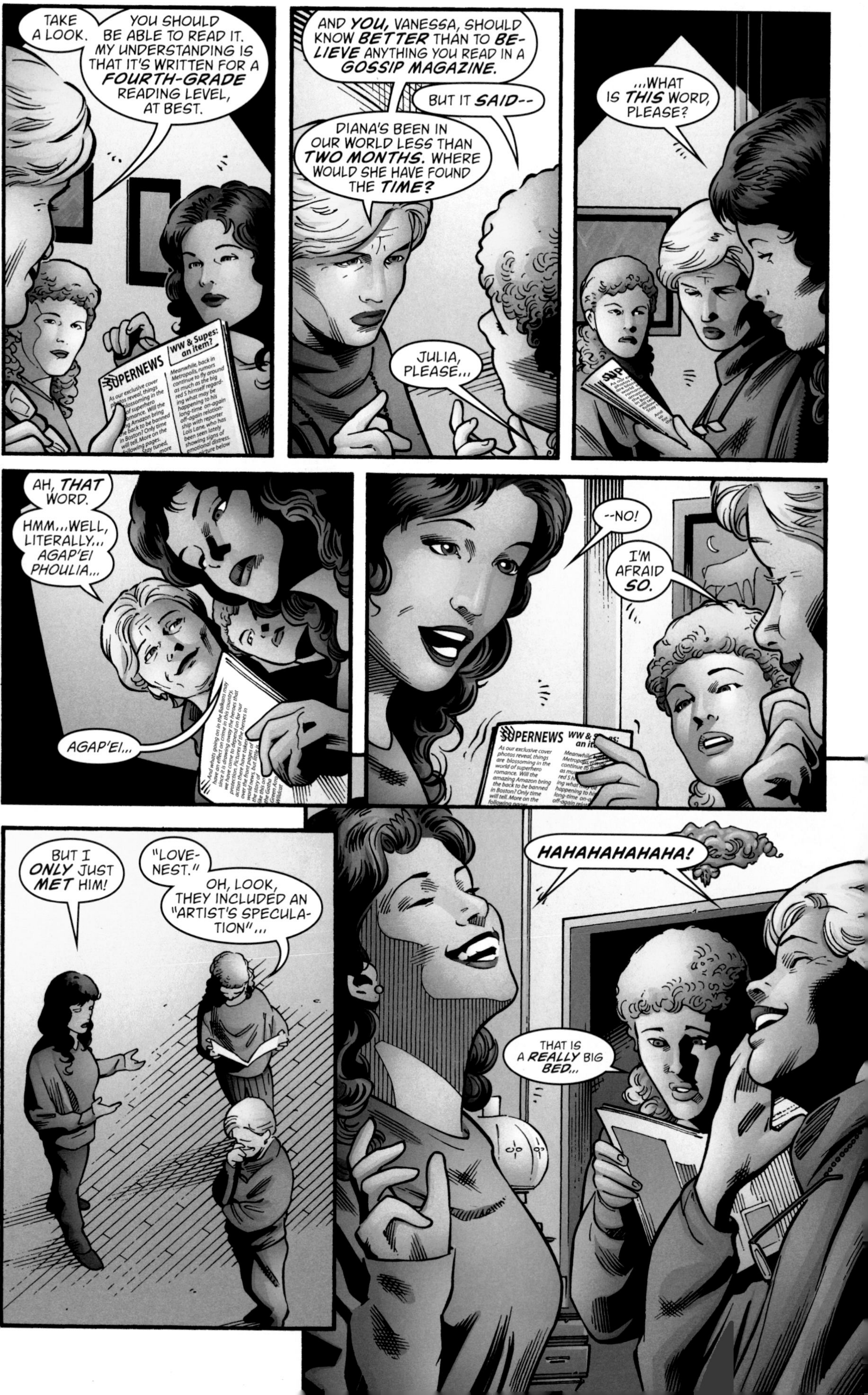
TAKE A LOOK.
YOU SHOULD BE ABLE TO READ IT. MY UNDERSTANDING IS THAT IT'S WRITTEN FOR A FOURTH-GRADE READING LEVEL, AT BEST.
SUPERNEWS
WW & Supes: an item?
AND YOU, VANESSA, SHOULD KNOW BETTER THAN TO BELIEVE ANYTHING YOU READ IN A GOSSIP MAGAZINE.
BUT IT SAID--
DIANA'S BEEN IN OUR WORLD LESS THAN TWO MONTHS. WHERE WOULD SHE HAVE FOUND THE TIME?
JULIA, PLEASE...
...WHAT IS THIS WORD, PLEASE?
AH, THAT WORD.
HMM...WELL, LITERALLY... AGAP'EI PHOULIA...
AGAP'EI...
--NO!
I'M AFRAID SO.
SUPERNEWS
BUT I ONLY JUST MET HIM!
"LOVE-NEST."
OH, LOOK, THEY INCLUDED AN "ARTIST'S SPECULATION"...
HAHAHAHAHAHA!
THAT IS A REALLY BIG BED...

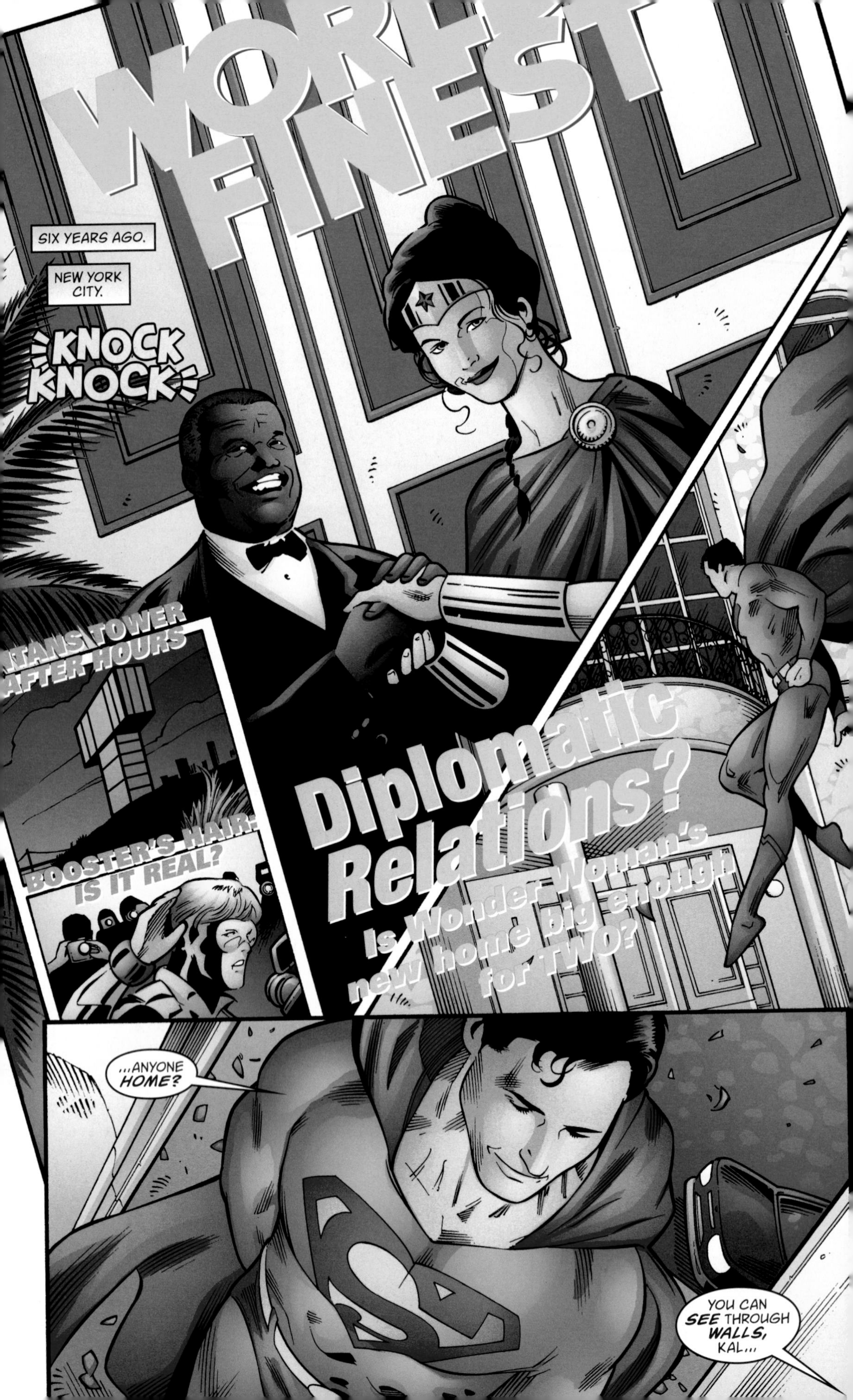
WORLD'S FINEST
SIX YEARS AGO.
NEW YORK CITY.
KNOCK KNOCK
TITANS TOWER AFTER HOURS
BOOSTER'S HAIR- IS IT REAL?
Diplomatic Relations?
Is Wonder Woman's new home big enough for TWO?
...ANYONE HOME?
YOU CAN SEE THROUGH WALLS, KAL...

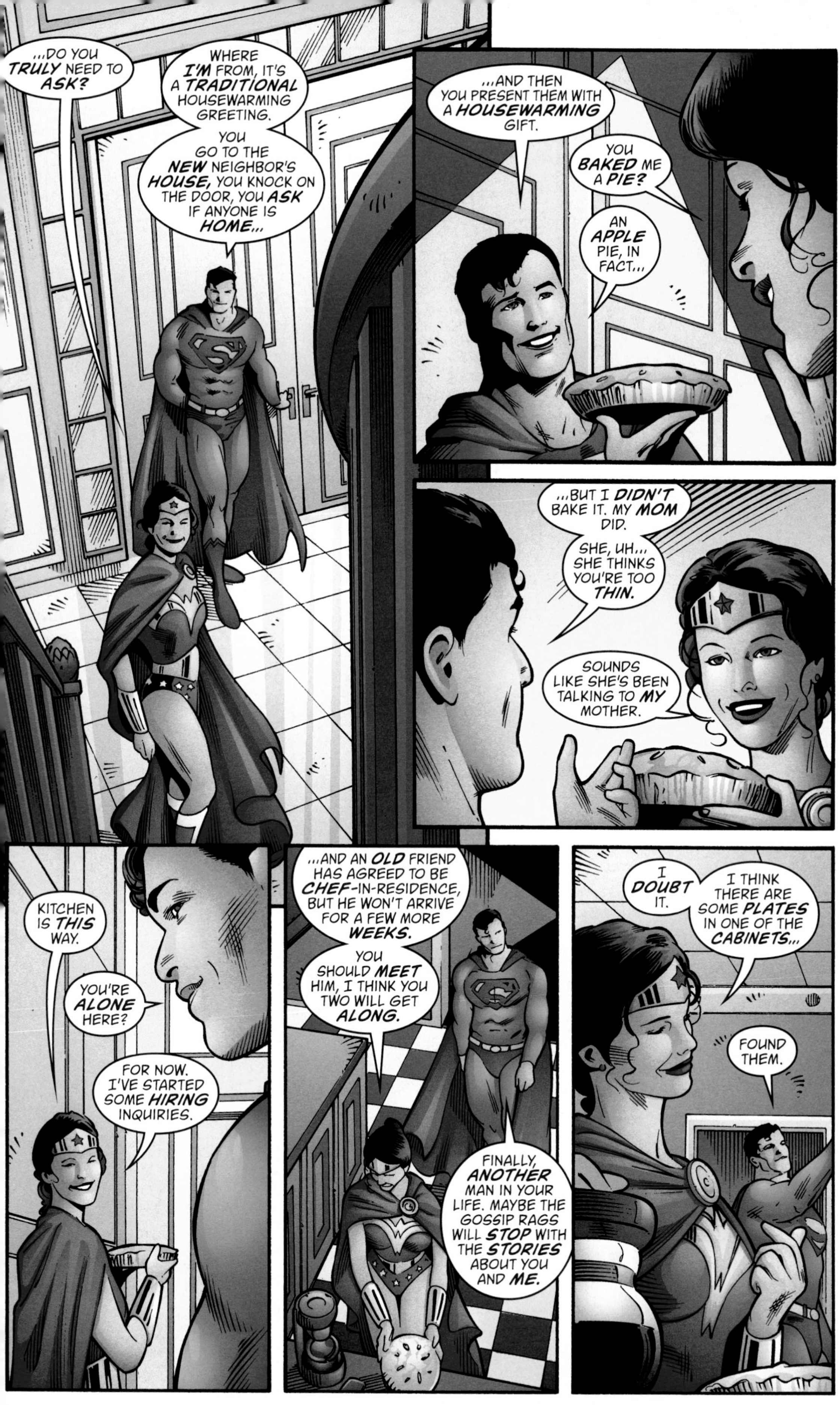
...DO YOU TRULY NEED TO ASK?
WHERE I'M FROM, IT'S A TRADITIONAL HOUSEWARMING GREETING.
YOU GO TO THE NEW NEIGHBOR'S HOUSE, YOU KNOCK ON THE DOOR, YOU ASK IF ANYONE IS HOME...
...AND THEN YOU PRESENT THEM WITH A HOUSEWARMING GIFT.
YOU BAKED ME A PIE?
AN APPLE PIE, IN FACT...
...BUT I DIDN'T BAKE IT. MY MOM DID.
SHE, UH... SHE THINKS YOU'RE TOO THIN.
SOUNDS LIKE SHE'S BEEN TALKING TO MY MOTHER.
KITCHEN IS THIS WAY.
YOU'RE ALONE HERE?
FOR NOW. I'VE STARTED SOME HIRING INQUIRIES.
...AND AN OLD FRIEND HAS AGREED TO BE CHEF-IN-RESIDENCE, BUT HE WON'T ARRIVE FOR A FEW MORE WEEKS.
YOU SHOULD MEET HIM, I THINK YOU TWO WILL GET ALONG.
FINALLY, ANOTHER MAN IN YOUR LIFE. MAYBE THE GOSSIP RAGS WILL STOP WITH THE STORIES ABOUT YOU AND ME.
I DOUBT IT.
I THINK THERE ARE SOME PLATES IN ONE OF THE CABINETS...
FOUND THEM.

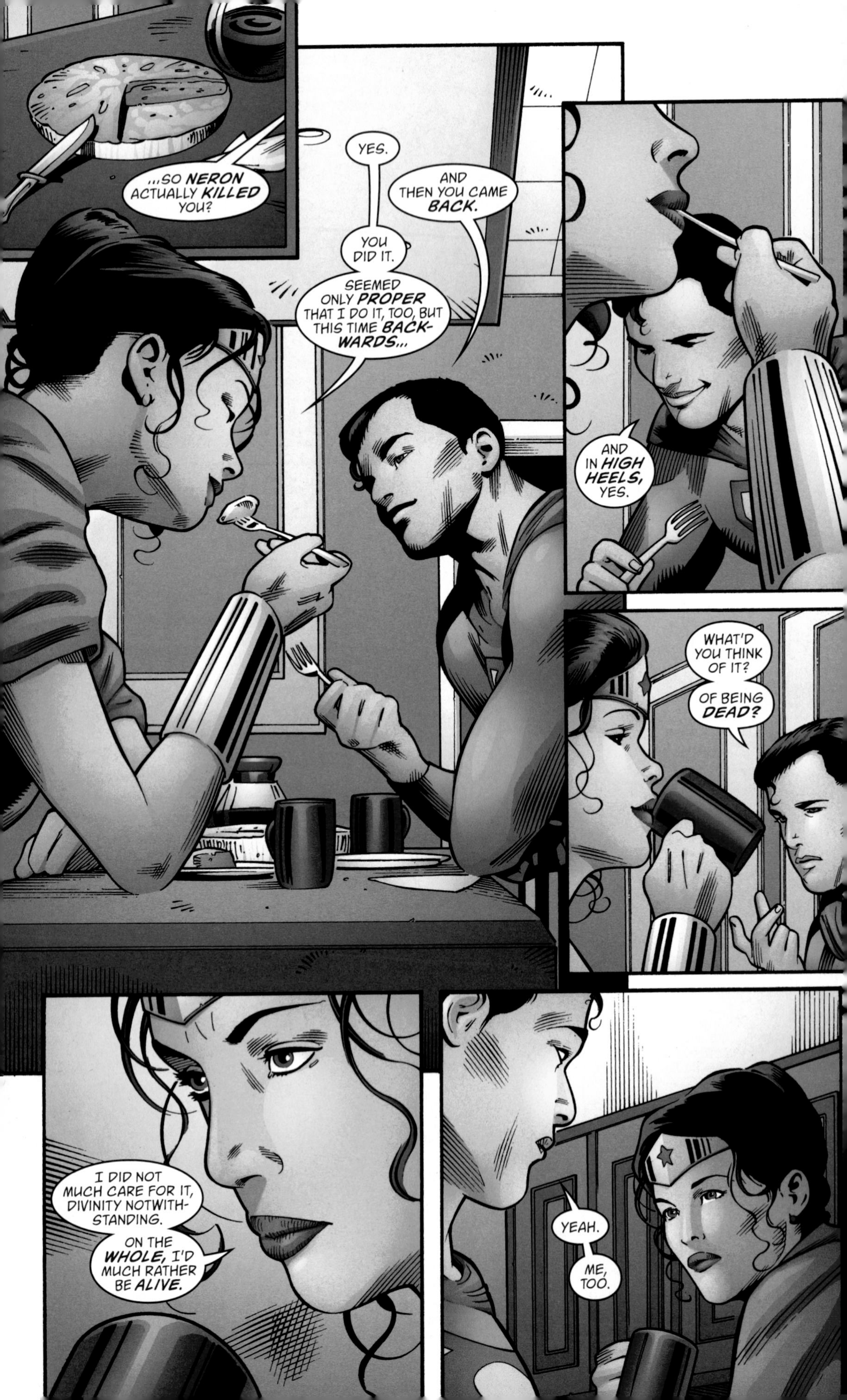
...SO NERON ACTUALLY KILLED YOU?
YES.
YOU DID IT.
AND THEN YOU CAME BACK.
SEEMED ONLY PROPER THAT I DO IT, TOO, BUT THIS TIME BACK-WARDS...
AND IN HIGH HEELS, YES.
WHAT'D YOU THINK OF IT?
OF BEING DEAD?
I DID NOT MUCH CARE FOR IT, DIVINITY NOTWITH-STANDING.
ON THE WHOLE, I'D MUCH RATHER BE ALIVE.
YEAH.
ME, TOO.

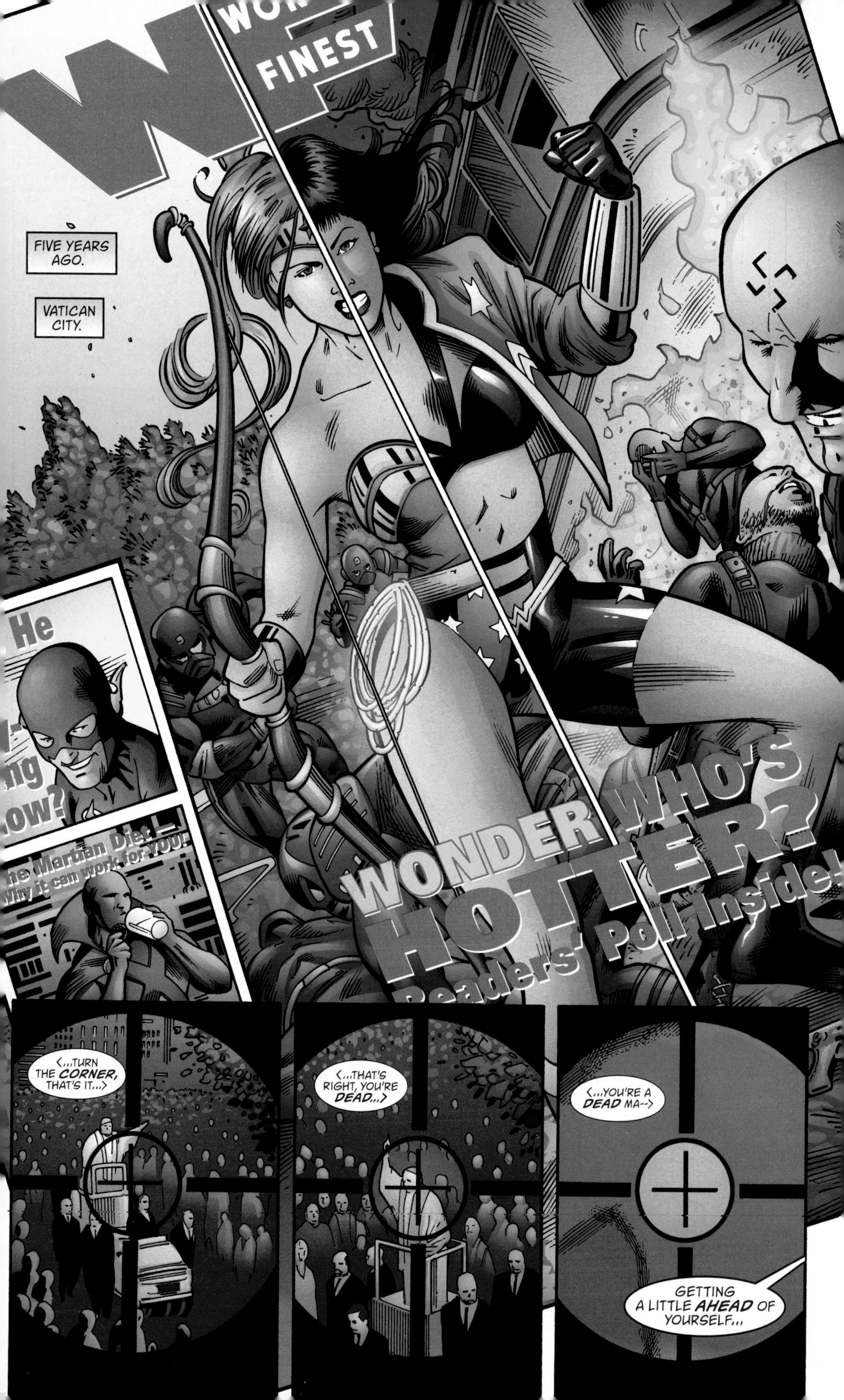

WORLD'S FINEST
FIVE YEARS AGO.
VATICAN CITY.
He
The Martian Diet — Why it can work for you!
WONDER WHO'S HOTTER? Readers' Poll Inside!
<...TURN THE CORNER, THAT'S IT...>
<...THAT'S RIGHT, YOU'RE DEAD...>
<...YOU'RE A DEAD MA-->
GETTING A LITTLE AHEAD OF YOURSELF...

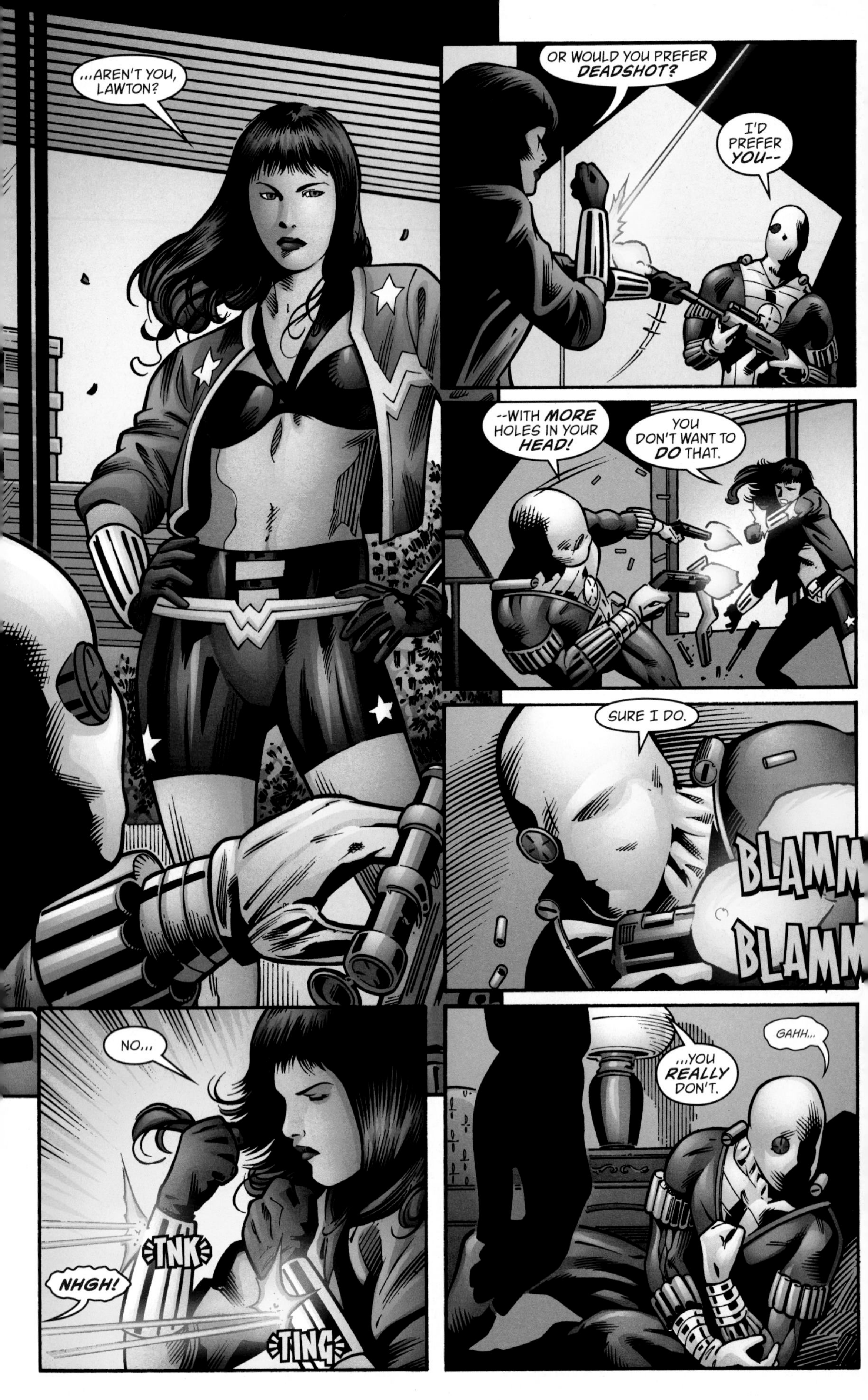

...AREN'T YOU, LAWTON?
OR WOULD YOU PREFER DEADSHOT?
I'D PREFER YOU--
--WITH MORE HOLES IN YOUR HEAD!
YOU DON'T WANT TO DO THAT.
SURE I DO.
BLAMM
BLAMM
NO...
TNK
NHGH!
TING
...YOU REALLY DON'T.
GAHH...

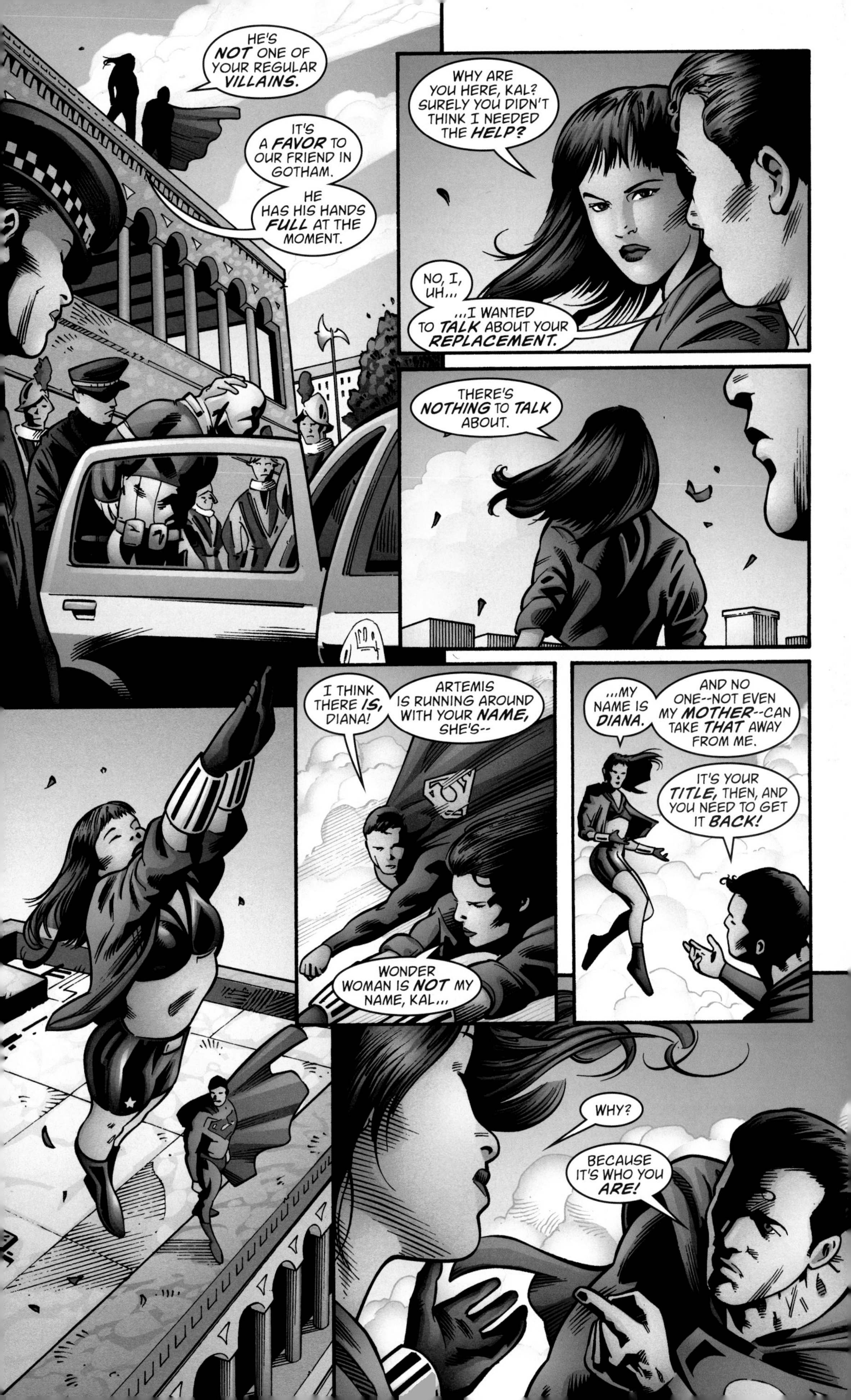
HE'S NOT ONE OF YOUR REGULAR VILLAINS.
IT'S A FAVOR TO OUR FRIEND IN GOTHAM.
HE HAS HIS HANDS FULL AT THE MOMENT.
WHY ARE YOU HERE, KAL? SURELY YOU DIDN'T THINK I NEEDED THE HELP?
NO, I, UH...
...I WANTED TO TALK ABOUT YOUR REPLACEMENT.
THERE'S NOTHING TO TALK ABOUT.
I THINK THERE IS, DIANA!
ARTEMIS IS RUNNING AROUND WITH YOUR NAME, SHE'S--
WONDER WOMAN IS NOT MY NAME, KAL...
...MY NAME IS DIANA.
AND NO ONE--NOT EVEN MY MOTHER--CAN TAKE THAT AWAY FROM ME.
IT'S YOUR TITLE, THEN, AND YOU NEED TO GET IT BACK!
WHY?
BECAUSE IT'S WHO YOU ARE!

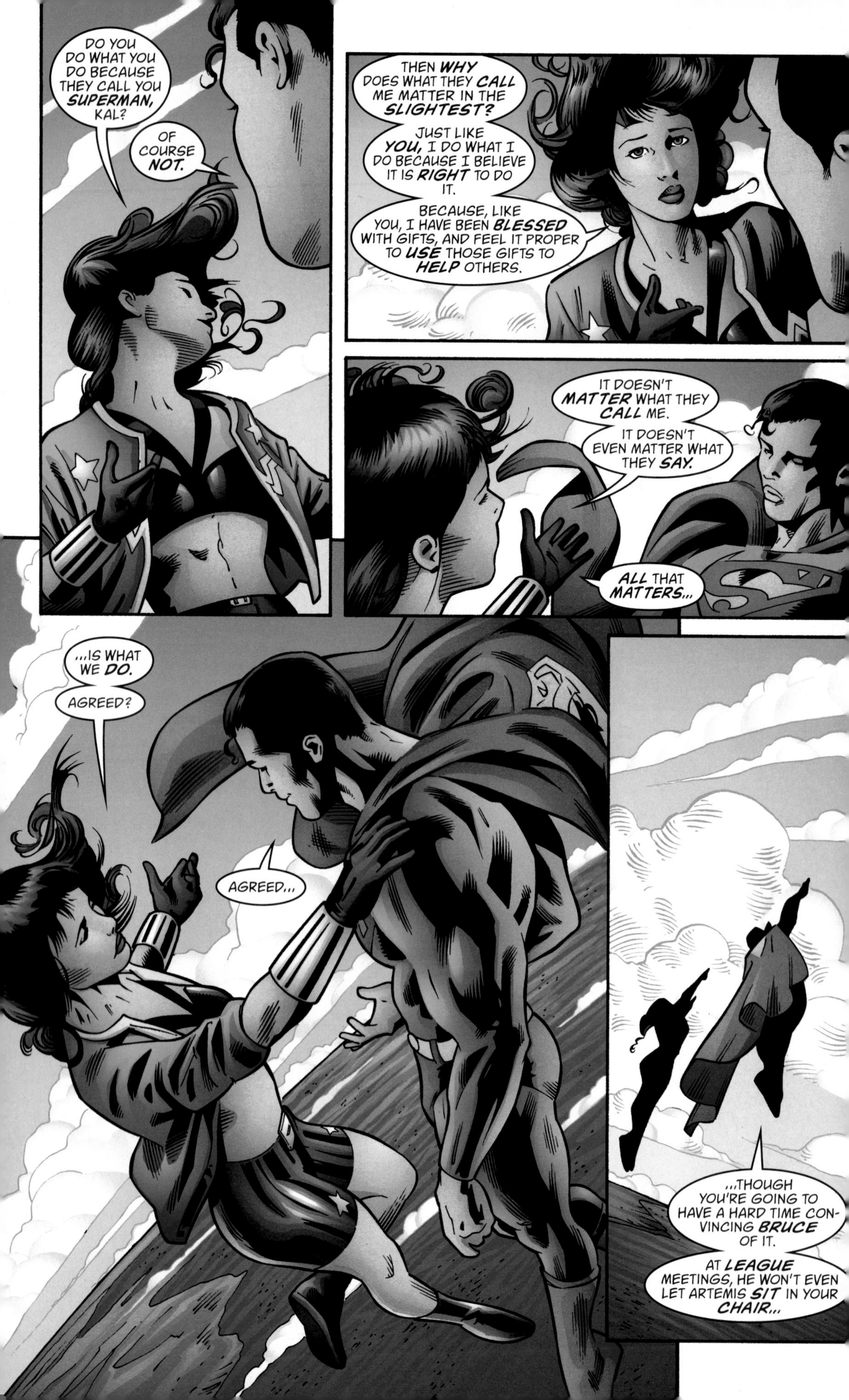
DO YOU DO WHAT YOU DO BECAUSE THEY CALL YOU SUPERMAN, KAL?
OF COURSE NOT.
THEN WHY DOES WHAT THEY CALL ME MATTER IN THE SLIGHTEST?
JUST LIKE YOU, I DO WHAT I DO BECAUSE I BELIEVE IT IS RIGHT TO DO IT.
BECAUSE, LIKE YOU, I HAVE BEEN BLESSED WITH GIFTS, AND FEEL IT PROPER TO USE THOSE GIFTS TO HELP OTHERS.
IT DOESN'T MATTER WHAT THEY CALL ME.
IT DOESN'T EVEN MATTER WHAT THEY SAY.
ALL THAT MATTERS...
...IS WHAT WE DO.
AGREED?
AGREED...
...THOUGH YOU'RE GOING TO HAVE A HARD TIME CON-VINCING BRUCE OF IT.
AT LEAGUE MEETINGS, HE WON'T EVEN LET ARTEMIS SIT IN YOUR CHAIR...

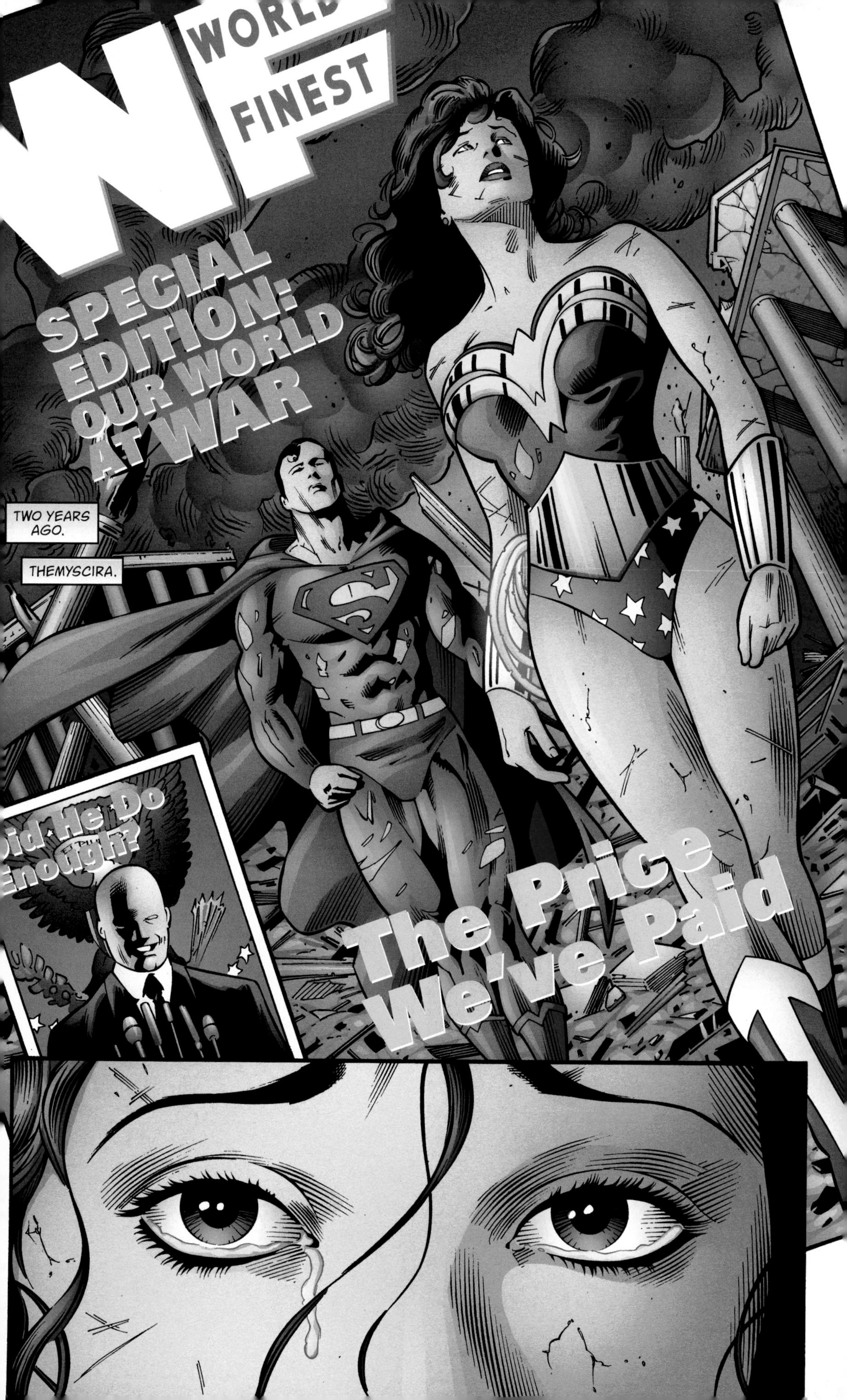
WORLD FINEST
SPECIAL EDITION: OUR WORLD AT WAR
TWO YEARS AGO.
THEMYSCIRA.
Did He Do Enough?
The Price We've Paid

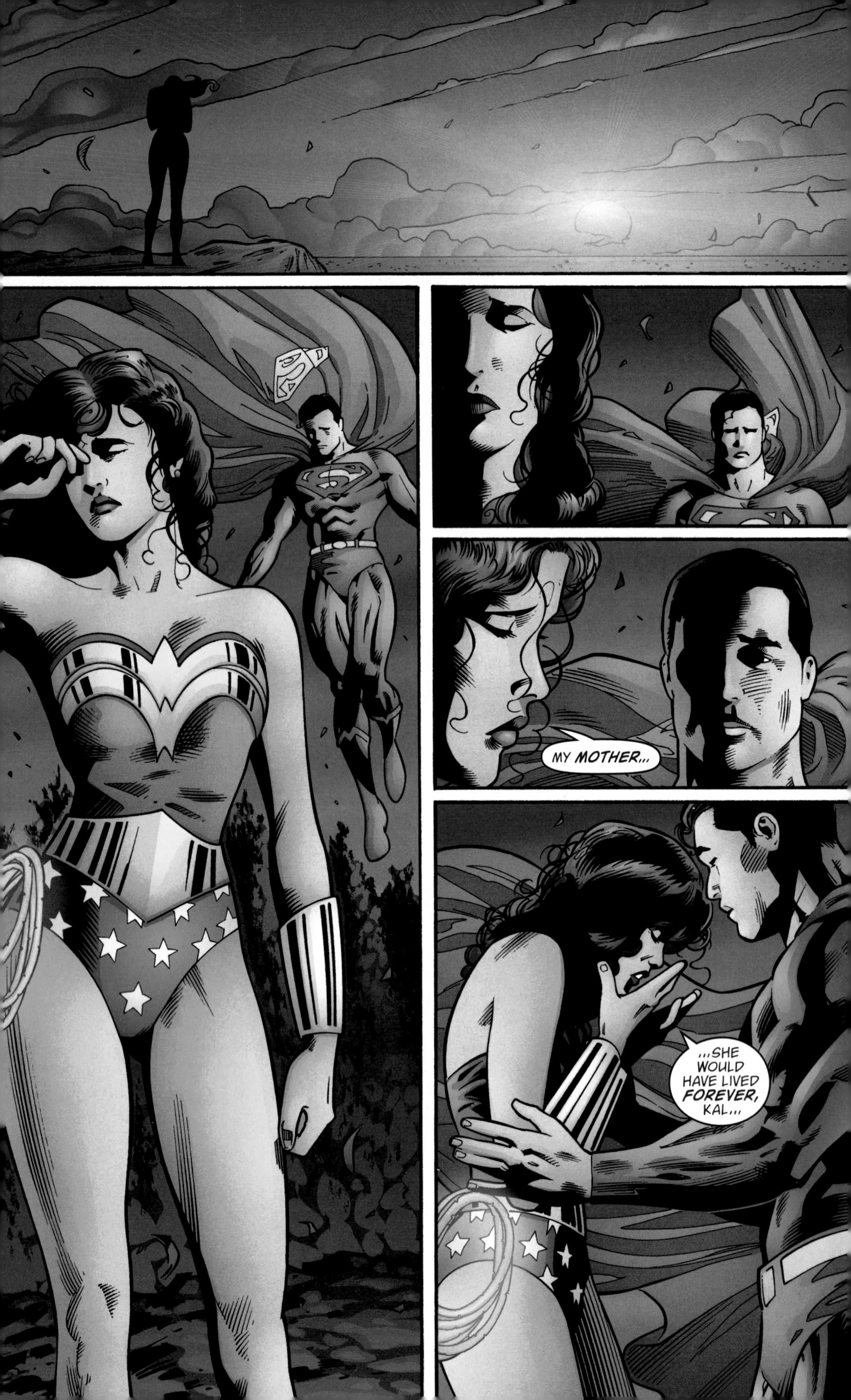
MY MOTHER...
...SHE WOULD HAVE LIVED FOREVER, KAL...

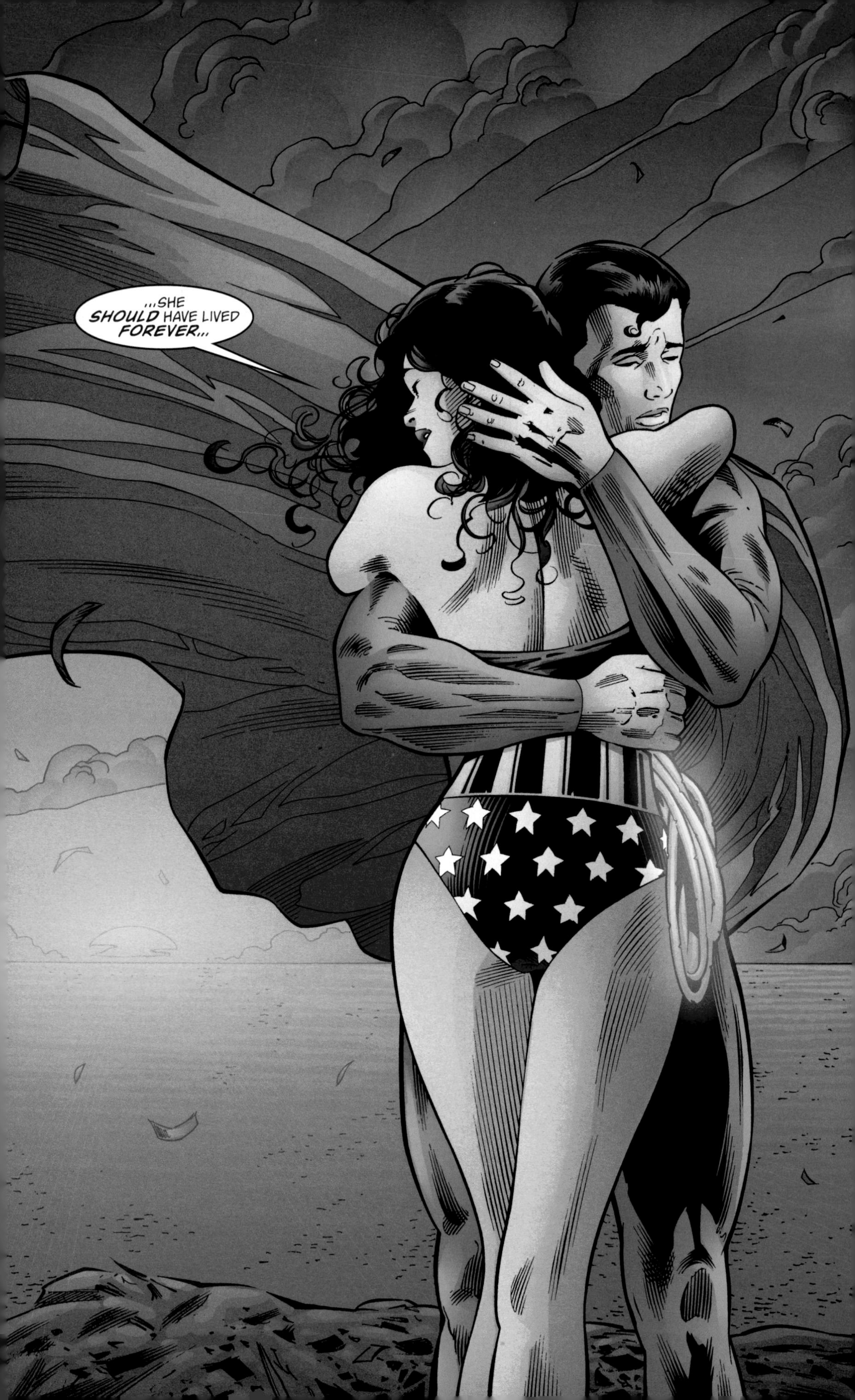
...SHE SHOULD HAVE LIVED FOREVER...

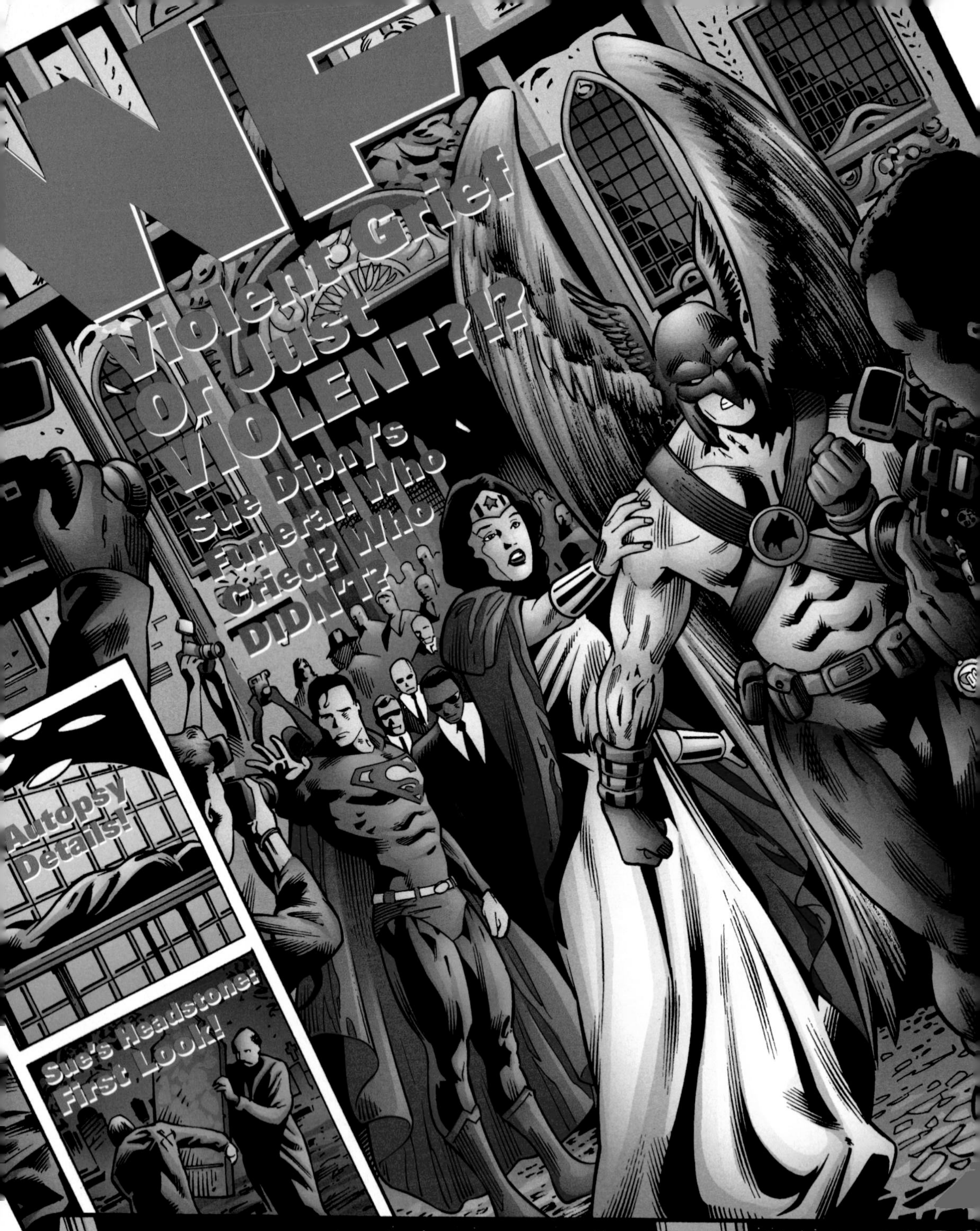
WF
Violent Grief or Just VIOLENT?!?
Sue Dibny's Funeral: Who Cried? Who DIDN'T?
Autopsy Details!
Sue's Headstone: First Look!

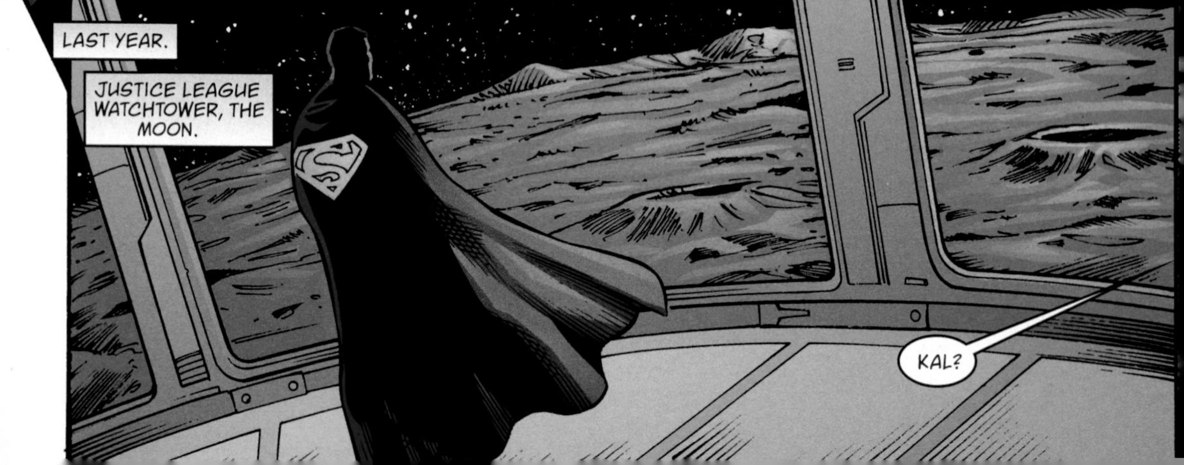
LAST YEAR.
JUSTICE LEAGUE WATCHTOWER, THE MOON.
KAL?

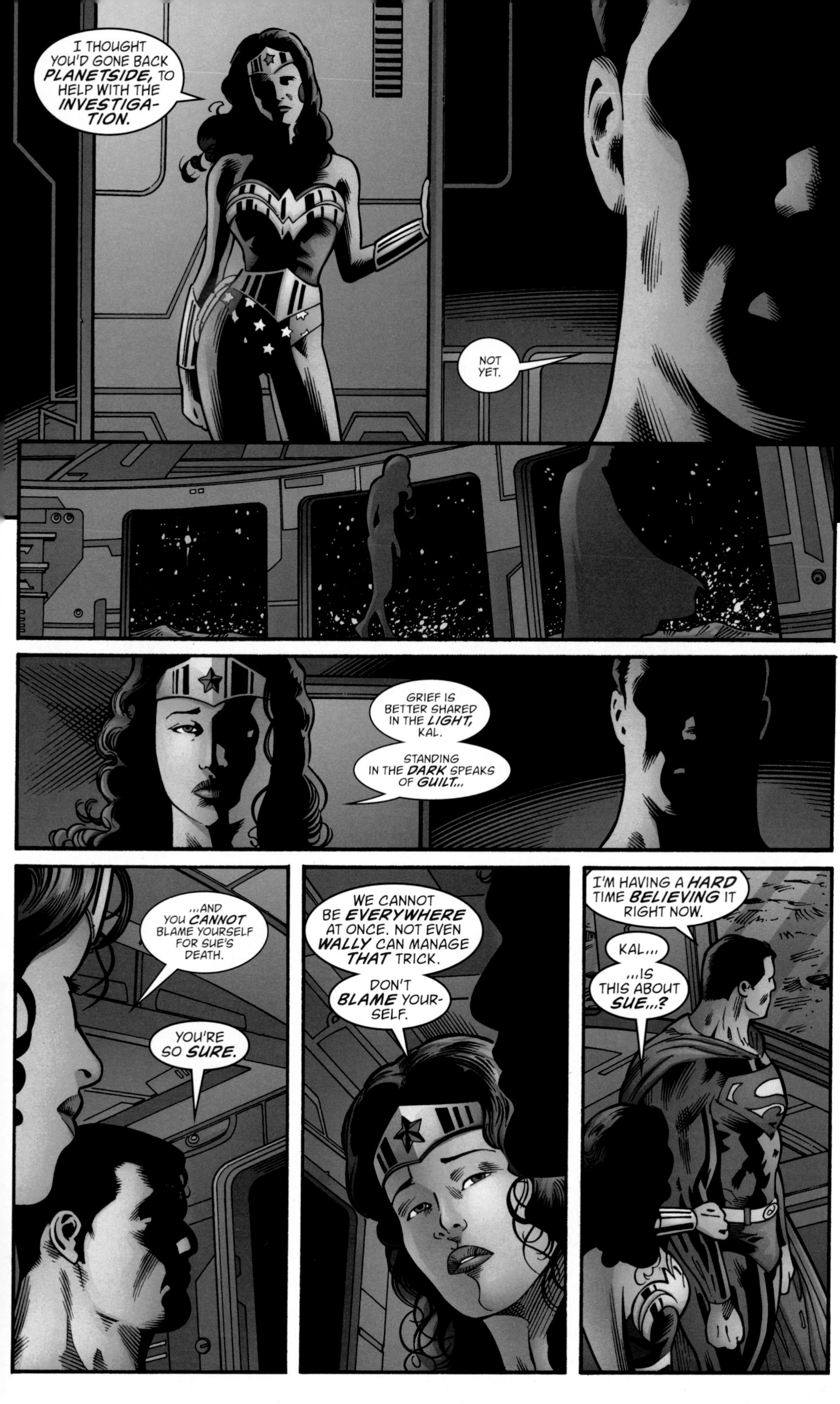

I THOUGHT YOU'D GONE BACK PLANETSIDE, TO HELP WITH THE INVESTIGATION.
NOT YET.
GRIEF IS BETTER SHARED IN THE LIGHT, KAL.
STANDING IN THE DARK SPEAKS OF GUILT...
...AND YOU CANNOT BLAME YOURSELF FOR SUE'S DEATH.
YOU'RE SO SURE.
WE CANNOT BE EVERYWHERE AT ONCE. NOT EVEN WALLY CAN MANAGE THAT TRICK.
DON'T BLAME YOURSELF.
I'M HAVING A HARD TIME BELIEVING IT RIGHT NOW.
KAL...
...IS THIS ABOUT SUE...?

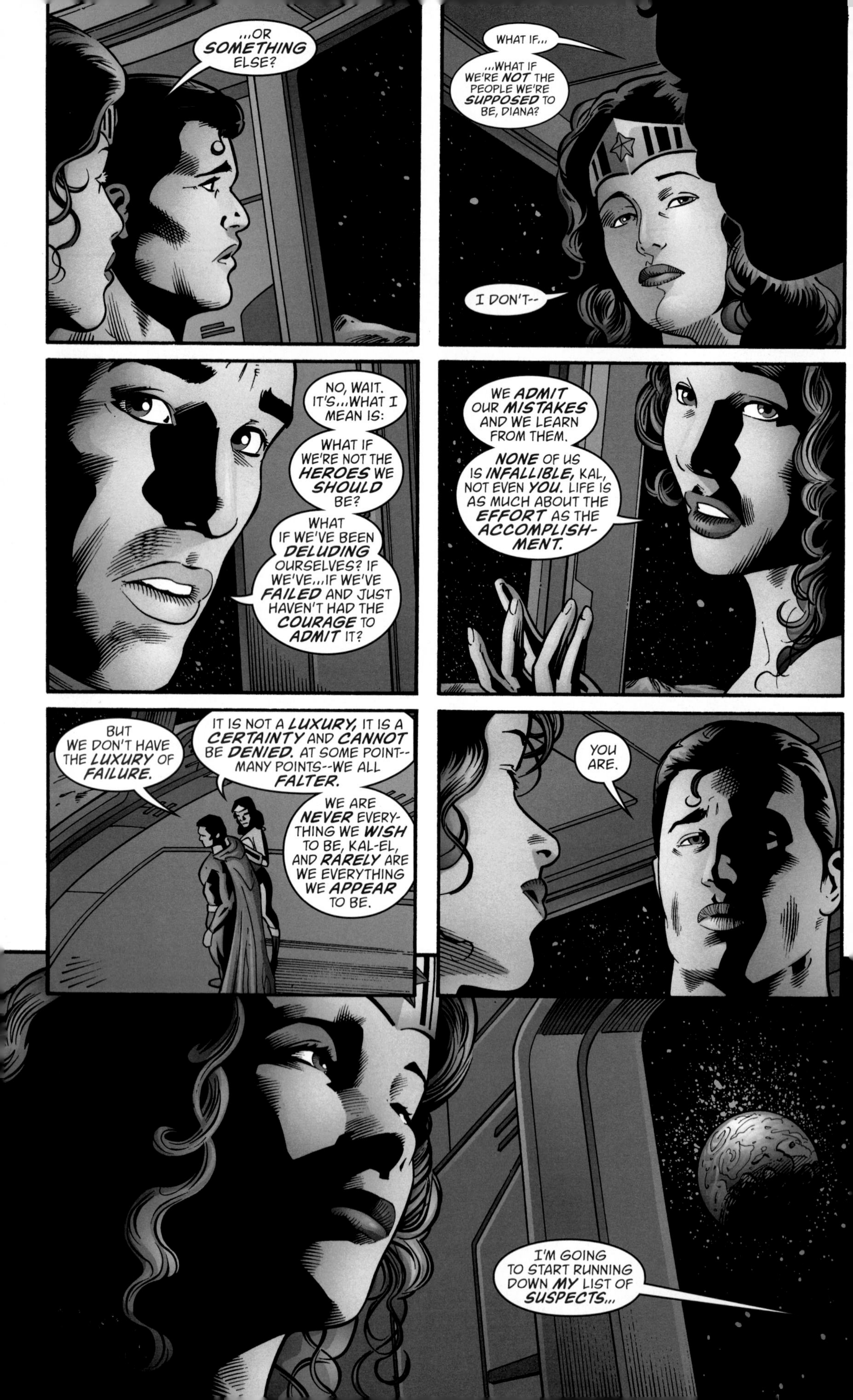
...OR SOMETHING ELSE?
WHAT IF...
...WHAT IF WE'RE NOT THE PEOPLE WE'RE SUPPOSED TO BE, DIANA?
I DON'T--
NO, WAIT. IT'S...WHAT I MEAN IS:
WHAT IF WE'RE NOT THE HEROES WE SHOULD BE?
WHAT IF WE'VE BEEN DELUDING OURSELVES? IF WE'VE...IF WE'VE FAILED AND JUST HAVEN'T HAD THE COURAGE TO ADMIT IT?
WE ADMIT OUR MISTAKES AND WE LEARN FROM THEM.
NONE OF US IS INFALLIBLE, KAL, NOT EVEN YOU. LIFE IS AS MUCH ABOUT THE EFFORT AS THE ACCOMPLISH-MENT.
BUT WE DON'T HAVE THE LUXURY OF FAILURE.
IT IS NOT A LUXURY, IT IS A CERTAINTY AND CANNOT BE DENIED. AT SOME POINT--MANY POINTS--WE ALL FALTER.
WE ARE NEVER EVERY-THING WE WISH TO BE, KAL-EL, AND RARELY ARE WE EVERYTHING WE APPEAR TO BE.
YOU ARE.
I'M GOING TO START RUNNING DOWN MY LIST OF SUSPECTS...

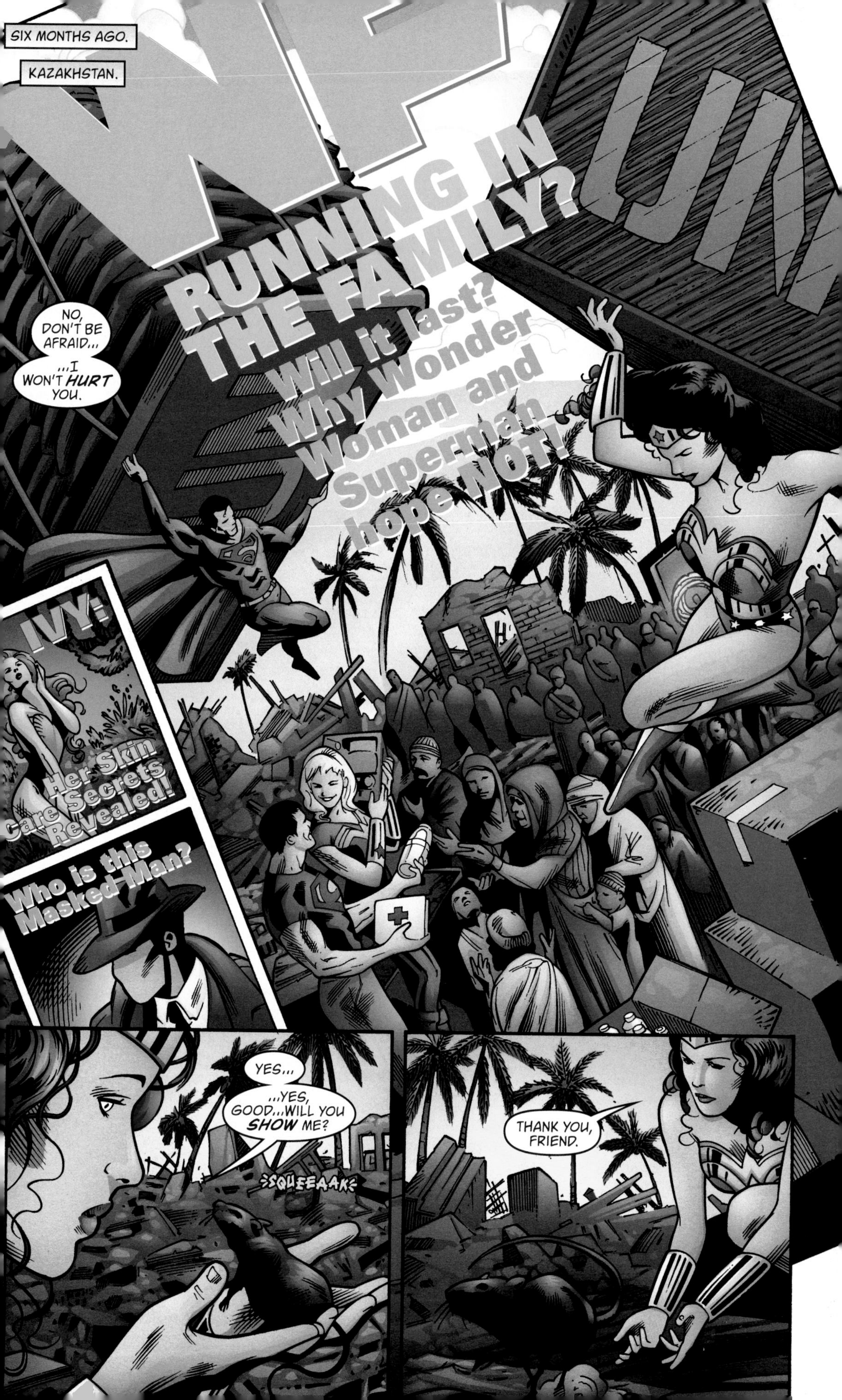

SIX MONTHS AGO.
KAZAKHSTAN.
RUNNING IN THE FAMILY? Will it last? Why Wonder Woman and Superman hope NOT!
NO, DON'T BE AFRAID...
...I WON'T HURT YOU.
IVY: Her Skin Care Secrets Revealed!
Who is this Masked-Man?
YES...
...YES, GOOD...WILL YOU SHOW ME?
SQUEEAAK
THANK YOU, FRIEND.

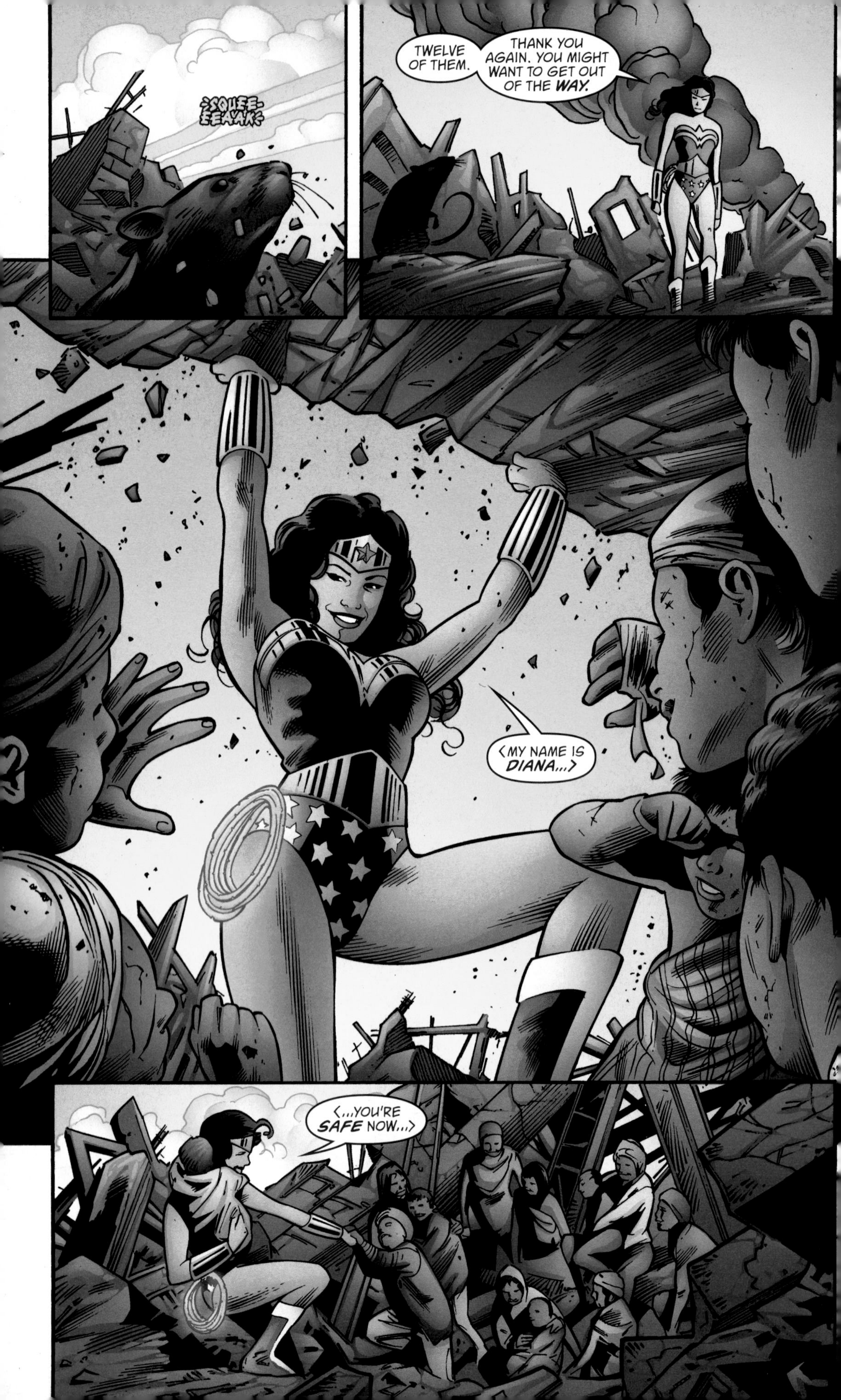
SQUEE-EEAYAK
TWELVE OF THEM.
THANK YOU AGAIN. YOU MIGHT WANT TO GET OUT OF THE WAY.
‹MY NAME IS DIANA...›
‹...YOU'RE SAFE NOW...›

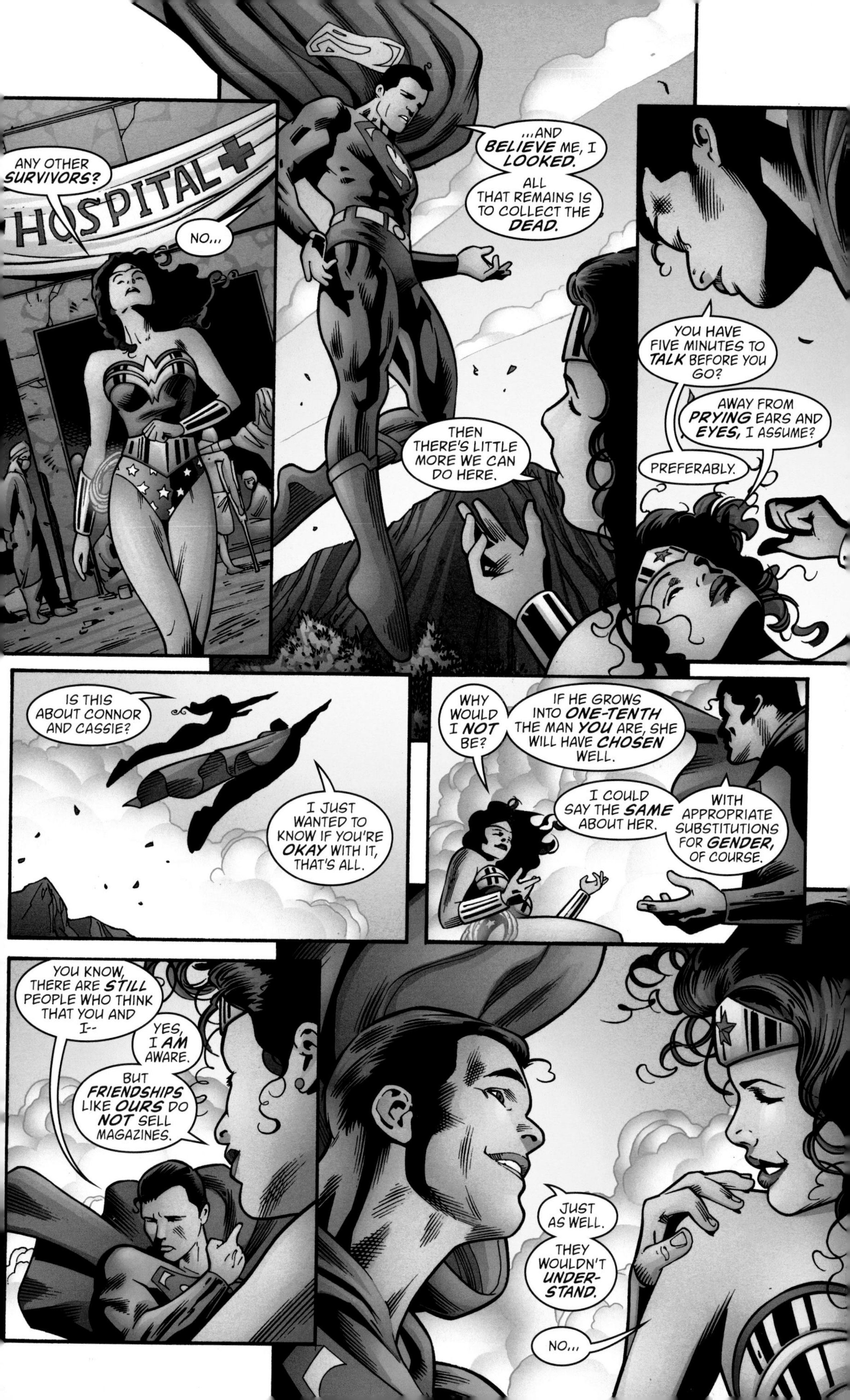
ANY OTHER SURVIVORS?
HOSPITAL
NO...
...AND BELIEVE ME, I LOOKED.
ALL THAT REMAINS IS TO COLLECT THE DEAD.
THEN THERE'S LITTLE MORE WE CAN DO HERE.
YOU HAVE FIVE MINUTES TO TALK BEFORE YOU GO?
AWAY FROM PRYING EARS AND EYES, I ASSUME?
PREFERABLY.
IS THIS ABOUT CONNOR AND CASSIE?
I JUST WANTED TO KNOW IF YOU'RE OKAY WITH IT, THAT'S ALL.
WHY WOULD I NOT BE?
IF HE GROWS INTO ONE-TENTH THE MAN YOU ARE, SHE WILL HAVE CHOSEN WELL.
I COULD SAY THE SAME ABOUT HER.
WITH APPROPRIATE SUBSTITUTIONS FOR GENDER, OF COURSE.
YOU KNOW, THERE ARE STILL PEOPLE WHO THINK THAT YOU AND I--
YES, I AM AWARE.
BUT FRIENDSHIPS LIKE OURS DO NOT SELL MAGAZINES.
JUST AS WELL.
THEY WOULDN'T UNDER-STAND.
NO...

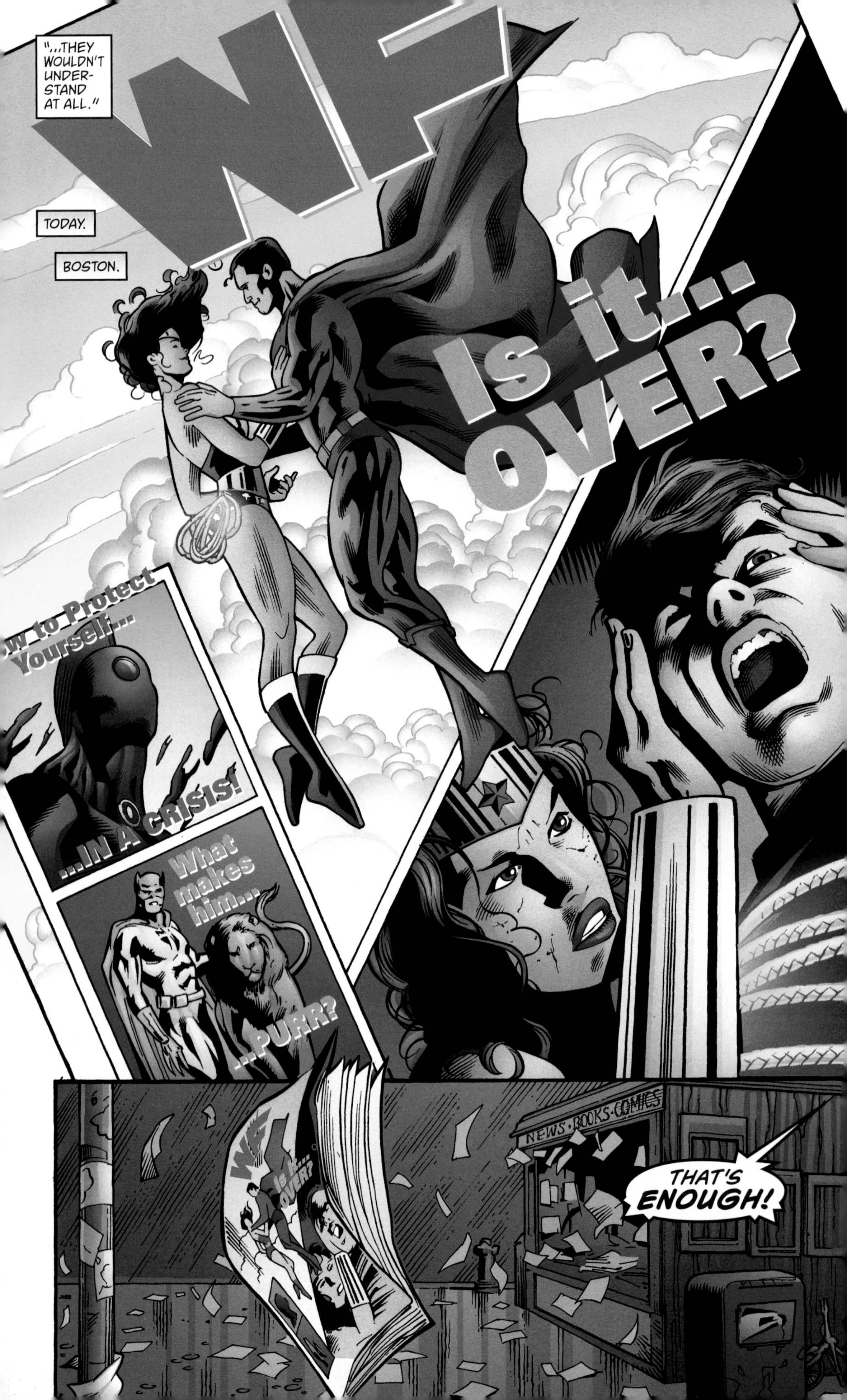
"...THEY WOULDN'T UNDER-STAND AT ALL."
WF
TODAY.
BOSTON.
Is it... OVER?
w to Protect Yourself...
...IN A CRISIS!
What makes him... ...PURR?
NEWS · BOOKS · COMICS
THAT'S ENOUGH!

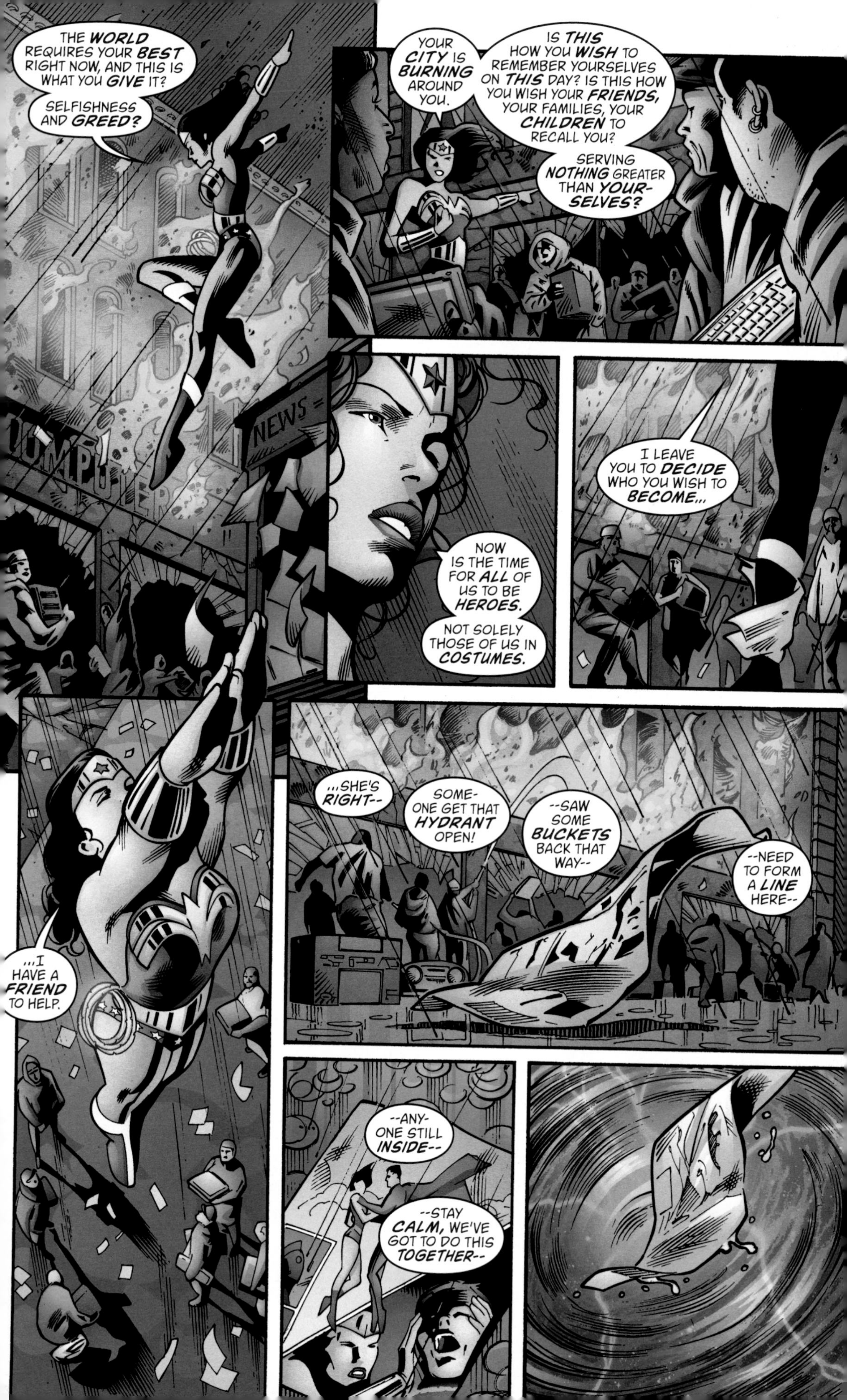
THE WORLD REQUIRES YOUR BEST RIGHT NOW, AND THIS IS WHAT YOU GIVE IT?
SELFISHNESS AND GREED?
YOUR CITY IS BURNING AROUND YOU.
IS THIS HOW YOU WISH TO REMEMBER YOURSELVES ON THIS DAY? IS THIS HOW YOU WISH YOUR FRIENDS, YOUR FAMILIES, YOUR CHILDREN TO RECALL YOU?
SERVING NOTHING GREATER THAN YOURSELVES?
NEWS
COMPUTER
NOW IS THE TIME FOR ALL OF US TO BE HEROES.
NOT SOLELY THOSE OF US IN COSTUMES.
I LEAVE YOU TO DECIDE WHO YOU WISH TO BECOME...
...I HAVE A FRIEND TO HELP.
...SHE'S RIGHT--
SOME-ONE GET THAT HYDRANT OPEN!
--SAW SOME BUCKETS BACK THAT WAY--
--NEED TO FORM A LINE HERE--
--ANY-ONE STILL INSIDE--
--STAY CALM, WE'VE GOT TO DO THIS TOGETHER--

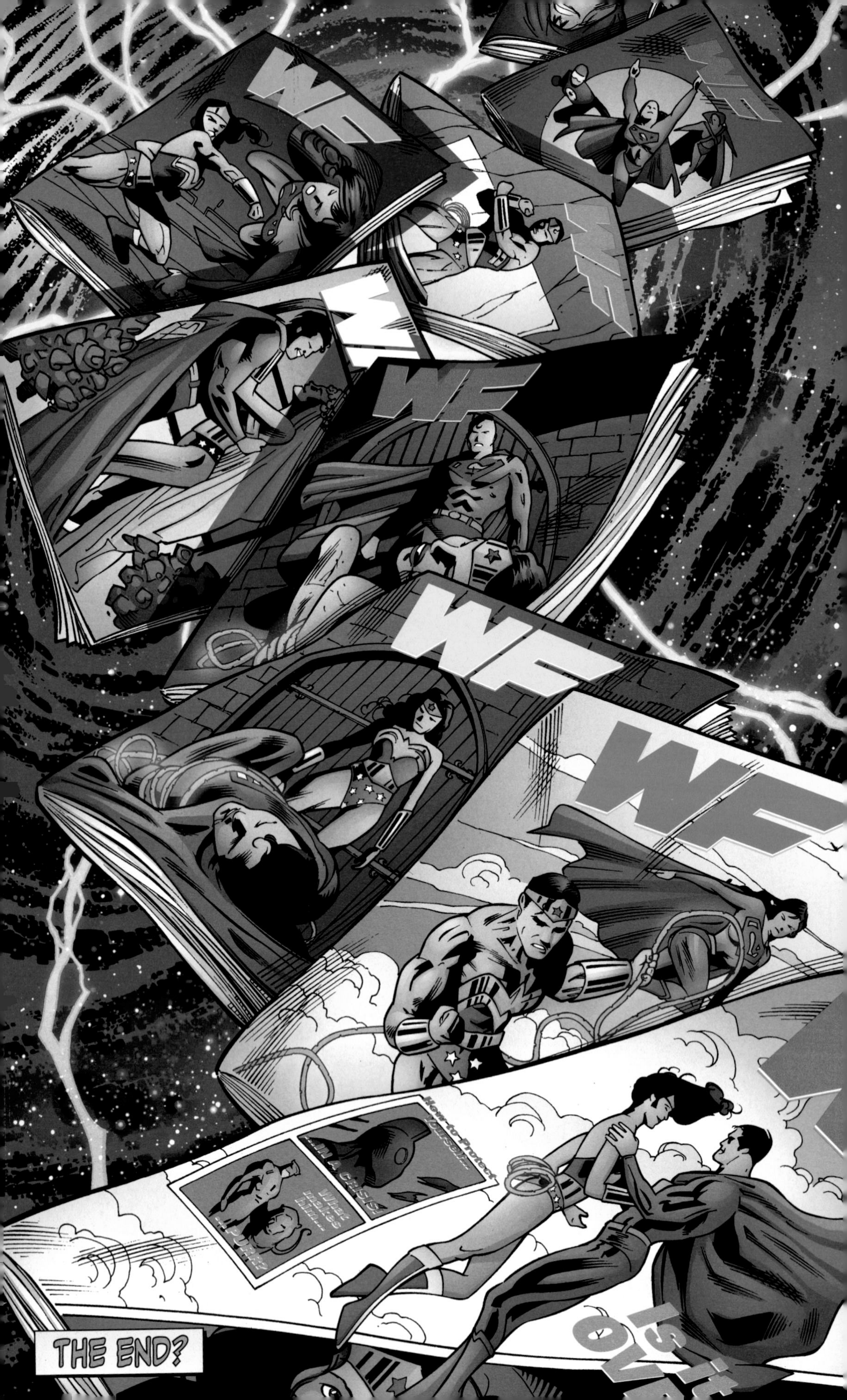
How to Protect Yourself...
...IN A CRISIS!
What makes him...
...PURR?
IS IT
THE END?

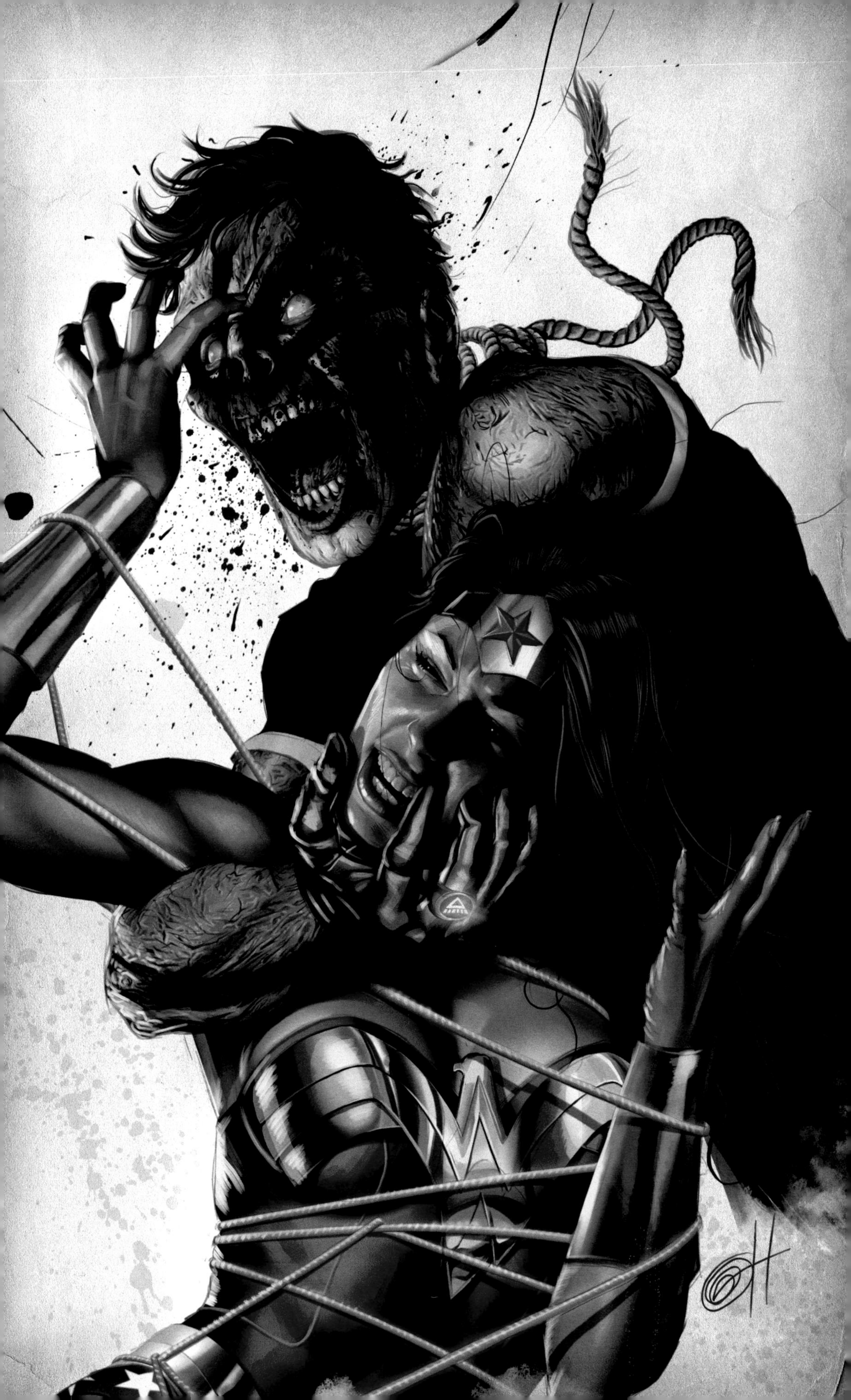

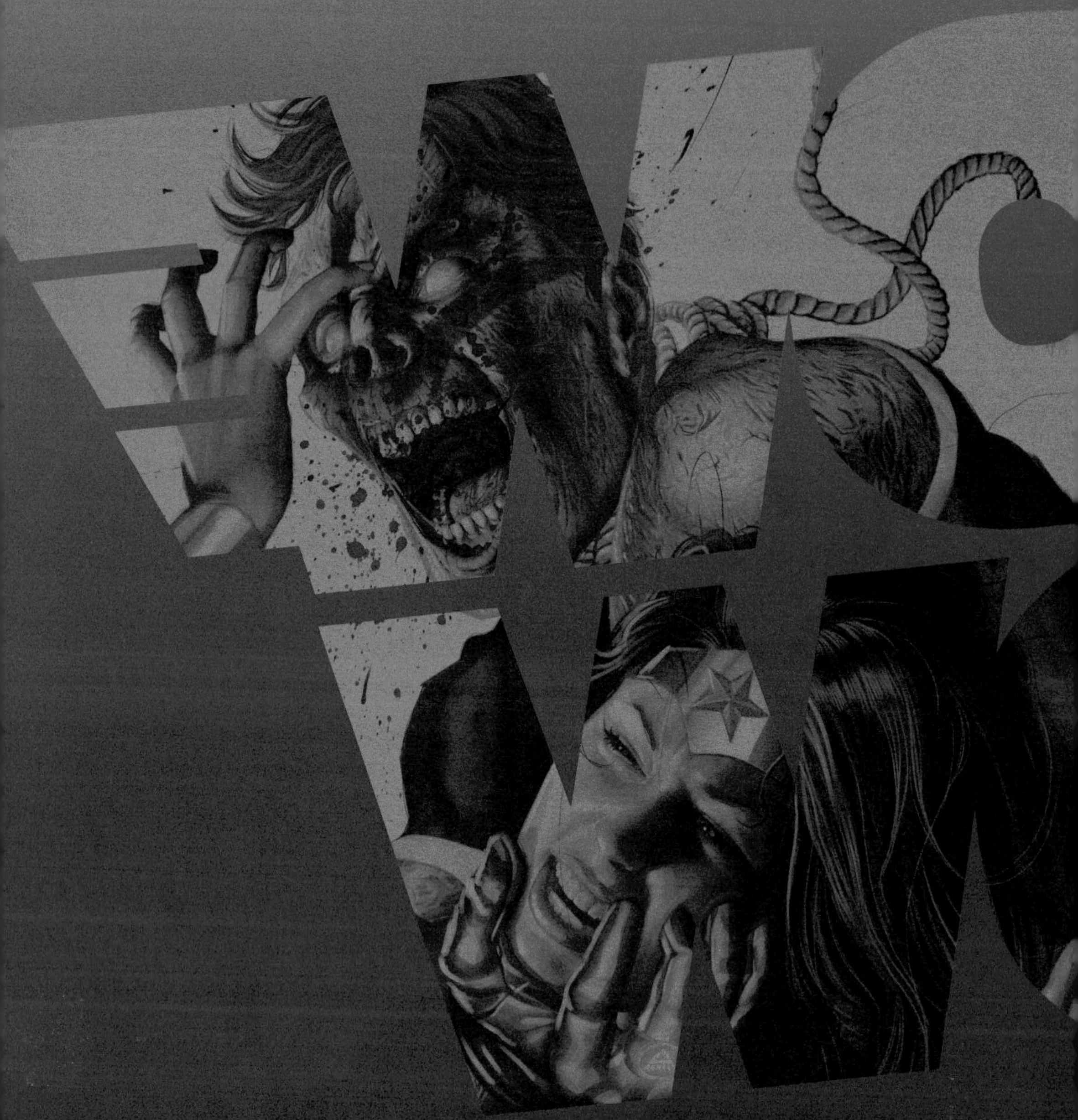

"WONDER WOMAN: BLACKEST NIGHT PART ONE"

Greg Rucka – *writer*
Nicola Scott – *pencils*
Prentis Rollins, Jonathan Glapion, Walden Wong and **Drew Geraci** – *inks*
Nei Ruffino – *colors*
Travis Lanham – *letters*
Greg Horn – *cover*

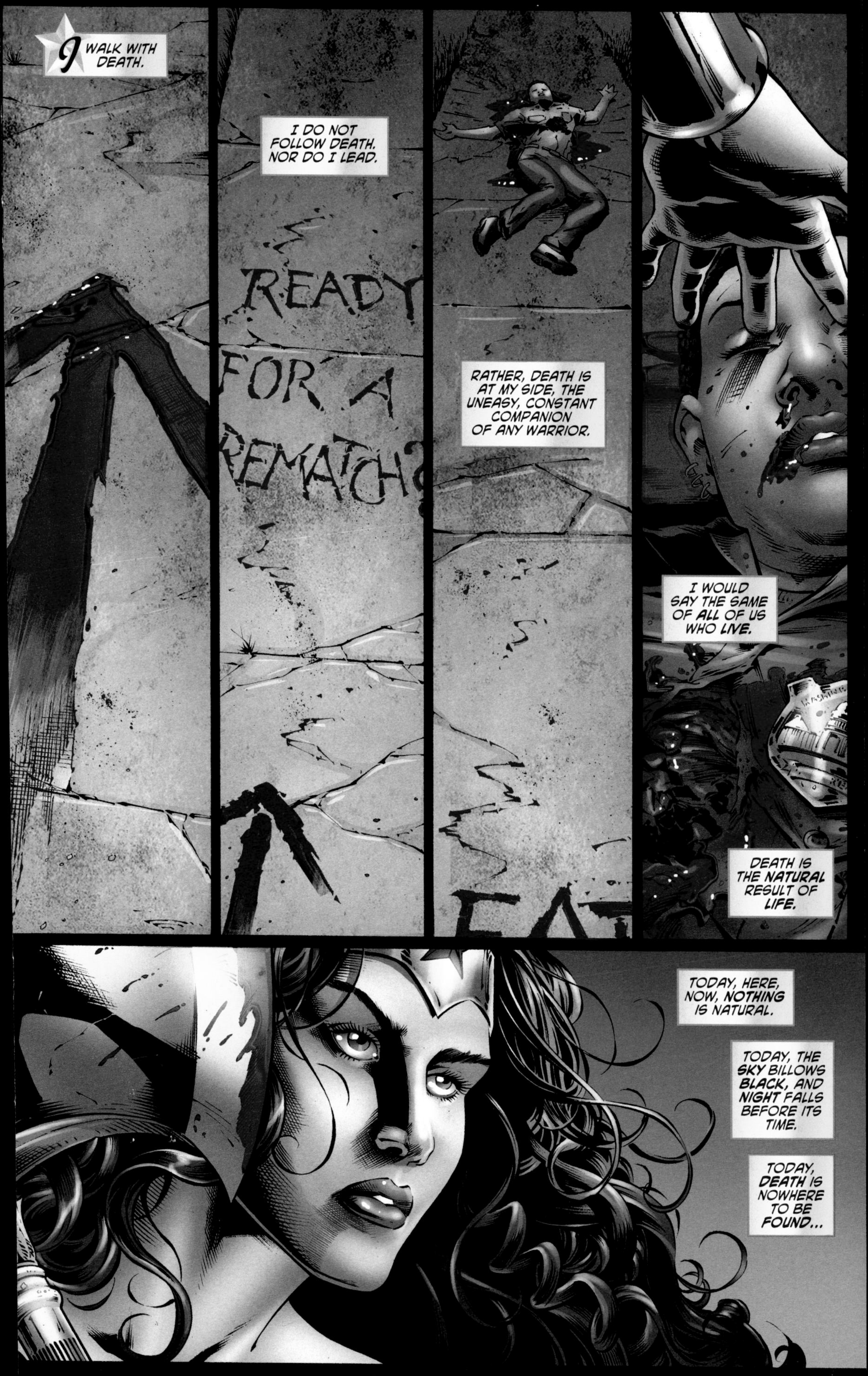
I WALK WITH DEATH.
I DO NOT FOLLOW DEATH. NOR DO I LEAD.
READY FOR A REMATCH?
RATHER, DEATH IS AT MY SIDE, THE UNEASY, CONSTANT COMPANION OF ANY WARRIOR.
I WOULD SAY THE SAME OF ALL OF US WHO LIVE.
DEATH IS THE NATURAL RESULT OF LIFE.
TODAY, HERE, NOW, NOTHING IS NATURAL.
TODAY, THE SKY BILLOWS BLACK, AND NIGHT FALLS BEFORE ITS TIME.
TODAY, DEATH IS NOWHERE TO BE FOUND...

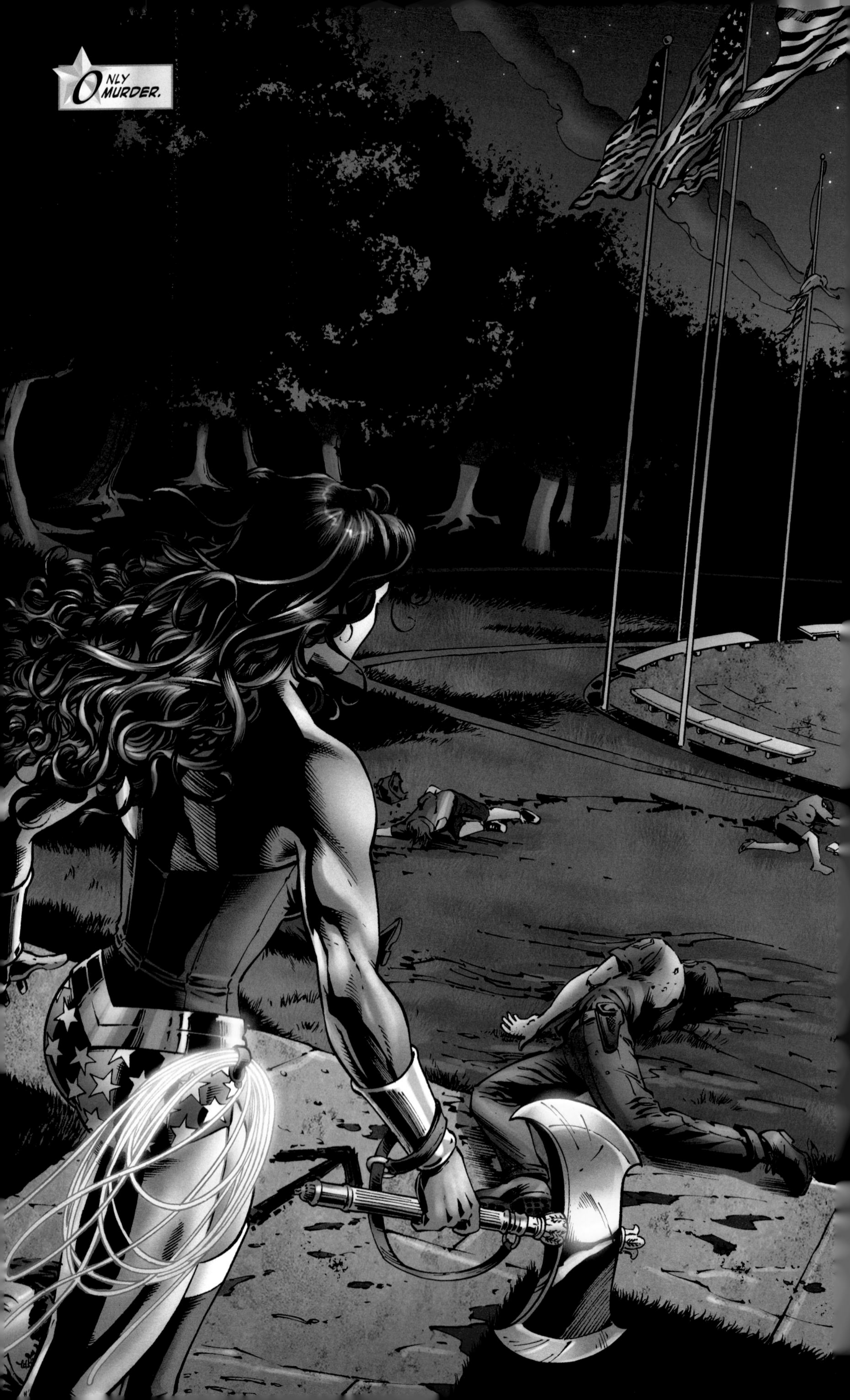
ONLY MURDER.

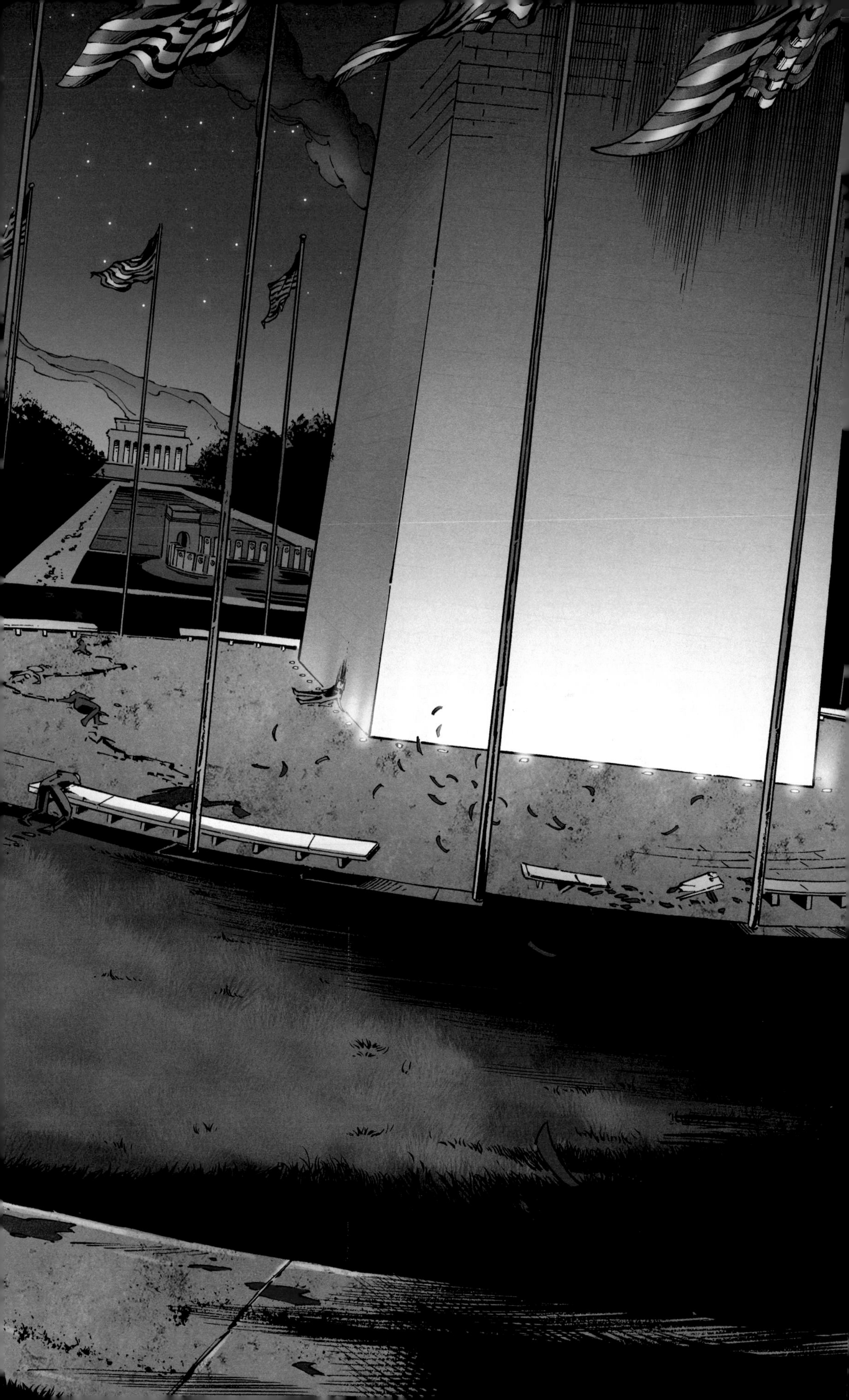

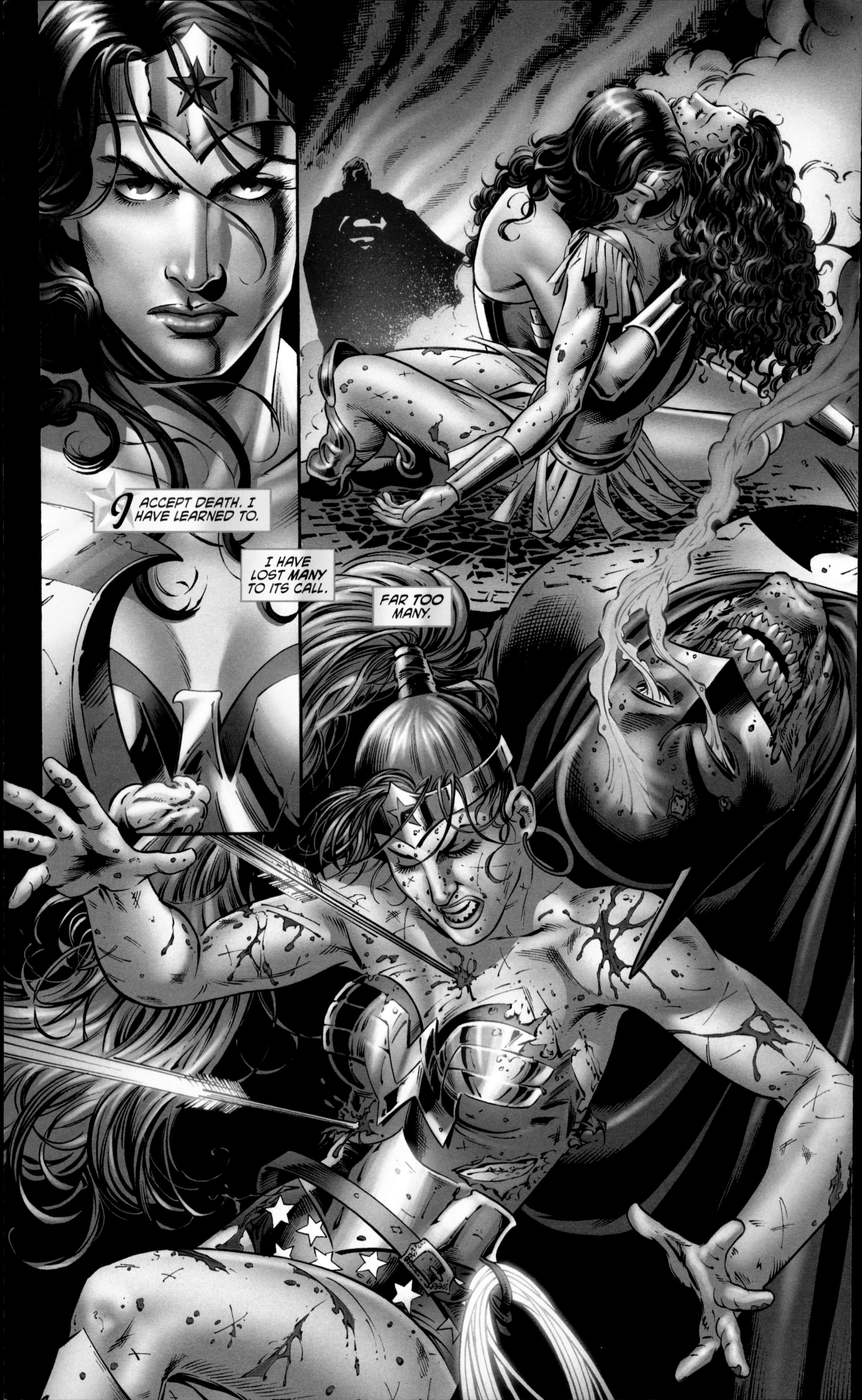
I ACCEPT DEATH. I HAVE LEARNED TO.
I HAVE LOST MANY TO ITS CALL.
FAR TOO MANY.

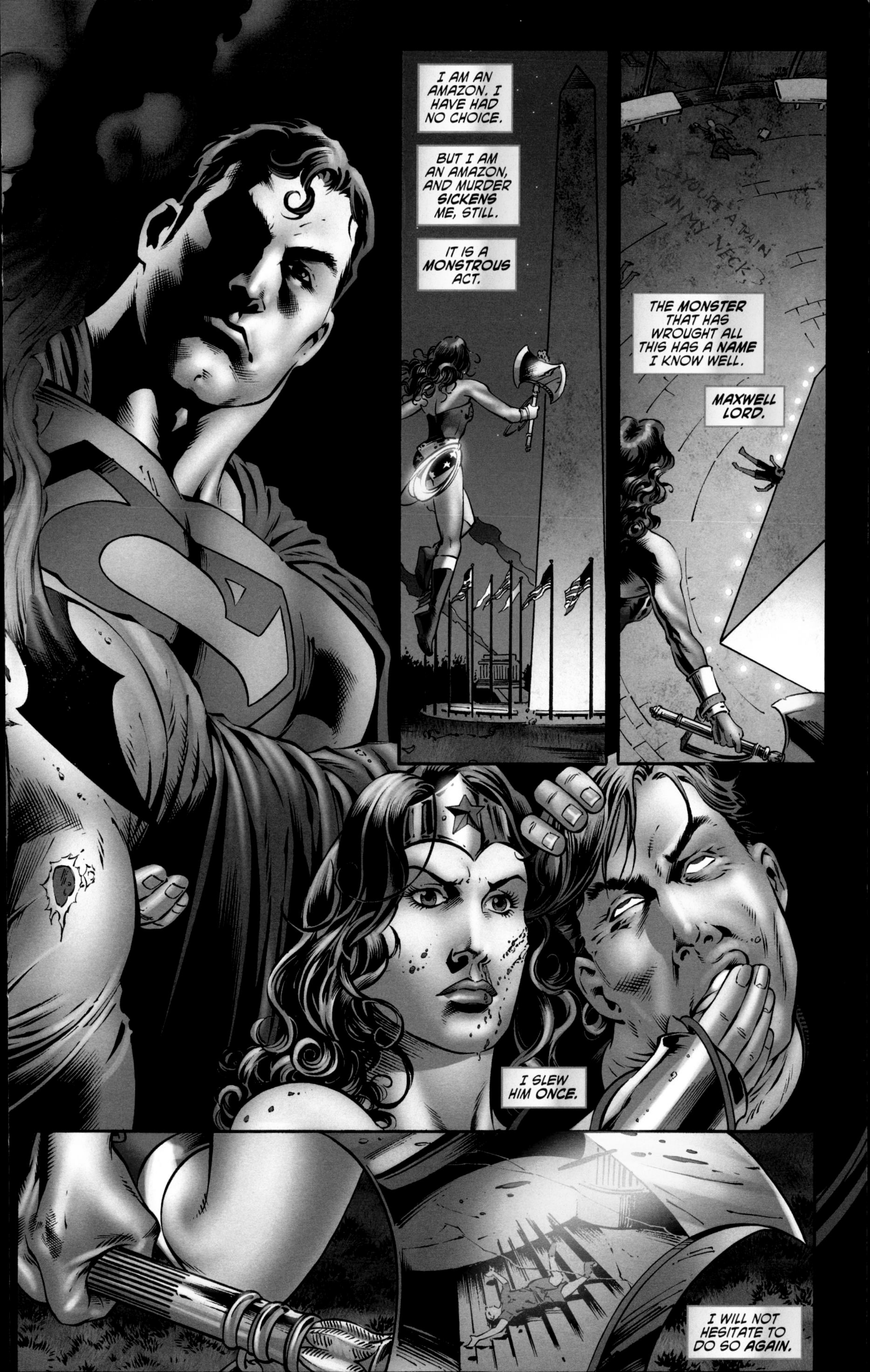
I AM AN AMAZON. I HAVE HAD NO CHOICE.
BUT I AM AN AMAZON, AND MURDER SICKENS ME, STILL.
IT IS A MONSTROUS ACT.
YOU'RE A PAIN IN MY NECK
THE MONSTER THAT HAS WROUGHT ALL THIS HAS A NAME I KNOW WELL.
MAXWELL LORD.
I SLEW HIM ONCE.
I WILL NOT HESITATE TO DO SO AGAIN.

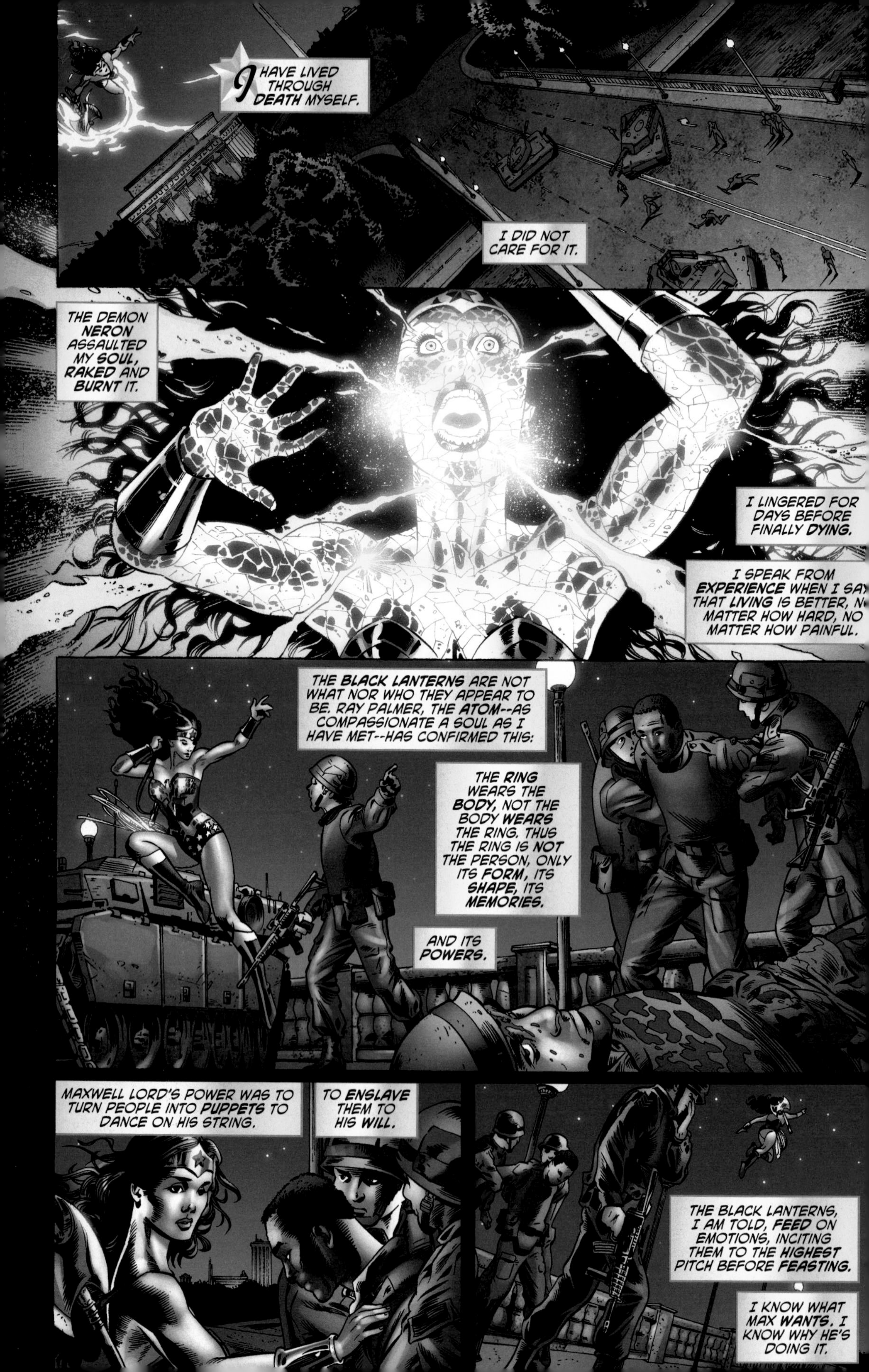
I HAVE LIVED THROUGH DEATH MYSELF.
I DID NOT CARE FOR IT.
THE DEMON NERON ASSAULTED MY SOUL, RAKED AND BURNT IT.
I LINGERED FOR DAYS BEFORE FINALLY DYING.
I SPEAK FROM EXPERIENCE WHEN I SAY THAT LIVING IS BETTER, NO MATTER HOW HARD, NO MATTER HOW PAINFUL.
THE BLACK LANTERNS ARE NOT WHAT NOR WHO THEY APPEAR TO BE. RAY PALMER, THE ATOM--AS COMPASSIONATE A SOUL AS I HAVE MET--HAS CONFIRMED THIS:
THE RING WEARS THE BODY, NOT THE BODY WEARS THE RING. THUS THE RING IS NOT THE PERSON, ONLY ITS FORM, ITS SHAPE, ITS MEMORIES.
AND ITS POWERS.
MAXWELL LORD'S POWER WAS TO TURN PEOPLE INTO PUPPETS TO DANCE ON HIS STRING.
TO ENSLAVE THEM TO HIS WILL.
THE BLACK LANTERNS, I AM TOLD, FEED ON EMOTIONS, INCITING THEM TO THE HIGHEST PITCH BEFORE FEASTING.
I KNOW WHAT MAX WANTS. I KNOW WHY HE'S DOING IT.

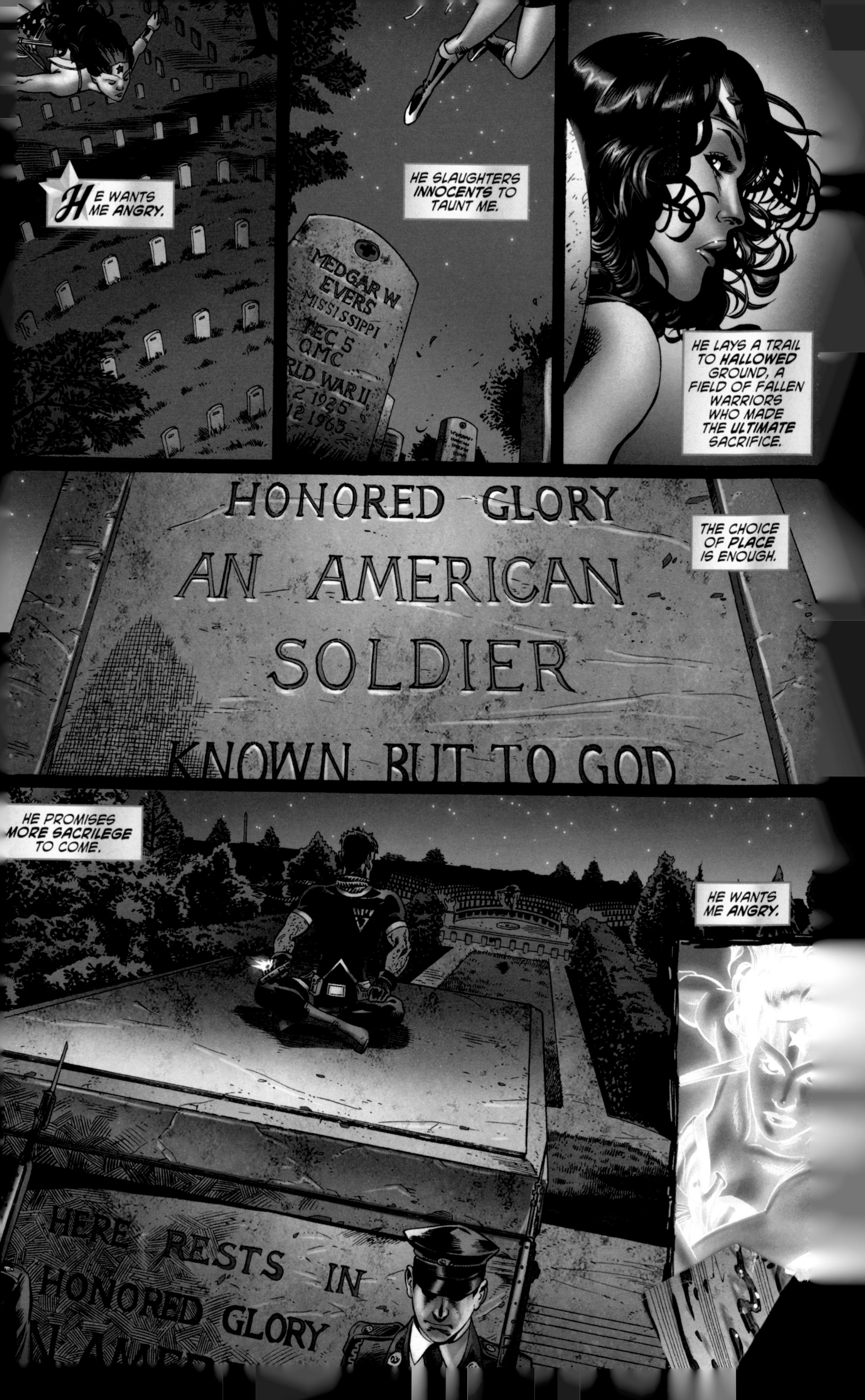
HE WANTS ME ANGRY.
HE SLAUGHTERS INNOCENTS TO TAUNT ME.
MEDGAR W EVERS MISSISSIPPI TEC 5 QMC
HE LAYS A TRAIL TO HALLOWED GROUND, A FIELD OF FALLEN WARRIORS WHO MADE THE ULTIMATE SACRIFICE.
HONORED GLORY
AN AMERICAN SOLDIER
KNOWN BUT TO GOD
THE CHOICE OF PLACE IS ENOUGH.
HE PROMISES MORE SACRILEGE TO COME.
HERE RESTS IN HONORED GLORY
HE WANTS ME ANGRY.

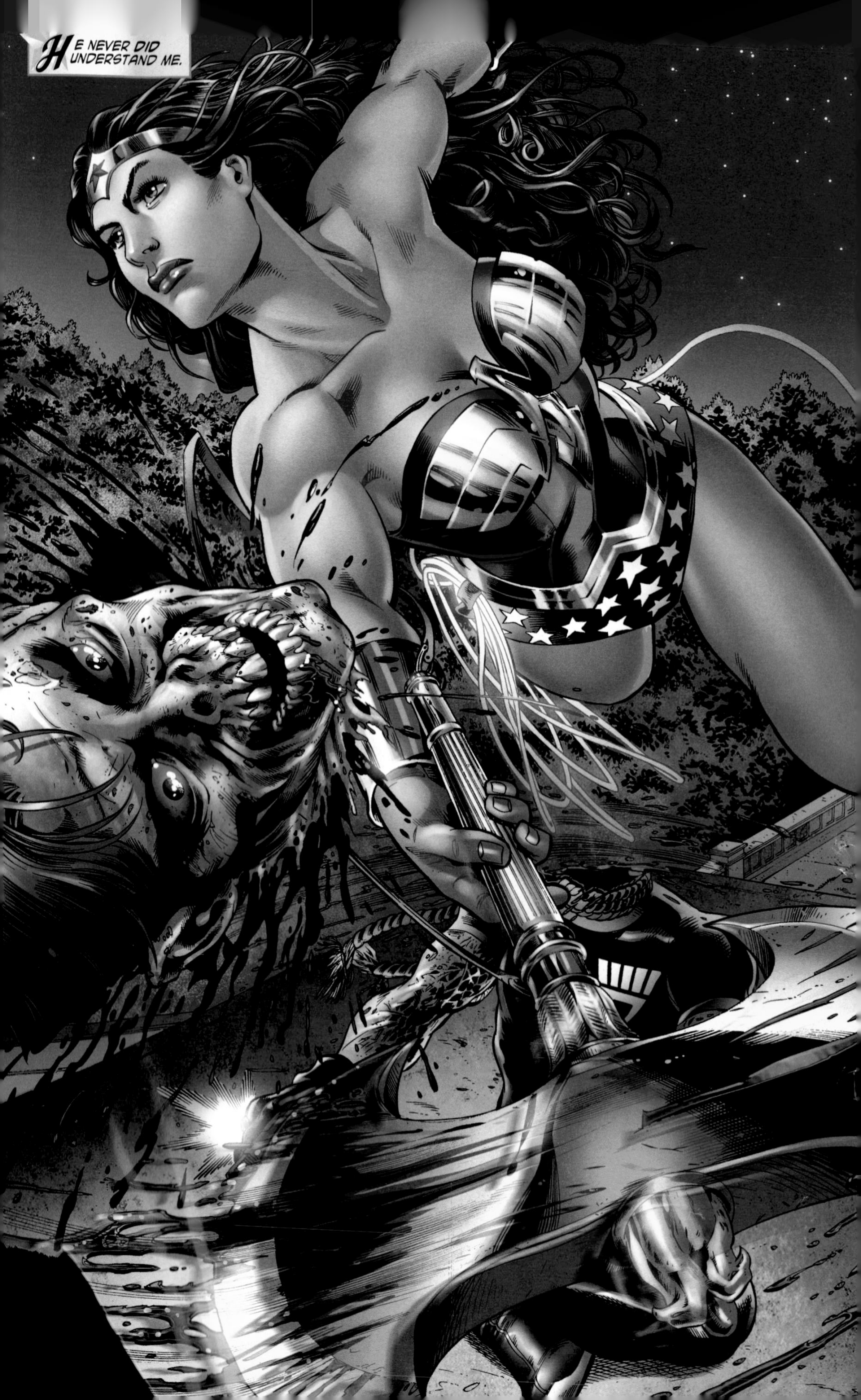
HE NEVER DID UNDERSTAND ME.

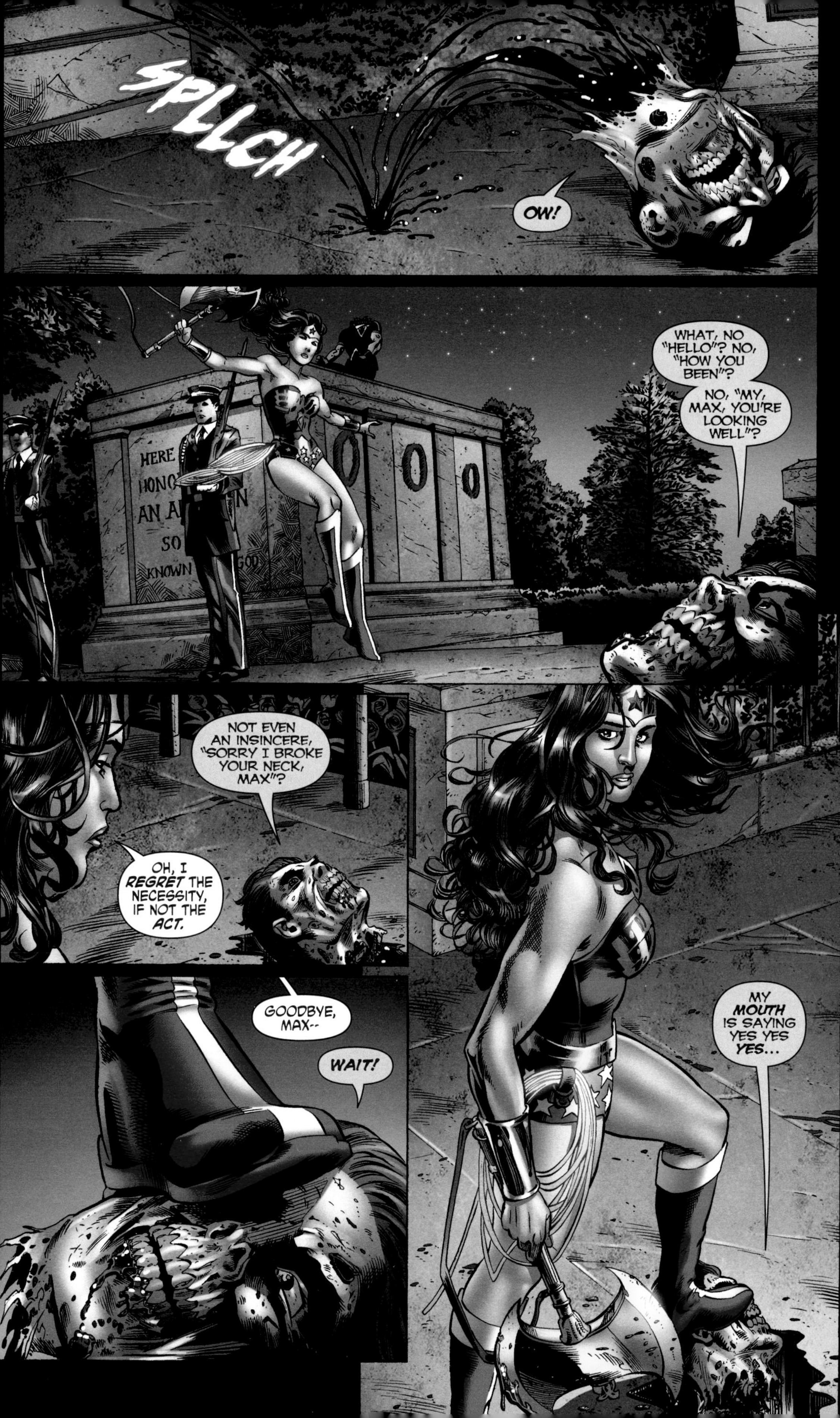
SPLCH
OW!
WHAT, NO "HELLO"? NO, "HOW YOU BEEN"?
NO, "MY, MAX, YOU'RE LOOKING WELL"?
NOT EVEN AN INSINCERE, "SORRY I BROKE YOUR NECK, MAX"?
OH, I REGRET THE NECESSITY, IF NOT THE ACT.
GOODBYE, MAX--
WAIT!
MY MOUTH IS SAYING YES YES YES...

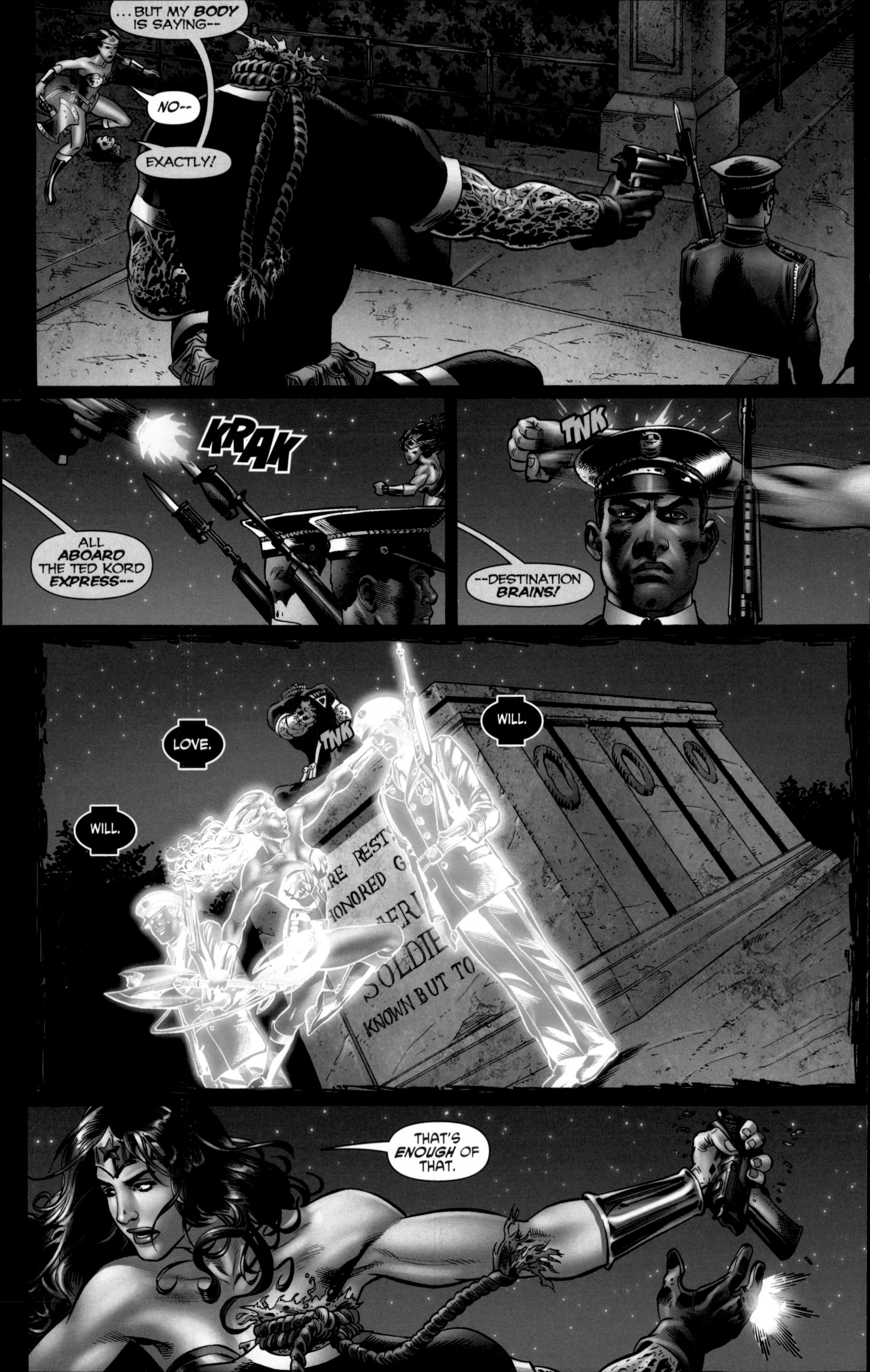
...BUT MY BODY IS SAYING--
NO--
EXACTLY!
KRAK
ALL ABOARD THE TED KORD EXPRESS--
TNK
--DESTINATION BRAINS!
LOVE.
TNK
WILL.
WILL.
THAT'S ENOUGH OF THAT.

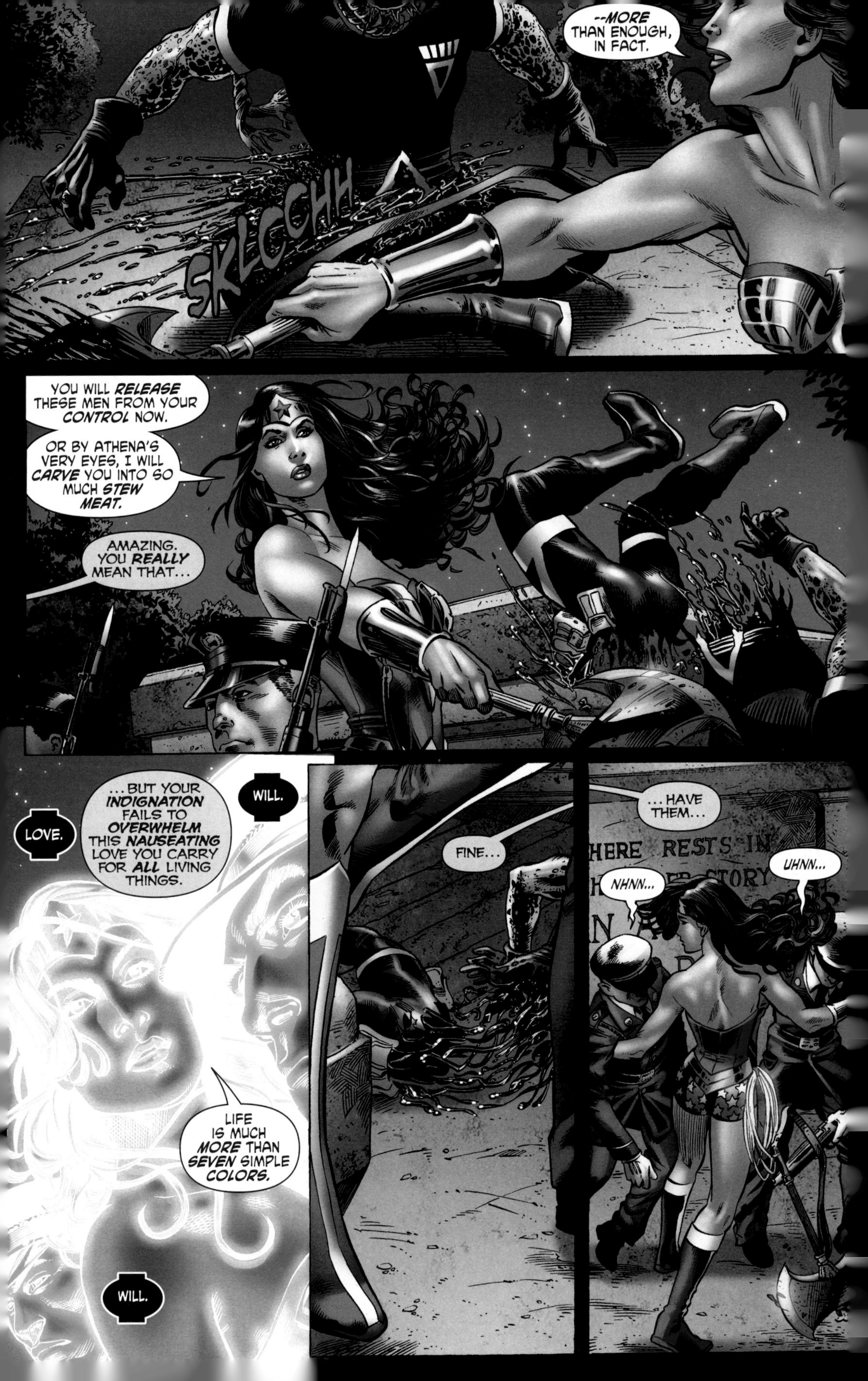
--MORE THAN ENOUGH, IN FACT.
SKLCCHH
YOU WILL RELEASE THESE MEN FROM YOUR CONTROL NOW.
OR BY ATHENA'S VERY EYES, I WILL CARVE YOU INTO SO MUCH STEW MEAT.
AMAZING. YOU REALLY MEAN THAT...
LOVE.
...BUT YOUR INDIGNATION FAILS TO OVERWHELM THIS NAUSEATING LOVE YOU CARRY FOR ALL LIVING THINGS.
WILL.
LIFE IS MUCH MORE THAN SEVEN SIMPLE COLORS.
WILL.
FINE...
...HAVE THEM...
HERE RESTS IN
NHNN...
UHNN...

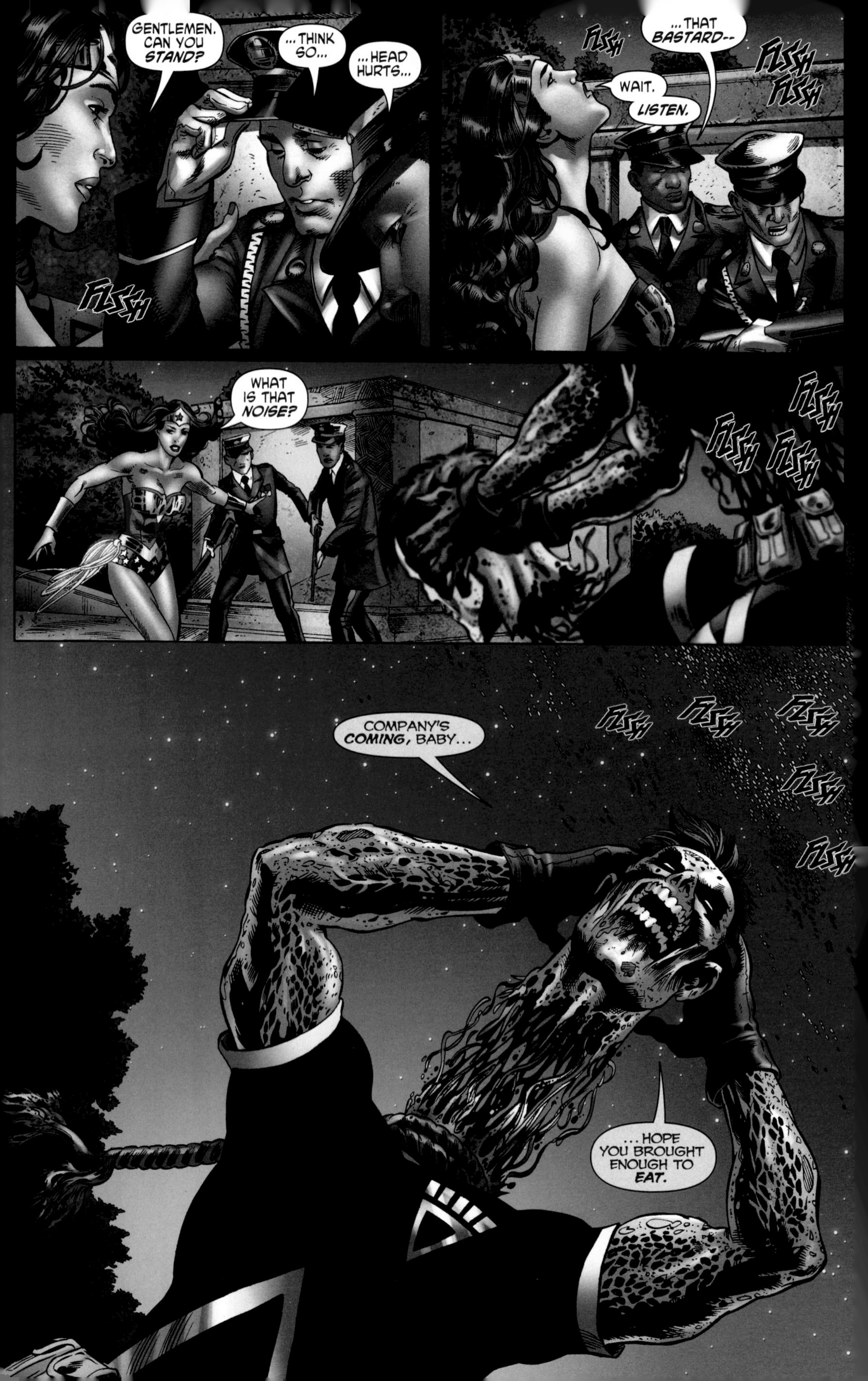
GENTLEMEN. CAN YOU STAND?
...THINK SO...
...HEAD HURTS...
FLSSH
FLSSH
...THAT BASTARD--
WAIT. LISTEN.
FLSSH FLSSH
WHAT IS THAT NOISE?
FLSSH
FLSSH
FLSSH
COMPANY'S COMING, BABY...
FLSSH
FLSSH
FLSSH
FLSSH
FLSSH
...HOPE YOU BROUGHT ENOUGH TO EAT.

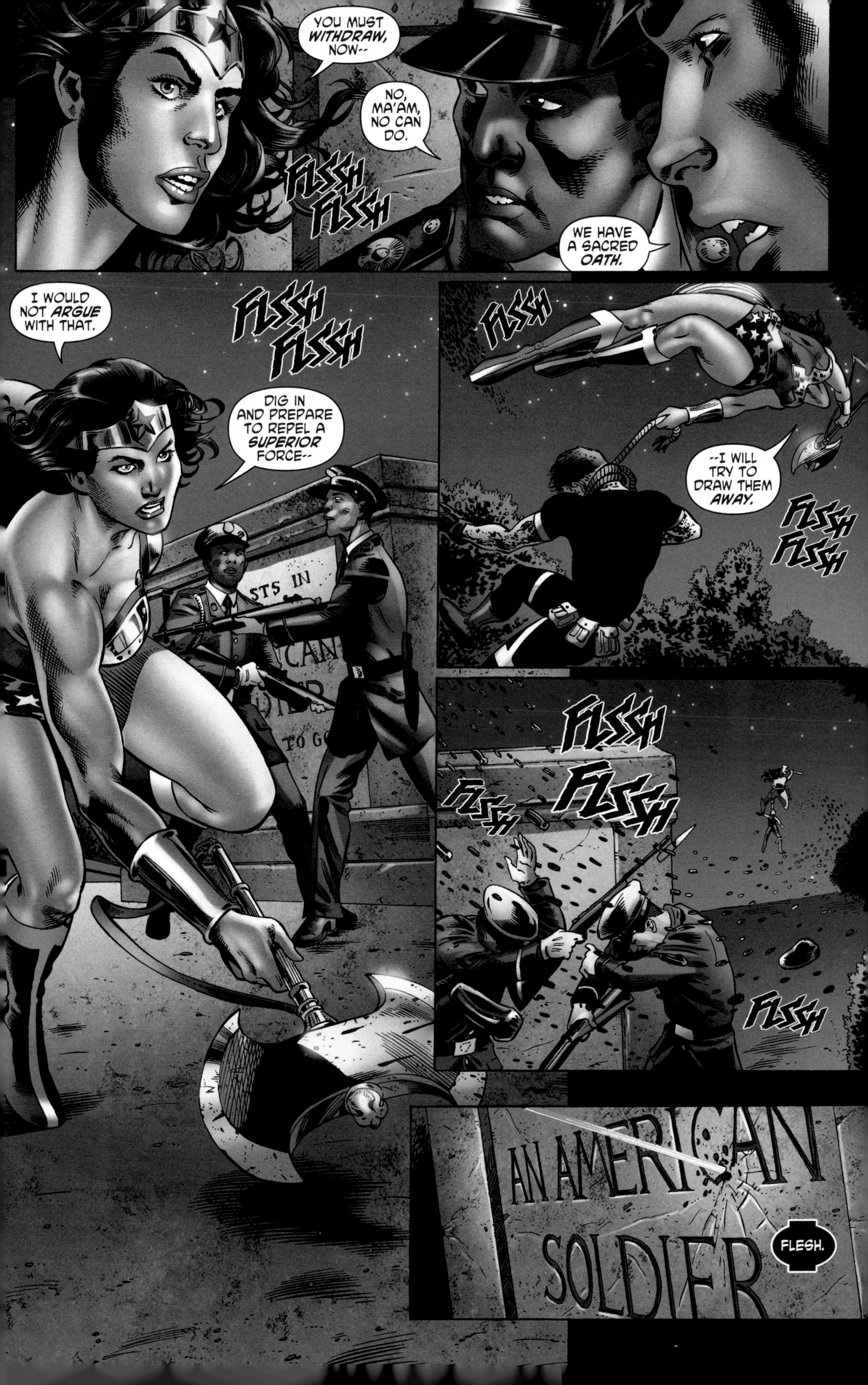

YOU MUST WITHDRAW, NOW--
NO, MA'AM, NO CAN DO.
FLSSH FLSSH
WE HAVE A SACRED OATH.
I WOULD NOT ARGUE WITH THAT.
FLSSH FLSSH
DIG IN AND PREPARE TO REPEL A SUPERIOR FORCE--
FLSSH
--I WILL TRY TO DRAW THEM AWAY.
FLSSH FLSSH
FLSSH
FLSSH
FLSSH
FLSSH
AN AMERICAN SOLDIER
FLESH.

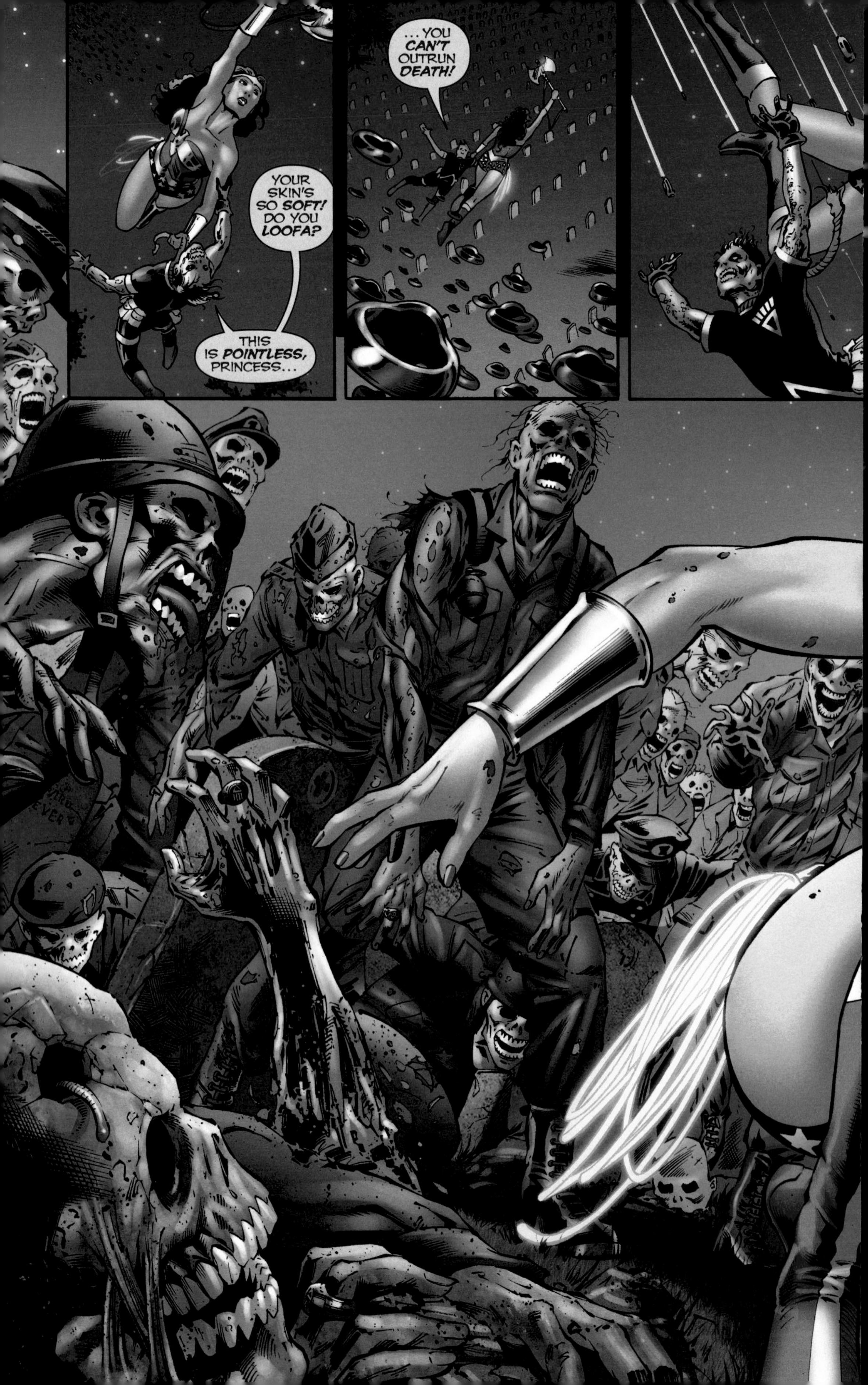
YOUR SKIN'S SO SOFT! DO YOU LOOFA?
THIS IS POINTLESS, PRINCESS...
...YOU CAN'T OUTRUN DEATH!

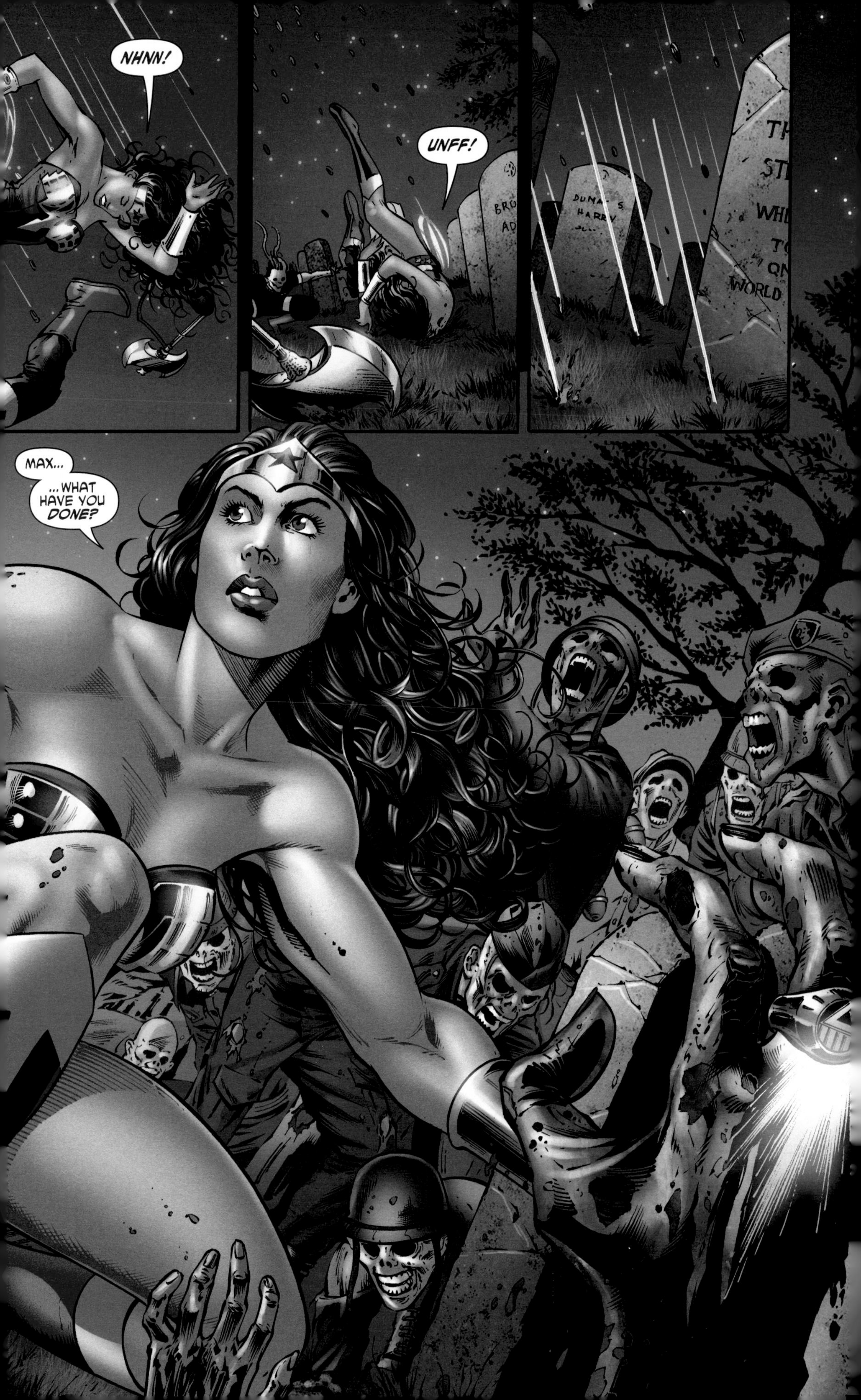
NHNN!
UNFF!
MAX... ...WHAT HAVE YOU DONE?

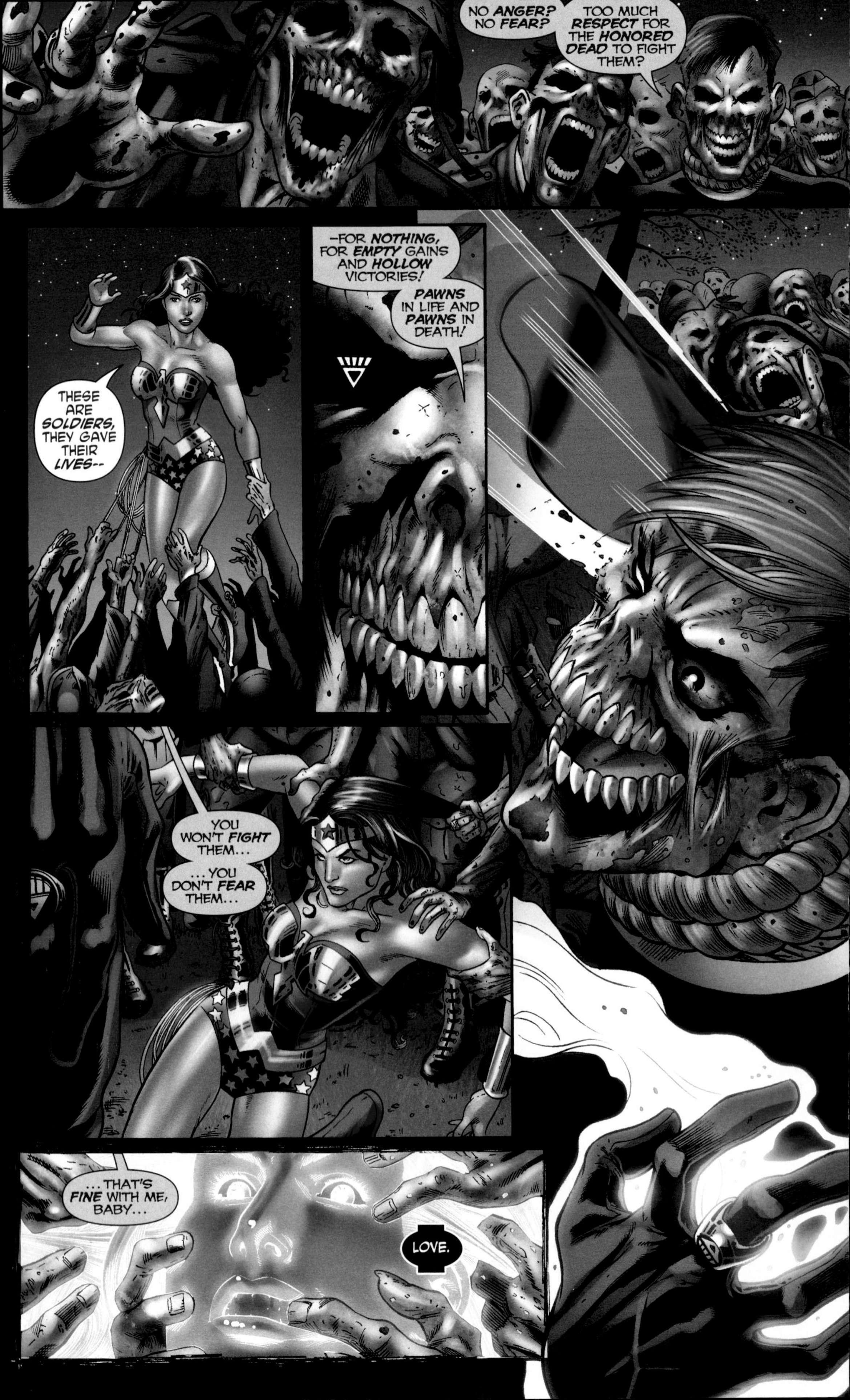
NO ANGER? NO FEAR?
TOO MUCH RESPECT FOR THE HONORED DEAD TO FIGHT THEM?
THESE ARE SOLDIERS, THEY GAVE THEIR LIVES--
--FOR NOTHING, FOR EMPTY GAINS AND HOLLOW VICTORIES!
PAWNS IN LIFE AND PAWNS IN DEATH!
YOU WON'T FIGHT THEM...
...YOU DON'T FEAR THEM...
...THAT'S FINE WITH ME, BABY...
LOVE.

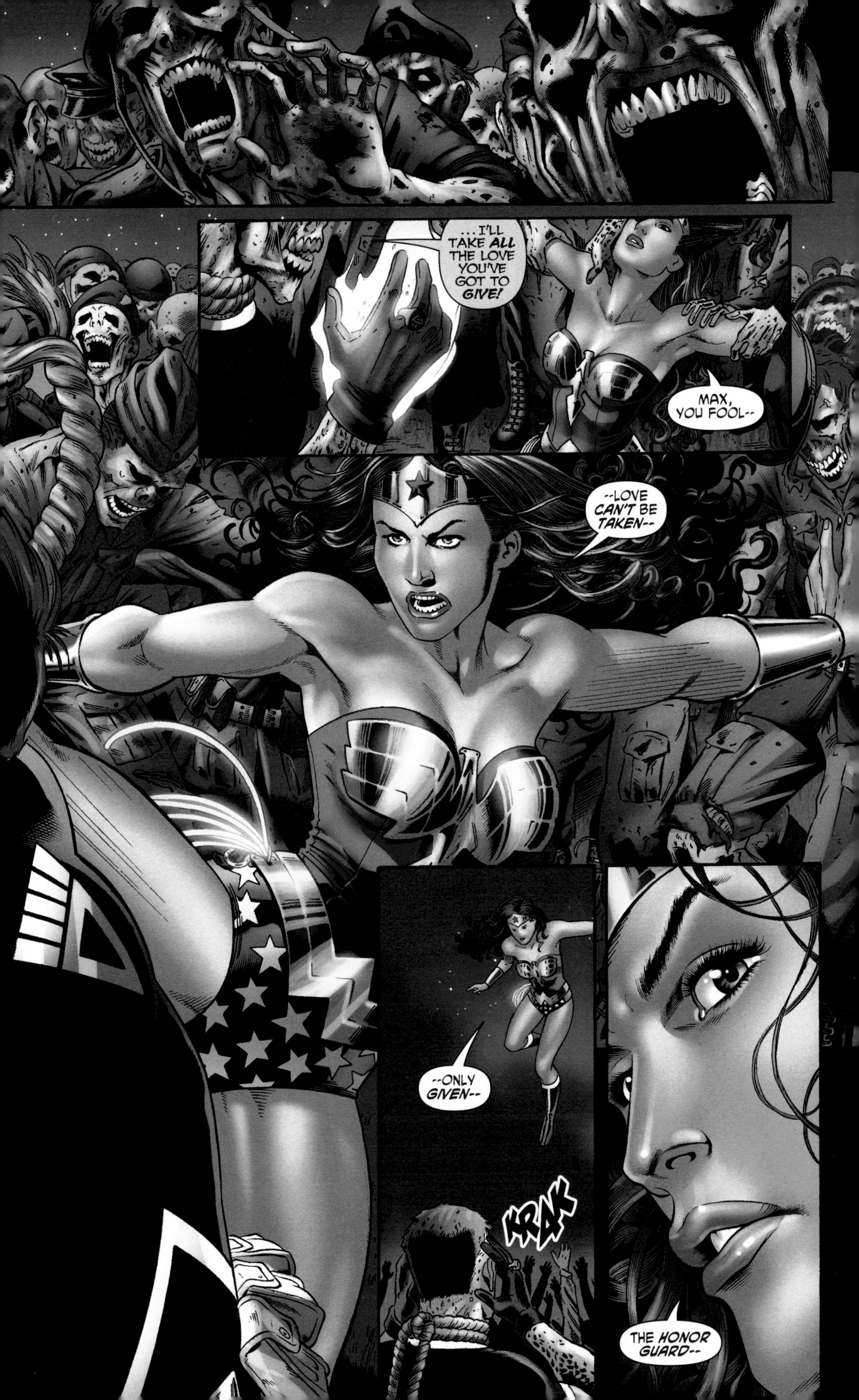

...I'LL TAKE ALL THE LOVE YOU'VE GOT TO GIVE!
MAX, YOU FOOL--
--LOVE CAN'T BE TAKEN--
--ONLY GIVEN--
KRAK
THE HONOR GUARD--

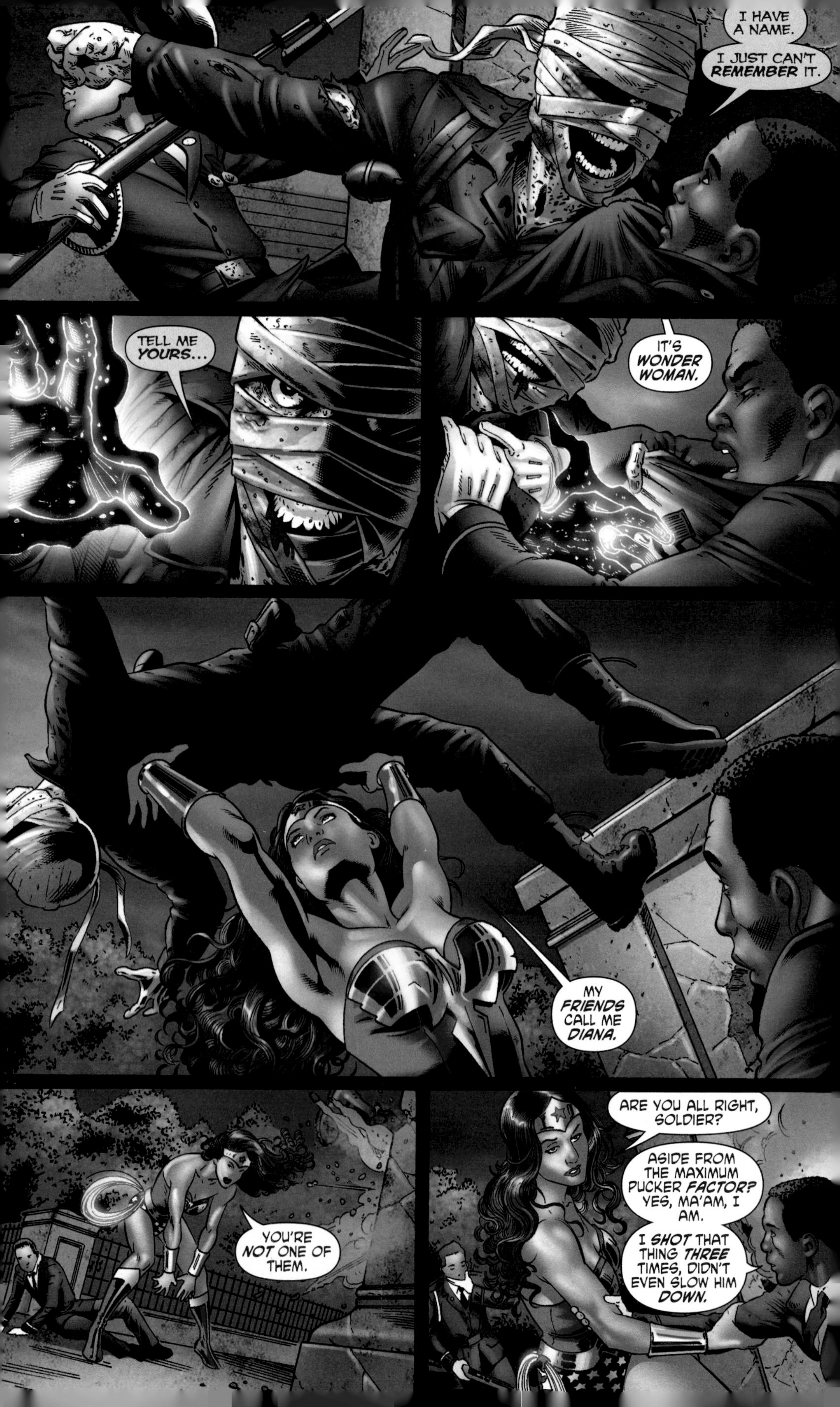
I HAVE A NAME.
I JUST CAN'T REMEMBER IT.
TELL ME YOURS...
IT'S WONDER WOMAN.
MY FRIENDS CALL ME DIANA.
YOU'RE NOT ONE OF THEM.
ARE YOU ALL RIGHT, SOLDIER?
ASIDE FROM THE MAXIMUM PUCKER FACTOR? YES, MA'AM, I AM.
I SHOT THAT THING THREE TIMES, DIDN'T EVEN SLOW HIM DOWN.

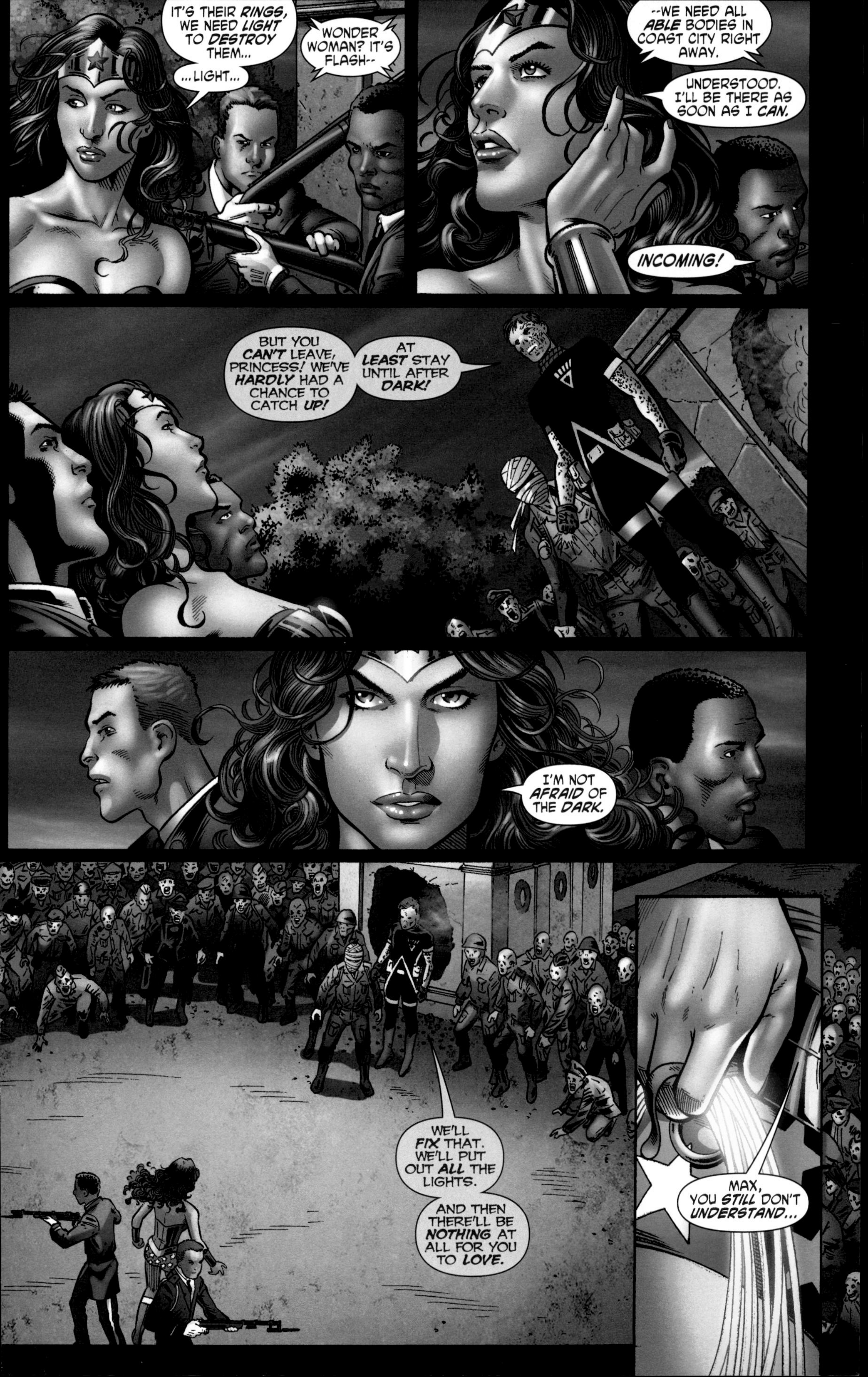
IT'S THEIR RINGS, WE NEED LIGHT TO DESTROY THEM...
...LIGHT...
WONDER WOMAN? IT'S FLASH--
--WE NEED ALL ABLE BODIES IN COAST CITY RIGHT AWAY.
UNDERSTOOD. I'LL BE THERE AS SOON AS I CAN.
INCOMING!
BUT YOU CAN'T LEAVE, PRINCESS! WE'VE HARDLY HAD A CHANCE TO CATCH UP!
AT LEAST STAY UNTIL AFTER DARK!
I'M NOT AFRAID OF THE DARK.
WE'LL FIX THAT. WE'LL PUT OUT ALL THE LIGHTS.
AND THEN THERE'LL BE NOTHING AT ALL FOR YOU TO LOVE.
MAX, YOU STILL DON'T UNDERSTAND...

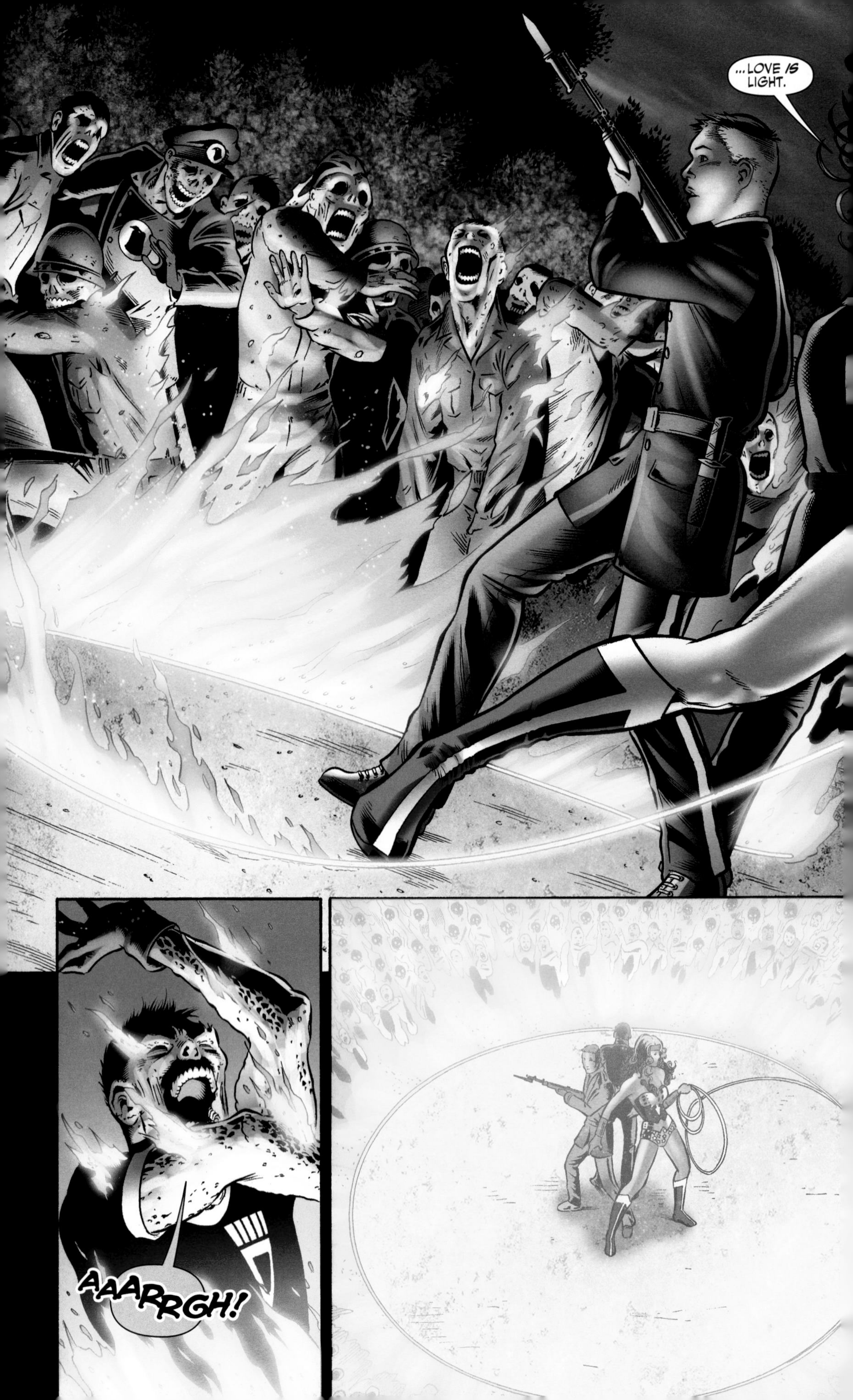
...LOVE IS LIGHT.
AAARRRGH!

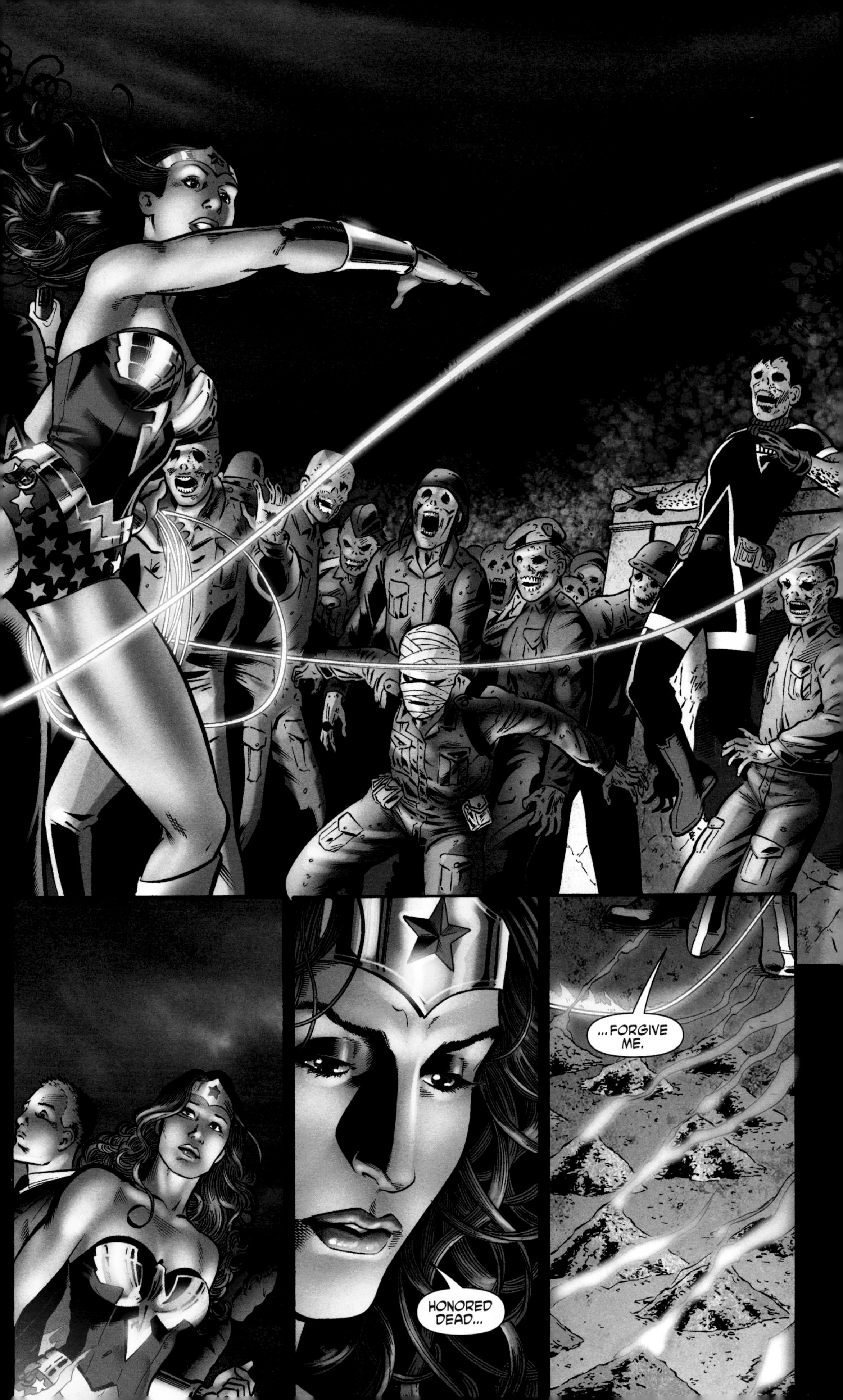
HONORED DEAD...
...FORGIVE ME.

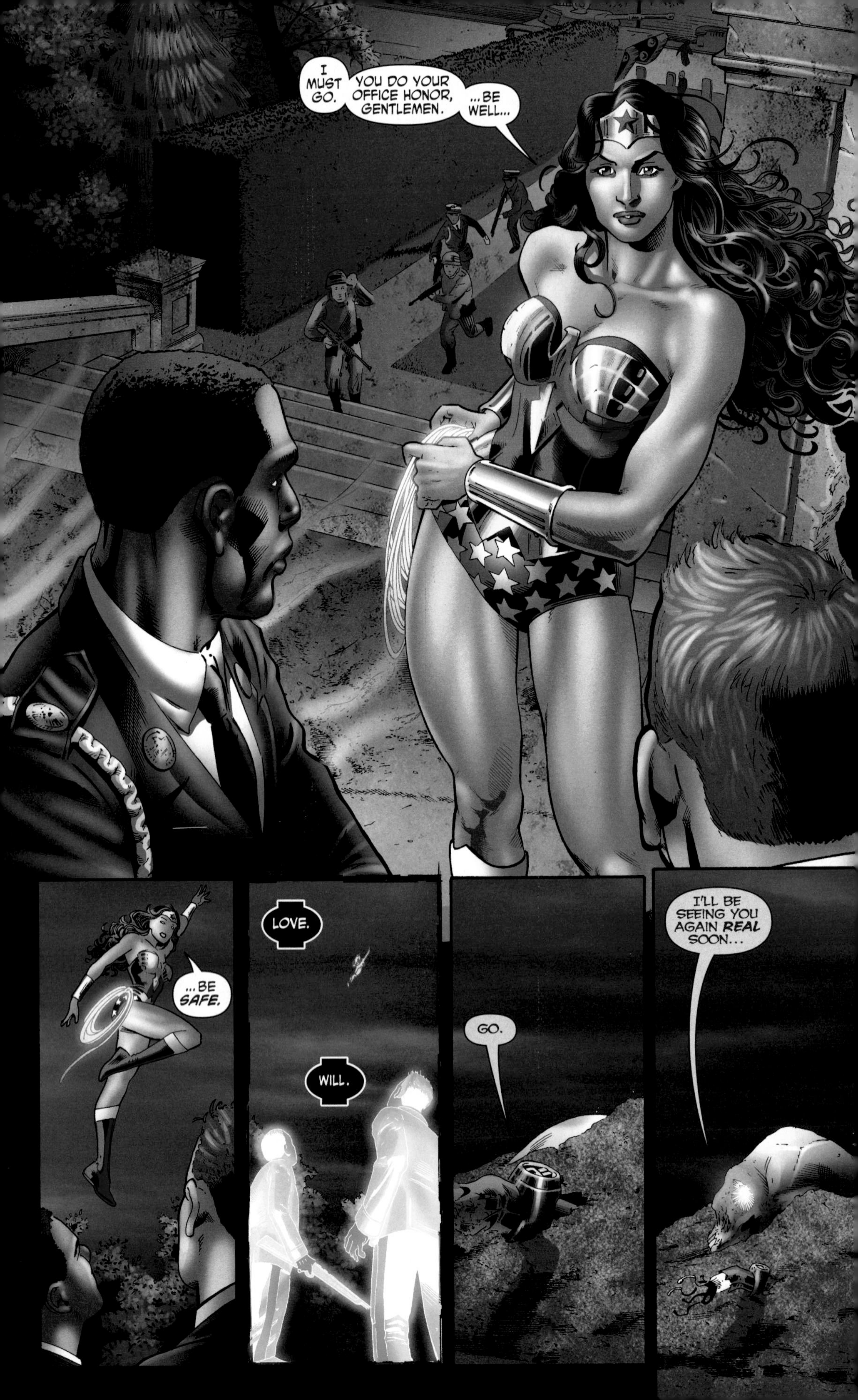

I MUST GO.
YOU DO YOUR OFFICE HONOR, GENTLEMEN.
...BE WELL...
...BE SAFE.
LOVE.
WILL.
GO.
I'LL BE SEEING YOU AGAIN REAL SOON...

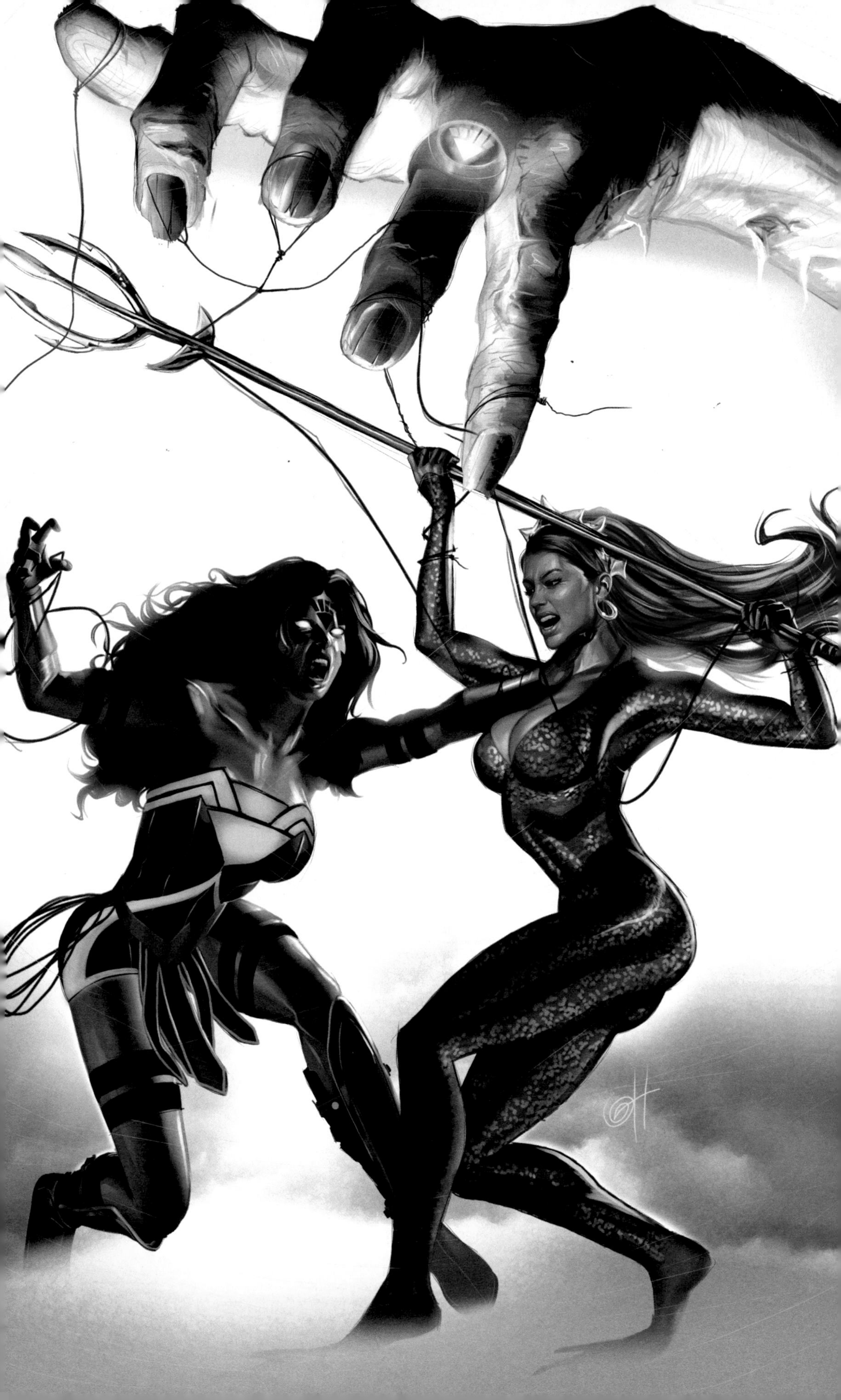

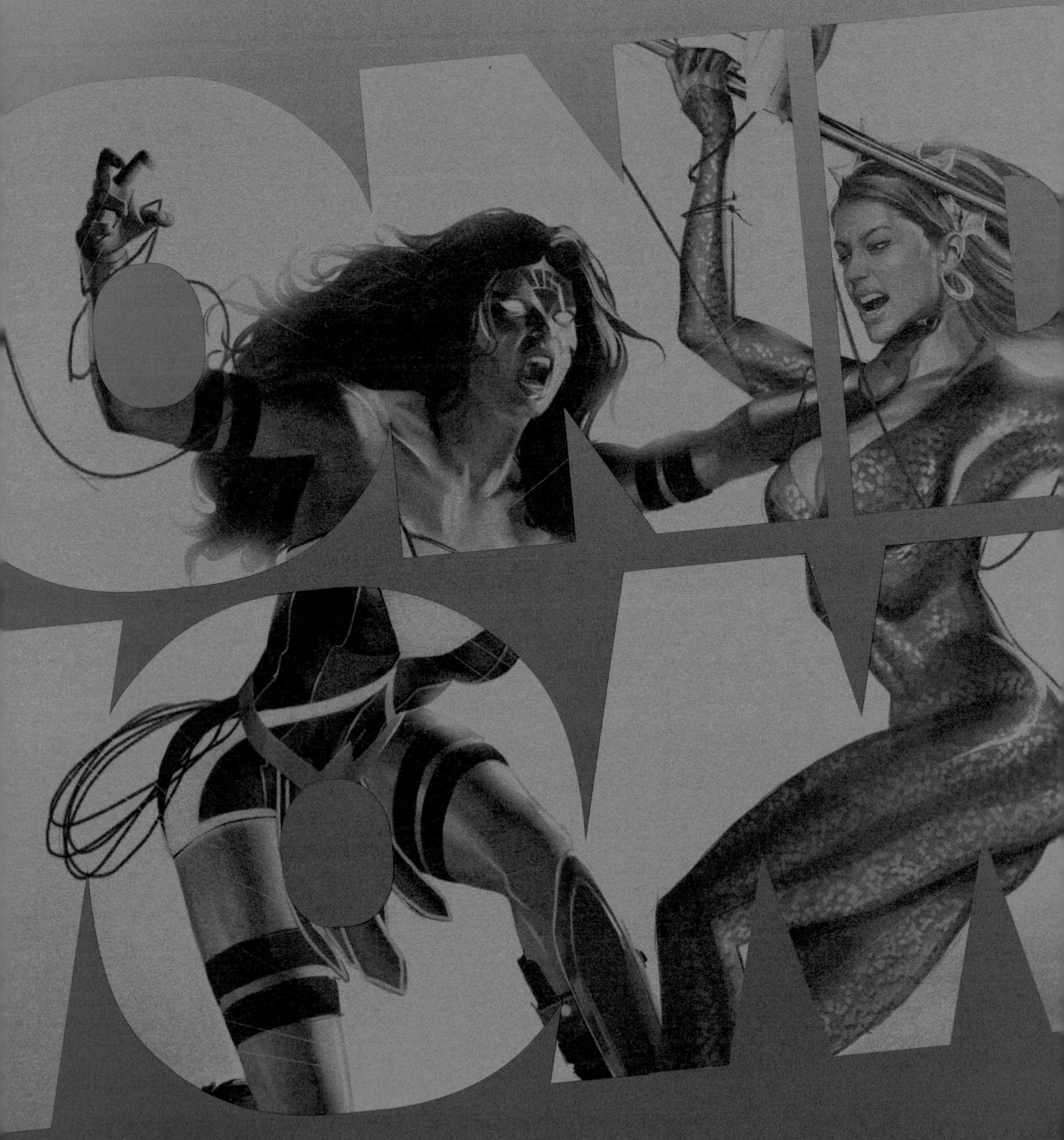

"WONDER WOMAN: BLACKEST NIGHT PART TWO"

Greg Rucka – *writer*
Nicola Scott and **Eduardo Pansica** – *pencils*
Jonathan Glapion and **Eber Ferreira** – *inks*
Nei Ruffino – *colors*
Travis Lanham – *letters*
Greg Horn – *cover*

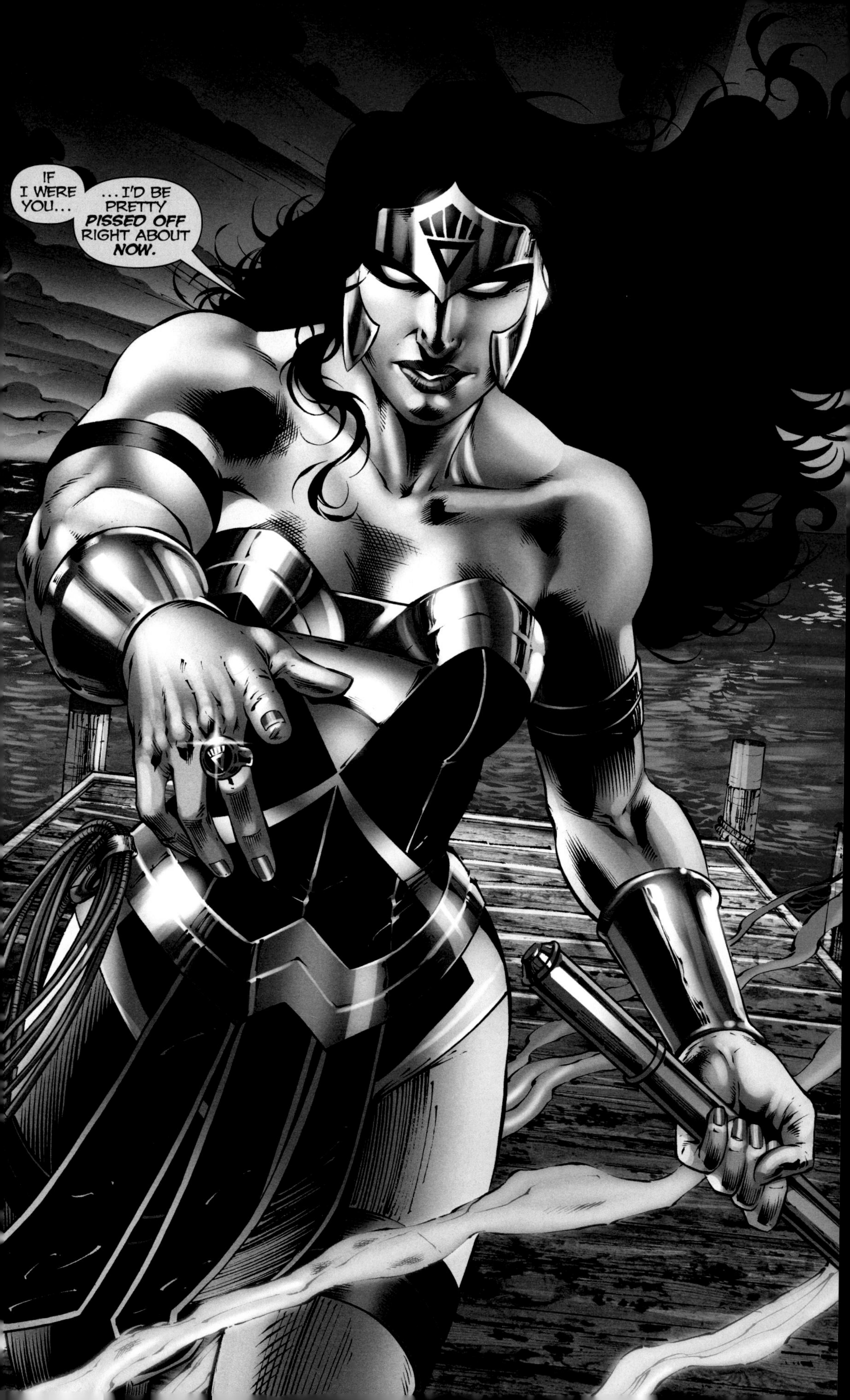
IF I WERE YOU...
...I'D BE PRETTY PISSED OFF RIGHT ABOUT NOW.

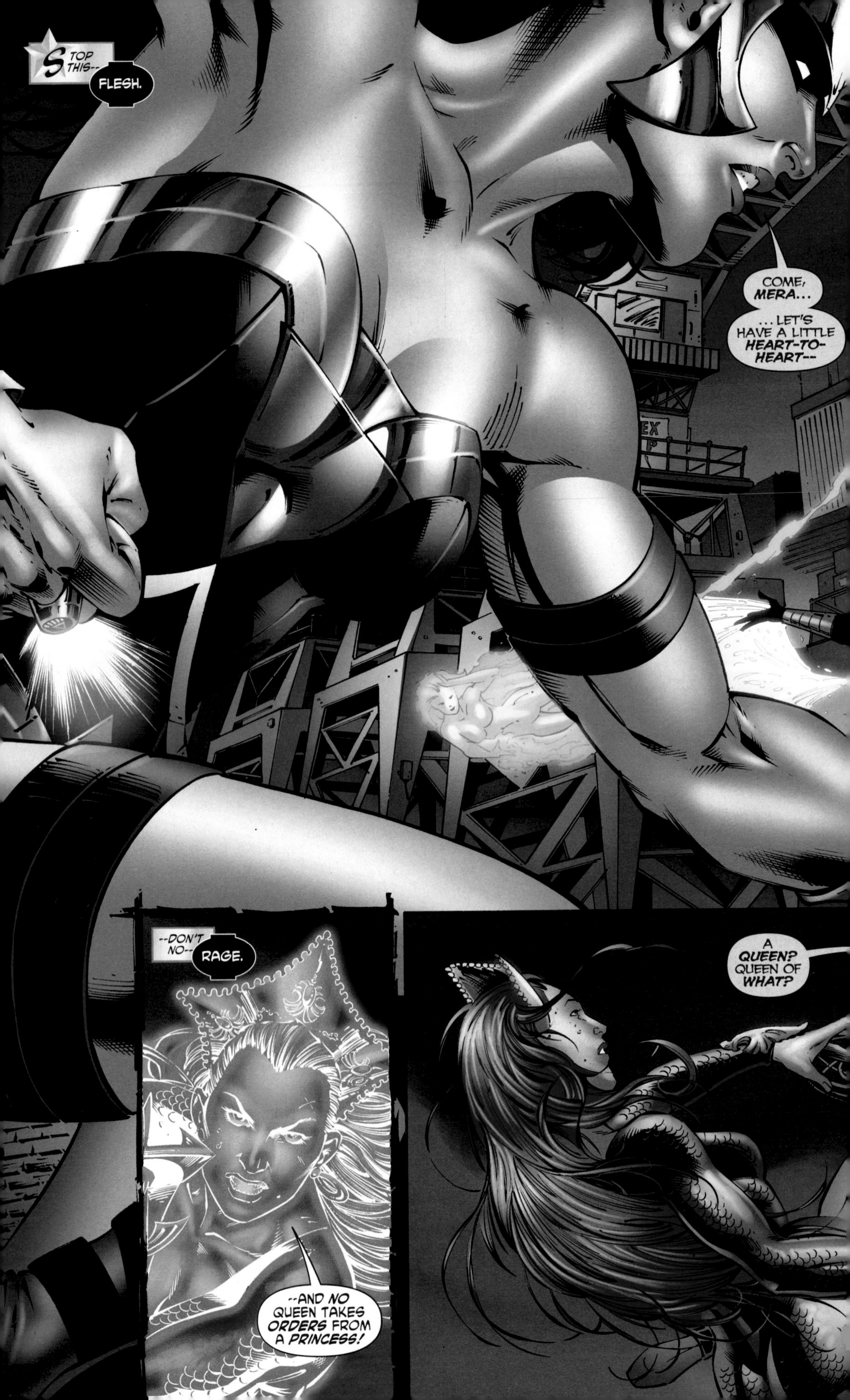
STOP THIS--
FLESH.
COME, MERA...
...LET'S HAVE A LITTLE HEART-TO-HEART--
--DON'T NO--
RAGE.
A QUEEN? QUEEN OF WHAT?
--AND NO QUEEN TAKES ORDERS FROM A PRINCESS!

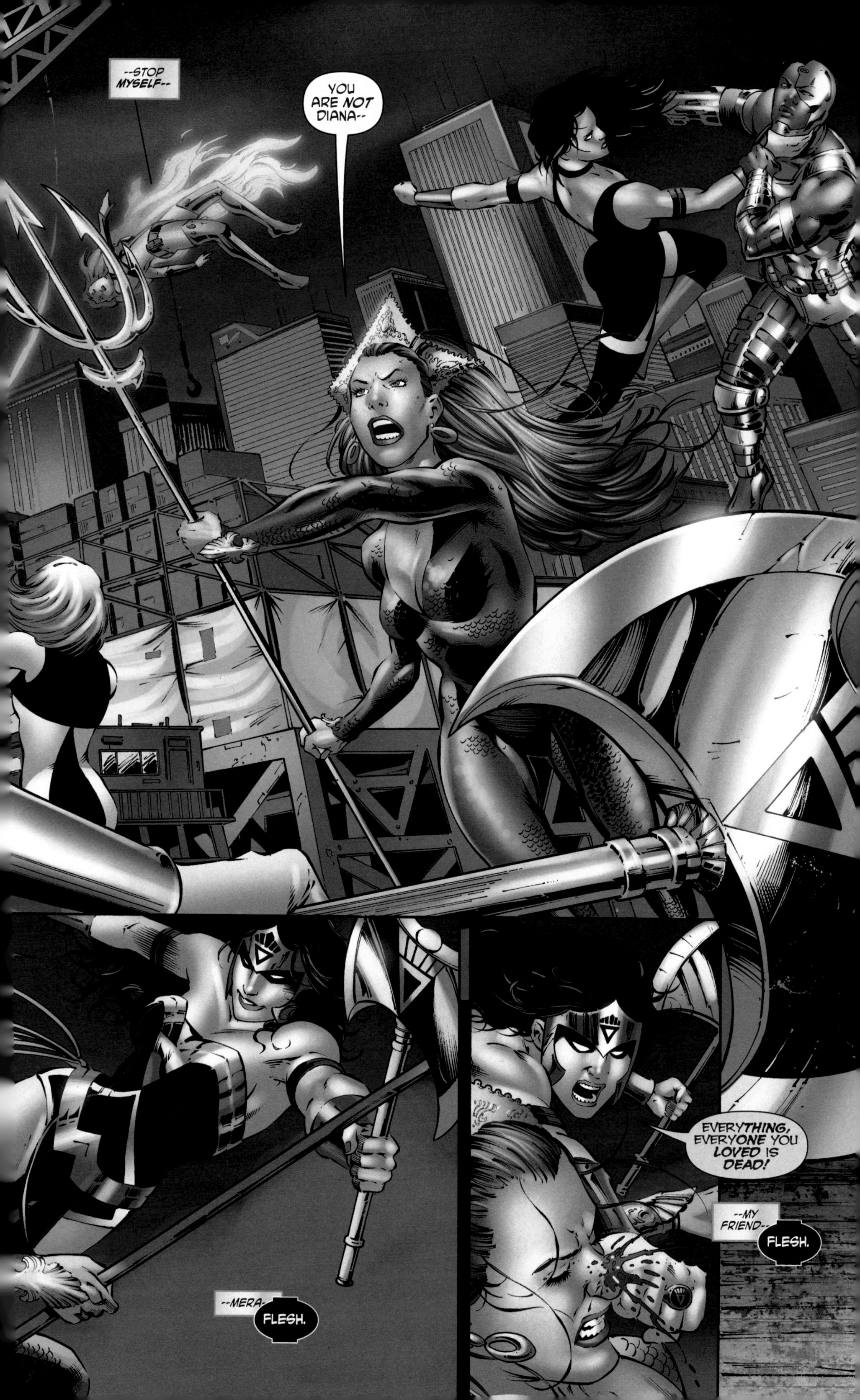
--STOP MYSELF--
YOU ARE NOT DIANA--
--MERA--
FLESH.
EVERYTHING, EVERYONE YOU LOVED IS DEAD!
--MY FRIEND--
FLESH.

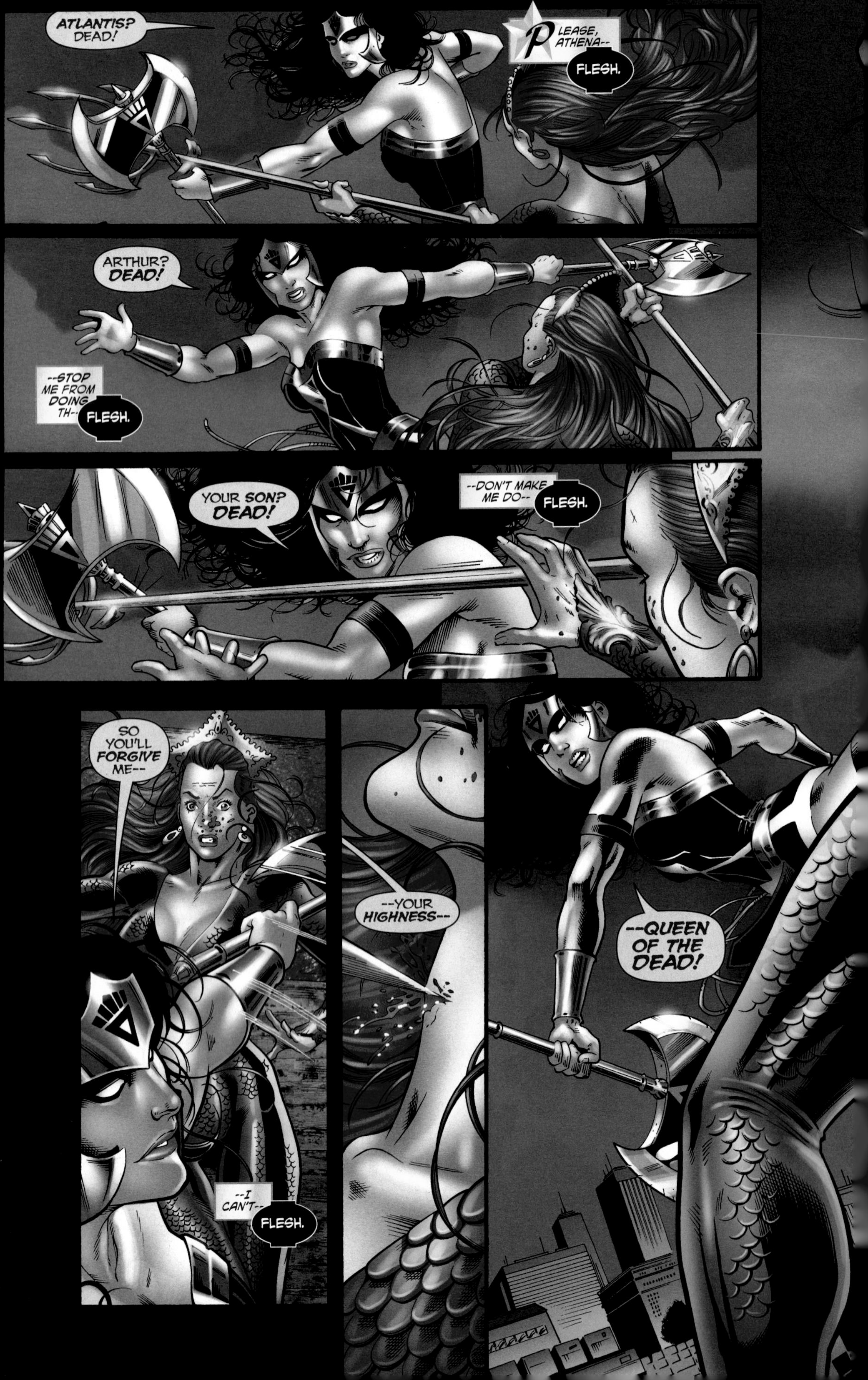
ATLANTIS? DEAD!
PLEASE, ATHENA--
FLESH.
ARTHUR? DEAD!
--STOP ME FROM DOING TH--
FLESH.
YOUR SON? DEAD!
--DON'T MAKE ME DO--
FLESH.
SO YOU'LL FORGIVE ME--
--YOUR HIGHNESS--
--QUEEN OF THE DEAD!
--I CAN'T--
FLESH.

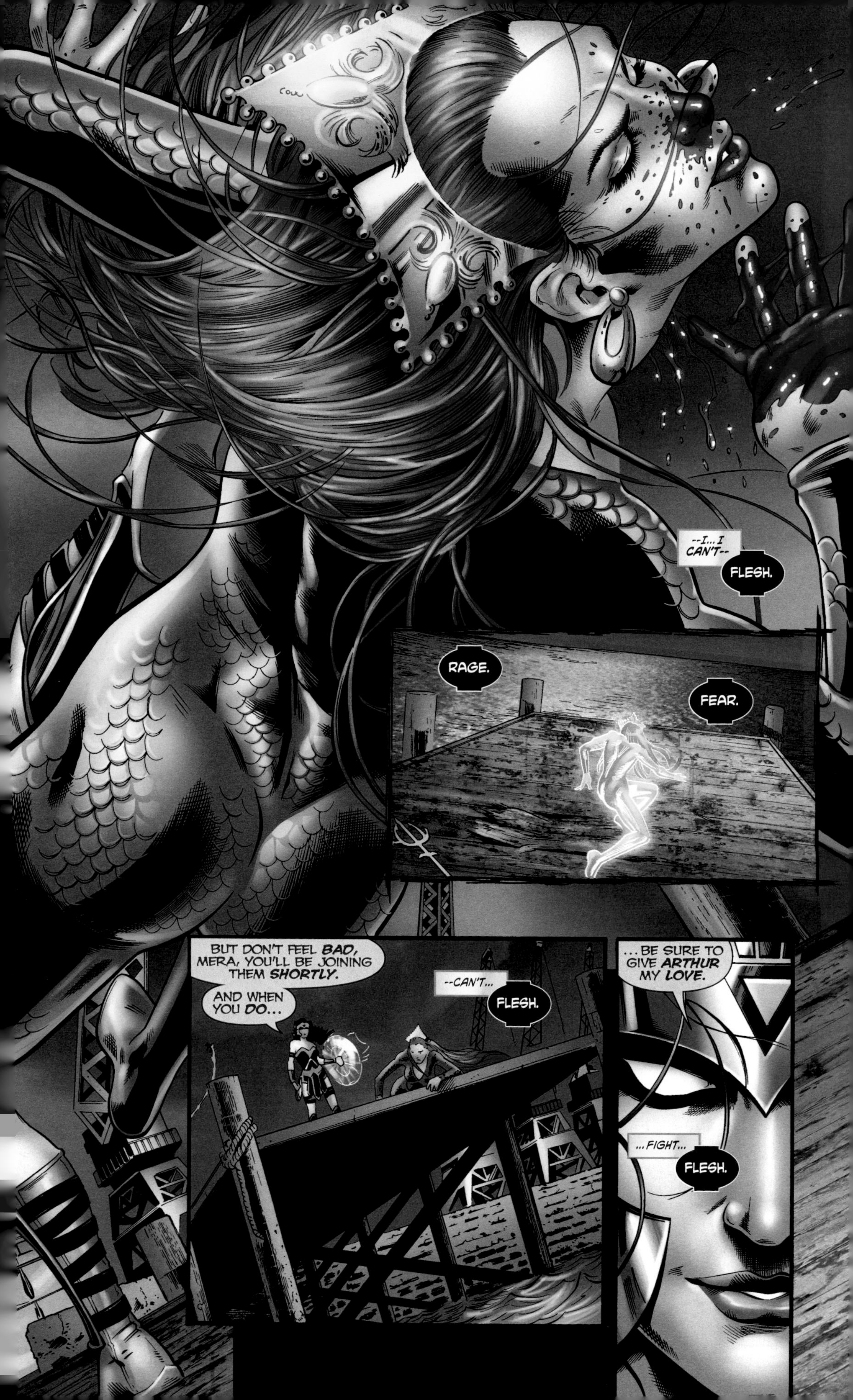

--I... I CAN'T--
FLESH.
RAGE.
FEAR.
BUT DON'T FEEL BAD, MERA, YOU'LL BE JOINING THEM SHORTLY.
AND WHEN YOU DO...
--CAN'T...
FLESH.
...BE SURE TO GIVE ARTHUR MY LOVE.
...FIGHT...
FLESH.

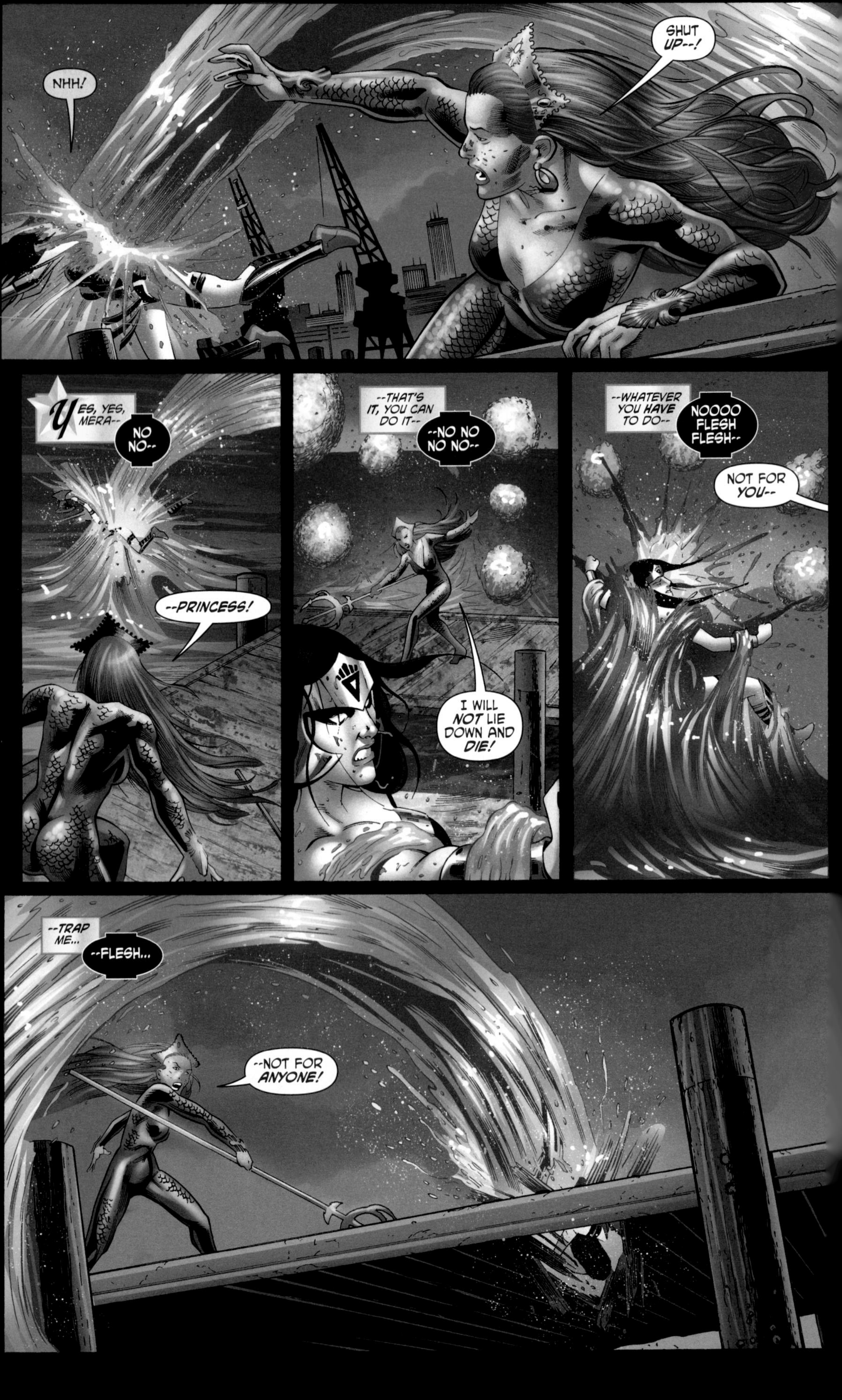
NHH!
SHUT UP--!
YES, YES, MERA--
NO NO--
--PRINCESS!
--THAT'S IT, YOU CAN DO IT--
--NO NO NO NO--
I WILL NOT LIE DOWN AND DIE!
--WHATEVER YOU HAVE TO DO--
NOOOO FLESH FLESH--
NOT FOR YOU--
--TRAP ME...
--FLESH...
--NOT FOR ANYONE!

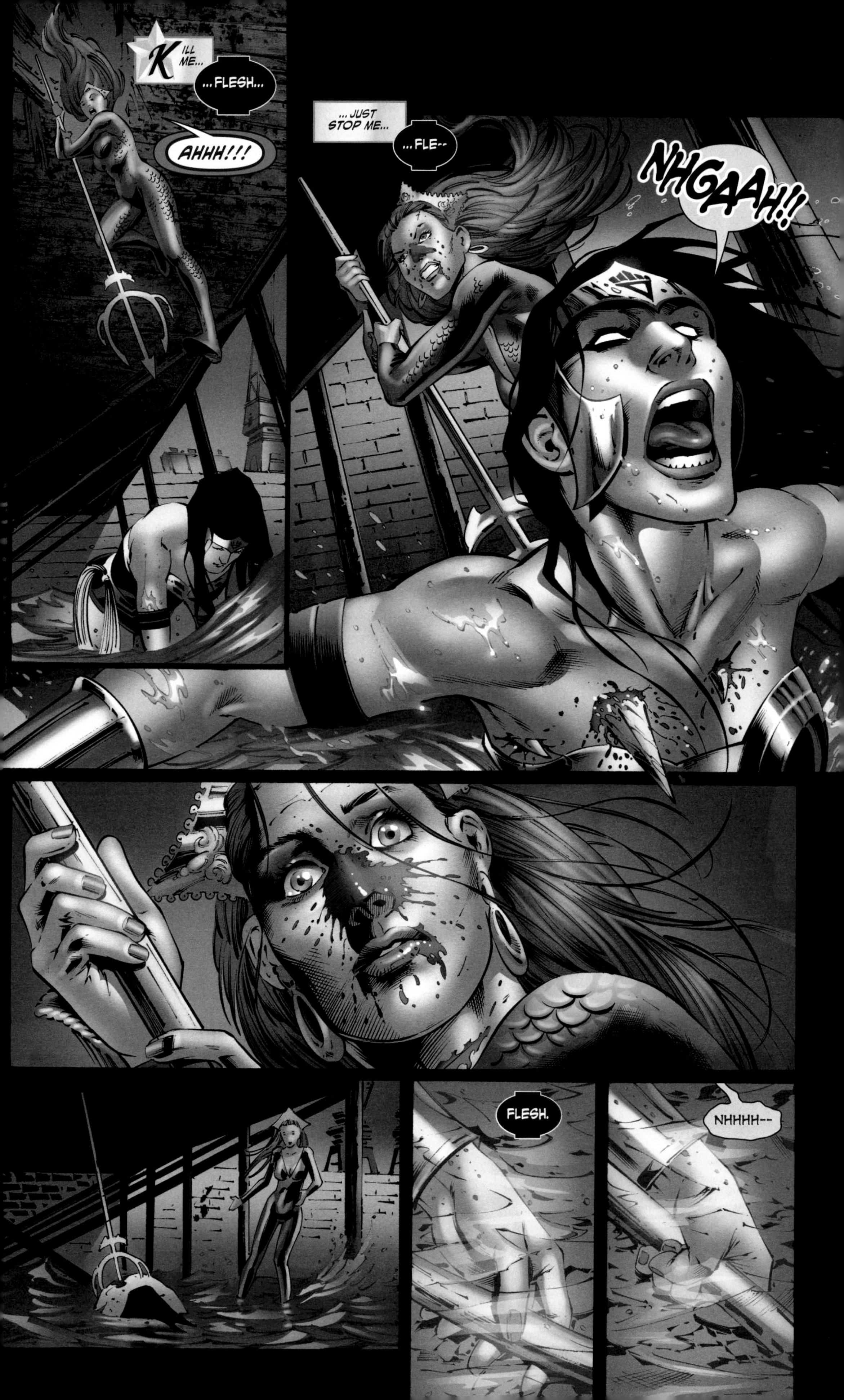
KILL ME...
...FLESH...
AHHH!!!
...JUST STOP ME...
...FLE--
NHGAAH!!
FLESH.
NHHHH--

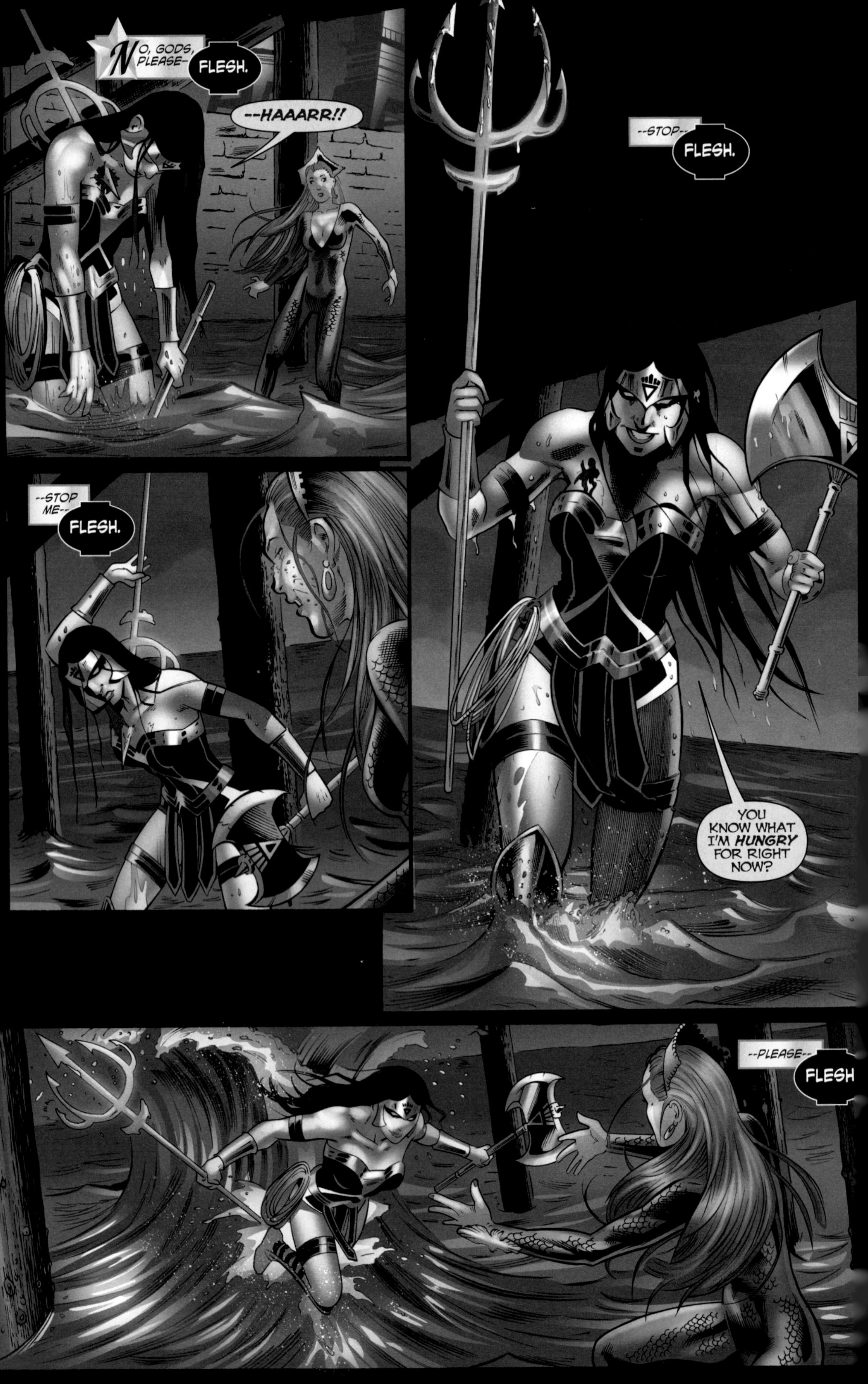
NO, GODS, PLEASE--
FLESH.
--HAAARR!!
--STOP--
FLESH.
--STOP ME--
FLESH.
YOU KNOW WHAT I'M HUNGRY FOR RIGHT NOW?
--PLEASE--
FLESH

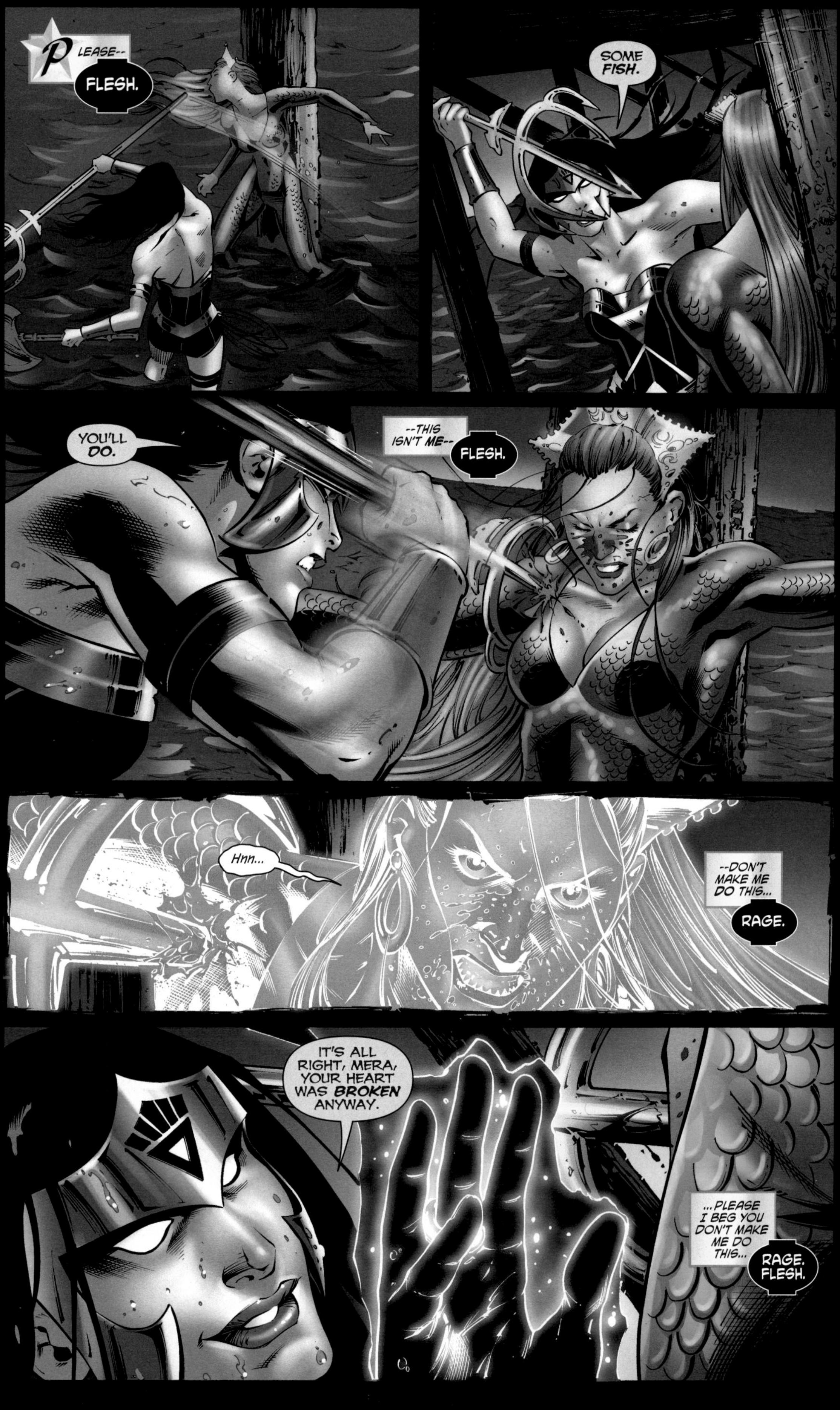

PLEASE--
FLESH.
SOME FISH.
YOU'LL DO.
--THIS ISN'T ME--
FLESH.
Hnn...
--DON'T MAKE ME DO THIS...
RAGE.
IT'S ALL RIGHT, MERA, YOUR HEART WAS BROKEN ANYWAY.
...PLEASE I BEG YOU DON'T MAKE ME DO THIS...
RAGE. FLESH.

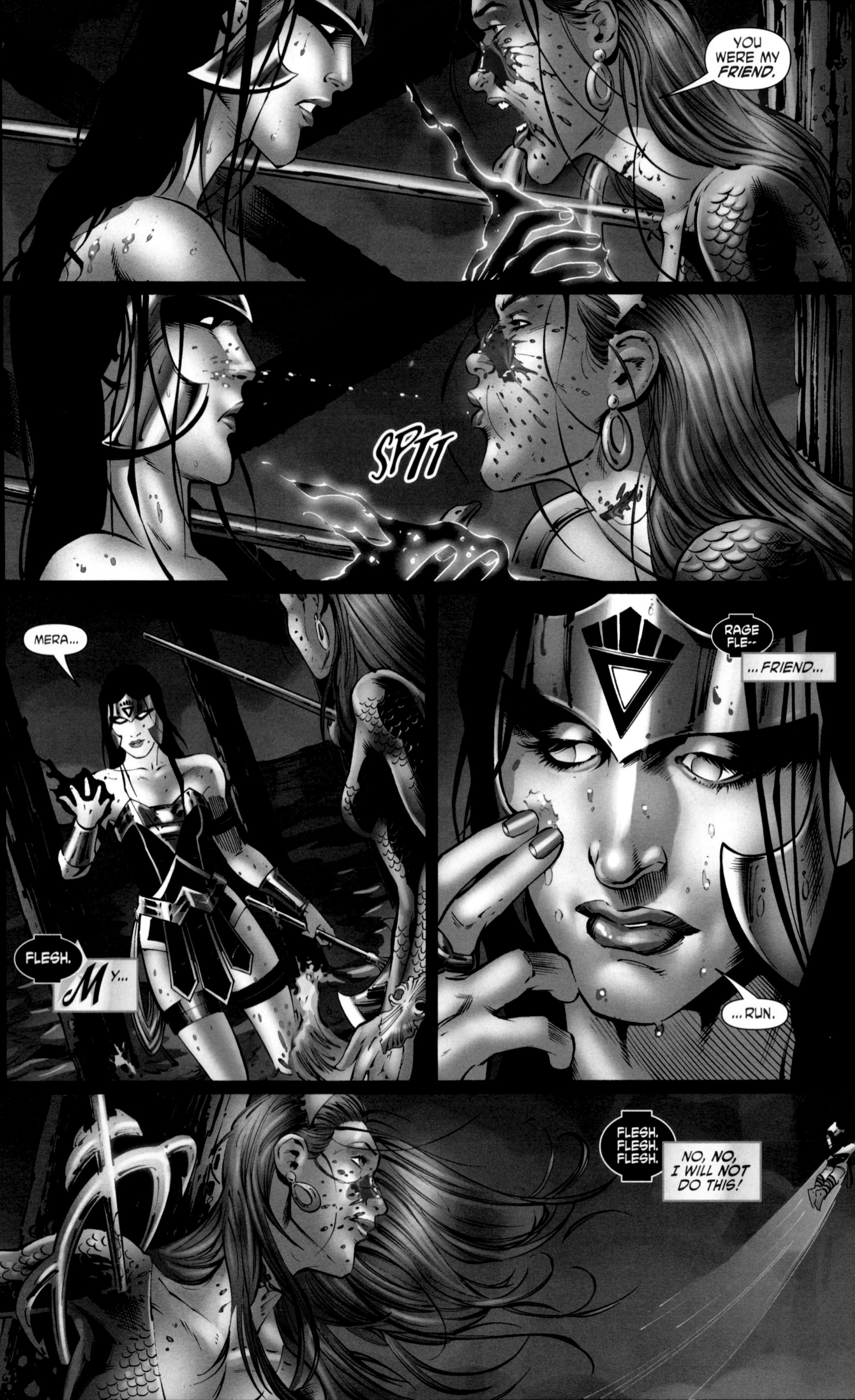

YOU WERE MY FRIEND.
SPTT
MERA...
FLESH.
MY...
RAGE FLE--
...FRIEND...
...RUN.
FLESH. FLESH. FLESH.
NO, NO, I WILL NOT DO THIS!

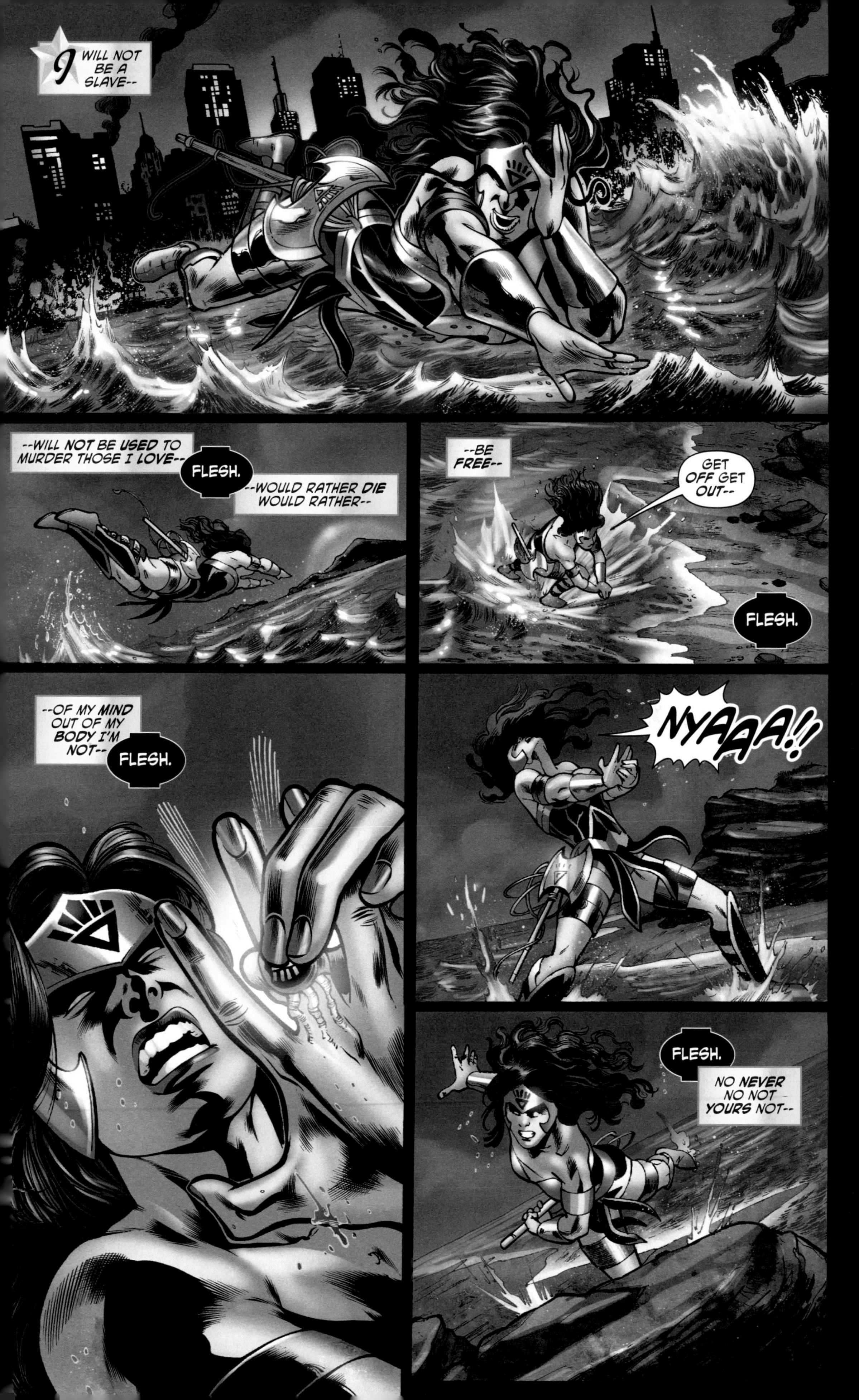
I WILL NOT BE A SLAVE--
--WILL NOT BE USED TO MURDER THOSE I LOVE--
FLESH.
--WOULD RATHER DIE WOULD RATHER--
--BE FREE--
GET OFF GET OUT--
FLESH.
--OF MY MIND OUT OF MY BODY I'M NOT--
FLESH.
NYAAAA!!
FLESH.
NO NEVER NO NOT YOURS NOT--

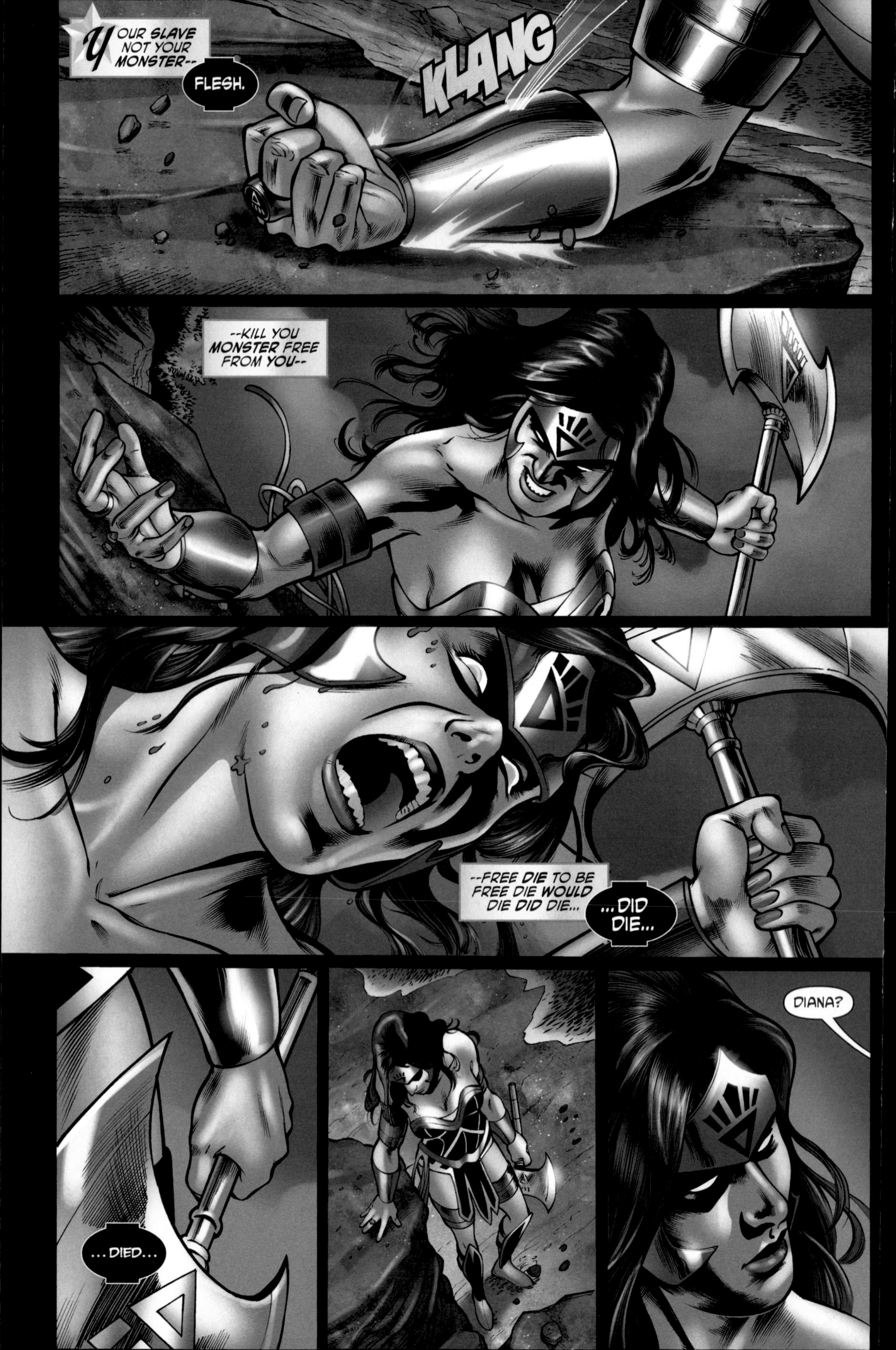
YOUR SLAVE NOT YOUR MONSTER--
FLESH.
KLANG
--KILL YOU MONSTER FREE FROM YOU--
--FREE DIE TO BE FREE DIE WOULD DIE DID DIE...
...DID DIE...
...DIED...
DIANA?

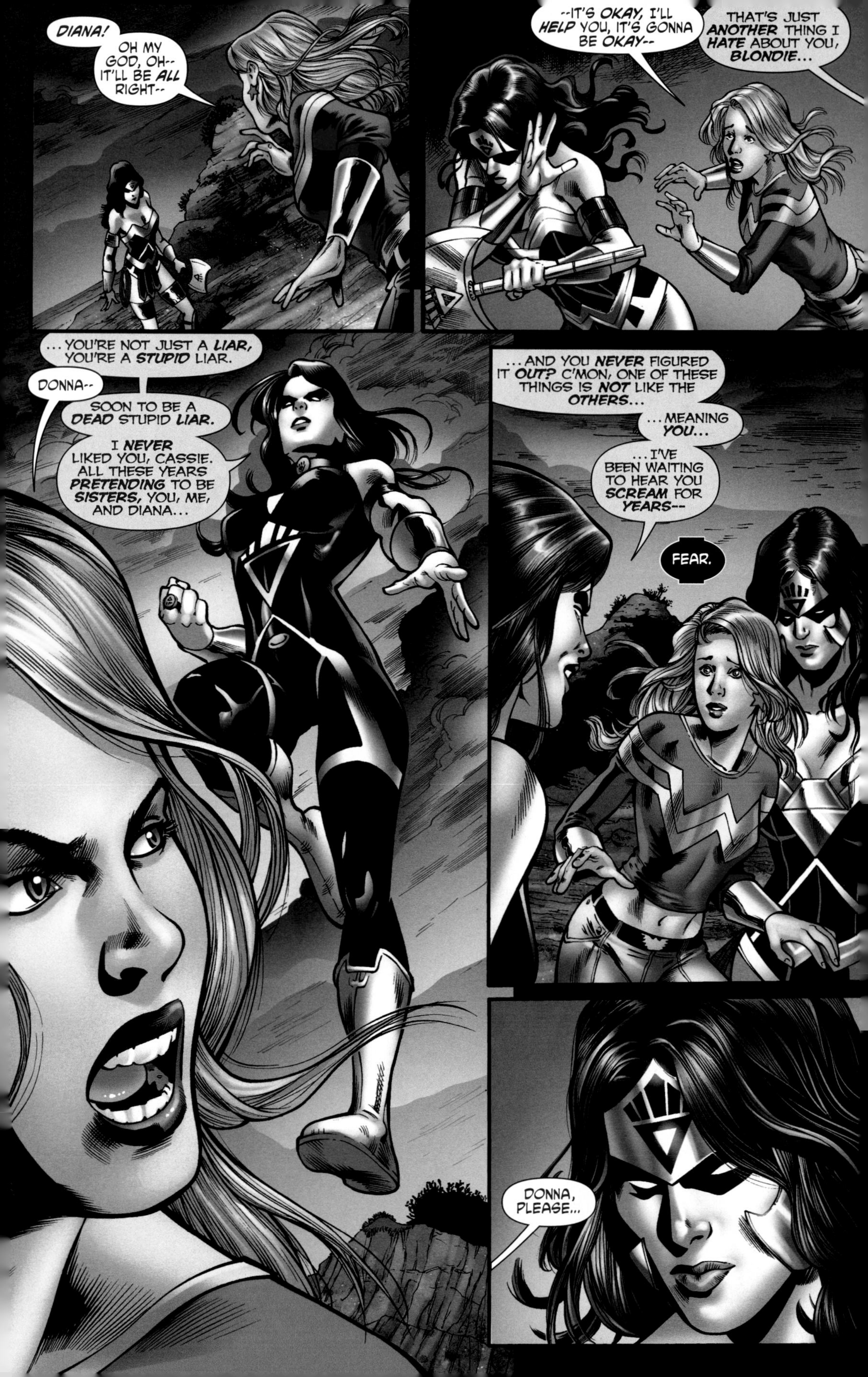
DIANA!
OH MY GOD, OH-- IT'LL BE ALL RIGHT--
--IT'S OKAY, I'LL HELP YOU, IT'S GONNA BE OKAY--
THAT'S JUST ANOTHER THING I HATE ABOUT YOU, BLONDIE...
...YOU'RE NOT JUST A LIAR, YOU'RE A STUPID LIAR.
DONNA--
SOON TO BE A DEAD STUPID LIAR.
I NEVER LIKED YOU, CASSIE. ALL THESE YEARS PRETENDING TO BE SISTERS, YOU, ME, AND DIANA...
...AND YOU NEVER FIGURED IT OUT? C'MON, ONE OF THESE THINGS IS NOT LIKE THE OTHERS...
...MEANING YOU...
...I'VE BEEN WAITING TO HEAR YOU SCREAM FOR YEARS--
FEAR.
DONNA, PLEASE...

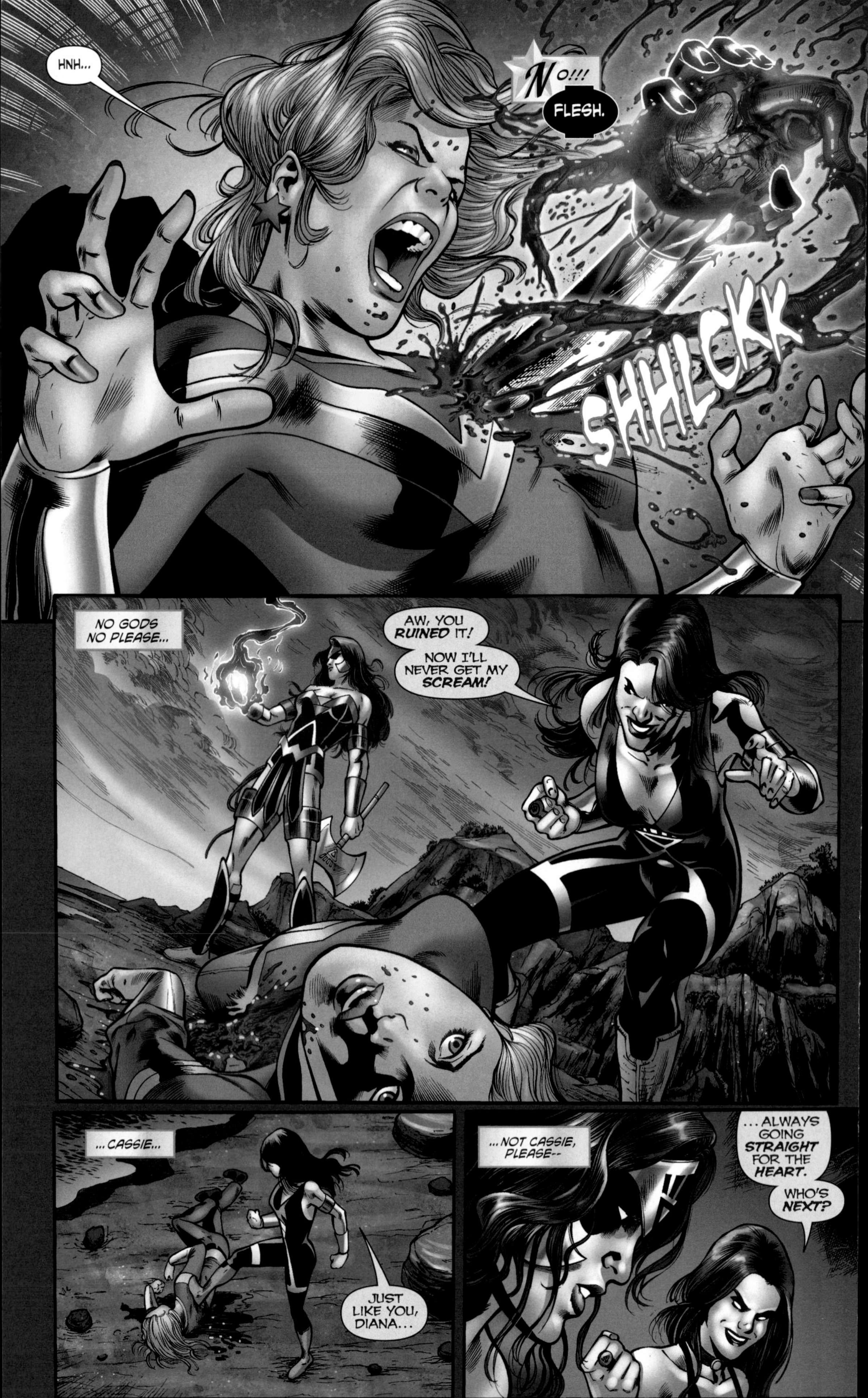

HNH...
NO!!!
FLESH.
SHHLCKK
NO GODS NO PLEASE...
AW, YOU RUINED IT!
NOW I'LL NEVER GET MY SCREAM!
...CASSIE...
JUST LIKE YOU, DIANA...
...NOT CASSIE, PLEASE--
...ALWAYS GOING STRAIGHT FOR THE HEART.
WHO'S NEXT?

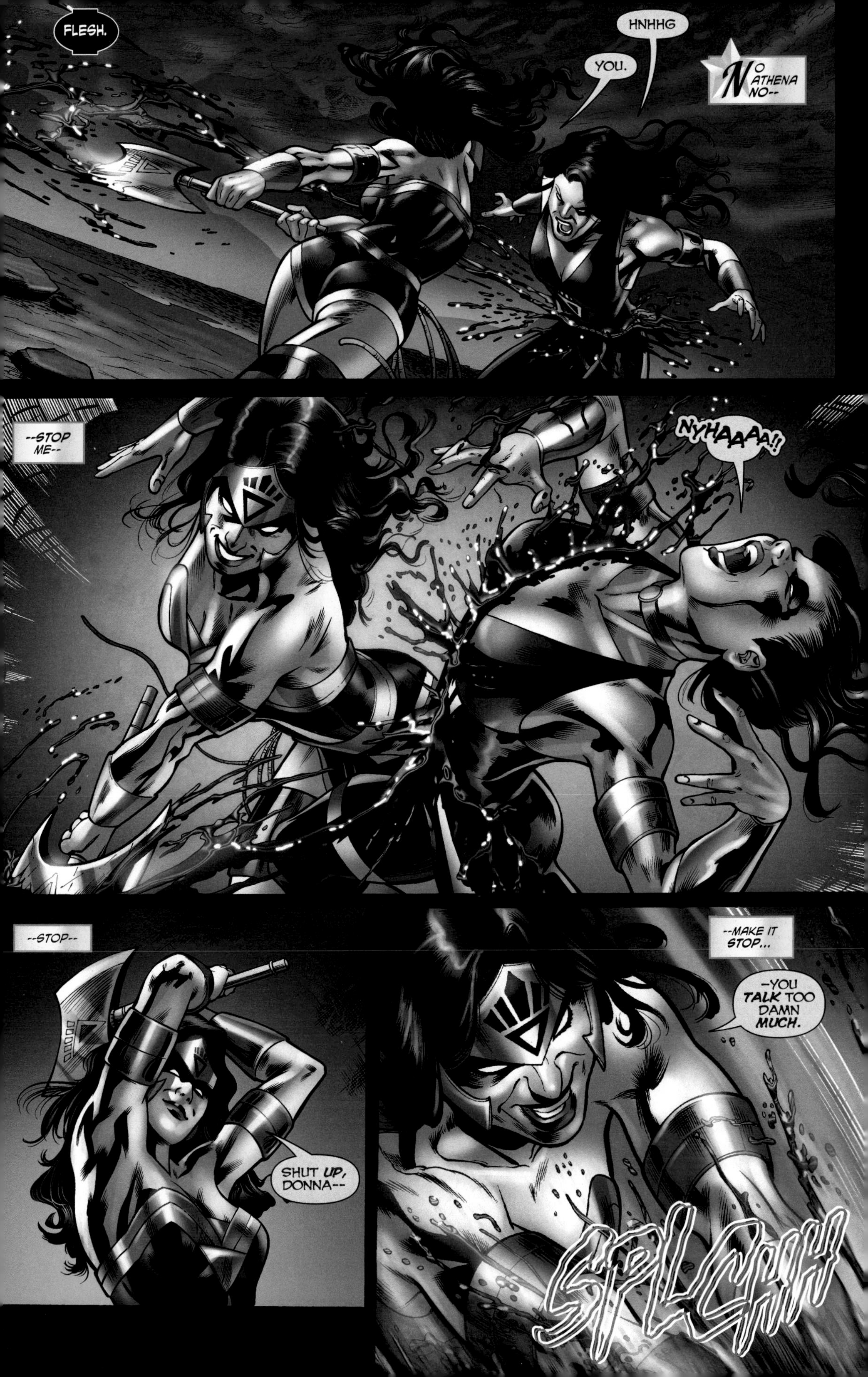
FLESH.
HNHHG
YOU.
NO ATHENA NO--
--STOP ME--
NYHAAAA!!
--STOP--
--MAKE IT STOP...
SHUT UP, DONNA--
--YOU TALK TOO DAMN MUCH.
SPLCHH

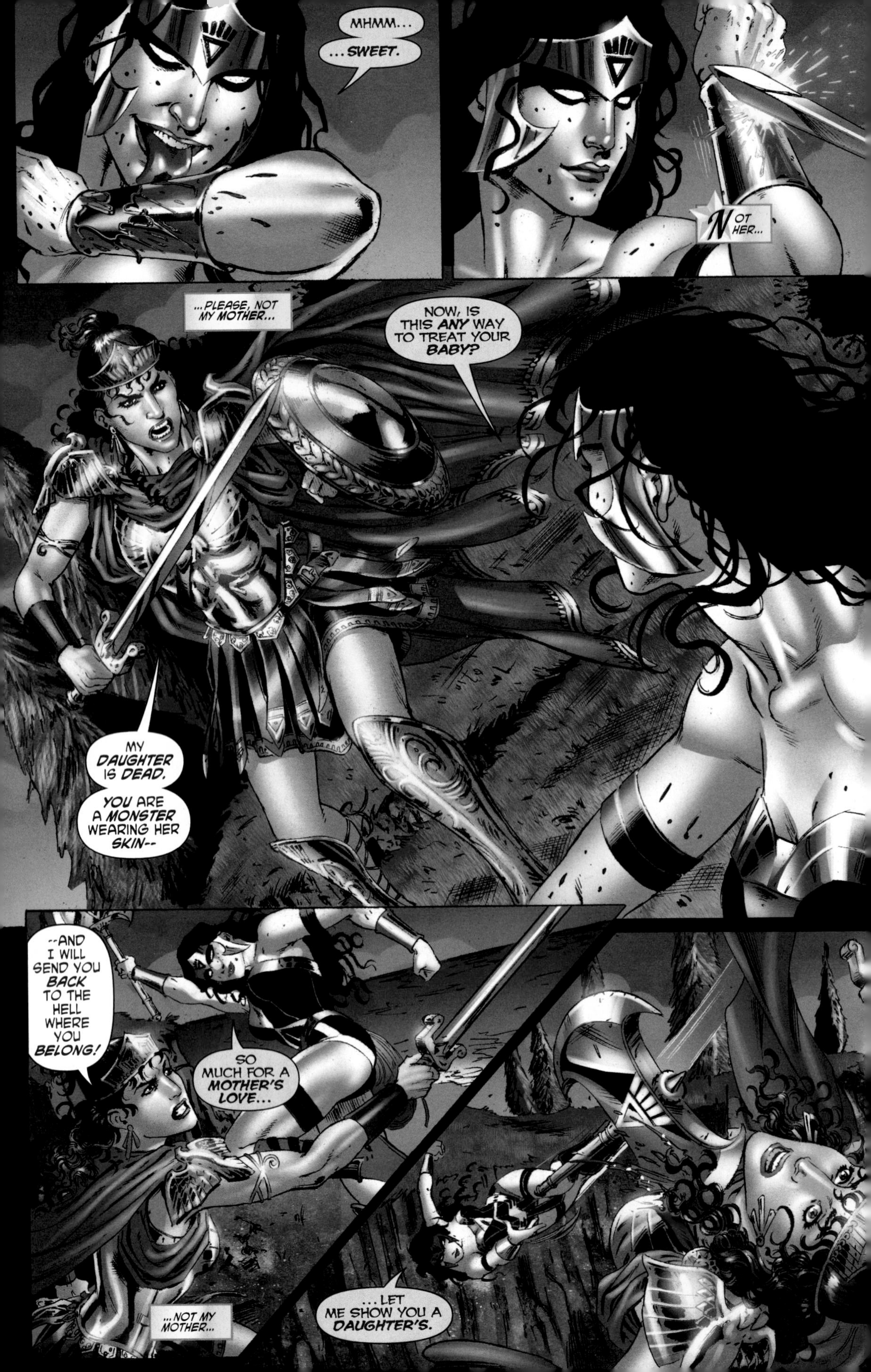
MHMM...
...SWEET.
NOT HER...
...PLEASE, NOT MY MOTHER...
NOW, IS THIS ANY WAY TO TREAT YOUR BABY?
MY DAUGHTER IS DEAD.
YOU ARE A MONSTER WEARING HER SKIN--
--AND I WILL SEND YOU BACK TO THE HELL WHERE YOU BELONG!
SO MUCH FOR A MOTHER'S LOVE...
...NOT MY MOTHER...
...LET ME SHOW YOU A DAUGHTER'S.

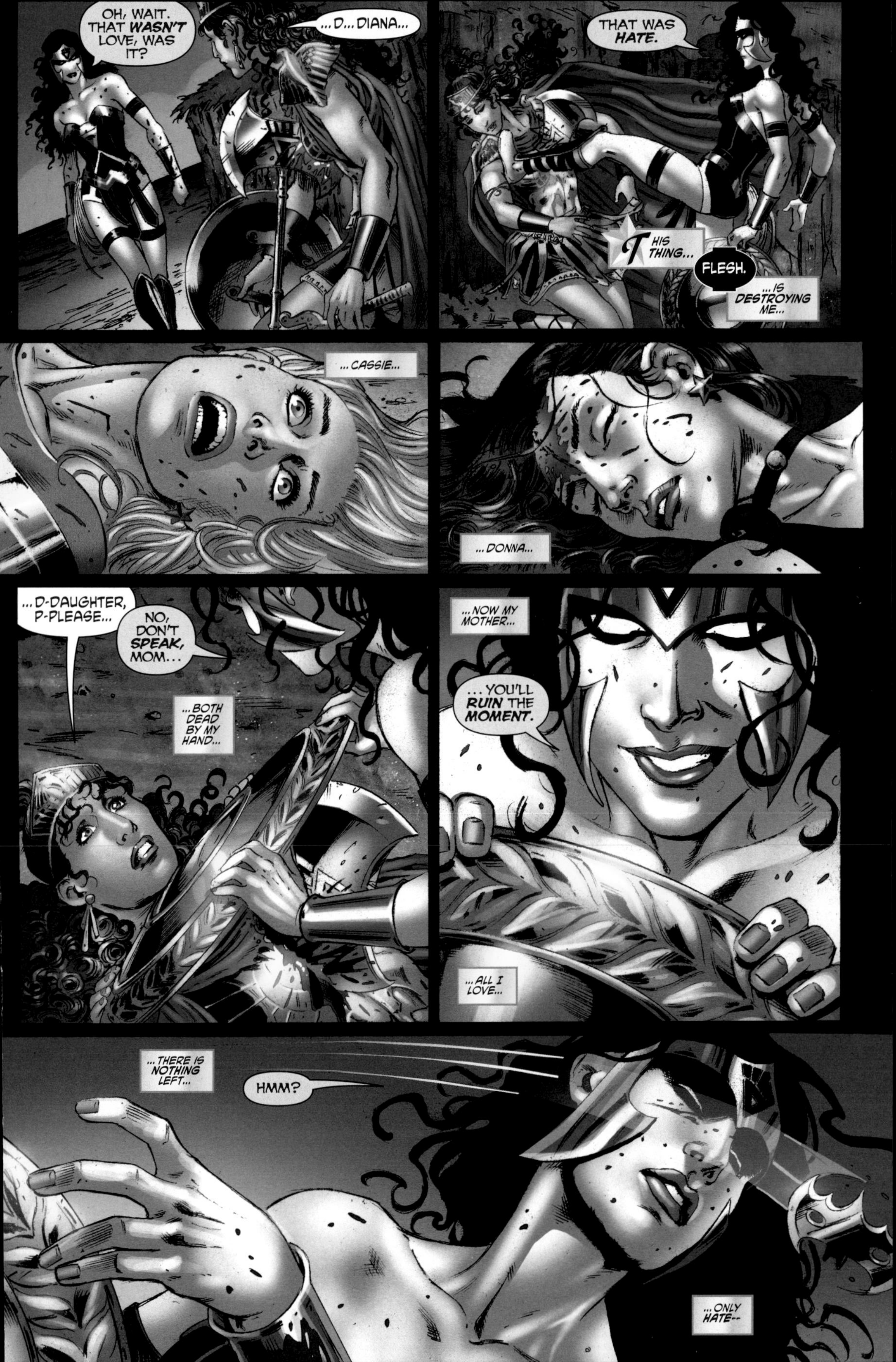
OH, WAIT. THAT WASN'T LOVE, WAS IT?
...D...DIANA...
THAT WAS HATE.
THIS THING...
FLESH.
...IS DESTROYING ME...
...CASSIE...
...DONNA...
...D-DAUGHTER, P-PLEASE...
NO, DON'T SPEAK, MOM...
...BOTH DEAD BY MY HAND...
...NOW MY MOTHER...
...YOU'LL RUIN THE MOMENT.
...ALL I LOVE...
...THERE IS NOTHING LEFT...
HMM?
...ONLY HATE--

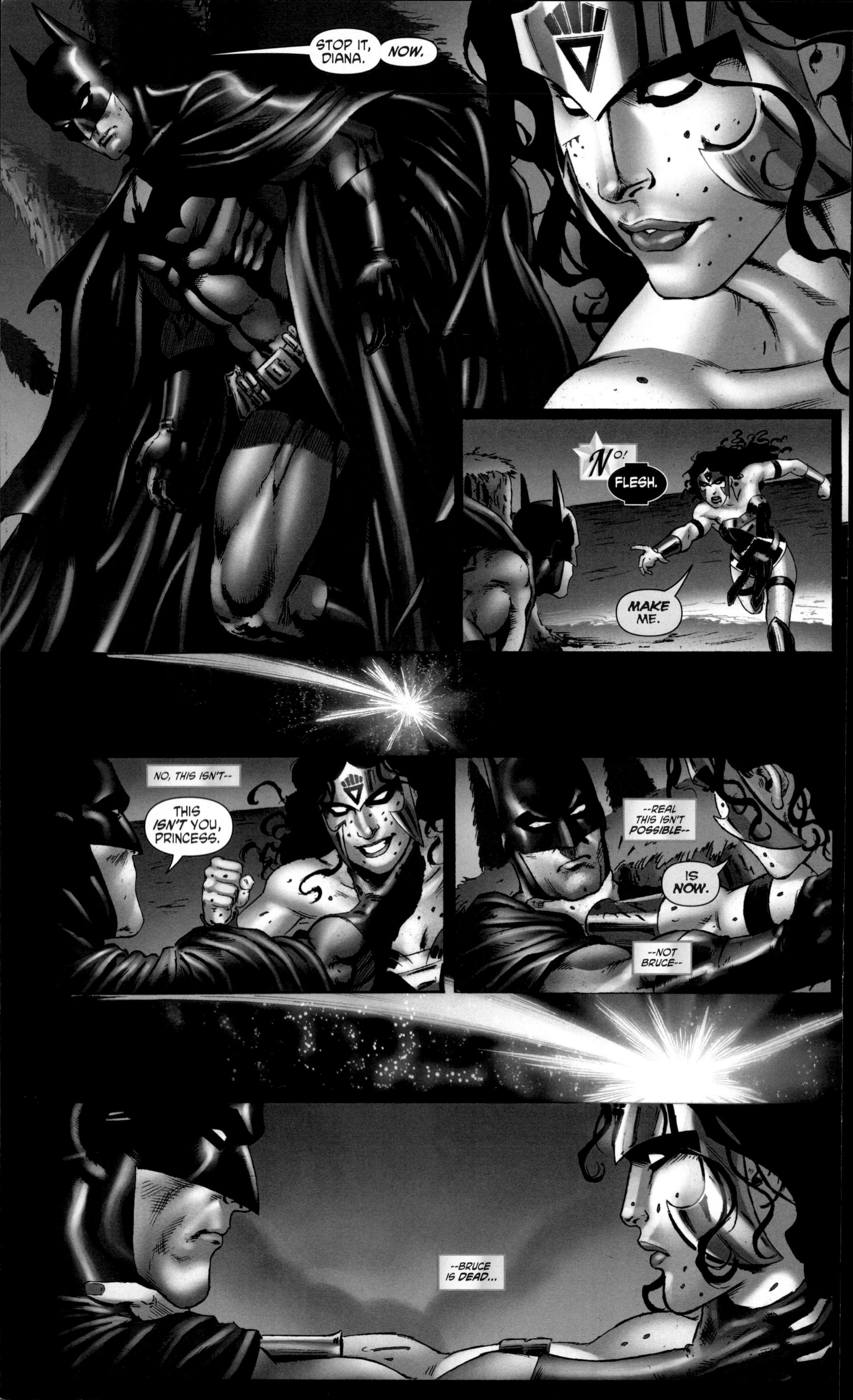
STOP IT, DIANA.
NOW.
NO!
FLESH.
MAKE ME.
NO, THIS ISN'T--
THIS ISN'T YOU, PRINCESS.
--REAL THIS ISN'T POSSIBLE--
IS NOW.
--NOT BRUCE--
--BRUCE IS DEAD...

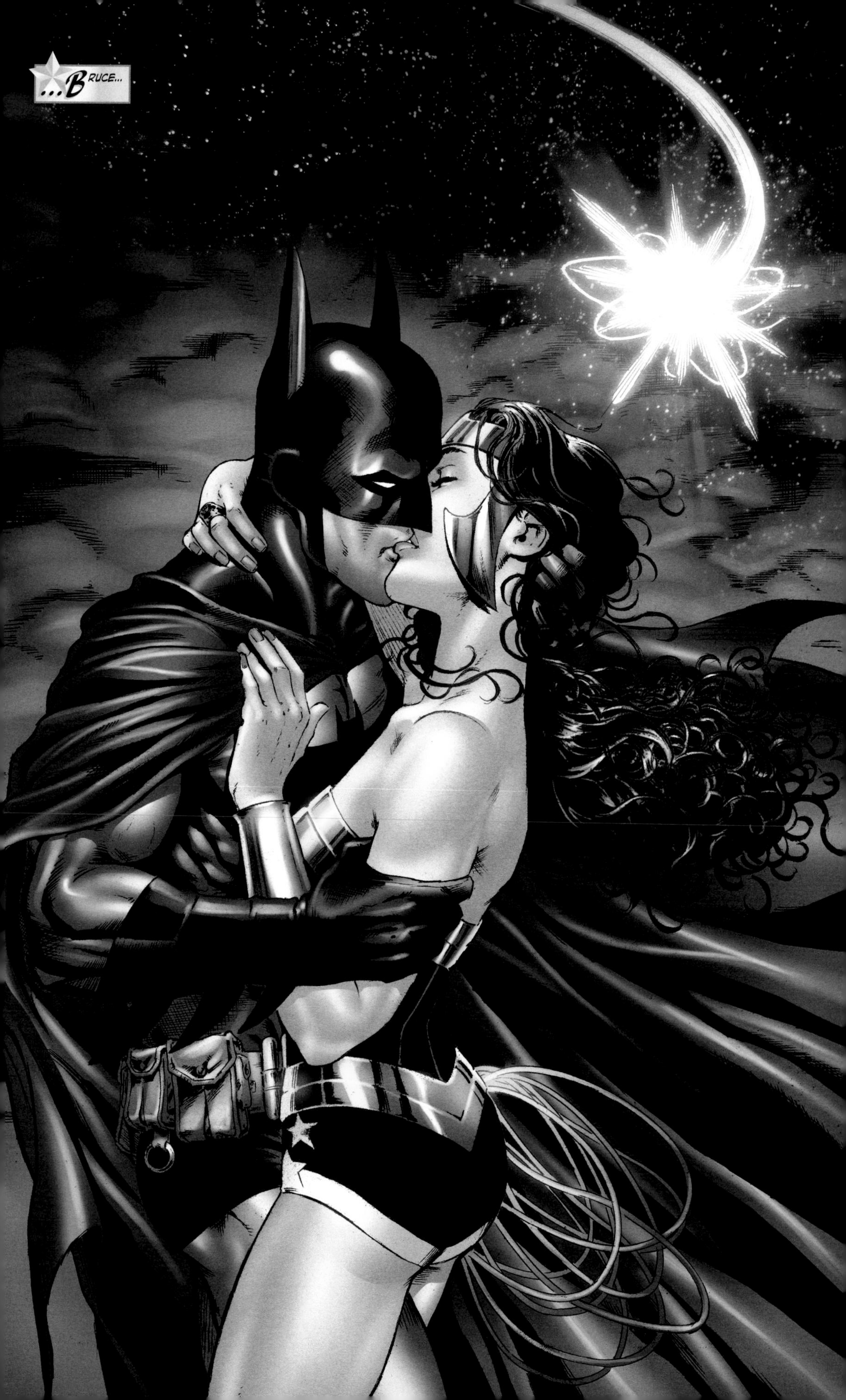
...BRUCE...

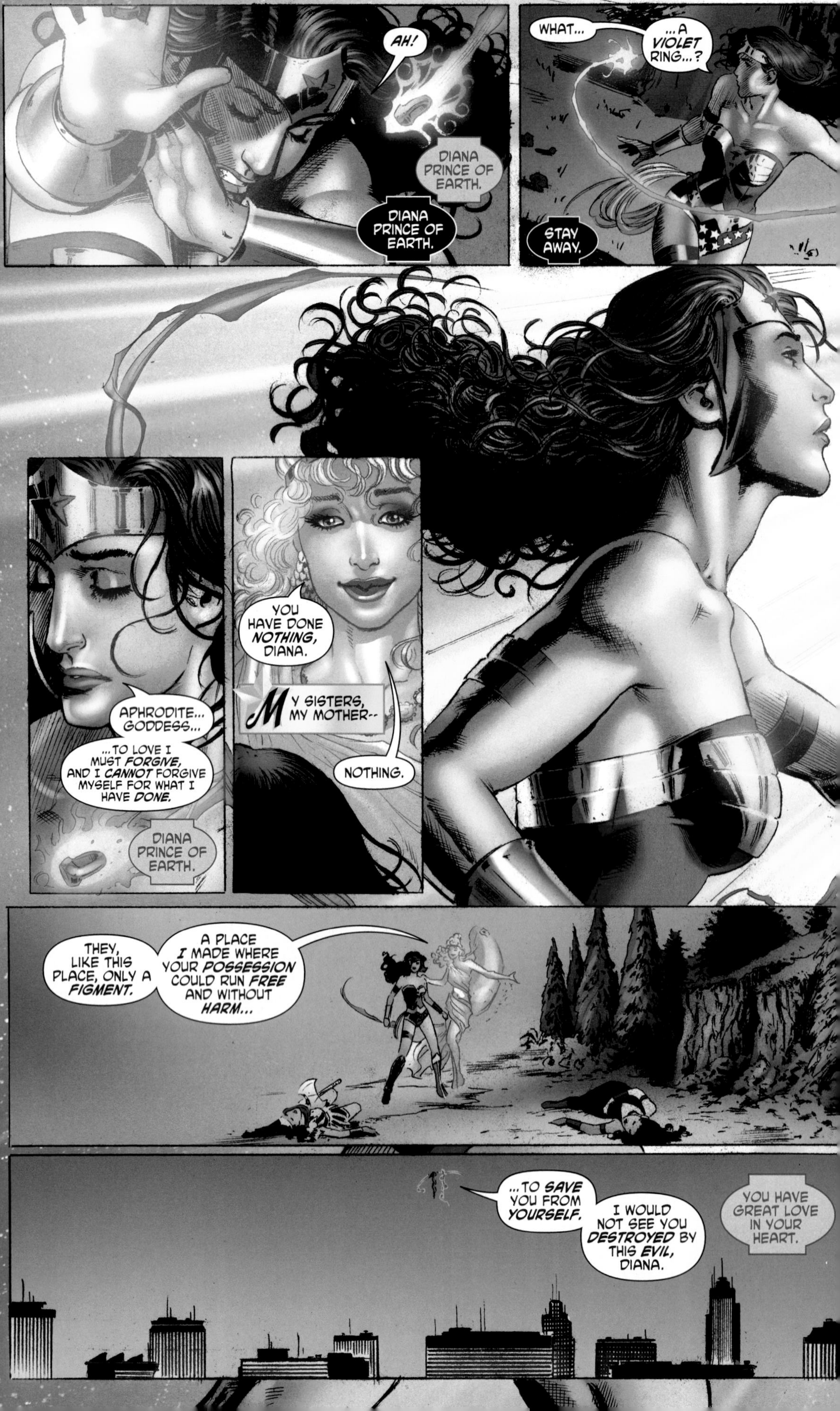
AH!
DIANA PRINCE OF EARTH.
DIANA PRINCE OF EARTH.
WHAT...
...A VIOLET RING...?
STAY AWAY.
APHRODITE... GODDESS...
...TO LOVE I MUST FORGIVE, AND I CANNOT FORGIVE MYSELF FOR WHAT I HAVE DONE.
DIANA PRINCE OF EARTH.
YOU HAVE DONE NOTHING, DIANA.
MY SISTERS, MY MOTHER--
NOTHING.
THEY, LIKE THIS PLACE, ONLY A FIGMENT.
A PLACE I MADE WHERE YOUR POSSESSION COULD RUN FREE AND WITHOUT HARM...
...TO SAVE YOU FROM YOURSELF.
I WOULD NOT SEE YOU DESTROYED BY THIS EVIL, DIANA.
YOU HAVE GREAT LOVE IN YOUR HEART.

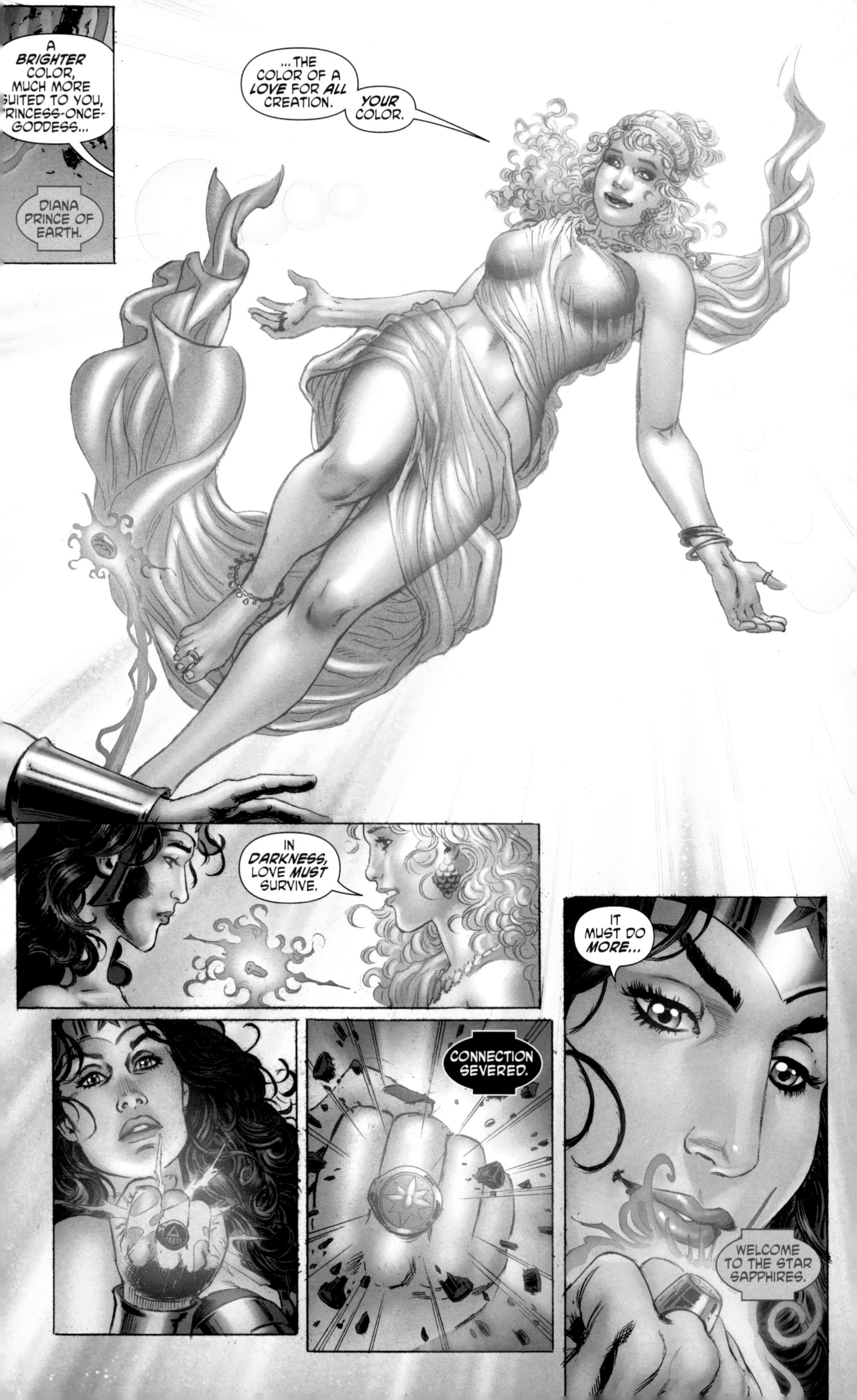
A BRIGHTER COLOR, MUCH MORE SUITED TO YOU, PRINCESS-ONCE-GODDESS...
DIANA PRINCE OF EARTH.
...THE COLOR OF A LOVE FOR ALL CREATION.
YOUR COLOR.
IN DARKNESS, LOVE MUST SURVIVE.
IT MUST DO MORE...
CONNECTION SEVERED.
WELCOME TO THE STAR SAPPHIRES.

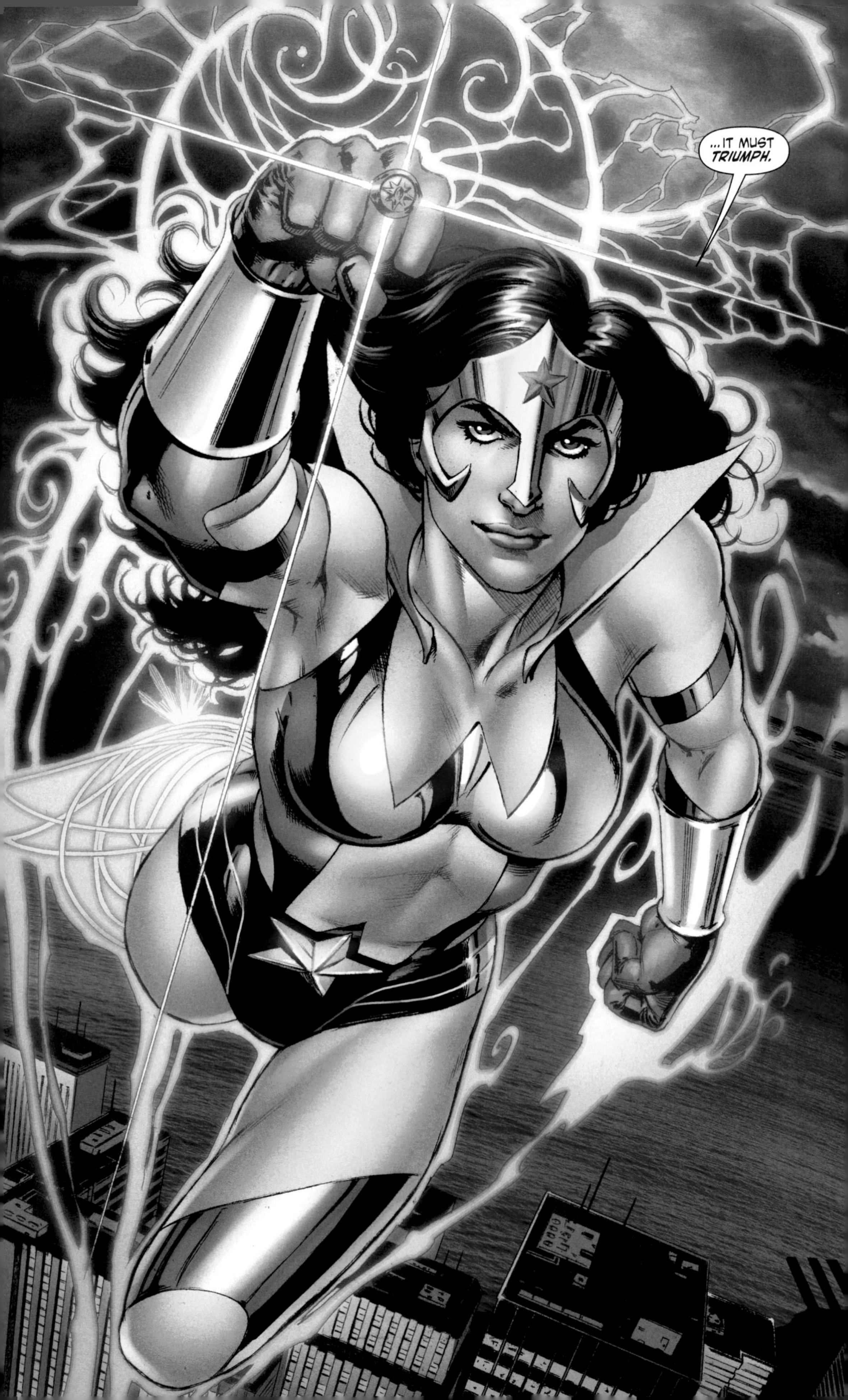
...IT MUST TRIUMPH.

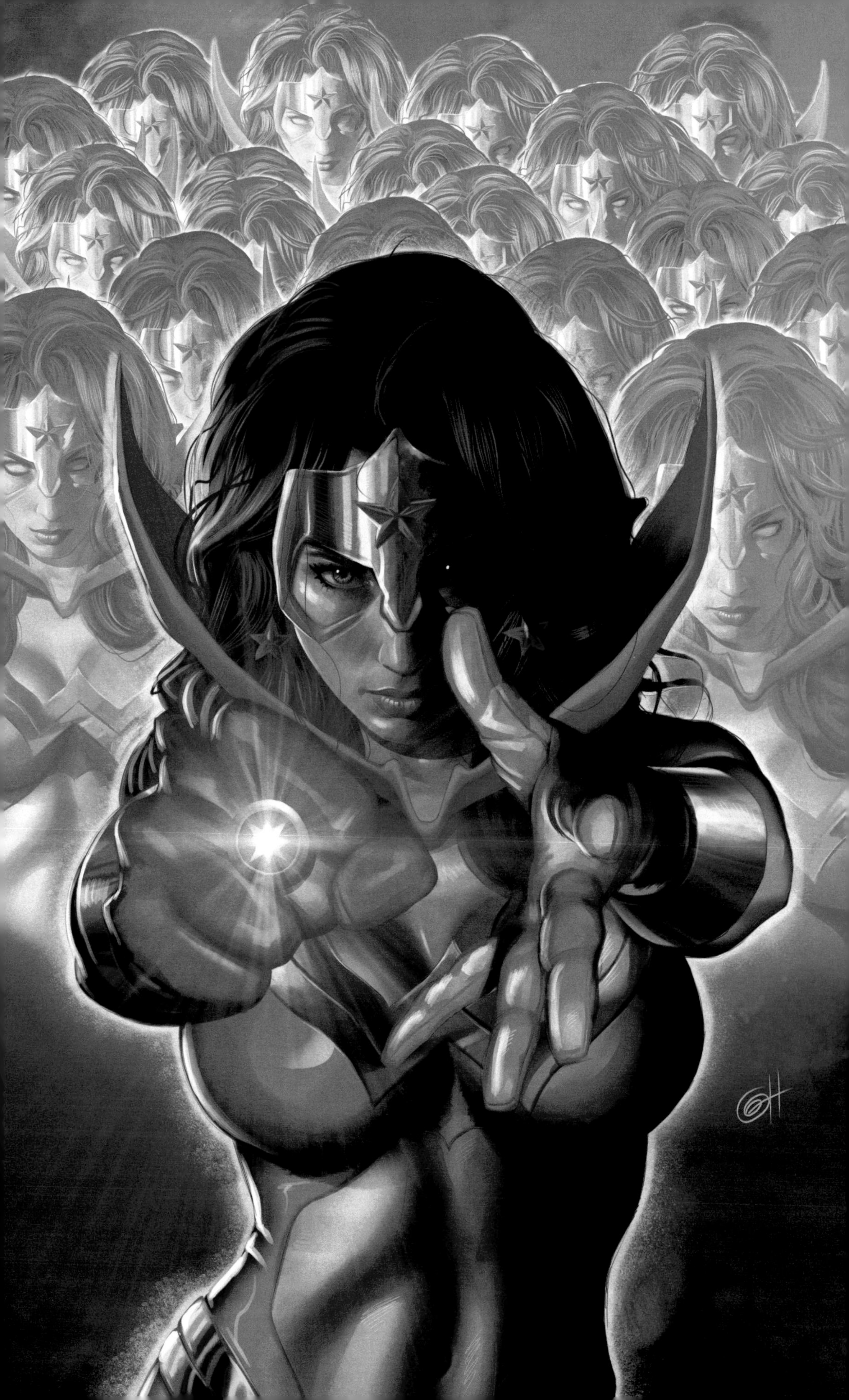

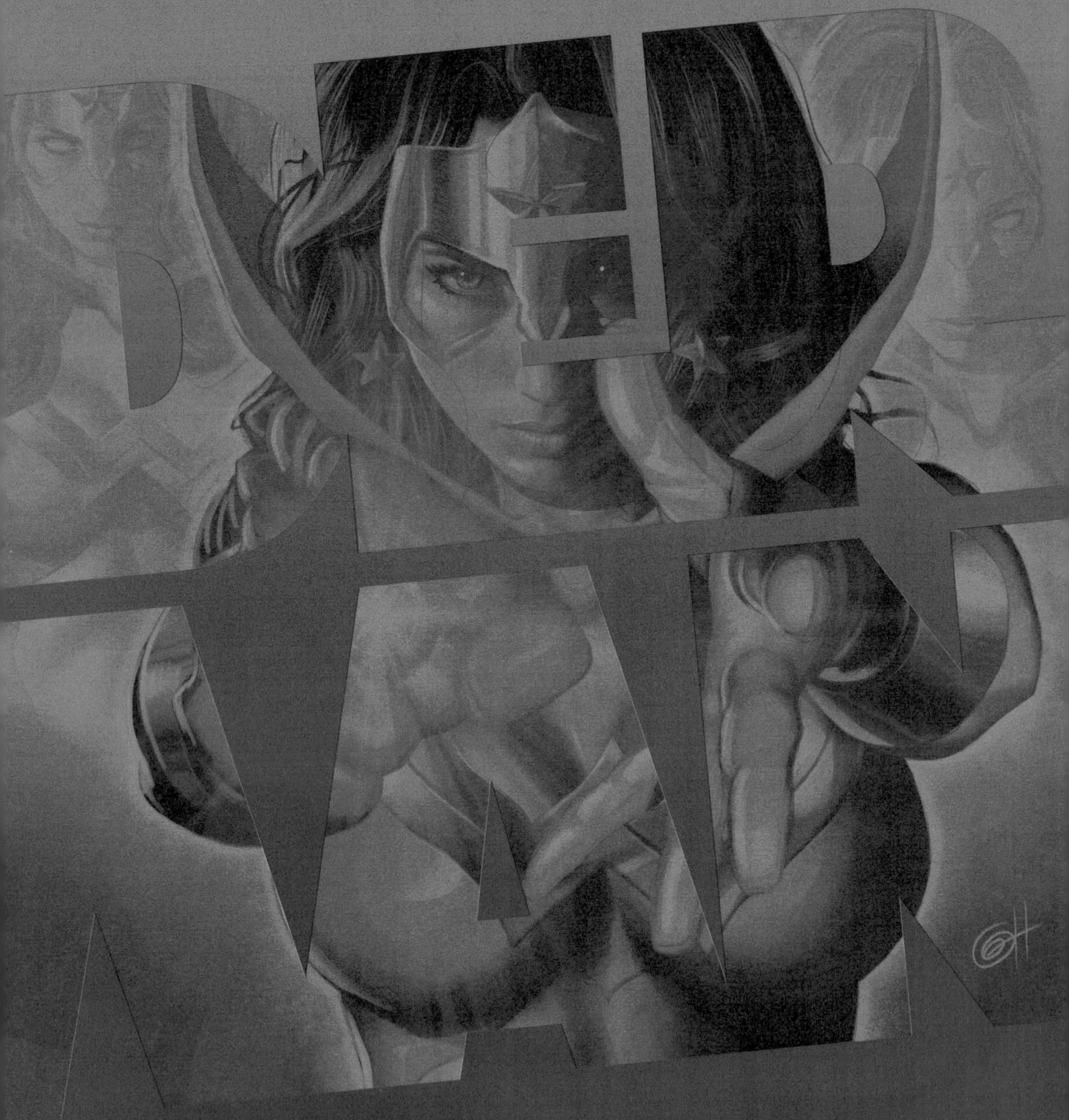

"WONDER WOMAN: BLACKEST NIGHT PART THREE"

Greg Rucka – *writer*
Nicola Scott – *pencils*
Jonathan Glapion – *inks*
Nei Ruffino – *colors*
Travis Lanham – *letters*
Greg Horn – *cover*

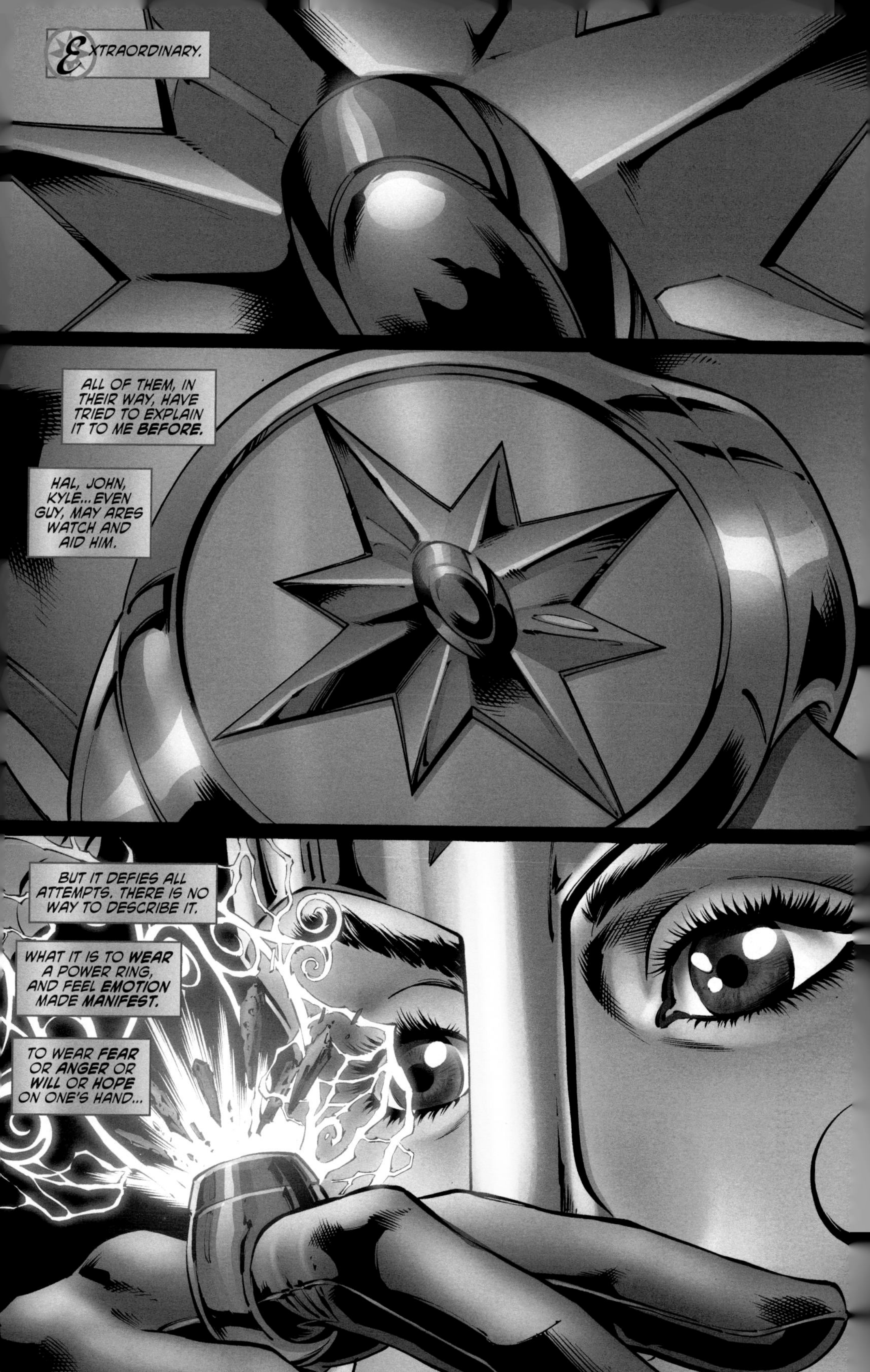
EXTRAORDINARY.
ALL OF THEM, IN THEIR WAY, HAVE TRIED TO EXPLAIN IT TO ME BEFORE.
HAL, JOHN, KYLE...EVEN GUY, MAY ARES WATCH AND AID HIM.
BUT IT DEFIES ALL ATTEMPTS. THERE IS NO WAY TO DESCRIBE IT.
WHAT IT IS TO WEAR A POWER RING, AND FEEL EMOTION MADE MANIFEST.
TO WEAR FEAR OR ANGER OR WILL OR HOPE ON ONE'S HAND...

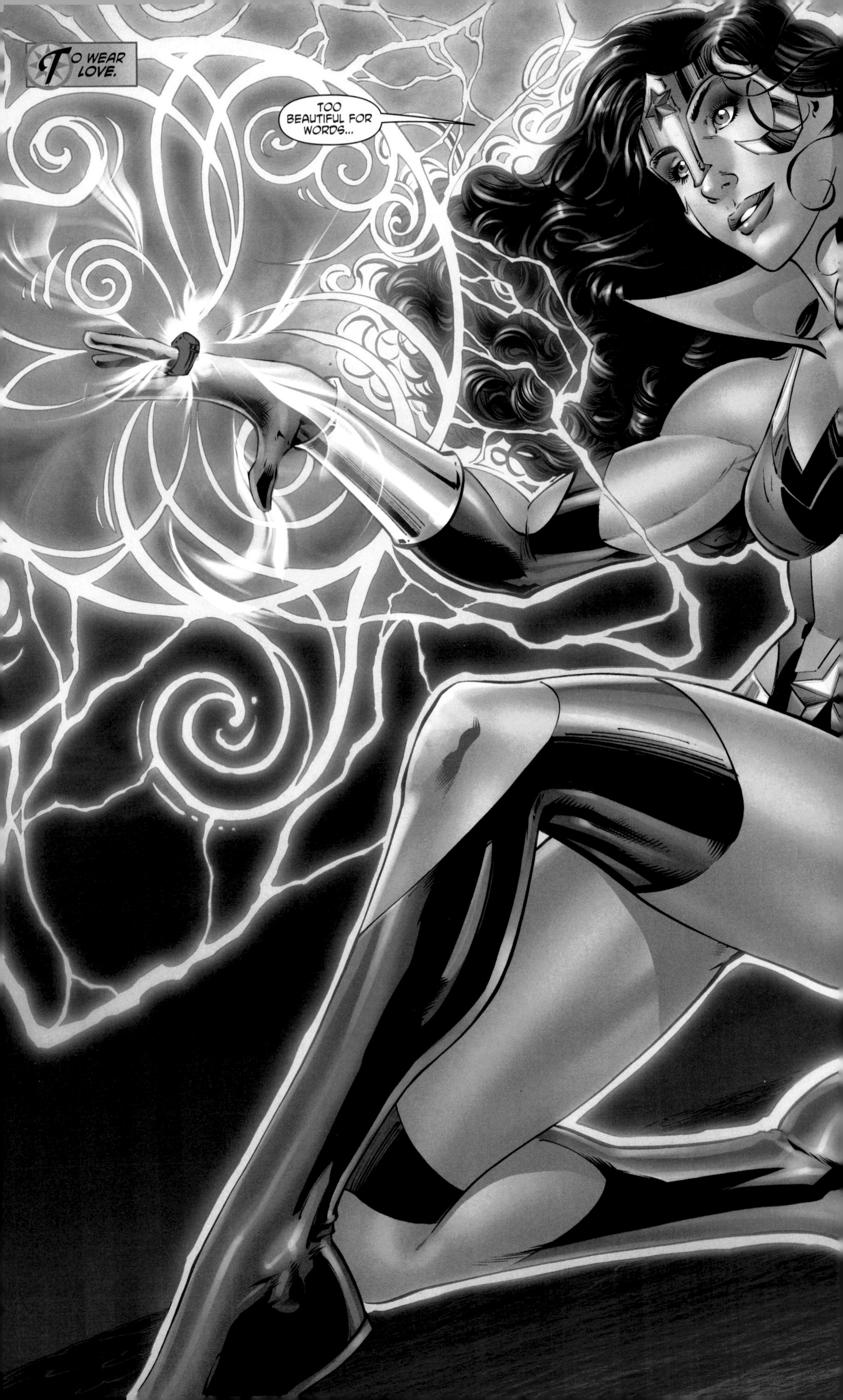
TO WEAR LOVE.
TOO BEAUTIFUL FOR WORDS...

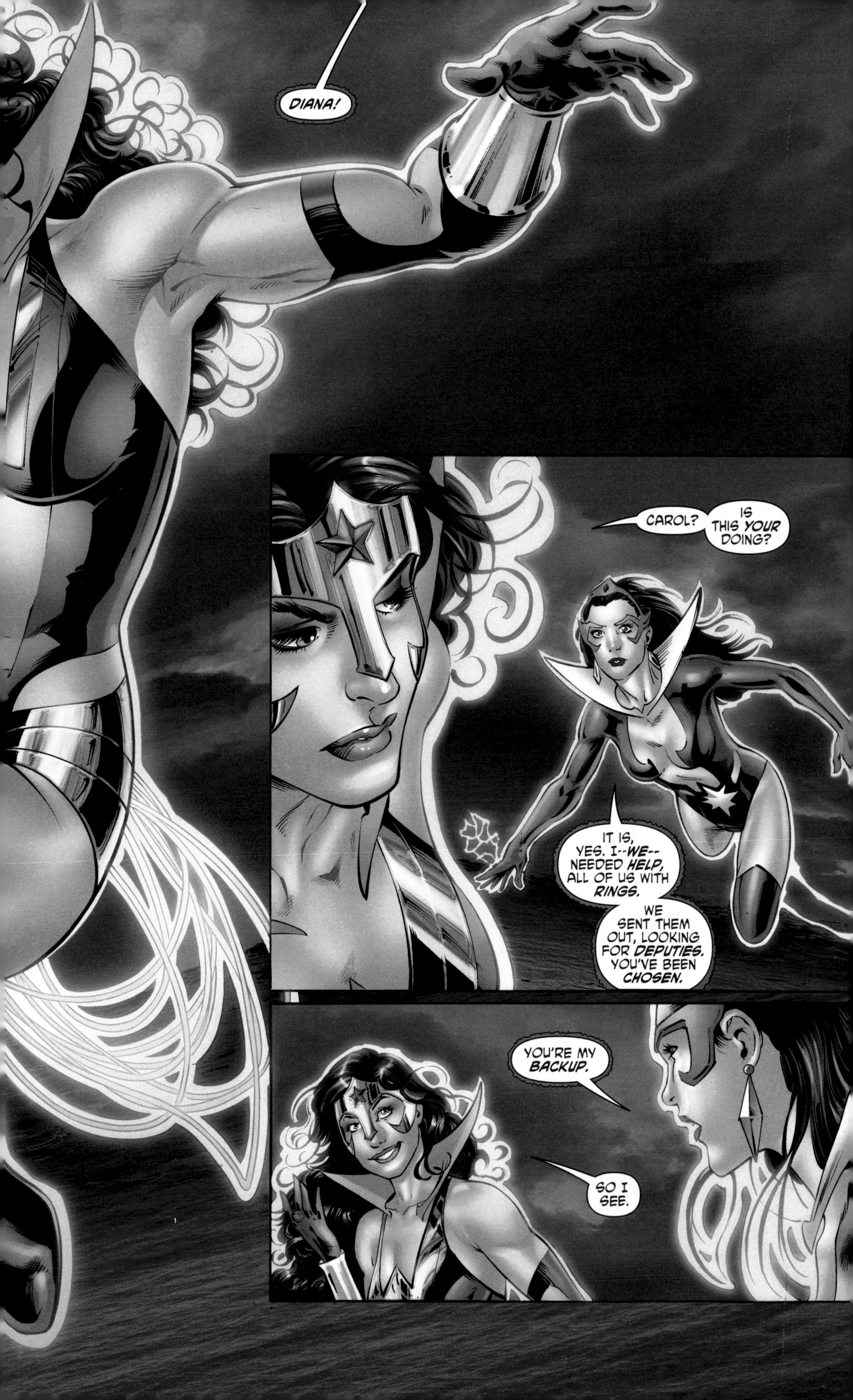
DIANA!
CAROL?
IS THIS YOUR DOING?
IT IS, YES. I--WE--NEEDED HELP, ALL OF US WITH RINGS.
WE SENT THEM OUT, LOOKING FOR DEPUTIES. YOU'VE BEEN CHOSEN.
YOU'RE MY BACKUP.
SO I SEE.

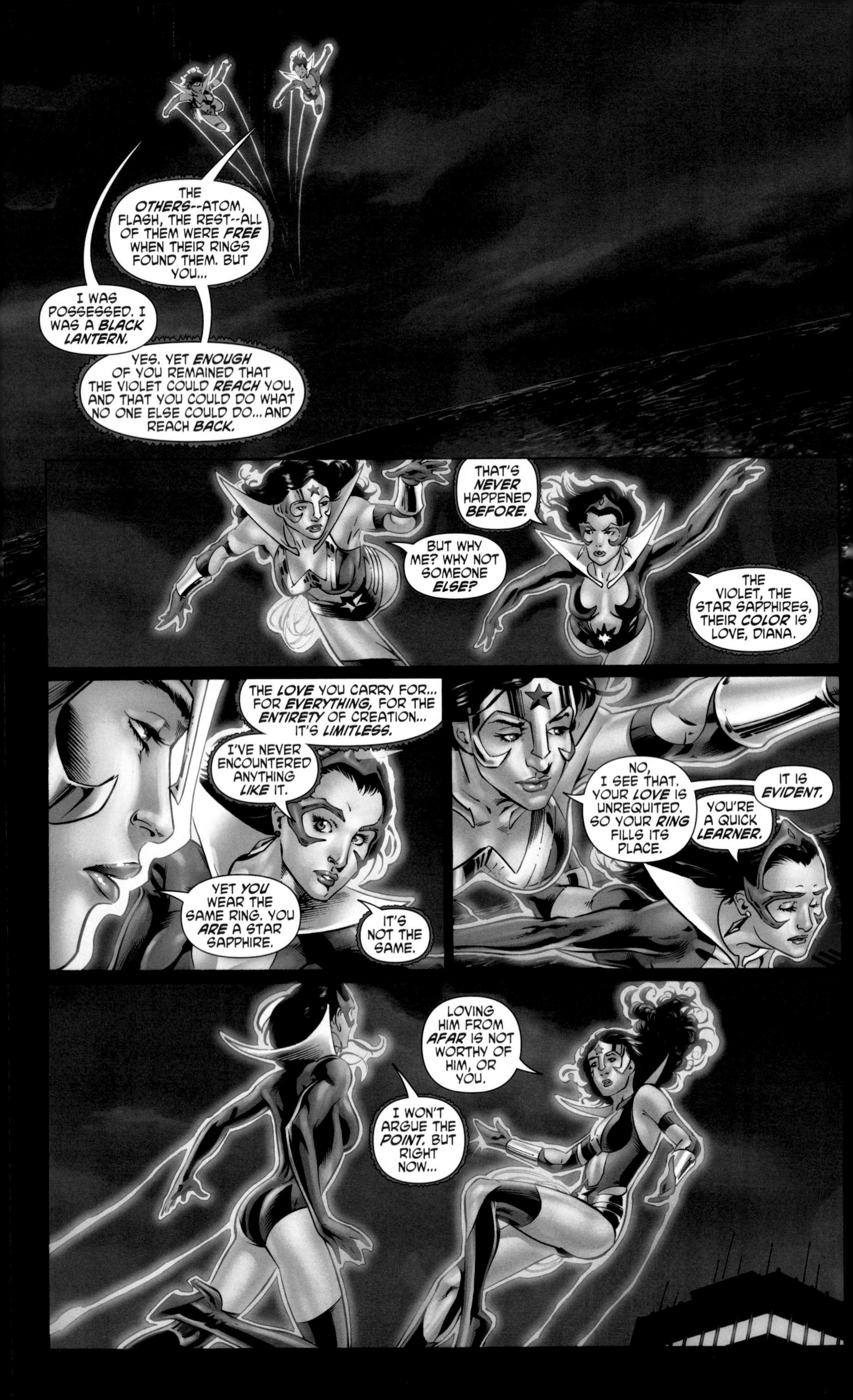
THE OTHERS--ATOM, FLASH, THE REST--ALL OF THEM WERE FREE WHEN THEIR RINGS FOUND THEM. BUT YOU...
I WAS POSSESSED. I WAS A BLACK LANTERN.
YES. YET ENOUGH OF YOU REMAINED THAT THE VIOLET COULD REACH YOU, AND THAT YOU COULD DO WHAT NO ONE ELSE COULD DO...AND REACH BACK.
THAT'S NEVER HAPPENED BEFORE.
BUT WHY ME? WHY NOT SOMEONE ELSE?
THE VIOLET, THE STAR SAPPHIRES, THEIR COLOR IS LOVE, DIANA.
THE LOVE YOU CARRY FOR... FOR EVERYTHING, FOR THE ENTIRETY OF CREATION... IT'S LIMITLESS.
I'VE NEVER ENCOUNTERED ANYTHING LIKE IT.
YET YOU WEAR THE SAME RING. YOU ARE A STAR SAPPHIRE.
IT'S NOT THE SAME.
NO, I SEE THAT. YOUR LOVE IS UNREQUITED. SO YOUR RING FILLS ITS PLACE.
IT IS EVIDENT.
YOU'RE A QUICK LEARNER.
LOVING HIM FROM AFAR IS NOT WORTHY OF HIM, OR YOU.
I WON'T ARGUE THE POINT. BUT RIGHT NOW...

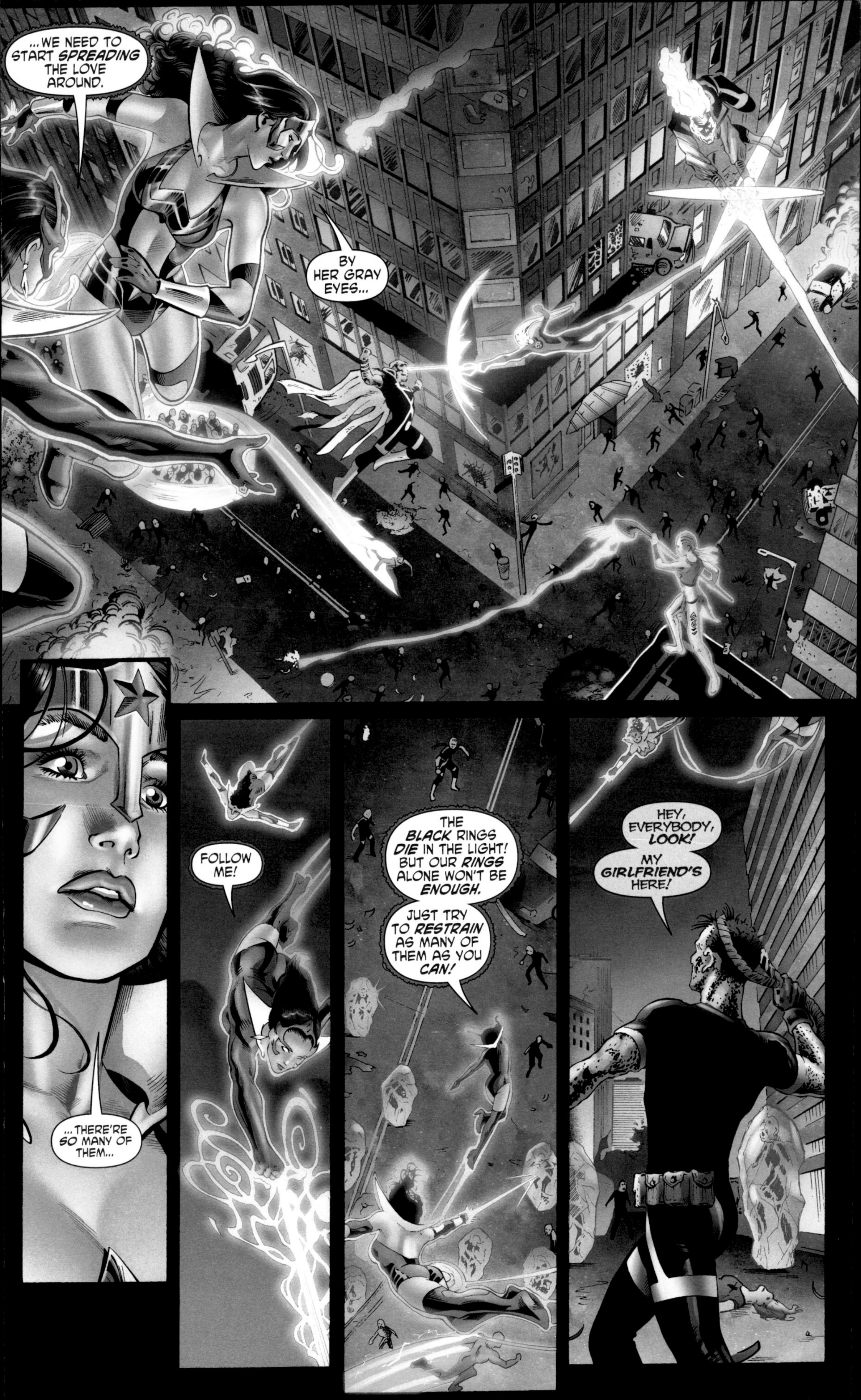
...WE NEED TO START SPREADING THE LOVE AROUND.
BY HER GRAY EYES...
...THERE'RE SO MANY OF THEM...
FOLLOW ME!
THE BLACK RINGS DIE IN THE LIGHT! BUT OUR RINGS ALONE WON'T BE ENOUGH.
JUST TRY TO RESTRAIN AS MANY OF THEM AS YOU CAN!
HEY, EVERYBODY, LOOK!
MY GIRLFRIEND'S HERE!

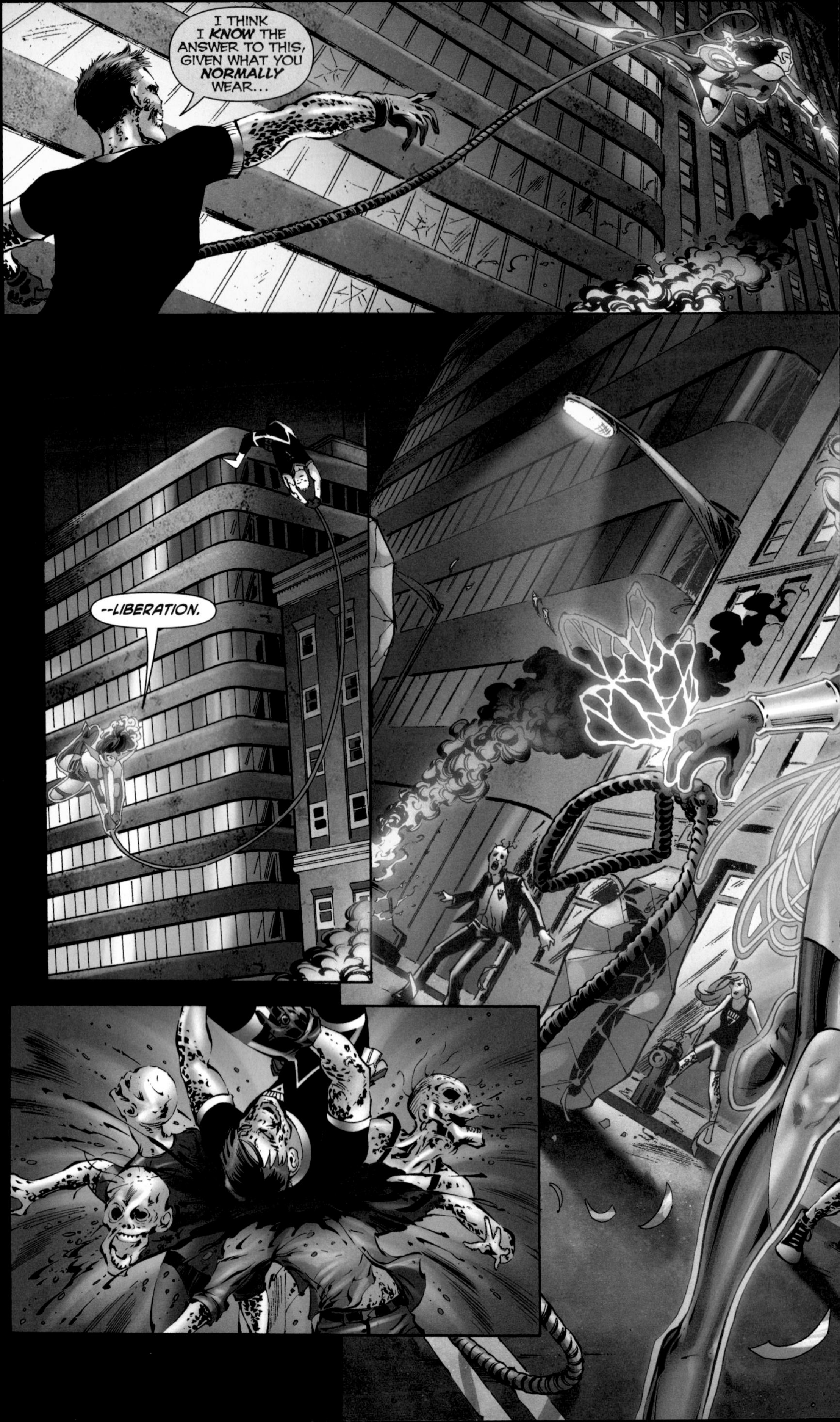
I THINK I KNOW THE ANSWER TO THIS, GIVEN WHAT YOU NORMALLY WEAR...
--LIBERATION.

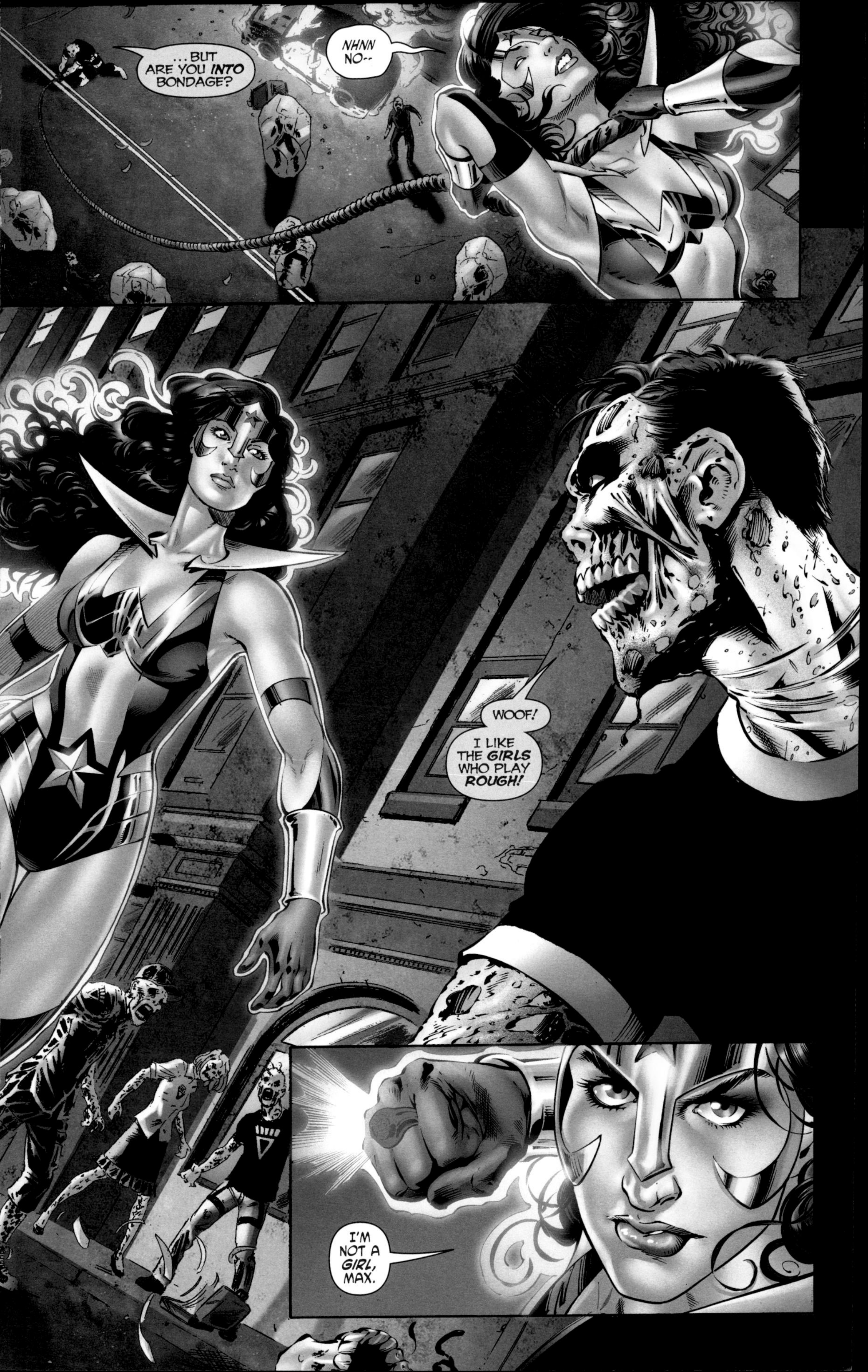
...BUT ARE YOU *INTO* BONDAGE?
NHNN NO--
WOOF!
I LIKE THE *GIRLS* WHO PLAY *ROUGH!*
I'M NOT A *GIRL,* MAX.

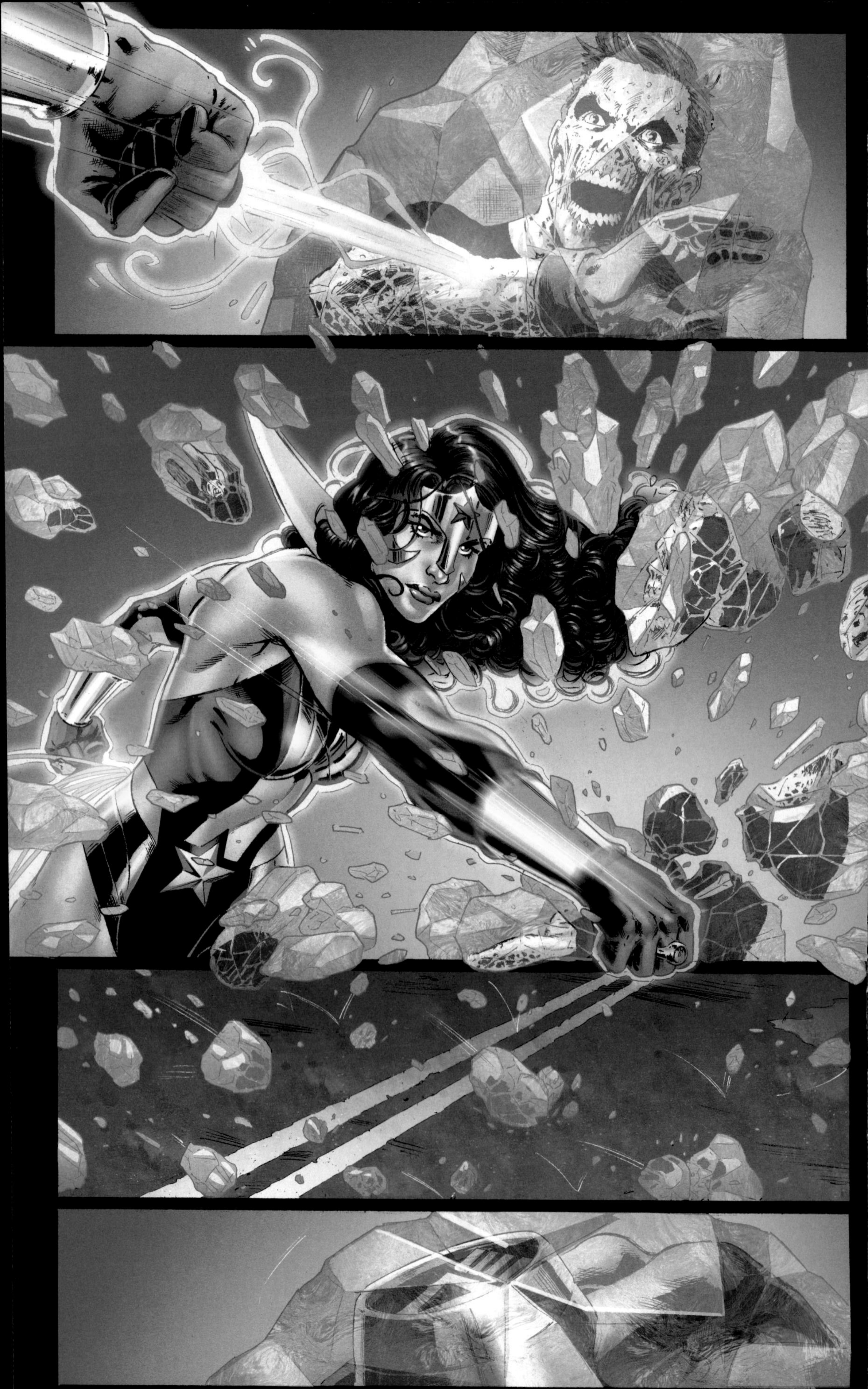

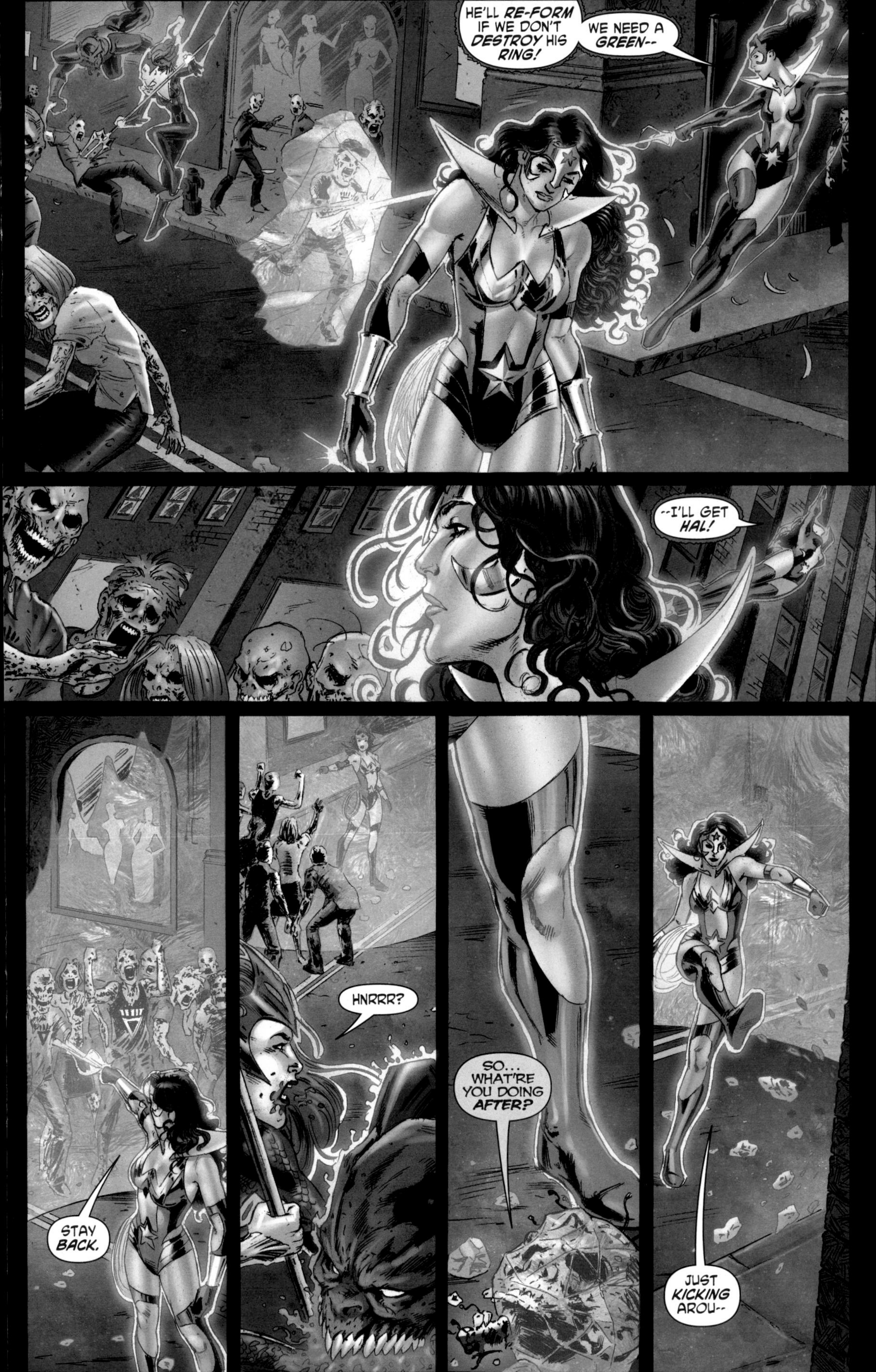
HE'LL RE-FORM IF WE DON'T DESTROY HIS RING!
WE NEED A GREEN--
--I'LL GET HAL!
STAY BACK.
HNRRR?
SO... WHAT'RE YOU DOING AFTER?
JUST KICKING AROU--

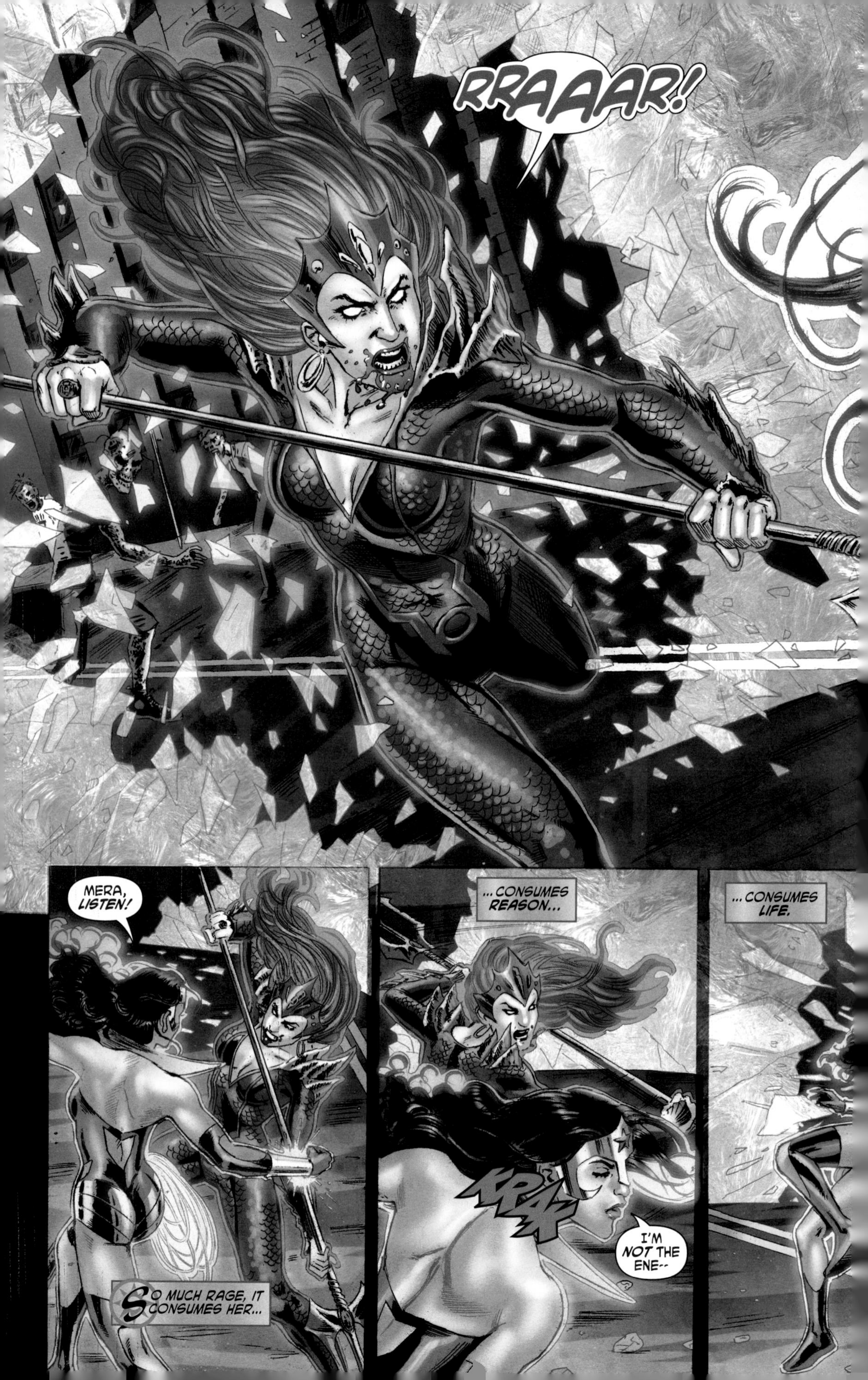
RRAAAR!
MERA, LISTEN!
SO MUCH RAGE, IT CONSUMES HER...
...CONSUMES REASON...
KRAK
I'M NOT THE ENE--
...CONSUMES LIFE.

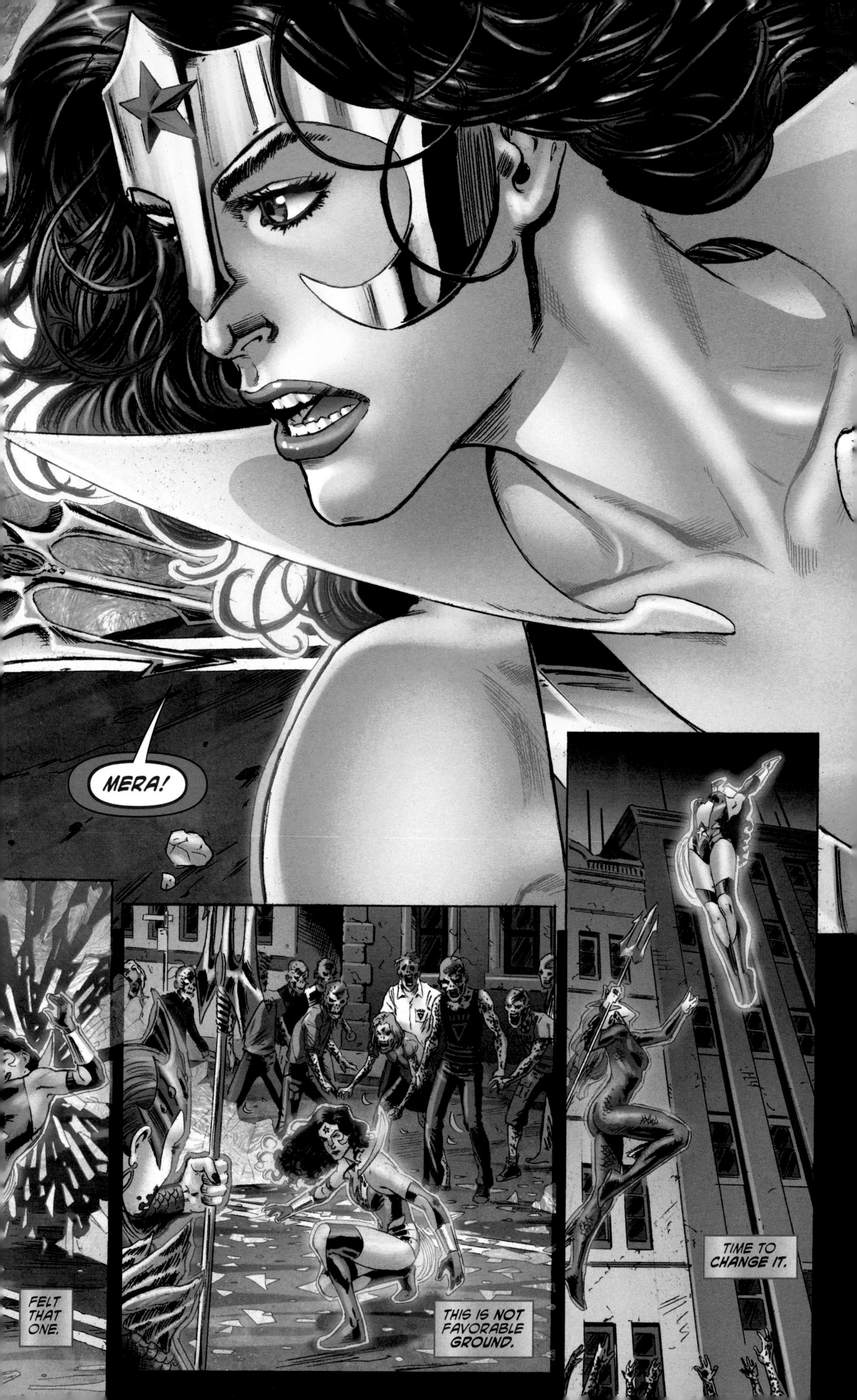
MERA!
FELT THAT ONE.
THIS IS NOT FAVORABLE GROUND.
TIME TO CHANGE IT.

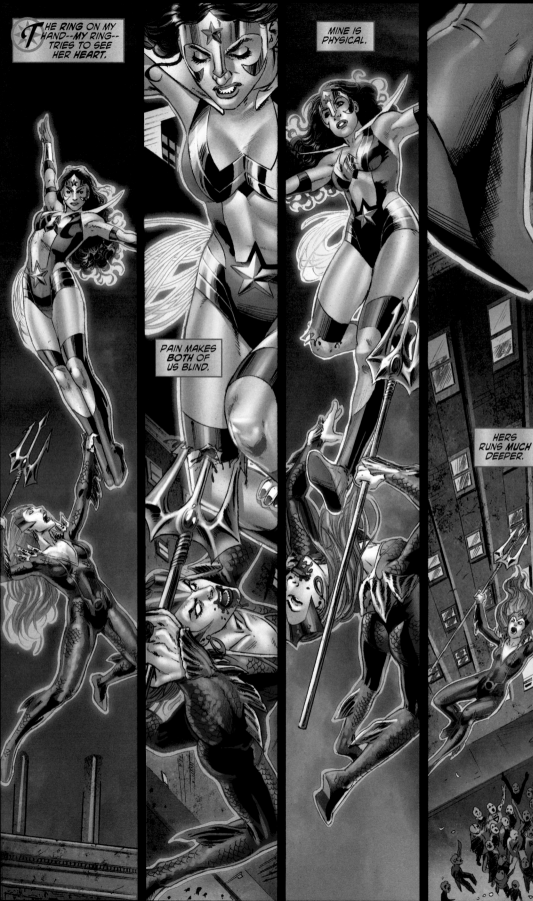

THE RING ON MY HAND--MY RING--TRIES TO SEE HER HEART.

MINE IS PHYSICAL.

PAIN MAKES BOTH OF US BLIND.

HERS RUNS MUCH DEEPER.

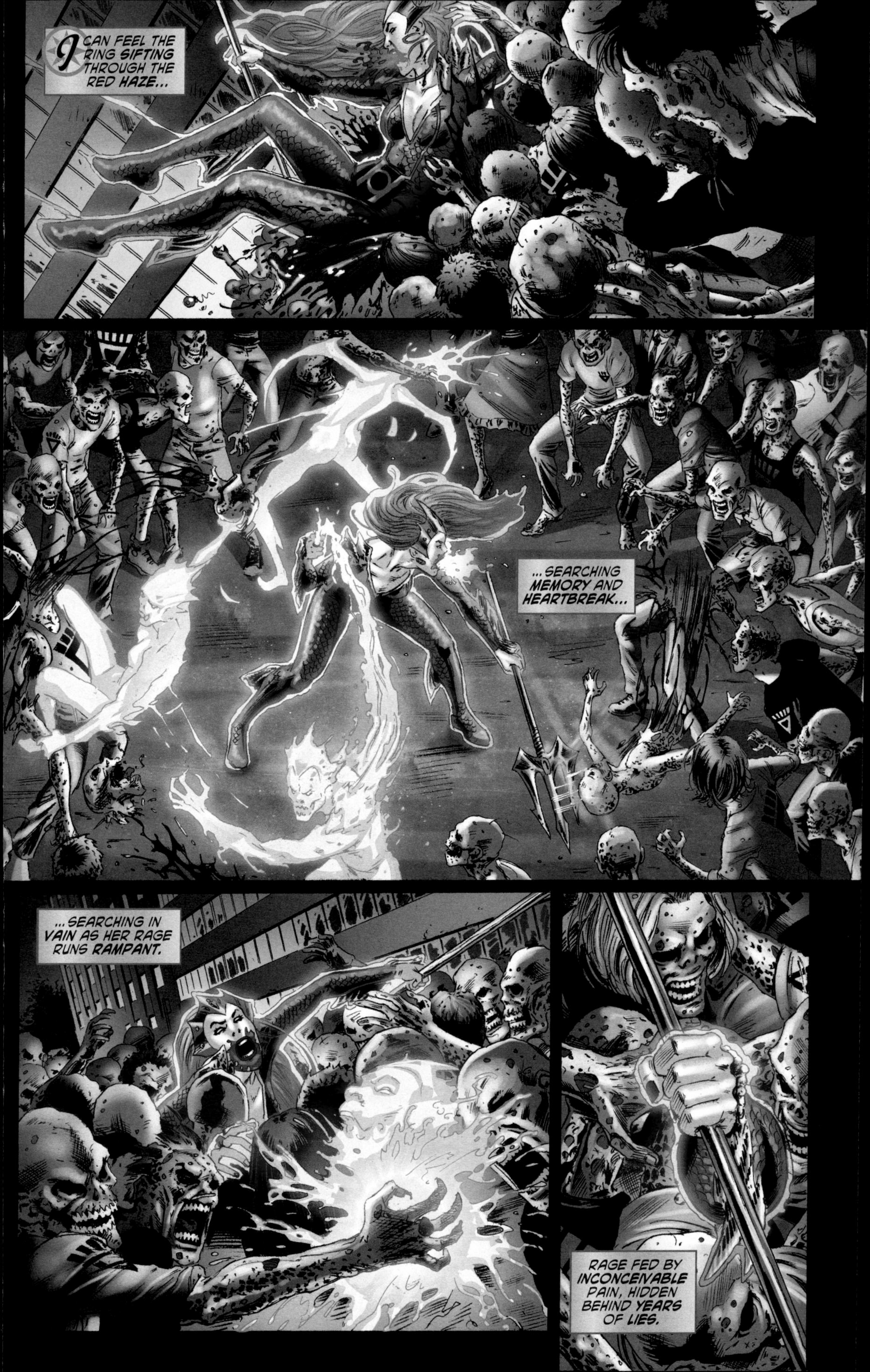
I CAN FEEL THE RING SIFTING THROUGH THE RED HAZE...
...SEARCHING MEMORY AND HEARTBREAK...
...SEARCHING IN VAIN AS HER RAGE RUNS RAMPANT.
RAGE FED BY INCONCEIVABLE PAIN, HIDDEN BEHIND YEARS OF LIES.

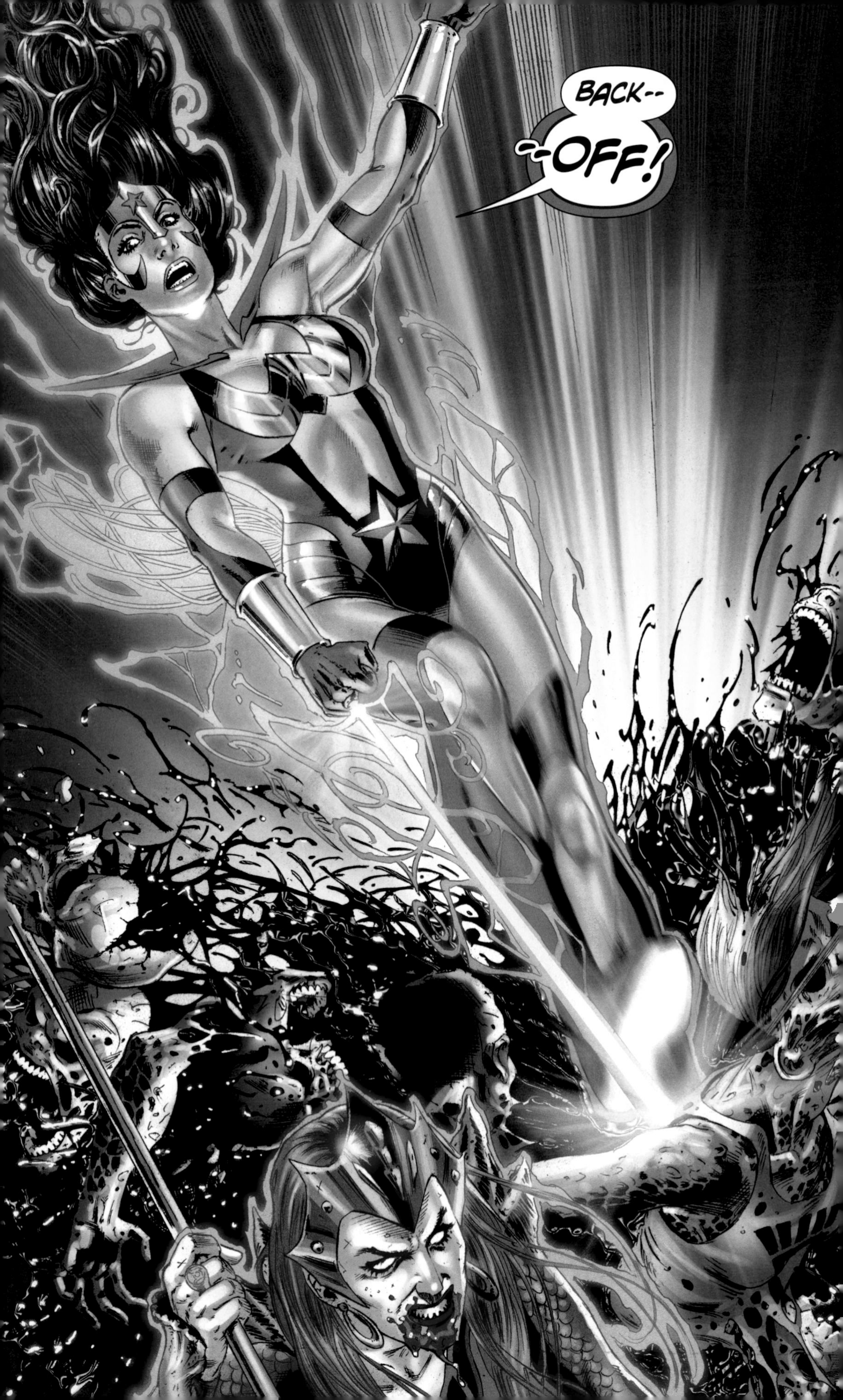
BACK--
--OFF!

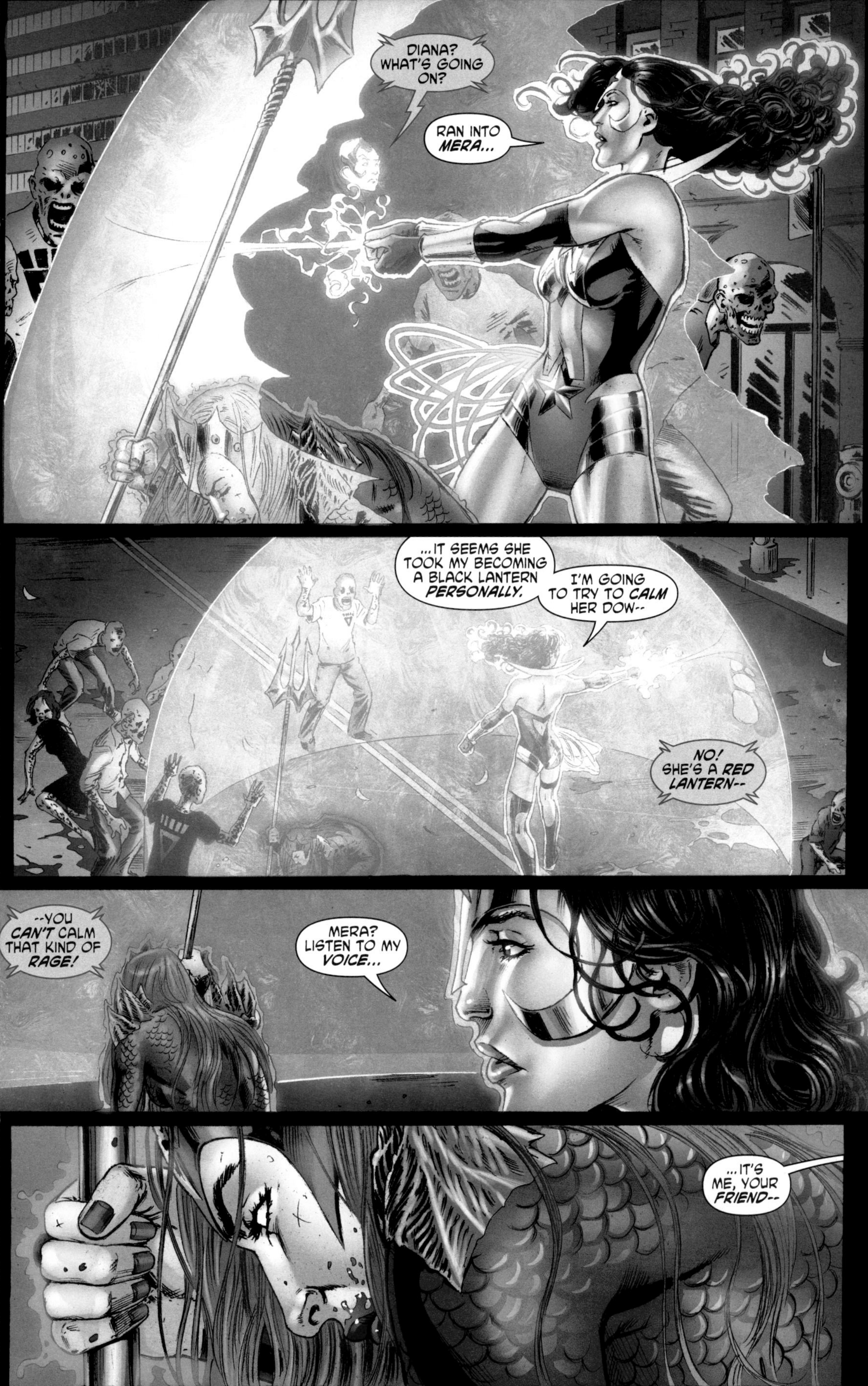
DIANA? WHAT'S GOING ON?
RAN INTO MERA...
...IT SEEMS SHE TOOK MY BECOMING A BLACK LANTERN PERSONALLY.
I'M GOING TO TRY TO CALM HER DOW--
NO! SHE'S A RED LANTERN--
--YOU CAN'T CALM THAT KIND OF RAGE!
MERA? LISTEN TO MY VOICE...
...IT'S ME, YOUR FRIEND--

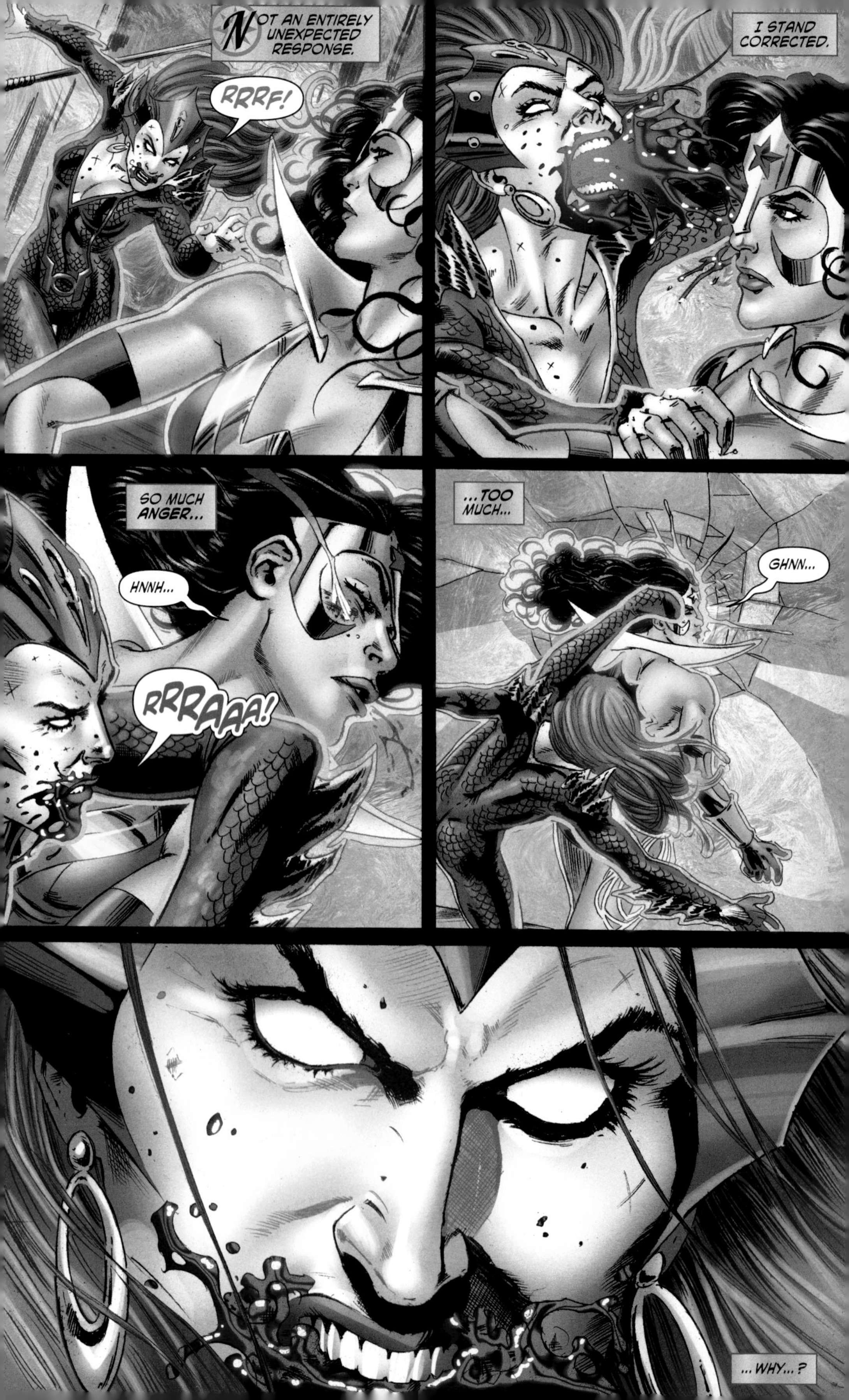
NOT AN ENTIRELY UNEXPECTED RESPONSE.
RRRF!
I STAND CORRECTED.
SO MUCH ANGER...
HNNH...
RRRAAA!
...TOO MUCH...
GHNN...
...WHY...?

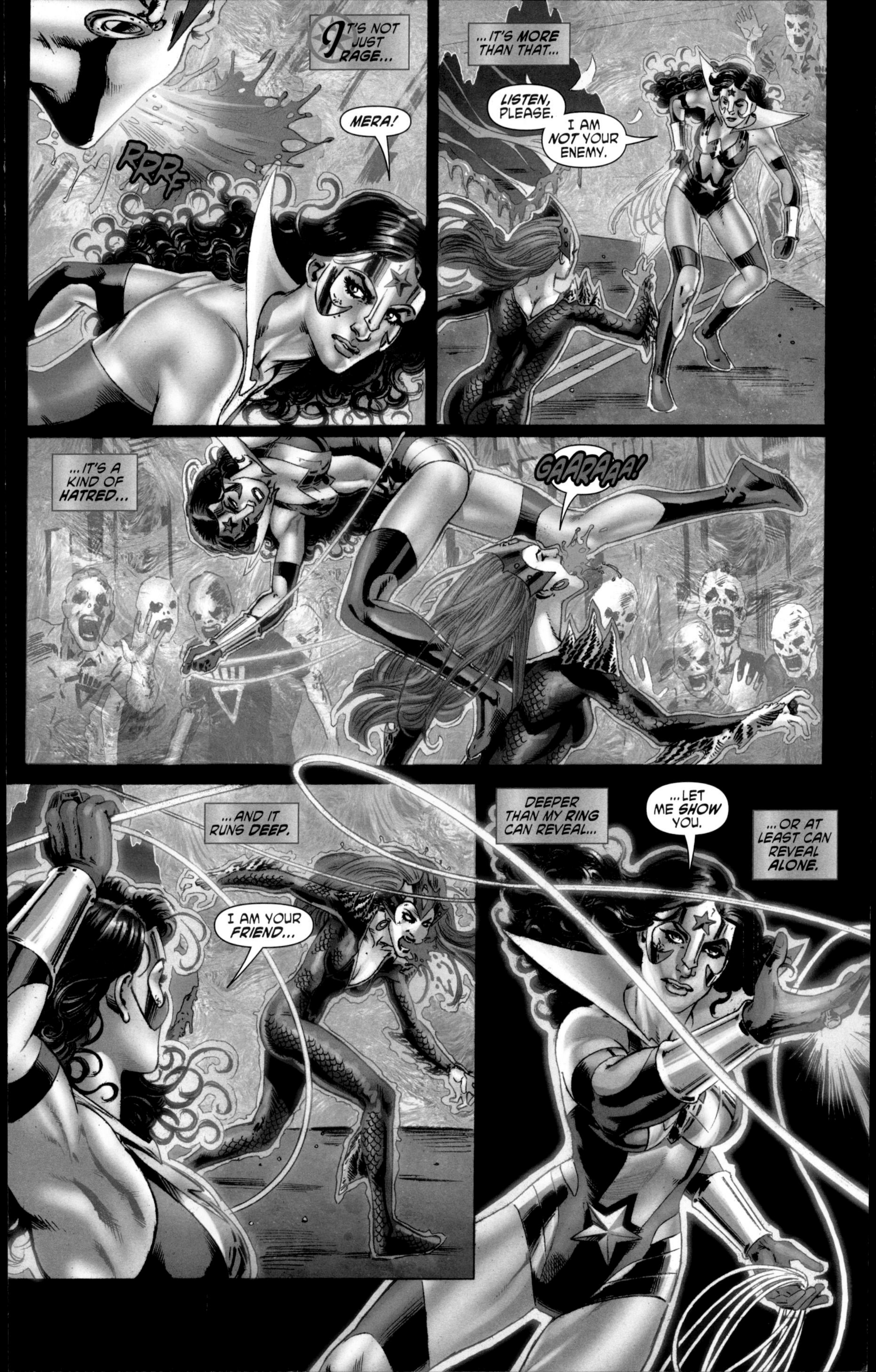
IT'S NOT JUST RAGE...
MERA!
RRRF
...IT'S MORE THAN THAT...
LISTEN, PLEASE.
I AM NOT YOUR ENEMY.
...IT'S A KIND OF HATRED...
GAARAAA!
...AND IT RUNS DEEP.
I AM YOUR FRIEND...
DEEPER THAN MY RING CAN REVEAL...
...LET ME SHOW YOU.
...OR AT LEAST CAN REVEAL ALONE.

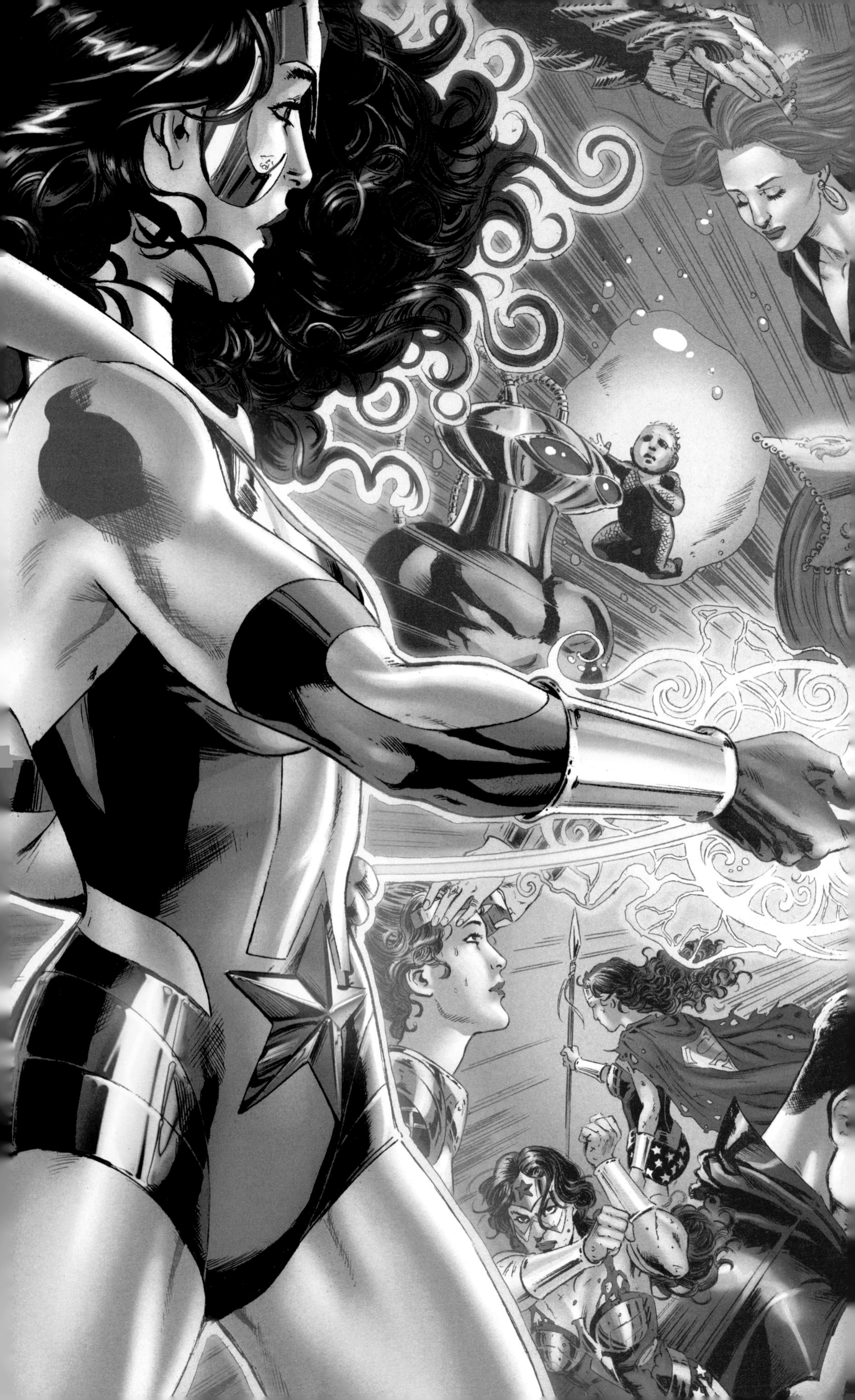

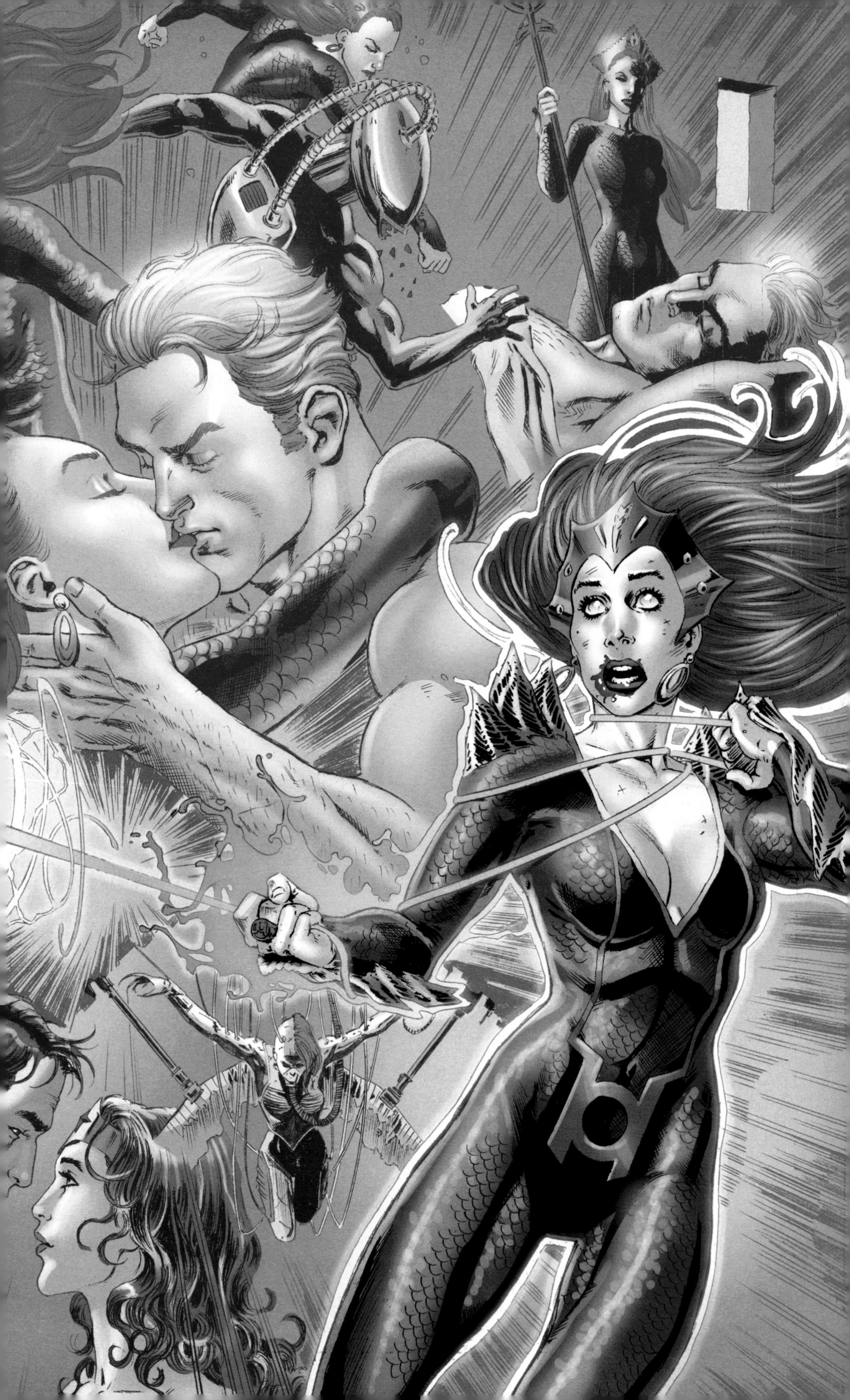

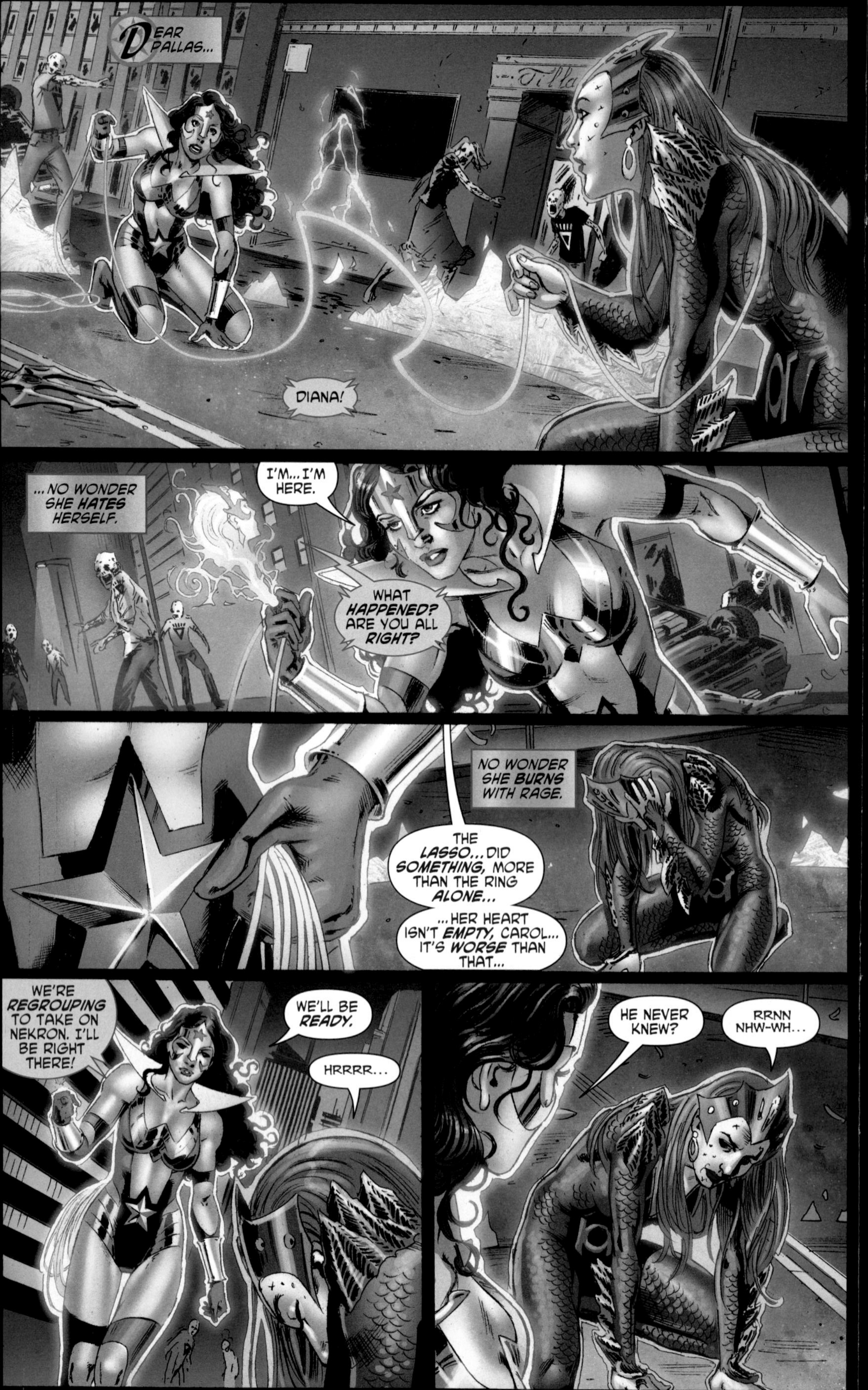
DEAR PALLAS...
DIANA!
...NO WONDER SHE HATES HERSELF.
I'M...I'M HERE.
WHAT HAPPENED? ARE YOU ALL RIGHT?
NO WONDER SHE BURNS WITH RAGE.
THE LASSO...DID SOMETHING, MORE THAN THE RING ALONE...
...HER HEART ISN'T EMPTY, CAROL... IT'S WORSE THAN THAT...
WE'RE REGROUPING TO TAKE ON NEKRON. I'LL BE RIGHT THERE!
WE'LL BE READY.
HRRRR...
HE NEVER KNEW?
RRNN NHW-WH...

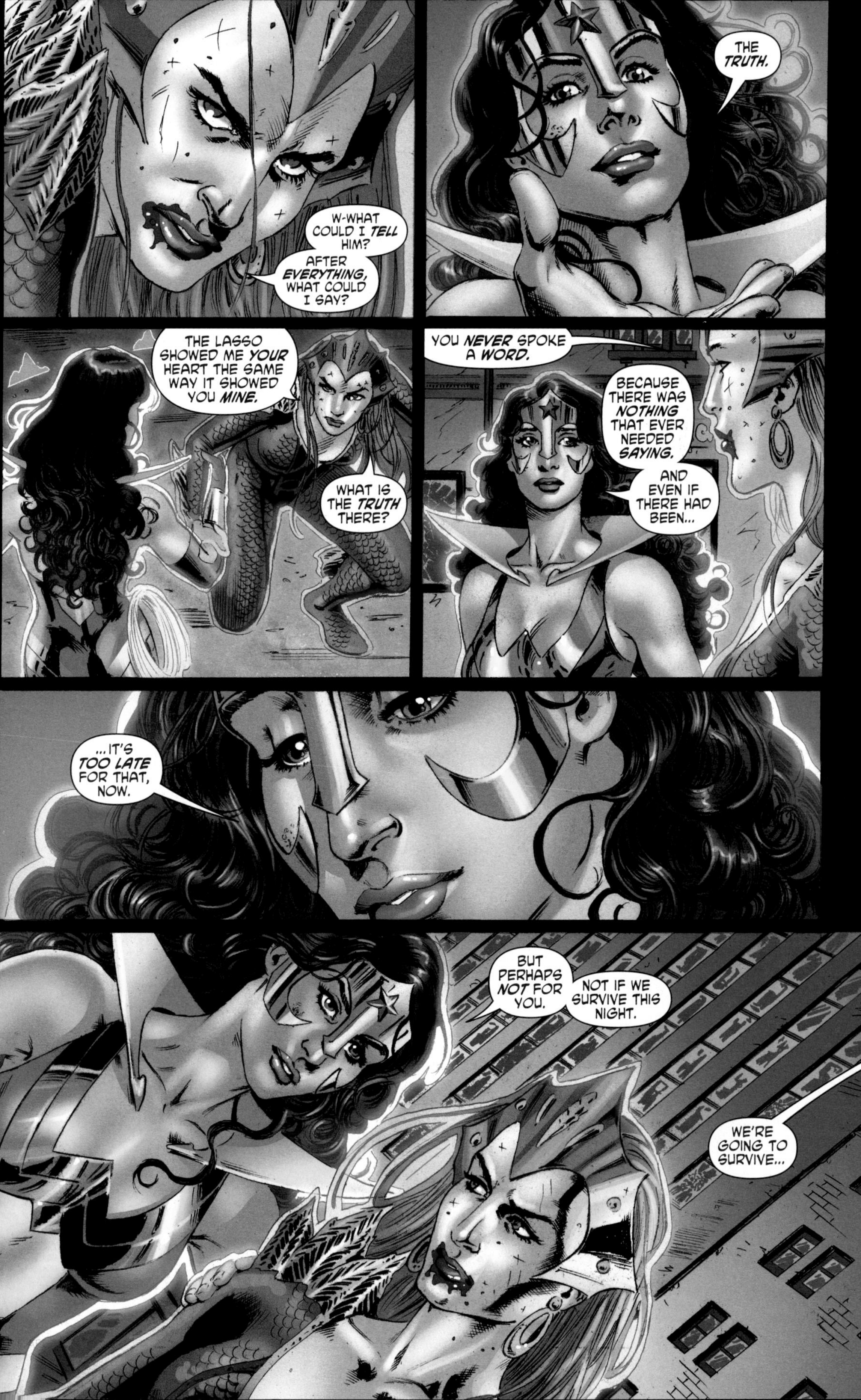
W-WHAT COULD I TELL HIM?
AFTER EVERYTHING, WHAT COULD I SAY?
THE TRUTH.
THE LASSO SHOWED ME YOUR HEART THE SAME WAY IT SHOWED YOU MINE.
WHAT IS THE TRUTH THERE?
YOU NEVER SPOKE A WORD.
BECAUSE THERE WAS NOTHING THAT EVER NEEDED SAYING.
AND EVEN IF THERE HAD BEEN...
...IT'S TOO LATE FOR THAT, NOW.
BUT PERHAPS NOT FOR YOU.
NOT IF WE SURVIVE THIS NIGHT.
WE'RE GOING TO SURVIVE...

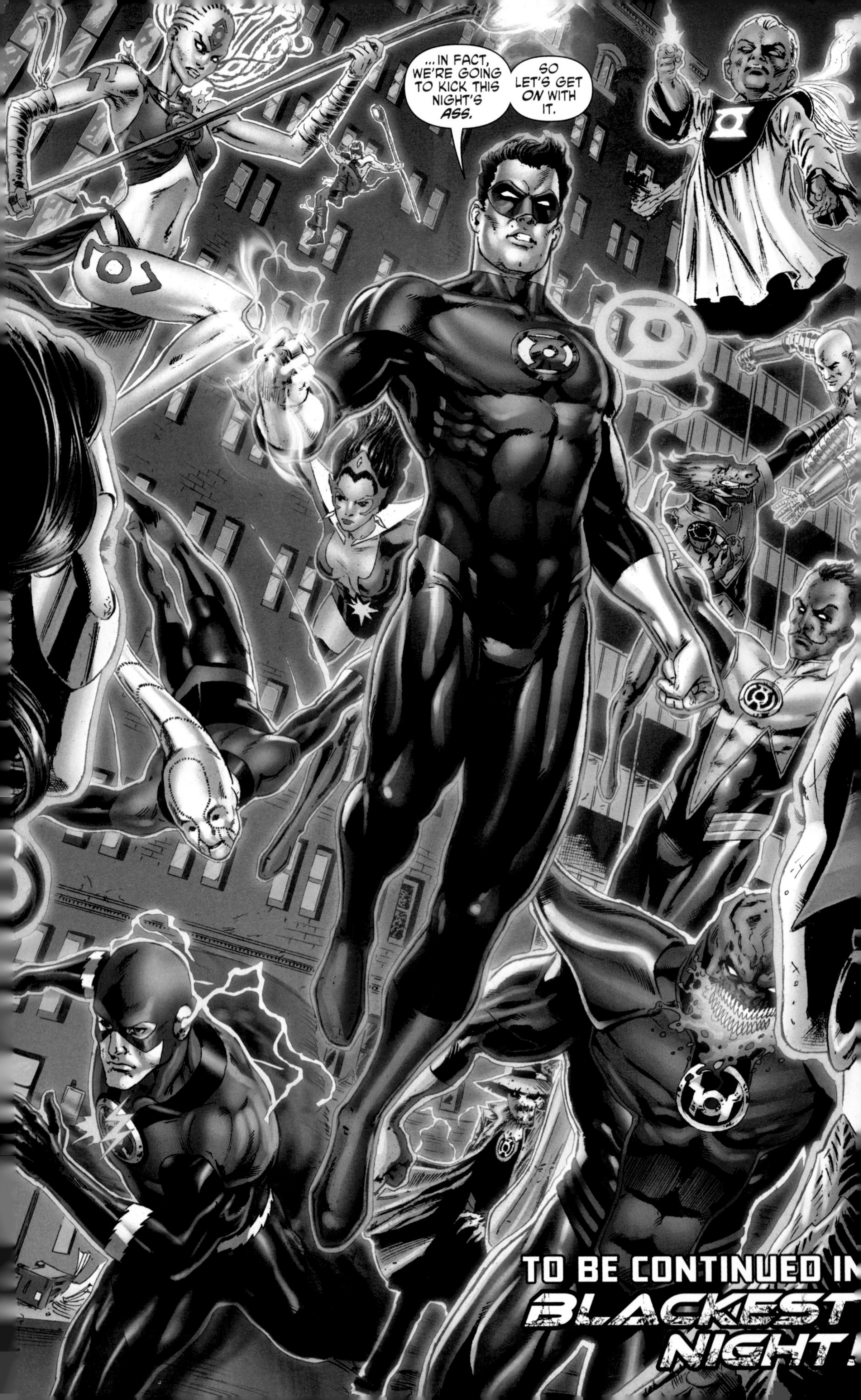
...IN FACT, WE'RE GOING TO KICK THIS NIGHT'S ASS.
SO LET'S GET ON WITH IT.
TO BE CONTINUED IN BLACKEST NIGHT!

WONDER WOMAN #219
second printing cover by JOSÉ LADRÖNN

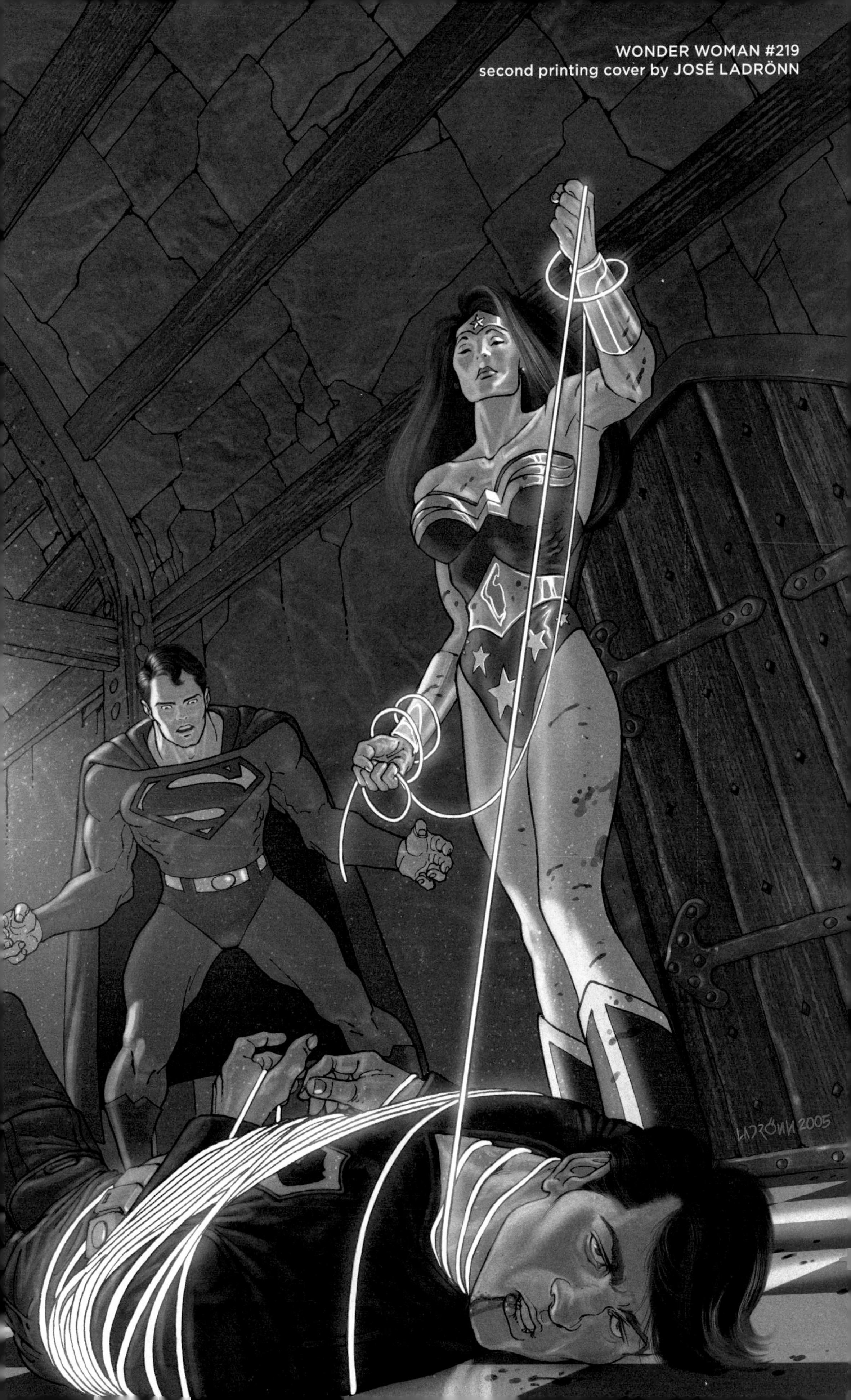
LADRÖNN 2005

BLACKEST NIGHT: WONDER WOMAN #1
variant cover by RYAN SOOK

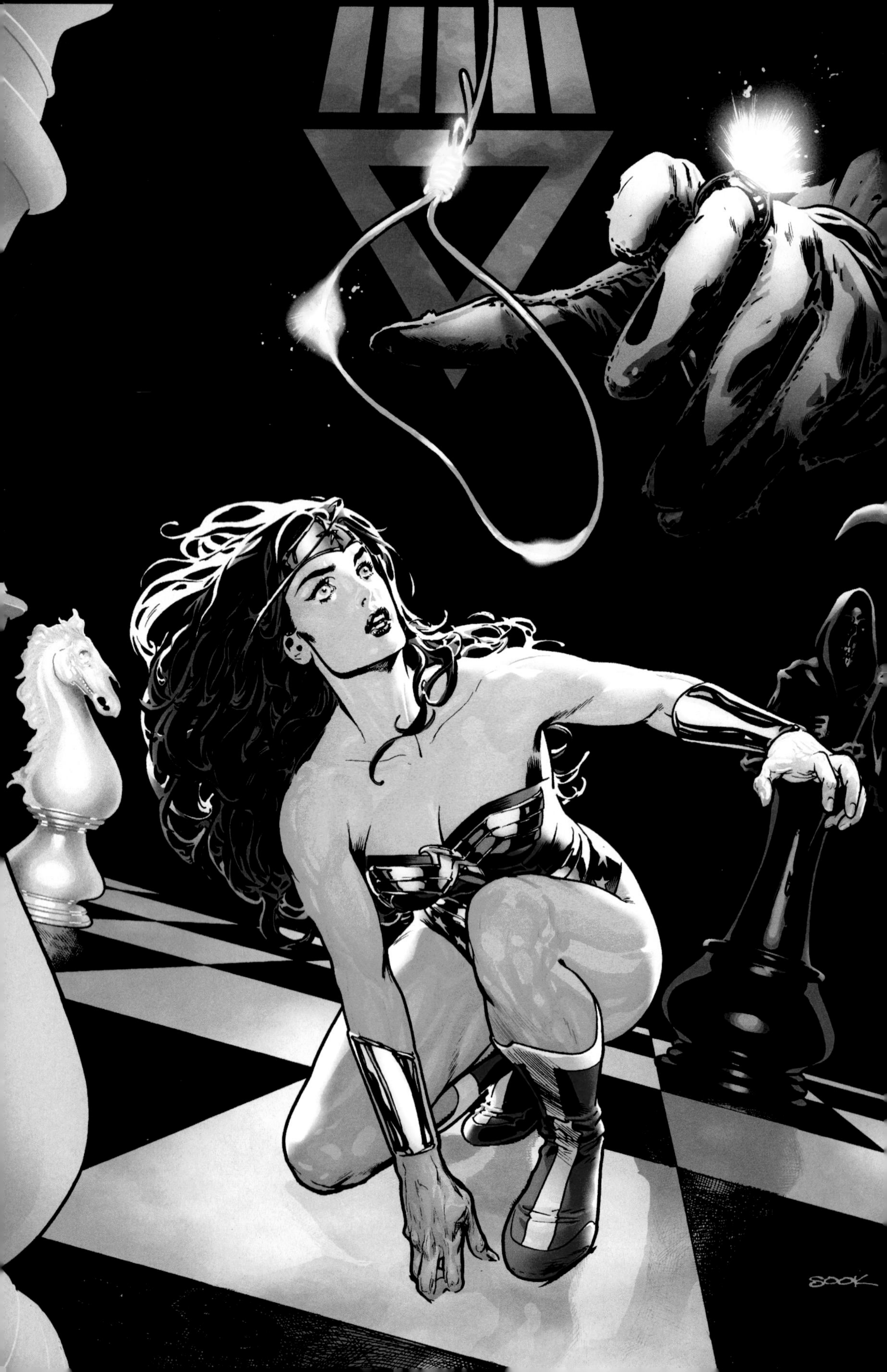
SOOK

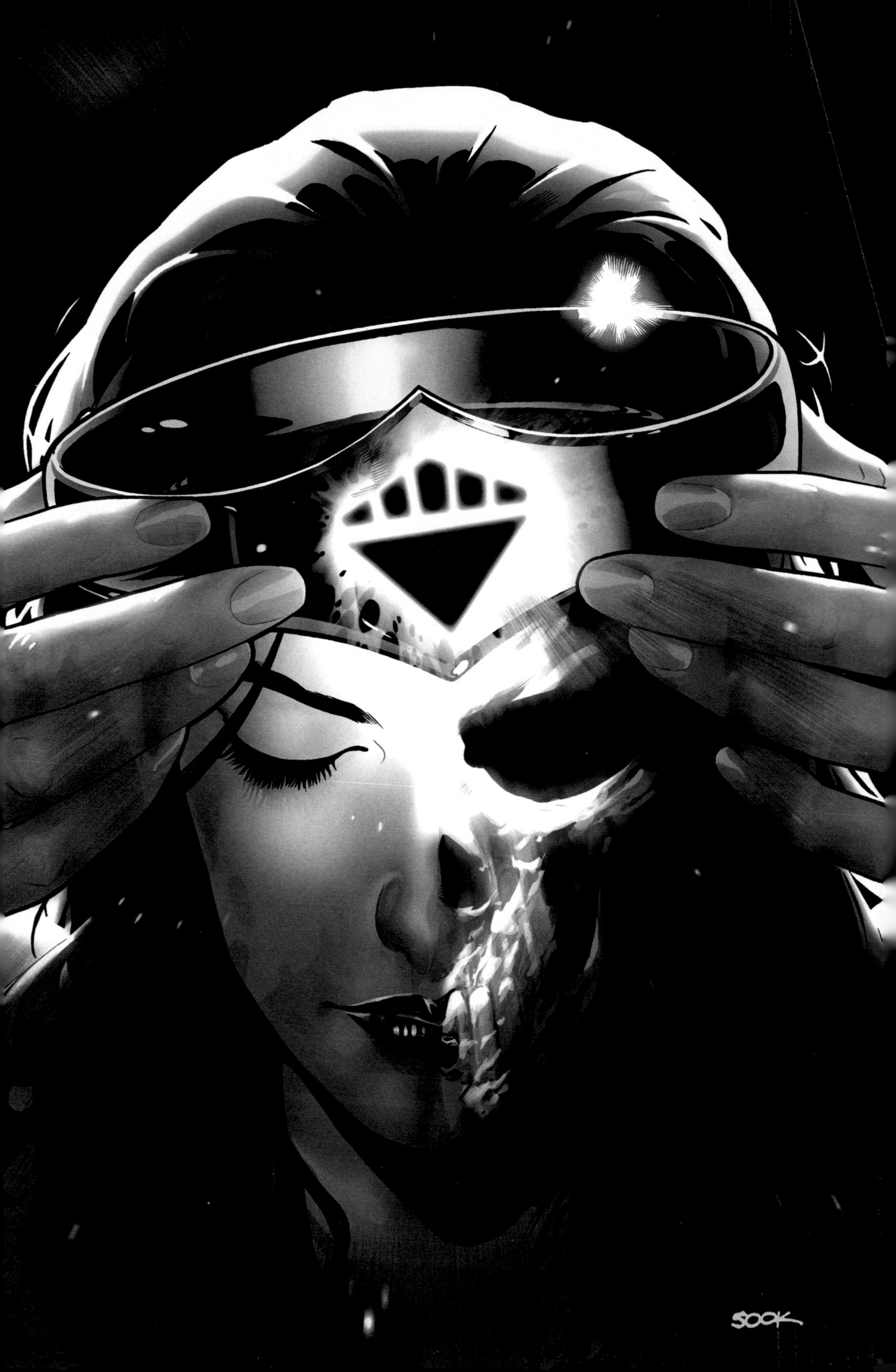
SOOK

BLACKEST NIGHT: WONDER WOM
variant cover by RYAN .

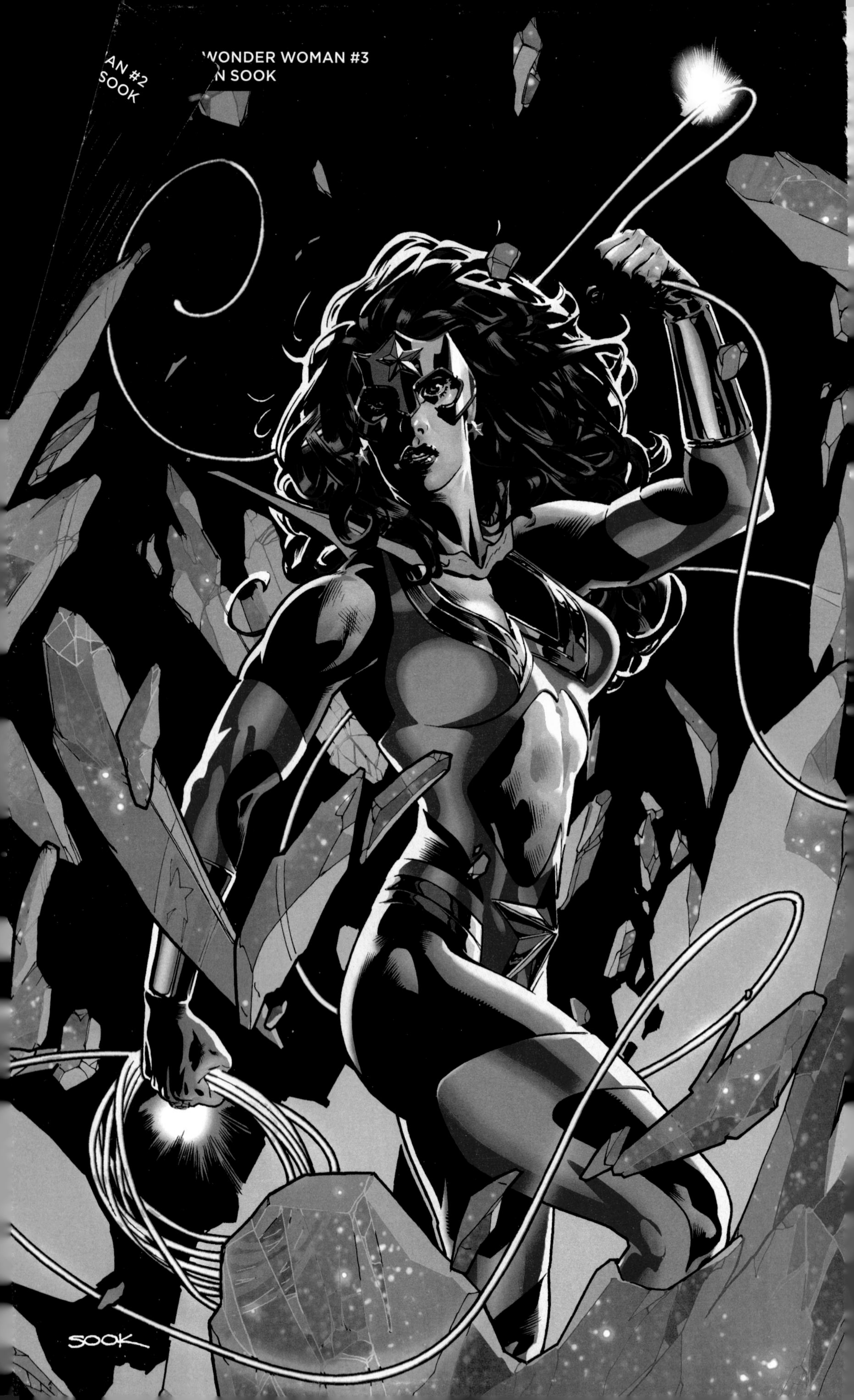
WONDER WOMAN #3
SOOK